한국에서의 영문학

한국에서의 영문학
― 1940년대 한국 사회와 문학 ―

李仁秀 글 모음

정리 李誠一·李誠元

한국문화사

李仁秀 (1916–1950)

아내 玄丙辰(1916~1998)과

I 죽은 이의 埋葬

四月은 殘酷한 달이기에
죽은 땅에서 라일락을 길러내고
記憶과 情欲을 뒤섞어 버프리며
잠자는 뿌리를 봄비로 깨우다.
겨울은 우리를 품속에 안어
忘却의 눈(雪)으로 땅을 덮어주며
배빠든 球根으로 가냘픈 生命을 이어주었건만
여름은 난데없이 스타안벨거세의 湖水를
넘어

몰어오는 소낙비와 더부러 우리를 쫓았거니.
우리는 나무밑에 몸을 의지했다가
볕을 마지하야 庭園에 들어가서
커되를 마시면서 이야기하고 한 睡間을
보냈었다.

난 露西亞사람 아니애요. 出生은 리투
아니아 이지만 純獨逸血統인 걸요.
그리구 어렸을제 四寸되는 皇太子집에서
슬매를 태배주마고 한켄 무섭드군요.
말력 말력 꼭 부자버 하고 四寸은 소리치드니

T. S. Eliot의 *The Waste Land* 번역 육필원고 첫 장 (1948)

荒蕪한 벌판은 등지고
물기슭에 앉아 고기를 낚는 나
내 땅을 다시 한번 다사려 볼거나?
둔든 다리는 무너지다 무너지다 무너지다
「그리하야 그는 洗練키는 불 속으로 몸을 더져」
「언제나 나는 제비처럼 되랴」
— 아 제비야 제비야
「아키텐의 王子는 廢墟된 塔 속에 있어」
나는 이 破片을 주어 뫃아
나의 滅亡에 對備하였나니

그렇다면 나는 너희들 비위에 맞을걸.
히어로니모는 다시금 미쳤다.
「다타— 다야드밤. 담야타.
  샨티— 샨티— 샨티—」

끝

T. S. Eliot의 *The Waste Land* 번역 육필원고 마지막 장 (1948)

The Vertex

Lee Yook-Sa (1905-44)

Lashed by the bitter season's scourge,
I'm driven at length to this north.

Where numb circuit & plateau merge,
I stand upon the sword-blade frost.

I know not where to bend my knees,
Nor where to lay my faltied steps,

Nought but to close my eyes and think
Of winter as a steel rainbow.

李陸史의 '絶頂' 영역 육필원고(1947)

차례

제1부: 영문학에 관한 글

英文學에 反映된 二十世紀 前半의 思潮 ·· 3
아이로니와 W. H. 오든 ·· 26
T. S. 엘리어트의 古典主義 文學論 ··· 34
近代 英詩 小史 ·· 58
〈오셀로〉 小考 ·· 69

제2부: 영어 연설문, 논설문, 수필

Statement by Dr. John M. Chang before the First Committee of the Third
  Session of the United Nations General Assembly (on 7 December 1948) ········· 75
Aesthetic Achievements of Korea: An Historical Survey of Classic Art ········· 89
A Brief Survey of the Present Condition of Korea ··································· 111
Our Naval Defense ··· 118
Inside Cloud Cuckoo Land: A Parallel Account ····································· 124
Plea for a Moral Education ·· 128
Democracy in the Orient: From a Non-Political Point of View ············· 138
Letters to the Editor, *The Seoul Times* ·· 165
Last Thoughts of a Dying Politician: Sermon of the Body to the Soul ······· 187
Editorial Restatement ·· 191
Subtle Corridors of History ··· 192
Moral Burden of the Aid Agreement ··· 194
Military Training at Schools ·· 196
Apology for Mayor Yun ··· 199
Absent Thee From Felicity Awhile ·· 201
One Man's Comment ··· 203
Kit-Cat Club Views on UNCOK: An Imaginary Dialogue ····················· 205
Thoughts after the Funeral Service of Mrs. Underwood ······················ 213
Home Thoughts From Abroad ·· 214
In Retrospect ·· 219
Apologia Pro Se ·· 220
"No Comment" ·· 222
The Students' National Guard: Its Purpose and Function ···················· 224
Chain of African Imposture ··· 233

Rightly to be Great when Honour's at the Stake 235
Cui Bono? 240
Cry Cry What Shall I Cry? (A Dialogue) 242

제3부: 한국문학 英譯
MODERN KOREAN POEMS

Han Yong-un (韓龍雲, 1879–1944)
  Mountain Abode (山居) 251

Cho Myŏng-hŭi (趙明熙, 1894–1938)
  A Prayer (無題) 252

Kim So-wŏl (金素月, 1902–1934)
  Wild Flowers of the Mountains (山有花) 253
  Sak-ju-ku-sŏng (朔州龜城) 254

Yi Sang-hwa (李相和, 1901–1943)
  Does Spring Come Also to These Ravished Fields? 255
  (빼앗긴 들에도 봄은 오는가?)

Chŏng Ji-yong (鄭芝溶, 1902–1950)
  In the Glen of Ku-sŏng-dong (九城洞) 257
  Stars (별) 258
  Sorrowful Image (슬픈 偶像) 259
  Homeward (歸路) 260

Yi Yuk-sa (李陸史, 1904–1944)
  The Vertex (絶頂) 265

Kim Ki-rim (金起林, 1908–?)
  The Fountain (噴水) 266
  Rain (비) 267
  Incantation of the Owl (올빼미의 呪文) 269
  Dusk (黃昏) 270
  Spring Comes without a Telegram (봄은 電報도 안 치고) 271

Yu Ch'i-hwan (柳致環, 1908–1967)
  Sun of My Life (日月) 273
  Flag (깃발) 274
  Head (首) 275
  Rock (바위) 276

P'i Ch'ŏn-dŭk (皮千得, 1910–2007)
  A Child's Fear (어떤 아기의 근심) 277

Life (生命) ·········· 278

Sŏl Jŏng-shik (薛貞植, 1912–1953)
- *Sunflower* (해바라기) ·········· 279
- *Gong* (鐘) ·········· 280
- *Sunless Land* (太陽 없는 땅) ·········· 282
- *With a Brew of the Bitter Sunflower Wine* (해바라기 쓴 술을 빚어 놓고) ·········· 284
- *The Wrath of Heaven* (諸神의 憤怒) ·········· 286

O Jang-hwan (吳章煥, 1918–1948)
- *Funeral Cortège* (喪列) ·········· 289
- *Christmas* (聖誕祭) ·········· 290
- *The Way to Father's Grave* (省墓 가는 길) ·········· 292

Kim Kwang-gyun (金光均, 1914–1993)
- *At the Nok-dong Burial Ground* (綠洞墓地에서) ·········· 294
- *Autumn Scene* (秋日抒情) ·········· 295

Yun Dong-ju (尹東柱, 1917–1945)
- *Primeval Morn* (太初의 아침) ·········· 296
- *Counting the Stars at Night* (별을 헤는 밤) ·········· 297
- *Another Home* (또 다른 故鄕) ·········· 299

Sŏ Jŏng-ju (徐廷柱, 1915–2000)
- *The Heat of Yellow Corn* (麥夏) ·········· 301
- *The Leper* (문둥이) ·········· 302
- *Self-Portrait* (自畵像) ·········· 303
- *Midday* (대낮) ·········· 305
- *A Post-Card* (葉書— 東里에게) ·········· 306

Kim Ch'ŏl-su (金哲洙, 1910–?)
- *Mountain Swallow* (山 제비) ·········· 307

Han Ha-un (韓何雲, 1920–1975)
- *The Demonstrations* (데모) ·········· 309

Pak Mog-wŏl (朴木月, 1916–1978)
- *Annual Ring* (年輪) ·········· 310

Pak Du-jin (朴斗鎭, 1916–1998)
- *Beneath the Blue Sky* (푸른 하늘 아래) ·········· 311

Cho Ji-hun (趙芝薰, 1920–1968)
- *Mountain Lodge* (山房) ·········· 312
- *Shedding of the Petals* (落花) ·········· 313

VERSES FOR THE YOUNG

Yun Sŏk-jung (尹石重, 1911–2003)

- *Half Past Four* — 314
- *The Postman and the Leaves* — 315
- *Day and Night* — 316
- *Shadow* — 317
- *Dewdrops* — 318
- *Child that Lost His Way in Snow* — 319
- *Lotus Leaves* — 320
- *The Train's a Fool* — 321
- *Horsie that Sleeps Standing* — 322
- *Child and Acorn* — 323
- *Where Do They Play?* — 324
- *Stream and Tree* — 325
- *Hempen Sandals and Wooden Clogs* — 326
- *Lullaby* — 327
- *O Reindeer* — 328
- *The Child and the Wind* — 329

SHORT FICTION

Kim Dong-ni (金東里, 1913–1995)

- *The Rock* (바위) — 330

Yi Sang (李箱, 1910–1937)

- *The Wing* (날개) [Translation unfinished] — 339

제4부: 현대영시 번역

T. S. 엘리어트 (T. S. Eliot, 1888–1965)

- 荒蕪地 (*The Wasteland*) — 349
- <荒蕪地> 飜譯 肉筆原稿 — 366
- 바람 부는 밤의 狂想曲 (*Rhapsody on a Windy Night*) — 387
- 聖灰 水曜日 I (*Ash Wednesday* I) — 390

G. M. 홉킨스 (Gerard Manly Hopkins, 1844–1889)

- 봄과 落葉 (*Spring and Fall*) — 392
- 별을 헤는 밤 (*The Starlight Night*) — 393
- 필릭스 랜들 (*Felix Randal*) — 394

W. B. 예이츠 (William Butler Yeats, 1865–1939)
- 제2의 강림 (*The Second Coming*) ········ 395
- 비잔티움으로 뱃길을 뜨다 (*Sailing to Byzantium*) ········ 396
- 肉體와 靈魂의 對話 (*Dialogue of Self and Soul*) ········ 398

해롤드 몬로 (Harold Monro, 1879–1932)
- 쓰라린 祭壇 (*Bitter Sanctuary*) ········ 401

T. E. 흄 (T. E. Hulme, 1883–1917)
- 가을 (*Autumn*) ········ 400
- 템스 江畔 (*The Embankment*) ········ 405

D. H. 로런스 (D. H. Lawrence, 1885–1930)
- 熱帶 (*Tropic*) ········ 406
- 除夜 (*New Year's Night*) ········ 407
- 南國의 밤 (*Southern Night*) ········ 408
- 平和 (*Peace*) ········ 409
- 뱀 (*Snake*) ········ 410

에즈라 파운드 (Ezra Pound, 1885–1972)
- 어쨌든 그들은 싸웠지 (*Those Fought in Any Case*) ········ 414

지그프리드 써쑨 (Siegfried Sassoon, 1886–1967)
- 臨終 (*The Death-bed*) ········ 416

H. D. (H[ilda] D[olittle], 1886–1961)
- 더위 (*Heat*) ········ 418

이디스 씨트월 (Edith Sitwell, 1887–1964)
- 間奏曲 (*Interlude*) ········ 419
- 비엘지바브 卿 (*When Sir Beelzebub*) ········ 420

윌프레드 오웬 (Wilfred Owen, 1893–1918)
- 더 큰 사랑 (*Greater Love*) ········ 421

허버트 리드 (Herbert Reed, 1893–1968)
- 크라나크 (*Cranach*) ········ 423

로버트 그레이브스 (Robert Graves, 1895–1985)
- 歲月 (*Time*) ········ 424

C. D. 루이스 (Cecil Day Lewis, 1904–1972)
- 죽음에 바치는 序曲 (*Overtures to Death*) ········ 425

루이스 맥크니스 (Louis MacNeice, 1907–1963)
- 聖誕祭에 題한 牧歌 (*An Eclogue for Christmas*) ········ 429

W. H. 오든 (W. H. Auden, 1907–1973)
- 西班牙 1937년 (*Spain, 1937*) ········ 435

無名의 市民 (*The Unknown Citizen*) ·············· 439
스티븐 스펜더 (Stephen Spender, 1909–1995)
　　　貧民窟의 小學校 敎室 (*An Elementary School Classroom in a Slum*) ·············· 441
　　　君主의 最終的 理論 (*Ultima Ratio Regum*) ·············· 443
찰스 매지 (Charles Madge, 1912–1996)
　　　星座가 만남 (*In Conjunction*) ·············· 444
조지 바커 (George Barker, 1913–1991)
　　　여름의 牧歌 (*Summer Idyll*) ·············· 445
딜런 토머스 (Dylan Thomas, 1914–1953)
　　　태양 없는 곳에 (*Light Breaks Where No Sun Shines*) ·············· 447
데이비드 개스콘 (David Gascoyne, 1916–2001)
　　　假想 人物 (*The Supposed Being*) ·············· 449

제5부: 창작시, 희곡

Variations on the Theme of Despair: Before and After August, 1945 (A Poem) ·············· 455
Love at Phillippi (A Conversational Melodrama in Three Acts) ·············· 460

부록:

Gregory Henderson, "Insoo Lee and His Cloud Cuckoo land" ·············· 545
University of London, Faculty of Arts, B. A. Examination for
　　Internal Students, 1940, Honours in English Studies List (Photo copy) ·············· 548
Testimonial of R. W. Chambers, Quain Professor of English Language & Literature,
　　University College, London (Photo copy) ·············· 549
Testimonial of Edith C. Batho, M. A., D. Lit., Reader in English Literature
　　in the University of London (Photo copy) ·············· 551
Biographical Note on the Author (By the editors) ·············· 553
After Compiling Our Father's Writings ·············· 554
李仁秀의 年譜 ·············· 556
아버님의 文集을 펴내며 ·············· 557

제1부
영문학에 관한 글

英文學에 反映된 二十世紀 前半의 思潮*

[筆者註: 厖大한 今世紀의 英文學 思潮를 年代順으로 敍述할 自信이 없어서 斷層的으로 나타나는 몇몇 特徵을 들어 보기로 하였다. 또렷한 論述 段階를 일부러 지어서 쓴 것은 아니로되, 굳이 全體의 테두리를 밝힌다면 아래와 같다.

　1. 機械産業과 文學의 技巧
　2. 精神分析學과 本能의 文學
　　가. 潛在意識의 文學
　　나. 性의 文學
　3. 科學思潮와 知性의 文學
　　가. 社會意識의 文學
　　나. 歷史意識의 文學
　4. 兩次大戰과 文學의 倫理
　　가. 求神의 文學과 新浪漫의 思潮
　　나. 共産主義의 文學的 限界

題目이 大膽함을 스스로 부끄러워하나, 提示의 責任이 筆者에게 있지 않았던 것을 自慰로 삼는 바이다.]

I

플라톤의 對話篇 <파이드루스>에서 哲人 소크라테스는 書籍에 關하여 아래와 같은 놀라운 말을 하였다.

---

* 이 글은 을유문화사 발행 <學風> (1950년 3월호), 5–28페이지에 실렸다. <學風> 편집진이 계획한 특집의 큰 제목은 <20세기 문명의 회고와 전망>으로, 활자화 된 이 논문의 제목은 <今世紀前半의 思潮: 英文學에 反映된 것을 中心하여서>이나, 육필원고상에서의 제목은 <英文學에 反映된 二十世紀 前半의 思潮>이다. 여기서는 육필원고에 나타나는 제목을 택하였다.

"冊이라면 무슨 깊은 뜻이나 가진 듯이 이야기하는 것인줄로 당신은 생각함직도 합니다. 그러나 冊이 말하는 것을 理解할 양으로 그 內容을 따져 본다면, 언제나 똑같은 한가지 이야기를 되풀이하는 데 그친다는 것을 당신은 깨다를 겝니다."

비록 著述에 興味를 느끼지 못하고 오로지 입심으로만 一生을 버티어 살았다는 소크라테스라 할지라도 그의 말이 全然 無根한 獨善만은 아니었으리라고 생각된다. 더구나 위의 引用文을 二十世紀의 文學에 適用한다면 누구나 首肯할만도 한 達觀이라 하겠다. 個個의 作家가 '되풀이'하느냐 않느냐 하는 論點은 姑捨하고라도 二十世紀에 들어서면서부터는 우선 著述이라는 精神活動마저 이미 一種의 '機械産業'이 되어버린 듯한 느낌이 顯著하기 때문이다.

文學이 機械産業化하였다 해서 勿論 거기에 反映될 '思潮'가 없다거나 單一해졌다는 것은 아니다. 英文學에 있어서 現代처럼 思潮가 複雜多端한 時代는 아직껏 없었다. 機械産業이라면 우리는 곧 그 結果로 보아 '大量生産'이라는 特徵을 聯想한다. 그러나 그것보다도 먼저 前提삼을 것은 機械가 精密해야만 機械産業이 可能하다는 點이다. 그러기에 現代作家는 自己의 創作活動의 밑천이 되는 機械—卽, 言語의 技巧와 表現의 手法—부터 가장 的確하고 가장 精密한 것으로 만들려고 辛苦하는 것이다. 이 뼈에 맺히는 苦心이야말로 過去의 西歐文學에서 보기 드문 現代文學 全體에 걸칠 特色의 하나이다. 傳道者의 말마따나 "太陽 밑에 새로운 것 없다"는 內容에 關한 苦衷도 없지는 않겠으나, 神靈만 잡힌다면 어느 作家치고 讀者 大衆—또는 曠野—에 외칠 메씨지가 없을 바도 아니다. 다만 二十世紀 作家들이 유달리 技巧問題를 에워싸고 實驗과 焦燥를 거듭하는 그 背後에는 表現할 內容과 思潮問題도 반드시 同時에 內包되어 있으므로 兩者를 聯關시켜서 論함이 適當하다.

詩人 엘리어트(1888–1965)는 그의 <파운드論>(1932)에서 다음과 같이 말했다.

"詩人의 努力은 想像의 그라프 위에 그려진 두 線을 따라 나아간다고 볼 수 있다. 그 첫째 線은 技巧에 卓越하도록 하는 끊임없는 意識的 努力이니, 다시 말하면, 自己가 참말로 表現할 만한 것을 가질 그 瞬間을 爲하여 그의 媒介를 不斷히 發展시키는 것이다. 또 한 線은 그의 普通人間으로서의 發達科程, 卽 經驗의 蓄積과 消化에 不過한 것이다.... 어쩌다 이 두 線이 어떤 絶頂에서 交叉하게 되면, 거기에 傑作이 생긴다. 換言하면, 經驗의 蓄積이 凝結하여 藝術의 素材가 되고, 多年間 쌓은 技巧의 訓練이 適切한 媒材를 마련한다. 그 結果, 媒介와 素材, 形式과 內容을 分揀하기 어려운 어떤 것이 생긴다."

이러한 指摘은 대수롭지 않은 말 같지만, 特히 現代英文學에 나타나는 創作活動의 傾向에 비추어 볼 때 意味深長한 觀察이라 하겠다. 詩나 散文에 있어서 現代처럼 作家의 연장이요 밑천인 言語의 行動과 波長을 理論的으로 探索하고 意識的으로 實驗해 본 時代는 적어도 英文學史上 없었을 것이다. 리차즈(1893-1979) 같은 文學評論家가 <意味의 意味>(1923)니, <文學批評의 原理>(1924)니, 또는 <修辭學의 哲學>(1937)이니 하는 著述에서 文學의 밑받이를 言語의 心理的 機能에 두려 한 것도 결코 偶然이 아니었다. 都是에 語義學이라는 科學이 言語學의 重要한 部門을 이루게 된 것도 近年의 일이라 하겠지만, 文學을 言語의 技術로 보는 見解도 아주 最近에 頭角을 나타내게 된 새로운 現象이라 하겠다. 그만큼 文學도 精密機械의 産業이 되었으며 또 그만큼 現代作家는 낡은 言語에 沈滯된 價値觀을 否定하거나 或은 疑訝해 하는 것이다. 詩人 오든(1907-1973)이 <四角形과 楕圓形>(1948)이라는 詩論 短章에서 아래와 같이 말한 것은 現代의 創作態度 全般을 端的으로 反映하는 感銘 깊은 觀察이다.

"'당신은 왜 詩를 쓰려 하오?'라는 質問에, 젊은 作家가, '나는 말하고 싶은 重要한 것을 가졌기 때문이오,'라고 對答하면, 그는 詩人이 아니다. 만일에 그가, '나는 말에 홀린 者라, 말이 이야기하는 것에 귀를 기우리기 좋아하오,'라고 對答한다면, 그는 詩人이 될 싹이 多分히 보이는 사람이다."

엘리어트도 비슷한 意見을 累累히 强調하여 왔다. 非但 詩뿐이랴? 散文作家 조이스(1882-1941)나 버지니아 울프(1882-1941)도 마찬가지다. 現代文學의 스핑크스라 할 만한 <율리씨즈>(1922)처럼 말의 칫수와 무게와 소리와 外延과 內包를 샅샅이 뒤져내어서 極度로 言語를 活用하는 作品은 또 없을 것이다. 構想도 構想이려니와 作家의 努力은 우선 言語의 探擇에 있다는 것이 現代英文學의 걸어온 길이었고, 그러므로 해서 言語의 技巧問題를 어떻게 解決하느냐가 現代文學의 重要한 思潮의 하나이다. 적어도 젊은 世代에 크나큰 影響을 미치었다는 作品 乃至 作家는 擧皆가 그의 말솜씨 때문이라 하여도 過言이 아니다.

詩와 散文으로 나누어서 具體的인 例를 몇가지 들기로 하자. 近代英詩가 十六世紀 後半부터 確固한 技巧的 地盤을 갖추게 된 以後로, 詩의 韻律學(프로소디)이 詩文學 評論의 重要한 部門을 차지해 온 것은 事實이지만, 在來의 韻律學은 자칫하면 類型의 命名에 그치는 定言的인 同時에 演繹的인 判斷이었고, 韻律의 實際 資料를 分析的으로 究明하여 韻律의 本質에까지 歸納하는 硏究는 드물었다고 할 수 있다. 그런데 이 轉換의 標石이 될 만한 著述에 詩人 브리지스(1844–1930)가 쓴 <밀튼의 韻律法>(1893, 改正 1921), 英文學者 쎄인즈버리(1845–1933)의 <英詩韻律史>(1906–1910)와 <英散文韻律史>(1912), 詩人 애버크롬비(1881–1938)의 <英詩韻律의 原理>(1923), 그리고 美國詩人 러니어(1842–1881)의 <英詩의 科學>(1880) 等을 들 수 있다. 例外없이 읽기 힘든 冊들이고, 그만한 豫備知識이 없으면 서뿔리 詩를 쓰지 못할 것이라는 느낌을 갖게 되는데, 이는 豊富한 遺産을 물려받은 現代英語詩人들에게 共通으로 부과된 課業이다.

한 마디로 要約하면, 英詩의 韻律에 두 가지의 基本形式이 있다. 美國의 詩人 칼 샤피로(1913–2000)는 그의 韻文 <詩論>(1945)에서 말하였다. "英詩의 律調는 두 가지의 形式을 取할 수 있고, 두 가지밖에는 取하지 못한다. 하나는 눈(眼)으로 세는 것, 또 하나는 귀(耳)로 세는 것이다." 二十世紀 英詩가 過去의 그것과 다른 點의 하나는 漸次 귀로 세는 方向으로 律調가 再調整되는 데 있다. (이것 亦是 페이터의 "모든 藝術은 音樂의 狀態로 接近한다"는 名言의 反證이라 할까?) 홉킨스(1844–1889)의 遺稿詩集(1918)이 던져 준 所謂 '스프링 리듬'을 보든지, 1910–1920年代에 많은 衝動을 준 '自由詩' 운동의 자취를 보든지, 또는 엘리어트 같은 詩人이 쓴 '블랭크 버스'를 보든지, 다 마찬가지의 現象을 말하는 것이다.

귀로 세는 律調는 結局 日常 會話體의 文章을 前提한다는 것으로 歸元하고 만다. 旣往의 英詩에서 가장 代表的인 律調의 單位는 音程이 위로 치미는 抑揚格('아이앰브스')이었다. '아이앰브스'를 가장 完全히 發達시킨 '블랭크 버스'에 있어서는, 마치 海邊에서 波濤를 보는 것과 같은 莊嚴을 느끼는 것이었다. 그러나 이 雄壯이 現代人의 生活 템포에는 맞지 않는 點이 많다. 極度로 緊張된 末梢神經膜을 가지고 '스타카토'로 살지 않으면 안 될 現代人의 呼吸에 그만한 精神的 餘裕와 生에 對한 安全感이 없는것이다. 高氣壓 속에서 허덕이는 焦燥와 眩氣症이 現代生活의 礎盤이므로, 따라서 現代詩의 韻律도 音程이 아래로 떨어지는 揚抑格('트로키이')이 아니면, 북을 치는 것과 같은 強한 액센트의 連續이다. 이를 發見하여 새로운 藝術的 效果를 거둔 功勞가 現代詩人에 있다. 美國詩人 맥클리이쉬(1892–1982)가 그의 詩劇 <恐慌>(1935)의 序文에서 다음과 같이 언급하였을 때, 그것은 現代英詩의 特殊性을 알려주는 關鍵이라고 생각된다.

"블랭크 버스의 律調와 우리나라 口語의 律調는 正反對 되는 것이다. 블랭크 버스의 律調는 幅이 넓고, 느릿느릿하고, 高尙하고, 雄壯하다. 筋肉的인 아이앰브스의 걸음거리로 씩씩하게 나아간다. . . . 이에 反하여 오늘날 美國사람 말의 律調는 筋肉的이 아니고, 神經的이며, 悠長하지 않고, 興奮된 것이며, 威勢堂堂한 것이 아니라, 躍動的인 것이다. . . . 事務室이나, 工場이나, 거리에서, 서로 熱中하여 이야기하는 이 나라 사람들의 말소리는 액센트 높은 音節에서 아래로 처지는 것이고, 셰익스피어의 戲曲에 나오는 人物의 말소리처럼, 강한 액센트의 音節로 올라가는 것이 아니다."

言語 律調가 이와 같이 바뀌어지는 根本 動機는, 機械文明과 이에 따르는 都市意識에 있다고 할 수 있는 만큼, 이 動向이 必然的으로 英文學—特히 英詩—에도 나타나는 것은 當然한 現象이다.

II

무엇보다도 二十世紀 散文作家들이 開拓해 준 새로운 世界는 潛在意識과 無意識의 斷層이라 하겠다. 이미 十九世紀 末葉부터 톨스토이나 도스토에프스키 같은 作家가 各其 다른 方法으로 人間의 知性을 拒否하는 創作態度를 取해 왔었고, 베르그손 같은 哲學者도 <物質과 記憶>(1897)이니 <創造的 進化論>(1906)이니 하는 著述에서, 마찬가지로, 知性의 爲主性을 懷疑해 왔었던 것이다. 記憶의 世界가 信仰을 잃은 現代作家에게 가장 알맞은 素材를 提供하게 된 由來는, 프루스트의 厖大한 作品 <잃어버린 時代를 다시 찾아서>(1913-1927)만 보더라도 알 수 있지만, 그러나 무엇보다도 心理學者 프로이드나 융이나 아들러가 물려준 精神分析學 乃至 心理學의 科學에서 이를 찾을 수 있다. 프로이드의 著 <꿈의 意味>가 1900년에 發表되었다는 事實부터가 뜻깊은 일이 아닐까?

프로이드의 決定論的 精神療法이 斯界의 專門家보다 차라리 門外漢을 相對로 삼는 理論의 展開였고, 그의 論據가 醫學보다는 오히려 神話, 歷史, 宗敎 等에 있었기 때문에, 文學에 끼친 影響이 더욱 直感的인 것이었다. 小說家 로런스(1885-1930)가 쓴 論文 <精神分析과 無意識>(1921), <無意識의 판타지아>(1922) 等을 보든지, 또는 조이스의 小說 <젊은 藝術家의 肖像>(1916)에서, <율리씨즈>를 거쳐, <피니건스 웨이크>(1939)로 展開되는

心理措寫의 技巧를 보든지, 버지니아 울프가 가위 完璧을 기했다고 볼 수 있는 '意識의 흐름'의 手法을 보든지, 要는 精神分析學이 가져다 준 科學의 思潮의 背景이 아니었던들, 二十世紀가 자랑하는 小說의 心理措寫는 一時的인 流行에 그치고 말았을는지도 모른다. 하기야 프로이드가 있었기 때문에 조이스가 생긴 것은 아니다. 作家의 創作情神이란, 어떤 科學의 抽象에서 出發하여 演繹하는 것은 아닐 게다. 人物을 創造하고, 具現하려는 作品의 世界를 構想하다가 보면, 偶然히도 어떤 科學의 眞理와 一致하는 수는 있을 망정, 프로이드의 '이드'가 곧 조이스의 '불루움'이라는 것은 아니다. 科學者의 學說 '이디푸스 콤플렉스'가 햄리트라는 創造人物을 考證하는 한 方便은 될 망정, 沙翁의 作品 自體가 '리비도'에 關한 科學知識을 確認하는 證據物이 될 수는 없는 것과 마찬가지다.

엘리어트의 未完成 詩劇 <苦憫하는 스위이니>(1932)에서 젊은 두 男女가 아래와 같은 對話로 人生을 論하는 諷刺的 場面이있다.

    女: 뭐예요?
    男: 낳아서 性交하고 죽는것.
       그것뿐야. 그것뿐, 그것뿐, 그것뿐.
       낳아서 性交하고 죽는 것.
    女: 싫증나겠네.
    男: 싫증나고 말고.
       낳아서 性交하고 죽는 것.

이에 프로이드의 精神分析學이 提起한 文學의 課題로서 性의 文學을 들지 않을 수 없다. 느끼하리 만큼 感傷的이고 偏狹하던 빅토리아 時代의 고리타분한 性道德에 叛旗를 들고 나선 것이 새삼스레 今世紀에 始作된 現象은 아니다. 이미 1880-1890年代에 發表된 하아디(1840-1928)나 또는 메레디스(1828-1909)의 小說에서도 이를 엿볼 수 있었고, 今世紀의 初期 作家들, 즉, 웰스(1866-1946), 골스워지(1867-1933), 모옴(1874-1965), 베네트(1867-1931), 무어(1852-1933), 버틀러(1835-1902), 기씽(1857-1903) 等, 其他 群小 作家들에서도 反빅토리아의 思想은 充分히 나타났었다. 그러나 性의 中産小市民的인 道德觀의 멍에를 完全히 벗어나서 그 自體가 獨立한 새로운 人生觀의 밑받이가 되고, 따라서 創作文學의 對象이 되기는 로런스에 이르러 비로소 볼 수 있는 것이었다.

如干 굳은 信念을 갖지 않고서야 <채털리 夫人의 사랑>(1928)을 세 번이나 다시 썼으랴? 죽은지 滿二十年 되는 오늘날 와서 새삼스레 로런스가 淫猥文學家이냐 아니냐 하는 皮相的 考察은 되풀이할 必要조차 없다. 그는 最後의 浪漫主義 作家였고, 極端의 道德家였기 때문에, 끝끝내 豫言者의 非運을 冒免치 못하였던 것이다.

"내사 내사 아니어라. 속속들이 불어 주는 바람의 所爲러니,
거룩한 바람이 새 時代의 方位로 불어 주도다."

曠野의 아우성이 아니고 또 무엇이랴? 實生活에 있어서 純潔하기 짝이 없는 性格이었고, 그의 遺稿作品 <죽은 사람>(1931)에서 復活한 예수의 心境을 措寫하는데 누구보다도 的確한 洞察力을 가졌던 그가 무엇 때문에 性을 이와 같이 崇尙하였던가? 로런스의 人生觀을 가장 要約하여 알려 주는 著述로 死後에 發表된 <黙示錄硏究>(1931)를 들 수 있다. 그 結論에 다음과 같은 一節이 있다.

"人間으로서 가장 神秘스러운 것은 산다는 것이다. 꽃이나 짐승이나 새와 마찬가지로, 사람으로서도 最古의 勝利는 가장 生氣있게, 가장 完全하게 사는 데 있다. 未生者나 死者가 무엇을 알든지간에, 그들은 肉體에 사는 아름다움과 神秘를 알지 못할 것이다. 이미 죽은이는 死後를 걱정할지로되, 肉體 속에 사는 그 壯한 '이 자리'와 '이 瞬間'은 우리의 것이며, 그나마도 暫時밖에는 누릴 수 없는 우리의 것이다. 우리는 산 코스모스의 化身의 一部分으로서 肉體에 살고 있다는 데 對해 마땅히 欣喜雀躍의 춤을 추어야 할지어다. 내 눈이 내 몸의 一部分이듯, 나는 太陽의 한 조각이니라. 내가 大地에 通함을 내 발이 잘 알고 있을 바에 내 피는 바다에 通하는도다."

'낳아서 性交하고 죽는 것'이 內包하는 完全한 虛無와는 正히 對蹠되는 生의 哲學이라 하겠으나, 로런스의 이른 바 性의 文學은 絶望的인 理想主義였기 때문에 究竟은 가장 峻嚴한 슬픔의 文學에 歸一하는 것이었다. 지긋지긋한 悲壯의 精神에 사무치는 것이 今世紀의 文學임에 틀림이 없다.

III

不可思議의 後光이 자꾸만 사라져 가는 것을 目擊하는 現代人은 生의 '健全性'을 懷疑한다. 世紀의 作品 〈파우스트〉는 書架에서 먼지만 들쓰게 되고, 作家 自身은 무슨 僞善者나 된 듯이―괴테에게 僞善이 全然 없었던 것은 아니지만―敵對視하는 것이 일쑤다. 차라리 現代人의 귀에는 티 이 휴움(1883-1917)의 말("우리 一生은 大部分 단추를 끼웠다가 뺐다가 하는 데서 가고 마는 거야. 참말로 그래"라고 하는 黑房秘曲)이 몇 갑절 더 솔직한 告白인지 모르겠다. 저고리 단추라면 或 高尙한 맛도 있다 하려니와, 바지 단추는 유달리 수줍음을 느끼는 弊端에 不過하다. 이 精神의 分裂病은 科學이 가져다 주는 副産物이 아닐까? 前記 리차즈의 말을 다시 한 번 빌리면,

"確證된 事實과 受諾할 수 있는 假想과의 差異가 [過去의 人間]에게는 그다지 뚜렷하지 않았다고 보는 것이 妥當할 것이다. 오늘날은 달라졌다. 그러한 假想을 믿는다 할지라도, 頭腦가 明哲한 사람이라면 相當한 苦憫과 相當한 不屈의 努力을 거치지 않고는 그것을 믿지 않을 것이다. 여러말 할 것 없이 徹頭徹尾한 懷疑主義者란 歷史에서 새롭게 보는 現象이다. 過去의 不信任者는 大槪 같은 範疇 안에서 다만 다른 信仰을 가졌기 때문에 異端을 信奉했던 것이다." (〈文學批判의 原理〉)

그러므로 完全한 懷疑는 完全한 批判精神 밖에 주지 않고, 따라서 現代의 創作精神에는 批判精神의 거미줄에 걸린 잠자리와 같은 몸부림의 眞髓이다.

이 몸부림이 두 갈래로 發露된다고 볼 수 있다. 그 하나는 自我意識이요, 또 하나는 歷史意識이다. 勿論, 全體를 支配하는 것은 理智性이다. 自我意識은 위에서 論한 精神分析學의 文學에 미친 影響과 同一한 問題이므로 다시 길게 論할 必要가 없다. 여기서는 今世紀 文學의 社會意識에 나타나는 理知性과 歷史意識의 思潮를 簡單히 敍述해 보기로 하겠다.

일찍부터 쇼오(1856-1950)가 舞台를 說敎壇으로 삼아 感傷의 偶像破壞者로 自認하고 나서서 左衝右突하던 것을 이제 와서 回顧해 보면, 結局 自己陶醉의 空砲가 아니었던가 하는 疑心이 떠 돈다. 兩次大戰에 시달린 現代人은 쇼오의 說敎文學과 整形文學에서 어떤

메씨지를 求하기보다는 차라리 그의 青山流水같은 말의 奇才에 感歎하는 面이 더 많다. 政治, 社會, 經濟, 宗教 等, 손에 안기는 대로 그가 휘두르는 理智的인 批判의 칼은 매섭기는 하나, 現代가 單純한 칼춤[劍舞]에 興味를 느낄 階梯가 아니라는 것을 젊은 世代는 더 잘 알고 있다. 知性의 文學도 좋고, 社會의 腐敗를 고칠 萬病通治藥도 좋다. 그러나 理智의 自瀆은 싫증나는 노릇이다. 쇼오가 물려준 批判의 精神과 理智의 文學이 할 任務를 다 하였다고 해서 그 任務가 적었다는 것은 결코 아니다. 쇼오의 論戰은 文學의 領域 밖에서 더욱 보람있었다고 볼 수 있다. 社會 改革熱과 義憤이 새삼 수世紀에 일어난 것이 아님을 잘 알고, 또 아무리 떠들어도 歷史는 갈 길을 간다는 것도 잘 알고 있으므로, 現代作家는 自己의 活動 範圍를 훨씬 좁혀서 謙讓한 創作 態度로 나서는 것이 아닐까? 藝術과 社會問題를 混線하지 않도록 努力한다고 해서 그들이 '藝術至上'을 다시 信奉한다는 것은 아니리라. 政治, 經濟, 社會의 밑받이가 될 價値觀이 確立된다손 치더라도, 이미 分裂된 精神狀態에 있어서는 히스테리컬한 自我意識의 助長밖에는 되지 않고, 또 그럼으로서 그 價値觀이 몇곱 더 悽慘하고 熱度가 높아지는 것이지만, 그렇다고 作家가 스스로의 苦憫 속에서 건져 낸 價値觀을 第三者의 個人이나 또는 範疇를 달리하는 一般社會, 政治, 經濟問題에 强要하려고 서두르지는 않는다. 그만큼 現代作家는 自己 力量과 存在를 잘 아는 正直하고 수줍은 사람들이다. 엘리어트는 아아놀드와 페이터에 關한 論文(1930)에서, '藝術 至上'이 한 主義로 成立이 된다는 것은 疑心스러우나, 萬若 이것을 한 主義라 할 수 있다면, 藝術家는 제 할 일에 熱中해야 한다는 訓戒로 볼 수 있다는 點은 오늘날까지 妥當性을 띤다"고 말했는데, 엘리어트의 이 말은 適切하고 悲壯한 告白이라 하겠다.

마찬가지 理論이 小說家 웰스에도 適用될 수 있다. 툭하면 社會改善의 秘訣을 提唱하고 科學思潮에 立脚한 豫言과 說敎를 입심있게 하는 그의 天才는 다시없는 樂天主義에 屬하는 것 같은 印象을 준다. 디킨스의 創作精神의 再現인 듯도 싶던 그의 初期의 實寫主義的 天才는 뒷전이 되고, 그는 일찍부터 멀리 思潮의 世界를 헤매어, 或은 科學, 或은 歷史學, 社會學, 生物學을 通하여 '호모 싸피엔스'의 앞날을 警告하는데 主力을 集中하였다. 悲觀論이라면 悲觀論이겠지만, 그의 메씨지의 骨子는 結局, '판타시아'의 世界에 屬하는 것이 아닐까? 이렇게도 '호모 싸피엔스'의 責任이 重且大할진대, 그것을 누가 堪當해 낼 수 있으랴? 때는 이미 늦었다는, 沈滯와 自己苛責의 느낌이 남을 뿐이다.

마아크 스테이즈는 말했다. "죽음, 우리가 完全히 俗化하는데 아직 成功하지 못한 것은 이것뿐이야. 勿論 하기 싫어서 그런 건 아니지만, 우리는 恰似 옛 城砦를 헤매는 개와도 같아. 無限量의 콩팥을 가지고 뛰어 다니면서 石像마다 다리를 쳐들고 깔기고자 하는 짐승이야. 大槪는 뜻대로 돼. 藝術, 宗敎, 英雄主義, 사랑— 다 한 번씩 우리가 歷訪했다는 表示로 名銜을 놓고 왔지. 그러나 죽음, 죽음만은 건드리지 못했어. 그 石像은 아직까지 우리가 더럽히지 못했어. 그러나 進步는 如前히 進步하고 있는 걸. . . . 더 큰 希望과 殖産하는 將來. . . . 죽음이 忠實을 지킨다는 걸 생각하니. . . 慰安도 되이. 모든 것이 사라져 없어질 망정 죽음은 忠誠을 지킬 테야."

헉슬리(1884-1963)의 中年作 小說 〈눈멀어 가자〉(1936)에서의 一節이다. 現代 知識의 尖端을 걷고 가장 綜合的인 思考方式을 가졌음에도 不拘하고 그가 이렇게 죽음을 希求한다는 것은 곧 現代人으로서의 그의 精神이 不調整 狀態를 벗어나지 못하였다는 反證이다.

創作小說은 勿論이려니와 그가 現代文明을 總批評하는 著書 〈目的과 手段〉(1936)만 보더라도 그의 知識人으로서의 時代批判이 얼마나 辛辣한가를 엿볼 수 있다. 現代人이 깊은 關心을 가진 모든 問題—社會改革의 效能과 限界, 暴力과 社會改革, 計劃社會, 現代國家의 本質, 中央集權과 地方分權, 自治精神의 倫理的, 政治的 地盤, 戰爭과 그 原因, 敎育問題, 實踐宗敎와 信仰問題, 파씨즘과 共産主義 等等—을 아무리 嚴密히 檢討하여도 시원스러운 解決策이 별로 없고, 있다면 佛道에서 말하는 無執着의 精神밖에 없다는, 一種의 時代錯誤的 悲觀論으로 決論지운다. 그의 批判은 破壞的인 面에 比하여 建設的인 面이 약하다. 勿論 이것이 헉슬리의 罪는 아니다. 그가 아무리 冷徹한 理性으로 時代를 批判하여도 時代는 귀를 기우리지 않는 탓이다. 哲學者 화이트헤드가 말하듯, "事物에 秩序가 있다는, 特히 自然에 秩序가 있다는, 本態的인 信念이 널리 普及되어 있지 않은 限, 산 科學이란 存在할 수 없다."(〈科學과 現代世界〉(1927)) '산 科學'도 重要하지만, '秩序'가 더욱 重要하기 때문에, 헉슬리 같은 知識人도 挫折의 慢性病으로 呻吟하는 것이다. 1940年來로 그가 헐리우드 附近의 沙漠 속에 居住하여 암소를 기르면서 每週 쓰와미 프라바난다의 門下에서 힌두 經書의 講義를 듣고, 瑜伽의 修行으로 瞑想하며, 베단타 哲學會의 機關紙에 寄稿할 글만 쓰고 있다는 것은, 그의 知性이 志向할 論理的 結論으로는 너무나 가냘픈 데누망이 아닐까 한다. 그가 創作小說에서 諷刺한 社會相은 아직도 現代人의 딜레마로 남아 있다. 原子彈 問題의 解決策으로 그가 〈科學과 自由와 平和〉(1946)를 著述하였지만, 原子 問題는 如前히 世紀의 宿題로 남아 있다. 그러나 그의 創作의 全體는 現代人의 理性의 傳記와도 같은 二十世紀의 '天路歷程'에 該當하는 것이라고 하겠다.

"主義思想의 衝突은 災厄이 아니라 機會"(<科學과 現代世界>)라고 前記 화이트헤드는 말하지만, 其實 이런 見解는 模索하는 哲人의 理想論이고, 創作하는 作家로서는 그가 具現할 知性과 感性, 經驗과 價値觀 모든 것의 統一의 秩序를 爲하여 적지 않은 不幸이 아닐 수 없다. 今世紀 英詩人인들 列外일 理가 萬無하다. 그들인들 科學과 社會現實이 가져다주는 頑强한 事實의 世界, 客觀의 世界를 어떻게 하면 主觀의 世界에 融和 시키느냐 하는 課題를 에워싸고 辛苦하지 않을 수 없으리라. 아무리 쌘터야나 같은 哲人이 "우리는 主觀的 見解와 主觀的 信念에 가득찬 獨白의 世界에 살고 있다"고 慰安의 말을 한들, 現實을 正視하는 詩人이라면 이러한 잠꼬대의 世界로만 滿足하지 않을 것이다.

그러나 어느 모로 보면 詩人의 課題는 散文作家의 그것과도 또 좀 다르다. 小說에서는 人物(한 經驗體)과 人物이, 또는 人物과 環境(提示된 한 事實體)이 서로 얼키고 설켜서 作品이 進展되는 동안에 플롯트, 或은 액션이라는 價値觀의 成長過程이 드러나게 되므로, 저절로 作家 自身의 世界觀(主觀的 假定과 客觀的 事實이 融和하여 이루는 價値體系)이 나타나게 된다. 그러나 詩作品에 있어서는 그러한 境遇도 많지만, 때로는 單純히 言語가 象徵하는 어떤 이미지와 이미지가 一定한 律調의 테두리 안에서 서로 交叉하여 한 官能的 秩序의 複合性을 이루는 수도 있다. 어떤 社會的 또는 科學的 事實이 作家의 判斷機能에 介在하여 한 結論的인 '理念'(아이디어)을 詩人이 表現하는 수도 있지만, 同時에 그런 事實을 意識함으로써 作家의 心鏡에 反影되는 '感覺'(쎈씨빌리티)만을 表現함으로 滿足하는 수도 있다. 그러므로 詩人의 이른바 世界觀은 散文作家가 追求하는 그것과 반드시 同一할 수는 없다. 詩作品 自體의 實在와 그것을 創作한 主體의 實在와 混同하지 않도록 하자는 것이다. 키이츠의 말마따나, "詩에는 性格이 없다"고 해도 過言이 아니리라.

이 點을 구태여 여기서 밝히고자 하는 理由는, 今世紀의 英詩人들이 社會 思潮를 어떻게 反影하느냐 하는 點을 論及하고자 하기 때문이다. 大體로 二十世紀 英詩는 資本主義的 中産文化의 崩壞를 알리는 社會的 危機에 處한 不安文學에 屬하는 것이라고 우리가 直決處分할 수도 있다. 假令 엘리어트의 <荒蕪地>(1922)는 戰後의 幻滅과 支離滅裂해 가는 現代人의 意識을 表白하는 作品이라고 決論지을 수도 있으리라. 그러나 作家 自身은 이를 論駁하여 아래와 같이 말했다.

"나는 '世代'라는 말을 싫어한다. 이 말은 過去 十年 동안 符籍과 같이 씨워져 왔다. 내가 <荒蕪地>라는 作品을 썼을 적에 比較的 讚美하는 評論家의 한 사람이

評하기를, 내가 '한 世代의 幻滅'을 表現했다고 말했다. 이것은 넌센스다. 내가 或은 그네들이 幻滅을 느낀다는 自己欺瞞을 그네들을 代身하여 表現해 주었는지는 모르나, 그것은 나의 意圖한 바가 아니었다."

또 그의 '聖灰水曜日'(1930) 以後의 後期作은 懷古的이고 逃避的인 카톨리씨즘의 냄새를 풍기는 作品으로, 現代의 勞動問題와 國際紛爭에는 何等 도움이 되지 않는다고 非難할 수도 있으리라. 그럼에도 不拘하고 現代 詩人들이 擧皆가 時代의 思潮를 反影하는 가장 根本的인 特殊性이 있다. 이는 곧 그들의 詩言語에 나타나는 科學性과 理知性이다.

科學은 結局 對象의 多樣性을 同一性으로 歸納하는 抽象의 學問이라고 볼 수 있다. 一般 藝術의 分野에 있어서도 이 抽象의 傾向을 또렷이 볼 수 있으니, 例를 들면, 英詩의 言語가 最近으로 내려올수록 抽象化해지는 現象을 본다. 結果는 뻔하다. 抽象名詞가 作品에 많이 나오는 것은 勿論이려니와, 이에 본받아서 具象名詞조차 抽象的인 行動을 取하는 것이 일쑤다. 門外漢으로서 피카소의 手法을 云云함은 輕率한 노릇이 아닐 수 없겠으나, 이 抽象의 傾向은 現代 西歐 藝術의 全面에 걸친 特徵이 아닐까 한다. 現代英詩가 難解하다는 非難도 應當 받을 만큼 現代의 作品은 秘傳的인 純理念의 舞踊과 같은 印象을 준다. 詩人 예이츠(1865–1939)는 말하였다.

"우리는 抽象의 心紋과 歸納的인 概括과 數學의 公式밖에는 모른다. 허기야 新聞의 論說이나 政府의 統計가 가져다 주는 荒廢도 이런 것일 줄 짐작되지만. 그러므로 두 個의 抽象이 같이 食卓에 앉아 점심을 먹을는지도 모를 노릇이다. 그러나 우리가 自然이라고 일컫는 이미저리, 卽 感覺의 世界는 어떠하냐? 우리는 同時에 깨어 있고, 자고 있는지도 모를 노릇일레라."(옥스포드 版, <現代英詩選集>(1936), 序文)

예이츠의 말이 半은 首肯이고 半은 反抗이라 하겠지만, 예이츠인들 이 時代의 思潮에 따르는 수밖에 없다는 것은 그의 後期作品의 創作態度가 充分히 證明하는 바이다. 또 젊은 詩人 오든은 예이츠보다 한 걸음 더 나아가서 詩를 '知識의 遊戲'라고 規定한다. 藝術에 遊戲心理가 內在함은 古來의 本質이라 하겠으나, 왜 現代詩가 구태여 '知識'의 遊戲가 되지 않고는 못 배길까? 그만큼 現代詩에는 腦髓作用이 不可缺한 要素가 되어 버렸다. 腦髓作用도 官能의 世界에 못지 않은 感覺이 되고 經驗의 媒介가 될 수 있다는 것은 現代詩─아니

現代藝術 全體一가 充分히 證明하는 바이다. 知性이니 感性이니 하고 分類하는 方法은 이미 낡았다. 經驗體로서의 人間은 이미 音樂의 樂譜와같은 組織機關이 되고 말았다. 散文에 있어서 '意識의 흐름'의 手法과, 韻文에 있어서 抽象의 隱喩法과는 結局 同一한 創作精神의 各各 다른 發露라고 볼 수 있는 것이다.

中世時代의 三學이 文法學, 修辭學, 論理學이었다면, 現代文學人의 三學은 經濟學, 心理學, 그리고 社會學일 것이다. 現代作家로서 이 三學이 가져다 주는 社會意識과 自我意識과 歷史意識의 三者를 等閑視할 수는 없다. 勿論 全體의 公分母는 科學이라는 主知主義의 批判精神이겠다.

그러나 여기서 말하는 歷史意識이란 王朝의 興亡盛衰라든가, 權勢를 휘두르던 偉人의 立身揚名을 가리킴이 아니라, 人類學, 比較民俗學 또는 比較宗敎學 等의 硏究에서 오는 人類 文化의 밑받이에 對한 意識을 말하는 것이다. 現代英文學에 가장 큰 影響을 준 斯界의 著者로 제임스 프레이저 卿(1854-1941)을 들 수 있다. 民俗, 神話, 禮式 等의 原始信仰에 對한 그의 論攷를 例擧할 必要는 없지만, 年代上으로 現代英文學과 聯關하여보면 興味를 끄는 바가 없지 않다. 그의 傑作 <金枝>는 1890年에 처음 出版되었으나, 1900年에 改正되었고, 1915年에 全 12券으로 增補되었으며, 1936年에 追加篇이 나왔다. 그밖에 <野蠻人의 慣習과 信仰과 言語> (1907), <토테미즘과 異族結婚>(1910), <死者의 崇尙과 永生信仰> (三券, 1913, 1922, 1924), <舊約의 民俗>(1918), <人間과 神과 永生>(1927), <불의 根源에 對한 神話>(1930), <原始宗敎에 있어서의 死者에 對한 恐怖>(三券, 1933, 1934, 1936), <原始時代의 宇宙開闢進化論>(1935) 等이 있다. 프레이저 以外에도 제씨 웨스튼(1928年死)과 같은 女流 民俗學者가 中世時代의 로맨스와 原始的 民俗과의 關係를 밝혀서 <荒蕪地>의 構想에 크나큰 影響을 주었다는 것은 엘리어트 自身이 告白하는 바이다.

"歷史意識은 過去의 過去性 뿐만 아니라 過去의 現在性까지 알아야 할 것을 內包한다"고 主張한 엘리어트는 非但, "호머 以來의 歐羅巴文學 全部와 그 支流의 하나인 自國文學이 同時的 存在와 同時的 秩序를 構成한다"는 精神 밑에서 創作할 뿐만 아니라, 究竟은 人間性 自體에 對한 歷史意識을 뼈 속에 지니고 글을 쓴다. 그렇기 때문에 그의 이른바 信仰詩라는 것도 單純히 어떤 制度化한 敎理를 追慕하고 祈願하는 在來式의 信仰詩가 아니다. 그보다 좀 더 깊은 씸볼리즘이 숨어 있는 것이다.

性質은 若干 다르나 씸볼리즘의 面에 있어서는 마찬가지라고 할 수 있는 것이 예이츠의

神話的 씸볼리즘이다. 위에서 引用한 예이츠의 말로도 明白하지만, 그는 終始 科學의 抽象性에 滿足을 느끼지 못하였기 때문에 神話의 世界에서 이를 補充하려 했던 것이다. 얼핏 생각하면, 이것이 一種의 逃避인 것도 같으나, 其實 예이츠는 後期로 내려올수록 單純한 '魔術'의 世界나 잠꼬대의 超自然主義로만 創作生活을 하려 하지는 않았던 것이다. 그가 抗拒한 것은 分析科學의 氾濫이었고, 人生 自體의 逃避는 아니었다. 抽象的이고 흔히 無價値한 科學體系에 對하여 그는 具象的인 象徵의 世界를 代置하려 辛苦하였던 것이다. 적어도 한 作家의 創作精神에 '쎈시빌리티'의 統一이 뚜렷이 나타난다면 우리는 섯불리 탓할 수 없으리라. 評論家 리처즈는 科學의 價値觀과 感性의 價値觀을 混同하지 않도록 警告한 바 있다. 卽, 과학의 命題가 한 '스테이트먼트'라 할진대, 藝術의 命題는 한 '쓔도스테이트먼트'라고 論攷한다 (<科學과 詩> (1926)). 詩人 예이츠는 차라리 兩者를 '神話'라는 綜合體系에다 結合시키려는 것이다. 특히 그의 後期作의 '神話'는 知性과 感性이 完全히 渾和하였다는 點에 있어서 그의 詩가 현대적이고 (初期作에 비하여) 恒久性을 띠는 것이다.

> "나는 天稟이 무척 宗敎的인 사람이다. 헉슬리[譯註: T. H. 헉슬리; 올더스 헉슬리가 아님]와 틴덜로 因하여 내가 幼年時代의 純直한 宗敎를 빼앗기게 됨으로부터… 나는 새로운 宗敎와 가위 絕對不可誤한 詩傳統의 敎會를 마련하였다. 哲人과 神學者의 도움을 若干 얻어서 詩人과 畵家들이 代代로 물려준 옛 이야기 보따리와 옛 사람들과 옛 情緖를 처음 表現된 그대로 고스란히 옮겨 놓은 새 信仰을 創造하였노라."

예이츠는 1925年에 發表한 散文 著述 <幻想>에서 이처럼 告白하였다. 同著에서 그는 또 말하였다.

> "나의 想像機能으로 하여금 自由롭게 創造하고, 創造한 것과, 또는 創造할 수 있는 모든 것이 唯一한 歷史의 一部分, 卽 人間魂의 一部分이 될 수 있도록 容許하는 思想의 體系를 나는 希求하여 마지않았다."

예이츠가 世紀末의 創作 零圍氣, 특히 佛蘭西의 象徵派 詩論에서 出發한 것은 事實이지만, 그가 좁은 象徵主義에 滿足하지 않고 더 큰 '思想의 體系'인 神話의 世界를 追求하였다는 것은 그의 歷史意識의 正當한 發露라 하겠고, 아울러 그의 後期作이 現代人의 苦惱을

代辯하는 所以라 하겠다.

IV

그러나 現代는 이미 進化向上의 時代와 知性의 時代를 지나서 戰爭의 時代로 들어갔다. 아무리 물샐틈없는 完璧을 期한 價値觀이라 할지라도 戰爭이라는 妖魔의 饗宴에 부딪치면 다 水泡로 돌아가고 만다. 아무리 '호모 싸피엔스'의 抱負와 任務를 積極的으로 내세운들, 또는 消極的으로 印度哲學의 三昧境에서 現實을 黙視한들, 또는 예이츠와 같이 象牙塔 속에서 神話를 構想하며 비잔티움의 文明을 그리워한들, 또는 엘리어트와 더불어 카톨리씨즘의 世界에 들어가서 단테의 煉獄을 내것으로 삼은들, 都是에 安息이라는 福은 누릴 수 없는 것이 현대인의 運命이다. 結局 흄의 洞察이 옳았었다. 그이 亦是 '戰死'라는 環境의 아이로니를 免치 못한 것을 回顧할 때, 그의 말이 유달리 深刻하게 들리는 것은 아닐까?

"사람이란 高度로 組織된 케이오스에 不過하고, 어느 刹那에나 다시 케이오스로 돌아갈 天性을 가졌다."

또는,

"哲學體系와 倫理體系는 우리가 安樂椅子에 앉은 瞬間에만 可能하고, 더러운 어린 아이를 안고 滿員된 뻐스를 탈 때는 벌써 無意味함을 알 수 있다."

그는 遺稿集 <摸索>(1924)에서 그렇게 말하였다. 現代人의 精神分裂症은 動機가 그렇게 單純치 않다. 이것이 知的인 原因에서 오는 수도 있을 것이다. 知識이 分業化하고 專門化하면 知識의 發達도 외줄기로 發達하므로 結果的으로 보면 人間精神이 一元的이 아니고 多元的인 世界에 살게 된다. 또는 이 分裂이 神學的인 動機에서 오는 수도 있으니, 善惡觀이 뒤집히는 데 起因하는 面도 있다. 끝으로 또 이것이 政治的 理念의 相馳에서 오는 수도 있으니, 對立하는 社會的 乃至 經濟的 秩序의 暗鬪로 因하여 分裂이 생기는 수도 있다. 그러나 戰爭은 이 모든 것의 都合보다 훨씬 더 큰 힘을 가진 精神的 危機를 提示하는 것이다. 어느모로 보면 現代文學은 다 戰爭文學의 類型에 屬한다고 하리만큼 戰爭과 平和는 현대인의 咀呪이고 다모클레스의 칼인 것이다. 宗敎改革의 뒤를 이어서 現代精神이 確立된 代價로 西歐는 150年 동안 피비린내 나는 戰爭에 突入하였다 하지만, 今世紀의 兩次大戰은 이의 比類가 아니다. 더더구나 무엇을 報償으로 싸우는지 目標부터가 虛無孟浪하다. 一次大戰 때에는 '戰爭을 없애기 爲한 戰爭'이라는 大義名分이나마 내걸 수 있었지만, 二次大戰 때에는 當時의 英國 外相 헬리팩쓰 卿이 國會에서 質疑答辯으로 '戰爭을 이기기 爲한 戰爭'이라고 우물쭈물 詭辯을 吐하는 수밖에 없었다.

實로 文學上으로 볼 때에는 詩人 윌프리드 오웬 (1890–1918)이 手帖에 적어 두어 後日 自己의 詩集의 序文으로 하려고 헛되이 計劃하였던 斷章이 現代의 戰爭을 要約한 絶叫가 아닐 수 없다.

"이 冊은 英雄에 關한 것이 아니다. 英詩는 아직 英雄을 論하기에 適當치 않다. 이 冊은 또 行動이나 祖國이나 榮譽, 榮光, 힘, 威力, 權勢 같은 것으로 이야기하는 것도 아니고, 다만 戰爭을 取材한 것뿐이다. 나의 主題는 戰爭이며 戰爭의 凄慘이다. 詩는 凄慘에 있다. 그러나 이 輓歌는 아무런 意味로나 이 世代에 慰安이 되는 것이 아니다. 或 다음 世代에 慰安이 될는지는 모른다. 오늘날 詩人이 할 수 있는 것은 警告밖에 없다. 그러므로 참다운 詩人은 眞實해야 한다."

오직 詩뿐이랴? 文學은 '凄慘'(pity)에 있고 오늘날 文人은 '警告'밖에 할 수 없는 노릇이다. 그러면 이 '凄慘'을 어떻게 '警告'하느냐가 問題다.

짧은 一生을 被害妄想症으로 쫓겨 다니다가 結局 바다에 빠져 自殺한 美國 詩人 하아트 크레인(1899–1932)은 그의 遺稿에서 아래와 같이 말한 一節이 있다.

"이리하여 나는 헬렌이 電車에 탄 것을 보았노라. 디오니소스 酒神에 바치는 그의 宮廷의 饗宴과 그 淫姦은 째즈 樂園이 장단 쳐 주는 메트로폴리탄 屋上 庭園으로 자리를 바꾸었으며, 트로이 陷落의 카타르시스는 恰似 最近 大戰에 본 듯 싶었다....

"오늘날 詩人이 當面한 問題는 참 어려운 것이다. 頹廢한 文化에서 人間 價値觀의 再調整을 向하여 世界는 激動하고 있으므로, 무슨 確固不動한, 또는 精神的인 波紋이나 信念을 일으킬 만한, 共通된 術語와 言語의 公分母가 거의 없어졌다. (敎會를 包含한) 過去의 거룩한 神話는 正面이 무너져 버려서 그럴듯한 揶揄조차 할 必要가 없어졌다. 그러나 그 傳統의 大部分은 아직도 살아 있다. 關聯性이 있든 없든 數많은 細目이 偶然的으로 結合하는 心理的 關係, 比喩, 戒律 等等에서 이를 볼 수 있다. 이것은 擧皆가 우리의 共通된 經驗의 一部分이요, 우리의 經驗이 自己規定을 할 때, 또는 自己擴張을 할 때, 쓰여지는 經驗 自體의 用語이다.

"그러므로 過去나 傳統과의 因緣을 斷絶하려는 意識的인 計劃은 感傷的 誤算인 듯 싶다.... 詩人은 冊이라든가, 其他 自己 身邊에 있는 모든 實在的 資源을 마음껏 活用할 權利를 가졌다. 다만 그는 自己의 感性과 經驗의 試金石을 鞭撻하여 옳은 命題와 細目을 取捨選擇하도록 할 따름이다. 그가 成功하느냐 또는 쓸데없는 考古學으로 低落하느냐는 여기에 매었다....

"나는 '모더니티'라는 單純한 標榜에 別다른 價値를 두지 않는다. 運命이 自己에게 强要하는 情熱과 經驗과 反省의 實狀에 속임없이 反應하고 感性이 可能한 最大限度로만 反應함으로써 詩人은 偶然的으로 自己時代를 充分히 規定 지을 수 있을 것이다....

"그러나 單純히 摩天樓나 라디오의 안테나나 汽笛이나 其他 우리 時代의 皮相的 現象만을 자주 이야기함으로써 時代의 定義가 내려진다고 어리석게도 自己欺瞞하는 것은 寫眞을 그리는 것과 다름없다. 우리 經驗의 根本 要素인 이러한 事物과 그밖의 要素가 우리에게 던져주는 有機的 效能에 우리가 屈服하고 이를 檢討하며 吸收하는 條件 밑에서만 於是乎 興味있는 것과 意味深長한 것이 나타나리라고 나는 생각한다."

引用이 길어진 듯하나 現代 作家의 戰爭에 對한 態度는 이 一節에 充分히 反映된 것으로 생각된다. 反戰思想이니 厭世哲學이니 하는 말은 너무 皮相的이고 公式的인 觀察이 아닐까 한다. 무어니 무어니 해도, 현대의 戰爭文學은 어떤 口號나 슬로간을 내거는 文學이 아니다. 兩次大戰의 生地獄을 겪어 나오는 人間性의 苦悶相을 그릴 따름이다. 淨化되어 煉獄에서 生을 누릴 수 있다면 千萬多幸이고, 天國은 애당초부터 바라지도 않은 것이라고 現代人은 생각한다.

戰爭 自體를 믿는 것은 戰爭犯罪者의 所任이고 文人이 할 일은 아니다. 英國의 哲人 제럴드 허버드(1889-?)의 말마따나 現代는 '機械中毒的 宇宙論'에 支配되는 時代로서 宇宙가 盲目的으로 돌아가다가 窮局에는 自律的으로 沈滯하여 滅亡하는 한 機械에 不過하다는 抽象도 一理가 있는 見解라 할 수 있다. 또는 小說家 헉슬리처럼 戰爭의

原因을 糾明하여,

1. 日常生活의 倦怠가 戰爭으로 말미암아 一掃됨으로 뭇 사람이 戰爭을 좋아한다. (戰時의 自殺率은 平時의 三分之二에 不過하다.) 뿐만 아니라, 戰時에는 生活이 簡素化해지고, 意味를 띠게 되고, 生活의 活潑로 因하여 生活이 潤澤해지고, 性生活의 制約이 많이 없어지고, 또 日常 新聞에 煽情的인 報道가 많아지므로 戰爭을 좋아한다.
2. 敵에 對한 憎惡心이 强해짐에 따라 自己自身에 對한 傲慢心이 커지므로 感情的 滿足을 느낄 수 있다. 擬人化한 國家 民族이 超人間的인 神聖不可侵性을 띠게 된다.
3. 軍備 自體가 必然的으로 恐怖心을 일으키므로 이 恐怖心을 除去하기 爲해서라도 더 새로운 武器를 마련해야 하고, 가장 有利하다고 생각되는 어떤 瞬間에 반드시 戰爭이 터지고야 만다.
4. 戰爭에는 이것을 保長할 만한 이데올로기가 반드시 있어야 하고, 이 理念이 한 通俗的인 宗敎의 代用物이 되므로, 大衆은 好戰的이다.
5. 勝利에 따르는 榮譽가 있기 때문에 戰爭은 魅力이있다.
6. 領土慾이 同伴하기 때문에 戰爭이 좋다.
7. 外國市場을 確保하는 方便이 되기 때문에 戰爭이좋다.
8. 武器製作者에게 絶好의 機會가 되기 때문이다.

等 等이라고 말할 수도 있다. 그러나 이러한 冷血的인 分析보다도 戰爭이 現代文學에 던져 주는 課題는 좀 더 深刻한 데 있다.

　現代文學은 人間精神의 失神 狀態를 그리는 文學이라고 흔히들 말한다. 그러나 '失神'은 '求神'을 前提하기 때문에 價値있는 것이다. 西歐 文明의 地盤은 有神論에 있고 無神論에 있지 않다. 앞으로 이 本質이 어떻게 變遷할지 우리가 알 바 아니로되, 現代의 科學 戰爭이 그 本質을 뒤흔들고 있음에는 틀림이 없다. '누우메논'의 世界를 渴望하는 西洋文明이 科學의 溫床인 '페노메논'의 世界와 그의 必然的 所産인 自然主義의 倫理觀을 虎視眈眈하는 것은 當然한 노릇이다. 今世紀의 思潮에서 이를 가장 端的으로 代表하는 것이 이른바 어빙 배비트(1865-1933)를 核心으로 한 '휴머니즘'이다. 비록 배비트는 美國의 學者라 할지라도 그의 論旨는 엘리어트 같은 文人에 끼친 影響이 컸으므로, 이에 略述하겠다.

　自然科學과 社會科學의 標石이 되는 베이컨과 루쏘의 基本 理念을 배비트는

〈民主主義와 指導精神〉(1924)에서 아래와 같이 批判한다.

> "過去의 모든 警告를 無視하고 또 다시 한번 自然主義의 허구렁에 빠지게 된 우리는 第一原則부터 그릇된 世界에 살고 있다는 結論을 내리지 않을 수 없게 되었다. 우리가 威脅을 느끼는 이 文明의 破綻은 希臘, 羅馬 時代의 末期에도 비길 수 있는 것이다. 指導者들은... 이미 自然主義에 屈服하여 道德의 原則까지 干涉하게 되었다.... 道德의 原則을 干涉한다는것은 究竟 人間의 內制力까지 꺾어 버리는 結果를 招來하는것이다.... 베이컨式 自然主義가 過去를 否認하는 所以는 더 한層 積極的의인 批判의 立場에서 自己를 事實의 世界에다 確立시키려는 뜻에서 나온 것이다. 그러나 사람의 內制力이란 우리가 考慮에 넣어야 할 가장 重要한 '事實'의 하나이다. 루쏘式 自然主義가 傳統의 束縛을 떨쳐 버린 것도 自己의 '이매지네이션'을 強化하려는 意圖에서 나온 것이다. 그러나 內制力이 없는 限, 사람의 '이매지네이션'도 單純한 '애너키'로 歸元한다. 베이컨主義者나 루쏘主義者는 어느 外在的인 힘이 自己自身과 自己의 知覺機能 사이에 介在하는 것을 싫어했다. 그러나 이 內制力은 決코 抽象的이거나 外在的인 것이 아니라 內在的인 것이다."

善과 惡의 葛藤이 社會制度에 있지 않고 個個人의 가슴 속에 있으므로, 善惡의 責任을 環境에 묻지 말고 倫理 判斷의 基準을 個人에 두지 않으면 안 된다는 思潮는 結局 在來의 基督敎의 唯一神論에 論據하는 思潮이다.

배비트가 하버드大學 時節의 恩師였고, 그의 主張이 現代 思潮에 對한 迫力있는 反抗이었던 것을 엘리어트는 公認하지만, 後者는 한 걸음 더 나아가 배비트의 論理의 飛躍과 危險性을 指摘 아니 할 수 없을 만큼 求神의 態度에 徹底한 摸索人이다. 哲學家 브래들리를 論하는 글(1926)에서 엘리어트는 말했다.

> "道德과 宗敎가 같은 것은 아니다. 그러나 어느 限界를 넘으면 兩者를 別個視하여 다룰 수는 없는 것이다. 徹底한 倫理體系는 表面的으로나 內面的으로나 神學 體系가 되는 것이며, 따라서 宗敎 없이 完全한 倫理의 理論을 세우려 하더라도, 그는 亦是 宗敎에 對한 어떤 獨特한 態勢를 取하는 것을 意味한다."

그는 또 휴머니즘의 弱點을 들어 그의 배비트論(1927)에서 다음과 같이 論하였다.

"(이 自制의 理論)은 政治的 및 宗敎的 無秩序에 對한 打開策은 된다. 政治的인 면에 있어서는 이를 承認하기가 쉽다.... 그러나 正統 宗敎의 '外部的' 制約이 軟弱해짐에 따라 個人이 自己 自身에게 주는 '內部的' 制約으로 이를 代用할 수도 있는 것이라고 배비트氏는 생각하는 모양이다. 나의 解釋이 옳을진대 그는 프로테스탄트의 널판을 가지고 카톨릭의 演壇을 만들려고 꾀하는 것 같다. 本是가 個人主義者이고 個人主義 思想의 自主性을 固守하려는 그는, 國家나 民族, 또는 世界 全體에 適用할 수 있는 무엇을 마련하려 애쓰는 것이다."

自然科學에서는 理想主義者가 되고, 道德에서는 現實主義者가 된 現代의 知性에 叛旗를 들고 나서는 點에 있어서는, 배비트나 아놀드나 엘리어트나 다 외로운 同志들이다. 그러나 求神의 努力이 없는 倫理觀이 배비트의 휴머니즘이라면, 敎理의 訓練이 없는 基督敎의 感情만을 讚美하는 것이 아놀드의 宗敎觀이다. 엘리어트는 이에 反하여, "基督敎에 關한 큰 過誤는 그것이 무엇보다도 敎理와 理智의 問題인 것을 宗敎와 感情의 問題로 삼는 데 있다"고 그의 散文 著書<基督敎 社會의 理念>(1939)에서 主張하여 範疇의 混同을 警戒함으로써 求神의 思想體系를 摸索하여 온 것이다.

이 摸索이 創作詩에 如實히 나타남으로써 그의 後期作은 새로운 價値를 띠는 同時에 現代人의 煩惱相을 代辯하는 作業인 것이다. 그의 神秘主義的 信仰詩가 第二의 中世紀 時代를 알리는 指針이라 斷定하는 評論家도 없지 않다. 中世時代라고 반드시 暗黑時代는 아니다. 엘리어트 곧 <荒蕪地>라는 通念은 이미 二十五六年前의 이야기다. 事實上 <荒蕪地>보다는 그의 1930年代 以後의 作業에 훨씬 더 큰 安息이 있고 光明이 있는 것이다. 信仰이 表面化하지 않는 <荒蕪地>야말로 暗黑時代에 마땅한 絶望의 아우성이다.

이것 또한 새로운 浪漫의 싹이 트는 徵兆가 아닐까? 적어도 第二次大戰 直前부터 登場하기 始作한 英詩人들—특히 '新黙示派'를 代表하는 헨리 트리이쓰(1912-1966), 제이 에프 헨드리(1912-?) 같은 作家들—은 1930年代에 登場한 오든 一派의 大學靑年式 社會主義의 諷刺的 傾向을 떠나서 새로운 浪漫의 着想과 懷古的인 音樂의 詩言語를 發見하고 있는 過程에 있다. 트리이쓰가 1946年에 詩全集을 냈을 때 한 말이 興味있다.

"(一部 評論家들은) 내가 飛行機나 爆彈에 關하여 詩를 써야 될 것이라고 느꼈었다. [譯註: 그는 大戰中 空軍에 服務하였음.] 6年 동안이나 戰爭에 시달려 보면 그렇게 되지도 않는다. 하루에 23時間동안 戰爭을 먹고 마시고 자고 하면, 나머지 짧은 餘暇에는 戰爭을 잊어버리고 쓰고 싶은 詩를 쓰도록 容認해야 할 것 아닌가?"

또 오든, 스펜더 一派와 때를 거의 前後하여 出現한 딜런 토머스(1914-1953)도 分明히 新浪漫의 思潮에 젖은 新進 作家이다. 系譜上으로 본다면 토머스의 創作精神은 예이츠, 씨트웰 女史, 월터 델 라 메어 等의 直系라고 할 수 있다. 또 "萬里長城과 내 가슴 사이에 亡命이 있어"라고 노래하는 조지 바커(1913-)도 近年에 보기 드문 純叙情詩人이다. 바커 亦是 1935年頃부터 이미 알려진 詩人이지만, 그는 오든, 스펜더, 루이스의 政治性과 豫言的 雄辯體를 取하지 않고, 무너져 가는 文明 自體와 自己 自身을 渾和시켰기 때문에 作品도 따라서 敎訓的이 아니고 劇的이며, 雄辯的이 아니고 抒詩的이며, 革命的이 아니고 悲劇的이었던 것이다.

佛蘭西의 評論家 쥴리앙 벙다(1867-)는 그의 名著 <識者의 叛逆>(1927)에서 아래와 같이 현대 知識人의 政治熱을 分析하였다.

"오늘날 政治熱은 다른 熱情에 比하여 現今 以前에는 볼 수 없던 程度의 普遍性과 論理性과 均一性과 的確性과 聯關性과 壓倒性을 띠고 있으며, 過去에 볼 수 없던 自我意識性을 갖추게 되었다. 個中에는 在來에 公認되지 못하던 것도 이제 와서는 意識에 오르게 되어, 떳떳하게 人間의 本質的 情熱과 合勢하게 되었다. 또 個中에는 過去 어느 때보다도 더 純粹한 情熱로 化하여, 于今 차지하지 못하던 道德面에 있어서 人間의 理性을 支配하게 되었으며, 數百年來로 자취를 감추었던 神秘主義的 性格을 띠게 되었다. 모든 政治熱은 이데올로기의 體系로 밑받이되어, 科學이라는 名目下에 그네들의 行動의 絶對的 價値와 歷史의 必然性을 宣布할 理念의 根據를 마련한다. 表面에 있어서나, 內面에 있어서나, 空間的 價値에 있어서나, 奧義的 迫力에 있어서나, 오늘날의 政治熱은 于今 歷史에 보지 못하던 完璧의 段階에 이르게 되었다. 現代는 根本的으로 政治의 時代다."

벙다의 攻擊 對象이 共産主義 뿐만이 아니라 파씨즘, 帝國主義, 民族主義까지도 包含한 모든 政治熱임에는 틀림 없다. 그러나 그의 著述이 知識人에 對한 攻駁이므로 우리는 우선 共産主義를 생각하게 된다.

　現代 英文學에 나타나는 左翼 思想은 일찍이 쇼오가 페이비안 協會의 創立(1884)에 因緣을 맺은 以後부터 꾸준히 내려 온 것이라고 하겠으나, 政治가 一般 文人의 焦燥한 關心에 오르게 된 것은 一次大戰을 겪고 난 얼마 뒤의 現象이다. 1930年代에 登場한 젊은 詩人들이 옥스퍼드 大學을 中心으로 하여 政治意識을 새로운 詩言語의 이디엄으로 삼은 까닭은 어디 있었을까?

　젊은 오든 世代는 이디스 씨트웰(1887-1964) 女史나 또는 로라 라이딩(1901-) 女史의 瑤池鏡式 詩言語에다가 政治 演壇의 雄辯體를 加味하여 엘리어트나 예이츠의 壯重한 求心的 創作精神을 揶揄하는 듯이 일부러 遠心的인 익살로 現代文明의 晩鐘을 울렸다. "革命思潮는 上流階級의 思想이며 지나친 詩의 洗鍊에 對한 反撥이다"라고 라이딩 女史와 로버트 그레이브스(1895-)는 그들의 共著 <現代詩 槪說>(1927)에서 말했거니와, 事實에 있어서 그들의 맑씨즘은 새로운 이미지와 術語를 提供하는 한 技巧의 方便에 不過하였던 것이다. 그들의 맑씨즘은 이제 와서는 녹슬은 戰利品으로 書齋에 陳列할 지난 날의 遺物이다. 設或 그들이 맑씨즘에 立脚하여 現代文明의 崩壞를 豫言하고 諷刺한다 치더라도, 文人이 豫言者然하는 習性은 너무나 十九世紀的인 態度이기 때문에 現代人은 이에 귀를 기우리지 않는다. 또 諷刺文學도 未來의 어떤 理想國을 假想하여 現在를 諷刺함은 諷刺文學의 本質에 어긋나는 것이다. 왜냐하면 諷刺文學은 確固한 傳統과 널리 普遍化한 價値觀이 試金石이 되어서야 비로소 可能한 文學의 類型이기 때문이다. 蜃氣樓가 價値判斷의 尺度가 되기는 어려운 노릇이다. 其實 쎄실 데이 루이스(1904-1972)도 이 點을 밝혀서 그의 現代詩論 <詩에 對한 希望>(1934)에서 아래와 같이 말하였다.

　　"그러나 한 刺戟物로서 共産主義를 利用하고 (中産文化에 對한) 不快感을 鎭定시키기 爲한 一種의 方便으로 생각하고 그것을 한 私的 信仰으로 理解하는 限, 그 生命은 짧을 것이고, 皮相的일 수밖에 없다. 精神的 苦痛이 없어지고 살아 生前에 누릴 個人의 平和만을 希求하는 文人에 對하여는 共産主義의 要求條件이 너무나 命令的인 것이며 너무나 變通性이 없는 것이다."

예이츠 自身도 그의 現代英詩 選集의 序文에서, 젊은 詩人들이 共産主義者라고 自稱하지만, "나는 그들의 作品에서 公認된 共産主義 哲學을 發見할 수 없으며, 實踐共産主義者는 그들을 拒否한다"고 論斷하였다.

智慧의 女神 미네르바의 올빼미가 黃昏에 그 날개를 편다는 警句는 哲人 헤겔의 말이었던가? 西歐文明에 黃昏이 왔다고 速斷하는 것은 아니로되, 미네르바의 올빼미가 到處에 날개를 펴고 있는 것은 英文學에서도 足히 볼 수 있는 事實이다. 이런 現段階에서 文人들은 어떤 創作態度를 取하고 있는가? 제각기 다르겠지만, 여기 詩人 오든의 感銘 깊은 말을 引用함으로써 이 拙稿를 끝맺고자 한다.

"쌀롱과 카페의 時節도 이미 지난 날 이야기이며, 熱狂的인 反動者가 卓越한 派黨을 지었던 것도 이미 옛 일이다. 文學運動도, 聲明書도, 다 쓸데없는 노릇이다. 各其 詩人은 孤立한 것이다. 그렇다고 해서 그가 홀로 한 구석에서 神秘롭게 짜증을 낸다는 것은 아니다. 오히려 그는 以前보다 더욱 社會的인 生活을 할는지도 모른다. 그러나 그 社會的인 生活은 詩人으로서가 아니라 뭇 이웃 사람의 一員으로서 하는 것일게다. 自己의 才技에 關한 限, 그는 홀로 守直하며 아무와도 合勢하지 않는다. 當代의 同僚 詩人들과 合勢하는 일은 더더구나 생각할 수 없다." (<四角形과 楕圓形>)

아이로니와 W. H. 오든*

'無名의 市民 J. S. O3. M. 378의 英靈을 爲하여 祖國은 삼가 이 大理石의 紀念塔을 세우노라'라는 作品에서 詩人 오든은 아래와 같은 追悼詩를 現代人에게 바쳤다.

"統計局의 調査에 依하면 그의 身分은 公民으로서 何等의 汚點이 없었던 것이 分明하고 그의 品行에 關한 모든 調會는 비록 表現은 낡었을 망정, 現代的으로 解釋해서 그가 聖人이였다는데 모두가 意見이 一致한다. 그는 오로지 弘益社會에 一生을 바쳐 餘念이 없었기때문이다. 戰爭期間을 빼놓고 그는 隱退할 때 까지 職場을 工場에 두어 한번도 罷免된 일이 없었고, 雇傭主인 「파지」發動機 有限會社에 좋은 成績을 남기였다. 그렇다고 同僚에 背信하거나 變態的인 見解로써 망나니 노릇도 한 일이 없었던 것은 그의 勞組가 報告한 바와 같이 (勞組의 報告는 信憑할만 하다) 組合費를 忠實히 냈다는 事實과 社會心理學 調査部員들의 審査 結果 그가 同僚間에 評이 좋았고 술도 한잔 씩은 하였다는 事實로써 足히 알 수 있는 것이다. 그가 每日 新聞도 熱心히 사 봤으며 廣告에 對한 反應도 남과 조금도 다름이 없었으리라고 言論界에서는 確信하는바 있다. 그의 名義로 加入된 保險證券을 보면 保險에도 빈틈이 없었고, 保健證을 보면 그가 한번 入院하였다가 完治되어 退院하였던 事實이 分明하다. 그가 또 月賦制度의 長點을 잘 理解하여 現代人의 生活必需品인 錄音器와 라디오와 自動車와 冷藏庫를 가졌었다는 것은 生産業者의 調査部 뿐만이 아니라 生活改善會에서도 確證하는 바이다. 興論調査部員들도 滿足을 느낀 것은 그가 그때 그때에 옳은 意見을 主張하였다는데 있으니, 平和時에는 平和를 부르짖었고 戰爭詩에는 出征하였던 것이다. 結婚하여 그는 人口에 다섯의 子孫을 보태주었으니 優生學者의 言明에 依하면 이것은 그 世代의 어버이로서 가장 알맞은 數爻라고 한다. 한편 子女의 敎育方針에 關하여 그는 何等의 是是非非를 論한 일이 없었다고 敎員들은 報告한다. 그가 果然 自由로웠드냐? 幸福하였드냐?는 問題는 都是에 語不成說인 것이, 萬若에 무슨 그릇됨이 있었던들 우리는 必然코 이것을 報告로 들었을 것이기 때문이다."

散文으로 飜譯해 놓으면 原文의 칼날같은 辛辣味가 많이 없어지지만, 作家가 노리는

---

* 이 글은 <詩文學> 二輯 (趙芝薰 編輯, 1950), 20–34페이지에 실렸다.

現代의 社會相은 대개 짐작된다. 어느 모로 보나 現代는 '아이로니'의 時代임에 틀림없다. 이른바 文明은 計劃社會로 나아가므로 現代人은 公民證을 부적처럼 품에 지녀야 하고, 統計局을 비롯한 뭇 調査機關은 그의 身元을 報告할 法的 權利를 갖게 되며, '게페우'나 '게스타포'나 '씨아이디'는 民衆의 지팽이가 되는 것이다.

그러나 '아이로니'가 眞摯한 詩人의 取할 態度인가 아닌가는 서뿔리 斷定 못할 問題인상 싶다. 이에 關聯하여 '젊은 詩人에게 보내는 書翰'의 第二信(1903年4月)에서 릴케는 말하되,

"事物의 깊이를 찾으시라. 아이로니가 거기까지 내려가지는 못 합니다. 이리하여 당신이 거룩한 事物의 벼랑끝까지 가까이 오시거든 곧 이 아이로니의 態度가 스스로의 本性에서 必然的으로 우러나는 것인지 살펴보시라. 嚴肅한 事物에 對할제 당신의 態度가 偶然的인 것이라면 아이로니는 사라지고야 말 것이요, 萬若에 참말로 당신의 天性에 內在하는 것이라면 아이로니도 峻嚴한 道具로서 힘을 얻어 당신의 藝術을 가꾸어 낼 온갖 연장 가운데에 떳떳한 자리를 차지할 것이다."

事物의 깊이를 探索하고 生의 낭떨어지를 일삼아 거닐어 좀체로 眩氣症을 느끼지 않는 詩人 오든의 아이로니가 차라리 後者에 屬하는 편이였기 때문에 그의 作品은 過去 二十年 동안의 '時代精神'을 大辯하는 것이 되였다고도 볼 수 있다. 그러나 이것은 좀 더 깊이 생각할 必要가 있는 問題이다.

앞서 엘리어트는 現代人의 苦悶相을 두고 "네가 아는 것 다만 산산이 부셔진 形象의 쪼각 조각"이라고 豫言한바 있었거니와 이 榮譽롭지 못한 豫言의 번거로움과 주체스러움을 記錄해 논 것이 오오든의 詩라 하겠다. 그렇다고 그의 創作精神이 '다다'는 아니다. 幻滅이 밑받이 되는 諷刺도 있고, 文明을 한 '뉴로우씨쓰'로 보아 이를 嘲弄하는 惡魔主義的 偶像破壞도 있으나 '다다'가 내거는 完全한 니힐리즘이라던가 故意이며 組織的인 無倫理와 無秩序, 理性의 破門같은 것은 그가 일삼지 않는다. 演壇의 雄辯體에다 悲劇的인 넌쎈스를 加味하고 秘傳的인 象徵에다가 '캇트·글라스'와 같은 技巧를 보태서 아이로니의 效果를 이루는 것이다. 1930년에 첫 詩集을 내고 爾來 全集을 1945년에 내기까지에 여섯卷의 詩集과 두卷의 紀行文集는(詩를 包含함)과 네篇의 詩劇을 發表하였으며 1946年에는 <不安의 時代>라는 牧歌 形式의 長詩를 냈거니와 그동안에 作者가 希求하는 '救濟'의 世界는 달라졌다고 볼수 있으나, 그의 手法과 말솜씨는 一貫한 것이 있으니 곧

아이로니라는 總稱으로 이를 일컬을 수 있다.

同僚詩人 매크니이쓰는 그의 評著 <現代詩>(1938)에서 오든의 創作世界 乃至 態度가 프로이디어니즘과 맑시즘에서 온 것이라고 밝힌 다음 이를 아래와 같이 分析하였다.

> "이 두가지로 因하여 世界의 모든 細部가 그에게는 뜻 깊어지는 것이다. 心理學者로서의 오오든에게는 거의 무엇이든지 (1) 治療를 要하는 病的狀態('뉴로씨스')의 例示나 象徵이 된다. (2) 또는 '뉴로씨스'가 善을 만들어 내는 過程의 例示나 象徵이 되는 것이다. 모든 進步向上은 病的인 不安定狀態에서 생기는 것이라고 오오든은 믿기 때문이다. 또 한편 맑시스트로서의 오오든에게는 거의 모든 것이 (1) 敵과 反動의 産物로서, 싸우지 않으면 안될 惡이거나 (2) 頹廢한 過去의 遺物로서, 한때는 善이었을는지 모르나 이제 와서는 尊敬과 愛情을 느끼면서도 慨歎해야 할 惡에 不過한 것이며, (3) 또는 앞날을 열어주는 더나은 事態의 前兆가 아니면, 이 세가지 類型中의 한가지를 表識하는 象徵이 되는 것이다."

그럴법도 한 論法이고 見解로서도 그럼직한 것이 없지 아니하다. 그러나 問題는 善과 惡의 限界線이며 '敵'과 '反動'의 規定이며 '앞날'의 '더 나은 事態'가 무엇이냐는 것이다. 모든 外界의 事實體를 象徵으로 보는 것도 首肯할 수 있고, 文明의 進步가 病的인 不安定狀態에서 생긴다는 見解도 트집 잡기 어려운 노릇이겠고, 싸우지 않으면 안 된다는 말도 詩人으로서 當然한 達觀이라 하겠다. 그러나 그 治療方法을 맑시즘에 두었다는 것은 詩人으로서 너무나 질게 서든 焦燥의 心境—그야말로 '뉴로씨스'의 發露—이라 아니할 수 없다. 왜냐 하면 詩人은 世界나 人間性을 뜯어고치는 治療法을 提示하는 일보다도 治療를 要하는 世界나 人間性 自體를 疑視하여 이를 的確하게 反影하는 일이 더 繁迫한 使命이기 때문이다. 詩人이 豫言者의 탈을 섯불리 쓰지 못 한다는 事實은 이미 十九世紀가 證明하였다—그들은 擧皆가 꿀과 젖이 흐르는 福地를 期約하였건만 其實은 그것이 "모퉁이를 돌아서 이내 내닫는다"는 煉獄이였고 決코 '빛나는 地域'이 아니었다. 그랬기에 오오든도 一九三六年의 詩集에 收錄된 作品<抽象風景>에서 아래와 같이 썼을 것이리라.

> 곡식이 골짜기에서 썩는다는 所聞을 들었다
> 거리는 이내 헐벗은 山으로 連함을보았기

모퉁이를 돌아서면 물이 내닫고

섬나라로 뱃길을 뜬 그들은 破船했음을 알기에

우리는 이 굶주리는 都市의 創設者를 祝福하노니

祝福은 우리들의 슬픔의 形象 (第一節 譯)

    네거리에 서서 交通整理를 하는 巡警도 特殊한 訓練이 必要하거늘, 하물며 善과 惡의 交叉點에 자리 잡아 人類의 갈길을 가리키는 사람은 천고에 몇도 없는 聖者의 所任이오, 詩人은 차라리 感性과 表現力이 날카로운 機關으로서, 스스로의 想像과 創造의 機能으로 하여금 언제나 流動性을 띠운 自我의 世界—'經驗體'라 해도 좋고 '個性'의 小宇宙(microcosm)라 해도 좋다. 命名은 어떠 하리?—와 時時刻刻으로 豹變하면서도 언제나 固定性을 띤 外界—'客觀'의 大宇宙(macrocosm)—또는 否定못할 '事實體'라 해도 좋다. 이 兩者의 世界에 다리[橋]를 놓아 中間에 介在하기가 일수인 眞空狀態를 없애므로써 어떤 秩序와 有機性—이른바 '美'—을 띠도록 마련하는 活動이 곧 詩人의 맡은 바가 아닐까 생각한다. 詩人이 줄 메씨지는 作品 自體이고, 其他의 것은 作者 或은 讀者가 任意로 取捨選擇하는 '希望的 觀察'인 듯 하다. '詩的인 素材'라는 꼬리표를 붙은 事實體가 따로 없을 바에 '詩的인 思想'이 있을 턱이 없다. 作品이라는 '씬택시스'—希臘語로 '秩序있는 配置'의 뜻이라 한다—에 모든 것이 完全히 반죽만 되면 그만일 게다. 다만 現代와 같이 外界의 事實體가 너무나 벅차고 機械科學으로 말미암아 生活感情이 가위 눌리듯 痲痺되어 있으면 創作藝術이 希求하는 '融和'도 어려워질 것은 事實이다.

    詩人 오든이 무슨 '이즘'을 내걸든지 相關은 없지만, 要는 그의 맑시즘이 반죽이 덜 되었기 때문에 詩人으로서 未及한 點이 綻露된다. '敵'과 '反動'을 諷刺하되 이를 分明히 糾明치 않기때문에 그의 '맑시즘'은 優柔不斷의 未凝結狀態로 곁돌게 된다. 흐리멍덩한 視野를 具現하려는 藝術家로서의 自己矛盾을 스스로 意識하므로 그는 結局 아이로니의 手法을 擇하는 것이다. 어리벙하게 抽象化된 惡은 說敎壇이나 新聞社說에서는 攻擊할 수 있겠지만, 作品에서는 이것이 가장 的確하게 具象化됨으로써 비로소 攻擊의 對象이 되는 것이다. 詩的인 價値를 노리는 것이 '宣傳詩'의 本質이다. 過去의 諷刺詩는 敎訓的인 目的을 達成하면서도 詩的인 具象化, 客觀化가 方法이 되었기 때문에 作品으로서 빈틈이 없었다. 事實上 社會 諷刺詩가 成立할랴면 十八世紀 初葉과 같이 물 샐 틈없는 倫理觀과 藝術觀이 確立되어, 이것이 곧 個別的으로 具象化된 惡을 치는 標準이 되며 出發點과 歸着點이 됨으로써 비로소 可能한 것이다. 漠然한 未來의 유토피아—맑시즘이 命題삼는

窮局의 世界도 이 範圍를 벗어나지 못 하리라—를 尺度로 하여 現在를 測量하기는 어려운 노릇이라는 文學의 常識을 그의 同僚詩人 데이 루이스는 現代詩 評著 <詩에 對한 希望>(一九三四)에서 指摘하는 바 있다. 유토피아 文學 치고 아이로니의 手法을 빌리지 않은 作品은 거의 없거니와, 오오든의 아이로니도 亦是 自己의 加擔할 隊列이 確實치 않다는 느낌에서 생기는 것으로 볼수 있다. 이런 點으로서도 그가 一九四一年에 發表한 長詩集을 <二重의 人物>이라고 부른 것이 單純한 偶然이 아니었다고 생각된다.

"現代詩人은 前世代의 詩人도 하지 못한 일을 할수 있다. 卽, 가장 嚴肅한 瞬間에 自己自身을 嘲笑하는 일이다!"

로러 라이딩과 로버트 그레이브스 兩詩人이 共著한 <現代詩槪觀>(1927)에서 引用한 말이다. 이 '아이로니'의 態度에는 여러 가지 原因이 있겠으나 特히 留意할 點은 旣往에 詩와 이웃四寸關係를 맺었던 宗敎나 哲學 따위의 精神科學이 現代에 와서는 專門化하고 分業化하는 傾向에 있으므로 詩도 따라서 제 갈 길을 외로히 가게 된다는 것이다. 그러므로 詩의 技巧가 날카로워질 뿐 아니라 內容조차 아슬아슬하게 된다. 十九世紀에 比해 現代詩는 分明히 덥석거리지 않은 편이다. 더구나 詩人은 聽衆을 많이 잃어버렸기 때문에 스스로의 어릿광대 노릇을 하기가 일수다. 또한 浪漫以後의 作家들은 '詩人'이라는 人間에 興味를 느끼는 편이 많았지만, 現代에 와서는 '詩'라는 作品과 '詩人'이라는 作者를 分離해서 前者에 關心을 더 많이 둔다. 事實上 詩人이라는 存在처럼 殺風景한 人間은 드물는지도 모를 노릇이다. 詩人이 風流客 노릇하는 時代는 이미 지났다. 理性이 매섭게도 날카로운 오오든이 이를 모를 리 없다.

그러나 오든으로서 가장 深刻한 '아이로니'는 그가 一九三九年에 美國으로 國籍을 옮겼다는 것과 아울러 그때부터 宗敎問題에 創作의 力量을 기우리게 되였다는 事實에 있다. 일찌기 엘리어트가 英國으로 亡命해 갔던 報復인지는 모르나, 美國은 오든의 歸化를 몹시 반겼던 모양이다. 戰爭中에 엘리어트는 每週 이틀밤씩 事務室 屋上에서 火災監視員으로 밤샘을 하며 <荒蕪地>에서 노래했던 句節—

산 넘어엔 또 무슨 都市가 있길래
보라빛 저녁 하늘에 發砲하고 改革하고 爆發하는게냐
무너지는 塔 들

>   예루살렘 아테네 알렉산드리아
>   비엔나 런던
>   虛無하구나

―을 새삼 回想하는 듯, 또한 다른 角度로 戰爭에서 이미지를 얻어 詩人의 苦衷을 말했다.

>   내 바야흐로 스무 해를 살아와 生의 한복판에 서있나니
>   大部分은 虛送한 스무 해 두 戰爭 사이의 歲月
>   말을 쓰는 공부에 애를 닳우었건만 試驗마다 번번히 全혀 새로운 出發이요 다른 種類의 失敗였거니
>   말에 이기고 보면 이미 말할것이 없어지고
>   스스로 즐겨 말하고 싶어 하는 方法도 아니였기
>   그러므로 冒險마다가 새로운 始作이요
>   흐린 情緖의 흐터진 無秩序와
>   訓練없는 感情의 編隊 속에서
>   언제나 退步一路의 낡은 武裝으로써 表現 못 할 것을 空襲하는 일…
>
>   (<四重曲>의 一節)

블릿츠 戰爭 터에서 멀리 떠나, 오든은 엘리어트와 같은 '悲劇'의 사무침을 일부러 輕快한 '喜劇'의 水準으로 끄어 올려 같은 戰爭을 아이로니의 手法으로 그렸다.

>   政治情勢로 因하여 요즈음
>   지붕없는 집이 꽤 많고
>   醉하지도 않았거니와 잠들지도 않은 사람들이 鄕村에 헤졌고
>   追後 通告 있을 때까지 모든 航海는 取消되고
>   書信에 여러 말 하는것이 賢明치 못하고 普通以下로 줄곧 繼續되는 요새 氣溫에 男女兩性은 이제 强者와 弱者가 되였다 할진데 그것은 이 季節로서는 조금도 非常한 일이 아니며 그것 뿐이라면 우리가 收拾할 길도 있으리라. 水災와 火災, 草原의 旱魃, 王子의 暴壓, 遠洋의 海賊, 肉體의 苦痛과 財政의 悲哀 이런거야 우리가 다 겪어온 災殃으로 골백번 當해 본 찌꺼기이다.…

더구나 이 一節이 <聖誕祭 오라토리오>(1945)의 信仰詩에서 나오는 것이기 때문에 아이로니는 한 層 더 짙어진다.

오든은 그의 詩論 短章 <四角形과 楕圓形>의 卷頭에서 다음의 警句를 引用하여 自己의 立場을 밝혔다.

"우리는 楕圓形을 만들어 四角形 위에다 세웠다. 이것이 우리의 勝利요 우리의 慰安이다." (버지니아 울프)

또

"成熟─어려서 놀 적에 가졌던 進擊을 도로 찾는 것"(니이체)

또

"그는 宗敎家가 되고 싶어 하면서도 詩人으로 남아 있다. 따라서 그는 不幸히도 神을 사랑하는 것이다."(키에르케골)

四角形이라는 確固不動한 事實의 世界에다 楕圓形이란 藝術을 아슬하게 세웠건만, 이것은 어느 刹那에 쓰러질는지 모르는 焦燥의 象徵이요, 따라서 善과 惡의 苦鬪에서 善이 勝利한다고 豪言壯談하는 文明도 제 멋에 겨운 탓이라고 할 수 있겠다.

"요즈음은 新聞의 編輯局長이 신이 날때다. 歷史는 만들어지며 人類는 前進하고 있다. 世界에서 第一 큰 水道가 建設 途中에있고 濕地排水工作兼 土壤保護委員會에는 近々 共同報告書를 提出하게 될 것이며, 貿易景氣의 循環이나 物價高騰의 匪線에 對한 問題도 專門家들은 거의 解決된 것으로 보고 있는 터이다. 最近에 斷行된 外人制限과 自由主義的 猶太人에 關한 法規도 이미 國民士氣에 좋은 影響을 미쳐주는 바 있다. 하기야 西海에는 아직도 海賊이 出沒하고 北方 野蠻人들의 膨脹하는 勢力이 若干 不安感을 던지고 있으나 우리는 이 危險을 모르는바 아니요 迅速히 武裝을 하고 있는 터이라 適當한 時期에는 다 解消될것으로, 오로지 共同利益과 共同權利에 힘을 뭉치면 우리의 偉大한 帝國은 앞으로 千年동안 平和安全을 누릴것이다. 우리가 孤獨을 모르고 언제나 허둥지둥 바쁘게 지난다면 或은 우리가 아는 것이 眞實이라고 믿어질는지도 모른다. 그러나 속는 사람은 아무도 없으니 적어도 밤낮 속지는 않는다. 沐浴湯에서나 地下鐵 車間에서나 또는 아닌 밤중에 우리는 不運이 아니라 惡이라는 것을 빤히 알고 있으며, 우리가 逃避하는 完全國家라던가 無國家狀態라는 것도 우리의 刑罰의 一部分임을 잘 아는 터이다." (<聖誕祭 오라트리오>의 一節 原文詩)

맑시즘을 버리고 天主敎로 入敎한 오오든은 如前히 아이로니의 手法을 지니고 있다. 그의 知性은 兩棲動物의 그것이기 때문이다. 또 知性이 發達된 現代人으로서 兩棲動物 아닌 사람이 없는 까닭으로 해서 오오든의 作品이 現代感情에 맞는 것일는지도 모른다. 1941年에 發表한 詩集부터 오오든은 18世紀의 포우프를 仰慕하여 어떤 '秩序'로 돌아가려는 努力이 뚜렷이 보인다. "남과의 싸움에서 우리는 雄辯學을 마련하고 自己自身과의 싸움에서 詩를 만들어 낸다"는 詩人 예이츠의 말마따나, 앞으로 오오든이 어떻게 하여 참다운 믿음의 詩를 써서 善과 惡을 分明히 하고 美를 的確히 具象化할 것인가가 興味깊은 問題이다. 목청을 높이지 않고 雄辯을 마련하던 그의 아이로니가 앞으로 어떻게 進展될 것인가? 그는 이미 믿음의 길을 擇擇하였다. 그는 또 "神이 萬若 詩人이였던들 或은 詩를 深刻히 생각하였던들... 人間에게 다 自由意思를 주지 않았을 것"이라고 <四角形과 楕圓形>에서 말하였다. 自由意思가 없는 詩人, 더구나 天主敎人 오오든이 벌써 神秘主義의 境地를 헤매는 秘傳의 詩言語를 創造하는 過程에 놓여 있다는 것은 그의 最近作 <不安의 時代>에서도 엿볼 수 있다. 그러나 神秘主義라고 덮어놓고 좋다는 것은 아니다. 아이로니의 精神이 어떻게 될것인가? 이것이 窮局의 難關인듯 싶다. 왜냐하면 그가 일찌기 西班牙 內亂에 題하여 쓴 傑作의 結末 처럼,

"별은 죽었고 짐승조차 눈을 감았다
우리는 일을 맡아 외로히 남아 있으나 歲月은 짧고 歷史는
敗北者를 불상히 여길망정 도웁거나 容恕는 못 하리라."

T. S. 엘리어트의 古典主義 文學論

[筆者 註: 이 論文은 "T.S. 엘리어트의 古典主義"라는 題目으로 지난 八月에 朝鮮英文學會 月例報告會에서 發表한 拙稿의 一部分이다. 評論에 나타나는 엘리어트의 古典主義思想은 文學論에서 出發하여 現代文化를 支配하는 모든 思想과 信仰의 價値論까지 浸透하는 點에 있어서 在來의 古典主義思想과 特異한 것이 있다. 여기에서는 紙面 關係로 그 前半 '文學論'만 아래의 順序를 좇아 考察하기로 한다. 써 놓고 보니 어중띠고 未備한 點이 많음을 스스로 느낀다. (1948年 9月)]

I. 序論:

브륀티에르(Brunetière)가 提示한 古典主義와 二十世紀文學의 課題

'古典的'이니 '浪漫的'이니 하는 말이 文學批評에서 함부로 쓸 수 없는 까다로운 用語가 되어있는 것은 이 두 말이 提示하는 價値觀이 單純히 文學의 領域에만 局限할 수 없는 複雜한 것을 內包하는 까닭이다.

그러나 르네상스 以後의 西歐文學에서 이른바 古典文學이라 하면 十七, 十八 兩世紀에 걸쳐 約 百年 동안에 全盛을 이룬 파리와 런던의 集中된 社會를 相對로 한 文學을 가리키는 것은 文學史에서 周知의 事實이다. 프랑스의 브륀티에르(1849-1906)가 쓴 <浪漫과 古典>이라는 論文은 이 時代에 나타나는 文學의 特性을 들어, '秩序,' '透明,' '均衡,' '適度,' '風趣'라는 몇몇 가지를 指摘하며 要約하여 '中庸의 德'이라고 斷定하였다. 허버트 그리어슨이 영국의 케임브리지 大學校에서 '古典과 浪漫'(1923)이라는 講義를 할 때에도, 브륀티에르의 말을 다시 修飾하여 '理智,' '內容과 形式의 均衡,' '功績의 意識' 等의 말로 이 古典文學의 特徵을 說明하였으며, 괴테가 말하는 '健實의 槪念'을 引用하여 論證하였다. 더욱 브륀티에르는 古典作家가 되는 세 가지의 具備條件으로 다음을 꼽았다.

첫째, 말이 充分히 發達되어 그 遺産이 豊富해야 하고,
둘째, 作品이 그때의 國民精神을 充實히 表現해야 하고,
셋째, 作品의 形式이 圓熟한 것이어야 한다.

이러한 批評은 十七, 十八 世紀의 文學에 該當하는 限, 트집잡기 어려운 定論일 것이다. 그러나 이 尺度를 그대로 二十世紀文學에 適用하기는 쉬운 노릇이 아니다. 二十世紀는 十九世紀의 燦爛한 浪漫의 遺産을 가지고 있는 때문이며, 그뿐만 아니라 過去의 數많은 傳統을 同時에 享有하는 까닭이다. 르네상스 以後의 英詩만 하더라도 (셰익스피어를 絶頂으로 하는 詩劇의 傳統을 제쳐 놓고) 十六世紀의 스펜서가 이룬 傳統, 十七世紀의 단과 밀튼이 남기고 간 메타피지컬과 밀튼의 遺産, 十七, 十八世紀의 드라이든과 포우프가 이룬 오가스트 時代의 遺産, 그리고 十九世紀의 浪漫傳統, 其他 여러가지의 傳統이 얼키고 설켜 있는 現狀인 만큼, 엘리어트같은 詩人이 萬若 루이 王朝나 드라이든과 포오프 時代의 古典主義를 그대로 追從했던들, 그는 한 懷古의 踏襲에 不過할 것이고, 歷史를 逆行하는 行爲일 것이다. <荒蕪地>가 出版된 1922年은 1579年의 <牧羊者의 月曆>이나 1798年의 <리리컬 밸러즈>와 더불어 劃期的인 詩傳統을 만들어 낸 轉換의 礎石이 되는 해[年]라 할진대, 詩人 엘리어트의 古典主義는 十七八世紀의 詩人이 可謂 絶對的인 信條로 믿었던 古典主義와는 本質的으로 다름을 알 수 있을 것이다.

三百年 英詩史에서 말의 遺産이 豊富하지 않다고 主張할 사람은 없을 만큼 英詩는 發達할 대로 發達했다. 그러나 詩는 언제나 새로운 生命力을 가진 말을 써야 한다. 아무리 彈力있는 말일지라도 오래 쓰면 낡아지고 因襲的인 惰性만 남게 된다. 近年에 와서 英詩人들이 온갖 方法으로 말의 實驗을 하려 애쓰는 것도 여기 起因한다. 完全히 빅토리아 時代의 詩人이면서도 G. M. 홉킨스(1844-89)는 브라우닝 以上 몇 倍 가는 大膽한 言語의 實驗家였기에 브리지스가 遺稿를 1918年에 出版하자 큰 波動을 일으켜 現代詩에 이바지한 바 많았고, 散文에서 조이스가 革命的인 言語의 實驗을 한 것도 같은 現象에 屬한다. 그밖에도 許多한 例가 많거니와, 要는 旣成된 낡은 言語만으로는 到底히 自己의 過敏하고 深刻한 感覺과 思想을 담지 못한다는 것이 現代詩人의 共通된 느낌이고, 따라서 허버트 리드가 <英詩發達論>(1928)에서 指摘한 바와 같이 現代詩人은 워즈워스가 부르짖던 '表現의 誠實性'을 具現하려는, 卽 經驗을 的確히 客觀化하려는, 一大 試鍊의 過程 속에 있다고 할 수 있다. 이런 實驗期에 있어서 브륀티에르가 생각하는 類型의 古典은 成立하기 어려울 것이다.

다음 '國民精神의 發揮'를 두고 보더라도 이것을 作品判斷의 標準으로 삼기에는 너무나 漠然하다. 19世紀 前半까지도 英文學은 比較的 孤立하여 獨自性을 發揮하며 國民生活과 直接 關係를 맺어서 存續할 수 있었다. 그러나 後半부터 佛文學과의 交流가 또다시 緊密하여지면서부터 作家는 過去의 英國作家들이 물려준 世界 안에서만 살 수는 없게 되었다. 現代作家는 오히려 플로베르, 보들레르의 藝術觀에 洗禮를 받아, 어떤 社會生活의 反影보다는 더 根本的인 人間性 乃至 藝術性의 표현에 힘쓴다. '完璧'을 藝術의 崇高한 對象으로 생각하는 峻嚴한 潔癖性이 作家를 괴롭게 한다. 더구나 詩人의 이런 高踏的인 創作態度는 그로 하여금 俗世界를 등지게 하고, 따라서 그의 作品은 生活의 暴露와 自己苛責의 悽慘한 記錄이 되는, 卽 內在世界의 客觀化를 理想으로 하는 結果를 자아낸다. 一般 社會生活과 遊離되는 限이 있더라도 이 理想은 犧牲치 않겠다는 固執이 생긴다. 詩創作의 努力 自體가 時代에 對한 叛逆쯤 되어 버린 오늘날, 詩人은 當代社會에서 追放 當한 不遇者라고 自認하는 境遇가 많다. 엘리어트 自身도 母校 하바드 大學의 招聘으로 1930-33年에 C. E. 노오튼 詩講座를 맡아 講義할 때, "詩는 生涯가 아니고 얼빠진 者의 장난이다"라고 말한 적이 있다. 勿論 이런 創作態度가 正當하냐 健全하냐 하는 것은 別問題다. 다만 그런 狀態에서는 브륀티에르가 要求하는 둘째 條件이 成立하기 어렵다는 것이다.

끝으로 詩라는 形式조차 20世紀의 精神狀態에 맞는 것일지 疑惑을 갖게 된다. 評論家 존 미들튼 머리(John Middleton Murry)는 <詩와 評論>(1920)에서 다음과 같이 이 不安感을 指摘하였다.

"오늘날 우리들은 누구나 다 이 詩라는 問題에 關하여 우리들 獨特한 方法으로 근심을 하고 있다. 五十年前까지도 브라우닝이 테니슨이나 스윈번보다 더 偉大한 詩人이냐 아니냐 하는 것이 是非거리였는데, 오늘날 問題는 分明히 더 根本的인 것이고, 內容조차 더 虛無孟浪해진 듯하다. 우리는 밤낮 '詩란 무엇이냐?'하는 點을 異常한 半意識的인 方法으로 討議하고 있는데, 그것은 詩作이 놀랍게도 多産한 이 現代에 살고 있음에도 不拘하고 거기에서 別로 所得이 없었다는 不安感에 휩쓸려 있기 때문이다. '시는 그 自體가 目的'이라는 主義가 우리를 滿足시킬 段階는 이미 지났으므로 이 詩的 活動에 對한 더 充足한 辯護를 찾아 우리는 漠然히 硏究하고 있다. 우리의 詩的 價値論이 混沌狀態에 빠졌다는 豫感이 널리 퍼져 있기 때문에 우리는 不安을 느끼는 것이며, 따라서 어떤 標準이 다시 한번 樹立되며 適用되어야 하겠다는 切實한 欲求가 있다고 생각된다."

한편 美國 評論家 에드먼드 윌슨도 그의 評論集 <三重의 思索家>(1938)에서 "韻文은 없어지는 手法이냐?"라는 題目으로 二十世紀와 詩의 形式 問題를 考察하였다. 韻文과

散文의 本質과 目的이 다른 것은 事實이지만, 在來의 文學史的 現象으로는 韻文으로 쓸 것을 散文으로 쓴 境遇보다는, 散文으로 쓸 수 있음직한 것을 韻文으로 쓴 편이 더 많았다. 그러나 十九世紀부터 새로운 詩의 觀念이 생겨서, (1) 한편으로는 詩에 對한 先驗的 觀念으로 말미암아 極端에 이르러서는 셸리의 말처럼, "詩人은 이 世上의 숨은 立法者"라는 結論까지 생기고, (2) 또 한편으로는 詩的 想像力의 本質을 究明함으로써 콜러리지가 말하듯, "長篇의 詩는 全部가 다 詩로 될 수도 없는 것이고 또 되어서도 안된다"는 생각이 普遍化하여, 드디어 포우는 "긴 詩는 또다시 流行하지 않으리라"고까지 豫言한 바 있었고, 아놀드 亦是 詩의 絶妙한 아름다움은 한 줄[行]이나 한 句節에서도 찾아볼 수 있다고 말하였다.

十九世紀 以後의 文學의 動向을 가리키는 分岐點에 서 있는 플로베르에 關하여 윌슨은 아래와 같은 말을 하였다.

"단테가 플로베르보다 더 偉大하기는 하나, 플로베르도 단테와 같은 階級의 作家라는 것은 누구나 認定하는 바이다. 다만 다른 點은 플로베르의 時代에 와서는 단테와 같은 作家도 그의 꿈을 韻文의 敍事詩로 쓰지 않고 散文의 小說로 썼을 따름인 것이다. 플로베르가 다른 時代에 살았다면 <聖 안토안의 誘惑>을 散文이 아니라 詩로 썼을 것임에 틀림없다."

마찬가지로 D. H. 로런스가 百年前에만 살았더라도 그의 短篇小說은 詩로 되었을 可能性이 많고, 버지니아 울프의 手法 亦是 過去에 詩人이 쓰던 手法에 近似한 것이었으리라 상정해 볼 수 있다. 詩의 形式에 制限이 많이 생기고 詩의 領域이 좁아들어 가는 것이 現代의 傾向인 것 같다. 오늘날 一流 詩作品이 擧皆 敍情詩인 原因의 하나도 여기 있고, 또 詩文의 律調나 手法이 散文의 그것에 接近하여 가는 傾向이 漸次 뚜렷이 나타나는 것도 같은 現象이라고 볼 수 있다. 詩보다 散文이 一般 社會生活에 더 密接한 有機的 關係를 맺고 있다 해서 詩의 機能이 頹廢하였다거나 또는 詩가 不必要한 것이 되었다는 것은 아니다. 다만 詩라는 形式이 普遍性을 잃었다는 것뿐이다. 事勢不得已하여 孤立한 立場에서 적은 聽衆을 앞에 두고 詩를 쓰는 現代 詩人들이야말로, 싼타야나가 말하듯, "우리는 主觀的 見解와 主觀的 信念에 가득찬 獨白의 世界에 살고 있다"고 하겠지만, 作家치고 스스로 孤立을 좋아하며 自己의 외침이 民衆에 들리기를 바라지 않는 者는 없을 것이다. 社會가 詩人을 容納치 못할 程度로 詩人이 無用의 存在가 된 것이 아니라, 詩가 社會生活에 浸透 못할 만큼 社會가 機械와 經濟의 獨占舞臺로 되어 버린 것일게다. 要는 現代라는 文學史的 階段에

處해서 브륀티에르가 말하는 따위의 古典主義란 成立하기 어렵다는 點을 거듭 强調하는 바이다.

II. 엘리어트의 古典主義的 歷史感

일찍이 엘리어트는 <自由詩 論考>(1917)라는 論文에서 아래와 같이 말한 적이 있다.

"어떤 藝術家가 間或 스스로 생각지도 않은 사이에 偶然히 한 手法을 發見한다고 치자. 그리고 이 手法이 自己 周圍에 있는 二流者의 그것과 根本的으로 다를 뿐더러, 自己의 偉大한 어느 先驅者의 方法과도 本質的인 要素만 빼놓고는 모든 點에 있어서 特異한 것을 가진 方法이라고 하자. 이럴 때 새로운 것을 남은 몰라준다. 몰라주면 攻擊心이 挑發되고, 攻擊을 하려면 主義 學說이 必要하다. 理想的인 社會狀態라면 좋은 새것이 좋은 묵은것에서 辯論과 學說의 必要 없이 自然的으로 자라난다고 想像할 수 있다. 이런 社會는 산[生] 傳統을 가진 社會다. 게으른 社會에서는—實上, 社會란 게으른 것인데—傳統은 恒時 迷信으로 墮落하며, 따라서 새것에 對한 激烈한 刺戟이 必要하게 된다. 藝術家와 그 一派는 自己의 學說과 自己의 辯論에 制約과 拘束을 받으므로, 이런 事態는 그에게 나쁜 것이다."

이 一節은 엘리어트 自身의 批評的 立場을 밝혀 주는 率直한 告白이라고 하겠다. 그가 일찍부터 發見한 手法이 特異하였고, 이것을 批評으로 理論化하여 辯護하려 애썼기 때문에, 그의 作品과 評論도 表裏一體하고, 그가 主張하는 持論에는 終始一貫한 것이 있기는 하지만, 때로는 自繩自縛의 結果를 빚어내는 境遇도 없지 않다. 이것을 그의 古典主義思想에 비추어 考察하여 보자.

엘리어트 文學論의 核心이 되는 思想은 '傳統'에 關한 것일게다. '傳統'을 論하는데 重要한 文獻은 그가 1917년에 執筆하여 1919년에 發表한 論文 <傳統과 個人의 才能>일 것이다. 이 評論에서 엘리어트는 '傳統'을 分析하여 但只 우리 前代의 風習을 盲目的으로 繼承하는 것을 意味함이 아니라고 밝히고 나서, 다음과 같이 말하였다.

"傳統은 爲先 歷史感을 意味하는 것이고, 누구든지 25歲 以後까지 詩作을 繼續하려는

者에게는 이 歷史感이 반드시 있어야 할 것이라고 말할 수 있다. 歷史感은 過去의 過去性뿐만 아니라 過去의 現在性까지 알아야 할 것을 內包한다. 自己當代를 뼈속에 지니고 글을 쓸 뿐만 아니라 호머 以來의 歐羅巴文學 全部와 그 支流의 하나인 自國文學이 同時的 存在와 同時的 秩序를 構成하고 있다는 느낌을 가지고 글을 쓰게 하는 것이 歷史感이다. 歷史感을 지님으로써 作家는 傳統的 性格을 띠게 되는 것이고, 아울러 一時的인 것과 永遠的인 것, 一時性과 永遠性을 兼한 것을 느끼게 된다. 또 한편 歷史感을 가짐으로써 作家는 그 時代에 있어서의 自己의 地位와 當代感을 깊이 意識하는 것이다."

따라서 作家는 單獨으로는 意味가 없는 것이고, 新舊의 作家를 聯關시켜 評價하는 데에 비로소 그의 重要性이 나타나는 것이라고 指摘한다. 新舊의 聯關이란 무엇인가?

"새로운 한 作品이 創造될 때에 생기는 變動은 過去의 모든 作品에 對하여 同時에 생기는 變動이다. 이미 存在하는 傑作은 그 自體가 한 理想的 秩序를 形成하고 있는 것이며, 새로운—참말로 새로운—作品이 參加함으로써 그 秩序에 變化가 생긴다. 이미 存在하는 秩序는 新作品이 오기 前에도 完全한 것이다. 그러나 새로운 것이 添加된 다음에도 秩序가 存續하려면 現存하는 全秩序가 아무리 些少한 것이라도 조금씩 變化하는 것이며, 따라서 全體에 對한 各個 作品의 關係, 均衡, 價値가 再調整되는 것이다. 이것이 곧 新舊의 一致 調和이다."

以上 두 引用文에서 엘리어트의 古典主義에 關한 基本理念을 다음과 같이 추려 要約할 수 있겠다.

첫째, 歷史感은 但只 過去의 基準을 尺度로 現在를 재는[測量하는] 것뿐만 아니라, 過去가 現在를 調整하듯, 現在도 過去를 調整하는 相互的 關係를 意味한다. 엘리어트 自身의 創作詩에도 그 用語와 構想이 過去詩人의 語句나 歷史의 故事에 依存하는 點이 많기 때문에, 全體의 效果는 單純한 懷古만은 아닌 새로운 聯關性을 갖게 된다. <荒蕪地>같은 極端의 作品에 引用된 句節만으로도 全歐羅巴文學을 網羅하다시피 한 느낌이 있다. 聖經은 勿論이려니와, 셰익스피어, 단테, 버질, 오비드, 스펜서, 키드, 웹스터, 마벨, 골드스미스, 보들레르, 제라르 드 네르발, 베를렌, 聖 오거스틴, 헤르만 헤세, 바그너, 심지어는 印度의 古典 우파니샤드, 어린이의 童謠까지 나타나 있지만, 全體의 效果로 보면,

擧皆 內在的 必然性에서 나온 것이고, 일부러 自己의 學識을 자랑한다거나 억지로 技巧를 부리는 것은 아니다.

둘째, 新舊가 同時的 存在와 同時的 秩序를 構成하고 있으므로 兩者가 交織이 되어 생기는 結果가 곧 文學의 發展이다. 따라서 作家의 '獨創'이라는 것도 歷史感을 떠나서 있을 수 없고, 또 퍽 微弱한 關係에 지나지 못한다는 것이다. 1933年에 美國 버지니아 大學에서 講義한 <異神을 찾아서>에서 엘리어트는 '獨創'에 對하여 이렇게 말하였다.

"分明히 藝術家의 獨創에 對한 關心은 消極的인 것이라 할 수 있다. 즉, 이미 흠집 없이 完全히 表現된 것을 重複하지 않도록 努力할 따름이다.... 또 잊어서 안될 點은, 어느 한 作家가 獨創性으로써 이바지할 수 있는 것은 實로 퍽 적은 것이며, 또 그것이 그 作品 全體에 對해서도 매우 微弱한 關係에 지나지 못한다."

요컨대 現代作家들이 歷史感이 적기 때문에 獨創을 自負하고, 獨創을 爲한 獨創을 讚仰하는 傾向의 弊端을 指摘한 것이다.

셋째, 엘리어트의 古典主義 思想의 基本이 되는 理念의 하나로서, 藝術 全體의 理想的 秩序는 進展하면서도 一定不變하다는 點이다. 進展하면서도 變하지 않는다는 말은 矛盾처럼 들릴는지 모르나 藝術의 理想的 秩序를 追求하는 그의 形而上學的 古典主義의 理念으로 볼진대 矛盾이라 할 수는 없을 것이다. 같은 論文―<傳統과 個人의 才能>―에서 엘리어트는 "[歷史感을 가진 詩人]은 藝術이 絕對로 進步 向上은 하지 않지만, 藝術의 材料는 늘 一定치 않다는 明白한 事實을 알아야 할 것"이라고 말하여, 所謂 浪漫主義의 藝術觀과 對蹠되는 觀點을 强調한다.

넷째, 歷史感으로써 藝術의 過去意識과 現代意識을 나란히 發展시키려면, 作家는 創造와 批評을 分離해서 생각하는 傾向에서 벗어나야 한다는 것이다. 흔히 兩者를 別個視하여 前者는 情緒的 想像力의 所産이요, 後者는 理智的 判斷力의 成果라고 보는 傾向이 많으나, 實地에 있어서 創造와 批判이라는 두 機能은 對立할 性質의 範疇가 아니라고 엘리어트는 생각한다. 兩者는 竝存할 수 있을 뿐더러 竝存하는 것이 應當하다고 본다. 批判精神 없이는 歷史感을 갖기가 可謂 不可能하기 때문이다. 假令 그는 <詩의 批評에 關하여>(1920)라는 論文에서 다음과 같은 아나톨 프랑스의 말을 引用하였다.

"批評은 모든 文學形式中에 最後의 것이며, 究竟 모든 文學形式을 吸收해 버릴지도 모른다. 批評은 遺産이 豊富하고 傳統이 오래된 文明社會에 가장 適合한 것이며, 특히 知識慾이 많고 賢明하고 練磨된 사람들에게 適當한 것이다. 批評이 繁盛하려면 다른 모든 文學形式 以上의 敎養을 要한다."

그리고 나서 엘리어트는 여기 담겨 있는 見解를 論駁하였다. 엘리어트는 批判的 才能과 創造的 才能을 分離하는 것은 有害한 생각이라고 論證하며, "現代를 두고 보더라도 좋은 詩를 쓰기에 不利하다고 생각될 만한 條件은, 좋은 評論을 쓰는데도 不利한 條件이라고 斷定해도 無妨하다"고 단언하였고, 또 事實上 가장 有益한 批評은 詩人 自身이 쓴 評論이라고 主張하였다.

엘리어트는 이 問題를 機會 있을 때마다 論하였다. <評論의 實驗>(1924)에서도 "創作과 批判은 同時代에 盛하지 않는다"는 在來의 槪括은 너무 皮相的인 것이고, 批判的 機能을 抑壓함으로써 創作이 더 나아질 것은 없다고 力說하였다. 또 그가 하바드 大學의 노오튼 詩學 講座를 맡아 英文學에 있어서의 詩와 評論의 關係를 論할 때에도 "評論은 創作精神이 衰頹할 때에 盛한다"는 通念을 攻擊하였다. 또 <評論의 機能>(1923)이라는 論文에서도 다음과 같은 適切한 말을 한 적도 있다.

"매슈 아놀드는 이 두 가지 機能을 너무 簡單히 區別해 버리는 것 같다. 그는 創作의 努力 自體에 있어서의 批判의 重要性을 無視한다. 果然 어느 作家든 創作에 바치는 努力의 大部分은 批判的 努力이니, 고르고, 結合하고, 構想하고, 削除하고, 고치고, 試驗하는 수고는 創作的인 同時에 批判的이다. 訓練 받은 能熟한 作家가 自己의 作品에 바치는 批判이야말로 가장 緊要하고 崇高한 批判이다."

한마디로 要約하면, 創作의 過程은 理智的 批判을 超越한 것이라는 浪漫思想의 通念을 歷史感이라는 命題로 多少라도 制約하려는 것이 엘리어트의 생각일 것이다. '獨創'의 槪念이 氾濫하면 奇拔한 것만을 찾게 되고, 溫故의 精神이 稀薄해질 것이며, 客觀的인 牽制가 없으므로 主觀的인 放縱으로 墮落할 것을 엘리어트는 憂慮한다. 르네상스 以後의 西洋文化를 만들어낸 中産階級은 古代의 希臘文化나 中世의 基督文化에 지지 않을 燦爛하고도 纖細한 文化를 남겨 주었다. 그러나 理智的 分析의 天才를 가진 이 豊富한 西歐文化도 綜合의 恩典을 받지 못한 까닭으로 드디어 걷잡을 수 없는 支離滅裂의 悲運을 免치 못하게 되었다. 헤겔의 말대로, 知慧의 女神 미네르바의 올빼미는 저녁에 날개를 편다. 또 事實 저녁 노을이 하루의 가장 아름다운 때라고도 할 수 있다. 그러나 저녁은 저녁이다. 敎養이 末梢神經에까지 스며든 엘리어트같은 사람이 이것을 모를 리 없다. 그러므로 그는 體得하기 어려운 歷史感이라는 綜合의 眼目으로 文學傳統을 收拾하여 제멋대로 放縱하는 傾向을 牽制하려는 것이다. 그러나 時代的으로 보아 이미 그의 외침은 曠野에서 들려오는 목소리의 格이 아니라 할 수 없다.

III. 엘리어트의 古典主義的 個性滅却論

<異神을 찾아서>에서 엘리어트는 確乎한 傳統이 없는 文學의 動向을 分析하여 두가지의 弊를 들었다. 그 첫째는 見解가 極度로 個人主義化하는 動向이요, 둘째는 文學이 擔當할 任務의 限界에 關하여 一定한 公認된 原則이 없다는 것이다.

中産階級 文化의 精神的 地盤이 個人主義라는 것은 누구나 首肯할 것이다. 個人主義로 말미암아 人間은 모든 本能的 欲求를 具現시킬 自由를 얻는다고 믿는다. 自我에 內在하는 個性의 自由스러운 發揮가 中産文化의 꿈이다. 이 꿈의 英雄的 代辯者가 文學에서는 셰익스피어의 햄리트, 밀튼의 쎄이튼, 디포의 로빈슨 크루소, 워즈워스의 '나'라는 主人公, 셸리의 프로메테우스, 바이론의 차일드 해롤드, 괴테의 파우스트, 브라우닝의 쏘델로, 하디의 나폴레온, 조이스의 스티븐 디딜러스, 엘리어트의 프루프록 등이다. 몇 例에 不過하나, 中産文化의 骨子가 經濟面에서는 自由市場이듯, 精神面에서는 自由人의 個性이라는 것은 틀림없는 사실이다. 그 文化의 相續者인 엘리어트도 이 個性이라는 問題를 깊이 생각지 않을 수 없었다. 엘리어트는 歷史意識을 가지고 藝術의 理想的 秩序와 權威에 順應해야 한다는 古典主義의 立場에서 이 個性의 滅却論을 主張한다.

1923년에 J. M. 머리와 論爭이 벌어졌을 때, 엘리어트는 <批評의 機能>에서 다음과 같이 말했다.

"머리氏의 論點은 分明하다. "카톨리씨즘은 個人 밖에 있는 絶對的인 精神的 權威를 表象하며, 이 原則이 文學에 있어서는 또한 古典主義의 原則"이라고 그는 말한다. 이것이 勿論 카톨리씨즘과 클라씨씨즘의 全貌는 아니로되, 머리氏의 理論이 展開되는 範疇 內에서는 論駁할 餘地가 없는 定義라고 하겠다."

'個人 밖에 있는 精神的 權威'를 믿는 엘리어트는 浪漫主義者가 唯一한 權威로 생각하는 '心聲,' 俗稱 '個性'이라는 것을 不信任한다. 이에 關하여 그가 初期에 쓴 論文 <傳統과 個人의 才能>은 이미 워즈워스의 <리리컬 밸러즈> 序文처럼 너무나 有名한 宣言書가 되어 버렸지만, 그 한 句節을 다시 引用해 보기로 하자.

> "事實上 創作의 過程이란, 그때 그때에 實在하는 自我를 굽혀서 더 價値있는 것에 服從하는 것을 意味한다. 作家의 發展이란, 끊임없는 自我 犧牲이요, 끊임없는 個性의 滅却이다."

浪漫主義가 膨脹的인 動向이라면, 古典主義는 制約的이며 凝縮的인 動向이라 하겠다. 浪漫은 個性을 探求하는 것이니, 作家는 唯一無二한 自我意識을 充分히 表現함으로써 藝術의 任務를 다하였다고 自認할 것이다. 그리고 個性에는 貴賤 優劣이 없는 만큼 個性만 獨特하고 表現만 絶妙하면 어떤 作品이든 優劣이 없이 똑같은 藝術的 價値를 지닌다는 생각이 浪漫의 論理的 結果로 나타난다. 따라서 應當 神에만 屬한 '完全'을 사람에게 歸屬시킨 나머지 '個性'이라는 虛僞物이 생긴다. 이 虛僞物에 對한 偶像崇拜를 藝術에서 除外할 것을 엘리어트는 主張한다.

> "實際로 詩에 있어서 새로운 感情을 表現하려고 이것을 찾는 것은 奇矯를 犯하는 過誤이다. 그릇된 데에서 神奇한 것을 찾으려다가 畸形的인 것을 發見할 것이다. 詩人의 任務는 新奇한 感情을 찾아내는 것이 아니라 普通感情을 材料로 삼아 이를 詩로 만듦으로써 實際의 感情에는 全然 없는 感情을 表現하는 것이라야 한다. 그러므로 直接 經驗하지 않은 感情이라도 많이 經驗한 感情과 같이 利用할 수 있다. 따라서 '平靜狀態에서 回想된 感情'이라는 워즈워스의 말은 不正確한 公式이다. . . . 實踐的 活動의 人間에게는 '經驗'이라 생각되지도 않는 數많은 經驗이 凝結 集中하는 것이 創作의 過程이다. 그리고 이 凝結은 意識的으로 深思熟考해서 되는 것은 아니다. . . . 拙劣한 詩人은 마땅히 意識的이어야 할 境遇에 無意識的이며, 反對로 無意識的이어야 할 境遇에 意識的인 수가 많다. 이 두 過誤가 다 그를 '個性的'으로 만들어 주기 쉽다. 詩는 感情의 解放이 아니고, 感情에서의 逃避다. 個性 人格의 表現이 아니라, 個性 人格으로부터의 逃避인 것이다. 그러나 個性과 感情을 가진 사람이 아니면 그것으로부터 逃避한다는 意味를 모를 것이다."

위 언급에 나타나는 엘리어트의 態度는 浪漫의 主情的, 煽情的 藝術觀에 對한 挑戰인 만큼 多少 極端에 흐르는 感이 없지 아니하나, 그의 古典主義의 觀點으로 본다면, 至當한 말이다. 하긴, 浪漫도 옳은 것이라면, '나'라는 主觀을 先驗的으로 超越하는 것을 意味할 것이다. 키츠가 "詩의 性格에 關하여 말하자면, 그것은 그 自體가 아니고, 自體도 없는 것이다. 그것은 모든 것인 同時에 虛無이다. 詩에는 性格이 없다"고 말한 것처럼, 詩 自體의 實在를 詩를 쓰는 主體의 實在와 混同해서는 안된다는 點을 엘리어트도 主張한다. 이 問題는 그의 重要한 論點의 하나인 만큼, 再三 말을 바꾸어서 强調한다. 엘리어트는 <詩의 用途와 評論의 用途>(1933)에서도 다음과 같은 말을 하였다.

"詩가 設使 '傳達'의 한 形式이라 한들 傳達되는 것은 詩 그 自體이고, 그 詩 속에 들어간 經驗이나 思想은 다만 附隨的으로 傳達될 따름이다. 詩의 存在는 詩人과 讀者의 中間에 있다. 그 實在는 單純히 作家가 表現하려 하는 實在도 아니고, 또 그 作品을 쓸 때 經驗하는 實在도 아니고, 또는 讀者나, 讀者의 立場에서 作家 自身이 作品을 읽을 때 얻는 實在도 아니다. 그런고로 어떤 詩든지 그 意味가 무엇이냐 하는 問題는 얼른 생각하기보다 훨씬 어려운 問題다. 詩의 意味는 詩人이 計劃하는 것도 아니고, 또는 讀者가 생각하는 것도 아니다. 또 詩의 機能도 作家가 意圖하는 것이나, 讀者가 事實上 받는 影響에만 局限되는 것이 아니다."

이와같이 詩는 그 自體가 儼然한 實在이고, 그 속에 나타나는 '個性'은 附隨的인 實在이므로, 詩는 感情과 個性만을 培養함으로써 誕生하는 것이 아니라, 非個性的인 感情이 內在한다는 것을 指摘한다. 1928年 <단테論>에서도 단테와 괴테를 比較하여 이 問題를 다른 角度로 考察한다. 이 두 詩人은 다 哲學的 詩를 썼지만, 두 作品의 思想의 背景이 되는 哲學과 作品과의 關係에는 多少 差異가 있다. 卽, 단테가 人間으로서 믿는 信條인 스콜라哲學 體系는 이것을 詩로 옮겨 놓음으로써 哲學의 價値가 詩的 價値로 變한다. 그러나 괴테가 人間으로서 믿는 信條는 作品에서도 그대로 價値를 變하지 않고 人間의 信條로 남아있다. 換言하면 <파우스트>의 哲學은 人間 괴테의 個性의 投射에 不過하므로, 人間 괴테의 信條와 詩人 괴테의 信條를 分離할 수 없을 만큼 同一體다. 그러나 <神曲>에 나타나는 人間 단테와 詩人 단테의 信條는 이것을 區別해서 생각할 수 있을 만큼 非個性的인 峻嚴한 藝術感의 支配를 느낀다. 그런고로 <파우스트>를 읽을 때는 人間 괴테의 個性과 人格이 讀者와 作品 사이에 侵入하기 때문에 詩 自體의 鑑賞을 흐리게 한다. 단테에 있어서는 그의 傳說的, 神話的 象徵을 仲介로 한 自然觀 또는 道德觀이 完全히 詩라는 統一體에 融合하여 있으므로 讀者의 立場에서 본다면, 그의 思想이 '哲學的 信念'의 與否가 아니라 '詩的 肯定'의 問題라고—이 結末이 엘리어트의 獨特한 論法이다.

> "이것이 카톨릭敎와 같은 統一된 傳統的 敎理 道德 體系의 有利한 點이다. 그 體系를 提要하는 어떤 한 個人과 分離해서, 믿지 않으면서도 解得하고 肯定할 수 있는 統一體系인 까닭이다."

'現代 異端의 敎本'이라는 副題目을 건 <異神을 찾아서>에서도 이 個性 問題가 考察되는데, 特히 道德의 觀點에서 아래와 같은 意味深長한 말을 하고 있다.

> "道德이 傳統과 正敎上의 問題가 아니고, 換言하면, 敎會의 不斷의 硏究와 指導로써 形成되고, 是正되고, 鼓吹되는, 社會의 慣習問題가 아니고, 個人 各自가 自己의 道德을 손수 體系化하지 않으면 안 될 때가 되면, 그때부터는 個性이라는 것이 놀랄 만큼 重大하게 되는 것이다."

많은 現代作家는 制度的 關心과 客觀的 信條의 拘束을 느끼지 않는 强烈한 個性이기 때문에 '自己表現'을 爲하여 글을 쓰는데, 그중에도 하디같은 作家를 顯著한 例로 들 수 있다.

> "하디의 人物의 大多數는 그들의 感情이 激發하는 刹那에 비로소 살아난다고 할 수 있다. 이 極端의 主情主義는 頹廢의 徵候라고 생각된다. 過激한 感情은 그 自體 안에 어떤 高尙한 것을 內包한다고 믿는 것이 浪漫時代의 基本理念의 하나이다. 그러나 사람은 極度로 興奮하였을 때 가장 實在的이라고 斷言할 수는 없다. 激한 肉體的 感情은 그 自體가 사람과 사람을 區別하지 않고 도리어 똑같은 狀態로 만드는 경우가 많다. 또 그 熱情은 主人公이 다른 平靜狀態에 나타내는 그의 性格이나 行動과 關聯시켜서 비로소 意味있게 되는 것이다. 뿐만 아니라 强烈한 情熱은 굳센 사람에 있어서만 재미도 있고 興味도 있는 것이다. 더구나 道德的 抵抗과 苦悶이 없다면, 그것은 아무 意味가 없는 것이다."

이와같이 浪漫主義의 個性 崇尙에 叛旗를 들어 藝術의 非個性的 本質을 力說한다. 앨릭 웨스트의 著書 <危機와 評論>(1937)에서도 엘리어트의 例를 들어, 作品에 나타나는 主體가 '나'가 아니고 '우리'라는 手法은 中産文化의 새로운 轉換期의 手法이라고 指摘한 바 있거니와 社會와 個人이 排他的인 抽象의 實體가 아니라, 個人이 社會 속에 있는 것과 마찬가지로, 社會도 個人 속에 있다는 生活의 有機性을 暗示하는 것 같다. 그러나 그의 評論에서는 理智的 立場에서 이처럼 個性滅却論을 主張하지만, 그의 作品에서는 自我意識을 完全히 벗어났다고는 볼 수 없다. 무어니 무어니 해도, 엘리어트는 19世紀의 浪漫思想의 相續者의 한 사람이요, 世紀末 文學의 經路를 밟아 온 사람이기 때문에, 그의 創作의 重要한 主題의 하나로서 '自我意識의 內向'을 들 수 있다. 疲勞와 幻滅은 懷疑와 否定을 가져다 주는 것이요, 이 懷疑와 否定의 무거운 짐을 지고 混亂에 빠진 中産文化의 荒蕪地를 거닐며 支離滅裂한 自我意識의 破片을 주어 모아 再建을 꾀하는 엘리어트의 딜레마는 現代人의 悲運을 代表하지 않는다고 볼 수 없다. 그러기에 그의 古典主義도 結末에 가서는 그가 排擊하는 浪漫思想과 合致된다고 볼 수 있다. 다음과 같은 앙드레 지드의 말에 담겨있는 洞察은 엘리어트에게도 適用될 수 있을 것이다.

"로맨티시즘과 클래씨시즘 사이의 싸움은 各個人의 精神 속에도 있다는 것을 잊어서는 안된다. 이 싸움에서 비로소 作品이 誕生하는 것이다. 古典主義的 作品은 內在的 浪漫主義를 克服하여 秩序와 適度가 勝利한 것을 이야기하는 作品이다. 그리고 이 爭鬪가 苛酷하면 할수록 作品은 더 아름다운 것이다. 萬若 作品이 始初부터 秩序整然하면, 그것은 生氣도 없고 興味롭지도 않을 것이다."

따라서 그의 詩的 發展은 이 딜레마와 苦境에서 어떻게 하면 벗어날까 하는 解脫의 記錄이라고 볼 수 있다. 'Prufrock'을 爲始한 初年作에서 'Gerontion'을 엮은 1920년 詩集으로, 1922年의 'The Waste Land'로, 1925年의 'The Hollow Men'으로, 1927年 以後 隨時에 發表된 'Ariel Poems'로, 그리고 1930年의 'Ash Wednesday'로, 네 篇의 詩劇을 거친 다음 1943年에 나온 'Four Quartets'에 이르기까지 그가 걸어온 길은 解脫의 努力이 자아낸 悽慘한 記錄이거니와, 이에 對한 더 詳細한 考察은 다음 機會로 미루기로 한다.

이와같이 個性을 根本的으로 否定하려 애쓰는 엘리어트는 作家의 創作機能을 어떻게 規定하는가 하는 問題가 興味있는 것이다. 그는 經驗하는 人間과 創作하는 精神을 分離해서 생각하려 하기 때문에, 創作의 原料가 되는 感情과 經驗을 完全히 消化해서 새로운 複合物로 만드는 機能을 創作의 過程이라고 斷定한다. 따라서 詩人의 마음을 한 容器에 比喩하여 그 그릇에 담기고 蓄積되는 모든 經驗과 語句와 心象의 여러가지 構成分子가 融解 結合되는 刹那에 생기는 複合의 熱度와 壓力이 강렬하면 할수록 偉大한 詩가 탄생한다고 말한다.

"詩人은 表現해야 할 個性을 가진 것이 아니라, 어떤 特殊한 機關을 가진 것에 不過하다. 이 機關으로 말미암아 여러가지 印象과 經驗이 獨特한, 豫想치 못한 方法으로 結合한다. 人間으로서 重要한 印象과 經驗은 그의 詩 속에서는 그다지 重要치 않을 수도 있는 것이고, 詩에서 重要한 것이 人間, 個性에서는 微弱한 任務밖에는 못할런지도 모른다."

이와 같이 말하여 詩作의 客觀的 機能을 강조한 것이다.

個性滅却論에 立脚한 限, 엘리어트의 詩人機關論도 首肯할 수 있는 理論이다. 더구나 그 自身의 創作手法에 비추어 본다면 妥當性을 띠지 않았다 할 수 없다. 그는 학창시절에 아서 시몬스의 著述 〈文學의 象徵運動〉을 耽讀하고 새로운 天地를 보는 듯한 感動과 啓蒙을 받았다고 하며, 또 "1908-9年頃에 내가 쓰기 始作한 詩形式은 쥴 라포르그와 엘리자베스 時代 後期 戱曲의 硏究에서 얻은 것"이라고 告白한 것을 보더라도, 그의 手法이 象徵派 詩人의 그것과 비슷한 點이 있다. 象徵派 詩人의 手法은 表現이 아니라 啓示의 手法을 써서 現代人의 複雜微妙한 心理를 傳達하는데 성공한 것이라고 볼 수 있다. 칼라일은 그의 〈衣裳哲學〉에서 "象徵에는 隱蔽가 있으면서도 啓示가 있다. 그러므로 沈默과 言語가 共同作用을 함으로써 二重의 意味가 생긴다"고 말하였는데, 이 名言은 엘리어트의 創作에도 該當한다고 보겠다. 또 日本詩人 工田敏은 〈海潮音〉의 序文에서 다음과 같은 말을 하였다.

"象徵의 用途는 이의 도움을 빌려서 詩人의 槪念에 類似한 心理狀態를 讀者에게 주는 데 있고, 반드시 同一한 槪念을 주려 애쓰는 것이 아니다. 따라서 象徵詩를 鑑賞하는 者는 自己의 感興에 應하여 詩人도 말 못하는 言語로 表現 못할 妙趣를 翫賞할 수 있다. 따라서 한篇의 詩에 對한 解釋은 各其 見解를 달리할 수 있으되, 要는 但只 類似한 心狀을 喚起하는데 있다."

여기 言及된 事實을 엘리어트의 手法에서도 볼 수 있는 것이니, 이미지가 어떤 감정의 觀念的 統一을 주며, 여러 이미지를 綜合한 全體의 形式은, 論理的 理性이 아니라 詩에 內在하는 藝術的 理性에 順應하여 한 思想의 統一體를 만들어 주는 것이다. 한 이미지가 다음 이미지와 融合하고, 또는 奇想天外의 方法으로 새로이 凝縮 結合하여 意外의 視野를 보여주는 그의 手法은 그의 詩人機關論에 맞는 手法이다. 이에 關한 더 細密한 考察은 나중 機會로 미루기로 한다.

끝으로 또하나의 例를 들어 엘리어트가 말하는 詩의 客觀的 機能을 例示하고자 한다. 엘리어트는 <햄리트>를 평하여 셰익스피어의 가장 成功한 傑作이라기보다는 藝術的으로 失敗한 作品이라고 斷定한다. 그 까닭은 主人公이 具現하려 하는 감정이 그 本質上 到底히 客觀的으로 表示되지 못할 問題를 다루기 때문에 解釋에 곤란한 人物이고, 따라서 괴테는 第二의 베르테르로 만들어 버리고, 콜러리지 亦是 自己 自身과 같은 人格으로 解釋해 버리는 不純한 結果를 자아낸다. 그러니까 엘리어트는 이 作品을 '文學의 모나리자'라고 일컫는다.

"藝術의 形式으로 感情을 表現하는 唯一한 方法은 '客觀的 聯關物'을 發見함으로써 되는 것이다. 다시 말하면, 그 獨特한 感情을 表示할 公式이 될만한 몇가지의 目的物과 어떤 環境과 一連의 事態가 있어서, 感覺的 經驗으로 그쳐야 할 이 外部의 事實이 提供될 때에 感情이 卽時에 喚起되도록 해야 할 것이다."

이런 觀點에서 <햄리트>를 作品으로 살펴본다면, 果然 主人公이 解決해야 될 課題나 그의 行爲가 자아내는 플롯에 客觀的으로 理解하기 어려운 要所가 內包된 까닭으로, 엘리어트가 前提로 하는 古典主義的 立場에서는 藝術的 滿足感을 주지 않는 作品이라고 할 수 있다.

IV. 엘리어트의 古典主義的 價値觀

여태까지 考察해 온 엘리어트의 古典主義의 이모저모는 다 文學의 테두리 안에서 생기는 問題이고, 또 文學의 範疇 안에서만 生命이 있는 問題다. 그러나 文學은 사람이 만들어내는 人生의 記錄인만큼, 生活과 分離해서 따로 간직해 둘 神聖不可侵한 것은 아니다. 藝術至上主義로 自足하던 時代는 이미 歷史에 屬하는 것이요, 文學이 解決해야만 할 生活의 問題는 如前히 한 宿題로 남아있다. 그리고 이 宿題의 根本的인 解決은 언제나 다름없이 價値問題와 이 價値가 結論지어 주는 信仰의 問題로 돌아가고 말 것이다. 이를테면 生活을 純物質로 換算하여 經濟問題라고 한들, 經濟問題를 追窮하면 政治問題와 合流하는 것이고, 政治問題는 다시 思想問題로 돌아가며, 思想은 마지막으로 價値問題와 信仰問題로 歸着하고 말 것이다. 엘리어트의 古典主義思想이 文學의 領域에만 滿足치 않고, 그가 文學과 哲學, 神學에서 받은 均衡있는 敎養과 纖細한 思考力을 가지고 文學의 國境을 넘어서 한 價値體系를 樹立하려고 애쓰는 理由도 여기 있다.

그의 價値觀을 把握하는데는 먼저 그가 어떤 時代相을 抵抗하는가를 檢討할 必要가 있다. 말할 것도 없이 엘리어트가 느끼는 괴로움의 하나는 現代의 知識에 統一性이 없다는 것이다. 求心的인 核心이 없는 現代 知識의 運命을 슬퍼하는 것이 그의 詩를 一貫하는 重要한 테마의 하나라는 것은 거듭 말할 것도 없다. 大學時節의 그의 恩師 죠지 산타야나가 말하듯이, 知識은 無識을 退治함으로써 解決되는 것이 아니며, 思想만이 知識의 全貌는 아니고, 언제나 그 思想의 統一的 用途가 究竟의 標準일 것이다. 現代의 中産文化는 實驗科學에 土臺를 둔만큼 歷史에 例를 보지 못한 稀貴한 文化이언만, 極致에 達한 多元的인 '分析'을 一元的으로 '綜合'할 힘이 없고, '分裂'을 '收拾'할 方途를 잃어 버린 不幸에 빠져 있다. 現代人은 '宇宙'—'universe'—에 살지 않고 '多宇宙'—'multiverse'—에 살고 있는 不運을 가졌기 때문에, 焦燥에서 不滿으로, 不滿에서 疲勞로, 그리고 失望으로 循環하며, 어수선한 每日을 되풀이하고 있다. 엘리어트의 創作과 評論에 直接 間接으로 나타나는 基本理念의 하나로, 그가 私淑하던 思想家 흄(T. E. Hulme)의 말을 빌리자면,

"哲學體系와 倫理體系는 우리가 安樂椅子에 앉은 瞬間에만 可能하고, 더러운 어린애를 안고 滿員인 버스에 오를 때는 벌써 無意味함을 알 수 있다."

"사람이란 高度로 組織된 케이오스에 지나지 못하고, 어느 刹那에나 케이오스로 돌아갈 天性을 가졌다."

이런 생각이 二十世紀에 새삼스레 생긴 것은 勿論 아니고, 일찍이 르네상스 後期의 英文學에서 이미 暗示된 中産文化의 必然的 運命이지만, 第一次大戰後의 英文學에 顯著히 나타나는 事實인 만큼, 엘리어트도 그 咀呪를 안 느낄 수 없다.

둘째, 現實政治에 對한 그의 批判도 苛酷한 것이 있다. 그가 1922년부터 十六年동안 主幹을 맡았던 〈크라이테리온〉에도 現實政治와 政治理念을 많이 論한 바 있거니와, 1939年 1月號로 同雜誌가 廢刊될 때 그가 쓴 廢刊辭의 一節에서 그의 着眼點을 엿볼 수 있다.

"내가 지난 八·九年 동안 漠然히 느껴온 것은 (그리고 나의 생각이 얼마나 漠然했고 얼마나 混濁했느냐 하는 것은 나의 主幹辭가 뼈아프게 證明할 것이다) 表面的으로나 內面的으로나 아무런 살아있는 政治哲學이 없기 때문에, 이 나라(英國)가 將次 逢着할지 모를 險惡한 危機라는 것이었다. 이 要請에 對應하여 佛蘭西의 文筆家들은, 不幸히도 그들의 思索이 아직껏 思想的 統一과 秩序를 가져오지 못하였다고는 할지라도, 우리들보다 더 活潑하였다. 옳은 政治哲學은 옳은 神學을 意味하는 것이며, 옳은 經濟는 옳은 倫理學에 매인 것이라고 나는 생각해 왔다. 그 結果, 當初에 뜻했던 文學雜誌의 테두리 밖에 있는 問題에 置重하게 된 點도 없지 않다. 回顧하건대, 나는 코멘테이터로서 너무 지나치게 共産主義理論에 나의 漫談的인 關心을 바친 것 같다. 그러나 나는 그 理論이나 또는 無理論을 評하였을 따름이고, 政治的 豫言에 從事하지 않았다는 것을 確言할 수 있다. 나는 主로 英國에서 생긴, 또는 英國으로 浸透해 온 政治理論에 關心을 두어 왔다. 그리고 (이 나라에서) 局部的으로 提供된 파씨즘의 類型은 그다지 큰 理智的 關心을 일으키지 않았다고 볼 수 있거니와, 그보다 더 重要하게 생각되는 點은, 保守主義의 바탕에 파씨즘을 접붙이기에는 適應性이 不足한 反面, 共産主義는 自由主義의 뿌리에 쉽게 자랄 수 있기 때문에 盛해지는 것이다."

現代政治의 頹廢를 暴露하는 證據로는, 統一의 美名下에 偶像崇拜가 旺盛하고 힘의 原則과 憎惡, 屈服의 哲學이 氾濫하여, 倫理의 原動力이던 '個人'과 '自由意思'는 團體의 힘을 構成하는 機械論的 單位와 統計的 材料밖에 안된다는 것이다. 道德觀에 立脚한 엘리어트가 國家, 階級, 또는 神化한 個人 等 많은 偶像의 무리가 勢力에 醉해서 無道德을 犯하는 現實政治를 黙過하지 않는 것은, 그의 諷刺詩 〈코리올란〉이나, 詩劇 〈大聖堂의 殺人〉에서도 볼 수 있다.

두 作品 中 後者는 〈荒蕪地〉에 못지 않은 엘리어트의 傑作일 뿐더러 希臘戲曲의 形式을 갖춘 古典的 作品으로 밀튼의 〈샘슨 아고니스티즈〉에 비견할 作品이므로, 그 모티프를

簡略히 紹介하여 現實政治에 對한 作家의 觀察을 살펴보기로 한다.

主人公 토마스 아 베케트는 十二世紀 英國史에 나오는 헨리 二世의 名宰相이었는데, 그가 캔터베리 大僧正으로 任命되자, 俗世의 權勢를 排擊하고 敎會의 地盤을 굳히는데 힘을 다 했다. 마침내 僧侶階級은 國王의 裁判 權限 밖에 있다는 베케트의 主張이 動機가 되어 國王과 敎會 사이에 軋轢이 생겨, 베케트는 職場을 떠나 佛蘭西에 避身한지 七年만에 다시 國王과 和解하여 1170年 12月 2日에 다시 캔터베리로 돌아왔다. 劇의 事件進行은 그가 돌아온 때부터 始作된다. 그런데 그 和解는 이름뿐이요, 언제든지 再燃할 運命을 띤 것이었기 때문에, 드디어 12月 29日 밤 國王의 從者 네 명의 騎士가 베케트를 暗殺할 目的으로 캔터베리에 侵入해 國王의 이름으로 그를 脅迫하며 그의 敎法的 權限을 굽힐 것을 強要한 끝에, 騎士들은 聖堂 안에서 그를 죽인다. 엘리어트는 이 史實에서 카이사와 하느님, 俗世의 權勢와 信仰의 權勢의 永遠한 軋轢을 그려내며, 勢力政治의 無慈悲로 말미암아 籠絡되는 人民의 悲慘을 描寫한다. 劇中에 캔터베리 婦女子들로 構成된 코러스는 엘리어트가 쓴 詩 가운데 가장 悲劇的이며 崇高한 슬픔의 노래일 것이다.

셋째, 自然主義思想에 對한 抗拒를 들 수 있다. 制度와 因習을 깨뜨리고 太初의 生活慾을 鼓吹하여 經驗의 直接性을 強調하는 데 浪漫思想이 이바지한 바는 컸다. 自然으로 돌아가게 하는 生의 無限한 精力을 讚美함으로, 한 經驗에서 또 한 經驗으로 끊임없이 流轉하는 生의 過程 自體가 目的이 되어, 窮極의 達成보다 窮極의 追求를 生의 價値라고 가르친 것이 浪漫思想이다. 浪漫이 現實世界를 度外視하고 꿈의 世界로 들어가는 面도 있지만, 그 自然主義의 論理는 自然科學과 社會科學을 북돋는 溫床이 되었다. 한편 '페노메논'의 世界를 觀察하는 自然科學은 '누메논'의 象徵的 世界를 돌보지 않기 때문에 사람의 감정을 制約할 힘을 갖지 않았다. 또 한편 人間은 本質的으로 善한 動物이라 믿으며, 罪惡의 責任을 社會制度와 環境에 轉換시키는 浪漫思想의 前提를 받아들임으로써, 社會科學은 倫理 判斷의 基準을 個人에 두지 않고 社會 思潮에 두는 傾向을 갖게 된다. 이 두 傾向을 엘리어트는 古典主義的 立場에서 抗拒한다. 그는 흄의 理念을 支持하여 人間은 本質的으로 局限된 力量을 가지고 訓練을 通해 겨우 向上할 듯 말 듯하다고 믿는다. 이 點에 있어서 엘리어트는 그의 恩師 어빙 배비트가 <民主政體와 指導力>(1924)에서 主張한 바에 共鳴한다. 卽,

"在來 神學의 基本理念이 사람은 神에서 墮落했다는 것과 마찬가지로, 루쏘의 根本 思想은 사람이 自然에서 墮落했다는 것이다. 이와같이 루쏘가 만들어 낸 神話의

根底에는 새로운 二元論이 確實히 들어있다. 在來의 二元論은 善과 惡의 葛藤을 個人의 가슴에 두고, 人類가 樂園에서 墮落한 以後로는 惡이 늘 優勢하므로 사람은 謙遜해야 한다고 말했다. 루쏘에 와서는 이 葛藤이 個人에서 社會로 移轉된 것이다."

라고 말하며 이에 起因하는 道德的 弊害를 아래와 같이 指摘한다.

"過去의 모든 警告를 無視하고 다시 한번 무서운 自然主義의 허구렁에 빠지게 된 우리는, 第一原則부터 그릇된 世界에 살고 있다고 結論짓지 않을 수 없게 되었다. 우리가 威脅을 느끼는 이 文明의 破鏡은 希臘, 로마의 末期에... 견줄 수 있다.... 指導者들은, 그 程度의 差異는 多少 있으나, 이미 自然主義에 屈服하여 道德的 原則에까지 干涉하게 되었다.... 道德的 原則에 干涉한다는 것은 究竟 人間의 內制力까지 꺾어 버리는 結果가 되는 것이며, 이는 必然的이라고는 할 수 없으나 大概는 傳統의 智慧와의 決裂이 招來한 것이라 하겠다. 베이컨式 自然主義者가 過去를 否認한 것은, 더 한층 積極的이며 批判的인 立場에서 自己를 事實의 世界에 確立시키려는 뜻에서 나온 것이다. 그러나 사람의 內制力이란, 우리가 考慮해야 할 가장 重要한 事實의 하나이다. 루쏘式 自然主義者가 傳統의 支配를 떨쳐 버린 것도 自己의 想像力을 強化하려는 意圖에서 나온 것이다. 그러나 이 內制力이 없으면 사람의 想像力도 單純한 混沌의 狀態로 돌아간다. 베이컨主義者나 루쏘主義者는 어느 外在的인 힘이 自己自身과 自己의 知覺機能 사이에 介在하는 것을 싫어했다. 그러나 이 內制力은 決코 抽象的이고 外在的인 것이 아니라, 內在的인 것이다."

自然科學과 社會科學의 標石이 되는 베이컨과 루쏘의 基本理念을 이와같이 批判하고, 아울러 人間行動을 制約하는 精神的 自制의 必要를 強調하는 點에 있어서는 배비트나 엘리어트나 마찬가지라고 하겠다. 그러나 엘리어트는 배비트의 휴머니즘을 全然으로 是認하는 것은 아니다. 그 理由는 배비트가 宗敎를 否認하는 傾向이 있기 때문이다. 過去의 歷史에 비추어 宗敎는 휴머니즘과 別個로 끊임없이 存續해 왔지만, 휴머니즘은 隨時로 盛했고, 또 盛할 때는 반드시 宗敎와 竝立하였기 때문에 兩者를 分離해서 생각할 수 없다는 것이 엘리어트의 持論이다. 그는 <F. H. 브래들리論>(1926)에서 다음과 같이 말했다.

"道德과 宗敎가 같은 것은 아니다. 그러나 어느 程度를 넘으면 兩者를 別個로 取扱할 수 없다. 徹底한 倫理體系는 表面的으로나 內面的으로나 神學體系가 되는 것이며, 따라서 宗敎없이 完全한 倫理의 理論을 세우려 하더라도, 그는 亦是 宗敎에 對한 어떤 獨特한 態勢를 取하는 것을 意味한다."

이런 觀點에서 배비트를 考察한다면, 그가 宗敎없는 휴머니즘을 論하는 論理의 飛躍과 危險性을 指摘하지 않을 수 없다. 그러므로 엘리어트는 그의 <배비트論>(1927)에서 휴머니즘의 弱點을 들어 다음과 같이 警戒한다.

"[이 自制의 理論]은 政治的 및 宗敎的 無秩序에 對한 打開策이라 하겠다. 政治的인 面에 있어서는 이를 承認하기가 쉽다.... 그러나 正統宗敎의 '外部的' 制約이 軟弱해짐에 따라 個人이 自己自身에게 주는 '內部的' 制約으로 말미암아 이를 代用할 수도 있는 것이라고 배비트는 생각하는 것 같다. 나의 解釋이 옳을진대, 그는 프로테스탄트의 널판으로 카톨릭의 演壇을 만들려는 것 같다. 本是가 個人主義者이고, 個人主義思想의 自主性을 固守하려는 그는, 國家나 民族, 또는 世界全體에 適用할 수 있는 무엇을 만들려 애쓰는 것이다."

그렇다면, 배비트가 集中攻擊하는 自然主義의 渦中에 不知中 스스로 휩쓸려 들어갈 危險性이 많음을 엘리어트는 指摘하는 것이다.

끝으로, 위의 自然主義 批評과 關聯해서 엘리어트의 價値觀을 考察하는 데 重要한 點이 또 하나 있다. 要約하여, 範疇의 混同에 對한 그의 反對的 態度라 할 수 있다. 19世紀가 犯한 가장 큰 思想의 錯誤는, 物質的 進步가 저절로 道德的 進步를 가져다 준다는 생각이었다. 이 錯誤가 世界大戰으로 말미암아 暴露된 것은 事實이다. 19世紀가 굳게 믿었던 '聯關'의 法則과 '進步'의 原理는, 20世紀에 와서 그 普遍妥當性을 多少 잃었다고 볼 수 있는 것이, 歷史와 認識에는 聯關도 있지만 '中絶'도 있는 것이고, 文明이 必然的으로 더 나은 方向으로만 前進하지 않는다고 믿어진 때문이다. 그러면 存在와 價値를 混同하는 이 過失의 哲學의 張本人은 누구인가? 미들튼 머리(Middleton Murry)는 그의 論文 <The Cry in the Wilderness>(1920)에서 이를 헤겔(Hegel)에게 묻는다. 歷史上의 모든 事實과 人間精神의 모든 活動이 다 같이 靈魂의 正當한 發露라고 생각하는 過誤, 實在的 現實은 合理的이며, 歷史的인 것은 理想的과 같다는 데 內在하는 過誤, 事實上 있는 것과 마땅히 있어야 할 것을 同一視하는 過誤, 이런 것을 綜合하여 엘리어트의 恩師였던 산타야나(Santayana)도 反對的 立場을 取한 것은 그의 글 <The Two Idealisms>에 나타난다. 림보에 있는 소크라테스로 하여금 對話 形式으로 獨逸의 理想哲學을 아래와 같이 論駁케 한다.

"이리하여 너희들은 物理에서는 理想主義者가 되고, 道德에서는 現實主義者가 되었다. 그 結果 어느 두 部門을 보든지 너희들의 哲學에는 健實性도 眞理도 없다. 理性의 混同이 너희들 哲學者의 共通된 遺産이니, 그의 思想體系는 姑捨하고라도, 아직껏 그의 判斷力은 좋든 궂든 無條件하고 어떤 迷惑하는 怪物의 痲醉力에 빠져 버린 것이다. 邪神을 崇尙함은 野蠻의 根本要素이러라. 그러므로 獨逸의 헤라클리투스가 스스로 造作한 絶對無限者의 惡魔性에 끝없는 興을 느껴, 그 魔術을 덮어놓고 神의 特性인 척 했을 때, 그는 둘도 없는 滋味있는 野蠻人이었다."

이러한 極端의 見解가 哲學的으로 成立되느냐 안 되느냐는 알 바 아니로되, 다만 여기서 指摘하고자 하는 點은 산타야나의 感化를 받았다고 볼 수 있는 엘리어트도 이런 範疇의 混同을 싫어하는 것만은 事實이다. 그는 哲學의 訓練을 받은 사람이지만, 文壇에 나선 後로는 純哲學的 論文은 쓴 일이 없다. 그러나 그의 哲學的 訓練이 文學論文이나 그가 主幹하는 <Criterion>誌에 이따금 暗示되고 있는 것은 分明하다. 많은 例 中에 한두가지만 들기로 하자. 그의 <블레이크 論>(1920)의 結論에 아래와 같은 그의 古典主義的 立場을 밝혀 주는 대목이 있다.

"[블레이크]의 天才가 要求하였으나 不幸하게도 지니지 못한 것은, 公認된 傳統的 思想의 體系였다. 이것이 있었던들, 그는 自己造作의 哲學에 沒頭하지 않았을 것이며, 詩人으로서의 問題에 關心을 集中했을 것이다. 思想과 感情과 꿈이 뒤범벅이 된 것은 <Also Sprach Zarathustra>와 같은 著述에서도 보는 現象이다. 이런 混同은 무엇보다도 라틴文化의 美德은 아니다."

또 한편 매슈 아놀드와 월터 페이터에 對한 論文(1930)에서도, 範疇의 混同을 警戒하는 態度가 나타난다. 아놀드가 '文化'라는 칼을 들고 當時의 '필리스티아'에 對한 社會批判에 외로이 싸웠던 功勞에 우리는 한 '同志'로서 感服은 하지만, 그를 '指導者'로서 推仰할 수는 없는 것이라고 말했다. 왜냐 하면, 그는 宗敎哲學의 理智的 訓練이 적음에도 不拘하고 툭하면 宗敎를 論하는 傾向을 가졌었기 때문이다. 1939年에 出版한 著述 <The Idea of a Christian Society>에서 엘리어트는 "基督敎에 關한 큰 過誤는, 그것이 무엇보다도 敎理와 理智의 問題인 것을 宗敎와 感情의 問題로 삼는 데 있다"고 指摘하였다. 또 "基督敎社會와 異敎社會를 區別하는 것은 情熱이 아니라 敎理에 있다"고 하여, 感情이 信仰生活을 潤澤하게 하기보다는 混濁하게 한다고 主張한다. 아놀드는 敎理 없는 基督敎를 前提하고 基督敎의 感情만을 讚揚하는 까닭으로, 結果는 어빙 배비트의 휴머니즘과 같은 얼치기 宗敎가 된다고 그는 論斷한다.

"아놀드의 散文 著述은 '文化'에 關한 것과 '宗敎'에 關한 두 部門으로 나눌 수 있거니와, 그의 基督敎에 關한 著述은, 基督敎 信仰이 文化人에게는 勿論 不可能하다는 것을 거듭 되풀이할 따름이다. 이 著述은 싫증나게도 消極的이다. 그러나 그 消極性에는 特殊한 것이 있다. 卽 基督敎의 感情은 信念 없이 保存할 수도 있는 것이고, 또 그리 保存해야만 한다고 主張하는 것이 그의 目的이다. 이런 前提에서 사람에 따라 두 種類의 結論을 지을 수 있다. 卽 첫째로, 宗敎는 道德이라는 것과, 둘째로, 宗敎는 藝術이라는 結論이다. 아놀드의 宗敎運動은 宗敎를 思想에서 分離시키는 結果가 되고 만다."

이 點에서 아놀드는 칼라일이나 러스킨과 같은 部門에 屬하는 作家이며, 페이터도 아놀드 思想의 繼承者로 볼 수 있다. 페이터의 耽美主義도 究竟은 不完全한 人生倫理觀에 不過하며, 宗敎를 藝術에 合流시키려는 純粹하지 못한 努力이라고 엘리어트는 본다.

"'藝術至上'이 한 主義로 成立된다는 것은 疑心스러우나, 萬若 이것을 한 主義라 할 수 있다면, 藝術家는 제 할 일에 熱中하여야 한다는 訓戒로 볼 수 있다는 點에서는 오늘날까지 妥當性을 띤 것이로되, 그 主義가 觀衆이나 讀者나 聽衆에 對해서는 何等의 妥當性도 없었던 것이고 또 있을 수도 없는 것이다."

要는 페이터의 文學史的 地位도, 分裂된 精神科學을 다시 綜合하려는 十九世紀의 한 一時的 現象이라고 規定할 수 있을 것이다. 그러므로 엘리어트는 그의 古典主義에 立脚하여, 宗敎는 끝내 宗敎로서만 意味가 있는 것이고, 道德이라든가, 感情이라든가,

藝術이라든가, 또는 哲學이나 科學이라든가 하는 範疇와 混同되는 것을 反對하는 것이다.

以上 몇가지의 抗拒的인 態度에 나타나는 엘리어트의 價値觀은 必然的으로 그의 宗敎觀과 一致하는 結果에 到達한다. 그의 古典主義가 單純히 文學의 領域에 그치지 않고 信仰의 境地에까지 미치는 것이 또한 在來의 古典主義와 다른 點이다. 이에 그의 宗敎觀을 좀 더 詳細히 考察해 보기로 하자.

V. 엘리어트의 宗敎觀

엘리어트가 1927年에 英國市民이 된 무렵에 그는 앵글로 캐톨릭敎에 入敎하였다. 이듬해 1928年에 그는 論文集 <For Lancelot Andrewes>를 出版하여 文壇을 놀라게 하였다. "文學에서는 古典主義者, 政治에서는 王權主義者, 宗敎에서는 앵글로 캐톨릭"이라고 自己의 信條를 宣言한 이 冊의 序文은 20年이 지난 오늘날 도리켜 생각해 보면 너무 지나치게 是非거리가 되었던 것이다. 이 句節을 引用하여 엘리어트 攻擊을 일삼는 讀者는 그 다음에 나오는 대목을 아울러 記憶해야 할 것이다.

"첫번째 말은 뜻이 完全히 模糊하고, 자칫하면 생색만 내기 쉬운 말이라는 것을 내가 모르는 바 아니다. 둘째 말은 아직 正確한 規定을 내리지 않았고, 더구나 헛 생색보다 더 나쁘다고 볼 수 있는 '얌전빼는 保守主義'와 混用되기 쉬운 말이라는 것도 알고 있다. 셋째 말의 定義는 내가 그 責任을 가로맡을 것이 안된다."

이처럼 엘리어트는 이 세 術語를 警戒해서 썼음에도 不拘하고, 文壇의 新刊 評者들은 이것을 한 슬로간으로 惡用하여 그를 攻擊했던 것이다. 그의 立場이 勿論 英國이라는 歷史와 社會의 背景을 떠나서 普遍妥當性을 띤 것은 아니라는 點을 여기서 미리 밝혀둔다. 그가 다른 歷史的 傳統 아래 살았던들 그의 持論은 두말 할 것도 없이 懷古的 感傷主義에 빠지는 叛逆의 妄發에 지나지 못할 것이다. 여기서 다만 우리가 考察하고자 하는 것은, 그가 英國國敎를 信奉하게 된 것은 그의 古典主義의 論理的 歸着點이라는 것을 밝히는데 있을 따름이다.

宗敎―더구나 카톨릭敎―에서 儀禮形式을 除外할 수는 없는 것이지만, 儀禮形式이 宗敎의 全貌는 아니다. 許多한 사람에게는 信仰이 阿片이겠지만, 그렇지 않은 少數의

例外도 있을 것이다. (大衆의 믿음에는 언제나 阿片의인 面이 있다.) 宗敎가 現實逃避의 길을 열어준다지만, 個人에 따라서는 現實正視의 길이 되지 않는다고 어찌 斷定하랴. 엘리어트처럼 透徹한 洞察力과 正直한 理智力의 소유자가 敎會에 들어갈 때에는 制度化한 信仰의 虛僞를 모를 바 아니고, 허름한 安息을 求하려 하는 것도 아닐 것이다. 그가 <Thoughts after Lambeth>(1931)에서 告白한 바와 같이, 絶對로 現存하는 敎會 그대로를 是認하고자 하는 것은 아니다.

"지난날 敎會를 죽인 가장 나쁜 原因의 하나로, 十八世紀 以來 上流와 中上流階級 및 向上階級이 敎會를 政治的으로든, 行世를 위함이든, 반드시 있어야 할 것으로 알고, 이것을 認定한 것을 들 수 있다."

그러므로 오래 文壇의 知識階級에서 놀다가 敎會로 들어간 自身은 形言할 수 없는 孤立을 느낀다고 告白한다. 또 美國의 學者 노먼 포어스터(Norman Foerster)가 編纂한 論文集 <휴머니즘과 아메리카>(1930)에 엘리어트가 寄稿한 글 <휴머니즘 없는 宗敎>에서도 그는 制度化한 敎會의 腐敗性을 숨김없이 暴露하여 이를 警告하는 말을 했다.

"理想的인 世界는 理想的인 敎會이겠지만, 우리가 人間性을 조금이라도 아는 以上, 神品制度라는 것은 腐敗할 可能性이 많고 愚昧에 墮落할 것은 事實이고, 宗敎的 信仰이라는 것을 無批判的, 盲目的으로 對한다면, 頹廢와 迷信의 危險性이 많을 뿐더러, 人間의 精神은 人間의 肉體보다 훨씬 더 게으른 것이며, 西藏의 聖者社會란 形言할 수 없이 低級한 것이라는 事實을 뻔히 알 것이다."

엘리어트는 카톨릭敎의 神學的 敎理를 자주 言及하지는 않는다. 또 敎理 自體를 論議하는 것이 그의 目的은 아니다. 創作에 있어서는 自己의 暗澹한 永遠의 슬픔의 精神이 生의 枯渴을 正視하여 善惡의 正態를 알고 謙虛의 心理로 돌아가는 信仰心理의 괴로움을 記錄했으나, 그의 散文評論에서는 敎理의 理智的 土臺에서 본 自己의 價値觀을 이따금씩 暗示했을 따름이다. 여기에는 그의 散文에 나타나는 宗敎觀과 文學에 있어서의 古典主義와 聯關있는 部面만 簡單히 考慮해 보기로 한다. [미완]

近代 英詩 小史

"The traditions of poetry, in fact, is nothing but the accumulation, from countless ages of experiment, of the knowledge how to make language approximate most closely to the infinite variety of imagination."

—Lascelles Abercrombie, *The Theory of Poetry*

I

드디어 歐羅巴的 水準에 達한 듯싶던 十四世紀 末葉의 英詩壇도 Geoffrey Chaucer (c. 1340-1400), William Langland (c. 1332-c. 1400), John Gower (c. 1325-1408), 세 사람이 거의 때를 같이하여 죽은 後로는 分明히 한 고비를 넘어 다시 退步의 길로 들어섰다고 할 만큼 다음 150年間은 英詩를 爲해서 유달리 創作情神이 貧弱한 時期였다. 量으로만 따진다면 十萬行을 넘게 쓴 詩文學의 長距離 選手 John Lydgate(c. 1370-1450)도 있었고, Prince Hal의 버릇을 고칠 目的으로 長篇의 政治說敎詩를 쓴 Thomas Hoccleve(c. 1368-c. 1446)도 있었고, 또는 文法, 論理, 修辭의 三學(Trivium)과 算術, 幾何, 天文學, 音樂의 四學(Quadrivium)의 따분한 敎育論을 厖大한 알레고리로 韻文化한 Stephen Hawes(1474-c. 1523)도 있었다. 그러나 冷靜히 評價해서 그들의 文學史的 生命은 오로지 Chaucer를 詩聖으로 섬겼다는 點에서 오는 것이다. '꿈의 모티프'와 알레고리, 그리고 敎訓的인 '이야기 시'(narrative verse)가 아니면 詩가 되지 못한다는 固陋한 생각에 젖어 있었기 때문에, 英詩는 오랫동안 中世的인 遺風을 씻어 버리지 못하였다. '中世的'이라고 반드시 나쁜 것은 勿論 아니지만, 아무리 훌륭한 것이라도 한 매너리즘으로 頹廢하면 답답한 노릇이다. 게다가 英語 自體가 偶然히도 그 무렵에 中世英語로부터 現代英語로 옮겨가는 過渡期에 놓여 있었던 關係로 그들의 律調는 더욱 절름거리는 것이었다.

하기야 북쪽 스코틀랜드에서는 제임스 1세(1394-1437)가 다 같은 초써의 模倣이면서도 純情과 經驗에서 우러나는 페이소스에 가득 찬 長詩를 썼었고, Robert Henryson(c. 1430-1506)은 이미 二百年前에 佛蘭西의 La Fontaine을 豫想케 하는 fables를 많이 썼으며, 또 한편 William Dunbar(c. 1460-c. 1520)는 Villon이나 Burns에 못지않은 질기고도 씩씩한 새로운 詩의 言語를 發見하였던 것이며, Gavin Douglas(c. 1474-1522)는 素朴하면서도 줄기찬 言語로 베르길리우스의 *Aeneid*를 飜譯까지 한 事實이 있다.

實로 15世紀 乃至 16世紀 前半이 英詩 遺産에 보탬이 될수 있었다면, 이는 곧 (1) 上記 'Scottish Chaucerian'들이 거둔 功績, (2) ballad 文學의 生産, (3) John Skelton(c. 1460-1529)이 發見한 새로운 諷刺詩들의 技巧, 그리고 (4) 엘리자베스 時代에 絶頂을 이룰 詩劇의 앞길을 터주었다는 것, 이 네 갈래를 들 수 있을 것이다. 그러나 (1)은 事實上 傍系에 屬하는 英詩에 지나지 못하며, (2) ballad의 詩文學은 매우 重要하긴 하나, 아직도 潛伏狀態의 庶民文學으로서, 이것이 올바른 英詩의 主流에 合해지기는 비로소 十八世紀 後半에와서 "medieval revival"이 文學의 口號가 된 以後, 即 Thomas Percy(1729-1811)가 *Reliques of Ancient English Poetry*(1765)를 編纂하여 詩壇에 크나큰 衝動을 주게 된 以後의 이야기라고 봄이 正當하다. 그리고 (3) Skelton은 果然 奇拔한 天才로서 "Skeltonics"라는 稱號까지 足히 받음직한 스타일을 發見하였다. 그러나 그의 詩才는 Samuel Butler(1612-80)나 Jonathan Swift(1667-1745)의 그것과 마찬가지로 언제나 英詩의 正統과는 동떨어진 特異한 奇才로 남을 것이다. 'Skeltonics'가 辛辣한 諷刺詩에 알맞은 'hot jazz'와 같은 手法인 것은 事實이다. 그러나 反面에, 껑충 現代로 뛰어와 W. H. Auden(1907-1973)과 같은—詩를 "a game of knowledge"로 規定하는—詩人들에게 그 手法이 새삼스레 硏究된다는 것은 Skelton이라는 詩人이 아무 '時代'에도 屬하지 않음을 反證함을 말한다고 볼 수 있다. 그리고 끝으로, (4) 戱曲藝術의 發達을 促進하였다는 觀察은 누구나 트집잡지 못할 또렷한 史實이지만, 이 時代가 우리의 關心에 오르는 까닭은 엘리자베스 時代에 彗星과 같은 詩人들이 쏟아져 나왔기 때문이지, 결코 그 時代의 作品 自體에 이렇다 할 뛰어난 詩的 價値가 있어서 그런 것은 아니라고 하겠다.

歐羅巴 大陸에 있어서 十五世紀라면 곧 Cosimo de Medici(1389-1464)와 그의 孫子 Lorenzo Il Magnifico(1449-1492)가 눈부실 만큼 새로운 文化를 育成하고 있던 르네상스의 時期다. 이름난 學者 Ficino (1433-99), Pico della Mirandola (1463-94), Scaliger (1484-1558), Erasmus (c. 1466-1536), 詩人 Poliziano (1454-84), Ariosto (1474-1533), Villon (1431-c. 1465), Aretino (1492-1556), Marot (1495-1544), 散文作家 Castiglione (1478-1529), Machiavelli (1469-1527), Rabelais (c. 1494-1553), 等等—其他 우리가 르네상스와 聯想하는 畫家, 思想家, 航海家의 群像은 말할 것도 없거니와—거의 다 同時代의 사람들이다. 이때 英國은 무엇을 하고 있었던가? 罪가 純全히 文人에게만 있었다고 볼 수는 없다. 하찮은 百年戰爭(1337-1453)의 끝장을 보자마자 더 한층 어지러운 '장미전쟁'(1453-85)으로 突入하여 눈코 뜰 새가 없었던 것이다. 또 Caxton(c. 1422-91)이 1476년에 Westminster에서 印刷業을 始作하였다고 하지만, 그가

印刷한 著述이란 Chaucer나 Lydgate의 作品이 大部分이었다. Hallam의 말을 빌리면, "[In] a literary history it should be observed that the Caxton publications are more adapted to the general than the learned reader, and indicate but a low state of learning in England" (Hallam, *Literature of Europe*. I, iii)라고 할 수 있다. 이에 比하면, 1490年에 베니스에 와서 有名한 Aldine Press를 創設하고 그리스 作家 27名의 著述 96券을 우선 刊行한 Aldus Manutius(1450-1515)의 功績이 얼마나 더 보람있는 노릇인가? 어느 모로 보나 英國은 Victor Hugo가 말하는 "bringing out from the darkness that ransomed captive, the human mind"라는 새 情神이 뒤늦게 싹튼 것이었다. 特히 詩에 있어서 그렇다. 이 時代가 英文學에 이바지한 것은 오히려 散文이 아닐까 한다. Malory(fl. 1470)의 *Morte d'Arthur* (1485), Thomas a Kempis(1379-1471)의 名著 *De Imitatione Christi*의 英譯版 (1503), Froissart(c. 1337-c. 1404)의 *Chronicles* 英譯版(1523-25), William Tyndale(c. 1495-1536)의 英譯 <新約>(1525), Miles Coverdale(1488-1568)의 英譯 聖書(1535), 그밖에 Thomas More(1478-1535)의 몇몇 著述은 英散文史에 두고 두고 남을 것이다.

그렇기 때문에 *Tottel's Miscellany*(1557)는 英詩를 爲하여 여러가지 意味로 劃期的인 出版物이다. 310편의 詩가 收錄된 가운데 130여편은 작가미상이요, 96편이 Sir Thomas Wyatt(c. 1503-42)의 作品이고 40편이 Earl of Surrey(c. 1517-47)의 作品이다.

1527年에 Wyatt가 外交使節로 로마에 갔다가 歸國하면서 그는 英詩에 새로운 몇가지의 形式을 가져왔다. Sonnet, ottava rima, terza rima가 그것이다. 形式도 形式이려니와 그는 또 참다운 '궁정인'('courtier', 즉 Castiglione가 말하는 'cortegiano')은 自身의 母國語로 훌륭한 詩를 써야 한다는 르네상스的인 信念을 굳게 하고 돌아왔다. 그뿐 아니라 外國에서 모방해 온 詩形式을 가지고 英國人이 英語로 Petrarca나 Marot나 Aretino나 Seralino에 못지 않은 훌륭한 作品을 쓴다는 것은 二重으로 愛國的이라는 抱負를 품고 돌아왔다. 이 두가지 野心은 Spenser를 거쳐 Milton에 이르기까지 일관되게 흐르는 르네상스的 思想이다.

西洋 近代詩에 있어서 '定型詩'가 얼마나 重要한 發見인가 하는 것은 우리가 얼른 생각하기보다는 複雜한 問題다. Wyatt가 Sonnet를 紹介한지 300년이 지난 다음에도 Wordsworth는 "Scorn not the Sonnet"라고 부르짖었거니와, 이 定型詩가 어떻게 發生하여 어떻게 써지고 어떻게 變해 갔느냐 하는 考察은 곧 詩 自體의 歷史라 해도 過言이 아닐 만큼 重要한 問題이다. 詩學者 Abercrombie(1881-1938)는 다음과 같이 말한다.

"I do not think anything like prescribed form is to be found earlier than the troubadours: the discovery of its possibility is perhaps the most conspicuous relic of the exquisite civilisation of Provence. The Greeks had, of course, a passion for strict and noble form; but Greek form was always appropriate to and varying with the poetic occasion." (*The Theory of Poetry*)

12世紀의 Provence 詩人 Arnault Daniel을 Dante가 '*il miglior fabbro*'('the better maker')라 일컬은 것도 결코 妄論이 아니다. 마찬가지로 Wyatt가 Petrarca를 비롯한 여러 詩人으로부터 새로운 詩形을 받아들인 것은 英詩를 위해 결코 헛된 一時的인 流行이 아니었음을 우리는 여기서 밝혀야 한다.

Wyatt의 쏘네트 31편 가운데 열 편은 Petrarca 시의 飜譯이고 나머지는 擧皆가 習作이다. 그렇다손 치더라도 史的으로 본다면 중요한 習作이다. 그의 또 한가지 功勞는 英詩의 리듬을 音樂的으로 確立했으며 現代人이 쉽사리 알아 볼 수 있는 純粹한 詩의 言語를 찾아냈다는 것이다.

    And wilt thou leave me thus,
    That hath loved thee so long,
    In wealth and woe among?
    And is thy heart so strong
    As for to leave me thus?
        Say nay, +say nay!
("And wilt thou leave me thus?" 第二節)

Henry Howard, Earl of Surrey의 詩가 本質的으로 Wyatt보다 나을 것은 별반 없지만, 그는 Wyatt의 前轍이 가르친 바가 컸다. 詩形式으로 이바지한 點은, 첫째, 'Petrarchan sonnet'에 對한 이른바 'Shakespearean Sonnet'를 創造하였다는 것과, 둘째, 그가 *Aeneid* 第2券과 第4券을 英譯함에 있어 英詩에서 처음으로 'blank verse'를 썼다는 것, 이 두가지 사실이다. 'blank verse'의 發見이 얼마나 큰 功獻인가에 대해서는 Shakespeare를 論할 때 더 詳細히 언급하겠다. "Look in thy heart and write"라고 Sidney가 읊은 바 있거니와, Wyatt와 Surrey가 보인 詩作 態度의 '現代性'은 私的 情感을 노래했다는 사실이다. Saintsbury (1845-1933)는 다음과 같은 언급을 하였다.

The absence of the personal note in medieval poetry is a commonplace, and nowhere had that absence been more marked than in England. With Wyatt and Surrey English poetry became at a bound the most personal . . . the most 'introspective' in Europe. There had of course been love poetry before, but its convention had been a convention of impersonality. It now became the exact reverse. . . . Although allegory still retained a strong hold on the national taste, and was yet to receive its greatest poetical expression in *The Faerie Queen*, it was allegory of quite a different kind from that which in the *Roman de la Rose* had taken Europe captive, and had since dominated European poetry in all departments, especially in the department of love-making. . . . (*Elizabethan Literature*)

設使 *Tottel's Miscellany*가 대수로운 詩集이 아니었다고 하더라도 이미 1549年부터 主日마다 아무나 들을 수 있었던 *Book of Common Prayer* 의 純粹한 言語와 律調에 詩人들이 感染되지 않았을 理는 萬無하다. 그럼에도 不拘하고 Elizabeth 女王이 즉위하고 난 뒤 20年間 一流 詩人이 출현하지 않은 까닭은 어디 있을까? 結局은 세 가지 理由를 들 수밖에 없다. 첫째, 一種의 妥協案으로 國敎會敎條 *Thirty-nine Articles*(1560)를 制定하기는 했지만, 宗敎的 暗鬪가 여전히 繼續되어 오래도록 精神生活에 暗雲이 끼어 있었다는 것, 둘째, 英語의 'accidence'는 어느 程度 確定을 보았지만, 어휘가 아직도 流動狀態에 있었다는 것, 셋째, 詩의 'accentual prosody'가 미처 'doggerel'의 痼疾에서 完全히 벗어나지 못하여 'poulter's measure'와 같은 얼치기 韻律이 通用되고 있었다는 것을 들 수 있다.

勿論 'poet'는 아닐망정 'rhymester'의 資格은 충분한 群小作家들이 많기는 하였다. *Tottel's Miscellany*를 본받은 *A Hundreth Sundrie Floweres*(1573), *The Paradise of Dainty Devices* (1576), *A Gorgeous Gallery of Gallant Inventions*(1578), *A Handful of Pleasant Delytes*(1584)와 같은 詩選集이 많이 流行되었고, *Mirror for Magistrates*(1559)와 같은 Lydgate流의 英國史 詩集도 愛讀되었다. 前記 *Miscellanies*에서 가장 注目할 만한 詩人에 George Gascoigne (1542–77)이 있고, 後者 *Mirror for Magistrates*에서는 Thomas Sackville(1536–1608)이 第一 關心을 끄는 作家이다. 그러나 Gascoigne이 아무리 앞날을 내다보는 作家라 할지라도 그는 結局 確固한 스타일을 찾아내지 못하였기 때문에 試鍊期의 詩人임에 틀림없고, 한편 Sackville은 그가 쓴 'Induction'(1563)이 아무리 印象깊은 作品이라 할지라도, 그의 手法이 前世紀에 屬하는 알레고리에 그치는 만큼, 그는 한 懷古的 詩才라 아니 할 수 없다. Spenser

自身에도 알레고리가 없었던 것은 아니지만, 이미 時代는 알레고리만으로 滿足할 수 없는 보다 더 큰 技巧를 要求하였던 것이다.

Ovid의 *Metamerphoses*(1567)가 더 重要하였다고도 볼 수 있다. Sackville의 'Induction'은 마치 James Thomson(1834-82)의 名詩 "The City of Dreadful Night"(1874)와 같은 範疇에 드는 作品이다. 印象에는 남지만 時代의 흐름과는 동떨어진 느낌이 없지 않다.

II

무엇 때문에 Spenser(1552~99)가 "the second father of English poetry"니, "a poet's poet"니 하는 讚辭를 받느냐 하는 問題는 英國人이 아니고서는 對答하기 어려운 問題일런지도 모른다. 그만큼 Spenser는 英國的인 存在이며, 특히 엘리자베스 時代 英國의 컨텍스트를 떠나서 理解하기 어려운 存在이다. 英國의 르네상스를 代辯하는 詩人으로 Shakespeare를 꼽는 것은 勿論 當然한 노릇이지만, 적어도 Shakespeare는 엘리자베스 時代 英國의 컨텍스트가 아니라도 우리가 能히 理解할 수 있는 詩人이다. Spenser는 그렇지 않다고 하여도 過言이 아니다.

올바르게 Spenser를 評價하려면 먼저 그가 어떠한 詩的 眼目을 가지고 詩作에 着手하였는가를 밝혀야 한다.

*Tottel's Miscellany*의 原動力이 Petrarca(1304-74)에 있었고, 또 Petrarca가 英詩에 끼친 影響이 엘리자베스(1558-1603) 朝 末期까지 繼續된 것은 事實이다. 그러나 Petrarca는 이미 2世紀 前의 詩人이었다. *Tottel's Miscellany*와 <牧羊者의 月曆>(1579) 사이에는 20年의 差異밖에 없었지만, Spenser가 登場함으로써 英詩의 標榜하는 詩的 對象은 飛躍的으로 '現代化'하여져 當代의 大陸 詩人들, 즉 Ronsard(1524-85), Du Bellay(1522-60), Tasso(1544-95)가 아니면 거의 當代라고 할 수 있는 詩人 Ariosto나 Marot였다는 點이 Spenser에 있어서 놀라운 事實의 하나이다. 詩人 Spenser의 出發點은 Petrarca가 아니고 Le Pleïade였다는 것과, 그의 宿願이 Aristo나 Tasso를 凌駕하는데 있었다는 것이 英詩史의 새로운 現象이다.

그가 'humanist poet'로 自處할 수 있었던 보람도 여기에 있다. 그의 詩作修業은 Virgil이나 Milton에 못지 않을 만큼 完全하였다. 르네상스 詩文學의 '宣言書'라고도 할 수 있는 Du Bellay의 名著 *Défense et Illustration de la Langue Française*(1549)의 理論을

그는 그대로 Shepherd's Calendar에서 實踐에 옮겨 英詩를 "rascally rhymers"의 손에서 救出하였다. 그뿐인가? Aeneid를 쓰기 前에 Eclogues를 쓴 Virgil의 前例를 그대로 좇아, Faerie Queene을 쓰기 前에 Shepherd's Calendar를 쓴 것이 결코 偶然의 一致가 아니라면, 또 "long planning and beginning late"라는 Milton의 告白이 Spenser에도 適用될 수 있다는 것 亦是 單純한 臆說은 아니겠다. 詩人 Spenser에서 이 르네상스的인 野心을 除去할 수 없으리만큼 엘리자베스 時代는 'romantic epic'을 憧憬하였던 것이다.

Shepherd's Calendar가 Lyrical Ballads나 The Waste Land에 견줄만한 大膽한 作品임은 周知의 事實이거니와, 이에 나타나는 獨創性은 곧 Spenser의 詩的 地位를 알리는 關鍵이므로 여기 그 몇가지를 들지 않을 수 없다. 첫째, Spenser는 말에 陶醉한 詩人임을 알 수 있다. 方言, 古語, 廢語, 造語, 할 것 없이 自由自在로 實驗하였기에 Ben Jonson(c. 1573-1637)은 Spenser가 "writ no language"라고까지 말하며 酷評하였던 것이다. 둘째로, 그는 이 作品에서 무려 14種의 metre를 썼으되 그 中에 5種은 自身이 創造한 것이고, 2種은 英詩에서 처음 보는 것이었다. 또한 6種의 形式—即, love-lament, *débat*, roundelay, fable, paean, dirge—을 다루는 솜씨가 非常하였다. 셋째로, 그가 이와 같이 지나칠 만큼 獨創에 힘을 기울였음에도 不拘하고, 그의 'syntax'—즉 詩想의 展開—는 언제나 透明하고 고르다는 點을 指摘해야 할 것이다. 實로 이 點은 그의 어느 作品에서나 볼 수 있는 特徵이다. Grierson(1866-1960)이 한 "Syntactically Spenser is one of the easiest of English poets"라는 말도 至當한 評이다. Mother Hubberd's Tale(1591)과 같은 Chaucer風의 諷刺詩를 보든지, Colin Clout's Come Home Again(1595)과 같은, 英詩에서 보기 드문 "well-bred conversation"의 文章으로 된 作品을 보든지, 또는 祝婚歌의 最高峰이라 할 수 있는 Epithalamion(1595)과 Prothalamion(1596)을 보든지, 要는 Spenser의 文章은 언제나 水晶처럼 맑다는 것을 알 수 있다. 끝으로 또 한 特徵은 그의 思潮이다. Puritanism에 가까운 Protestant Christianity를 그가 信奉하였다는 것은 <牧羊者의 月曆>에서도 또렷이 나타나는 바이거니와, Spenser가 르네상스 詩人으로서 特色을 發揮할 수 있었다는 點은 그의 精神的 地盤이 어느 한쪽으로 치우치지 않았기 때문에, 이것이 可能하였다고 말할 수 있다. 英文學者 Elton(1861-?)도 이 點을 밝혀 다음과 같이 말했다.

> He has no compact body of dogma like Milton. Many streams of thought float along in his mind together, mixing when they may. He may be said to have several religions. His Protestant Christianity adjusts itself easily to the doctrines of Plato;

and in these he appears, quite early his course, to have found a refuge from his melancholy mood. . . .

(*The English Muse*)

이런 複合性이 없었던들 Spenser는 *Faerie Queene*과 같은 傑作을 쓸 수 없었을 것이며, 또 *The Four Hymns*(1596)와 같은 Platonic-Protestant 哲學詩를 썼을 理 萬無하다. 前者가 後代 詩人에게 至大한 影響을 준 事實은 다 아는 터이려니와, 後者가 思想的으로나 藝術的으로 卓越한 '哲學詩'의 嚆矢라는 事實은 作品을 읽어보면 누구나 首肯할 것이다. 그만큼 Spenser는 르네상스와 宗敎改革의 思潮를 反映하는데 成功한 詩人이다.

그러나 '모든 길은 로마로 通한다'는 格으로 그의 모든 群小作品은 오로지 *Faerie Queene*을 爲한 練習에 不過하다 하여도 좋을 만큼 이 作品은 重要한 傑作이다. 前半은 1590年에, 後半은 1596年에 出版되었지만 其實 19年 동안 힘을 기울인 三萬六千行이나 되는 力作이고, 그나마도 半밖에 쓰지 못한 未完成品이다. 完成 未完成은 姑捨하고 우리가 여기서 따질 것은 作家의 構想과 手法이다.

Sidney와 마찬가지로 詩의 目的을 "delightful teaching"에 둔 Spenser는 이 作品에서 '紳士道의 龜鑑'이 될 만한 敍事詩를 쓰는 것이 目標였다. 表面에 나타나는 構想人物은 道德的 德目들이고 그들이 取하는 行動은 *Pilgrim's Progress*에 못지 않은 道德的 알레고리이지만, 이 道德的 알레고리의 裏面에는 當時의 英國歷史의 斷層을 內包한 政治的 歷史的 알레고리가 겹쳐 있다. 이 두 줄기를 *Morte d'Arthur*와 같은 騎士道的 로만스의 形式으로 表現하되, 作家의 窮極目標는 *Orlando Furioso*에 비길만한 "善과 惡의 永遠한 戰爭"을 命題로 삼는 敍事詩를 쓰는 데 있다. 알레고리와 로만스와 敍事詩, 세 文學 形態 사이를 交錯하는 思想의 根底 亦是 알송달송한 것이다. 칼빈적 基督思想이 있는가 하면 俗化한 아리스토텔레스 思想도 있고, 또 Ficino가 流行시킨 플로렌스 플라토니즘도 찾아 볼 수 있다. 어느 모로 살펴 보나 거미줄과 같은 異彩로운 構想이다. W. B. Yeats(1865~1939)는 그의 Spenser 論에서 이렇게 말하였다.

He was always to love the journey more than its end, the landscape more than the man, and reason more than life, and the tale less than the telling.

이 特質은 Spenser 뿐만 아니라 어느 程度 英國의 詩才 自體에서 볼 수 있는 要素가 아닐까? Keats(1795-1821)나 Byron(1788-1824)의 長詩를 보든지, 甚至於는 Pope(1688-1744)의 *Moral Essays*의 設計圖나 Wordsworth(1770-1850)의 *Prelude* 以後의 大計劃을 보든지, Yeats의 말이 含蓄하는 바가 더욱 큰 듯하다. Spenser를 '詩人의 詩人'이라고 Hazlitt(1778-1830)가 讚美한 것도 결코 偶然이 아니다. 그러므로 Spenser의 天才를 爲해 'Spenserlian stanza'보다 더 適合한 律格이 없었던 것이며, 그의 繪畵的 詩才를 發揮하는데 있어서 *Faerie Queene*보다 더 알맞은 構想이 있을 수 없었다. 作家 스스로가 이야기를 重要視하지 않았을 바에야 讀者가 굳이 탓할 것이 못 된다. 끝없이 展開되는 꿈속같은 敍景과 아울러 千態萬象의 調和를 이룰 수 있는 韻律, 이 두가지가 完全히 結合된 作品이기에 *Faerie Queene*은 두고 두고 後代 作家들의 硏究對象이 되고 남는 것이다.

國運이 날로 膨脹해 감에 따라서 1590年代부터 英詩도 獨特한 方向으로 發展을 보게 되었다. Romantic epic을 通해 愛國意識을 鼓吹하겠다는 Spenser의 뜻을 繼承하여 詩人들이 歷史詩('historical poems')를 이 무렵에 많이 썼다는 것이 다른 時代에서 보기 드문 現象의 하나이다. 이른바 '歷史詩'가 비록 '敍事詩'와 類型을 달리한다 할지라도 그 뜻한 바는 共通된 點이 많다. Shakespeare 自身도 이 무렵에 歷史劇을 연달아 썼다는 것이 興味있는 事實이다. 이름난 歷史詩人들의 作品으로 다음의 몇 가지를 들 수 있다. 길이가 一萬行이나 되는 William Warner(1558-1609)의 長詩 *Albion's England*(1586-1606)를 오늘날 읽을 사람은 별로 없겠지만, 그 當時에는 호메로스에 比較되던 作品이었고, 實은 십팔世紀에 特히 愛讀되었다. 當代의 評論家 Francis Meres(1565-1647)는 Warner를 Spenser와 함께 屈指의 'heroic poet'으로 꼽았던 것이다. 또한 같은 範疇에 들 수 있는 詩人에 Samuel Daniel(1562-1619)이 있다. 그는 多方面에 詩才를 發揮하였으나, 自身은 薔薇戰爭을 取材한 七千餘行 되는 長詩 *Civil Wars*(1595, 1609)를 가장 力作으로 생각했던 모양이다. 오늘날 우리가 Daniel에서 取할 點은 內容보다는 그의 淡淡한 文章인 듯하다. 散文과 詩의 中間을 걷는 無色透明한 文章—Coleridge(1772-1834)가 말하는 '中立的 言語'('neutral language')—도 亦是 詩의 言語가 될 수 있음을 Daniel이 證明한다. 그러나 누구보다 意識的으로 스펜서의 創作精神을 標榜한 作家는 Drayton(1563-1631)이겠다. 多藝多能한 作家였던 만큼 歷史詩도 이루 列擧하기 어려울 程度로 많이 썼다. 그 中에 特히 *England's Heroical Epistles*(1597) 같은 長詩는 그 時代의 趣味를 엿볼 수 있는 作品의 하나이다. Drayton이 얼마나 "Merrie England"를 사랑하는 典型的 엘리자베스 時代의

作家였던가는 그의 最大力作 *Poly-Olbion*(1622年 完成)으로도 이를 足히 알 수 있다. 都合 三十部 近 一萬五千 行이나 되는 이 厖大한 作品의 內容은 그 副題目이 如實히 나타낸다.

"A Chorographical Description of all the Tracts, Rivers, Mountains, Forrests, and other parts of the Renowned Isle of Great Britain, with Intermixture of the most Remarkable Stories, Antiquities, Wonders, Rarities, Pleasures, and Commodities of the same."

鄕土愛도 이쯤 되면 罔惻한 狂症밖에는 안 되지만, 要는 Drayton이 Spenser의 'romantic epic'에 對한 野心을 繼承하지 않았던들 그가 이와 같은 千古에 남을 畸形의 長詩를 쓰지 않았을 것이다.

以上 略記한 바와 같이, Spenser의 敍事詩 傳統은 얼마동안 特殊한 方向으로 展開되다가 그만 앞길이 막혀 버렸다. 더구나 Arthurian romance를 素材로 한 敍事詩라면 Spenser의 作品이 고작이라는 通念이 있었기 때문에, 다음에 올 敍事詩人 Milton(1608-74)까지도 한동안 Arthur의 傳說에서 取材하려 망설이다가 結局 抛棄하였던 것이다. 그러나 *Shepherd's Calendar*를 契機로 하여 이루어진 'pastoralism'은 Spenser 當代 뿐만 아니라 꽤 오랫동안 確固한 詩風으로 남았다. 'Pastoral elegy'만 하더라도 *Lycidas*(1637), *Adonais*(1821), 또는 *Thyrsis*(1867)와 같이 英詩에 오래 繼續된 것이라고 볼 수 있다. 그러면 이 pastoralism이 Elizabethan 詩風에 어떤 特徵을 띠었던가를 暫時 살펴보기로 하자.

Elizabeth 時代의 pastoralism에 두가지의 遺産을 찾아 볼 수 있으니, 그 하나는 이른바 'Sicilian'이요, 다른 하나는 'Arcadian'이라 하겠다. 前者는 紀元前 3世紀의 希臘 詩人 Theocritus가 Sicily의 田園生活을 그린 三十餘篇의 牧歌(idylls)에서 始作된 것이라 한다. 이미 Theocritus에서 '田園詩'의 手法인 (1) singing-match, (2) dirge, (3) love-complaint를 볼 수 있다. Virgil(70-19 B.C.)은 이를 다시 繼承하여 그의 'bucolic eclogues'에서 새로이 (4) panegyrics(讚辭)의 傳統을 添加하였다. 羅甸語 詩人 Mantuan(1448-1516)은 Petrarca가 發見한 (5) satire의 技巧를 完成하여 素朴한 田園生活과 腐敗한 社會面을 相剋시켰다. 이 모든 要素가 Spenser에도 同時에 나타나는 結果로 그의 'shepherd'는 (1) 때로는 moralist가 되고, (2) 때로는 poet의 性格을 띠고, 또 (3) 때로는 lover로 나타나는 것이다. 特히 Elizabeth 時代의 pastoralism에서는 其二와 其三의 性格이 가장 濃厚하다.

그리고 'Arcadian' pastoralism은 散文 로만스 *Daphnis and Chloë*를 썼다는 紀元 四世紀 乃至 五世紀의 希臘 小說家 Longus에서 始作되어 伊太利의 Boccaccio(1313-75), Sannazaro(1458-1530), 또는 葡萄牙의 Montemayor(c. 1521-61) 等을 거쳐 英國의 散文 로만스 作家인 Sir Philip Sidney (1554-86), Robert Greene (c. 1560-92), Thomas Lodge (c. 1558-1625) 等으로 傳해 왔다. 大槪 이런 散文作品 가운데 珠玉같은 抒情詩가 挿入되었던 것이다. 'Shepherd Corydon'이니 'Shepherdess Phyllis'니 하는 稱號는 다만 二八靑春의 男女 'lad'나 'lass'와 同意語로 쓰여졌으므로 結果는 뻔하다.

> There is little realism in the Elizabethan Arcadia; it is the country of a townsman's dream, where eternal summer dwells and lovers are always a-Maying. . . .
> (Grierson and Smith, *A Critical History of English Poetry*)

要컨대 Pastoralism이 Sicilian 이건 Arcadian이건 純情을 '노래'하는데 있어서는 매일반이므로 이 牧歌的 傳統이 Elizabeth 時代의 抒情詩才를 얼마나 潤澤하게 하였는가를 알 수 있다.

이와 아울러, 일찍부터 流行하던 "Miscellanies"가 1590年代에 들어서면서부터 유달리 많이 刊行된 것을 보더라도 마찬가지 傾向을 알려주는 것이다. 例컨대 *Breton's Bower of Delites*(1592), *The Phoenix Nest*(1593), *The Passionate Pilgrim*(1599), *England's Helicon*(1600), *England's Parnassus*(1600), *Belvedere*(1600), *Davison's Poetical Rhapsody*(1602)같은 抒情詩 選集을 들 수 있다. 뿐만 아니라, 當時의 英國음악은 歐羅巴에서 最高水準을 자랑하던것이었던 만큼, 有名한 作曲家들—William Byrd(c. 1538-1623), John Dowland(c. 1563-c. 1626), Thomas Morley(1557-c. 1603), Thomas Campion(1567-1620), John Daniel (Samuel Daniel의 아우) 等—이 作曲은 勿論이려니와 흔히 作詩까지 하여 'Song-books'를 많이 發表하였던 것이다. [미완]

<오셀로> 小考*

作家 셰익스피어에 對해서는 옛날 黃喜 政丞의 人生觀밖에 옳은 것이 없을 상 싶다. 톨스토이가 말하듯이 가장 군소리가 많은 詩人이 셰익스피어라는 見解도 그럴법한 노릇이고 또는 許多한 셰익스피어 禮讚者와 더부러 이를 偶像化하여 最高의 入札價格을 부르는 사람도 一家見을 이룬 사람이라 하겠고 이 兩極의 矛盾을 矛盾으로 看破하는 사람도 옳다고 하겠다. 콩을 퐅이라고 우기지만 안하면 그만이다. 荒唐無軌한 이 詩劇의 天才에 對해서는 解釋의 '正道'가 있을수 없다. 그러므로 모로가도 서울만 가랬다는 金言이 셰익스피어의 舞臺藝術論에 알맞은 말이다.

寫眞쟁이가 한 장의 寫眞을 찍을랴면 對象의 距離와 周圍의 光線을 생각해서 露光의 시간을 調整해야만 이른바 '焦點'이 맞는다고 한다. 비록 凡庸한 比喩라 하겠으나 이 세 原則을 作品 <오셀로>에 適用해 보면 그 舞臺藝術의 複合性과 特殊性을 大略 앎즉도 하다. 時時刻刻을 客觀化되어 찍혀지는 寫眞이 戲曲의 終幕에 가서 어떠한 全體的인 心紋을 이루도록하는 것이 劇作家의 任務라 할진대 具現할려는 人物과 人物即 對象이 어떻게 交叉하며 그들의 台詞나 그들의 行動하는 場幕의 雰圍氣—即光線—이 어떠한 이미지를 투영하여주며 또 그들의 밑받이되는 情熱이 어떠한 고비와 액션—即 露光이 時間을 겪어서 最後的인 카타르시스의 現像이 이루워지나? 하는 몇몇가지 斷層的 考察이 없이는 伸縮性있는 셰익스피어의 藝術을 알기어렵지 않을가 생각된다.

외줄기의 플롯트만 가지고는 作品을 쓰지 않는 것이 셰익스피어의 常習이다. 여러 줄기가 竝進하면서 서로 얽혀 한 바탕을 이루는 것이다. 作品 <오셀로>에 나타나는 男女 乃至 夫婦關係만 해도 너댓 種類가 있어—오셀로와 데스디모나, 이아고와 에밀리아, 캐씨오와 비앵카, 로더리고와 데스디모나, 그리고 假想的인 캐씨오와 데스디모나—各其 存在面을 달리하면서도 한 核心을 싸고 도는 螺旋運動이다. 아내를 죽이는 것도 두 가지로 對照가 된다. 勿論 最後的인 對蹠는 오셀로와 이아고이다. 셰익스피어의 四大悲劇中에서도 이처럼 善惡의 葛藤이 個個의 人物로 具象化된 作品은 없다. 모든 否定의 原理—憎惡, 죽음, 恐怖, 生의 더러움 等等—을 表白하는 惡이 다른 作品에 있어서는 苦憫體(主人公)의 主觀과 渾然一體하여, <햄리트>의 幽靈이라든가 <맥베스>의 魔女라든가 <리어>의 暴風雨와 같은 自然 또는 超自然과 合勢됨으로써 惡의 觀念이 가위 象徵的으로 具現되어 作品 全體의 雰圍氣를 支配하게 된다. 그러나 <오셀로>에 있어서는 이러한 象徵이 全然없고

---

* 이 글은 劇團 女人小劇場의 셰익스피어 祭 제7회 공연작품인 吳華燮 譯 <오셀로>의 팜플레트에 실렸다.

오로지 이아고라는 이웃 四寸 人物을 通하여 惡이 具現되므로, 따라서 이 悲劇에 있어서의 善惡의 葛藤은 더욱 齷齪하고 더욱 醜惡하고 窒息하리만큼 답답한 性格을 띄우게된다. 問題꺼리의 손수건 조차 巫女가 짠 것으로 魔力이 접힌 神秘스러운 것이라 하지만, 우리가 舞臺에서 볼 수 있는 것은 한 쪼각의 헌깊에 지나지 못한 것이다.

詩人코울러리지는 <햄리트>의 幽靈과 <맥베스>의 魔女를 評하여, "前者는 興奮시키는 것이 目的이고, 後者는 이미 興奮된 心理狀態를 表白하는 것이 目的"이라고 말했거니와, 이와같이 主人公의 主觀과 幻像과 客觀의 事實體가 渾和하여 惡의 觀念이 表現되지만, <오셀로>에서는 독사같이 惡辣하고 배암의 혀끝 같이 날랜 한 人間으로서 表現되므로, 그 比重을 보아 셰익스피어는 이아고에게 千 줄 以上의 臺詞를 주고, 오셀로에게는 千 줄보다 훨씬 적은 臺詞를 주며, 데스디모나에게는 不過 三百九十줄밖에 주지 않는다. 그뿐 아니라 이아고는 大部分 散文으로 말하는데 비해, 오셀로는 氣絶하는 場面―四幕一場―에서 暫時 散文으로 말할 뿐이요 데스디모나는 終始 韻文으로만 말하는 均衡만 보더라도 作者의 意圖하는 바를 알 수 있다.

그러나 무엇보다도 作品 全體의 雰圍氣를 알리는 關鍵은 그 詩言語가 內包하는 이미지에 있다. 疑妻症이라는 感情이 가장 動物的인 感情인 同時에 第三者는 무어라고 形言할 수 없는 醜惡한 感情이라는 것은 말할 必要도 없다. 따라서 학자 캐롤라인 스퍼어전 女史가 指摘한 바와같이, 作品 <오셀로>에 나오는 比喩, 隱喩의 이미지는 擧皆가 下級動物이 서로 죽이고 淫亂한 가운대 으르대는 데서 뽑은 것이다. 쉬파리 떼가 엉긴다는 둥, 개가 싸운다는 둥, 끈끈이로 새를 잡는다는 둥, 당나귀 코를 꿰어 끈다는 둥, 거미가 파리를 잡는다는 둥, 개새끼를 두들겨팬다는 둥, 불알을 깐다는 둥, 其他 살쾡이, 이리, 염소, 원숭이를 자주 들먹여서 殘忍한 苦痛相과 淫蕩한 雰圍氣를 알리는 것이 이아고의 臺詞이다. 이에 젖어 純?한 사랑이 더럽혀진 後로는 오셀로도 '염소 떼, 원숭이 떼들!' 하고 咀呪하며 징글맞은 ?蟲, 두꺼비, 악어같은 下級動物이 자주 그의 臺詞에 오르내린다. 그밖에 樂器의 나사를 늦추어 音程을 破壞한다든가, 毒藥이 몸에 단다든가 하는 이미지가 이아고의 입에서 나오는것도 當然한 노릇이다.

한갖 깨끗한 이미지로는 主人公의 사랑에 關聯된 바다의 이미지가 있을 뿐이다. 이런 意味로도 戱曲의 骨子는 베니스를 떠나 아슬하고도 浪漫的인 바다를 건너 一同이 싸이프러스로 옮겨 온 第二幕부터 始作된다고 볼 수 있다. 오셀로가 데스디모나를 만나 하는 말―"아, 나의 靈魂의 기쁨이여! 風浪 끝에 이러한 平穩이 올진대, 바람은 불어 죽엄을 깨워 일으켜도 좋으리…" (二幕一場) 오셀로가 이아고의 誘惑에 빠져 굳은

決心을 할 때 하는 말―"얼음장 싸늘한 湖水와 거센 물결이 썰물됨이 없이 프로폰티크와 헬레스폰트의 기슭을 씻어 오직 줄기차게 나아가는 폰투스의 바닷물처럼 나의 피비린 생각은 暴流를 이루어 뉘우침이 없으리니, 사랑의 보금자리로 물러서지 않으리라...." (三幕三場) 오셀로가 아내를 죽인 뒤에 하는 말―"나의 나그네는 이에 끝나니, 이곳이 나의 마지막 航海의 目的地요 寄港地러니..." (五幕二場) 몇몇 例에 불과하다.

"나의 難關은 幕을 올렸다가 내렸다가 하는데 있다"고 詩人 티 에스 엘리어트가 告白하였거니와 現代 舞台에서 셰익스피어 作品을 上演하는데도 가장 어려운 問題의 하나는 어디서 幕을 내리느냐 하는 것이다. 폴리오 全集에 表示된 機械的인 場幕의 區分은 그대로 盲從할 必要조차 없다.

中間幕을 내림으로써 一旦 액션의 抛物線은 끊어지게 된다. 끊으면 勿論, 戱曲 全體의 律動의 形象이 깨어진다. 입센 以後의 散文戱曲과 달라서 셰익스피어의 戱曲은 우리의 聽覺을 通하여 들어오는 詩言語의 波長과, 登場人物의 情熱과 情熱이 凝結하므로 우리의 想像力에 스며드는 空間의 心紋과, 一定한 連續性을 띠고 굵은 波濤처럼 밀고오는 액션의 呼吸, 이 三者가 步調를 맞추어 나가는 가운데서 作品 全體를 抱擁할 수 있는 한 다이내믹한 螺旋運動의 核心體를 우리에게 주는 것이다. 그러므로 그의 時間은 硏究家들이 累累히 말하듯이 韻律('rhyme')의 問題가 아니라 템포의 問題요, 地理的 空間의 問題가 아니라, 心理的 空間의 問題이다.

現實的으로 보아, 作品 <오셀로>는에 無理한 것이 많다. 評論家 그랜빌 바커가 지적한 바와 같이 싸이프러스로 場面이 옮겨진 二幕一場에서 不過 白八十 줄 남저지 進展되는 사이에 土耳其 艦隊가 暴風雨에 難破하고 캐씨오의 배가 入港하고, 데스디모나와 이아고가 到着하고, 마지막으로 오셀로가 無事히 入港하여 夫婦가 再會한다는 것은 非現實的이라고 트집 잡을수 있으리라. 또는 이아고가 誘惑을 始作하여 그날 밤중 쯤해서는 이미 데즈디모나가 죽는데, 이아고는 말하기를, 최근에 캐씨오와 같이잔 일이있었다는 둥, 오셀로는 캐씨오의 키쓰를 아내의 입술에서 보지 못했다는 둥 하여 相當한 時日의 經過가 있었던 것 같은 印象을 준다. 한 줄의 예에 지나지 않으나, 요는 셰익스피어의 時間이 懷中時計에 依한 時間이 아니라 감정에 呼訴하는 액션의 템포와 呼吸이 問題라는 것이다.

이와같이 伸縮性있는 心理的 波長과 둥근 曲線의 리듬으로 戱曲 <오셀로>를 본다면, 大略 네 번의 呼吸을 두고 進展될 것이다. (i)베니스의 場面 (第一幕 全部) (細分하여 두 呼吸, 即 (1) 港內의 場面 (2)布告文부터 캐씨오가 醉中亡身하기까지) (iii) 中心이되는 액션, 即 三回로 빨리 演出되는 誘惑의 場面―三幕 始作에서부터 四幕 二場 까지, 될 수있는 대로

細分하지 않고 숨 돌릴 餘裕없이 一瀉千里로 나가는 것이 累積의 效果를 이룰 듯하다) (iv) 끝까지―四幕 三場에서부터 끝까지―(細分하여, 세 呼吸 (1)버들 노래 場面,(2) 夜半 騷動,(3) 끝場面). 그러나 위와같은 考察은 結局 作品의 메타피직크요, 上演됨으로써 비로소 이것이 한 피직크로 化하는 것이다. 舞臺 藝術의 보람도 이에있는 것이다. 演出되는 瞬間이 戲曲 作品으로서는 가장 重要한 瞬間인 것이다.

제2부
영어연설문, 논설문, 수필

Statement by Dr. John M. Chang
Before the First Committee of the Third Session
Of the United Nations General Assembly
(7 December 1948)

[This is the typescript of the speech Professor Insoo Lee wrote at the request of the leaders of the nation to be delivered at the General Assembly of the United Nations on December 7, 1948. It was read by Dr. John M. Chang, the Korean delegate to the U. N., and was recorded on a tape and reproduced as a typescript to be kept in the U. N. archive. Sixty years later, Professor Lee's daughter's son, Quentin Kim, then a doctoral student at Julliard, was invited to play the piano for the international guests who gathered for a party held at the residence of the U. N. Secretary-General, Mr. Pan Ki-mun, in New York, on December 17, 2008. After the event Quentin, remembering what his grandmother wrote in her memoir, asked the U. N. personnel in charge of the archive to locate and make a copy of the typescript of the speech for him. The U. N. archive still keeps the typescript reproduced from tape-recording.]

Honorable Chairman,

To speak before the distinguished representatives of the sovereign nations of the world gathered in this Committee of the General Assembly of the United Nations is a great honor for me. Since we, thirty million Koreans, regard the United Nations as our greatest hope, we present our cause before you with confidence. This noble organization bears within itself the collective conscience of mankind, and I am humbled to be the one who speaks before it on behalf of justice and liberty for the ancient Korean nation now reborn.

Throughout our unbearable years of bondage, the Korean people kept ever burning their deep longing for restoration of sovereign independence never to be surrendered to their fate. Some delegates in this room, whose homelands for a time were ruled by an invader, can share more intimately the ardent feeling of the Korean people. But all delegates, whose nations are founded on devotion to liberty, understand our feelings. Surely, love of liberty is the most compelling emotion shared by all, all men. The crying memories of men's constant struggle for freedom, which surround us in this beautiful city of Paris, are powerful evidence of that fact. In the Pantheon, on the heroic statue commemorating the Convention Nationale, are inscribed words, which precisely express the feelings of the people, whom I have the great honor to represent: "vivre libre ou mourrir."

The Korean people have suffered greatly in the past. The crushing defeat of the Japanese enemy in the recent war, however, prepared the way for re-establishment of our national sovereignty. The war is more than three years past, the Japanese have long since gone home, yet our freedom remains incomplete. We urge you to act within your proper power to give the General Assembly's support to the government of the Republic of Korea. We are confident that with such support most free nations will recognize our government. The General Assembly's approval of our government, followed by wide-spread recognition, will profoundly strengthen the support even of those Koreans who were not permitted, by objection by one foreign power, to participate in the popular elections, on which our Republic is based. In reality, we request very little: only that you should acknowledge us first, who have conformed in every way to your stipulations, the same privileges which you acknowledged for other nations, large and small.

We have not had the privilege of welcoming many of you to our country, since it is far from most of your homes. I can tell you, however, that Korea is a beautiful country of rugged mountains, narrow, cultivated valleys, and swiftly flowing streams. We have an ancient civilization, an ancient history of sovereignty and independence, and a common language, complete racial homogeneity, and clearly recognized frontiers. We, Koreans, deeply love our land, as each of you must love yours. There are no people anywhere more passionately devoted to the cause of their national independence than the people of Korea. It is true, I am sad to say, that we have some disloyal citizens willing to turn our national heritage of our fatherly nation in accordance with the foreign dialectical propaganda. We even have some relegated citizens willing to murder their fellows for the advancement of the interest of a foreign country. Yet I ask you how many of you, free nations' representatives here, do not have such a fifth columnist. I cannot show you, however, that such persons are few in number, and that where they exercise power, they do so through the military will and the assistance of a foreign government, against the will of the overwhelming mass of the Korean people. The degree of terrorism which they sometimes execute is completely disproportionate to their numbers or their ultimate effect. But a wholly overwhelming majority of Korean people, regardless of differences in politics of economic theory, are united in patriotic love of the country.

During the forty years of Japanese domination, our people never surrendered their faith in ultimate freedom. We maintained an active movement for independence at home and abroad during the whole period. For 25 years, Korean soldiers were in the field of Chinese territory against Japanese. Our Prime Minister, Yi Beom-seok, is one of the many who fought the Japanese from the early 1920's until the Japanese capitulation in 1945. Our long, bitter war, gentlemen, did not commence as it did for some of you on December 7th, 1941, nor on June 22nd, 1941, nor on September 3rd, 1939, nor on July 7th, 1937, nor even on September 18th, 1931. Long before those never-to-be forgotten dates, our patriots were fighting and dying in the struggle for our freedom. Our people were suffering under the conqueror's heels years before the Nazi and Japanese blitzkriegs had erupted over Europe and the East. We have had enough suffering, enough oppression, enough rule at the hands of aliens.

Now, we have our Republic, our constitution, our government. Our circumstances are far from perfect, but surely, the Assembly would not deny us the exercise of the liberty open to us simply because one member of the United Nations has defied the Assembly. Surely, we who come before you with clean hands, with no ambition beyond that of liberty, with no request but that this Assembly should approve of our conformity to the will of the Assembly, will not be penalized, will not be rejected because one power has defied the Assembly's clear mandate.

The international pledges for Korean independence and sovereignty are so numerous that no one contests our facts-like rights. At Cairo in 1943, the British, Chinese and American governments, through their great war-time leaders, pledged the establishment of Korean independence as one of their common aims. At Potsdam, in July 1945, the United States, the United Kingdom, and China, with the subsequent adherence of the Soviet Union, again pledged themselves to establish the Korean independence, and presented this objective as one of the surrender demands upon the Japanese government. The Japanese did surrender on these and other terms. When the war with Japan ended, Russian troops entered Korea from the north, while American troops came into the south by sea to take Japanese surrender. We welcomed them, Americans and Russians alike as liberators. On those days of great joy and high emotions, few of us thought that our liberators were to settle down and stay on indefinitely once the Japanese had gone home. But stay they did. The joint Soviet-American occupation of Korea became intolerable from the beginning.

The military dividing line was arbitrarily established at the 38th parallel, a line without political, topographical or economic meaning. This military line swiftly froze into a barrier against the flow of commerce, of persons, of railway and highway traffic of every kind from one part of our country to the other. Parents were divided from their children, raw material from factories, food from consumers, at the parallel itself, farm's work cut into two, and the local irrigation projects seriously disrupted. Gentlemen, this monstrous severance of our country was response to no act, contemplation or decision of the Korean people or any of their representatives. We had no part in it, and it is we, the innocent, who still suffer from so many evils which have flowed from this monstrous division. In fairness, I should say that once having become a party of this division of Korea, the United States government did all in its power to lift this dreadful barrier, both by the appeals from its Commanding General in Korea and in several conferences, notably in the U.S.–U.S.S.R. Joint Commissions of 1946 and 1947. The United States attempted to establish political unity, or at the very least, an amelioration of the economic paralysis of that dreadful parallel. The Russians, on the other hand, refused to consider any political unification which would not in effect establish the communist party in control. Failing at political agreement, they did not even discuss the relaxation of the cruel economic barricade. We, Korean people, had no part in and no responsibility for the division of our country. This cruel division was imposed upon us. That dreadful division and the problems flowing from it still confront us.

The obvious injustice done to the Korean people caused the General Assembly of the United Nations on November 14th, 1947 to adopt two resolutions on Korea. The first called upon the General Assembly to hear the elected representatives of the Korean people in regard to the Korean problem. The second called for the United Nations Temporary Commission in Korea to proceed to Korea, to observe elections, to consult with the elected representatives who would constitute themselves and the National Assembly, and then to consult with the national government which would be formed by that Assembly. The Soviet government boycotted the Temporary Commission—they refused either to permit any member of the Commission to proceed to North Korea or to receive its communications. To face this obstacle, the Temporary Commission conferred with the Interim Committee and received the permission to proceed with its work in the area open to its observation. The Temporary Commission has stated in its official report: "The results of the ballot of 10th May 1948 are a valid expression of the free will of the electorate in those parts of Korea which were accessible to the Commission and in which the inhabitants constitute approximately two thirds of the people of all Korea." Now more than two thirds of the Korean people, twenty millions of them, have held the elections under the United Nations' observation. They have set up a government now ruling themselves. Can any reasonable man urge that our government be disapproved, that it should not be recognized because a foreign power arbitrarily refused to permit the other third of our people to join the elections? Never in Korean history had we participated in popular elections. Yet the Korean people turned out *en masse* both to register and vote, approximately 80 percent of the potential electorate registry and over 95 percent of the registered electorate proceeding to the polls and casting their ballots in complete freedom and absolute secrecy. As the Temporary Commission has reported, "the elections were regarded as a step in the re-establishment of independence of Korea, resulting in the large percentage both of registration and of balloting." The Korean people yearned to have their own sovereign government, despite threats on their lives and murder of several candidates, election officials and over 100 police officers by communists who tried by every foul means to disrupt the elections. The men and the women of Korea went to the polls and voted in accordance with their convictions. At that occasion, I stood for election and had the great honor to be elected in my district, in the city of Seoul. Our alternate delegate Mr. Ki Young Chang, likewise was elected from his district in Kang-won Province. We, therefore, come before you responsive to resolution won on Korea of the General Assembly.

The elected representatives had assembled on May 31, 1948, as the Korean National Assembly. In due course, they considered, debated, and finally adopted the Constitution of the Republic of Korea. Under this constitution, the President, Dr. Syngman Rhee, and the Vice-President, Mr. Shi Young Lee, were elected, and the government was formed. This Government was inaugurated on August 15th, 1948, in a colorful ceremony at Seoul. At last, after 40 years of bondage, we had a government of, by, and for Koreans, based on the clearly expressed will of our nation. Since the establishment of the Government, negotiations were conducted between the Korean and the American governments, resulting in the transfer of governmental powers from the United States military authorities to the Government of the Republic of Korea. It is our aim to secure similar transference to the Republic of Korea from the occupation authorities north of the 38th parallel. Our brethren in the north, however, were barred from participating in the general elections, so taking their rightful part in the government. We, Koreans, well know that mere residence north of an artificial line has not made aliens and communists of the patriotic Korean people. The fact remains, nevertheless, that nearly one-third of our people remain in bondage. In our National Assembly, we hold vacant approximately one-third of the seats for such time as elections can be held in the north and our brothers can sit with us. This urgent desire of the Assembly for national unity was clearly expressed by resolution of the National Assembly on June 12, 1948, along those lines. We publicized it in the north by every means at our disposal. We used the radio extensively and the members of the national assembly personally broadcast the texts. A copy also was given to the Temporary Commission with the request that it be forwarded to the people of north Korea through appropriate channel.

The problems of unification of our country have been vastly complicated by the establishment, under Soviet sponsorship, of a communist dictatorship based in the northern city of Pyongyang supported by Russian-trained military forces. Initially, a small group of Korean communists, designated by the Russian military command, organized an administrative committee by declaring themselves in office. Subsequently, they renamed the communist party, and created numerous other organizations of various names, but all without exception under communist control. These communist leaders then conducted a so-called election for themselves. They placed their own names on a ballot and, on a given day, required all citizens to go to polling places to place that prepared list in a box. Neither the nomination nor the list was permitted. Those illegibly favoring the list, placed it in a white box, those presumably disapproving it, placed it in a black box. Communist party designated officials carefully observed the choice of the box. Fear of reprisals was such that few persons dared to drop the list in the black box. Such so-called elections have now been held three times in the area of Russian occupation. In every case, the elected have been the same.

The most recent display of these white and black boxes in the area of Soviet occupation was last August 25th. Last July, the self-appointed communist leaders in Pyongyang declared in force a Soviet typed constitution, and designated August 25th as the date on which so-called elections would be held under that so-called constitution. To the amazement of every resident outside of the zone of Russian occupation, the extraordinary claim was made. First over Pyongyang radio, and more recently at the rostrum of this General Assembly, by some delegates, that elections were also held in South Korea and that the new communist so-called government decreed at Pyongyang was inclusive of north and south. Such statements are an extraordinary departure from truth. At no time was any semblance of elections for the Russian sponsored communist body in Pyongyang held south of the 38th parallel. The only elections ever held anywhere in Korea were those observed on May 10th, 1948, by the Temporary Commission. The only elected representatives in or from Korea are those elected in the United Nations sponsored elections. No matter how contrary claims may be just in pressed list of statistics, they are fuddled. Any persons not selected in the United Nations observed elections who pretend to come before you as elected representatives of the Korean people not only perpetrate a fraud, but insult inaudible intelligence. During the month of August, 1948, at which time these same persons claimed they were being elected in South Korea, the Temporary Commission was in Korea. They saw no elections. The United Kingdom, China, France, and the United States had consular offices in Korea, and they saw no elections. The United States had an occupying force of both civilian and military, and they saw no elections.

I myself was serving in the National Assembly, and I saw no elections. Despite all this independent testimony, certain delegates sitting in this committee, as well as the members of a self-selected communist regime which they support, cynically proclaimed that 77.52 percent out of the people living south of the 38th parallel, that is, an actual 6,731,470 human souls, went out and voted in some so-called underground for that communist dictatorship in the north. Please contemplate this claim, Gentlemen, they expect you to believe that over six million people could go to the polls to vote secretly, and unseen by anyone. Well, there may be parts of the world where white becomes black, and black becomes white merely by assertion. This committee room is not such a place, nor is Korea such a place.

The essential facts are that the Government of the Republic of Korea, the national government of Korea, has been established as a result of the elections of last May 10, which were observed and approved of by your Temporary Commission. This is a Republic based on the constitutional safeguards of civil liberty and public participation in government, common to the democratic world. This Government actually exercises a jurisdiction over two thirds of Korean people, more than twenty million. This Government seeks, at the earliest possible time, to have popular elections held in the north, and reserved seats in the National Assembly in proportion to the northern population. The Government has the essential bases for economic stability and maintenance of public peace. This Government already has received the provisional recognition of the United States of America, the Republic of China, and the Republic of the Philippines. Following the approval of the Government of the Republic of Korea by the General Assembly, we look forward to wide-spread recognition and the establishment of normal diplomatic relations with most of the nations of the world.

Meanwhile we shall present our request for membership in the United Nations. We have been compelled to absent ourselves for so long from the society of nations that it is with a particular satisfaction that we now look forward hopefully to formal membership and active participation in the United Nations Organization.

Because of the conduct of the Soviet military forces and of the Korean communists acting under their direction, several millions of Korean citizens have been displaced from their homes, and have been forced to take refuge south of the 38th parallel. These people are from every stratum of society. They are farmers, dispossessed of farms worked by their families for generations; they are businessmen big and small; they are students and journalists and physicians and surgeons who would not subscribe to the confinement of a totalitarian society. They are land-holders, and they are workmen. It is impossible to find a common economic category for them. But they have one common aspiration. They all seek freedom. Some of these refugees stood for election last May 10, and were elected to the National Assembly from districts far from their home. One of them is a member of the cabinet, another, the vice-chairman of the National Assembly. We sympathize deeply with these our brothers, and we will help them to the limits of our abilities. We can well imagine, however, that such a large proportion of refugees creates serious economic dislocations.

Adequate security forces are required for our defense. While we have the sound base for our security in the loyalty and the determination of the Korean people, some time must pass before we can properly train and equip an adequate military force. The establishment of adequate security forces was one of the major concerns expressed by the General Assembly resolution last November. I assume this still remains a deep concern of the General Assembly. About two years ago, the United States armed forces in Korea began organizing a small constabulary to serve as auxiliaries to the police. Not until last spring, however, foreseeing the establishment of a Korean government responsive to the General Assembly resolutions did the United States authorities begin the expansion and the training of the constabulary as a regular military body. Currently there are some fifty thousand constabulary men under arms serving as the army of the Republic of Korea. But mostly they are in the early stage of training. Much time must elapse between a soldier's enlistment and the creation of a competent army. Then there is the problem of developing a solid core of competent non-commissioned officers, which also requires much time. We would be unrealistic not to call attention to the very large military forces which the Soviet army has been training and equipping for over three years in the northern part of our country and which will be in military position upon Soviet withdrawal.

The leaders of these forces are devoted to an alien philosophy, and supported by foreign government. Recently, their spokesmen of Pyongyang Radio have made repeated threats against the lives of our national leaders, and they have even proclaimed that the time will soon come when they will fly their alien flag over our national capital at Seoul. Despite their bombast, we do not believe that this communist army will attack if they know we are strong. They would view military weakness in the Republic of Korea, however, as an invitation to use their well-trained forces. It seems reasonable, therefore, that the General Assembly, the foster parents of the Republic of Korea, should view with friendly consideration our concern over the problem of having adequate time to train our security forces. We hope that the United States, which has shown continued good will toward our people and our Government, will give us further assistance, so that no security vacuum may occur during the training period of our armed forces. Until such time as our army can be adequately trained to execute its defensive mission, we ask that the United States retain a small technical force in Korea to serve both as a school force for the education of our soldiers, and to give the necessary moral backing to our troops during the training period. Our National Assembly has passed a resolution to that effect, and our Government likewise has made such a request. While it is clear that the question of further retention of the United States forces in Korea is to be perused first by the Korean government, it is one entirely for the United States to decide after Korean invitation. Yet neither the Korean government nor I believe the United States government would wish to act in this matter without the moral support of the free nations. I, therefore, urge the continued interest of the General Assembly in this problem and your moral support for such arrangements as may be made between my Government and the United States for the solution of this problem.

The Korean delegation has examined with great care the joint resolution on the Korean question submitted by Australia, China, and the United States. We regard it as a possible measure for the solution of Korean problems under the present circumstances. However, I will make specific comment on the following points. With regard to Paragraph 2, it is the conviction of our Government that it is that Government envisaged in the General Assembly resolution on November 14, 1947, and that it is only prevented from exercising full control and jurisdiction over the whole of its territories by *force majeure.*

Nevertheless, the whole sovereignty of the Korean nation resides in the Republic of Korea, which in due course will be able to exercise full control and jurisdiction of its whole territory. We desire, therefore, some suitable changes to be made to clarify and confirm our claims. It is the desire of our delegation that Paragraph 3 should be amended by the addition of the words, "bearing in mind the completion of the training and equipment of an adequate security force for the Government of the Republic of Korea."

We understand Paragraph 4(c) means that the United Nations Commission will be available for observation and consultation in the further development of representative government based on the freely expressed will of the people north of the 38th parallel. Whenever the Commission may have that opportunity, we long for that day. Meanwhile, in the Government of the Republic of Korea we have a representative government based upon the freely expressed will of the people, and with a democratic constitution as is testified by the Temporary Commission in their report.

We understand that Paragraph 8 calls upon Member States to refrain from any acts derogatory to the results achieved by the United Nations in assisting in the creation of the Republic of Korea, and any further results which the Commission may achieve in bringing independence to our unfortunate brothers to the north so that they may unite with us again in one nation.

We regret that Paragraph 9 does not use more precise language in calling for the recognition of the Government of the Republic of Korea by Member States. We do not understand why the word "recognition" was not used. But since that is the meaning of the Paragraph, we look forward to the pleasure of very early diplomatic relations with most of the nations represented in this august Body.

Naturally the question arises as to what can be done to erase that artificial, but terrible dividing line at the 38th parallel. It is my personal conviction and the belief of my Government that the greatest single aid to unification will be the approval by the General Assembly of the Government of the Republic of Korea and its subsequent general recognition. Such recognition will fulfill the natural and normal expectations of the people of Korea. Without the slightest doubt, it will attract the loyal adherence to the Republic of millions of men and women in the north. Every Korean in north and south will clearly understand the significance of such approval and recognition. In the meantime, it is wholly unfair to hold against us a geographical division imposed upon us without our prior acknowledgement or consent. It is totally unfair to demand of us an immediate solution of the disunity enforced upon us when in three years of tenacious efforts the United States of America could not find one. It is unfair to demand of us an immediate solution when a special commission of the United Nations themselves did not find one. But it is even more unfair to withhold from us, who for so long have been forced to live away from the rest of the world, the normal courtesies of diplomatic intercourses which are especially helpful to a newly reborn nation, simply because one member of the United Nations had defied the rest. Accept us, welcome us, let us be one with you, let us share with you the understanding and goodwill of the free world.

There has been hesitation on the part of some Members of the United Nations to approve of the Government of the Republic of Korea because at this date it is unable to include the northern part of its territory under its effective jurisdiction. Yet, this Government is the direct result of the carrying out of the mandate of the General Assembly of the United Nations as expressed on November 14, 1947. Any claimants to the governmental authority in the north exercise their claim in defiance of the United Nations.

For the General Assembly to fail to approve of the Government of the Republic of Korea as that Government contemplated in Resolution 2 on Korea, of November 14, 1947, because the Soviet government boycotted the work of the United Nations Commission, and because a self-appointed ruling body has established itself in the portion of Korea inaccessible to the representatives of the United Nations, would be to reward the guilty and punish the innocent.

It would be to place a premium on defiance of the mandate of the United Nations. Failure to give approval to the Government of the Republic of Korea because a communist regime has been established at Pyongyang, in effect would be an admission by the General Assembly that this defiant political group has the General Assembly's support.

We have complied with your mandate and direction of your Commission. We have established, and we shall maintain our independence and our sovereignty against any challenge. We now have our Constitution, our Republic, our National Assembly, and our Government. These we will never surrender. We will not betray the Korean people and no force of any kind, military or otherwise, shall be able to put a single one of us back into bondage alive.

I conclude this statement confident that the delegates of the free and liberty-loving nations of the world can not in good conscience refuse our claims. We ask you to approve our Government as that conceived of by the General Assembly in its resolution on Korea on November 14, 1947, and to recommend its recognition to the Member States of the United Nations.

I thank you.

(Reproduced from U. N. tape-recording)

註:

위의 글은 1948년 12월 7일 프랑스 파리에서 개최된 유엔 총회에서 당시 대한민국을 대표하여 참석한 장면 박사가 읽은 것으로, 당시 대한민국의 정치 지도자들의 요청에 의해 이인수 교수가 작성한 연설문이다. 유엔 총회가 진행되는 도중 녹음한 것을 타자하여 유엔 사무국 문서철에 보관하여 왔다. 그로부터 60년이 지난 2008년 12월 17일, 이인수 교수의 딸 성윤의 장남인 김정권이 줄리아드 음악원에서 박사과정을 밟던 시절, 반기문 유엔 사무총장의 관저에서 열린 외교관들의 모임에 초청받아 연주를 하게 되었고, 연주가 끝난 후 김정권은 외조모의 회고록을 기억하고 유엔 사무국 문서 보관 담당자에게 부탁하여 그의 외조부 이인수 교수가 작성한 연설문의 복사본을 입수하였다. 유엔 사무국 문서보관소에는 지금도 이인수 교수가 작성한 이 연설문의 타자본이 보관되어 있다.

李仁秀 교수의 아내 玄丙辰은 회고록에서 다음과 같이 적었다.

"[남편은] UN 총회에 보내는 한국 독립호소의 진정서를 작성했다. 당시 옵서버로나마 UN에 참석한 우리 대표들에게 크게 도움을 주는 자료가 되었단다. 물론 국내의 여러 정당에서 진정서를 보냈겠지만 영국 런던대학에서 오너(B. A. Honours)로 학위를 받은 영문학도의 능력을 누가 따를 수가 있었겠는가. 인촌 선생 하명에 의해 몇 날 몇 밤을 침식을 잊다시피 하여 작성된 진정서의 논리의 정연함과 문장의 유려함에 구구절절 읽는 이의 심금을 울리기에 족했겠지만, 하도하도 장문(長文)이고 이것을 복사하자니 시간은 너무도 촉박하고 해서 군데군데 뽑아서 복사한 것을 가지고도 UN의 전 회원에게 돌려서 그 결과는 마침내 만장일치의 박수와 갈채였단다.

포츠담 회담도, 얄타 회담도 목적은 약소민족해방의 보장이었지만, 그 시기에 그렇게 빨리 다른 약소민족들에 앞서서 그렇게 멋진 한국독립의 승인안의 통과는 오로지 인촌 선생께서 보내 주신 호소문이 아니었던들 UN에 참석한 한국대표들이 어찌 체면을 세우고 이렇게 귀국을 할 수가 있었겠느냐 하는 감사와 감격 어린 찬사를 인촌 선생이 받으시고, 우리 내외에게 들려주시는 것이었다. UN 대표 중의 한 분인 김활란(金活蘭) 박사는 인촌 선생님의 손을 잡고 놓지를 못하셨단다. 그 호소문을 보내 주심에 감격하시고 치하하시면서.

그런데 이 호소문의 원본을 인촌은 고이 간직하고 계셨다가 후일 이 교수의 구명운동에 쓰고자 백낙준 박사와 함께 한 자리에서 이 원본을 펴놓고 상담하는 자리에 당시 국방부 장관 신성모(申性模)에 의해 찢기어 없어졌음을 인촌은 통탄해 마지않으셨다. 그 어른이 오랫동안 와병중에도 우리 가족을 불러서 격려해 주시며, "내 병은 그때 얻은 것 같소" 하실 때, 나는 하늘이 또 한 번 캄캄해 옴을 느꼈다. 지각이 모자라는 사람에 의해서 우리나라 혼란기에 역사적인 문서를 망실 당하는 치욕의 변을 겪었던 것이다. 그러나 나는 짐작한다. UN 빌딩 안의 서류철에는 반드시 빛을 간수하고 남아 있으리라고 말이다." (<메마른 언덕에 꽃밭을>, 나남출판, 1998, 40-42면)

Aesthetic Achievements of Korea: A Historical Survey of Classic Art

[*Writer's Note:* This tentative essay on Korean art could not have been written without the valuable information derived from such notable works as: *History of Korean Art* (Seoul, 1948) by Professor Kim Yŏng-gi, of Ewha Women's University, Seoul (written in Korean); *History of Korean Art* by Andreas Eckardt, English translation by J. M. Kindersley (Oxford, 1929).]

Introduction

When in 1820 Thomas Love Peacock wrote whimsically on the Four Ages of Poetry, it was part of his intention to poke fun at the romantic excesses of his contemporary poets. Without any implication of satire, however, we could conveniently apply his notion of the Four Ages, rough and ready as it is, to the history of Korean art. If, as is frequently averred, Korean art achieved its classic grandeur and poise between the sixth and the tenth century, the four ages of Korean art appear somewhat as follows, corresponding roughly to the political development of the country:

Period of Assimilation (Iron Age): Beginning to the fifth century

Naknang	108 B.C.–A.D. 313
Koguryŏ	37 B.C.–c. A.D. 500
Paekje	18 B.C.–c. A.D. 500
Shilla	57 B.C.–c. A.D. 500

Period of Achievement (Golden Age): the sixth century to the tenth century

Koguryŏ	c. 500–668
Paekje	c. 500–660
Shilla	c. 500–935

Period of Refinement (Silver Age): the eleventh century to the sixteenth century

Koryŏ 918–1392
Chosŏn 1392–c.1600

Period of Sterility (Brass Age): the seventeenth century to the nineteenth century

Chosŏn c. 1600–1910

This paper proposes to trace the development of Korean art in the light of the above division, halting at the frontier of the modern period, whose new traditions and media are still in the making, and therefore difficult of appraisal. What has already become part of history can be considered on the basis of accepted knowledge, of which this paper is meant to be a summary recapitulation.

I. *Naknang* (Chinese: *Lolang*) (108 B.C.–A.D. 313)

Even though our legendary history is supposed to take us back over 2,300 years B.C., manifestations of formative arts go no further than the Naknang period. The seventh emperor Wuti of the earlier Han dynasty (206 B.C.–A.D. 9) colonized the northern half of the Korean peninsula in 108 B.C. Three 'provinces' out of the original four were lost some 30 years later, but one, i.e. Naknang, comprising chiefly the modern P'yŏng-an and Hwang-hae provinces, was held in control for some 420 years. Although there is still some controversy among Korean historians as to whether, if at all, any native element went into the formation of the Naknang culture, it can be fairly surmised that four centuries of Chinese infiltration, both political and cultural, must have proved a great stimulus in the assimilation of Chinese art of the earlier Han and the later Han (23–200). South West of P'yŏng-yang along the Taedong river are found remains of some 1,300 tombs, which testify to the whilom glory of Naknang culture. The finds in these tombs, which show high workmanship, notably in lacquer-work, gold, silver and other metal-work, are of importance to Korean art as much as to Chinese, in so far as Naknang, in our early history, brought into our midst the living culture of China, without which our great achievements in art at the time of the Three Kingdoms would be difficult to conceive as a matter of historical continuity.

II. *Koguryŏ* (37 B.C.–A.D. 668)

Koguryŏ's intercourse with China antedated that of Paekje or Shilla, for which two main reasons may be cited: (1) its geographical position, and (2) the influence of Naknang within its very territory. As early as 372, i. e. in the second year of the seventeenth king Sosurim (371–384) of Koguryŏ, the Chinese Buddhist monk Shuntao introduced Buddhism into Korea by bringing the gospels and image of Buddha. Koguryŏ was thus the first of the Three Kingdoms to come under the Buddhist influence, and the first to build a Buddhist monastery in 375.

Koguryŏ art, however, as seen in the mural paintings of the royal tombs, is less Buddhist in spirit than that of either Paekje or Shilla. It embodies the 'heroic' rather than the 'religious,' and to that extent, more 'pagan'; it is the most classic expression in our country of the Spartan vitality of the continental Northerners, where Shilla, and to a lesser degree Paekje, represents the Athenian sensibility of the oceanic Southerners. Fifteen tombs have so far been excavated, five of them being across the Yalu in modern Manchurian territory, where the ancient capital used to be located, and the rest in the vicinity of the Taedong river, whereto the capital had been moved in 427: five in Yonggang-gun, two in Taedong-gun, two in Kangsŏ-gun, one in Sunch'ŏn-gun. The former group would, therefore, be dated not later than early fifth century, thus proving to be among the earliest mural paintings in the Far East. Three of the latter group, "Tomb of the Four Gods" at Maesan-ri, Yong-gang-gun, "Tomb of the Four Gods" at Honam-ri, Taedong-gun, and "Tomb of the Celestial and Earthly Kings" at Sunch'ŏn-gun, show the same technique of painting as the former group, and would be dated not later than mid-fifth century. The rest come after this date, but not later than c. 550, which is the date for the latest tomb, i. e. "The Great Tomb" at Uhyŏn-ri, Kangsŏ-gun.

From a pictorial point of view, these tombs are of interest for (1) their ornamental designs and (2) their human and animal representation. Some of the favorite motives are: the lotus-flower motive, the wave or stem motive, the star or cloud motive with tongues of fire, the wheel motive, and the 'four leaves' motive. Human figures are well represented in such tombs as the "Tomb of the Four Spirits" at Maesan-ri, the "Tomb of the Dragon Spirit" at Hwasan-ri, Yong-gang-gun, the "Tomb of the Twin Pillars" at Chinji-dong, Yong-gang-gun. They show processions, sacrificial scenes, women in court dress, ox-carts escorted by soldiers, the king in state attended by dignitaries, deer-hunting scenes, etc. A tomb discovered in 1940 in the T'ung-gu district across the Yalu is noteworthy for its painting of fourteen men and women dancers.

Two of the most outstanding of these tombs are: "Tomb of the Twin Pillars" (c. 510) and "The Great Tomb" (c. 550). The former is not only richly peopled with human figures but also celebrated for "the harmony and vital strength" of the decorated pillars, which, in the words of Eckardt, "is nothing short of wonderful" (p. 124). The latter has no representation of human figures, but is justly famous for its depiction of the four legendary animals that symbolize the four cardinal points of the zodiac: the blue dragon (east), the white tiger (west), the two red griffins (south), and the blue-black tortoise (north). The painter's presentation of these unearthly creatures is one "fearful symmetry" of sinewy motion and fiery flight: the imaginative freedom in the motion of the dragon, the breezy swing in the flight of the griffins, the sinewy strength of the tiger reminding one of Blake's Tiger, and the sublime struggle of good and evil depicted in the deadly embrace of the tortoise and the snake. Koguryŏ art of the sixth century proved its dynamic power of artistic imagination in these works.

The gap that follows such achievements of the sixth century is really a curious vagary of history. For not till nearly a century after these mural paintings in the royal tombs do we hear of another great name in Koguryŏ art, which by then had undergone a complete change in spirit. In 610 a Koguryŏ monk, Tamjing (Japanese: *Donjo*) went over to Japan to paint the frescoes of Horyuji, Nara. His twelve frescoes, Buddhist in conception, are of the greatest value in the history of "Japanese" art. There were other Koguryŏ painters, besides Tamjing, who partook in the pioneering of art in Japan.

A unique example of Koguryŏ calligraphic art has remained in the famous memorial tablet of King Kwang-gae-t'o (391–412), which was erected in 414 to commemorate his conquest of neighboring tribes and his martial feats against Japan conjointly with Shilla. The *Li-shu* style in which it is written is comparable with the best of the contemporaneous Eastern Tsin (317–420) in China.

III. *Paekje* (18 B. C.– A. D. 660)

Because of Koguryŏ blocking the northern pathway, Paekje trafficked with China across the Yellow Sea. Buddhism was first introduced in 384. By the sixth century it had permeated through every phase of cultural life in Paekje. It was the twenty-sixth king Sŏng (523–554), a most enthusiastic Buddhist, who first introduced Buddhism into Japan in 552. Many artist-monks, architects, sculptors, painters, metal-workers and tile-makers went over to Japan to build the Horyuji in the early part of the seventh century, which remains to this day a great monument of Far Eastern art and a testimony to the once glorious culture of Paekje. When the first queen-ruler of Shilla, Sŏndŏk (632–647), was building the nine-story pagoda of the Hwang-yong-sa temple, she had more than two hundred artists and craftsmen from Paekje working for her.

Yet, this once flourishing art of Paekje is no more to be seen in *this* land, except for a single five-story pagoda at Puyŏ, its ancient capital, some half a dozen small Buddhas in gold or bronze, fragments of tiles, and bits of gold ornaments. By a strange irony of history, the pagoda, commonly known as Paekje Pagoda, was erected in memory of the victorious T'ang general who had incurred the downfall of Paekje in 660 jointly with Shilla. The cause for this almost complete destruction must be sought in the geographical position of Paekje; almost every traffic of war in subsequent Korean history added to her fate of loot and destruction.

The best expression of Paekje art must indeed be sought in the world-renowned Horyuji of Japan. The Kondo or 'Sermon Hall' is now a museum of statues and frescoes, mostly of Korean origin. The five-story tower pagoda is of the same style as that of the Pŏpju-sa pagoda, though this is of a much later date (the fifteenth century). Writes Eckardt on the architecture of Horyuji (p. 30):

> What chiefly strikes us in all these Horyuji architectural monuments is the
> elegance and majestic serenity which broods over them. A frequent sign of

great age is the almost straight roof line: only slightly sprung at the corners; another is, as in the Horyuji, the perfect symmetry and delicately proportioned harmony of the different parts, which gives the building not only a monumental, but also a classical character. Even if we were unaware that the architects of these magnificent monuments were Koreans, we could deduce it from the serene, classical lines and forms.

History has recorded names of some of the outstanding artists from Paekje who went over to Japan to spread their art: for example, Insara, a painter, who went to Japan in 463; Paekka, another painter, who crossed the sea in 587; Prince Ajwa, son of King Widŏk (554–598), who went over to Japan in 597 and painted the famous portrait of Shotoku Taishi; and Hasŏng, afterwards naturalized Japanese, who excelled in portrait and landscape painting.

IV. *Shilla* (57 B. C. – A. D. 935)

Whereas the civilizations of Koguryŏ and Paekje died out in the zenith of their glory, that of Shilla was to grow slowly but surely and to leave a permanent cultural heritage to the people of Korea. The golden days of Shilla will always remain the object of our imaginative longing, not only because they were golden but also because we all have the legacy of Shilla "felt in the blood, and felt along the heart." It is not enough to say that Shilla found the perfect medium of artistic expression in Buddhism; the point to remember is that she could blend into a perfect whole what was native with what was foreign. And she was able to achieve this union partly because her south-easterly position, with natural barriers of mountains and sea, exempted her from the power struggle, but chiefly because her amicable relationship with T'ang added greatly to her inborn southern mellowness for aesthetic development.

Shilla art may be conveniently divided into two periods by the date of the unification of Korea in the latter seventh century. Buddhism came into Shilla through Koguryŏ in the early half of the fifth century. By 528 the twenty-third king Pŏp-hŭng (514–540) had adopted it as a state religion. During the sixth century there arose in or near

Kyŏngju some sixty Buddhist temples, of which the most celebrated was Hwang-yong-sa, begun at the time of the twenty-fourth king Chinhŭng (540–576), and completed ninety years later in 645. In the same year the queen-ruler Sŏndŏk, already referred to, had the observatory built, which remains today the oldest of its kind in the Far East.

Most of these architectural monuments the Mongol invaders of 1238 burnt down, and the Japanese invaders of 1592–1598 further devastated what was left. The sculptures of the sixth and seventh centuries met with the same fate. There are only a few extant Buddhas of the earlier Shilla period, of which the Maitreya Buddhas now in the Dŏksu and the National Museums, Seoul, are justly famous, and testify amply to the high craftsmanship of early Shilla which was in no way inferior to the Kwannon sculptors of Paekje, so well represented in Japan. The numerous bas-relief stone sculptures in or near Kyŏngju foreshadow the great Sŏkkuram art of the next century, notably the three-Buddha-group at Am-bang-gok, and the Inwang or Dvarapala excavated from a tomb west of Kyŏngju (now in the Dŏksu Museum).

Excavation of Shilla tombs, which was seriously taken up by the Japanese government from 1916, has revealed more works of handicraft than the tombs of Koguryŏ or Paekje—probably due to the fact that the structure of Shilla tombs was less accessible to plunder or the ravages of war. The undertaking was capitally rewarded in 1922 when a gold royal crown was discovered, followed by some 200 or more items of handicraft mostly wrought with gold and precious stones. Just as sculpture was to be the representative art of the later Shilla period, so handicraft may stand for the earlier, if we make allowances for the accidental factor that what is best preserved may not necessarily be the most typical. The point to be borne in mind is that such profusion in handicraft could not have been an isolated phenomenon in the aesthetic achievements of the earlier Shilla period.

The three centuries of united Korea under Shilla (668–935) happened to coincide with the brilliant period of the T'ang dynasty (618–906) in China. Culturally Shilla had everything to gain. Indeed, the two civilizations, taken together, may well claim to be called the Renaissance of the Far East.

Of the many architectural monuments that belong to this period, the most typical is Pulguk-sa of Kyŏngju, which, being founded by the afore-mentioned King Pŏp-hŭng, was rebuilt in 751 after the T'ang style of architecture by Kim Tae-sŏng, minister to the thirty-fifth king Kyŏngdŏk (742–765). It took twenty-five years to complete. Though the building was restored after the Japanese invaders had burnt it down, the original layout still remains, including the stone bridges and the two pagodas. There are some dozen extant pagodas of this period, dispersed among various localities: Kyŏngju (2), Iksan (1), Ch'ungju (1), Kimch'ŏn (1), Kurye (1), Yŏju (1), Andong (2), Hyŏpch'ŏn (1), Yangsan (1), and Tongnae (1). It is easy to deduce that these pagodas, as symbols of the Buddhist faith, are only a small part of the total sum of the pagoda-art that flourished in the later Shilla period.

In sculptural art, however, the Rock Cave Temple of Sŏkkuram alone is enough to represent the whole art of the later Shilla period. Built by the same Kim Tae-sŏng at the same time as the monastery of Pulguk-sa, it bears the palm not only in Korea but in the whole of the Far East. What adds to its value is the fact that, unlike those in China, it was an artificially constructed cave. Detailed descriptions have so often been lavished on this Cave Temple that repetition seems unavoidable in writing about the calm beauty and symmetrical arrangement of the sculptured figures. Suffice it here to give their names. To the entrance of the rotunda stand twelve bas-reliefs: four knights, two Indian deities (Dvarapala), two temple-warders (Vajrayaksa), and four kings of heaven (Vesurabana); in the rotunda stand fifteen bas-reliefs surrounding the colossal Sakya Buddha, and above them in niches eight smaller Buddhas and Bodhisattvas, the fifteen figures being: four Bodhisattvas (Munju-posal, Pohyŏn-posal, Kwanseŭm-posal, Taeseji-posal), ten disciples of Buddha (Arhats), and one Eleven-headed Kwannon. Writes Eckardt on the architecture of Sŏkkuram (p. 48):

> Architecturally, more interest attaches to the structural design of this unique cave-temple, which for refined and methodical execution is without parallel in the Far East. Neither the Chinese nor the Japanese cave-temples show the same structure; it is perhaps safer to look for the prototype in the Chaitya of Krishnagiri-Kanheri in India. In the Korean Sŏkkuram, the long row of columns is, it is true, missing, as is the hall almost twenty-five meters in length; but the same clean-cut general idea remains. The antechambers would also, apart from the position of the two

outer pillars, to a certain extent coincide. On the other hand, the Korean temple, especially the rotunda, is in spite of similarities so entirely different, that it can be cited with a clear conscience as Korean.

In general handicraft, the later Shilla period does not show the richness of the earlier. The main reason is that, as Buddhism penetrated more and more into the national life, cremation became the accepted mode of burial, with the result that excavation is less enlightening for the later period than the earlier, except for fragments of urns or tiles of curious design. A more interesting aspect of handicraft in a specialized form, however, is seen in the bronze bells. The oldest surviving bells of the Far East come from the Shilla period, notably the bells at Sang-won-sa (725) and at Pongdŏk-sa (771). The celestial figures usually represented in the bells symbolize the delight of resounding gong-sound, which wafts them into the clouds of music.

Throughout this golden age of Buddhist sculpture only one artist has come down in history by name. According to *Samguk-yusa,* a book of history and legend of ancient Korea compiled by a Koryŏ monk, Il-yŏn (1206–1289), in the latter part of the thirteenth century, one Yangji, a mid-seventh century monk of the time of Queen Sŏndŏk, was famous for his mastery of Buddha sculpture.

In pictorial art, on the other hand, Shilla has nothing left but a few names of painters and their legends. From the earlier period, only one is known: Solgŏ of the mid-sixth century, who painted the frescoes at Hwang-yong-sa (with the common enough legend that his pines deceived the very birds of the air), and who was also renowned as a painter of Kwannon and Yuma. From the later period three names are known: Kim Ch'ung-i, a warrior-artist of the time of King Wŏnsŏng (785–798), whose art was acclaimed in T'ang itself; and two monks, Jŏnghwa and Hongkye, of the time of King Kyŏngmyŏng (917–924), famous as painters of Samantabhadras (Pohyŏn-posal).

Names of some fourteen calligraphists of the Shilla period can be traced in memorial tablets and bells, etc., of whom the most renowned were: Sŏlch'ong, a great scholar of late seventh century; Kim Saeng (710–c. 790), a Buddhist monk whose calligraphy was the counterpart of Solgŏ in painting; and Ch'oe Ch'i-won (856–915), the great scholar-poet who studied in T'ang and died a recluse.

V. *Koryŏ* (918–1392)

The silver age of Koryŏ art that followed was essentially a continuation of Shilla in that it was mainly Buddhistic in content and aristocratic in spirit. These characteristic features were especially prominent in the first three centuries of the Wang dynasty until the harassing years of the recurrent Mongol invasions, which began in 1231, causing the temporary removal of the capital from Songdo to the island of Kanghwa (1232–1270). Just as the golden period of Shilla art had coincided with T'ang, so the first three, and the best, centuries of Koryŏ art until the twenty-second king Kangjong, i. e. from 918 to 1213, were more or less contemporaneous with the Sung civilization (960–1279) in China.

How Buddhism formed the basis of this period may be seen from the following data alone. The founder of the dynasty, Wang-gŏn (918–943), is recorded to have built some sixteen Buddhist monasteries in the capital. There were no less than fifty bonzeries in or near Songdo. The carving of Buddhist sutras in woodblocks, which was begun in 1021 under the auspices of the king Hyŏnjong (1010–1031), was continued again from 1086 through the effort of the prince-monk Ŭich'ŏn (who had traveled widely in Liao, Sung, and Japan) during the reign of the thirteenth king Sŏnjong (1084–1094). These woodblocks, which covered over 10,000 sutras, the Mongol invaders destroyed; but the carving was resumed in 1236 and completed in 1251, covering some 6,500 sutras with a total of 163,000 blocks. Now preserved in the monastery of Haein-sa, they form the oldest and the most comprehensive collection of carved Buddhist sutras in the world.

And yet, only half a dozen specimens of Koryŏ architecture have survived the war flames. Particularly noteworthy is "the Hall of Infinite Life" (Muryangsujŏn) of Pusŏk-sa in Yŏngju, which is today the oldest wooden building in Korea, having been constructed in the latter part of the seventh century and rebuilt during the reign of King Ch'ung-yŏl (1275–1308). Stone pagodas and lanterns have survived better. We have still in good condition some twenty pagodas and eight lanterns from the Koryŏ period. A new development in the pagoda art is the predominance of hexagonal and octagonal types, which, unknown in the Shilla period, are attributable to the influence of central Asia through the political impact of the Mongol dynasty, Yüan (1260–1368), in the early thirteenth century.

In sculptural art Koryŏ shows a sad decline from Shilla. There are not a few stone Buddhas of the Koryŏ period; the most conspicuous perhaps is the so-called Maitreya Buddha of Ŭnjin, which was begun in 968, taking thirty-eight years to complete. Aesthetically, it is but a monstrosity (total length c. seventy feet), but its very eccentricity has been the cause of its fame. Far more satisfying aesthetically is the wood-carved Amida-Buddha of Pusŏk-sa, which dates back to the latter thirteenth century, proving to be the oldest specimen of wood-sculpture extant today in Korea.

The best expression of the aristocratic spirit in the art of this period is undoubtedly the ceramic art, which reached its culmination in the mid-eleventh and twelfth century, i. e. between the eleventh king Munjong (1047–1083) and the eighteenth Ŭijong (1147–1170). If sculpture was the embodiment of the Shilla spirit, ceramic art may be said to be the consummate expression of the Koryŏ spirit. What is to be noted in the Koryŏ pottery is its variety and workmanship, its controlled grace and inward glow. The technique, originally learnt from Sung, completely overshadowed that of the Chinese masters, notably in the production of the celadon. In the words of Eckardt again (p. 166):

> The coloring of later Chinese and Japanese works may be finer; but the Koryŏ pottery singles itself out by its richness of form, its attractive monumental repose and restraint, its classical symmetry and noble proportions; to these may be added a refined feeling for quiet colors and chaste aloofness, and a certain dreaminess which is peculiar to the whole nation.

The jade color of the celadon was known in China as the 'secret' or 'forbidden' color, because its use was allowed only to the royalty. The chief categories of the Koryŏ celadon are:

"Sun-ch'ŏngja" ('Pure' celadon), produced before the seventeenth king Injong (1123–1146)

"Ŭmgak," or ornamented with indented lines

"Yanggak," or ornamented in bas-relief

Pieces without ornament

"Mulhyŏng," or shaped after certain objects

"Kamhwa-ch'ŏngja," or "Sanggam" (*Shokan* in Japanese pronunciation), produced first between Injong and the nineteenth king Myŏngjong (1171–1197), and continued till the twelfth to fifteenth century in the form of pierced-work. This was the most original part of Koryŏ pottery. The incised surface was filled with white kaolin or black clay, rubbed smooth, fired and glazed

"Hŭkhwa-ch'ŏngja," or "Hoe-Koryŏ" (*E-Korai* in Japanese), produced in the last third of the dynasty. Dark-brown color was over-painted with brush in bold lines

"Hwakŭm-ch'ŏngja": gilt ornamentation applied to No. 2

"Chujŏm-ch'ŏngja": reddish-brown tint ("chicken-blood" color) applied to Nos. 2 and 3

Kilns of the Koryŏ period are known to have existed in the following *gun*s (counties): Kangjin, Kwangju (South Chŏlla); Puan (North Chŏlla); Kyŏngju (North Kyŏngsang); Taejŏn, Ch'ŏng-yang, Poryŏng, Puyŏ (South Ch'ungch'ŏng); Ansŏng (Kyŏnggi); Song-hwa, Haeju, Ongjin, and Shinch'ŏn (Hwanghae).

Only eight paintings have come down from the Koryŏ period, four of which are known to be in Japan. They are mainly Buddhist in content. The justly celebrated fresco at Pusŏk-sa is by an unknown artist. *Kŭn-ik-sŏ-hwa-jŭng*, the book of Korean painters and calligraphists compiled by Mr. O Se-ch'ang, represents some twenty-four painters of the Koryŏ period. The more famous ones, in chronological order, are:

Yi Yŏng: Flourished in the early twelfth century. His paintings were admired by the Sung emperor as well as by the Koryŏ king Injong

Myŏngjong: Third son of Injong, and the nineteenth king (1171–1197). Noted for landscapes

Chŏng Hong-jin: Flourished in the mid-twelfth century. Noted for bamboo-paintings

Yi Ja-sŏng: A soldier-painter and calligraphist who flourished in the mid-twelfth century

King Ch'ungsŏn: The twenty-sixth king (1309–1313) who studied painting and calligraphy at the court of Yüan. Noted for his subsequent influence

Yun P'yŏng: Flourished in the early fourteenth century. Noted for landscapes

King Kongmin: The thirty-first king (1352–1374). Noted for landscapes and calligraphy. Two hunting scenes painted by him are still extant in the Dŏksu and National Museums

The gradual departure from Buddhism for a new form of aristocratic taste, which is a marked feature of the ceramic art, and to a lesser extent, of the pictorial art, is further evidenced in calligraphy. It is a historical fact that the Koryŏ dynasty had encouraged Confucianism side by side with Buddhism. As early as 958 the Chinese system of state examination was formally adopted; King Sŏngjong (982–997) favored the Confucian philosophy of government to the extent of enforcing it. By the time of Munjong and the fifteenth king Sukjong (1096–1105) Confucianism was in a flourishing condition with ever-increasing energy. This tendency, together with the rapid deterioration of Buddhism into a syncretistic superstition, naturally had a telling effect on calligraphy, not to mention learning in general. This art, which is still represented by seventy odd extant specimens of inscriptions on memorial tablets and temple frames, can be traced back to some forty-five different artists of all periods throughout the dynasty. But since the culmination of calligraphic art falls with the next dynasty, it should here be noted only cursorily that this art gradually assumed an importance hitherto unknown in the history of Korean aesthetic development. Art, which had been for centuries the embodiment of religious aspirations, became from the middle years of the Koryŏ period an expression of cultured taste and acquired leisure. It is in this sense that Koryŏ art began as a continuation of Shilla art but ended with many elements of the next phase of art under Chosŏn.

VI. *Chosŏn* (1392–1910)

The suppression of Buddhism, which had frequently been advocated by the

Confucians of the previous dynasty, was carried out to the letter with the foundation of the new dynasty, notably from the third king T'aejong (1401–1418) onwards. Art of the Chosŏn dynasty, therefore, derived its energy from a single source of inspiration: Confucianism. It is generally supposed that the new dynasty thereby brought about a 'revolution' in art; actually, it would be more correct to say that the new era merely carried to its logical conclusion what had already been foreshadowed in the previous. As the shift of emphasis crystallized under Chosŏn, it effected an attitude towards art that was humanistic rather than religious, and, in potentialities at least, inclusive rather than exclusive. Confucianism, however, had its own drawbacks for art: the danger of emotional sterility, inherent in the rational philosophy of Confucianism, led eventually to a new kind of exclusive mannerism and esoteric subjectivity, devoid of all social content and organic life. When faced with Confucianism, artistic activity must inevitably suffer from its excessive formalism on the one hand, and its emotional asceticism and frugality on the other.

Art of the Chosŏn dynasty may be divided into two periods with the Japanese invasion of 1592–1598 forming the divide. The first period shows by far the greater achievements. The great wave of humanism, together with the close cultural intercourse with Ming (1368–1644), led to encyclopedic compilations and publications in history, geography, classics, music, Buddhist gospels, and state codes, etc., under the successive humanist kings T'aejong (1401–1418), Sejong (1419–1450), Sejo (1456–1468), and Sŏngjong (1470–1494).

Although the sixteenth century carried on the humanistic tradition by producing a number of great scholar-statesmen, symptoms of political decadence had already begun to appear in the repeated wholesale 'purges' (1498, 1504, 1519, 1545) of scholar-politicians, foreshadowing the great factional strife of the seventeenth century and after. It is true that ceramic art, which had been revived under the fourth king Se-jong, reached a second peak of culmination since Koryŏ during the troublesome reign of the fourteenth king Sŏnjo (1568–1608). But by then the tide of fortune had begun to turn; and after the Japanese had wrought havoc and confusion on our heirlooms, the Manchus followed suit in further destruction (1625, 1636).

A brief heyday of cultural achievement in comparative peace followed between the seventeenth king Hyojong (1650–1659) and the twenty-second Chŏngjo (1777–1800). But our relationship with Ch'ing (1644–1912) was hardly comparable, either in intimacy or in fruitfulness, to what we had enjoyed with T'ang, Sung, or Ming. A feeling of estrangement and isolation seems to have crept into our cultural contacts with Ch'ing. From this mood of detachment we might have evolved a national culture of our own, and achieved another revival of art during the latter half of the Chosŏn dynasty; but instead, we fell heir to the disease of 'hermitage' by the deadweight of political corruption, factional strife, chronic poverty, emotional impoverishment, and the crust of pseudo-classic formalism. After 1800 we witness a sorry decline in the creative vitality of our people.

A marked characteristic of architecture in the Chosŏn dynasty is its unprecedented variety: palaces, gates, pavilions, memorial halls, Confucian mausoleums, shrines attached to tombs, Confucian schools, etc, besides a fair number of monasteries in the mountain recesses. Though many of them were rebuilt after the Japanese invasion, they adhere to the older styles of architecture in which Korea does not show much change through the centuries. In formal beauty, the architecture of the Chosŏn dynasty is comparable to the best of the earlier dynasties, but perhaps not in detailed finish.

Three stone pagodas come down from the latter half of the fifteenth century, of which the white marble pagoda (1467) at what used to be the Won-gak-sa, Seoul, is by far the most classic example of sculptural art of the Chosŏn dynasty. It is justly celebrated for its rich representation of Buddhist theocracy.

Buddha sculpture naturally shows a marked decline, though among the recognized masterpieces may be counted, from the earlier period, the wood-carved Vairochana Buddha of Haein-sa (South Kyŏngsang), and from the later period, the wood-carved Maitreya Buddha (with three attendant Buddhas) of Kŭmsan-sa (North Chŏlla), and the wood-carved Bodhisattva (c. 1765) of Pohyŏn-sa (North P'yŏng-yang). But none of them can equal the best Buddhas of the Shilla period or the Amida-Buddha of Pusŏk-sa, Koryŏ period.

The same could be said of Buddhist painting, which showed only a vulgar reproduction of raw colors, effeminate lines, and mechanical conception. Among the large number of Buddhist paintings only half a dozen show artistic worth and noble workmanship: Maitreya Buddha (1627) of Muryang-sa (Puyŏ), Kwannon Bodhisattva (1700?) of Kŭmsan-sa (Kimje), Sakya Buddha (1722) of Ch'ŏnggok-sa (Chinju), Loshana Buddha (1741) of Ssanggye-sa (Kimch'ŏn), Sakya Buddha (1765) of Pohyŏn-sa (Yŏngbyŏn) and Buddha group (1800?) of Yongju-sa (Suwŏn). The last was painted by Tanwŏn, of whom more later.

Ceramic art, however, was to reap another remarkable achievement in the early half of the Chosŏn dynasty. Just as Koryŏ had excelled in celadon, so white porcelain saw the fullest development from the time of King Sejong down to the end of the sixteenth century. The cause for this change in taste for *paekja*, or white porcelain, may be said to be threefold: (1) a parallel change in the ceramic art of Ming from that of Sung, (2) the pervasive influence of Confucian asceticism, and (3) the preference for subdued light-tinting which is said to be inherent in the Korean aesthetic temperament.

The important varieties of white porcelain technique are four: (1) "Mumun" or "So-mun" (undecorated), (2) "Shich'ae" (ornamental color applied), (3) "Yanggak" (decorated in relief), and (4) "Tonggak" (pierced-work). The ornamental patterns are both variegated and ingenious; particularly noteworthy are the symbols of long life (sun, moon, hill, water, cloud, pine, bamboo, crane, tortoise, deer, etc.) and those of wealth and happiness (peonies, grapes, etc.).

Celadon also underwent a change of technique and became *hwa-mun-ja-gi* (*mishima-de* in Japanese). The light inward glow of the Koryŏ celadon gives way generally to a duller, iron-gray tint; and the points or lines of decoration are punched out and filled in with clay, as in the Japanese *mishima-de* of mid-sixteenth and seventeenth centuries. The main varieties of Korean *mishima,* which flourished from the thirteenth to the sixteenth century are: (1) *kak-hwa-mun-gi* (*hori-mishima* in Japanese), where the pattern is indented; (2) *kam-hwa-mun-gi* (*shokan-mishima* in Japanese), a modification of the *sanggam* technique; (3) *pyŏn-p'il-hwa-mun-gi* (*hake-mishima* in Japanese), where the pattern is boldly treated with a brush; and (4) *kye-ryong-gi,* so called after Mount Kye-ryong of South Ch'ungch'ŏng Province which specialized in this production, a variation of the Hoi-Koryŏ technique.

That Korean potters virtually founded the pottery industry of Japan is an undisputed historical fact. The Japanese invading generals saw great potentialities for enriching their aristocratic life and the cult of the tea ceremony. Many of our artists, who settled in Japan either by inducement or of their own accord, created new traditions of pottery—another important contribution made by Korea to Japanese culture. Some of the names known are: one Edo Shinkuro (Korean name unknown), taken home by Kato Kiyomasa, founded the Edo Yaki, and later, being invited by Kurota Nagamasa, founded the Takatori Yaki; Yi Kyŏng (Jap. Korai Saemon), brought to Japan by Mori Terumoto, founded the Hagi Yaki; one of his disciples, Kwon Ch'ang-gi (Jap. Kurasaki Gombei), enriched the Izumo Yaki; Ku Kwan, taken home by Matsuura Shinzunobu, founded the Hirato Yaki; some twenty potters, headed by Pak Pyŏng-i, were taken home by Shimazu Yoshihiro, and founded the famous Satsuma Yaki; Yi Sam-p'yŏng founded the Arita Yaki; a Korean by the Japanese name of Agano Kizo founded the Agano Yaki and the Yatsushiro Yaki; and so on.

The most important contribution to art that Confucianism made during the Chosŏn dynasty was in calligraphy and painting. The twin arts, by tradition, were not only considered in the self-same stretch of imagination but also thought to be one with moral character, learning, and wisdom. They had the common laws of aesthetic application, and the common purpose of moral enhancement. As the Yüan calligraphist Chao Meng-fu (1254–1322) said: "The method of painting lies yet in the 'eight fundamental strokes' of writing. If there is one who can understand this, he will realize that the secret of calligraphy is really the same." And as the Ming artist Wen Chen-ming (1470–1559) said: "If one's moral character is not high, his art will also lack style." It is thus but natural that Confucianism in Korea should also have produced an unprecedented number of eminent artists in both fields.

Some 430 calligraphists are known to have flourished during the five centuries of Chosŏn. Their works are naturally far better preserved in original albums, hangings, screens, tablets, etc., than the works of their predecessors of the Koryŏ period. As the art developed through the centuries, audacity and individuality became the distinguishing features of the Chosŏn dynasty calligraphy, just as smooth grace and elegance were the characteristics of Koryŏ calligraphy. The style of Chao Meng-fu, which flourished during the Koryŏ period, continued to hold sway until the end of the fifteenth century, when our close contact with Ming led our subsequent artists to study the styles of such

Ming artists as Wen Chen-ming and Tung Ch'i-ch'ang (1555–1636). Prince Anp'yŏng (1418–1443), third son of King Sejong, was a consummate artist and promoter of the Chao Meng-fu style. Sŏng Su-ch'im (pen-name: Ch'ŏngsong), who flourished late in the fifteenth and the early sixteenth century, was our pioneer in introducing the Ming style. But the one who must receive the palm for the early Chosŏn period is Han Ho (Sŏkbong) (1543–1605), who, though schooled in the Chao Meng-fu style, developed a characteristic style of his own, so much prized in China and Japan as well as in Korea. Even after the seventeenth century, when in China the change of dynasty had brought with it new schools of calligraphy, Korea adhered to the older Yüan and Ming masters, developing its own individual technique. The most representative calligraphists of the later Chosŏn period are: Yun Sun (Paekha) (b. 1680, and flourished in the early eighteenth century), Yi Kwan-sa (Wŏn-gyo) (1705–1777), Kang Se-hwang (P'yoam) (1713–1791), and Kim Jŏng-hŭi (Ch'usa) (1786–1856). The work of the last-mentioned Kim Jŏng-hŭi is, indeed, the crowning glory of Korean calligraphy. None but a veritable genius could have achieved his free and unrivalled mastery of the brush and his deep scholarship.

Painting, as a part of the accomplishment of a scholar-artist, assumed a new direction in the Chosŏn period, which produced over four hundred painters of merit. The founder of the dynasty instituted in 1392 a royal academy, 'Tohwawŏn,' modeled after the Chinese organization of a similar nature; and one of the assigned tasks of its members was to paint portraits of the royalty. But the influence of Tohwawŏn was never strong enough to counteract the tendency, created by the overwhelming number of lay scholar-artists, of looking down upon the use of colors as a 'lesser,' and even 'vulgar,' art. These upheld the otherworldly art of 'the Southern school' at the expense of the realistic technique of 'the Northern school,' regarding the India ink painting as the earmark of refinement. This tendency asserted itself early in the dynasty, and as time passed, scholar-poet-painters aspired more and more to the aesthetic notions of Sung poets like Su Tung-p'o (1035–1101), who said: "Poetry has painting in it, and painting, poetry." The heyday of their art fell between the reigns of the nineteenth king Sukjong (1675–1720) and the twenty-first, Yŏngjo (1725–1776). This subjectivity itself became conventionalized in turn, and duly brought about its decline.

In the earlier period of the dynasty, the Northern school produced three great artists: An Kyŏn (Hyŏndongja), who flourished in the early fifteenth century, painter of the famous 'Dream' landscape, depicting the unearthly scene which Prince Anp'yŏng is said to have seen in a dream; Kang Hŭi-an (Injae) (b. 1419), the versatile artist who flourished in the fifteenth century, though he himself despised the art as being 'vulgar'; and Yi Sang-jwa (Hakpo), the landscape painter who flourished in the latter half of the fifteenth century. Three artists in India ink of the Southern school who were hailed as 'the three pinnacles' were: Hwang Jip-jung (Yŏnggok) (b. 1533) who excelled in vine and grapes; Yi Jŏng (Tanŭn) (b. 1541) who excelled in bamboo; Ŏ Mong-yong (Sŏlgok) (b. 1566) who excelled in plum blossoms. The only woman artist of Korea belongs also to this century: Shin Sa-im-dang (1512–1559), mother of the famous scholar Yi Yi (Yulgok) (1536–1584), excelled in birds and flowers.

The galaxy of master-painters that crowded the latter centuries compensated for their relative debility of aesthetic energy by their esoteric way. Korean painting reached a high mark from the late seventeenth century into the eighteenth. Landscape and 'genre' painting were the two categories of highest achievement. The masters in 'hill and water' landscapes were: Chŏng Sŏn (Kyŏmjae) (1676–1759) who is rated the greatest master in Korean landscape; Shim Sa-jŏng (Hyŏnjae) (1707–1769), a disciple of Chŏng Sŏn, who introduced the Chinese 'sublimity' into his landscape; Kang Se-hwang (1713–1791), the calligraphist-painter already mentioned; Choe Puk (Sŏngjae), who flourished early in the eighteenth century; Yi In-mun (Yuch'un) (1745–1821), who is famous for his horizontal twenty-eight-foot long landscape; Kim Hong-do (Tanwŏn) (b. 1760), who, with Chŏng Sŏn and Shim Sa-jŏng, was one of the three most versatile painters of the latter period; Yi Bang-un (Kiya), who flourished late in the eighteenth century; and Yi Han-ch'ŏl (b. 1808), who is also known as a portrait painter. There were three 'genre' painters who depicted the customs and modes of daily living in a light vein: afore-mentioned Kim Hong-do (Tanwŏn); Kim Tu-ryang (Namni) (1696–1763); and Shin Yun-bok (Hyewŏn), who flourished in the early nineteenth century--the Korean Hogarth. Three more names must be added for their unique qualities: Pyŏn Sang-byŏk (Hwajae), who was a great eighteenth-century master of cats and birds, continuing the art of another earlier famous painter of cats and dogs, Yi Am (Tu-sŏng-yŏng) (b. 1499);

Hŏ Yu (Sochi) (1809–1892), an expert in bamboos and peonies; and Chang Sŭng-ŏp (Owŏn) (1843–1897), who specialized in birds and flowers.

Conclusion

In any assessment of Korean culture, including art, we must be on our guard in two ways. First, our country has been regarded for generations as a quaint land of hermitage and squalor, engaged in its timeless dreams of hard-crusted medievalism. Taking up this sentiment as a ready means of political justification, the Japanese, with a definite axe to grind, distorted the picture further by condemning our whole culture as being imitative, parasitic, and moribund. Such a censure, even granting an element of truth in it as far as it goes, is, of course, not the whole truth. By an effort of historical imagination and perspective, we should try to see beyond the enervating influence of state-sponsored Confucianism, which brought about our decline from the seventeenth century onwards. And second, we should beware of the over-patronizing attitude, much as it may gratify our sense of pride as Koreans. A battle cry will always remain a battle cry: it can never be accepted blindly as a final verdict, as when Eckardt writes (p. 6):

> It is no exaggeration to aver that Korea is responsible for the production of by far the most beautiful, or rather, the most classical works of art in the Far East, differing both from the exaggerated and frequently distorted models of China, and from the often too sentimental and pattern-ridden degeneracy of Japan.

The fault of distortion and exaggeration, of sentimentality and pattern-ridden-ness is found as much in Korea as anywhere else. Such over-enthusiasm probably comes from an engrossment in some detached aspect of Korean culture. Our findings in Korean art will assume a deeper significance if we correlate them with the rest of the general pattern which we call Korean culture.

In tracing the development of Korean art, certain characteristics will suggest themselves as being common to all phases of our national life, political and cultural. As a consequence of our peninsular environment, our country has, throughout the ages, been both peripheral and central, solitary as it were in the midst of neighbors. It is the destiny of the periphery to be bathed in the twilight of the burning center. Had Korea occupied a more inland position on the Far Eastern continent, she would certainly have been absorbed into the burning center of the Chinese culture; but, unlike the Manchus, for instance, we have never lost our identity, nor proved a directive force in the enrichment of that civilization of the center. It is not enough to say that our culture has been derivative of the Chinese; in any examination of a culture, the point of difference should repay our study as much as those of similarity.

And yet, our intermediary position made our homeland the highway of traffic, political and cultural. Japan will always owe us a debt for transmitting Buddhism and Confucianism, not to mention our art. We were once a worthy sea-faring race. The people of Shilla had made the Yellow Sea "a small lake in front of their gate," founding innumerable colonies along the Chinese coast from Shantung to the Yangtse. Our traffic with the southern countries flourished as late as the fifteenth century. And to counterbalance this asset, we have always had the liability of being the chessboard of political conflict. To that extent also we have been central. The march of clashing armies, with the inevitable destruction attendant upon it, has been our fear and often fate throughout the ages. That is why, politically, we have shown such humiliating contrasts of adulatory submission and resilient independence, and culturally, such fertile genius for venturesome receptivity and inward centripetence.

If Chinese art may be said to excel in solidity of form, and Japanese in delight of color, Korean art must be said to stand for the capture of the fleeting moment in line. This is but natural in a land that knows it to be neither a fountainhead nor a terminus. If one is powerful and the next joyful, it is the characteristic of the last to be evanescent, and sorrowful.

It is not by accident of history alone that Korean art had discovered in Buddhism a lasting source of inspiration. Korean Buddhism never had adopted that aggressive, or that furiously mystical type of worship so prevalent in Japan, or that doctrinaire religiosity which is common enough on the Continent. It always stopped at the frontier of mellowness, providing itself to be a happy vehicle for embodying our inborn temperament of quiet yearning after that "Pure Land of the West."

It is not to say that Buddhism should be revived if we say that it played for centuries an indispensable role in Korean art. The 'aristocratic' age of art will never return again any more than the monarchical system of government will be restored again. The top-heavy vertical structure of our society, which Confucianism so doggedly persisted in upholding, has long since crumbled. And Buddhism, which today is as dead as the dynasties, which helped it flourish, is also but a museum piece of "passion reconsidered." Psychologically, we have long been ready for the horizontal, the democratic, structure of society, but for Japan, who by political force retarded its realization by nearly half a century. Art in this new age to come is bound to change, because the medium of art has changed. Though our artistic faculty will likely to remain the same, its achievement will be, we hope, of a different nature. For, in the words of Arnold Toynbee (*A Study of History,*' 1947, p. 49):

In primitive societies, as we know them, mimesis is directed towards the older generation and towards dead ancestors who stand, unseen but not unfelt, at the back of the living elders, reinforcing their prestige. In a society where mimesis is thus directed backward towards the past, custom rules and society remains static. On the other hand, in societies in process of civilization, mimesis is directed towards creative personalities who command a following because they are pioneers. In such societies, 'the cake of custom,' as Walter Bagehot called it in his Physics and Politics, is broken and society is in dynamic motion along a course of change and growth

(Wednesday, November 24–Wednesday, December 8, 1948, *The Seoul Times*)

A Brief Survey of the Present Condition of Korea

Introductory Remarks:

We Koreans are a homogeneous people, enjoying a long homogeneous cultural heritage of one language and one national sense. We have known class distinctions in the past, but no national division; we have had religious differences, but no internecine antagonism. It was none other than this strong communal feeling which found its logical expression in the nation-wide independence movement ten years after the annexation by Japan, and which underlay our ceaseless resistance of Japan's tyrannous rule for forty years, resulting in the recovery of freedom as the outcome of the Second World War.

Since the so-called Liberation, however, the Korean people are faced with a hitherto unknown misfortune and a menace in the form of the Iron Wall of the Thirty-eighth Parallel. This line, originally agreed upon as a line of demarcation for the enforcement by the two Allied Nations of the terms of surrender of the Japanese Army, has ended by becoming a frontier between the two stationary forces, whereby the country is faced with the grave menace of losing its integral life as a unified nation: namely,

1. The inability to interchange material resources—rich mineral and industrial products of the North and the abundant agricultural products of the South—has created a serious economic disruption that has rendered impossible a healthy. reconstruction of national economy;
2. The people have been deprived of the very minimum freedom of removal and intercourse; father and son, husband and wife, are living in harassed conditions of unnatural severance;
3. The political systems of the two regions differ so entirely as to create a feeling of being two separate alien lands. Whereas in the South the people enjoy comparative peace under democratic rule, those in the North are placed under communist dictatorship; and contrary to the proclamations of the Supreme Commander of the Allied Forces in the Pacific, their civil liberties and property rights have been trampled under foot, and decent citizens who do not blindly

accept the communist doctrine, are being branded and ruthlessly ostracized as "reactionaries," "pro-Japanese national traitors," etc. Furthermore, the farmers are suffering under a heavy burden of taxation in kind, amounting to seventy-to-eighty percent of their products. The refugees into the South, who literally stream by the thousands each day seeking to escape from this oppression, amply endorse the degree and extent of their dire misery.

In short, the Iron Wall of the Thirty-eighth Parallel has cut our country into two halves, destroying our homogeneity as a nation, undermining our wholesome economic structure, and proving a fundamental barrier to the unification of Korea; so that, if this condition is to be prolonged, August 15, 1945, will not be the day of liberation but that of eternal curse and woe.

The Communist Intrigue

With the stationing of the Soviet forces, North Korea is completely under communist dictatorship. Their so-called "People's Commission" is not of the people but of the communists, and their "democratic" free election not a reflection of the people's free will, but a disguise of the dictatorial machination of the Communist Party. Besides the Communist Party, alias the North Korea Labor Party, there are one or two political parties, e.g., the Chosŏn Democratic Party, the Chŏng-u-dang, etc., but only in name. All social organizations are but partisans of the communist cause. In the North there is neither an independence of the legislature, the executive and the judicature, nor sanctity of election, nor freedom of association. The civil liberties and property rights, that should form the basis of a state, are being denied and violated; and the farmers, whom they claim to have liberated, are in destitute conditions with over-taxation. Where human rights are undermined, there can be no freedom of religious worship or learning. The people in the North are suffering not only from economic ruin but also from mental and spiritual suffocation. This is the true character of the so-called "progressive" democracy.

It goes without saying that power in North Korea is being maintained by two factors—the forces of the Soviet Army, and the terrorist methods of the police. The reign of terror, which characterizes communism as well as fascism, is the diametrical opposite of the democratic ideals. The fact that the communists in North Korea, who only constitute fifteen percent of the Northern population, are nevertheless in power shows clearly to what an extent they are dependent upon a rule by force and fear.

The communists themselves, being human, realize the unnaturalness of their policies; but they feel themselves fully justified by their fanatic creed, which indoctrinates the liberation of the proletariat by means of ruthless subjugation under iron control for the purpose of accomplishing a world revolution. For them the end justifies all means, and they find it expedient to become a satellite, or even a confederation, of the Soviet Republic, which they look up to as the "fatherland" of the proletariat. The Korean communists are no exceptions to the rule. By turning the most opportune Thirty-eighth Parallel to advantage, they are turning North Korea into a base for Bolshevising South Korea as well as for assisting the Chinese communists to extend their power over Manchuria. This is clearly borne out by the fact that the Korean Communist Army has invaded Manchuria and the Chinese Communist Army has been stationed in North Korea. Further, the words of Major General Brown irrefutably corroborate this point. In his statement issued on August 25, he has declared to the effect that:

The South Korea Labor Party, and other political parties and social organizations under the banner of the South Korea Democratic National Front have from the beginning taken hostile stands against the South Korean Government and against the U. S., and have been a great impediment to the administrative functions in the U. S. zone by means of destructive intrigues and acts of unlawful violence. They have worked under the support and instruction of the North Korea Democratic National Front. Agitators dispatched from the North have repeatedly staged public seditions, and the politico-social bodies under the South Korea Democratic National Front have guided them.

In the light of such undeniable facts, it is self-evident that Russia's sinister designs in North Korea will not cease at Bolshevising the South of Korea, but will further make our country a base for controlling the whole of the Far East. And she has nothing to depend upon but the Thirty-eighth Parallel Iron Curtain.

Prospects of the Joint Commission

In the present state of affairs, the deadlock of the Joint Commission is only too natural, for the Soviet representatives seem to be desirous:

1. Of delaying as much as possible the establishment of a unified Korean democratic government involving the lifting of the Thirty-eighth Parallel, meaning planning to strengthen and enlarge the communistic hold upon Korea;
2. In case of establishing the unified Korean government, of interfering with our internal policy from the beginning by means of "Trusteeship," thereby strengthening the communistic power. Otherwise, there is no reason for refusing to take into consideration the opinions of Koreans themselves on a wide basis, and for excluding from consultation all membership bodies of the Anti-Trusteeship Combat Commission.

If the concrete provisions of the Moscow Decision are founded upon the Cairo Declaration, which in turn goes back to the principles of world peace laid down in the Atlantic Charter, it follows that the sacrosanct principle of the self-determination of nations is the corner-stone of the Moscow Decision also. This basic principle is indeed set forth in the first provision of the said Decision, of which the third provision—that of "trusteeship"—is but a substantiation of the first. If, however, the concrete method set forth in the third provision is at all ambiguous, or seemingly contradictory to the basic principle manifested in the first, it is then only too natural, as General Brown has pointed out in his historic statement, that Koreans should be given an opportunity to express their views in accordance with the ideals of democracy. Furthermore, if the Soviet interpretation of the much debated word "trusteeship" does not by any means infringe upon the independent sovereignty of our nation, then it is all the more necessary that she should invite those membership bodies of the Anti-Trusteeship Combat Commission, and endeavor to clear their fears, suspicions, and misunderstandings. Facts, however, are far otherwise. So long as she persistently adheres to her original intention of eliminating from consultation those political and social bodies, our misgivings will not be cleared, and we shall be given to doubting the very function of the Joint Commission.

If, therefore, the progress of the Joint Commission is to be re-scrutinized by the two governments at home, it is highly desirable that the U. S. should take new decisive measures by which the Korean question should either be settled among the Four Allied Powers concerned, or else be brought forth in the General Assembly of the U. N. and decided by world opinion. A fulfillment at the earliest possible date of the world pledge vouchsafing the independence of Korea is not merely the poignant desire of the Koreans themselves, but also a point of honor for the two great nations, and a key to establishing world peace in the Far East.

Some Observations upon the U. S. Military Government in South Korea

The Korean people have every cause to feel grateful for, and to trust in, the U. S. Military Government in South Korea. Not only have the U. S. Armed Forces been our true liberators, but also America has enjoyed the unique privilege of being a friendly nation both historically and factually. We know for certain that the U. S. has no territorial ambitions or political designs upon us and that she well live up to her pledge guaranteeing our sovereign independence. Through the unswerving efforts of General Hodge and his forces, we have progressed with great strides in many spheres of national activity—industrial, educational, social and political. Food shortage has somewhat been assuaged by imports from the U. S., and economic rehabilitation effected to a considerable extent. Public peace has been restored on a firmer basis, and the appointment of Koreans in administrative functionaries as well as the creation of the Legislative Assembly, though not wholly by election, is undeniable evidence of great progress.

Be it admitted, however, that sincerity alone is not enough. Due mostly to an insufficient knowledge of, and insight into, our condition and mood, past and present, the Military Government has inevitably committed some blunders, such as:

1. Frequent annulment or replacement of laws and ordinances, creating a general diffidence in the integrity of the administration;
2. Evils consequent upon the so-called "administration through interpreters";
3. Uncertainty and irresponsibility created by the indecisive transfer of administrative authority to the Korean civil servants;
4. Lack of administrative efficacy attendant upon red-tape-ism;
5. Corruption and graft due to slackness of morale; etc.

The most glaring fault, however, of the Military Government is to be found in the indecisiveness of policy, which undermines the general security of the whole administration. It must be admitted in all frankness that the officials in the Military Government are not directed by any definite guiding policy, with the result that they form no body politic but an assembly of individual officials who perform the daily routine work according to the political weather of the day. A salient example of this indecisiveness is the so-called coalition policy of the leftists and the rightists. The vague attitude which asserts that the left is good, the right also good, but the middle of the way is the best, tends only to confuse public opinion, with the inevitable consequence of increasing minority splits and factional animosity, which in turn creates political confusion and social disorder and unsettlement. The conciliation policy that changes with the change of political situations, is partly responsible for the strengthening of communism in South Korea. At a time when the sinister character of communism is being exposed to light and when the ideological differences are being more and more clearly demarcated throughout the world, one cannot but doubt the efficacy of such lukewarm conciliation policies.

If, therefore, the Military Government in South Korea is to handle the Korean problem under the guiding policy of the Truman Doctrine, the time-honored middle-of-the-way attitude must be changed for a firmer stand in closest co-operation with the Nationalist Camp. Only by supporting the conscientious nationalists, will the Military Government be able to relieve the present state of irresolution and confusion and to solidify peace in Korea.

Conclusion

A unified and independent Korea can hardly be expected from the Joint Commission as it now stands. We therefore propose in all earnestness that the Korean question be either put forth before the Four Great Powers or else before the General Assembly of the U. N., and at the same time, that we be given an opportunity of general election with the view to establishing our own democratic government by ourselves, and that the U. S. give us the necessary economic support in order to strengthen the democratic bases in our country, which will gradually raise the morale of the people and at the same time promote our voluntary aspirations towards the unification of Korea. There can be no wiser or easier solution for the Koreans except by appealing to their patriotic sentiment and their homogeneous culture.

Our Naval Defense
As Recounted by Home Minister Shin Sung–mo

[*Editor's Note*: Since this is an article based on private talks with Mr. Shin, full responsibility is with *The Seoul Times* for any views expressed herein that might be interpreted as contrary to the interests of the Government or the people. —The Woolgatherer]

A. No Axe to Grind

Since my belated homecoming in the early part of November last, I have been studying the problems of our naval defense in the light of its past achievements and future potentialities. Whatever observations that I may have made by investigation of the given data can, I believe, be expressed at this date with some candor because, now that my assigned task lies elsewhere, I need entertain no fear of being misconstrued that my thoughts are activated by a desire to gratify some personal ambition as a seaman.

I am by education a seaman; and it is true that a seaman on land does not necessarily find himself always in his elements. Had times proved not so emergent for the people of Korea, I would doubtless have served the state better and derived a greater degree of personal happiness by steering a ship on the open sea than by sitting in the uneasy chair of a red-tape ministry. Fond as people are of speaking metaphorically of "steering the ship of state," I myself am not well disposed to such an image because of the two-fold fear that those who think of government mainly in terms of such metaphors may easily become power-sick just as one gets sea-sick, and that they may unconsciously imagine the Republic of Korea to be a floating ship instead of a solid edifice! It is not long since I have taken up the difficult office of the Home Ministry but already people, both well-meaning and deeply concerned about the welfare of the people, have urged me implicitly to effect drastic changes in administration that are, as changes, nothing short of wonderful. With all due respect to their sincerity and sound advice, I know myself to be no Popeye the Sailorman, who upon a dose of spinach is known to achieve knockabout wonders. It is partly because I do not believe in success of the riffraff kind, even if that dose of spinach were to be given me by sanction of the people; but chiefly because my official duties as Home Minister include the control of the Police, to which it is deemed unwise to encourage the riff-raff.

I make this apology in detour because I wish to stress home the fact that whatever my present official capacity, I am by years of discipline of my own choice a seaman of modest pride, and that it is in this private capacity that I wish to speak here. Beyond that I have no axe to grind.

B. Labor of Love

It is important to refresh our memory of the various difficulties which the Korean Coast Guard has had to obviate since its legal establishment on June 15, 1946, by Section III of Ordinance No. 86 of USAMGIK. Though the Coast Guard was activated effective 14 January 1946 by this ordinance, it had been but a body in name prior to September 1946, with a poor enough skeletal organization, scarce floating equipment, unreliable communication network, and poor morale and discipline among the recruits of approximately 1300 including 75 officers. It was not until a group of Washington-dispatched Coast Guard personnel, headed by George E. McCabe, arrived in September 1946, that the arduous program of organizing and training was taken up effectively with collaboration of the then Lt. Com. Sohn Won Il. To them must be given the credit of having effected between September 1946 and February 1947:

1. Establishment of a working radio communications network.
2. Increase of two additional bases of operation at Kunsan and Pusan to the four already functioning: i.e., Inchon, Mokpo, Chinhae, and Mukho.
3. The setting afloat of the Coast Guard with serviceably-trained personnel to man 18 ships commissioned during the period.
4. Supervisory organization at Seoul Headquarters to attend to all problems of administration, including the trying task of co-ordination between departments.
5. Concentrate efforts on training of service force at Chinhae, for which purpose operations were removed to the nearby Pusan base.

6. Achievement of satisfactory results in the assignment of training duties to selected seamen on board U.S. destroyers in offshore patrol around South Korea.

As an operating branch of the Department of Internal Security, the Korean Coast Guard was charged with maintaining inshore and inter-island patrol of South Korean Coastal Waters. Its function so far has been of a negative kind, though a vital one: i.e., (i) prevention [. . .], and suppression of smuggling and piracy; (ii) conducting of rescue work in case of marine disasters; and (iii) assistance of other government departments in enforcing national shipping laws, rules, and regulations. What stands out, however, as an undeniable fact is that the Korean personnel, whether officers or enlisted men, would never have shown such enthusiasm, had they not had the implicit faith that the Korean Coast Guard would be the nucleus of our future navy. As such they have done, a praiseworthy service in the Coast Guard, even though as a navy they leave yet much to be desired.

With the establishment [of our republican] Government, when the Korean Coast Guard was [expected] to assume added responsibilities, the advisory personnel as of August 30, 1949, was reduced drastically to the number of 7 only, headed by Captain Harold L. Sutherland, whereas his predecessors, Captains McCabe and Perkins, had some 20 subordinates to help him. Captain Sutherland is carrying on a difficult work which can only be described as labor of love, at a time when the transition from the Coast Guard to the Navy requires more circumspection and vision than ever before.

C. Supply and Equipment

It is a fact of some significance that the FMAG makes no direct provisions or recommendations for the Korean Navy. It does not, of course, mean that the Army gets everything and the Navy none. One thing that can be said for our Department of National Defense, if nothing else, is that there exists no inter-services rivalry of any kind. But it does mean that the Navy has to get its supply through the Army channel, which ideally speaking is not the most efficient way for the Navy. And one among many of the valuable services which Captain Sutherland has rendered to our national defense is to put our Navy on a coeval basis with the Army in the eyes of the PMAG.

From its earliest days, the greatest difficulty facing the Coast Guard had been the supply and equipment problem. Looking back at this date, one cannot but marvel at the patience with which the Coast Guard has been built up. To instance but a couple of cases, in October 1946 two LCIs and six 45–foot picket-boats arrived from the Philippines; but none being operable upon arrival at Pusan, they had to be towed to Chinhae for overhauls. In August 1947 half a dozen YMS class vessels were received through Civilian Supply Program, stripped of all spare parts and tools. From the viewpoint of vessels, indeed, the growth of the Coast Guard seems to have virtually stopped with 1947, for all vessels, as of August 30, 1948, has been acquired before the end of the previous year. Half a dozen LCIs, some 15 or 16 YMSs, some dozen or more smaller craft of the Japanese Mine Sweeper type, some 20 odd forty-foot picket-boats, one patrol vessel, one YC, and half dozen tugs. . . this, with poor enough ordinance, might be considered a serviceable Coast Guard on the bare minimal scale, but only Lilliputian would in all seriousness accept it as a battle-worthy craft. Which means is effect that I am not the last man to feel the irony of entitling this brief article 'Our Naval Defense,'

D. Inspired Training

All material shortcomings, however, are well made up for by the inspired enthusiasm with which our officers and men are undergoing their training. The future of our Navy lies undoubtedly with their vision, discipline, and latent power.

With a hodge-podge of Japanese and U.S. equipment, our radiomen, for instance, have achieved a rare degree of efficiency and competence. The U.S. advisors of the Coast guard have found out to their pleasant surprise that radio training to our men presented a minimum of difficulty.

The batch of some 60 or more midshipmen who were assigned destroyer duties on board U.S. patrol destroyers have been highly praised by the commanding officers for their industry, eagerness, and their cooperation. It seems to me that every effort should be made by our Government to request SCAP for the continuation of some such program, which unfortunately seems to have been terminated in September 1947.

The authorized complement of the Coast Guard has been for 3,000 officers and men. All personnel, as of August 30, 1948, was kept within 5 percent of this authorized strength, with no reserves. Since then, however, the force has been greatly increased. By the end of this year, we may probably have a force of the regular establishment approximating ten thousand. What is vital, however, is not the quantity but the quality of the force, particularly of the officers.

E. Chinhae the Key Spot

For such palpable reasons our Navy is concentrating all its energies at present on the training of officers and men at Chinhae. Some 13 different schools virtually are gathered in this key Academy, besides the boot training and petty officer training by the Service Force the Shipyard, Supply Depot, Hospital, and Radio Station.

On December 15 last I had the good fortune to attend the graduation ceremony of 46 officers from the Academy. It was an occasion of official jubilation, which was fully justified; but to me personally it was also an occasion of private anxieties, which were equally well grounded. For the Academy which has so far produced some 110 graduates, leaves yet much to be desired. Fully aware as I am of the achievements which the Korean Coast Guard has scored against overwhelming odds during the past three years, I feel obliged to draw the public attention to the following desirable aspects:

1. As compared with deck training, a visible weakness lies in the training of engineers, both officer and enlisted personnel. We cannot afford to shrug away this fact by admitting complacently that Koreans are not adept mechanically. It has to be rectified at all cost for the healthy growth of our maritime defense power.
2. Though instruction is being carried out on an intensive scale, there inevitably ensue certain gaps, such as in gunnery and tactics, due to the shortage of competent instructors. Unless a group of special instructors from U. S. come to the aid of the Academy, it will be extremely difficult to carry on instruction on a balanced scale.

3. Five small vessels are at present in use for training purposes. Larger size vessels are considered absolutely necessary.
4. The shipyard is capable of doing good machine and foundry work, but it has to meet the inevitable shortage of supplies and materials as best as can by improvising in order to effect the necessary repairs.
5. Some time ago I as a private citizen ventured to make certain recommendations to the President regarding a proposed independent naval mission from U. S. for the purpose of training, developing, and equipping our Navy. Since it would not be to the interests of our Government to reveal the particulars of this much desired naval mission, I will only reiterate the importance thereof in the hope that it may be effectuated expediently. That, and only that, it is believed, can solve our imminent problems in sea defense.

Human memory is a short-lived thing. The people of Korea today are hysterically aware of the northern menace of the grisly Bear, but they are more or less oblivious of the potential menace from across the Channel, which will in due course be visited upon us if we do not heed to the building up of our sea defense. We are without exaggeration a century or more behind Japan in our sea-awareness. It is not for political reasons alone that the development of our sea-consciousness is urged. We shall indeed prove ourselves great fools if we were to hand over again to our jealous neighbor our rich resources in fishing industry. We should further prove ourselves to be shortsighted to rely upon our Army alone for national defense. A heavy militarization program often leads to consequences that are far from democratic, and a cumbersome army is likely to prove a traffic burden in times of peace, especially in a small over-populated country like ours, and in times of emergency, a ready political weapon of graver consequences than we may imaginably foresee. Building up a navy costs money. It was the government's verdict in the days of Admiral Yi Soon-shin. Though it still holds good as far as the verdict goes, we must also remember that the cost of building up a navy is in effect the cost of building up democracy in this country.

(*The Seoul Times,* January 15, 18, 19, and 20, 1949)

Inside Cloud Cuckoo Land: A Parallel Account
—Essay in Collocation—

In the heart of the metropolis, wrapped in the muffled drone of ever-increasing traffic that thrives on dollar petrol, guarded at the gates by vigilant policemen who hold the obvious conviction that trespassers of public peace are to be found only among pedestrians (seeing that these undergo a careful scrutiny of personal identification while any odd citizen in the shabbiest of taxis is permitted to pass free), stands the Capitol Building, breathing out in that over-peopled and restless capital an air of singular repose and forced dignity. It is, of course, a reality with the two coats of varnish, Liberation and Independence, gradually peeling off by four years of wear and tear. Inside, there is the same hubbub and the same shuffling of feet down the corridors, as pompous officials, less like servants of the people than commercial travelers, struggle to cope with the intricacies of meta-politics in a curious epoch of post-war vociferousness. A crowd of tired retainers awaits with mixed feelings the next stunning announcement from the Americans about a possible withdrawal of the occupation forces; in which case the blame for all posterity would go to the Americans for their having used this land as experimental ground for sowing the seed of democracy in dubious weather, and for their having never understood the time-honored custom of engaging fifteen men to squander the work of two. Nothing of this appears on the surface, however, for nothing in the Cloud Cuckoo Land ever does.

Along the dusty tram ways the molested willow trees of the avenue begin to bear the signs of having survived the winter; magpies fly overhead; urchins play marbles in street corners, mud color their own color; and this is the human center of the metropolis, squalid as it always was but nowadays more cynical, too. Here pathetic people from the country will stay in one-night bed-and-board hotels to submit their petitions, and slick and up-to-date young gentlemen from the city will sometimes make theatrical calls over the "Washington" telephone. Courting couples sit in smoky teahouses, sipping soda water, their faces more desperate and glum if possible than those of couples, similarly placed, in other countries. The occupation forces are much spoken of but rarely to be seen in parades, which have almost become the sole prerogative of the Students' National Guard; and the people gather before notice boards to see what the Metropolitan Police Chief has to "proclaim" for the day, all being ready, whatever their political color, to show the Presidential Car its due respect should it speed past, complete with sirens and armored tanks; and up and down the Ponjŏng highways of an evening saunter the Americans, conscious as ever of the need for buying jewelry and souvenirs, glancing with disgust at the miraculously surreptitious sales of things out of the quartermaster's warehouse, before returning to their billets, to whisky and soda, back numbers of *Esquire* and *Post,* and a polite disparagement of all around them.

Past the City Hall is a beehive of a building, mongrel in style and deficient in ornament, reputedly Western but in fact resembling the architecture of the West as much as a translated version resembles its original; this has naturally become the headquarters of the American Mission, since for better or worse it has good plumbing and central heating. The rooms are delightfully warm in winter and deliciously cool in summer; refreshments are readily available at all hours and offices are furnished with file boxes and ominous-looking maps of the Cloud Cuckoo Land, which create an atmosphere of strategic importance. I have had some memorable interviews against a background of such maps and filing cases and of shadowy figures who pester the visa officers with their languishing hopes of going to America; during one of them, indeed, I was definitely confirmed of my long-standing doubts that the American Mission must know far more of the affairs of the Cloud Cuckoo Land than the latter's own Government.

The people here live in a sunny little world of their own, fetched to work in sumptuous buses and in shiny motor cars fitted with heaters and coolers and, of course, radio, from efficiently run hotels and spacious homes furnished with odd trinkets of the Cuckoo Land and well cared for by a troupe of obsequious servants, a much envied job among the poverty-stricken natives. A former Japanese department store, converted as PX, used to furnish them with all the heart could desire; but this has been closed down for some time, presumably because, among other reasons, they discovered that much of the commodity on sale managed somehow to appear again at the native "PX" where things would fetch handsome prices. In the evenings they try to forget that they are stationed in this Cloud Cuckoo Land, by inviting each other to chatty gatherings, cocktail parties and innocuous games of poker; they have long since discovered the boredom of stooping to the folly of the *kisaeng* girls, and so they prefer to visit the Corps Theater in which to dump their nostalgia for home and the "march" of civilization. Never in their lives before, they acrimoniously agree, have they been so hard put to it, with their sense of burden that they must save this land of innocence and inefficiency from the Reds.

Very different from this, in outward appearance at least, is the world of average citizens of this land of squandered opportunity. In their offices, they shiver round a small charcoal brazier in winter, worrying about their parents in the "other" zone and their friends under police detention in this, and in the rainy season of the summer they grumble about the menace of floods which will affect their ration. Plain boiled water takes the place of coffee and Coca-Cola: for luncheon, there is no Glorified Hamburger or Apple Pie à la Mode, but cold rice and barley in a small tin box. They travel to work in rattling trams and buses converted from trucks, crowded in on each other like cattle, after first standing in a queue for anything up to an hour; and their free time is spent in selling out household valuables to buy cereals with, now that the ration has been reduced, if not entirely cut. The view of Mr. Pak on life in general and democracy in particular differs widely from those of Bud and Hank; and passing from a Ministry in the Capitol to the American Mission is like issuing from a marketplace into the quiet of a club lounge, where the typewriter taps away in falsetto to the droning undertones of the human voice.

But the metropolis hides its distress, as it hides its pleasure, vice, luxury and opinion, on the whole very completely. Ugly spots are there, if you care to look for them under your nose; the back streets at night, the war-time dugouts, the bridges over the open city sewage, where homeless beggars, old and young, and refugee mothers and babies sleep on the ground, and where the guttersnipes and pick-pockets gather for a smoke and a chat about their day's booty in trafficking, pimping, blackmail and theft; on the gay quarters of Myŏng-dong where, apart from the brothels, illegal but flourishing, a string of restaurants and coffee-houses, frequented by well-to-do brokers of luxury goods from Macao and Hong-Kong and by artists of belated bohemianism with no asset but their leisure to kill, prove at any rate that some seeds of nineteenth-century Western culture have fallen on abortive ground.

The normal sights of this unwieldy, ramshackle city, however, are of crowds of sulky people, hungry but not starving, shabby but fortunate enough in having inherited khaki jumpers from their foreign friends, thumping about their business on army boots, melancholy, apathetic and unfailingly aggressive: of thousands of new wooden shacks, fresh ones springing up almost as you watch, each the size of a sumptuous hen-house but still having its constitutional right to vote and its communal obligation to be called out for mass meetings: of poverty and self-assertiveness. Its despair is kept out of the way, as good manners require. (I.L.)

(Tuesday, May 24, 1949, *The Seoul Times*)

Plea for a Moral Education

One of the indisputable advantages of democracy is that we can wash our dirty linen in public. For some reason or other, however, very few people so far seem to have taken up this advantage in all seriousness. Leaders of our society are perhaps too much engrossed in home and international politics to give any other phase of our national life a consideration other than cursory. But it seems to me that there is altogether too much assertion of political ideals, and, in proportion, too little denunciation of the obvious sins of the world. Several reasons can be given for this: firstly, denouncing requires, by the very nature of it, far more moral courage than asserting, which in many cases is no more than a kind of attitudinizing; secondly, the ordinary ruck of politicians are all too careful not to offend the public; they may flatter in order to win favor, but they will not censure, even when it is a question of raising the tone of public life; and thirdly—this is the most serious charge against them—many of them are so intent upon grinding their own axe that their vision of life has been considerably vulgarized, not to say blinded, by some set of ready-made cheap notions and preconceived ideas. It is high time that we stopped fooling about with that two-penny-ha'-penny gift of lip service; for unless we learn to call a spade a spade, we can never hope for true democracy. And furthermore, unless we begin to do some real spring-cleaning of our own selves and our society, we are likely to be unworthy of that true democracy when it comes.

I do not think that I am guilty of a rhetorical exaggeration when I say that our present situation shows a kind of groveling pathos pervading our whole moral life. Certain symptoms are apparent which seem to point to a definite crisis. And unless some leader comes forth in a mood of prophetic denunciation to stir us out of our moral inertia, the chances are that we shall gradually and unwittingly drift into an amoral condition of national life, which will in the end render us impotent to seize our opportunities of regeneration. I do not of course for a moment wish to be understood that I am proposing to assume that prophetic attitude. I merely set down my thoughts which, if not sufficiently dispassionate to warrant some such ambitious epithet as 'analytical' or 'scientific,' are at least free from those luxuriant emotionalisms to which young people in their moods of inverted romanticism are frequently addicted.

It is one of the tribulations of being a buffer state that the political cross currents are apt to absorb to an unhealthy degree the greater part of its national energy. Such can be said of the present lot of Korea. The atmosphere of suspense, if not of deadlock, in our home and international politics is undermining our mental health and paralyzing our moral life. Politics are becoming so intricate that the ordinary public is beginning to think unconsciously that only politics will and can solve our national and individual problems. Every one seems to be waiting with a tacit assumption at the back of his mind, that things will be altered when our political situation gets settled down. Of course things will be altered. But, I submit, only political things, and not *all* things, and least of all, things pertaining to our national morality. Morality has a life of its own which is capable of functioning apart from politics, even in spite of politics. Politics settled, then, can we guarantee that our moral life will rehabilitate itself automatically, with no conscious effort whatsoever on our part? Politics settled, is the salvation of a nation to be a matter of course, a thing to be taken for granted? Politics settled, are we to assume that morality is well capable of looking after itself? The answer is more likely to be in the negative than otherwise. They are questions our leaders must set themselves to answer in a way that will win the implicit conviction of the people. The public needs a satisfactory guidance in such permanent questions as much as in temporary questions of politics.

Morality means different things to different people. It may mean those innumerable virtues in counterpart to those still more innumerable vices, petty and gross, of which our perennial infirmity makes us the victims. But when I say morality here, I have in mind something more fundamental. I mean that attitude of high seriousness which seeks for a purpose in the mysteries of life, that reverent frame of mind which thinks of life not only in terms of power, of politics and economics, but also of right and wrong, good and bad, in short, a mind that is capable of lambent idealism as much as downright realism. I maintain that this kind of mental outlook is not a thing that comes naturally to mankind, but something to be acquired with much discipline and deliberate exertion. And unless we learn to acquire this moral attitude towards life and the world, we shall not be going about the right way to achieve our ultimate ends, which are democratic freedom and national independence. For democracy, as I understand it, is one of the few existing political ideas which has this morality as an integral element of its make-up: as witness the inseparable relation between the Englishman's conception of democracy and his spirit of gentlemanship which form the brick and mortar of his view of life. It may be observed in passing that many of our political leaders fail to appeal to our conscience with anything like a compelling force precisely for the reason that they regard politics and morality as two entirely different entities. By so doing, they soon come to the end of their resources, and their politics are likely to become a question of calculated astuteness. What Korea needs today is a prophetic genius who will hold the nation in his confidence, rather than a political leader pure and simple who likes the game of power-politics for its thrilling adventure.

What is going to give us this moral training? What indeed? Take religion, for example.

In the Western countries, the Church is still the recognized guardian of human conduct. She is of course functioning less effectually than she used to. The Modern Mind knows, or thinks it knows, too much to be satisfied with any dogmatic or institutional scheme of life. Besides, a coarse wave of materialism, and a welter of strutting creeds have somewhat muffled our faith in Christian virtue. But then, dogmatic creeds and institutional smugness are not the whole truth about the Christian religion. Although it is difficult to point to a thing or things in pronouncing the quintessence of Christianity, this much at least can be said for it, that it teaches people to think that there is a purpose in the scheme of things, that unless we are constantly watchful of ourselves, we shall be unworthy of that purpose, and that there is in this world a thing called justice, which is natural if not supernatural.

But here in Korea, by a series of misfortunes in history, we have at present no religion far-reaching enough to be called national. Both Buddhism and Confucianism are steeped in a ritualistic convention and have little palpitating life inside the hard crust. They were antiquated long ago and serve merely, to the people at large, as anachronisms of bygone cultures. And as for Christianity, we have been interrupted, after a promising beginning, before getting as far as we might have liked. And within our recent memory, we associate it, not without resentment, with many of those second-rate missionaries whose sanctimonious airs and graces went so well with their complacent attitudes and condescending manners. We have had martyrs in the past, but they are now faint echoes heard in our dim memory. We have at present many people of genuine faith who are capable of some measure of spiritual leadership. But they seem to be singularly out of touch with the people, because they choose the contemplative mode of life in preference to the active, a natural result of the days of Japanese persecution. Some of them do take on the active life, but in an altogether undesirable direction.

There are men, in all countries and in all times, whose spiritual functions get perverted by being subjected to non-spiritual ends. But at this critical juncture of our barely-begun national life, our spiritual leaders should particularly be on their guard against this temptation. We have achieved a political revolution by the aid of the Allied Nations at a time when our country was at the nadir of its spiritual fervor. But political revolution alone is not enough: as witness our present state of affairs, which show up our impotence and want of direction. We must bring about a moral reformation to complete the job. And are we to bring about this moral reformation *also* by the sponsorship of the Allied Nations? In that case, we should be driven to make some hitherto unknown discoveries: for example, (1) we have such a wretched civilization that there is nothing in our heritage which can possibly be a source of our moral inspiration. Conceit is admittedly a vice, and self-denial a virtue in many cases, but I have never heard that abject servility was a virtue also. (2) Not only is God on the side of the Allied Nations, but also He has vested the Democrat President and the Communist Dictator with the powers of our spiritual salvation—a fact, which again manifests His all-forgiving Nature, for the latter is known to be singularly given to the habit of blasphemy in the profession of his political doctrines. But in all seriousness, we are in dire need of a fresh impetus in our moral strength. We see so many political leaders in the limelight, and so few, if any, moral leaders, that there is a serious danger for the younger generations of being misled to think that this is the normal condition in all countries and in all times. Our men of faith should no longer be content with a contemplative mode of life.

If religion has not a far-reaching voice in our national life, what other institution will take over the responsibility of looking after our morality? I can only think of Education. Here again, it is easy to rush in where angels fear to tread. Who can ever hope to say the last word about a never-ending process like Education? Who knows the 'fiat'? One can only hope to set down one's observations of the present condition of Education, and make some tentative guesses at its effect upon our national life.

Though it is uncomfortable in the extreme to admit it, let us put it point blank, because it is staring us in the face. In the one field where we should be pushing forward with a renewed hope and a fresh impetus, we are just plodding along inertly from sheer force of habit. Just when education should be most inspired, it is becoming more and more pedestrian. From this bare fact, we might be thought to be a very unimaginative race; but there we are; and no getting away from it.

It is a thousand pities that we Koreans should have got our ideas of modern education mostly from Japan. It can be fairly said that the fundamental error in the educational ideas of modern Japan, and for that matter of all non-democratic countries of the world, has been the implicit assumption that Education should serve the State, that it should be inspired by the State rather than inspire the State. It is naturally in such countries that people talk most often about the educational "policy," for policy it truly is, and nothing but policy. As might be expected, of course, this "policy" idea was carried to its extreme in Korea, since the sole end of the Japanese government lay manifestly in Japanising the Koreans by every means, subtle and crude, of disintegration and suppression of our racial sense. We can now look back and say that they have not, after all, succeeded in grafting upon us their preposterously superstitious myth of a culture; but we must admit frankly that they have reaped some success in devitalizing our educational efforts. Our educationists were drilled into accepting their strange philosophy of subjugation; and the duty of the schoolmaster was considered to be one of acquiescence, if not of blind obedience, but never of voluntary efforts.

It was after all a nightmare of an education. For decades we have not been allowed to take the slightest initiative; we have been expected to obey—no more, no less: for either would be taken as a sign of danger. Passion, let alone fanaticism, was a quality unknown, even undesirable, in such a scheme of things. Now all that has been changed overnight. And the nervous tension, relaxed all of a sudden, is telling upon us. The sigh of relief seems to be accompanied with a tired anemic feeling. We know that from now on we must take the initiative in all things and do constructive work with voluntary efforts. Education is not a thing that originates in the Bureau within the Capitol; it is something that springs from the heart of the teachers. We all know it, but because of our time-honored habit, we find that it is by no means an easy affair to switch off from the position of following, blindly following, to that of leading, thoughtfully leading. Our chronic inertia is the curse of the present day educationist.

Besides this psychological change, there is to be noted also a social change in two directions—with a not altogether happy consequence for education. First, with new vistas of life opening before us, many of our good educationists have departed for other spheres of activity. We need not necessarily regret this, so long as they do good work in their new lines. What is far more serious for education is the second aspect of the change: namely, those who have stayed on have been "promoted" somehow. The result has been a feeling of general contentment and self-complacency. Flushed with the pleasing sensation of advancement in life, we have let our expansive natures get the better of us. And when there is a prevalent atmosphere of all being well with us and also with the world, the chances are that we shall not get a renewed spirit of learning. Just when we should be thinking of education as a mission, a thing to be undertaken with passionate enthusiasm, many of us are thinking of it as a "career." These elated emotions, however, are gradually wearing off; we are slowly beginning to fear that perhaps we may have bitten off more than we can chew in one mouthful. We are waking to the knowledge that passionate enthusiasm is something quite different from sheer expansive emotionalism. Things are beginning to lose shape, because we have been laying out our goods too much, when we should have been stocktaking rather. When education loses its structural shape and its spiritual pattern, we know what its consequences will be. By their fruits ye shall know them.

We are making a grave mistake if we think to solve *all* our problems of education, notably of moral education, by means only of conferences, committees and sub-committees. They will solve *some* problems, but the greater part of the work will always remain to be done in actual practice, inspired by ordered passion and careful forethought. I am not denying the legitimate functions of our committees and sub-committees. They are, on the contrary, part of the indispensable machinery of government. I am only contending that our educationists must not shove the whole responsibility of education to the Government Bureau, as I have heard so many of them reiterate with a kind of mental shrug: 'Oh we can't do anything until our national educational policy gets settled!' If education, which is, by the very nature of it, a process and not a 'completed thing,' must wait for the formation of policies, I can only think that policies are damnable things because they prevent our educationists from getting down to solid work. Waiting with a vague hope, with our arms akimbo, will not give us anything, except a languishing habit, moral cowardice, and torpidity. This waiting attitude has an important side issue. Many of those who are engaged in adult education are so much in their high-hoping plane that they refuse to come down to the brass-tacks of education. They see many things to do, for example, correcting the manners of boys, inculcating the habit of cleanliness, and a thousand other little but important things. But somehow these little things seem to be below their dignity, and they refuse to stoop lower than their stiff-backed prestige will bend, so intent are they on looking after their career. The result is anything but educational. I was recently struck by the following words quoted in a book of William James:

> Plenty of people wish well to any good cause, but very few care to exert themselves to help it, and still fewer will risk anything in its support. 'Some one ought to do it, but why should I?' is the ever-re-echoed phrase of weak-kneed amiability. 'Some one ought to do it, so why not I?' is the cry of some earnest servant of man, eagerly forward springing to face some perilous duty. Between these sentences lie whole centuries of moral evolution.

The aptness of this criticism should drive us to shame.

It is impossible to ignore the deadly effect upon our moral education of the political antagonism, which is growing day by day and filtering into many phases of our national life that have nothing or little to do with politics. For aught we know, politics *may* have certain inherent paradoxes, makeshift expediencies, trapping machinations, and shameless duplicities. But these features must not influence education. When politics invade the domain of education, it is then that we must be on the lookout. Teaching is a free and honest activity of the soul, and must not be hampered by any set of political prejudices. When you find professors and teachers of social repute beating the tin-can music of cheap propaganda, and sentimental students dancing as if in an orgy to the tune thereof, you cannot but have some fears for the future of our national education.

There are two ways in which our political unsettlement is undermining the moral stability of our adult education. First, the educationist starts from an honest determination that politics shall not affect the educational activities one way or the other. He is full of good intentions—and so far, so good. But there come moments in our national life when this attitude of neutrality has a negative effect upon our public vigor by assuming a fear-bound psychology of non-committal. In this way his moral courage becomes weakened, and his educational aims and executions work at cross-purposes.

Second, by far the more detrimental of the two, certain political ideas are shaking the very fiber of our moral judgment, and corrupting the citadel of the human spirit. Is life, after all, nothing but a dirty business? I see no earthly reason why so-called progress should be attained at the expense of narrowing our vision of life by vulgar perversion of values, and rendering the human soul more ignoble than our fathers left it. One of the holy duties of education is to expose the human cant to ridicule. The vulgarity of learning was never so apparent in our country as today, when second-rate pedants, highly opinionated but not even pedantic enough to boot, are brandishing their borrowed syllogisms in fits and starts to explain away all the problems of human life and culture, as if the shortest cut to happiness lay in one steam-roller process of leveling out. The fourfold spirit of learning, which should be the critical spirit, the spirit of humility, of self-discipline, and of continuity, is alien to them. With their amoral outlook it is next to impossible to attempt anything like a true education, an education that aims at goodness of character, civil manners, reverence for nature and love of humanity, love of beautiful things and noble thoughts and deeds, and a training in unbiased judgment.

Such educationists are, so to speak, amphibious. They can swim in the muddy waters of politics, as well as walk on the dry land of education. But it cannot be denied that political passions are dissipating their vital energies to a considerable extent. These passions are harmful to education, because they are realist passions, accompanied by a strong disposition to action, and a thirst for worldly effect, and fanned by a hatred that is all the more coherent and precise for being based upon fixed ideas. If by education we want to turn out, within the shortest possible time, men and women who will do lip service to certain political jargons with no more imagination than a parrot is capable of, then we can be content with the present condition of learning, which is painted all over with realist politics and economics. If, however, our national education is to be a driving conscience and a permanent source of inspiration for many generations to come, it must be firmly planted on a moral basis now. We can hang all immediate results. We must look at least two or three generations ahead and keep our eyes fixed upon the distant horizon. We must never forget the havoc that the Japanese have wrought upon our spiritual life. We must shore some of the shattered fragments together against further ruin. It is our duty to save them from the possibility of complete annihilation, so that when our sons and grandsons take on the work, they will go a step further in the direction of not only preserving but also fertilizing our heritage. Right now, we must think of our educational work as a spiritual salvage campaign.

This, I submit, is neither sentimentalism nor humbuggery, as our more radical friends would lead us to believe. However degenerate our older civilization may be, we cannot just sweep it away with the broom of 'progressive' thought, hoping to build a more advanced civilization. If we do, the result will be anything but civilized, since violent means will always give birth to violent ends. In fact, it may be fairly said that civilization, if it is to be at all worthy of survival, must be a never-ending process of re-adaptation and re-adjustment to the ever-changing conditions of history. Our civilization is a fairly old one. It does not of course follow that its antiquity is a sign or proof of its goodness—good heavens, no. But it means at any rate that, with all our glaring defects, we are not totally blind to that "sweetness and light" which form the touchstone of the civilization of the West.

Unless we aim at an education that is sweet and true, we are likely to find our future as unhappy as our past. And this 'sweet and true' attitude comes only from that mental outlook which I have been describing by the term 'moral' seriousness. Without it, we cannot hope to progress in the true sense of the word. There is a fallacy in the common conception of progress: it is that progress in civilization is an unquestionable thing, whereas, actually, there is no sure guarantee that the human civilization is forward-bound only; history abounds in examples of its halting and back-sliding. Only conscientious effort can keep it up. And my thesis is that we Koreans are not exerting enough at present to warrant a surer and brighter future.

I have thus far given a more or less destructive criticism of our present state of learning, but it all leads in the end to the overwhelming question: What are our immediate concerns in the field of education, in particular, of adult education? This is a question that demands a constructive answer; and we all know that constructive criticism is much harder than destructive. Neither my experience nor my position entitles me to attempt such a serious task. However, I cannot refrain from suggesting just two more points which, in my opinion, are not receiving due attention in these days.

The first is that human decency should come before anything else. Our society needs healthy-minded, serviceable youths, men and women who will do better team-work than their predecessors, more open-minded and less bigoted, more tenacious and less sentimental, who will have learnt to acquiesce in the decision of the majority, who will have an inveterate sense of hearth and home, who will not jump to hasty conclusions about life and the world, who will believe that what gives us lasting happiness is honest work, and not dreams, or ideas, of prestige, or power, and who will have an unshakable faith in our just claim to our share of happiness as an independent nation.

The second point is that we should take more pains to inculcate the true spirit of freedom. Much of the coarseness of the younger generation comes from a misconception of the spirit of freedom. It requires careful thought and study. Absence of control does not give us freedom: life will never do without control. Liberty is not the same thing as license. Liberty means perhaps no more than that the responsibility of control is within us, and not without. I can do no better than end this article by a quotation from Earl Baldwin: "We have to remember that the price of liberty is eternal vigilance, and I may add, eternal knowledge, eternal sympathy, and eternal understanding." I can think of no harder task than what is demanded of us in this sentence.

(Friday, March 15–Tuesday, March 19, 1946, *The Seoul Times*)

Democracy in the Orient:
From a Non-Political Point of View

(A Talk Given at the Banker's Club, Seoul, Korea, October 30, 1947)

Introductory Remarks:
I come to praise democracy, not to condemn it:

For a Korean of my age and status, it is an undeserved honor and a rare privilege that I should have been offered this opportunity to speak to you this evening. If I were to begin my talk without an expression of gratitude, followed by some words of apology, I should be false to my present feelings.

I come indeed to praise democracy, not to condemn it; and I feel tonight that I can best thank the honorable members of this Club by saying that it is all to the good that our part of the world is at last learning something of that philosophy of human dignity known as 'democracy.'

Perhaps, as a student of literature, I have little or no business to overreach myself by taking up such a big subject as democracy. If I have any justification, it is twofold: (1) Because democracy in the Orient is a burning question of the moment, and one that concerns the future destiny of not only every nation but also every individual of the East as well as the West; (2) I have reason to suspect that the kind of contact which many Koreans make with you may perhaps lead you to draw half-true, if not false, pictures of our country, its people and its traditions.

I do not intend to whitewash Korea, and the bewildering mess that Korea represents today. Far from it. Rather is it my purpose to persuade you, if I can, to have a deeper insight that you may penetrate beneath your summary impressions of Korea and the Koreans. Speaking dogmatically, I believe that there are two main categories of Koreans who determine much of your impressions about our country: (a) the politicians and would-be politicians who have their own political axe to grind; (b) the businessmen and profiteers who are intent upon filling their private pockets. What obscures our sight is that the few good and the many evil are working at cross- purposes, whether in politics or in economics. If it is our business to work our way through this present mist of confusion towards a more permanent ideal, it is surely yours also, you who have come across the widest of seas to teach us the ideals of democracy both in theory and practice.

I will not pretend to speak from a political standpoint this evening. I propose merely to make a tentative attempt at a comparison of the mental and psychological background of democracy with the traditional culture and temperament of the East, in the hope that such a comparison might throw some light upon our present difficulties in assimilating on our part, and propagating on yours, the Western knowledge and experience designated in the term 'democracy.' Just as democracy came slowly to you, so it will come relatively slowly to us, much slower than you would perhaps expect, and certainly much slower than we ourselves would like. For various reasons, which I shall try to point out, democracy must have time to take root. I stress this obvious point, because you in Korea will have to be infinitely patient. Let me remind you of the words of King Lear: "Give me that patience, patience I need." I don't think that Koreans are fools, but if they are, you will have to suffer them gladly—for a while at least.

I do not wish to sound dogmatic, but the word 'Orient' or 'Oriental' in this paper refers chiefly to China and Korea, exclusive of Japan. Both culturally and politically, China and Korea may be said to present more or less similar problems, while Japan in many aspects offers difficulties of a somewhat different nature. It may even be axiomatic to hold that the fate of Korea will ultimately be bound with that of China. So much for apology.

(1) *Democracy on a Silver Platter*

"Most of the people in Asia have never known democracy. They may or may not want our type of democracy. Obviously all of them are not ready to have democracy handed to them next Tuesday on a silver platter. But they are determined to work out their own destiny under governments selected by themselves."

These are the words of the late Wendell Wilkie in his book, *One World.* To a Korean of today, Wilkie's pronouncements sound highly prophetic of our present national mood. Now that inevitable Tuesday has come, and in the political banquet of today democracy is the *pièce-de-résistance,* which we of the East have every claim to relish. Unfortunately, it is being served to us on a silver platter; and having only a pair of chopsticks each in our hands, we are not making a clean job of handling that substantial meat. I therefore propose to discuss in all frankness the problem of democracy in the Orient in the light of Wilkie's judgment.

(2) *New Wine into Old Bottles*

Certain aspects of political thinking, which have been characteristic of the Western man for hundreds of years, are more or less recent in the Orient. They should be considered, however cursorily, in evaluating democracy in the Orient.

Take nationalism, for example, which historically may be considered as the first embodiment of modern political naturalism. According to Renan, "The sentiment of nationalism is not a hundred years old in the world." History indicates that France before the Revolution was more 'provincial' than 'national,' and that Germany and Italy did not become 'national' until the latter part of the nineteenth century. Nationalism as such may very well be not more than a hundred years old; but it surely has a longer history behind.

Actually the growth of the national spirit was a direct outcome of the naturalistic trend of mind, which gradually characterized European political thinking since the Renaissance. Modern man began to be occupied with the things that were Caesar's for their own sake. Political naturalism, as opposed to supernaturalism of medieval theology, and its direct outcome, nationalism, therefore, seem to have been the common property of the Western man for a longer period than Renan indicates.

But here in the Orient, nationalism is only a recent phenomenon. Upon this question Lin Yu-tang says: "Within the orbit of the Chinese culture there has not been a rise of nationalism, but only of provincialism, which after all was what made peace within the empire possible for centuries." This is in the main also true of Korea. Nationalism, even as a vague sentiment, still less as a working philosophy of government, was never salient in the political history of our country, until—such is the irony of history—it was directly and indirectly fostered by the Japanese rule. If the sack of Peking in 1900, as Lin Yu-tang observes, goaded China into becoming a modern nation, the Japanese annexation of Korea ten years later was a *coup d'état* that humiliated us with a sense of helplessness before the organized machinations of modern statecraft.

For aught we know, the age of nationalism has already past in the West. The ideals of democracy can well exist without nationalism, and conversely, nationalism in its extreme form can exist without an atom of democracy. But when, in a country like Korea, nationalism has been a recent development, the people are not likely to drop it summarily. The immediate task for us is to find a way that will both meet with the ideals of democracy and satisfy our nationalistic cravings. The two can, I think, be compromised.

(3) *Whatsoever a Man Soweth*

Democracy cannot be dissociated from the historical sense. It was after centuries of experience and thoughtful modification that the modern Western man arrived at his present basic beliefs concerning the nature of himself and his universe. Take, as an example, the American democracy, which has a most direct impact upon our ways of thinking in present day Korea.

The words of Thomas Jefferson ("I did not consider it any part of my charge to invent new ideas altogether, and to offer no sentiment which had ever been expressed before") show that European philosophers had already formulated the ideals of the Declaration of Independence. Professor Northrop of Yale University makes this point clear in his recent book, *The Meeting of East and West*. The American mind of before and after 1776, he clearly shows, was fed on Locke's philosophy. Locke's own words in his essay, "Of Civil Government,"

"Man being, as has been said, by nature all free, equal, and independent, no one can be put out of his estate and subjugated to the political power of another without his consent,"

demonstrate how the two basic premises of Locke's theory of government and the Declaration of Independence are the same: that all men are born free and independent, and that the basis of government is in the consent of the governed. Whereas the Aristotelian man, by his very nature, participates in an hierarchical order which is "defined by an empirically determined teleological law of nature existing quite independently of the opinions and social conventions of men," the Lockean person, says Professor Northrop,

> "is . . . an independent, atomic, mental substance, knowable only in one's own self by subjective introspection, and having no conceivable or specified relations to other mental substances, or persons. Thus, in the essential nature of the Lockean person, there is no scientifically and philosophically grounded social relation joining him to other persons, independent of the private opinions of individual men, for the grounding of ecclesiastical or civil law. Consequently, nothing remains but to regard all laws as mere conventions, having their authority solely in the free consent of the majority."

The notion of personal liberty being inherent in the spirit of Protestantism, this postulate in political thought of the ideal, self-sufficient freedom and independence of the individual comes naturally to the Western man, but is unknown in the Oriental tradition, where the social unit is the family. If anything, the Oriental concept of man is nearer to the Aristotelian-medieval than the Lockean-modern concept. As Babbitt observes in *Democracy and Leadership,* "to be modern has meant practically to be increasingly positive and critical, to refuse to receive anything on an authority 'anterior, exterior, and superior' to the individual." This individualism, which is part and parcel of the Western man, is a very recent development in the Orient, and therefore we have not a little difficulty in adopting democracy as a working political system.

In relation to this recent development in the Orient of this conception of individual freedom, I should like to specify one aspect of Oriental political thought that bears some similarities with that of democracy. As Professor Vinacke points out in his *History of the Far East in Modern Times,* the Oriental ruler was an autocrat, who ruled by "the dictates of heaven"; but in practice,

> "he was expected to act responsibly in accordance with advice tendered by members of the Censorate and other higher-ranking official bodies. . . . In return for the autocratic power conferred on him by Heaven he assumed a definite responsibility for the maintenance of peace, order and comparative prosperity within the Empire. Thus if famine became widespread, the condition was held to be a result of some failure on the part of the Emperor. Famine, of course, would produce brigandage, and the gathering together of large bodies of armed men might easily result in rebellion against the Imperial authority. A successful rebellion would bring the dynasty to an end, and consequently would indicate that the 'mandate of Heaven' had been withdrawn."

This right of revolution, if not exactly an expression of the Western type of individual freedom, is at any rate based on a political freedom that is the essence of democracy. The same was true, in fundamentals, of Korea also.

(4) *Fairy Godmothers in Politics*

In connection with the Declaration of Independence, I should like to make one other observation that, to my mind, marks a sharp distinction between the Western mentality and the Oriental. We in Korea have our so-called Declaration of Independence, by which we commemorate that heroic outburst of passive resistance, which held the people spell-bound for a brief period beginning March 1, 1919. It was all the more a tragic gesture, because it was predestined to be a failure accompanied by suffering in general and martyrdom for the thirty-three representatives who signed the document and for several thousand of their followers. The value of the document today is historical and emotional rather than political. Is it because our memory of that lyrical outburst of national emotion is still fresh and vivid that even to this day we Koreans are inclined to think of political independence in an altogether too idyllic fashion? Or is it because our very constitution is that of a *rêveur*, that we so often put aside the brutal factual aspects of political independence? God knows, we have already paid a high enough price for our freedom to sing our national anthem and to make street demonstrations. In the world of realistic politics there are, I believe, no fairy godmothers that, with a wave of the magic wand, can satisfy our innermost and sacrosanct wishes. Ours, as a political document, is not a Declaration but a Declamation of Independence. Consider on the other hand the American Declaration of Independence. Whether there was so much galling tyranny on the part of the British Crown as to justify those piled-up grievances, is no concern here. The point is that the Declaration of Independence is packed with concrete charges of colliding *interest.* In comparison, our Korean document is but a lyrical expression of vague desires, with an overtone of glorious hope, but not without an undertone of desperation.

This endorses a crucial difference between the Western and Oriental basic ideas concerning the state. The Western man, though he believes in absolute individual freedom, is prepared to bind himself to a political organization called the state, because it protects and preserves his positive interests. For, in the words of Locke, unless the individual "seeks out and is willing to join in society with others who are already united, or have a mind to unite for the mutual preservation of their lives, liberties, and estates, which I call by the general name Property," his 'property' will be exposed to insecurities and dangers. The Western man's conception of the state is more concrete and legalistic, a direct outcome of social contract. That of the Oriental is inclined to be more of an abstract deduction. The truth is that, though we have had much experience in bad or indifferent government, we have not had much experience in really good government. Much of the time the people have been left to their own devices. It is therefore natural that our ordinary man in the street--he who should count most in the ballot box of democracy--should not have a clear positivistic *civic* sense. True enough, the Confucian doctrine enjoins a philosophy of government that is perhaps second to none for its ethical idealism. But it teaches the ruler how and in what spirit to govern, rather than the people how and in what attitude to *be* governed.

Let me quote in corroboration the words of the Cambridge philosopher and man of letters, G. Lowes Dickinson, writing as a Chinese resident of London at the beginning of this century (1901):

> "With you the function of government is so important and so ubiquitous that you can hardly realize the condition of a people that is able almost wholly to dispense with it. Yet such is our case. The simple and natural character of our civilization, the peaceable nature of our people. . . , above all, the institution of the family, itself a little state—a political, social, and economic unit—these and other facts have rendered us independent of government control to an extent which to Europeans may seem incredible. . . . Law, in a word, is not, with us, a rule imposed from above; it is the formula of the national life; and its embodiment in practice precedes its inscription in a code. Hence it is that in China government is neither arbitrary nor indispensable. Destroy our authorities, central and provincial, and our life will proceed very much as before. The law we obey is the law of our own nature, as it has been evolved by centuries of experience, and to this we continue our allegiance, even though the external sanction be withdrawn."

We must not be deceived by Dickinson's ironic method, by which he deliberately and exaggeratedly praises the Orient in order to expose what he sees to be the spiritual decay of the Western civilization. Nevertheless, he does explain satisfactorily the reason for the Oriental's weak civic sense.

In isolating this seemingly Oriental feature, I do not mean to suggest that democracy postulates a "ubiquitous" function of government. It is one of the axioms of democracy to hold that "that government is best which governs least." I mean rather to suggest that democracy must inculcate upon us a stronger, more organic consciousness of citizenship. It is perhaps because we are relatively lacking in this particular consciousness that we appear, to a Westerner particularly, to be such incorrigible individualists.

As a matter of historical fact, the absence of centralized government control had long been a characteristic of our society. The semi-autonomous structure of the provinces, the family system, leading to the village autonomy, and the powerful guilds of traders and artisans—all these were embodiments of essentially democratic traits in the East. China, I believe, still preserves these essential traits. Korea, on the other hand, being a small country with a keener susceptibility to foreign influences, and having experienced the all but complete submergence under the modern statecraft of Japan, has lost the greater part of these age-old fundamentals of democratic structure. If we are to start afresh, as we must, it will be more or less a new experience.

(5) *I Will Arise and Go Now*

In the last analysis democracy is based on a civilization whose medium of contact is primarily by word of mouth in public. It is difficult to conceive of the essential nature of democracy, be it the ancient type of 'direct' democracy or the modern 'representative' type, without the spirit of the marketplace, of publicity.

Now, this spirit of publicity might be designated by the epithet 'urban.' It would be, of course, too sweeping a generalization to say that 'urban' civilization is therefore the basis of democracy, simply because the most prominent feature of Western civilization happens to be 'urban' as a natural consequence of industrialism. America in 1776 was ninety percent rural, and Jefferson's idea of a perfect democracy was a government based on a free farming population, not economically dependent upon an employer's capital and machine. There certainly need be no necessary correlation between Urbanization and Democracy.

On the other hand, a comparison of the rural life of the West with that of the East seems to show a real difference. Your farmers, just as your city workers, live up to the spirit of publicity, the marketplace, by freely exchanging views and arriving at settlements in cases of colliding interest. To that extent they are more politically minded, and more 'urban.' Now in the East, rural life is more often considered in terms of complete seclusion, a retreat far from the madding crowd. To that extent we are less politically minded, and less 'urban.' In contrast to the urban civilization of the West, the basis of the civilization of the East is still rural, or agricultural. Says Lin Yu-tang:

"The ruling class not only came from the country but also returned to the country, as the rural mode of life was always regarded as the ideal. . . . For the rural ideal of life is part of the social system which makes the family the unit."

Lowes Dickinson's *Letters of John Chinaman* emphasizes this point also:

"In attempting to lay before you a characteristic scene of Chinese life I selected for the purpose a community of peasants. I did so because it is there that I find the typical product of our civilization. Cities, it is true, we have, and cities as monstrous, perhaps, as yours; but they are mere excrescences on a body politic whose essential constitution is agricultural. With you all this is reversed, and for that reason you have no country life deserving the name. . . . Whatever in England is not urban is parasitic or moribund. If, then, I am to give an impression that shall be candid and just of the best results of your civilization, I must turn from the country to the life of your great cities."

Though our cities show more and more signs of congestion, this rural basis of Oriental life will continue for quite a while until, perhaps, the industrialization of the country will be advanced enough to place agriculture in a secondary position. In any case, we in Korea have an almost proverbial expression, which reflects the importance of rural life as a mode of retreat: a man who has had some misfortune and experienced some form of disillusionment in life, generally says: "Ah well, I might as well now go to the country and dig some plot of ground."

(6) *Too Late to Mend*

The Western man believes that, to borrow a proverbial expression, it is never too late to mend. He is an idealist, always on the move and in quest. This is because he possesses what the philosopher Keyserling calls the dynamic ego-consciousness. He says:

"Even if we strip the Ego of all attributes, there still is left to it one peculiar character; we feel it as function, as energy, as dynamic being, as capacity for creation, for activity, as hesitancy between two possible forms of existence, as principle of rejuvenation, of quickening, of renewal, of free agency in the midst of circumstances."

For this reason, Keyserling argues: (a) man always lives forward; (b) he gazes steadfastly towards goals in front of him; (c) he can never find satisfaction in the moment; (d) he is wholly conscious of himself only in restless, ever-advancing, productive activity, not in flaccid idleness.

This is as true of nations as of individuals. As an example, take the Americans, of whom Charles W. Eliot, sometime president of Harvard, has said:

"He [The American] is usually the descendant of an immigrant or an immigrant himself. The immigrant, in many cases, was escaping from some sort of religious, political, social, or economic oppression. He was some kind of non-conformist, and he was dissatisfied with his surroundings and wished to better them. Therefore, he must have had an unusual amount of imagination, ambition, and venturesomeness. This is as true of the late comers to America as of the earlier comers. . . . Hence, by heredity, the white Americans of today—of whatever race or stock—have a fair chance to be by nature independent, bold, and enterprising."

On such a soil democracy can be a natural growth. But here in the Orient, things are somewhat different.

Faith in the perfectibility of man and his universe is not part of the traditional culture of the Orient. In the words of Lin Yu-tang, "The Chinese have a certain contempt for young enthusiasm and for new brooms that will sweep the universe clean." Elsewhere he said:

"Perhaps had our capacity for sufferance been smaller, our sufferings would also be less. As it is, this capacity for putting up with insults has been ennobled by the name of patience, and deliberately inculcated as a cardinal virtue by Confucian ethics."

It all boils down to the fact that Orientals are incorrigible realists, born and bred, rather than idealists. It is part of his defense mechanism. The great sage Confucius himself, who never aimed at being systematic, still less dogmatic, held constantly that an ethical proposition should primarily be in accordance with human nature. Ultimate questions, the eternal *why* and *wherefore*, which trouble the soul of the Western man, are only incidental to the Oriental mind, whose preoccupation is with the practical world of human conduct. His primary concern is the world of immediate practice, which to the Westerner can only be the result of metaphysical speculations in 'first principles' and 'prime causes.' Like a crass empiricist and agnostic that he was, Confucius evaded the question of the immortality of the soul, for example, in a way that can hardly be said to be satisfactory to the Western mind. When one of his disciples, Cha-ro (子路), asked him about death, the Master said, "How can one know of death, when one is ignorant of life itself?" (子曰 不知生 焉知死)

Where the Western man questions as to how he should save his soul in a theistic scheme of the universe, the Oriental seeks to find a sanction for appropriate conduct at the appropriate occasion in a man-centered mundane world. Let me quote Lin Yu-tang again:

> " . . . a certain hard-headedness characterizes the Chinese ideal of life. There may be imagination in Chinese paintings and poetry, but there is no imagination in Chinese ethics."

My purpose in dealing with this point at length is to show that political idealism, such as democracy, offers not a little difficulty to the Oriental temperament, which is realistic by circumstance, if not by birth.

(7) *What's Hecuba to Him?*

Side by side with realism there exists another Oriental trait that is not congenial to the growth of democracy as conceived in the West. It is the element of indifference or fatalism, which so often damps out the Oriental's spiritual urge for reform. The

Oriental too readily believes that a good government is one that does nothing. True enough, Emerson said something to similar effect: "The less government the better." But, coming from the mouth of America's 'champion of self-reliance,' that was spoken on the assumption of individual freedom. In the Oriental temperament, the attitude of *laissez-faire* in government is too often reflected in his chronic indifference. What Lin Yu-tang says of the Chinese is equally true of the Korean:

> "The Chinese people take to indifference as Englishmen take to umbrellas, because the political weather always looks a little ominous for the individual who ventures a little too far out also. In other words, indifference has a distinct 'survival-value' in China."

He adds: "Indifference is not a high moral virtue but a social attitude [made] necessary by the absence of legal protection." In his analysis of the Chinese character Lin attributes this ultimately to the influence of Taoism:

> "Taoism, in theory and practice, means a certain roguish nonchalance, a confounded and devastating skepticism, a mocking laughter at the futility of all human interference and the failure of all human institutions, laws, government and marriage, and a certain disbelief in idealism, not so much because of lack of energy as because of a lack of faith. It is a philosophy which counteracts the positivism of Confucius."

The destructive element in the nature of the Oriental man has trained him from time immemorial to look at the world, not as it ought to be, but as it actually is, in all its squalor and hopelessness. Being no visionary, he is not wont to see haloes around things; and the brilliantly wicked philosophy of Lao-tzu and Chuang-tzu, who preferred to speak in paradoxes, offers him a barrier of self-defense in a hostile world.

I do not mean to suggest that Taoism is a living religion among the Koreans as among the Chinese. I merely submit that the temper of Taoism is not wanting even among us. The justly celebrated *Book of Tea* by the Japanese man of letters, Okakura

Kakuzo, shows how Taoism, which blossomed forth in South China, found affinity with the Chinese Zen Buddhism, which the sixth Chinese patriarch Yeno (637–713) is said to have first founded in southern China. Through thus being connected with Buddhism, the idiosyncrasies of Taoism can be said to have subsequently influenced the whole of Asiatic life, even as far as Japan. Taoism or no Taoism, the Buddhist philosophy is in itself sufficient to have implanted the attitude of negativistic realism in the Oriental temperament. Certainly the spirit of downright realism is not the best kind of soil in which the idealistic doctrine of freedom and democracy can take root.

(8) *Tricks of the Trade*

In evaluating any Western thought, we should always go a step beyond the thumb-rules of dogma and consider the philosophic bases from which that specific dogma has grown. This is in the main the purport of Professor Northrop's argument in his chapter on 'The Meaning of Western Civilization.' In brief, he says that it is the mental habit of the Western man to arrive at a theoretical conception of his being and nature "by observation and scientific hypothesis." The typical Western knowledge is the theoretically conceived knowledge, which

> ". . . even when determined by empirically and experimentally controlled scientific methods, always affirms more. . . than bare facts by themselves provide. In short, scientific theory always asserts more than observation gives, and is not verified directly. . . by mere observation; instead, it is a hypothesis proposed *a priori*, verified in part at least indirectly through its experimentally checked deductive consequences. . . . This *a priori* is, however, a hypothetical *a priori*, subject to change in its formal as well as its empirical content; not a categorically or immortally certain *a priori*, even with respect to its formal concepts."

"Subject to change"—that is the wonder-working phrase! Because the Western man postulates more than the factual world provides, and because he is ever prepared to reconstruct, retest, and restate his premises, in short, because he possesses that glorious mental as well as psychological freedom of the imagination, he has been able to achieve what he has achieved of "genuine progress in the moral, political, and religious as well as in the mechanical and physical sphere."

Now, the Oriental mind is somewhat alien to this habit of thought. His imagination, when not bound by realism, is essentially idyllic. Consequently, its movement is in leaps and bounds. When, therefore, introduced to the Western knowledge, the Oriental runs the double risk of accepting it at its immediate face value alone, or else of accepting it as something "categorically and immortally certain." This risk is particularly blatant in the case of Western political thought, whether it is democracy or communism. He is too apt to think in a handful of ready-made terms. If it is Lockean political freedom, he says to himself, "Yes, the freedom to choose one's own civil representatives." If it is Marxian economic freedom, "Yes, the freedom to have enough to eat by social justice, which means class justice, which in turn means by proletariat dictatorship." And so on. I wish to goodness that things were as simple as that; for then, one could dispense with all the nerve-racking toil and trouble of trying to assimilate and shore together the scraps of wisdom and experience of bygone generations, and with a peaceful conscience one could be certain of drifting towards some "far-off divine event."

This much granted, we are not after all doing a bad job in learning the tricks of the trade, considering how late we entered the workshop of modern statecraft. Why bother our heads about the first principles of democracy, if we have learnt the technique? Thus, we are already being caught in the forces that we have liberated by taking to such claptraps of modern statecraft as the moralist Aldous Huxley enumerates in his *Ends and Means*: e. g., "organized lying" in the form of propaganda; "worship of such local divinities as the nation, the class, and even the deified individual"; passionate bigotry in ideology, for which men are prepared "to kill and to be killed"; perpetration of violence; terrorism legalized, opposition banned; "elaborate systems of police espionage"; Fascist planning to grab the power and to keep it; the nation "personified as a living being with passions, desires, susceptibilities"; the encouragement and exploitation of orgiastic crowd emotion; and so on. There is no need to enlarge this list of indictment, because it is common knowledge.

(9) *Minority Rule and Education*

It is common knowledge that in democracy the people must acquiesce in the opinion of the majority. This majority rule, however, is only possible when the people have attained a certain degree of more or less common political thought, which will have enabled them to arrive at that majority opinion. That is why democracy is impossible without an education, which will supply the people with that more or less common political thought. When the standard of education is uneven, or its scope limited, the probability is that there will be a number of minority opinions, which will defeat their own ends by working at cross purposes, and in the end dissipate the political energy of the people. The present condition of our country seems to be a case in point. Theoretically, a number of minority factions would mean minority rule, whichever party came into power. I do not say that the uneven standard of education is the sole cause of our bewildering number of political parties; I merely submit that it is one of the many causes.

Thus, the task of education in democracy should be to inculcate upon the younger generation such civic sense as what will guide the political destiny of their future to the best advantage. This does not mean that education should bring the younger generation into certain channels of political belief; for that would be propaganda rather than education. In the words of Bertrand Russell:

"Education as a political weapon could not exist if we respected the rights of children. If we respected the rights of children, we should educate them so as to give them the knowledge and the mental habits required for forming independent opinions; but education as a political institution endeavors to form habits and to circumscribe knowledge in such a way as to make one set of opinions inevitable. . . . The prevention of free inquiry is unavoidable so long as the purpose of education is to produce belief rather than thought, to compel the young to hold positive opinions on doubtful matters rather than to let them see the doubtfulness and be encouraged to independence of mind. Education ought to foster the wish for truth, not the conviction that some particular creed is the truth."

I see no harder task in the field of education than what is demanded of us in these sentiments.

(10) *Some Have Greatness Thrust Upon Them*

Democracy recognizes that "men are not equal as regards native capacity or acquired power" (C. W. Eliot), but it does not admit of inequality by birth or privilege. In the words of Shakespeare, it permits people to achieve greatness, but not to be born great or to have greatness thrust upon them. Unfortunately, in the hierarchical scheme of society, the traditional Oriental convention had too readily accepted the existence of social status. The convention, however, has now largely been exploded, as far as Korea is concerned. We no longer believe in the *yang-ban* class. Each man, in theory at least, stands or falls by his own merit. The old State Examination system, administered to choose government officials, was in its limited way founded on democratic principles; but it was exposed to corruption like any other system. At a time when the classical learning was a prerogative of the few, it naturally limited the opportunity to the few. On the other hand, by placing a great emphasis on learning as a necessary accomplishment, it taught men to respect letters embodying the Confucian ethics, and thus to look for good in the integrity of character rather than in the pursuit of wealth or in the love of power. Korean history abounds in edifying examples of ministers who lived in direst poverty. In its later development, however, the State Examination system ended by being formalistic, with other attendant evils of graft and corruption.

I shall but mention two such evil consequences. Because Confucianism teaches that the family is the basis of society, and that virtue should extend from the family, to the clan, and then to society in general, it lends itself easily to the evil of nepotism in government. Second, a bad government is bad for the people, but not so bad for the men in power. This state of things, when chronic, makes any government position a coveted object. In a truly democratic world, there should be no reason whatever why a tram conductor must be considered to be on a lower status of social function than a civil servant in the government. But facts are otherwise.

There is one other aspect of Oriental life that seems to take social inequality for granted. It is indicated in the makeup of such languages as Korean and Japanese. It is the use of honorifics. The subtle distinctions of vocabulary and predicate endings, by which we express our sense of respect, are good in themselves, except for the reverse side of non-respect that they necessarily involve.

(11) *A Comic Relief*

A Western man, especially an American, will raise the question at this point: "What about the status of women?" Yes, what about it? If there were no ladies present here, perhaps I would not have raised the question myself. Among men only, one does not feel the immediate compunction to speak about the status of women!

When Mencius said, "Between husband and wife there is distinction," he meant that the social functions of man and woman differ horizontally, as it were, rather than vertically. But 'the rut of pseudo-classic formalism' into which the Oriental mind has ever been in danger of falling, has made this difference of function one of spiritual inferiority and superiority. So, for a long time, the status of women in the East has been, and is, from a democratic point of view, "appalling." Man being essentially a more selfish creature than woman, he has readily accepted the most convenient notion that the world is made for him. Now, if this status is to be changed, as it must be changed, women of the East will have to strive hard. It is up to the women rather than the men to make them first repent of past folly, and then, to prove that women are created co-equal. Men are no saints, ready to give up at a week's notice the privileges that they have enjoyed so long. That is why women must strive hard. In the meantime, we must anticipate many a strange interlude and comic relief, such as the one depicted by H. H. Munro (Saki) in his short story, "Hermann the Irascible":

Hermann the Irascible, of Saxe-Drachsen-Wachtelstein, also nicknamed the Wise, sat on the British Throne in the second decade of the twentieth century, after the Great Plague had swept away the entire Royal Family. One day his Prime Minister revealed the fact that the votes-for-women suffragettes were disturbing all meetings throughout the country and trying "to turn Downing Street into a sort of political picnic-ground." The King contemplated the situation, and seating himself before the typewriter, said to his minister:

> "I will draft you a Bill, enacting that women shall vote at all future elections. While voting will remain optional for male electors, every woman between twenty-one and seventy will be obliged to vote at all future elections for Parliament, county councils, district boards, parish councils, municipalities, coroners, school inspectors, church wardens, curators for museums, sanitary authorities, police-court interpreters, swimming-bath instructors, market superintendents, and all other local functionaries. Pass the Bill through the two Houses and bring it to me for signature the day after tomorrow."

The Compulsory Female Franchise duly became an Act of Parliament, and the women were attending the polling station almost every day, "and weekend parties and summer holidays became gradually a masculine luxury." Now the No-Votes-for-Women became a formidable movement; once again meetings were disturbed, ministers mobbed, and policemen bitten. Still the Government obstinately adhered to its original conviction of universal suffrage. At last the women hit upon a happy idea. The Great Weep was organized, in which thousands of women in relay wept continuously in all public places—railway stations, tubes, buses, in concerts, theater performances, museums, Army and Navy Stores, in St. James' Park, etc.

The situation became unbearable. At last, the Prime Minister, "whose cook had wept into all the breakfast dishes," pleaded the case to the King once again. The wise King said: "All right, have it your way. There's a time for everything. Pass a measure through the two Houses depriving women of the right to vote, and bring it to me for Royal assent the day after tomorrow."

(12) *Inner Control*

I have thus far tried to show aspects of Oriental life that are seemingly incongruous with the ideals of Western democracy. I shall now turn to those ideals that are essentially common to both doctrines.

Babbitt says in *Democracy and Leadership*: "In the long run democracy will be judged, no less than other forms of government, by the quality of its leaders, a quality that will depend in turn on the quality of their vision." One of the central theses of the Confucian political doctrine is the question of leadership. The greater part of the fourteen books of Mencius may be said to revolve round the concept of a good ruler who does not betray the first principles of 'rule by virtue.' It may well be both feasible and enlightening to find parallels between the ideal ruler of Mencius and the philosopher-king of Plato. My poor knowledge in the Confucian classics makes me fear of over-simplification in defining the Confucian ideals of life and government. Nevertheless, certain aspects are so manifestly akin to the spirit of democracy that they do not require deep reading in the classics to be discovered even by a novice.

The ultimate goal to which Confucius aspired was the realization once again of the civilization of the Chow dynasty in the twelfth century B. C. He constantly dreamed about it, as testified in his own confession:

The Master said: "How old I must have grown. Not for a long time have I seen again King Chow in my dreams!" (子曰 甚矣 吾衰也 久矣 吾不復夢見周公)

In realizing the ideal spirit of the Chow civilization, namely 'propriety' (禮), he concluded, men must acquire the spirit of *Jen* (仁), which has literally been translated as 'man-to-man-ness,' but in spirit is the same as 'love' or 'benevolence.' *Jen* is the basis of Confucianism, both in theory and practice. *Jen* postulates the spirit of harmony and love between man and man.

Jen is a congenital virtue of every man—in the Confucian terminology, 'dictates of heaven' (天命). Confucius says of himself:

"At fifteen I aspired to learn. At thirty I entered upon practical life. At forty I was unmoved by temptation. At fifty I knew the dictates of heaven. At sixty my senses were in harmony with nature. At seventy I followed what my mind desired without trespassing the limits of propriety." (吾十有五而志于學 三十而立 四十而不惑 五十而知天命 六十而耳順 七十而從心所欲 不踰矩)

Now, the dictates of heaven are not something that are imposed from without, they come from within by means of introspection. Mencius said:

> "Every man has a sense of pity, and likewise a sense of shame, of respect, and of right and wrong. Sense of pity is man-to-man-ness; that of shame, integrity; that of respect, etiquette; and that of right and wrong, judgment. These do not come from without and disintegrate me. I have them with me from the beginning. It is only that I am not conscious of them. Therefore, I say: seek, and you shall obtain them; neglect, and you shall lose them." (惻隱之心 人皆有之 羞惡之心 人皆有之 是非之心 人皆有之 惻隱之心 仁也 羞惡之心 義也 恭敬之心 禮也 是非之心 智也 仁義禮智 非由外鑠我也 我固有之也 弗思耳矣 故曰 求則得之 舍則失之)

Confucius himself is emphatic on this point of introspection and inner restraint. Once one of his disciples asked about *Jen*:

> Yen-yuan asked about *Jen*. The Master said: "If by self-restraint you recover a sense of propriety, that becomes *Jen*. If one day you achieve this decorum by means of self-restraint, the whole world will be unified in *Jen*. *Jen* depends on oneself. How can it be said to depend on others?" (顏淵問仁 子曰 克己復禮 爲仁 一日 克己復禮 天下歸仁焉 爲仁由己 而由人乎哉)

The inner restraint, which Confucius urges, is further enhanced by his insistence upon the critical spirit. In other words, the principle of decorum innate in man, that is a check upon his expansive desires, must be constantly cultivated and rationalized by learning. He says: "To love *Jen,* and not to love learning, such instruction would indeed be folly." (好仁 不好學 其敎也愚) Similarly, Mencius urges this point with his characteristic sophistry:

> Mencius said: "*Jen* is man's innate nature, and integrity his way. If he deserts his way and follows not, if he discards his nature and knows not how to seek it again, pitiful is he indeed. A man who has fowls and dogs, knows how to seek them when

they go astray; but he knows not how to seek out his nature when that goes astray. The object of learning is none other than this—to seek out one's nature that has gone astray." (孟子曰 仁人心也 義人路也 舍其路而不由 放其心而不知求 哀哉 人有鷄犬 放則知求之 有放心而不知求 學問之道 無他 求其放心而已矣)

This double insistence on our conscience and our reason is a trait of the philosophy of democracy. Compare, for instance, the following words of Stuart P. Sherman with what has already been said:

"The ideal of the German is external control and inner freedom; the government looks after his conduct and he looks after his liberty. The ideal of the American is external freedom and inner control; the individual looks after his conduct and the government looks after his liberty. Thus, *Verboten* in Germany is pronounced by the government and enforced by the police. In America *Verboten* is pronounced by public opinion and enforced by the individual conscience. In this light it should appear that Puritanism, our national principle of concentration, is the indispensable check on democracy, our national principle of expansion. I use the word Puritanism in the sense given to it by German and German-American critics: the inner check upon the expansion of national impulse.

(13) *Law and Balance*

In practical ethics, Confucianism takes the five cardinal relations of human society, and inculcates the spirit of law and order:

(A) Between father and son there is filial love; (父子有親)
(B) Between ruler and subject there is integrity; (君臣有義)
(C) Between husband and wife there is distinction; (夫婦有別)
(D) Between the elder and the younger there is order; (長幼有序)
(E) Between friend and friend there is sincerity. (朋友有信)

Two of these (A and C) are relations within the family; two (B and E) without; and one (D) in both. Confucianism holds that filial piety is the basis of all human ethics: "Filial love and brotherly love—are they not the root of all benevolent actions?" (Legge's translation of "孝弟也者 其爲仁之本與") That is why *The Book of Filial Duty* (孝經), written, so tradition has it, by Tseng-tzu(曾子) at the express command of his Master, is one of the lesser Bibles of Confucianism.

In the Thirteenth Book of Mencius, there is an interesting dialogue that throws light upon two points: (1) that even the ruler must subject himself under the law; (2) that all other ethical laws are subservient to the law of filial duty:

> T'ao-ying asked and said: "If Shun rules as emperor, and Kao-yao serves as minister, and if Ku-sou (the Emperor's father) has committed an act of murder, what then should be done?" Mencius said: "There is nothing else to do but to arrest him." T'ao Ying asked: "Should not the Emperor, then, prevent him from so doing?" Mencius said: "How should even the Emperor be able to prevent it? A murderer must needs abide by the dictates of law." "And then, how should the Emperor act?" asked T'ao-ying. Mencius said: "The Emperor must discard his empire as if it were an old worn-out sandal, steal out his father, carry him on his back, and seek refuge along the seashore, where, forgetting about his empire, he should live in joy with his father for the rest of his life." (桃應問曰 舜爲天子 皐陶爲士 瞽瞍殺人 則如之何 孟子曰 執之而已矣 然則舜不禁與 曰 夫舜惡得而禁之 夫有所受之也 然則舜如之何 曰 舜視棄天下 猶棄敝屣也 竊負而逃 遵海濱而處 終身訢然 樂而忘天下)

Take the philosophy of Hsun-tzu (荀子) for another instance. His analysis of human psychology is diametrically opposed to that of Mencius. Briefly speaking, Mencius holds that human nature is inherently good, but that this goodness is often obliterated by 'desires' (欲), which spring from our physical senses in contact with the outer world. The key to improving our mind lies, therefore, in lessening our desires, which are the root of all evil:

Mencius said: "In improving one's mind, nothing is better than to decrease one's desires." (孟子曰 養心 莫善於寡欲)

Hsun-tzu(荀子), on the other hand, says that we have desires innate in us, which create 'disputes' (爭), which in turn create 'confusion' (亂), which ends in 'violence' (暴):

"Therefore, it is necessary that we should be placed under the influence of tradition and law and the guidance of decorum. Then, we shall act in humility, conform to sweet reason, and return to peace and order." (故必將有師法之化 禮義之道 然後出於辭讓 合於文理 而歸於治)

Thus, Hsun-tzu (荀子), in spite of his so-called heretical views on human nature, ends by upholding the supremacy of law and order, for which decorum and etiquette are the sole justification for encouragement.

Here again, the parallels with the ideals of democracy are not far to seek. We must, of course, remember that the motivating spirit behind the Confucian insistence upon the supremacy of law and order is somewhat different from that of democracy. Law is important for Confucianism because it fosters that mood which preserves the hierarchical order of society as has been laid down by convention and tradition. Law in democracy has its being because it safeguards the fundamental rights and dignity of man as postulated in the almost legalistic contract of society. Otherwise, the two may be said to merge for all intents and purposes. Professor Northrop writes, in discussing the "Unique Elements in British Democracy," as follows:

"The great protector of the liberties of the British individual is the law. This law goes back at least to the *Magna Carta* in 1215 and to the Common Law, which developed from the *Magna Carta*. It was this triumph of the Common Law, achieved over the centuries, which established the principle that the law is above the King or any executor of the government."

And he quotes the historian G. M. Trevelyan in corroboration:

"Victory of the Common Law preserved the medieval conception of the supremacy of law. . . . That medieval idea of the supremacy of law as something separate from and independent of the will of the executive, disappeared in continental countries. But in England it became the palladium of our liberties and had a profound effect on English society and habits of thought."

From this sense of law and order the Doctrine of the Mean is a natural growth. This doctrine, as formulated by Tzu-ssu (子思), and the democratic spirit of compromise and balance, have one thing in common—namely, the appeal to man's reasonableness. Though formulated by Tzu-ssu (子思), the ideal goes back, of course, to the Master himself. In the *Analects* (Book IV), it is written:

The Master called: "Sen! One spirit runs through my teaching." Tseng-tzu (曾子) answered: "Verily, Master." The Master went out. The other disciples asked what the Master meant. Tseng-tzu answered: "The essence of our Master's teaching is this—fidelity to oneself, and not to do to others what you would not wish others to do to yourself." (子曰 參乎 吾道一以貫之 曾子曰 唯 子出 門人問曰 何謂也 曾子曰 夫子之道 忠恕而而矣)

This is the epitome of reasonableness in ethics. Lin Yu-tang gives the reverse side of this aspect:

"The preference for daintiness over power in art has a physical basis in a man's lessened vitality and mellowed instincts, and the preference for reasonableness over aggressiveness in philosophy may be actually traceable to the rounded chin and the amorphous face. . . . When one cannot be powerful, one must choose to be dainty, and when one cannot be aggressive, one has to make a virtue of reasonableness. . . . That is what two-thousand years of kowtowing could do to a nation."

(14) *Benefit of the Doubt*

I wish to conclude this paper with a brief consideration of the historic role which democracy is playing throughout the Far East.

It is a role that did not have an auspicious beginning. With a wounded sense of pride, the Oriental man has witnessed the crumbling down of his scheme of valuation before the politico-economic system of the West, backed as it is by the stupendous forces of science and mechanical industry. He has ever suspected an unholy motive behind the Westerner's desire to proselytize and to trade. The politico-economic intrigue of regarding the whole of the Far East from the standpoint of military strategy or of trade market has always had a demoralizing effect upon his imagination. In short, he has felt the justice of Sun Yat-sen's righteous indignation, when he said: "The rest of mankind is the carving knife and the serving dish, while we are the fish and the meat." And then, to aggravate the situation, Japan quickly became a finished master in the art and craft of Western power politics, and lo and behold, she even beat, for a time at least, the Western nations at their own game. America herself, who is the least sinful of the powers, has not been exempt from the suspicion. A Korean in dejection, for example, be it frankly admitted, feels that neither of the two Roosevelts, Theodore at Portsmouth and Franklin at Yalta, were real benefactors to our cause, in so far as they placed expediency before fundamental principles.

But that is the darker side of the picture. On the brighter side are the Atlantic Charter, and the preachments of the Four Freedoms that will ever pluck at our heartstrings, together with what Wendell Wilkie calls America's 'reservoir of good will':

"All the people of the earth know that we have no sinister designs upon them, that even when we have in the past withdrawn from international affairs into a false self-sufficiency, it was without sinister purpose. And they know that, now we are in this war, we are not fighting for profit, or loot, or territory, or mandatory power over the lives or the governments of other peoples. That, I think, is the single most important reason for the existence of our reservoir of good will around the world."

Well and good. We of the Orient are prepared to believe this, provided the Americans do not sit back with self-complacency in the implicit and unquestioned belief that that 'reservoir of good will' will last forever. Being, as noted above, realists to the core, we are in the habit of judging things by the results rather than by the motives. We shall readily believe that America is full of good intentions, but we shall not be hood-winked by them if the execution of her declared ideals of freedom and justice turns out to be the old game of power-politics, of which we have cause enough to be sick and tired.

The prospect is, if you will, bright, but not clear. For set in immediate juxtaposition also are Russia's communistic ideology and a political realism of a somewhat different kidney. The horns of the dilemma are that both democracy and communism, as political *doctrines*, have 'survival values,' and that both offer equally crucial difficulties to the Oriental temperament and culture. Faced with the disintegration of the time-honored traditions and the impact of modern scientific thought of the West, and driven by chronic poverty, which has long characterized the moribund social structure of the East, the dislocated and the rebellious are marching to the almost fatalistic drumming of the philosophy of communism.

Why communism has such an appeal to the Oriental mind of the present, is a subject that requires a separate treatment. Suffice it here to point out merely the fact that we are going through a fearful and tumultuous test, from which we desire to emerge the wiser as well as the stronger. The process of that test will be slow and exacting. Its resulting pattern will not be easy to predict; for, like the wrong side of a tapestry, we have all the brilliant colors in every stitch, but we must turn it over in the perspective of history to see its intelligible design. Meanwhile, two things are more or less certain: first, ours can hardly be an exact replica of democracy as America conceives, any more than we want to have an exact replica of communism as Russia conceives; second, we shall not be led to identify peace with status quo, for in the words of Wendell Wilkie, with which I wish to end as I began:

> "In Africa, in the Middle East, throughout the Arab world, as well as in China and the whole Far East, freedom means the orderly but scheduled abolition of the colonial system. Whether we like it or not, this is true." (August 15, 1947)

Letters to the Editor of *The Seoul Times*

Sir:

For various reasons I have been led to ponder upon the present condition of national education in South Korea, which does not by any manner of means permit us to sit back in self-complacency.

Two whole years and more have elapsed since the Military Government laid down what are considered to be the basic principles of new education in this country. Two years in the history of an individual is nothing. Two years in the history of a hermit nation that has been accustomed to 'living and partly living' for over 4,000 years is still nothing. But two years in the history of a nation, caught in the throes of birth pang in the most critical of times, is something to give us sleepless nights.

The most significant symptom of unhealthiness in present day education is that things are once again assuming the colorless aspect of the routine and the humdrum. The flurry of excitement, which held us in tension for a year after 1945, has not died down. If things are on the move, people seem to be satisfied! One is too often reminded, in a slightly derogatory sense, of the words of Wordsworth: "I see what was, and is, and shall abide, Still glides the stream and shall for ever glide, The form remains, the function never dies."

Another significant symptom of unhealthiness is the insufficiency of cooperation between the National Department and the institutions of learning, both high and low. This is, in all likelihood, due to two causes: (1) that there is a prevalent feeling among the administrators and the school authorities, that the groundwork has been accomplished, and that there now remains the superstructure, the realization of the basic principles; (2) that, true to the spirit of democracy, all efforts in the realization of those principles must come voluntarily from the individual school and teachers, and that the proper task of the Department is the co-ordination, rather than the initiation of those various efforts.

I suspect that, if the groundwork is finished, it is in appearance only, and that there still is a great deal of spadework to be done. From the very nature of the thing, there can be no 'fiat' in education; we must ever be prepared to re-test and re-scrutinize. And this can only be attained through a closer co-operation between the Government and the schools.

According to a pamphlet released by the Department of Education, there are, or were until December 1946, no less than twenty-three different educational committees, with an aggregate total of 1,460 members. I should like to ask the Department: What has happened to all these committee activities? In all appearance, those committees are still extant.

I am not contending that the activities of these twenty-three committees should be revived. Nor, from the practical viewpoint, is it at all certain that they are the best possible kinds, being organized on such an extensive and cumbersome basis that they are difficult to wield. I am only contending that some form of committee activity should never cease. A standing committee of *select* membership for specific fields should be working persistently for the common good of the Department and the actual schools. In this way, the schools and colleges will not be left to their own devices; and the National Department will not only be alive to the best ideas but also to co-ordinate them to the best of advantage.

Granted, the committee idea may be over-done. In the words of a modern poet, it may well turn out to be: "Cry cry what shall I cry? The first thing to do is to form the committees: The consultative councils, the standing committees, select committees, and sub-committees: One secretary will do for several committees. . . ." Let the Director see to it that the committee does not cease at the nomination of members, or that the members do not just talk away the time for the sake of aiming their 'highly original' views. Let him see to it that they beat out their given problems to some *practicable* conclusion. Korea has already a surplus of schemers on paper.

As for the second cause I have mentioned, suffice it to say that if the schools themselves cannot take the initiative, then the Department must. It so happens that most of our schoolmasters have been so devitalized by the nightmarish philosophy of subjugation under the Japanese regime that they have lost their creative imagination to a greater extent than they perhaps realize. It is then the business of the National Department to be their driving conscience at all times until they have recovered their creative vitality.

Yours etc.

Vox Meditantis

(Monday, December 22–Tuesday, December 23, 1947, *The Seoul Times*)

Sir:

Your correspondent, who signs himself as 'Vox Meditantis,' has made some pertinent observations on what he calls the "significant symptoms of unhealthiness" in the present condition of national education in South Korea. In the main, I have nothing to say against his diagnosis. To my mind, however, there is a more significant aspect that seems to have escaped his attention. Kindly permit me to make myself clear, on the clear assumption that I write in the spirit of corroboration, and not of retaliation, with your thoughtful correspondent.

Education in Korea has been, and is to this livelong day, the handmaid of politics. Time was when education, in partnership with police espionage, had served the Japanese well enough in their efforts to graft upon us their fanatic myth of a culture. That nightmare was hardly ended, when the Communists took over the handy weapon and did what they could to turn student bodies into an organized political force. Now the table is turned, and the change of political weather has given rise to the rightist wire pulling, while the students remain what they have always been, easily gullible and far too readily excitable.

I have been informed by the Department of Education that one of the 'desirable qualifications' for the new Director is: 'Non-partisan politically.' For all intents and purposes, the late Director himself was non-partisan enough. Few can doubt that he, being a genial gentleman to his fingertips, tried his utmost to make the best of both political worlds. I regret, however, to submit that 'Non-partisan politically' sounds too much like the so-called middle-of-the-way slogan in politics. 'Non-partisan' is not enough; I should feel more at rest if it had been 'Independent of politics.'

I do not see why education cannot be independent of politics, rightist, leftist, or middle-of-the-road. If we respected the rights of the younger generation, we should beware of circumscribing their habits of thought in such a way as to make one set of political opinions inevitable. Even the middle-of-the-road opinion, qua *political* opinion, is no better or no worse than the rightist or the leftist as far as education is concerned, if education is to be a means to foster in the younger generation the independence of judgment and the desire for truth. Korea has enough people, as it is, who do but lip service to democracy, class equality, love of one's land, and the rest. Do we want our future generations to continue this lip service?

Students, as individual citizens, are entitled to have any political belief they wish. But their private affiliations must not interfere with the public functions of education by being organized into political bodies. But things have now reached a stage where the school or college has less control over the students than their own organizations, which in turn are watered in stock by political demagogues. The individual schoolmaster will most likely be ostracized, if he should attempt to eradicate the political element from his school. The only hope for him is in the Department; if an order should be issued from the National Department, to the effect that all student organizations of a *political* nature should be dissolved, the schoolmaster will feel greatly encouraged and strengthened in his efforts to purify his school.

Yours etc.

Vox Clamantis

(Wednesday, December 24, 1947, *The Seoul Times*)

Sir:

I have been told by an American gentleman, whose veracity I have no reason to doubt, that the British people found three faults with the American Expeditionary Force in Europe, that they are over-paid, over-sexed, and 'over here.' I myself am inclined to believe that, coming from the British, who have cause enough to be jealous of their English-speaking brothers, this is no serious indictment against the Americans in general. As a disinterested Korean, I see nothing wrong with being over-paid if the War Department in Washington has the money to give and to spare. And I have met with Americans who are as non-sexed as confirmed celibates. As for being 'over here,' I don't know that they are doing more harm than the Russians in North Korea.

What I do feel perturbed about, however, is the fact that many a good American, whether military or civilian, with a deep and sympathetic understanding of our people and culture, is continually leaving us for good, either for home or for Japan.

Knowing full well that the pursuit of happiness is one of the unquestionable rights of democratic man, a Korean has no right to complain of the Americans going home, since love of home is part of human nature. But when a true American friend of the Koreans is being moved to Japan, whether by order or by choice, there is, I think, a justifiable ground for protest.

No doubt, Japan is a better place to work in than Korea. It may well be that Japan offers better environment and more pleasure-resorts than Korea. Certainly Japan is nearer home than Korea. But such are too flippant reasons for an American to leave his work in Korea for that in Japan. America's political commitments in Korea were not made in a mood of gaiety, but out of a sense of solemn duty. Not only should an American in Korea be a Stoic of the first water but also should never permit himself to be in a frame of mind to compare Korea with Japan.

The departure of a good American to Japan is a double loss to Korea. Any favorable impression of Japan on the part of Americans has a negative effect on Korea. A conscientious Korean might even have an objection to Americans making vacation trips to the inland of Japan, for every American back from Japan has nothing but good to say about Japan.

It might be to the interest of the Commanding General and the Military Governor in Korea (not to mention the beneficial effect on the Koreans themselves) to have all American citizens on holiday leave visit Okinawa, Saipan, the Aleutian Islands, and other bleak spots of the Eastern hemisphere. Such a trip will not only prove instructive, but add to their sense of gratitude and relief that their assigned work lies here in Korea.

My immediate motive for writing this letter is that I am going to lose soon an excellent American friend, who is also a true friend of the Korean people. Nor is this my first experience of its kind. My further apprehension is that Korea may be in such a mess that all the good Americans will want to 'pull out' at the earliest possible hour. I hope that the Commanding General and the Military Governor will see to it that Korea is not left with only indifferent Americans.

Yours etc.
Vox Meditantis

(Thursday, December 25, 1947, *The Seoul Times*)

Sir:

Permit me to express my unexpected pleasure at having discovered a correspondent in your paper by the name of 'Vox Clamantis.' His salutary remarks on the undesirability of political wire pulling convince me that he is not only my fellow-thinker but, if he will pardon my liberty, a most welcome friend of mine.

In my humble capacity as a schoolteacher, I have frequently protested to my principal that politics is ruining the campus atmosphere, urging that something should be done about it, even if that something is of a drastic nature. But time and again he has politely evaded the issue by saying that things must be done at their appropriate time.

I believe in the sincerity of my principal. I have an implicit faith in his administrative vision. And I am prepared to wait patiently, if my patience is going to add at all to the cause of our education. But being a man under thirty, with little experience to boot, I feel my confidence somewhat shaken by the ominous presence of political prompters behind the amateur stage of young students.

If we intend merely to get a kick out of education, a political puppet-show would have quite as much entertainment value as any other, provided we make sure whom it is going to entertain. If it is to entertain the USAFIK, we should be trespassing upon the legitimate functions of the WVTP. If it is going to amuse the Korean people at large, I know for a fact that we are already over-harassed with worry to be in a mood to feel amused, least of all in education.

By all means let us have, within limits, many different kinds of student associations, ranging from the grave to the gay. Let the boys and girls call for a Less-Parents'-Association-Fee League, or a society for historical research into the abuse of flogging. Such will add piquancy to a teacher's life, which is at most a mug's life and not a career.

Ostensibly, student life is comparatively quiet recently. No more strikes at regular intervals, etc. That is a blessing, to be sure. But the snake has been only 'scotched.' Now a greater one is at loose, greater because it is legitimately authorized, and accepted full blown, issuing statements and counter-statements in the true manner born. Time will come when tit for tat will take place; and who is to guarantee what the tat will be?

If our educational leaders are thinking of glossing over the situation with a fuzzy conviction that Korea will muddle through the mounting crises, well and good. Doubtless, we'll muddle through and through, till we'll really be through with everything, including education. Individual effort will not amount to much. Some form of national order should be promulgated for the benefit of these unthinking children, who are seemingly let alone to play with fire.

In effect, I am only reiterating what my fellow-correspondent has already expressed deftly. I hope to be excused for this redundancy, because it is a point that deserves driving home.

Yours etc.
Vox Meditantis

P. S. Could you invite Vox Clamantis to continue writing on education? Henceforth, I propose to follow suit. Two is indeed company in this cactus-land of vainglory and dogmatism

(Tuesday, January 6, 1948, *The Seoul Times*)

Sir:

A number of Americans have confessed that Korea is a land of many mysteries. Admitting that this is true, I persuade them to think as I do, that since mysteries are so numerous, they no longer remain mysterious. I further add that the Military Government has added many more mysteries to our already cumbersome stock of mysteries; and they think I am pulling their legs!

As an instance, I should like to mention the methods by which Korean students are being sent abroad to study. What mystifies us all is the fact that America is helping Korea on a national basis, but picking our supposedly bright boys and girls on a purely personal basis.

Time and again, I have had to confess ignorance when asked by my students about the requirements for going abroad to study. Being uninitiated in the organization of the Military Government, I don't even know whether the work belongs to the Department of Education or of Foreign Affairs. Frankly, I can't get it out of my head that the whole thing belongs to the Department of Personal Affairs!

Being a woolgatherer, I have only lately discovered how a Korean student may get himself over to the U. S. to study. His qualifications are threefold: (1) Either, he must be well connected with an influential family; or, he must have had some experience in house-keeping at an American dependent house; (2) He should be endowed with a parrot's genius for sputtering out a few idiomatic sentences in English; (3) Some home-going colonel or missionary must take a *personal* interest in his future. With these conditions fulfilled, he will have a fair chance to sail by the next boat.

Korean students are what is euphemistically known as 'ambitious,' or in plainer monosyllables, 'full of vague hopes and dreams.' Ask any Korean student if he would like to go to America. Being sick at heart, he wants to pull out of this wilderness of a country—perhaps even before the Allied Armies! As an instinctive animal, he knows what he wants: go to America, come back with a qualified air of pomp, settle down to some key position in the government office, and 'enjoy' life.

With such high hopes, he will land in America, only to discover the unexpected truth that the freedom to enter Harvard, Yale, or Columbia is not included in the Four Freedoms, or guaranteed in the Cairo Declaration. But suppose, for the sake of argument, he does enter one of these world-famous universities, he will next be hounded to distraction by difficulty after difficulty. His delusions about his perfect mastery of the English language will be ruthlessly shattered. His purse will become lean. In this land of opportunity, he will be driven to resume his older mode of life, housekeeping, dishwashing, etc. Meanwhile, he will create a decidedly unfavorable impression on the university authorities, who will not only be most reluctant to take in Korean students in the future, but also find it expedient to dispose of the present one with some kind of courtesy degree.

We may well expect two evil consequences from this state of affairs: (1) The Korean student, after such hardships, will probably return home with a violent prejudice against the American academic institutions and social structure in general. This is something to worry about at a time when democracy stands or falls by education; and (2) there will be an inundation of courtesy degrees in Korea, of which we already have a surplus number. This overflowing may prove beneficial to America, because it will show America to be a land of courtesy and etiquette, but it will be no blessing to Korea. We want real specialists, and not specialists in name or by courtesy.

After much thought, I make bold to make the following proposals:

(1) Let the Department of Education initiate a state examination system by which all qualified students may compete for the privilege of studying abroad. The examination ought to lay special emphasis on English and the particular subject in which he intends to specialize. In this way not only the best will be chosen, but also they will be picked out on an impersonal and universal basis. The present system, if there is a system, does not guarantee either condition.

(2) For the time being, only graduate work should be permitted; so, the examination should be, on principle, open to graduate students of recognized universities and colleges.

(3) Science and technology should be given absolute priority. No doubt Korea needs theologians to teach us how to save our sinful souls, philosophers to meditate

on the ruins of time on a hungry stomach, musicians and dancers to perform Stravinsky's *Fire Bird*. But they are not going to construct our sewage system, or improve plumbing, still less give us hydroelectricity. Culture-craze is no longer a joke in modern Korea.

(4) Must the Department of Foreign Affairs put its finger in this pie also? By all means issue passports at the last moment. But let the Department of Education be the chief agency in this game: appropriating money, contacting American universities for scholarships, enrollment, etc.

(5) Send more *real* and *honest* students, and not vainglorious tacticians. How many Korean students have been sent to America since the late summer of 1945? I am not hinting at the fact that the number is small, or that North Korea has, according to rumor, dispatched students to Moscow by the hundreds. I myself don't fancy much the idea of packing off young boys and girls to walled citadels!

(6) The greatest handicap, the language difficulty, will partly be met with by a period, all be it brief, of intensive training at the American Language Institute.

Yours etc.
Vox Clamantis

(Monday, January 19, 1948, *The Seoul Times*)

Sir:

I was much struck the other day by an opinion expressed by 'Vox Clamantis' in your column, that "Culture-craze is no longer a joke in modern Korea." It has brought to my acute consciousness what has been worrying me vaguely and intermittently for these several months. The ironical implications of that sentence should cut deep into the mind of any conscientious thinker about education in South Korea.

I have so often heard Americans say that the Koreans are a culture loving people that I have come to suspect a slight leer in their civility. The fault lies largely, of course, in us: we not only love culture, but also dote on it, decidedly 'on this side idolatry.' This sounds like washing our dirty linen before the English-reading public. But that is precisely what I want to do. My hope is that the American advisors in the Department of Education will partake in this linen washing.

A careful study of the latest available statistics from the Department of Education shows the following evidences of culture-craze in higher education in South Korea. The total student enrollment, as of October 1947, in the 29 colleges and universities approved by the Department numbers some 20,500. Of those, *circa* 4,600, by far the largest single category, are enrolled in literature and language courses, foreign or native. Political Science, Law, Economics, Commerce, Philosophy, History, etc., together, have over 6,300 students; Medicine, c. 1,900; General Science, c. 1,800; Technology, c. 1,700;

Pharmacology, c. 1,050; Theology (including non-Christian), c. 800; Agriculture, Veterinary Science, Forestry, together, 720; Music and Fine Arts, c. 600; Fisheries, c. 230; and Dentistry, 210.

From these factual data, what morals can be deduced? It looks as if Korea is going to win nearly all the Nobel Prizes for literature in the not distant future. At worst, we should have any number of qualified interpreters who will greatly ease the arduous duties of the occupation forces! We can expect a fair crop of budding politicians and lawyers, who will no doubt know how to solve the impending question of unemployment among the politicians themselves. The accepted belief that Korea is an agricultural country is going to prove a fallacy, for we are going to have more sanctimonious pastors than farmers equipped with modern technical knowledge. As for fishing industry, which is supposed to have a promising future, it is going to be all but neglected, though leisurely officials in the Government, be it granted, will take to angling in the true-born manner of Isaak Walton. There is evidently going to be many diseases, otherwise our future doctors and chemists will be put out of work. And from the expected number of dentists, we shall obviously have to have strong enough teeth to chew not only rice but also grit with it, owing to the shortage of rice production.

In case I may be thought to falsify the picture, here are some further corroborative facts on the number of majoring courses open to students throughout the said 29 colleges and universities: Language and Literature, again the highest single category, 23; Political Science and Diplomacy, 10; Philosophy, Sociology, and Psychology, 10; History, 10; Economics, 8; Theology, including non-Christian, 7; Music and Fine Arts, 7; Commerce, 6; etc. On the Science side, Medicine, with 5 well-established colleges to itself, seems to be the only branch that is going 'full steam.' There are 4 colleges of agriculture, of which 3 are but recently established, or rather, in the process of being established. The number of majoring courses in Physics is 5; Chemistry, 6; Mathematics, 6; etc. Our country is supposed to have great potentialities in hydroelectricity; but only 2 courses are found in Electricity; in Engineering, 3. The mining industry is also said to have a prosperous future; but South Korea offers only 3 courses in Mining. And so on.

Where lies the root of all this evil? Several reasons, I think, can be given, of which the more important are:

(1) Psychological: Youth loves expansive emotionalism. To a young man Liberal Arts is really liberal, and Social Science furnishes him with a soapbox full of prophetic denunciation and panacea. Natural Science comes down to brass tacks. Damned uncomfortable.

(2) Economical: It is so much cheaper to run a college of Liberal Arts and Social Science. Not much equipment needed. Get a blackboard with a teacher to stand before it, and a lecture will be started in full swing, especially if the teacher has a talent for gabbling. That is why private endowments so often go in for Liberal

Arts and Social Science.

(3) Politico-historical: Until yesterday, the Japanese wanted Koreans to be only efficient clerks and lip-service men. They would furnish as few technical schoolsas possible, and further, admit as few Korean students as possible to those already established. Quite unwittingly, we are following the same old trend of education that Japan had initiated.

I do hope we shall no more be hoodwinked, or be sinned against, with such tactics. And unless a vital change takes place in higher education, we are going to have a flood of swelled-headed men with lively tongues who will want to 'enjoy' life, but an acute shortage of those silent technicians and servants to the state who will render that enjoyment possible.

One of the 'desirable qualifications' for the Director of the Department of Education is said to be: 'Demonstrated interest and understanding in scientific, vocational, and technical fields.' At least the Department could show 'demonstrated interest' in Science negatively, by *not* approving any *more* colleges of Liberal Arts and Social Science. We have enough of them in South Korea already. Why not call it a day?

Yours etc.

Vox Meditantis

(Tuesday, January 27, 1948, *The Seoul Times*)

Sir:

Having read in your column the latest letter by 'Vox Meditantis,' I do not know whether to rejoice or lament. I did not realize, until he raised the point, that there were as many as 29 colleges and universities in South Korea.

After further investigation, I have discovered the fact that 20 of them are located in Seoul, counting Seoul National University as one, which has 9 colleges. From this bare fact alone, we may well be justified in considering our capital city to be one of the most learned cities in the world. And this surely something to rejoice in!

I have asked several people why so many colleges of liberal arts or social science are springing up like mushrooms. Among the various interpretations, I have heard one enlightening remark. Apparently it pays to establish such a college. The present politico-economic condition of our country is so unsettled that a man with money runs an enormous risk in ordinary investments. If he earns money, he will be branded with the unpleasant title of 'Profiteer'; and the lack of social stability may reduce him to a state of bankruptcy at any unexpected moment. So he turns to education. Running a school, which does not require much equipment, is not only safer but also more honorable than, say, running a factory. He can whitewash his past sins, if any, and guarantee himself to go down to history as a benefactor of society.

I am not imputing such an unholy motive to all the donors. I am merely saying that we--the students, the parents, and the Department of Education--must beware of such double dealers.

Higher education should be concentrative at the best of times. By all means let us be expansive, even diffusive, in elementary and secondary education. Korea cannot yet afford to be diffusive in higher education. It will take some time before we can tighten up the universities and colleges that are comparatively well grounded with a fair history behind. Even the best of them are not living up to their fullest potentialities, owing to the shortage of good teachers, and the inadequacy of library equipment, to mention but two of the most glaring handicaps.

Two ways of tightening up may be imagined. First: Set up a much higher standard for approval by the Department of Education. The Association of Universities and Colleges can join with the Department in enforcing such a standard. What that higher standard ought to be, I am not qualified to speak. Second: Initiate a state examination system, whereby any prospective graduate from any of these 29 colleges and universities can, if he wishes, obtain an extra diploma for his specialized field of knowledge.

Our higher education has not yet reached the desirable stage of real specialization. If we go on at this rate for any length of time, we are almost certain to become but a nation of amateurs, in the bad sense of the word. Who denies that Korea is in dire need of specialists in every field? The democratic process of 'leveling out' is not without serious dangers, when it comes to specialized knowledge.

Both theoretically and practically, such man should stand or fall by his own innate capacity and acquired merit. In a well-established society, the graduate of one college can, by universal consent, be esteemed better qualified than that of another. But how are we to make such a distinction in our own country? The only remedy in our case seems to be a state examination system, by which each student will be able to test his own merit. This will further serve as a great impetus for studying harder in his undergraduate days. Can we, in all frankness, say that our college students today are very hardworking?

Yours etc.
Vox Clamantis

(Wednesday, February 4, 1948, *The Seoul Times*)

Sir:

Early this month our newspapers revealed the fact that some 104 students have so far been sent to the U. S. to do graduate work. On that very day I happened to read a copy of a letter sent from the Counselor for Foreign Students, Harvard University. The letter was such a staggering experience to me that the feeling of deep mortification, which I felt then, is still oppressing my memory. My plea is: Cannot our Department of Education do something about it, to remedy the awful situation?

Apparently two Korean students, Y and Z, had applied for admission to Harvard College. The Committee on Admission had to refuse in consequence of another Korean student, X, "who came to Cambridge last September with the *idea* of registering at the Harvard Law School. Upon his reporting, it was immediately apparent that, due to his grave lack of knowledge of the English language, he could not undertake any required schedule of courses at the college level, and certainly not at the graduate level necessary for the Law School. . . . Unfortunately, it is now apparent that X's competency in English is barely equivalent to about *first year in grammar school. . . . Harvard does not provide courses in elementary English. . . .* Also, unfortunately, X's financial status is very precarious in that he is practically without funds. . . . Accordingly, the Committee on Admission presently is withholding approval of the requests of Y and Z, at least until definite information can be submitted as to their abilities to speak English fluently and without hesitation, to write English freely and rapidly, and to comprehend spoken English with accuracy. While Harvard at present has some 664 foreign students enrolled from *65 different countries,* and endeavors to give them every reasonably favorable consideration both financially and scholastically, it will be appreciated if sponsors, before the departure for the U. S. of prospective Korean students, definitely establish their competency in English and their abilities to pay their own expenses at least until their eligibility for scholarships can be determined. . . ." (My italics)

The letter also quotes the latest regulations of the U. S. Immigration Service (as of August 10, 1947): one of the reasons for deportation being "Failure of a foreign student to maintain a full schedule of college courses, due to his lack of competency in English."

It looks as if your correspondent Vox Clamantis has proved himself to be a minor prophet of a kind, for he wrote on this very question in your issue of January 19 last, with exactly the similar forebodings and misgivings.

Though this is the first time that I have come across such a letter, I conjecture that similar letters must have reached our Department of Education from other universities also. It means that more and more universities are being closed to Korean students for a good many years to come. With their own soldiers returning to college life, and immigrants from poverty-stricken Europe preparing for a fresh start in life, can we honestly expect American universities to be bothered with megalomaniacs from Korea? The Americans are no saints and angels; they are but human.

I endorse every word of the letter by Vox Clamantis, already referred to, and give full support to his proposals. On the possibility of remedying the situation, the American Language Institute has great potentialities. But being unacquainted with the Institute, I do not trust myself to speak. Perhaps Vox Clamantis has more constructive observations to make on this.

Yours etc.
Vox Meditantis

(Monday, February 23, 1948, *The Seoul Times*)

Sir:

Having been referred to as "a minor prophet of a kind" by Vox Meditantis in his latest letter, I do not know whether to take the phrase as a compliment or as an indictment. Personally, I feel it is the latter, since his letters distinctly indicate an ironic turn of mind in him. Nor is a prophet, by the very nature of his being, anything but a cry in the wilderness: he may be shouting himself hoarse from the rooftop, but nobody will pay any attention to him. Anyway, I have no happy evidence so far to prove that my letters in your column are being read, except perhaps by Vox Meditantis, your own typist in the editorial office, and the civil censor.

Since I have been invited to write about the functions of the American Language Institute in relation to the question of sending our students abroad, I may be excused for bringing up the topic again to substantiate some of my observations made in the letter of January 19 last. I am not without misgivings, though. The public may suspect some secret motive, in the nature of jealousy, behind my insinuations. Actually, I have no such private intentions. I am already over 40 years of age, with heavy enough family obligations to boot, permanently settled in oblivion as a middle school teacher trying to make both ends meet on a meager income. I am a realist enough not to 'dream' of going to America to do 'graduate' work.

It is reported that when the Korean Educational Mission was sent to the U. S. in the summer of 1946, the honorable members of the Commission were greatly impressed by the importance that educational heads in the U. S. laid on an extensive training for our students as a prerequisite to studying in America. I should be much enlightened if the Commission could show clear evidence of having improved our language-training program since their triumphant return. The Commission, of course, performed an excellent diplomatic service. But it is my opinion, crude as it may sound, that education neither begins nor ends with diplomacy. As far as I know, the American Language Institute is the only recognizable agency that has *tried* to come down to brass-tacks.

I venture to submit, however, that the Institute has not reaped a full enough harvest. For one thing, it tries to put too many things in one basket. This is partly due to the fact that the Institute is the successor to the English School established in April 1946 for the prime purpose of giving short courses in spoken English to the Korean employees in the Military Government. Even after its transference in October 1946 from the Foreign Affairs Section to the Department of Education, the work is still being carried on. Korean civil servants with proficiency in English are indeed as needed today as in the early days of the Military Government. But it can be fairly said that the immediate needs have now been met with to set the wheel turning. The Institute can now surely dispense with the lesser duties of giving English lessons to the Military Government clerks and employees. In this sense every GI is virtually on the staff of the Institute! The Institute should have other fish to fry.

Frequent contact with the Supervisor of the American Language Institute convinces me that other higher objectives are kept in view by the Institute, of which the most vital are:

(1) Training our students planning to study in the U. S. "to attain at least the average level of English proficiency of freshman classes in American colleges before going to study." I still adhere to the original conviction that these students should be selected on a strictly national basis by means of a state examination system, and that for some time to come the American Consulate should not issue visas to our students, however well connected or personally sponsored, unless they have the *final* approval of the Department of Education. As shown in his last letter by Vox Meditantis, Korean students are proving something of a nuisance and a laughing-stock in the American universities. Personal disgrace is nothing. What matters is national disgrace. As a Korean proverb says, a lizard can make the whole stream muddy.

(2) Bringing about a reform in the method of English teaching in our country. Who denies the urgent necessity of a reform in this field? The basic tenure of the Institute is sound. The question is, as in all reforms, how can it be brought about and propagated? I venture to submit the following proposals:

Absolute priority should be given to teachers rather than to young men and women who like to dabble in English because they think it genteel to speak it, or because they want to get jobs in the Government. If possible, the latter category should eventually be excluded from enrollment.

The Department of Education should arrange a shift system, without regard to vacation or term-time, whereby teachers of English throughout the country should receive an intensive course in the new method of English teaching.

The English lessons on the Korean wireless should be designed for students rather than the general public. The now familiar dallying with English over the radio is ineffectual in propagating the new method of language instruction.

If possible, some periodical publication should be sponsored by the Department of Education as an organ devoted to the propagation of new language teaching methods.

New methods of testing and examining should be introduced as well as new methods of teaching.

In propagating the new methodology, the art of patient persuasion is very much needed. Our teachers are in a vulnerable position, both technically and psychologically. Telling them off bluntly in so many words—no grammar, no phonetics, no this, and no that—will only scare them out of their wits and create hostility, rather than good results.

Yours etc.
Vox Clamantis

(Thursday, February 26, 1948, *The Seoul Times*)

Last Thoughts of a Dying Politician:
Or,
Sermon of the Body to the Soul
By Fabricius Lee

No, no. What's the use of whimpering at the last moment? Anybody would think, by the way you moan and groan, that you had the bullet-shot and the scalpel, and not me. Rather than eat your heart out with indignation against the cock-eyed world or with self-pity for your unrealized potentialities, you should comfort yourself with a feeling of relief that you should have been considered worthy of assassination. Supposing that we were to live to a ripe old age of three score and ten, would you guarantee that posterity would honor us the more for it, that our protracted existence shall have been worthwhile? Now that we have not much more to live, what's the use of just being preoccupied with the impact of present pain and regret?

You have bossed me all these years; and I rarely complained. It is now my turn to tell you one or two things, not emotional claptrap but downright plain sense. I don't wish to kick up a fuss at the last moment. Whether our past may have been full of ups and downs, our present transition from life into death must be such an unhurried process that it shall deceive Eternity itself momentarily. There must be a complete surrender of our past willfulness. In timeless eternity, 'will' as we understand it is non-existent. For what ultimately is the human will but a sort of race with time, a sort of impatience to hurry things up? It seems that all these years we've been working up to this momentous crisis, preparing for this *ritardando*. Calm down and retrace the dark alleys of experience. That's what we need at this moment.

It always struck me as odd that you should have taken up politics for a career. With your inborn restlessness, and your perpetual crying for resolution with the brute facts of the world, you might have fared better as a critical writer of some sort, had you chosen to discipline your intellect and imagination in another and more painstaking way. I always felt a little sorry for you, in the same way that I should have felt sorry for the politics of Brutus. What politics requires is a cold calculation coupled with a strong sense of facts, neither of which you had enough to see you through a crisis. Besides, your contempt for the mob was always too explicit for the liking of those, who, as far as politics are concerned, remain what they always have been precisely for the reason that they must be humored to their faces and exploited behind their backs. The public will resent any leader to be too ahead of the time: by all means denounce, but not to the extent of wounding the pride of the public and showing up the mortifying spectacle of their ignorance.

What? Ah yes, you always trot out that excuse. The thing about Father and Mother: Father dying in exile, after seven years' wandering beyond the northern frontier, penniless; starvation in the cold of February. Consumptive. Fleeing for some abortive attempt at rebellion against the corrupt monarchy. Leaving us, and Mother, for good at the age of eight. Years of bitter hardship for Mother among the narrow strips of land in the lonesome valley. Then coming to the city for making a living by needlework. Misery in our puberty. And then the turning point of our whole life, soon after the invasion of the enemy troops. Oppressive heat of the summer evening. Two unshaven soldiers coming into the house for water. Looking at Mother and me alternately. Then only a timid young lad of seventeen. After muttering something to each other, one of them gripping me by the arm and leading me out of the house, while the other stayed. The instinctive feeling of horror that chilled down my spine, and the image of pollution and mutilation flashing across your imagination. Both being confirmed by Mother's disheveled look half an hour after. . . . It is since then, you say, that you swore to become a politician to fight against any kind of tyrannous power or external authority. To this livelong day I cannot help feeling that this is all very heart-rending, but somewhat far-fetched. If you were so attached to Mother, and her defilement such a staggering shock, why did you stop me, as you did, from doing something desperate at the very moment that my arm was being gripped? I was ready to fly at the throat of the beast; but you immediately threw cold water on me. Doesn't it show up in a way your inability to face reality as reality? My constant grievance with you is that you so often let yourself deliberately be caught in the mesh of your own Misery Absolute. Why the hell restrain me from immediate action, knowing as you did that I loved Mother really?

It was the same kind of thing with marriage. You know how happy I was with our first marriage with the ballet-dancer. Her beautiful, lithe, and leopard-like body, which responded so perfectly to the demands of my senses, was a sufficient justification for all her license. Hang it all, sensuality is but another form of zest for life. You never had a deep enough understanding of her. Consider her untimely death. Death in childbirth is as terrible as anything that can befall a human being. As you and I sat silent beneath the shower of her fitful pain and curses, I felt as if the whole firmament was staggering and the rooftop falling upon us; but you never lost your equanimity, with your secret comments: "Humiliating, all very humiliating!" As time passed, we would lie with strange bedfellows at nights. I cannot say that I ever enjoyed being a 'client.' But what I disliked more was your Shakespearean rag of a morning hymn on such occasions: "The expense of spirit in a waste of shame," etc. Why did you have to rub it in like that? My suspicion of your lack of understanding for women, was confirmed when you launched us on a second marriage with the widow of a rich merchant. Marriage for policy, eh? By Jesu, anything under the sun can be rendered political, from marrying down to wearing a certain kind of moustache, provided, of course, that you are prepared to make the woman as insignificant as the moustache. She's been a better wife than you a husband.

I've told you these home truths so often that I am only wasting what little energy I've got left in proving what a die-hard you are. Some things in your career you've done with a brilliancy amounting almost to a flourish; other things you've made a mess of, rent where you should have cut. Some of your guesses have been prophetic; and some plain bigotry. Let posterity be the impartial judge. The only point I wish to drive home is this: you've always made everything in life a stepping-stone to something else. For instance, you would read poetry and draw a moral that fits beautifully with your politics; you'd look at a landscape and see a corrupted society behind; you'd meet a man for the first time, and say to yourself that he'll make a good private secretary, and so on. All very ingenious, but somehow the public will smell out your insincerity sooner or later. You cannot become a politician just by keenness of intellect, a talent for lying, or a clear head for organization—though these things will take you quite a long way—any more than you can succeed in love-making to a woman just by talking suavely; there come moments when one must put one's whole body and soul into whatever work one is doing. It is in such moments that inspired work is done; and who would deny that inspired work is what counts in life? If your political career had been really inspired and sincere, the public would have been palpably aware of your inspired-ness, and perhaps surrendered themselves in blind confidence. And perhaps you might not have been assassinated, though that depends assuredly on the extent of corruptibility to which humanity is capable of at one stretch of time.

As soon as I stop breathing, you and I part. I know the direction I'm going in—worm-ward, proving no exception to the golden lads and the chimneysweepers. I don't know where you'll be going. If, as the time-honored legend has it, you are to seek salvation, the Road of Humility, which is said to lead to the Land of Forgiveness, must be walked on hands and knees, on genuflection, as they say. My man, you have been proud sometimes, to my thinking. True, when one is surrounded with depravities, one is likely to be eaten away to the altitude of the Self, and choose to live in a tub as a Greek eccentric once did in protest against the world because it is hardly good enough to warrant a palace. But such willful pride will not bring salvation; nor will the heroics of one who thinks he can mend the world in one *coup de grace*. The only thing to do is—what? I'm talking more like you than myself? All right, then, I'll shut up.

Hush, I hear footsteps. Wife and kid are coming. Poor creatures. Coming to weep over us, or for them. Let's not put up a poor show in front of them. Pity the living. Look at them, look! But for them, I should have been rather glad of this sudden death. Nay, in spite of them, I am myself rather glad of this sudden death.

(***Writer's Note:*** This is an entirely imaginary piece of writing, and has no bearing whatsoever on any of the Korean personalities, living or dead.)

(Monday, December 29, 1947, *The Seoul Times*)

Editorial Restatement

It is an empirical fact that fools rush in where angels fear to tread. In assuming the heavy responsibility of *The Seoul Times,* the editor feels it his first duty to confess his diffidence for the assigned work, knowing himself to be ill adapted, whether by aptitude or by discipline, to the world of journalism as such. If there is any justification at all, it is that Korea is at best a happy land of amateurs, and that *The Seoul Times* is a thoroughly local paper, with all the forgivable defects of provincialism.

For some time this paper has been generally assumed as being a bore and something of a political nuisance; it has not been entirely exempt from the fault of Atticus, whose inclination is to "Damn with faintest praise, assent with civil leer, And without sneering, teach the rest to sneer."

As to the paper being a nuisance, it should be stated clearly that the function of *The Seoul Times* does not lie in mud-slinging or in entertaining any sinister intentions, or for that matter, in whitewashing; for the simple reason that its indulgent readers, small in number and select in quality, are quite immune from propaganda in so far as they would rather have factual and exact information rather than its willful interpretation.

As to the paper being a bore, efforts will be made, within the circumscribed limit of poor English and of provincialism, to make it as readable as possible by endeavoring to give a true and balanced picture of the life lived by our people.

The Korean people, like any other, do not live all the time by current politics and economics alone. Important as news-reporting is, it is considered to be not wholly out of place for a paper of this kind to give periodical reviews of the social and cultural aspects of our national life, both past and present.

(Friday, December 10, 1948, *The Seoul Times*)

Subtle Corridors of History

When the late Neville Chamberlain returned from the Munich Agreement in late September 1938, the first words that he spoke on landing at a London airport were the words of Hotspur, "out of this nettle, danger, we pluck this flower, safety," punctuated with all the emphasis of "try, try, and try again."

The unification of divided Korea has already been tried three times officially and on an international basis, by the two Joint Commission Conferences of January 16—February 5, 1946 and May 21—October 18, 1947, and by the U. N. Temporary Commission since its first meeting at Seoul on January 12 this year in its praiseworthy efforts to carry out the General Assembly resolution of November 14, 1947. And now it has got to be tried again for the simple reason that the cause of unification is a life-and-death issue for the people of Korea.

The new resolution as adopted by the U. N. Political Committee on December 8 last is another decisive turn in the subtle corridors of our national history. From all juridical, diplomatic, and emotional considerations, it must be hailed as an event for jubilation.

Ultimately, however, it depends on the individual temperament how you take to the jubilation. Unless one is an optimist, who by description is a person who says, "So far, so good!" as he passes by the third story after jumping from a four-story building in his happy attempt to commit suicide; unless, that is, one is born only to see the rosy side of things, one cannot but take the jubilation in a controlled mood. With all the due emotions of heartfelt gratitude to our friendly nations, we must not gloss over the facts of the given situation, home and abroad, that are staring us in the face. The inevitable six votes. Harrowing arguments at cross-purposes. The eternal syncopation and tautology. The anticipated fear that North Korea may well slam its doors against the coming Commission, even though it "is authorized to travel, consult and observe throughout Korea." The further fear that the Commission will have no juridical body in the north to carry on consultations with, after the withdrawal of the Soviet occupying forces by December 30. The probable delay incurred by consultations on the part of the Commission with the interim committee "with respect to the discharge of its duties in the light of developments and within the terms of this resolution." The justifiable anxiety arising from the fear that *some* Koreans may not cooperate with the Commission, even though *all* Koreans are called upon "to afford every assistance and facility to the Commission in the fulfillment of its responsibilities." And so on *ad infinitum*.

We have had no shade of a doubt that the U. N. General Assembly has "regard to its resolution" of November 1947, and is "mindful" of the unaccomplished unification of Korea. Nor have we ever doubted that our Republican Government is the only "lawful" government as established by elections observed by the Temporary Commission. The greater issues, however, of the unity of jurisdiction throughout Korea, of the integration of all our security forces, of the removal of the present political, economic and social barriers, and of the withdrawal of the occupying forces at the earliest "practicable" date, all are still in a state of suspended irresolution.

Meanwhile, the Korean people, being great hopers by circumstance, if not by birth, will go on hoping with our implicit faith in the goodwill of the U. N. and the endeavors of our Government, we, the people, will go on "living and partly living." It may well be that history "gives when the attention is distracted/ And what she gives, gives with such supple confusion/ That the giving famishes the craving." Let us hope not.

(Vox Meditantis)

(Monday, December 13, 1948, *The Seoul Times*)

Moral Burden of the Aid Agreement

The two highlights of the week's news have undoubtedly been, on the political level, the U. N. General Assembly's approval of our Republic on December 12 by 48 votes to 6, and on the economic, the U. S.-Korean Agreement on Aid, which was signed on December 10 and ratified by the National Assembly on December 14 with an unanimous vote of 84 to 0. A greater measure of success could not have been attained for the political stabilization and economic rehabilitation of our Republic.

The general response of the Assembly to the Aid Agreement bears some comparison, upon recollection, to that awarded to the U. S.-Korean Agreement on Initial Financial and Property Settlement, signed exactly three months earlier on September 11 and given the Assembly's consent on September 18 by 78 votes to 28. Though the earlier agreement was part, and that an important part, of the transfer of governmental functions, in which we had more to gain than to lose, some 20 odd Assemblymen had shown an exceptional degree of nervous excitement, motivated by the fear of the so-called "infringement of sovereignty," and thereby gave the probable impression to our foreign observers that most Koreans were still suffering from that incurable disease of xenophobia which had been observed in us by Hendrik Hamel as early as 1653–1666, or else that we had something of the dog in the manger in our national traits! The same, somewhat over-sentimental reason was trotted out by more or less the same number of representatives in their recent debates on the Aid Agreement.

The real point of difference, in effect, lies in the fact that one was passed by 78 votes to 28, and the other by 84 to 0. Put in plainer terms of human nature, the 28 votes signify that one never likes to pay old debts, especially when one is as hard up as our Republic is, and the vote of 0, that we vitally need sustenance "to divert economic crisis, promote national economy, and insure domestic tranquility."

Plain sense dictates that we cannot go on being 'moral' and talk about 'sovereignty' on a hungry stomach. Plain sense further dictates that we must *not* forget to be really 'moral' after a fuller stomach. Both the Government and the people must live up to the responsibilities attendant upon the aid, which *qua* responsibilities are eventually of a moral nature rather than material. It might be asked, moral responsibilities to whom?

The answer is obvious: primarily to our people, of course.

An effective enforcement of the Agreement will call for our highest exercise of economic insight and administrative alertness. Most of the important articles in the Agreement pertain to the obligations on the part of our Government, notably Articles 2, 4, and 5. A well-planned program of collection and distribution of cereal products, a controlled monetary policy, a long-range plan of import requirements and export availabilities, to mention but a few from a layman's point of view, are alone enough to rack the first-rate brains of our country. If we start squandering the money, it will not be long before we become aware of ourselves wallowing in a debt far and away beyond our national budget.

The success or the failure of the program will ultimately depend upon the justice, with which we procure our material and technical demands of production, rather than of immediate consumption, the efficiency with which we effectuate an equitable distribution, and above all, the far-sighted vision with which we spend the special deposit in our National Bank. In the reciprocal execution of the aid, all priority must be given to the development of our export potentialities, whether in mineral resources, rice, or marine products, and to the implementation of power supplies. (For no amount of bone and flesh will be able to move without the circulation of blood.) To these double ends the two Governments concerned, and the individual technicians who have been or will be invited, must devote their fullest energy.

Besides attending to our power engineers, manufacturers, farmers, miners, and fishermen, we must look to the behavior of the two port authorities. For at the present state of affairs, foreign ships in and out of our ports seem to be putting up with a great deal of bullying impudence from half a dozen or more organized bodies. Never in the history of civilized foreign trade have 'youth' organizations been known to partake in the ordering of loading or unloading cargoes! The test of Anglo-Saxon patience is clearly not provided for in the Agreement. In any case, it rests not in our power to measure their capacity for putting up with trials and difficulties where trade interests are at stake. They are known to be finished taskmasters in that virtue. (The Woolgatherer)

(Friday, December 17, 1948, *The Seoul Times*)

Military Training at Schools

Recently our Ministries of Defense and Education have announced that some 260 gymnastics teachers in middle schools and colleges are scheduled to receive a 40 days' course in military training at our Taenŭng Military Academy, beginning from December 23. Coming back with the rank of sub-lieutenant, they will, in the capacity of commissioned officers attached to schools, start teaching military drill to our upper grade boys of middle schools and college students. The immediate purpose of this measure, as announced by the Government, is fourfold: (1) "solution of the critical situation" in our national affairs, (2) "defense of the fatherland," (3) "cultivation of the national spirit," and (4) "discipline in the organized spirit of submission."

We may roughly consider the first two objectives to be issues of national defense, and the other two, of education. Where such vital issues are at stake, however, we should stretch our foresight and hindsight to the widest range and to the minutest detail before arriving at any decisive policy.

Assuming that this plan is carried out both fully and satisfactorily, we can expect the following statistical results in rough estimation. The total number of secondary school boys, as of May 31, 1948, is 173,577. If, on the minimal scale, one fifth of them receive military training, the number will be over 34,700. The number of male college students as of the same date is 18,093. Even if we assume no increase of students since last March, the potential total of students receiving military training will be roundly estimated at over 52,800. This is a large item in manpower, though in itself it can hardly lessen the urgent necessity to speed up the strengthening of our standing army. Student bodies, however large, can never be substituted for the latter; they will always remain as extras, and likely to prove something of a deadweight in case of real emergency. A motley company of half-baked youth organizations and student bodies may well serve a political purpose, but not a military one.

The moral danger of student mobilization is inherent in the very fact that they are so easy to mobilize, physically or mentally. The immediate motive for deciding to incorporate military drill in school curricula is no doubt the sorrowful fact that many students, in a fit of mass hysteria, participated in the recent Yŏsu and Sunch'ŏn riots.

If, however, it is communism that we are up against, we must decide whether military drill is really the best educational method of dissuading students from coming under its influence. Is discipline in "organized action" and "submissive spirit" after all the best way to oppose communism? It is an established fact that communism in action makes full use of both. It may indeed be argued with some justice that one of the many reasons why communism comes so readily to our "younger generation" is their habituation to authoritarian discipline in the hands of the Japanese.

Military training at schools is not a new thing in this country. Any male Korean above the age of 18 and below 35 is already familiar with it from first-hand experience. But what most Koreans do not realize is the caution with which the Japanese enforced it in their own schools long before they introduced it into ours. Human memory being deceptive, one is apt to think that it was a feverish attempt, adopted overnight by the militarists, to serve their aims of aggression. Facts prove that it was a slow and painstaking process. By the Imperial Decree No. 135 of 1925, it was first ordained that officers in active service should be attached to schools of the secondary and higher levels to give instructions in military drill. Ten years later, in 1935, War Department Ordinance No. 22 sanctioned those officers to examine students before graduation and to issue certificates to those who should satisfy a strict standard, granting them certain privileges upon entering military service by conscription. In 1941, a joint ordinance (No. 1) of the War and Education Departments gave detailed regulations relative to the application of the said Imperial Decree. And it was not until 1942 that the Government-General enforced specific curricula in military drill in Korean schools (Instruction No. 29). These are but a few of the key dates that mark the slow evolution of the program undertaken by the supposedly quick-tempered Japanese militarists. Full twenty years they had exerted to reap a harvest at the sacrifice of education, and the harvest they reaped in 1945 was far different from what they had expected back in 1925.

The case of Japan is here cited not because of the fear that our Republic may indulge in any dreams of 'aggression,' which is absurd, but because of the misgivings that expediency, resolved in haste, may not always hit the target in aim. Communism, in theory and action, has a step-tight 'doctrine' behind it. If our purpose lies in the undermining of that doctrine, we must go about it by a painstaking process of enlightenment, moral and intellectual. A string of abstract words and nebulous concepts, however full of good intentions, will prove no saving grace in unraveling the intricacies of a given 'crisis' when it comes. Unless due precaution is taken in educating our younger generation in the spirit of voluntary cooperation rather than compulsory submission, mental equanimity rather than blind emotionalism, moral conviction rather than orgiastic hysteria, unless the Ministry of Education retains the final casting vote in matters relating to the development of the civic sense in the younger generation, we might expect an aggravation rather than a "solution of the critical situation" in our national affairs. (Vox Cassandrae)

(Tuesday, December 21, 1948, *The Seoul Times*)

Apology for Mayor Yun

It is refreshing for once in a long while to see a gentleman educated in England take up a responsible job in the administration of our unwieldy society. Much of the credit and the discredit of the three years of Military Government go to our American-educated Koreans, who seem more inclined to live in the sparkling overtones of life than in its drab undertones. By some irony of circumstance, for which America cannot be held responsible, we have witnessed several cases of excessive flourishes, of men who scorn to come down to the brass-tacks of administration because of their firm conviction that life should be spelt with a capital L. Too often they have misconstrued the virtue of denial and refusal, including self-denial and self-refusal, because they have not been fully aware of the two-edged truth of the dictum of a French poet: "As for living, our servants will do that for us." They claimed to be masters where they should have been servants, and vice versa.

One thing we can say for Mayor Yun: he will not make flourishes. Strutting histrionics simply are not in his temperament. A man of few words, he neither wears his heart on his sleeve, nor talks through his hat.

Nor would he indeed be permitted to make high-sounding promises as Mayor of Seoul. There is no glamour in his assigned task, because Seoul is far from being a glamorous city. Much of the Mayor's energy will be spent in the thankless task of endeavoring to give the citizens as few excuses for grumbling as possible, seeing to it that they do not go too hungry or cold, or over-taxed, looking after their sanitation, that the streets are clean and the sewerage working. Like a true servant of the people, he did not talk in abstract terms at his first press conference: he merely said that the maintenance of the city would require much money but that he would start from the least costly job of getting rid of the city garbage. That, to say the least, is being more to the point than promising to distribute candies.

One only hopes that his fundamental humility of spirit will permeate down to the last clerk of the City Hall and the District Offices, not to mention the Metropolitan Police. One has reason enough to fear that his subordinates may well abuse his 'sincerity' and 'honest endeavors.'

We make this apology for Mayor Yun with a clear conscience, because we know that he will be the most embarrassed person in town to hear of it. A reader with a distorted imagination might perhaps be misled to think that *The Seoul Times* is flattering the Mayor for some ulterior motive. It should, however, be made perfectly clear to our readers that *The Seoul Times* is not getting a penny out of the City or the Mayor, be it material or immaterial; nor does it mean to for a good long time to come!

(*The Disinterested Citizen*)

(Wednesday, December 22, 1948, *The Seoul Times*)

Absent Thee From Felicity Awhile

A year ago, when the U. N. Temporary Commission first arrived in Seoul on January 8, the people of Korea were wallowing in the Inferno of political dissonance and hysteria. The duties incumbent upon the Commission was to deliver this unhappy people out of the Inferno through the tortuous ways of eventual salvation. A year later, today, when the second Commission is arriving in Seoul, we find ourselves in the middle cycles of the Purgatorio, waiting for the days of promised beatitude in unification.

The Commission will be proudly aware of a great task accomplished; and yet a greater task remains to be achieved. They will further recall that last year's journey through the Inferno was more dramatic, because it was more crowded with human passions. This year's course through the Purgatorio will be more strained and less 'interesting,' because it will consist of the technicalities involving the subtleties of the Paradiso of a united Korea.

No Korean has to be told that Korea cannot long endure the present division of the country. We have put up with the plight for three and half years and have almost reached a stage of lethargic habituation, punctuated, however, with nightmarish fits of emotional frenzy arising from the tension of the grim reality. Our welcome of the Commission this time may not be so vociferous as last year. But we assume it tacitly that somehow the Commission must resolve us of our well-grounded fears. It will no longer serve our turn to say that North Korea has again slammed its doors against the Commission and that, therefore, the only thing to do is to shrug one's shoulders and bite at one's fingernails.

We recall the conclusion of the Second Report of the last Commission, approved by the Political Committee of the General Assembly on December 8 last, that although effective jurisdiction over the North is not exercised by the Republican Government, "this Government does provide a basis from which it may be possible to proceed to unification by peaceful methods of negotiation at least in the economic field where such unity is of vital importance." Here, at least, is a good place to start, with an economic unification, if not a political one. And we doubt not the Commission will lend its good offices with the greatest of patience in bringing together the two obstinate halves of our divided Korea.

Distasteful as it may be to admit of the realities, the internecine warfare, which the people and the Commission have feared all along, has already started in the form of riots and guerilla warfare in the hills and provincial towns of the South. Such a state of affairs is hardly to the credit of our Government, and certainly a source of wanton sufferings for the innocent people. That is why, even apart from the realization of unity in jurisdiction, the North and the South must come to some sort of terms by hook or by crook.

It is further felt that an atmosphere of orderliness will prevail to a much greater extent than last year in the coming consultations of the Commission with the Government. This certainly is a matter of some relief. But the Commission must not be satisfied with the official side of things only; they should at the same time be fully aware of the feelings and desires of the people as a whole in effecting the proposed measures reuniting this country. (I.L.)

(Thursday, February 3, 1949, *The Seoul Times*)

One Man's Comment

One of the undisputed advantages of democracy over dictatorship, be it Hirohitoite, Hitlerite, or Stalinite, is that we can poke fun at anybody we like, from God and the President down to the lowliest chimney-sweeper, provided it is kept within the decency of human comedy. And it usually happens that the easiest person to bait is the President because of the contrarious fact that he is created human and yet, especially in countries like our own, he is revered as the infallible [exponent] of oracular 'fiat.'

[I know I] should be the last [person to be led on] to detract President [Rhee's supreme] merits as head of our state. I would not, however, count myself among those that protest that the best way to serve him is by apotheosizing him. For one thing it would not be democratic, and for another, it would prove most tiresome for the President himself, a born fighter, to have suppliant choirs of the 'angelic' singing laudatory hymns day in and day out. I make this observation because I feel certain that the President himself would welcome any amount of fresh air in the form of a voice of minor dissent.

At a recent press talk with Mr. John Latrash, UP correspondent, our President is reported to have expressed the following views regarding the recent political developments in China. Asked as to how a coalition or a communist government would affect our Republic, he answered that we would not be affected "except in moral aspects," adding: " I do not believe the Chinese people will accept a puppet government and remain under it very long. Under all circumstances our communist neighbors should strictly keep out of our boundary. If not, we will have to push them out and go into Manchuria to protect the large colonies of our nationals there. Nearly a million of them are mostly nationalists, who need our protection."

It is particularly after reading the last two sentences that I feel like inserting a harmless ejaculation: "Oh but Mr. President! You're not thinking of sending an expeditionary force into Manchuria, are you?"

We in Korea of course would not, and could not, go out of our way to curry favor with a red China. But a fact is a fact, and cannot be brushed away with a curt nod. The tragic downfall of China's hero of the century is an event of such significance for the whole of the Far East that it deserves our closest and most dispassionate scrutiny. However great our attachment to the retired Generalissimo may be, we must make it perfectly clear to ourselves that politics is not a thing governed by the familiar axiom of "old books, old wine, and old friends." Why should the consensus of world opinion, which gave full support, moral and material, to Chiang until a couple of years ago, decide now to drop him like a hot plate? Thereby surely hangs a tale.

The President also speaks of a 'puppet' government in China before such a government is even formed. Much as I can appreciate his dislike of Communism, I still feel that we had better wait a little and see. AP reports from London that Britain's Ambassador to China, Sir Ralph Stevenson, will remain in Nanking and not follow the Chinese nationalist government to Canton. Is this because His Britannic Majesty's Government goes in for 'puppet' governments?

China and Korea are bound to each other almost by a 'natural piety.' The Chinese people do not become our friends or foes just because of a change of government leadership. We must ask ourselves why the most conservative of the Oriental peoples should decide to accept this change of leadership. If communists in China were made in the manner of Genesis: God said, "Let there be communists in the land of the Blue Dragon," the story might have a different cue; but the Chinese people, being realists to the core, don't move that way.

That is why we ourselves should learn a great lesson from this tragic end of China's hero. Rather than worry ourselves to distraction over our poor nationals in Manchuria, who are supposed to be crying for our 'protection,' we should devote our full energies to solidifying our own little Republic as a worthy bridgehead of democracy. And it might not be out of place in this context to remind ourselves of the ironical implication of our traffic rule, which phenomenally is an unfortunate but apt description of the general drift of the Korean people at the present moment: "Pedestrians to the left; Motor-cars and wagons to the right." (Iseen Loo)

(Friday, February 4, 1949, *The Seoul Times*)

Kit-Cat Club Views on UNCOK

Writer's Note: This is a purely imaginary dialogue, and has no reference to any actual personalities, Korean or otherwise.

B: You are quite right, C, in recalling the words of the U. N. Secretary-General Trygve Lie in his message to the new Commission on Korea, that it has taken upon itself one of the hardest and most delicate jobs that can be handled within the province of the U. N. But it seems to me that harping on this fact of difficulty will neither help the Korean people nor facilitate the work of the Commission.

A: Of course not. It is just one more aspect of that great challenge which democratic principles, as embodied in the U. N. Charter, have to face the world over. This struggle against Sovietism—I wouldn't even call it communism, because it is too generous a term for that specific type of political monopolism—is such a life-and-death issue for the very survival of civilization that one must be as ruthless as our very opponents. For it goes without saying that Sovietism thrives on leniency and hesitation.

D: I am an ignoramus, and have neither 'erudition' nor 'culture' to back me up in sanctioning me to use such ambiguous terms as 'democratic principles,' 'Sovietism,' 'political monopolism,' or 'survival of civilization.' A is at liberty, of course, to be as ruthless as he wishes in accusing communism of all the heinous crimes under the sun; presumably he has his grounds for doing so. But I do know this much: that the mere sound of 'civilization' does not convince me that I am living in the best of all possible worlds. I know little about 'political liberty'; but I do know what it means to have friends who are being hunted down the rat's alley. Nor do I know anything about 'economic equality,' but I for one am certain about the sensation of going on a hungry stomach, breathing the air of corruption. Call me what you will. I have not got the patience to talk about the prospects of the recently arrived Commission. They are not a host of angels and saints; they would presumably put their own government interests before those of the Korean people—I repeat, the people. So you can drop me altogether out of this fruitless discussion. Bootless talking is about the one great virtue that all Koreans seem to have; but it so happens that I wouldn't care to indulge in it myself.

C: You are deliberately falsifying the picture, D. With the exception of die-hards like you, we know for a fact that the U. N. Commission is not here to represent 'any sectional or national interests.' The saving grace of the Commission lies after all in the fact that it is essentially in the nature of a Good Offices Commission that it has assumed its activities since the end of January last. That is why we cannot afford to take such a disinterested attitude as you do. Can you honestly put up any longer with the present division of our country? Something has got to be done about this.

D: And what is that? Is talking going to help? Not on our level, surely!

C: I wouldn't be so dogmatic. The strongest pillar of the U. N., after all, as the Chairman of the Commission pointed out in his statement of policy (February 12), is 'an enlightened public opinion.' Now I grant you that ours may not be 'an enlightened public opinion,' but at least it is a public opinion, or some aspects of it. And I submit that it is our moral duty as Koreans to help the Commission by offering whatever opinion, good or bad, that we may have, even though our Office of Public Information told us some time ago (January 29) to pay particular attention to our p's and q's regarding the problem of unification.

D: What about 'an enlightened private opinion' or 'an underground one'? Don't bother to answer. Good day to you all. (*Exit*)

A: He flatters himself! As if we would even bother to answer him!

B: Come, A! We are not here to give vent to our ill humors. "Judge not, that ye be not judged."

A: Of course not, except that it would prove futile enough to cast such pearls as the words of the Gospel before a swine.

C: Or let me put it this way by quoting the words of the Chairman of the Commission at the Mass Meeting on February 12: "Stagnation and ignorance lead often to stubborn bitterness and from there the stage to conflict is all too easy." But coming back to our point, what in your opinion, A, can the Commission do to bring its high mission to a successful conclusion?

A: Speaking as an amateur—and we are a nation of amateurs—I myself attach much importance to the conclusion of the Report of the Temporary Commission as approved by the General Assembly, that our Republican Government "does provide a basis from which it may be possible to proceed to unification. . . ." That is why I felt greatly encouraged to hear the Principal Secretary of the Commission announce over the radio on February 9, that the Commission "does not desire to be a passive body but intends to pursue an active policy." This point was further stressed at the Public Meeting, at which it was urged that the task of the Commission, being in the nature of a continuation of the work of the Temporary Commission, was to bring about unified independence in our country "on the basis already established." I therefore feel fully justified in believing that the Commission can, and should, base its practical measures on the fact of recognition of our Republican Government by the General Assembly.

C: I agree with the main tenure of your argument, though I do object to your use of the word 'recognition.' I am no student of international law, but as far as I have read of the U. N. Charter and the text of the General Assembly Resolution of December 12 last, I have not come across the word "to recognize" or its noun form. Considerable confusion, if it be such, has been caused in this respect by the fact that we Koreans have only one word in current use to signify the content of Paragraph 2 of the said Resolution and the 'recognition' in the narrow sense of our Government by such individual governments as the British, the French, or the American. In the course of the Mass Meeting on February 12, for instance, this word cropped up several times as used in the first sense. The message to Secretary-General Lie spoke of our Republic of Korea as having been "recognized by the decision of the General Assembly." The Chairman of the National Assembly expressed the view in this address of welcome that the duties incumbent upon the Commission was "first to induce all things to surrender under the Government of the Republic of Korea, and second to fill up the 100 vacant seats in the National Assembly." It was announced also at the Meeting that the Commission was here "to lend its good offices for the unification of Korea under the Republic of Korea." From such announcements of semi-official weight, it is easy to surmise that the people may be under the general impression that the Commission is somehow 'accredited' to our Government—which is nonsense. I hasten to add that the Commission will be free to interpret such minor points as it pleases, and not necessarily as we please; but North Korea might make a ready use of it for the purpose of prejudicing the legitimate functions of the Commission.

A: I am not in a mood to quibble about the juridical interpretation of words. What I want to drive at is that I attach a great importance to the activities of Sub-Committee II, which is particularly directed to "study the development of representative government in Korea." Without prejudicing the honorable aims of Sub-Committee I, I still think that this Sub-Committee is up against a blank wall. Even if, for the sake of argument, Kim Il-sung does admit the Commission, or part of it, into the North, he will do nothing but impose his own terms, which will not only be unacceptable to our Republican Government but also thwart the very work of the Commission. Common sense further dictates that our Government, which has been declared 'lawful' by U. N., cannot be treated on an equal basis with the puppet regime of the North.

B: Your argument is tantamount to saying that 'the development of representative government' can legitimately be paraphrased as the 'extension of our Republican Government.' This might be feasible if the Commission had not created a Sub-Committee I, with specific instructions to explore all possible means of contacting with the North. I myself put more emphasis on Sub-Committee I; or if that is begging the question, let me say that I put *equal* emphasis on the two committees, upon whose interdependent activities the ultimate success or the failure of the Commission depends.

Your interpretation, carried to its logical conclusion, has one serious danger, namely, a headlong plunge into internecine warfare. Recently I came upon an American magazine, which reported a statement by one of our former ministers to AP on December 18 last year. He is reported to have said: "The minute the [Russian] occupation force leaves, we recognize the existence of no government above the 38th Parallel. We intend to extend our authority to that lost territory, and we want to do it peacefully. But if the people in North Korea resist the authority of the lawful Government, then we must conquer them." In the U. N. Charter we came across such words as 'negotiation,' 'enquiry,' 'mediation,' 'conciliation,' 'recommendation,' 'arbitration,' 'judicial settlement,' 'resort to regional agencies,' etc.; but we do not meet with words like 'conquest.' I am not implying that Koreans as a whole or in part are entertaining the thought of resorting to armed conflict for the purpose of unification. I do urge, however, that the work of Sub-Committee I is, if not a prerequisite to, at least an integrate part of, the study of "the development of representative government in Korea." You remember, in this connection, how the British Government recognized our Republican Government? Mr. Holt, then *chargé d'affaires*, writing to our acting minister of foreign affairs on January 19, said that Britain had recognized our "Republic as an independent sovereign state, whose territory is that part of Korean peninsula in which free elections were held under the observation of the U. N. Temporary Commission."

A: You are unwittingly distorting my meaning, B; I never said, "*Delenda est Carthago.*" I am merely saying that the General Assembly Resolution of last December is a decisive step forward to the goal of unified independence of Korea, and that the present Commission is here to find out with great caution where the next step may be placed. And being a realist, I still feel skeptical about the sincerity of Kim Il-sŏng's regime. They will have no scruples whatsoever in undermining the goodwill of the Commission and the security of our Republic. For aught we know, they may suddenly change their tactics, lift the iron curtain, to let the Commission in. And let us suppose, just for the sake of argument, that a general election by our own Election Law is duly held under supervision of the Commission. It is quite fair to suppose that at least 50 seats out of 100 will go to the very communists dyed in the wool. And think what tricks those 50 can play up in the National Assembly. It would be a nightmare of a republic, which has enough troubles already as it is. That is why we must guard jealously our 'lawful' rights as vested upon us by the General Assembly Resolution. We have three choices before us: Seoul *and* Pyŏng-yang; and Seoul *or* Pyŏng-yang, which means either two Seoul's or two Pyŏng-yang's. The first situation, as we have it today, is intolerable enough; but to have two Pyŏng-yang's would be a case of jumping from the frying pan into the fire. If we cannot have the best, we must choose the next best, and wait for the turn of the world tide. Korea is after all only one aspect of the world political crisis, or as the Indian delegate reminded us the other day, of a spiritual crisis for the whole of mankind.

C: For a realist, as you maintain you are, A, that to my mind is a fatalistic assumption to make. Things political must be kept strictly on the political level, and things Korean must not, if we can possibly help it, be raised to the level of humanity in general. Human reason is apt to be deceptive in that it flits about between two seeming opposites, the fear of the objective and the glorification of the subjective. Politically speaking, the Pyŏng-yang regime seems to be afraid of the will of the people, and at the same time, to revel in its self-righteousness. And who knows? The same might also be true of our Republican Government. By a series of historical accidents, we Koreans have unfortunately had little opportunity of realizing true personal freedom in the bilateral sense of political and economic equality. We know that it takes time and trial to exempt ourselves from the ordeal of autocratic governments; so the people are inclined to put up with them in docile resignation. We hear much of the ideological differences of North and South. But I doubt whether such differences are really found in the people as much as in the institutions that are supposed to reflect the will of the people and to look after their interests. To my mind, the will of the people has never been divided by what the Philippine delegate refers to as "that imaginary line." And here the Sub-Committee I can be of some help. Study the facts as they are, not as they ought to be, by coming down to the 'popular' level. On the political level, which presupposes definite 'interests' to protect, it is quite likely that the present Commission will not be able to go beyond the stage reached by the Temporary Commission. But on the social and cultural levels, the Commission might achieve some degree of success if it exercised enough patience and wisdom to consult with Koreans on a wider scope and variety than last year. Speaking bluntly, I should say that the man in the street, whether of Seoul or of Pyŏng-yang, is not concerned much with the mud-slinging debate over who should become his boss, so long as he is convinced that his will be an honest boss.

A: You are climbing up the ladder from the wrong end. How can you solve social, economic, and cultural problems without solving the political? You are essentially a dreamer.

C: I never pretended to be anything else but a dreamer.

A: Though your argument sounds persuasive enough, C, it is both impracticable and unauthorized. You seem to insist that the Commission should, without any regard to the two already existing governments, somehow base its judgment on "the freely expressed will" of the people—of those, as you say, who are not actually concerned with the protection of 'power' as such. There is no judicial way of knowing "the freely expressed will of the people," other than by an election. And we had it last May. On that rests the whole fabric of our Republic and the basis of the General Assembly's Resolution. Deny the validity of that election, and you deny our very Constitution. Furthermore, the so-called will of the people is an unruly thing, having no significance unless expressed by its delegated spokesman. And Heaven knows we in Korea have enough of those self-styled 'spokesmen' and self-appointed 'leaders.' The time for 'provisional' governments for Korea has passed. What is the unearthly use of going back on our one and the only 'lawful' government?

B: Perhaps I can answer that point better than C. No conscientious person like C would entertain any thought of denying the validity of our May election or the lawfulness of our government. It is only that the task of unification, as assumed by the Commission, requires the voluntary co-operation of the whole nation—nothing more and nothing less. The removal of the 38th Parallel is both a world issue and a national one. That is why the General Assembly "calls upon member states concerned, the Government of the Republic of Korea, and all Koreans to afford every assistance and facility to the Commission." It would be vanity on the part of our government to think that it can assume the *whole* responsibility of unification. The government could of course appoint governors for the five northern provinces, thinking that such a measure would help to unite Korea! To my mind it is nothing more than a case of *"La province, c'est moi!"* if such an axiom were possible. And it would be presumptuous on the part of the people to think that unification could be achieved *only* by their efforts, though some veteran politicians are a bit over-confident in this respect. Some common ground of compromise, with honor to everyone concerned—U. N., America, Russia, our Republican Government, the Pyŏng-yang regime, and the people of North and South—must be sought for by the symphonic genius of the Commission. By some such joint labor of love only can the work of unification be brought to a happy end. The Commission has got to work in two directions simultaneously: officially to bring about a peaceful negotiation between our Republican Government and the Pyŏng-yang regime, and unofficially by consulting with as many individuals and representatives of political, economic, social and cultural organizations as possible. This does not mean, however, that the Commission will best conduct its work by disregarding the status of our Republican Government as defined in the General Assembly Resolution. The chairman's statement of policy at the opening meeting on February 12 leaves no shadow of a doubt as to this unwarrantable fear. He clearly stated: "The Commission will bear in mind the status of the Government of the Republic of Korea as defined in the General Assembly Resolution."

A: Your argument sounds like a piece of circular reasoning.

C: The Korean problem is a vicious circle in any case. It depends ultimately on the top policy of Washington and Moscow. In the meantime, it is we who are suffering on the wheel of fire. And do we feel any the wiser for having sat through this argument? Perhaps D is right after all in anticipating the futility of bootless talking on our level.

(Tuesday, February 22–Friday, February 25, 1949, *The Seoul Times*)

Thoughts after the Funeral Service of Mrs. Underwood (March 22)

The visible expression of deep remorse on all the faces, celebrated and unknown, that were gathered in the small Sae-mun-an Church; and the droning solemnity of the voices that delivered the orations in humble tribute to the deceased lady; but "*Cui Bono?*" as the tag would say. Can noble sentiments exonerate us from the deed?

For, indeed, what is at stake is not sorrow as such but humiliation. The unfortunate death of Mrs. Underwood marks another milestone on the downward path of moral degradation that our society has been following palpably these several years. To think that 'Liberation' and 'Independence' and 'Representative Government' should occasionally be spelt with bullet shots of assassins is to be reminded of the fact that our so-called cultural heritage, which we so readily trot out with pomp and satisfaction, is no guarantee against cant and humbuggery.

If it were purely a matter of personal loss, one could afford to accept it in a mood of sober restraint. But to kill and bury with our own hands a lady who had known and loved our people and country, root, fruit and blossom, is to betray our very memory of the Underwood family and to pour upon our heads the indictment of "ingratitude, that marble-hearted fiend." Murder is murder, whether it be by accident or by calculation. And it is hardly the cue for any Korean, including Miss Mo, to comment thereon. (I.L.)

(Wednesday, March 23, 1949, *The Seoul Times*)

Home Thought From Abroad

By Iseen Loo, Our Imaginary Correspondent in London (March 10)

The more I attend the Commons debates here in Westminster, the more I am driven to confess a deep-rooted apprehension for the actual working of democracy at home.

Are we still flinging about on the rostrum of the National Assembly those well-worn rhetorical phrases that any college boy in a 'soap-box' mood can trot out with pat efficiency? Do our government officials still indulge in the innocent conviction that democracy is a religion of 'the heart,' when it is really a creed or stubborn fact and levelheaded reason? Do our Assemblymen still think that each member is party to himself? Do our ministers and bureau chiefs still live in the world of make-believe that the sum total of administration lies first and foremost in personnel appointment?

Such are the thoughts, ineffectual as they are, that distract my memory as I walk out of the Commons debates that invariably bear all the earmarks of enlightenment: orderliness, an absence of pomposity, sudden turns of humor by which the attacker and the attacked meet unexpectedly on the human level, and the tacit understanding of team-work.

But I moralize. Not that a bit of moralizing would hurt the Korean public. I have in mind two such recent debates, of which I might do well to give a brief account for the benefit of our own society. Since the current political problems of England are only distantly related to ours in Korea, I will choose from social topics that have a common human appeal, whether in London or in Seoul.

A. *Commons Debate of February 25*

I would indeed like to see, before I die, some member of our National Assembly introduce a bill prohibiting cruelty to animals. I say "before I die," because I suspect that such a wave of humanitarianism will have a long, long way to come before reaching our society, seeing that no Assemblyman is even dreaming of introducing a bill banning human torture. Meanwhile, I suppose, one has but to eat humble pie on the stock syllogism that, physical torture being unknown in democratic police and ours being a democratic police, there can be no torture in our democratic police. I hasten to add, of course, that I use the phrase "democratic police" as commonly accepted in our society, and do not worry my head over the semantic legitimacy of such a combination of words.

The Englishness of the debate of the Protection of Animals (Hunting and Coursing Prohibition) Bill was brought out by the fact (1) that the M. P.'s, true to their tradition of having led the world in kindness to animals, should have introduced such a bill at all, and (2) that the Bill should have lost its second reading by 214 to 101. The debate is particularly interesting when correlated with that of March 4 on the Bill for Painless Childbirth.

Mr. Cocks (Soc.), moving the second reading, said he was trying to speak for creatures that could not speak for themselves. When he cited, among the names of prominent people who supported the measure, that of Professor Laski, the Opposition burst out laughing.

"At any rate," retorted Mr. Cocks, "he survived a recent hunt." (*Laughter*)

He further referred to a report that fox hunters were going to ride down Piccadilly in protest against the Bill, and remarked: "I think it might have amused the late Mr. Oscar Wilde to see 'the unspeakable pursuing the uneatable' in the vicinity of Leicester Square." He argued that there was no reason why hounds and huntsmen should not be used with shooting parties organized by 'crack shots' from Aldershot. (*Conservative laughter*)

"The only reason I can suggest for that laughter," he remarked, "is that members opposite have not a very high opinion of the firing accuracy of the British Army." He suggested that, if Field-Marshal Montgomery were asked to clear the deer from a moor, he would soon do so.

Mr. M. Webb (Soc.), opposing the Bill, said that coursing was not merely a pursuit of idle playboys but the occupation of many ordinary people throughout the land. Opposition loudly cheered him when he declared:

"It is not our business, as the Mother of Parliaments, to do as some mothers do and say, 'Go outside, see what the people are doing, and tell them not to.' It is as important to stand up for the liberty of the subject in this House as to stand up against cruelty to animals."

Mr. Williams, Minister of Agriculture, said amidst derisive laughter from the Socialist benches: "A disquieting feature is the feeling in rural areas that this is a townsmen's attack upon the way of life of the countryside, and that the arguments of cruelty are merely a cloak for prejudice. They read about football matches with 80,000 people there. They know that special trains are put on, despite the fuel shortage, and that thousands of cars are present, all using dollar petrol." Ninety percent of those who followed the hunt, he said, never saw a fox and certainly never saw a 'kill.' It was a day out for them just as a cocktail party might be a day out for some Londoners.

The Bill left it to the Minister of Agriculture to specify alternative methods of destroying animals. "Very nice, thank you," he commented. "They are hunting the hunters now. They will be hunting me tomorrow." It was no part of Government policy to nationalize packs of hounds (*Laughter*) in case the Minister of Agriculture might feel that they were the most effective way to deal with excessive concentration of deer, hares or rabbits.

Earl Winterton (Cons.) insinuated that the supporters of the Bill were of two categories: "the Bloomsbury boys," and "those who required the attention of psychiatrists." The Bloomsbury boys under the patron saint of Oscar Wilde, he thought, opposed hunting, because it required courage, endurance and physical fitness—qualities that were anathema to them. (*Laughter*) To the latter category would belong the mentally unbalanced: "They are men and women who have suffered misfortune in their life and perhaps have not succeeded in attracting the other sex and who find in the solace and companionship of animals that which they cannot find through friendship with their own fellow men," he said, amid laughter.

He recalled a case in which a boy was charged with cruelty to a cat by throwing a stone at it. No less than fifteen women were reported to have fainted in court on hearing of the cruelty. He slyly asked: "Would they have fainted if they were told about the horrors suffered by human beings behind the Iron Curtain? Not one of them."

The Bill was defeated by a margin of 113 votes.

B. *Commons Debate of March 4*

Meditations on the private member Bill providing for Analgesia in Childbirth have led me to conclude that such a bill would be far too premature in our society, seeing that it will only encourage the increase of population in a country that is already over-populated! It is just as well that our husbands, no less than our wives, should have it firmly implanted in their minds that the pangs of childbirth are often indistinguishable from those of death.

The point of interest, however, in the Commons approval of the Bill is that the British M. P.'s should have succeeded in interpreting the so-called Freedom from Fear in its widest sense, namely, a freedom from not only 'political' but 'natural' fears. That pain must be eradicated from a truly democratic society goes without saying. And in our own case, the doctrine of painless society should be preached as much to the Ministry of Home Affairs, which looks after the conduct of the Police and the Youth Organization, as to that of Social Affairs, which attends to our national health.

The Bill in question places an obligation on hospitals and maternity homes to provide facilities for painless childbirth. The mover, Mr. Thorneycroft (Cons.), attacked the Government of insincerity, because Mr. Bevan, Minister of Health, was trying to stop the Bill on the ground that the Government were concerned with the development of the National Health Services as a whole, and that the isolation of portions of service would be likely to wreck the whole conception.

Mrs. Manning (Soc.), seconding, said that the House should by a stretch of imagination be mindful of the dawn of creation. She said:

"I would remind them of that very interesting operation—I do not know if I ought to call it Caesarian—performed on Adam. We are told that the man 'was put to sleep.' It is not surprising that while Adam was the first man to produce another human being, he was also the last." (*Laughter*)

Col. Hutchison (Cons.) said it would be a cynical commentary if the House accepted the Baiting of Animals Bill and the Docking and Nicking of Horses Bill, which dealt with animals, and refused one that dealt with human beings.

Col. Stoddart-Scott (Cons.), a doctor, supporting the Bill, said that even conservative women had labor pains.

Mrs. Ridealgh (Soc.) said, "Last week these benches were filled because of the sufferings of animals, but now they are practically empty because we are discussing the suffering of women."

The Bill was given a unanimous second reading amid cheers.

To conclude: The British Parliament is far away from our own National Assembly, whether geographically or spiritually. And I cannot be accused morally of being excessively pro-British for having admitted this, for the simple reason that my thoughts, for what they are worth, are essentially 'Home thoughts from abroad,' and not the other way round, and that neither the British Commonwealth at large nor myself as a humble citizen of Korea would have anything to gain from any thoughts or acts on my part which might be construed as 'pro-British collaboration.' If but a few of our government officials and our Assemblymen would by some odd chance get the gist of my argument in this correspondence, my purpose for having dispatched it will have been amply rewarded.

(Wednesday, March 30–Thursday, March 31, 1949, *The Seoul Times*)

In Retrospect

To think that *The Seoul Times* is older than the United States Army Military Government in Korea is to be reminded of the fact, of which we are but modestly proud, that it is the only English daily in Korea, edited and published by Koreans themselves, which has a file going back to September 6, 1945.

We have had various trials and vicissitudes for the past three and a half years, and we may expect more to come. We had started with high enough aspirations by dubbing it alias "the voice of Korea," but we know by now that, ours being a vociferous country, we have at least more than two voices, that of Seoul and Pyŏng-yang. If we still retain that unwarrantably ambitious sub-title, it is not so much because of self-conceit as of that human weakness for past memories. We have never been free from the fault of uncouth provincialism consequently; with all the best intentions, we have not infrequently been something of a bore in our manner of presentation. To counterbalance this shortcoming, however, we have always endeavored to be as factual as possible, knowing as we do that the select quality of our indulgent readers and the smallness of our circulation exempt us from the necessity to engage ourselves in propaganda as such, whether in the form of accusation or of gushing enthusiasm. In short, in a society that admits of little scope for the free play of tolerance, we have endeavored to live up to the stand of an independent paper.

It is not without some misgivings that we start the movable type printing from today, which by tradition is the April Fool Day. If our readers should feel that they are being fooled, the editorial office would feel the same, too. Judging from the way in which our compositors have to go through the laborious process of handpicking letter by letter, we may well expect, among other things, strange reforms in English spelling and syllabication! For such radical innovations, we can but ask for the indulgent sympathy of our readers. Meanwhile, we may feel somewhat justified in cheering ourselves with the highfalutin slogan that "*The Seoul Times* marches on."

(Friday, April 1, 1949, *The Seoul Times*)

Apologia Pro Se

It has recently been pointed out from official channels that *The Seoul Times* asks more questions at the UN Commission press conferences than any other news agency or paper in town, and that our stock-in-trade manner is "to alter from day to day the method of putting forward questions of similar content, and try to probe into the activities of the Commission by detecting and analyzing any discrepancies that might be found in the answers given."

It is difficult to determine whether this is meant to be praise or a censure. In either case it is a roundabout way of telling things. Certain inferences may be read into the foregoing paragraph, depending upon whether one reads it between the lines or accepts it at its face value. One may say that *The Seoul Times* is doing just what a free press should do; or that it is making a public nuisance of itself: that it attaches enough importance to the activities of the Commission to feel prompted to exercise all its resourcefulness in asking questions; or that it is not playing the game with its vicious habit of beating about the bush for any tit-bit of news from the Commission, which in any case is such a highly non-committal body that only by surreptitious means can any reporter get access to its secretive opinion.

If we have taken the liberty to ask as many questions as we have done, it is precisely because of our conviction that the UNCOK constitutes a vital element in the general pattern of our national life. That we have asked so many questions may also be due to the fact that we have made it a point of reading up all available UN literature on Korea in the original text rather than in a garbled translation. But to imply that we have approached the UN Commission with any deliberate intention of discomfiting the Government, or the Commission, or both, is indeed a gross misrepresentation. UNCOK is not, and should not be, a forum of calculated subterfuge: there can be no mincing of words on the part of the pressmen or the Commission itself.

If the authorities so desire, we are prepared to say, to ourselves and the public, at any moment's notice that mum's the word where the UNCOK is concerned. But in all eventualities we would much prefer to be dealt with plain words rather than to be told that a spade is not a spade but a thing of metal with which mischief-makers dig the earth of government and politics. (I.L.)

(Friday, April 8, 1949, *The Seoul Times*)

"No Comment"

Cardinal Newman's definition of a gentleman is such a difficult precept to follow these days in the midst of our Stygian gloom of front-page news and back-page gossip, that one often feels like hanging oneself in despair.

"The true gentleman carefully avoids whatever may cause a jolt in the minds of those with whom he is cast. . . he has no ears for slander of gossip. . . and interprets everything for the best. . . his disciplined intellect preserves him from the blundering discourtesy of better, perhaps, but less educated minds: who like blunt weapons, tear instead of cutting clean, who mistake the point in argument, waste their strength on trifles, misconceive their adversary and leave the question more complicated than they find it. . . ." Such sentences float in and out of one's memory, only to add to one's sense of mortification. They may of course be simply brushed aside as being worn-out tags of Victorian smugness. But then one must confess at times that Korea of 1949, whether politically or socially, has in many respects not even entered upon the evolutionary stage of Victorianism, so how can she be expected to have outlived it?

This is indeed a long prologue for a comment on the recent case of the Inspection Committee v. the Minister of Commerce and Industry. Since it was made public (April 4), more than a week has passed, and the public feels no wiser for having read all the statements and counter-statements. One can only moralize by saying that a storm in a ministerial teacup these days brings with it a feeling of nation-wide guilt, which, in the words of Lope de Vega, might be phrased as: "The only sin for man is to be born a Korean at all."

Any expression of opinion for or against the Minister would automatically involve us in the intricacies of our political kaleidoscope. We might therefore hope to be excused for "no comment" by a quotation from Shakespeare:

> Hamlet: Madam, how like you this play?
> Queen: The lady doth protest too much, methinks.
> Hamlet: O, but she'll keep her word.
> King: Have you heard the argument? Is there no offense in 't?

Hamlet: No, no, no offense i' th' world.

The only hope that we can justifiably cherish is that the case will not perturb or prejudice Mr. Hoffman in presenting his draft of the Korea-Aid Bill to the Congress at an early date. (I.L.)

(Wednesday, April 13, 1949, *The Seoul Times*)

The Students' National Guard:
Its Purpose and Function

Event of the Week

The great event of the week has undoubtedly been the meeting on April 22 of some 41,000 students at Seoul Stadium to inaugurate on a national scale the formal organization of the Students' National Guard. On the secondary school level: 30,000 boys and girls from Seoul City, 1,000 from Kyŏng-gi-do, and 700 from the other provinces (each province being represented by 100); on the higher level: 1, 650 from women's colleges, 3,050 from Seoul National University, 4,300 from other colleges and universities in Seoul, and 24 representatives of colleges in the provinces; grand total 40,774. Never in the history of Korean education have so many students of pure Korean extraction met in one place to celebrate and participate in one common cause. It can be said, if nothing else, that, for once in our national history, our student bodies have been organized into a united front, and that burning patriotism in the intractable bosoms of the young have been directed to a serviceable force in the defense of our national heritage and morning calm glory.

Historical Setting: Phase One

There has been some unjust criticism of our minister of education, Dr. An Ho-sang, for his policy of organizing the present student body on a national scale. It must, however, be readily admitted that any such censure is essentially in the nature of 'communist complaints' or of biased judgment, or of both, on the part of unthinking citizens.

Modern Korean education has suffered various misfortunes, which it is high time to rectify once and for all. The Japanese overloads—it is both convenient and highly justifiable to assume that all our sins, both political and social, originate from them—attempted by every possible means, subtle and crude, to graft upon us their preposterous pseudo-myth of a culture militant, by which they had hoped to disintegrate our time-honored tradition and national consciousness. It was after all a nightmarish experience, from which we reaped nothing but the habit of that two-penny-ha'-penny gift of lip-service, if not of utter spiritual anemia. One has but to recall the memory of the decade before Liberation to see what havoc in education has been wrought: the two deadly 'Instructions' of the Education Bureau of the Government-General in 1937, goading the Korean schools "to be thoroughly mindful of the current situation" and "to enhance and intensify the national (Japanese) sense"; the Korean Education Ordinance of 1938 (revised 1941) by Imperial Decree; the Elementary School Ordinance of 1941 by Imperial Decree; the Secondary School Ordinance of 1941 by Imperial Decree; the Military Drill Curriculum as enforced in Korean schools by Government-General Instruction of 1942; the Student Mobilization Ordinance of 1944 by Imperial Decree; the Korean Physical Aptitude Test Ordinance of Government-General, 1945; the War Time Education Ordinance of 1945 by Imperial Decree; and so *ad infinitum.*

The purpose of listing this catalogue of dead issues *ad nauseam* is not to draw a parallel with our present Students' National Guard. Nothing could be in fact further apart in purpose and motive. The one was a continued effort to strangle our national 'existence,' while the other is a bold endeavor to strengthen our national 'sovereignty.' In the one, education was made to serve an alien state; in the other, it is to be inspired by our own state.

Historical Setting: Phase Two

Whether education should inspire, or be inspired by, the state is a matter of controversy that has not yet been solved since the dawn of civilization. And since there can be no absolute standard of evaluating education other than the 'fiat' as governed by environmental needs, education will always remain a matter of practicable 'policy.' The fault of the Japanese lay not in the fact that they tried to enforce an education, which was one of policy first and last, but in the fact that their policy was an utterly *impracticable* one.

A similar criticism could in some measure be made of the democratic concept of education as propagated by the Military Government. The American advisors, with the best of their intentions, were reaching for the stars in a society of groveling sentimentalism. The arts of freedom and rational order, arrived at rationally, were something beyond our pale of educational experience. And lethargy being what it is, one of the seven deadly sins of man, what we had in retribution was the regrettable phenomenon of the wolf of dialectical materialism devouring all, or nearly all, the tender flesh of the younger sheepish generation; for if the wolf had the freedom to devour by sanction of the Hodge dynasty, the sheep no less had the legitimate freedom to *be* devoured.

Si Vis Pacem, Para Bellum

Our three years' experience in the education for freedom has thus taught us a bitter lesson. The question now remains: how are we to destroy that snake in the bush called Communism? Herein lies the historical basis and *raison d'être* of the Students' National Guard.

First: We must have a watertight organization to resist the communist organization; and since the latter thrives on social chaos and dislocation, we must replace them by some sort of order, even if it involves an order imposed by force. In a world of confused skepticism the appeal to reason is vain.

Second: We must strengthen corporate action by utilizing the herd mind, if nothing else. After all, we can instance no less an authority than the very president of New York State College for Teachers for justifying our new trend of thought: "Education is not even primarily intellectual, certainly not chiefly intellectual. It is the process by which the emotions are socialized." Socialization, or nationalization, of emotions of the young generation is indeed an ideal toward which all right-thinking educators should strive. And even if it so happens that a teacher or a headmaster should be condemned for entertaining any spurious interest in outmoded morals, or fictitious wisdom, or unwholesome intellect, he fully deserves such severity of criticism if and when it comes from those who have the

'true interest' of our country at heart.

Third: Inasmuch as education is a matter of policy, and will remain such, there can be no such postulate as 'good education' apart from good administration. One of the crucial errors of the Military Government days was to encourage 'good education' through mediocre administration. There were, for instance, as of December 1946, no less than 23 standing committees on various aspects of education, involving a total of 1,469 member personalities.

But what have they done? So far as the national Statute Book is concerned, there has been no enactment of their decisions, if any. They have confused the central and the peripheral, the essential and the trivial. It is, therefore, a source of some relief that Dr. An has come to the brass-tacks of educational administration by proving himself bold enough to execute with determination what most sound-thinking Koreans believe to be desirable. He further has the high advantage of having been trained in the science of accurate thinking and the method of manipulating abstract ideas with confidence and logic.

Underlying Principles of the Students' National Guard

The Prospectus of the Students' National Guard gives a fair and square picture of its underlying purpose, organization, and basic functions. Since it is an important document, we could not do better than to give an adequate translation of the essential points raised in the Prospectus.

"We are faced with a grave national crisis in consequence of the division of our land and the disintegration of our ideology, which have in turn caused the present social and cultural disorder and the sorrows of internecine hostility. We are therefore in duty bound to render ourselves to the cause of complete sovereign independence by enhancing the true national spirit and reinstating the dignity of the nation through a purified unification of ideological differences. It is for this reason that we propose, in accordance with the following compendium, to organize the student bodies into an ideologically unified whole, to be known as the Students' National Guard, and to strengthen their corporate discipline, both physical and mental, on the deep-felt conviction that they form the pith and kernel and the impellent force of the whole nation, and for the manifest purpose set forth herewith that they be called upon to protect their campus life and fatherland and to foster their practical ability to render their devotional services to the state."

Basic Principles of the Organization

(1) All teachers and students of both sexes above the secondary school level are to be incorporated in accordance with regional or categorical principles.

(2) It is to be organized in such a way as to achieve an organic unity with military training in schools.

(3) It is to be of various grades: (a) the Central or National, (b) the Seoul Municipal, and the Provincial, (c) the Local (i. e., of towns, *gun*s, etc.), and (d) of the individual school.

(4) It is to have the following officers on the National scale, all subsidiary units varying in proportion and degree:

The Commander, under the guidance of the President and the Premier, is to be the Minister of Education

Four Vice-Chairmen, consisting of the vice-ministers of Education, Home Affairs, and National Defense, and one other to be appointed from among school principals

Board of Council, to be appointed from among chairmen of Parents' Associations of school

Steering Committee, to be presided by the Minister of Education, with members to be appointed from among government officials, school principals, and representatives of social organizations

(5) A General Office, with Bureaus of General Affairs, Planning, Culture, Propaganda, Training, and Inspection, is to be created for discharge of clerical duties.

(6) Individual schools may organize its activities on some such pattern as the following:

(a) General Affairs (Sub-sections: Finance, Planning, Research, etc.)

(b) Propaganda (Sub-sections: Ideology, Debate, Propaganda)

(c) Discipline (Sub-sections: Military Drill, Defense, Labor)

(d) Physical Training (Sub-sections under games and sports of all kinds)

(e) Culture (Sub-sections: Research, Science, Literature, Fine Arts, Magazine)

(f) Welfare (Sub-sections: New Life Movement, Health and Sanitation, Distribution);

(g) Inspection (Sub-sections: Inspection, Information)

Guiding Principles and Disciplinary Tenets

(1) To foster the national spirit and to oppose communism by corporate discipline of mind and body

(2) To respect the spirit of mutual help and research among teachers and students

(3) To implant the spirit of labor service and frugal living

(4) To foster the spirit of obedience and law-abidingness

(5) To encourage physical fitness and wholesome morale

(6) To enhance the special qualities of our national culture by encouragement of the spirit of originality

With these objectives in view, the following practical measures are to be enforced:

(1) Mental training and research to be implemented by (a) lectures and speeches on current affairs, home and international, (b) meetings of self-examination and self-criticism, (c) discourses on historical figures of national stature, and (d) other special features of academic nature and artistic attainments.

(2) Physical training to be achieved by (a) gymnastics, military drill, and sundry sports, (b) marching, mountaineering, swimming, and endurance training against cold and heat, (c) fire drills and other mock drills.

(3) Discipline in corporate labor to be practiced by (a) voluntary labor service, (b) cattle-raising, cleaning, and repairs labor, and (c) issuing of organ papers or

magazines.

In the manipulation of these activities, special attention is to be paid to the following points:

(1) Not to use suppressive measures to thwart the burning desire for truth inherent in the young
(2) To foster the spirit of reasonable sweetness
(3) To award prizes and to punish with judicious prudence in accordance with the merits or demerits of students concerned
(4) To investigate carefully the thought-trends of students in general and particular
(5) To respect the voluntary and independent spirit of all concerned
(6) To cultivate the ideals of nationalism for the purpose of guidance of the young
(7) To endeavor to show good examples to the young on the part of responsible leaders
(8) To be always mindful of order and restraint in action, corporate or individual
(9) To have close contact with the students' families for the purpose of guidance and help
(10) To enforce the kind of discipline that is adequate to the various age, sex and physical condition of the students

Lack of space prevents any further amplification of these itemized measures. We can but hope, in all sincerity, for the grand success of the program that it fully deserves, since there is no jingoism whatsoever involved in it. (I.L.)

(Tuesday, April 26–Wednesday, April 27, 1949, *The Seoul Times*)

A Letter to the Editor

Sir:

As a schoolteacher of modest aspirations, I have read with some interest your lengthy article on the Students' National Guard in your issues of 26th and 27th. I must, however, confess that I still am at a loss to know whether you really meant it to be a eulogy or a criticism of the program.

You seem to have taken the unnecessary trouble of interpreting in the Minister's own terms what we are already given to understand. How could one praise or condemn any given program, unless one held, either implicitly or explicitly, a criterion of judgment other than that implied in the program itself? Almost every sentence in your article could be turned to prove that you were saying what you did not mean and you were not saying what you did mean.

If you took the trouble to make a statistical study of the program by some such method as the Gallup Poll among students and teachers in this country, you would at once know which way the public opinion tends as to the pros and cons of the whole stagecraft.

Yours etc.,
Fabricius L. Paek
Taehan Middle School
Seoul

Editor's Note

1. I meant exactly what I said, with full documentary grounds for saying it.
2. Your argument definitely begs for the indictment of "communist complaints."
3. There is nothing good or bad but thinking makes it so. This applies as much to theatrical claptrap as to genuine statecraft.
4. It is not my business to deal our judgments, which rests solely in the hand of the Minister himself, but merely to report.

5. Gallup polls are unreliable things. Think of the last Presidential election case in the U. S. Why should we in Korea bother about such futile setups?

Another Letter to the Editor

Sir:

Your article on the Students' National Guard is a shocking one. It is a matter of great surprise that *The Seoul Times* has come to entertain such a fascistic view on education.

Yours indignantly,
Cassandra

Editor's Note:

By 'shocking,' do you refer to the content of the article, or to the attitude in which the article was written? I cannot be held responsible for the former; and as for the latter, I wish to make it quite clear that I wrote it in all defense to the Minister that is due. I further insist that *The Seoul Times* has no 'views' on education to entertain, fascist, communist, democratic, militaristic, or otherwise.

(Monday, May 2, 1949, The Seoul Times)

Chain of African Imposture

From what I have gathered of the recent talk of the town, it looks as if the enemies of public peace are not only the rebels and rioters who molest the hilly provinces of the South, and the armed hooligans who discharge private might to prove public right, but also those pathetic creatures who hope for a pot of luck by writing the so-called "Chain of Good Luck" letters.

I myself have not so far had the privilege of receiving such a letter for the simple reason, of course, that the editorship of *The Seoul Times* is not a luck-bringing vocation at the best of times; but I have had quite a number of visitors in the office asking me to construe the general purport of the wretchedly spelt "Chain" letters. Since most of them were gentlemen of respectable age, somehow connected with the game of social repute and amateur politics in the heyday of the Military Government, I got the vague impression that here was indeed a lost generation of the Korean woebegone who were in secret need of some luck, be it from Africa or Tibet.

The earliest copies I had seen bore a long list of Japanese names, ending with a few Korean ones; which confirmed my old tenure that Korea has the incurable habit of importing many a strange custom from Japan, including neo-Shamanism, militarism, and physical torture.

A couple of days ago I received a letter, signed "Indignant," from U. S. Information Service, pointing out in the gravest of manners that hoodoo-ism was amongst us again, intimidating people into making under the threat of the direst misfortunes twelve copies of the "Chain" letter in order to send to twelve different people. "In our opinion," the letter concluded, "people originating and sending on such effusions should be tracked and prosecuted as being public nuisances of the worst kind preying on the susceptibilities of the weak mind and superstitions."

Is it worth getting so angry about? I thought. If after all the instructions of the Chain letter were carried out faithfully for a period, say, six months, it would no doubt spread like fire over the whole population of the Republic and add greatly to our general hopes of better luck in the days of gloom ahead, and also add handsomely to the actual revenue of the postal service!

I definitely thought his *saeva indignatio* to be somewhat excessive, for, as I stopped to peruse the names of those hapless luck-hunters (fellow sufferers, surely) in the enclosed specimen of the Chain letter, I discovered by chance what undoubtedly was the name of one of our ministers. If so, it was most consoling to think that he, for all intents and purposes, was striving for good administration as well as good luck. And that is a thing to be thankful for, to say the least.

It has further been reported to me that one of the typists in the office of the National Assembly is said to have typed as many as sixty copies a day of the same Chain letter. Lord only knows that our over-worked servants of the people need a modicum of good luck.

There can be only one irrefutable objection to the Chain letters, and that is the fear of spreading a false species of English. The linguistic changes which the Chain letter must inevitably undergo as it passes from hand to hand, are of such a haphazard nature that none of them could reasonably be explained by the existing laws of philology, other than the one pertaining to the English as spoken and written in this part of the world: namely, *Humanum est errare.*

It would be a matter of some discourtesy to reveal the names attached to the letter; for human nature being what it is, there would certainly ensue many a scene of jealousy and animosity if the luckless public were to discover that some of their privileged fellow citizens were having pots of good luck thrust upon them by this chain of African imposture.

I readily admit that good luck is good luck, whether one gets it by hook or by crook; at least, such is the legitimate conclusion that one can safely draw from the evidential data shown by our society, high and low. But I sometimes think—and that is my other reason for writing this lengthy article—that we might do well to exercise just a modicum of discretion in hunting for good luck at the expense of public peace. (I.L.)

(Tuesday, April 26, 1949, *The Seoul Times*)

Rightly to be Great when Honour's at the Stake

Weasel Word: A Digression

What has been proved cannot be disproved, for no amount of counter-evidence can have any weight against a certainty that is both plausible and glib.

The temporary suspension of *The Seoul Shinmun,* which was resolved at the Cabinet meeting of May 3, is already a dead issue as far as the actual progress of events local and national is concerned. Proverbial philosophy dictates that sleeping dogs are best left lying. But human sentiment induces us to meditate once more on that well-worn phrase—freedom of the press.

Though *The Seoul Shinmun* is considered the largest paper by our standard, it can still be argued that its suspension will make no material difference to our freedom of the press *in toto,* seeing that we still have fourteen odd daily papers and four news agencies in town entrusted with the duties of carrying on that "constitutional" privilege. And we could well leave it at that. But when errors are committed in the name of the freedom of the press, and the same errors are corrected in the name of the selfsame freedom, one cannot but suspect that "freedom" is a weasel word with no constant value or absolute standard. Did not after all a certain French lady stand once before a statue of Liberty in the streets of Paris and ejaculate: "Ah, Liberty, what crimes have been committed in thy name!" It probably was a mistake on the part of the human imagination in the first place to conceive of Liberty as a goddess standing glamorously on a pedestal; she would have been more truly represented as a spinster Humpty Dumpty sitting primly on a wall. For it is only after that Humpty Dumpty of a liberty has fallen or has been dragged down from the wall that we discover two disconcerting facts: that what has been shattered cannot be pieced together again, and that absolute freedom is still in the realm of dreams.

Argument at Large

It is instructive, if not rewarding, to review in all partiality the contents of the various statements that have been occasioned by the suspension of *The Seoul Shinmun*.

"The Government," said Mr. Kim Dong-sŏng in a press release in English on May 4, "does not want to be in the newspaper publishing business. As a matter of fact, complete freedom of editorial judgment has been left to the Editor of *The Seoul Shinmun*. Too often that privilege has been abused and the newspaper has printed stories clearly reflecting a support for the unlawful and totalitarian police state imposed upon our brethren in northern Korea through the force of Russian armies."

It is self-evident from this that the long-standing rumor about *The Seoul Shinmun* being planned for a Government organ paper is entirely groundless, for we have it on the authority of Mr. Kim to the contrary. And further, if there is any clear evidence of the paper shilly-shallying in support of the police regime of the North, mere suspension of a temporary nature is surely not enough; it should be completely closed down. For, as Mr. Kim makes explicit, "What will not and cannot be tolerated in any nation is attacks against the very structure of free government itself. The Republic of Korea is fighting for its life against foreign-directed Communist subversion. . . . Nowhere in the world can freedom of the press be interpreted as freedom to destroy the government. If, as the above words indicate, *The Seoul Shinmun* has been guilty of foreign-directed Communist subversion, there is no excuse whatever for being more lenient to this paper than to *The Kukje Shinmun*, which was completely banned some time earlier.

Mr. Kim further corroborates in a statement in Korean on the same day. "Inasmuch as we have advanced with rapid strides in the progress of home politics, economy and industry, newspaper enterprises are also urgently urged to heighten their general standard and to solidify their ethics of reporting to the extent that all reports which may be contrary to the interests of the nation must be handled with great circumspection on the part of editors and proprietors. It is therefore a matter of deepest concern that a paper should give distorted or exaggerated reports that may lead to an undermining of the national cause by creating a general feeling of bewilderment and uncertainty as to the realities of our complicated political, economic and industrial affairs in the early stages of our national rehabilitation. . . . All newspapers, news agencies and magazines both in the capital and the provinces are hereby admonished to refrain from any possibly anti-national attitude of news report resorting to the Communistic method of destruction and subversive intrigue. . . ."

More Argument at Large

Where by long social convention grandiloquence passes for argument and innuendo for stigma, such words naturally get under the skin of editors in town. Tamsuhoe, which is an association of all the editors in Seoul, submitted a petition to President Rhee on May 6. Except for two papers, which chose to withdraw from the association, sixteen papers and news agencies were represented in the petition.

In a document of over 1,100 letters and characters they stressed two main points. First: the Newspaper Ordinance of 1907, which furnishes the legal basis for the present measure to *The Seoul Shinmun,* "is totally unacceptable to the people of the new-born Republic of Korea insofar as it was an evil law created to serve the bayonet of Japanese aggression," and that the OPI director has shown no "concrete evidence" to corroborate his branding the paper as "anti-national" and "subversive." "Even in the application of a bad law the loss of equilibrium in punishing any social organization will create a general confusion in the public mind and prove most injurious to a healthy enlightenment of the renascent national spirit of the people in consequence of the wantonly curtailed freedom of the press." And second: the OPI director's insinuation in the form of admonition was most "unexpected" since "he seems to assume that all our press entertains thoughts of anti-national inclination and destructive subversion. Nothing could be more insulting to our dignity than such an assumption inasmuch as we enjoy the constitutional right (of free press) under a government that is bound to defend and foster that right."

Being to the manner born, newspaper editors are as capable as any of retaliating grandiloquence for grandiloquence. The curious thing is that both parties seem to lay the blame on each other for creating general "confusion" and "bewilderment." What is truth? Said Pontius, and like the wise man that he was, he did not wait for an answer. Plain reporters followed suit. On May 7 the Press Group attached to the Capitol submitted a long petition to the President, and on May 9 the Pressmen attached to the U. N. Commission did the same, each re-emphasizing from specific angles what

Tamsuhoe had already pointed out with polite rhetoric.

More Argument in Particular

When in answer to a pressman's question the President confessed his unawareness of the suspension, Mr. Kim Dong-sŏng, being referred to, issued another detailed statement on May 7. The catalogue of grievances is as follows:

The excellent equipment and large circulation of *The Seoul Shinmun* could have been put to better service by slight changes in the tone of editorial policy; statistical evidence shows that the paper has printed only 60 percent for last January, 43 percent for February, 53 percent for March, and 39 percent for April, of Government announcements and press releases; the Haeju Uprise incident was reported inconspicuously in one column (March 20); the President's inspection tour of Cheju Island was reported in one column, while another item on "the Vice-Chairman of a certain committee" was sensationally featured as top news in three columns with illustration (April 10); Foreign Minister Im's statement of Korea's U. N. Membership Claim was obscured in one column as if to signify an attachment of little significance thereto (April 10); the President's statement on the Soviet veto was placed in the nether half in two columns, when it really should have been placed as top item in three columns (April 12); on May 1 a large space was devoted to a feature item entitled "Meaning of May Day"; the President's important statement on a proposed U. S.-Korean Defense Alliance, which was treated with due importance in all the other papers, was not reported at all in this paper (May 3); while on May 4 the AFP item on the U. S. response to the said Defense Alliance was featured as top item; on March 16, a derogatory and agitating item on the actual condition of the rebel-torn areas was featured in three columns under a sensational heading (March 16); an item presumably aimed at the alienation of the people from the Government was arbitrarily concocted in a report entitled "Tension in Political Circles Before Announcement of a Certain Incident" (April 13); an attitude of belittlement was shown in the report in one column of the sufferings of North Koreans under Communist exploitation (April 12); and so on and on.

Where the Tree Falls

Under such a weight of evidence no claim, real or hypothetical, could be made. We must but hide our distress, as good manners require, and find comfort in the sagacity of the ancients--"Rightly to be great Is not to stir without great argument, But greatly to find quarrel in a straw When honour's at the stake,"--with thoughts of regret that Harvard has lost one more alumnus to the Communist camp in the person of Dr. Ha Kyŏng-dŏk. (I.L.)

(Thursday, May 12, 1949, *The Seoul Times*)

Cui Bono?

After a series of namby-pamby press releases from the UN Commission, such as the one (May 17) on its recent trip to Cheju Island, or its narrative (May 20) on its two months old letter to Kim Il-sŏng, it is refreshing to discover the UNCOK in the limelight once more with Dr. Luna's dramatic statement and the Commission's full-blown resolution on May 23.

So many browbeating remarks have recently been hurled into the air on the 'burning' question of the withdrawal of the U. S. occupation force, that one is inclined to lose track of the arguments, especially since the various reiterations for the last six months have shown only a pendulum swing of views.

The Government now brings forth in the sternest of manners the call to 'moral obligation,' always the Achilles heel for democracy, by reminding the U. S. of the joint commitments with Russia for having created the Thirty-eighth Parallel, a fact which does not require any reminding at this stage of Korean history.

Dr. Luna brings forth the rhetorical argument: "Do you know what the forty-five degree salute is?" We certainly do. To some extent we practice it even today, in 'liberated' Korea. And with the three years of Japanese occupation of Manila still fresh in his memory, he recalls that, as Assistant Minister of the Interior, he used to bow to a forty-five degree angle "every time I passed a Japanese sentry." (We Koreans ought to consider ourselves lucky that we did not have to do that to a sentry, reserving it only for occasions connected with the Imperial Personage, Palace or the Shinto shrine.) Rather than draw a parallel with the forty-five degree salute, Dr. Luna might have been more explicit in his reference to our Communist menace by pointing out that this would doubtless be a case of crawling on our hands and knees.

As for the Resolution, adopted by the Commission at its thirtieth meeting on May 23, it does not seem to clarify the issue in the least. The Commission resolves to assume "no responsibility regarding either the timing or the facilitating of the withdrawal of forces of occupying powers." Is not this what the Commission has been maintaining all along? (Cf. Press Release, April 25) and how does it differ from Par. 4 (d) of the General Assembly Resolution?

But there must be some reason for the Commission's coming forth with this resolution. Is it to be interpreted as an answer to President Rhee's statement on April 18 that the UNCOK "is being advised on the progress" of discussions "now underway" between U. S. and Korea concerning "a date in the course of several months" for the U. S. troop withdrawal, and that "its (UNCOK) advice and assistance are playing an integral part in these discussions"?

Whether the U. S. token regiment will go or stay, the Resolution will be interpreted in a favorable light for the U. S. Army, and not necessarily for the Korean Government. Now that the Commission has refused to play "an integral part," the balance of weight goes to the carefully planned policy of the U. S. Army, and not to the dictates of our clamor, official or unofficial. It is difficult at any time to hold the naïve assumption that the U. S. Army ever follows the whim of outsiders.

It is further difficult to understand the real significance of the two abstentions and the one against in the voting of the Resolution. What are France and Australia abstaining from, and what is India against? It is all very confusing in the extreme. (I.L.)

(Thursday, May 26, 1949, *The Seoul Times*)

Cry Cry What Shall I Cry?
A Dialogue

A: You are quite right, B, in saying that any opinion expressed publicly or privately on the current issue of the withdrawal of the U. S. forces from our country is likely to transform our soberest official into a fretful porcupine with every quill quivering. But that should not really deter us from saying what we really think.

B: Because we have a constitution guaranteeing the freedom of speech? Or might I further add, the freedom of gossip?

A: Granted our talk would not sound any better than futile gossip, since neither you nor I can be so self-complacent as to believe that our views may 'influence' the course of events one way or another with regard to the withdrawal. It so happens that I concur with the Government in believing that the withdrawal should not take place just now. And it also happens that you hold the contrary view. It would therefore be only too fair to say that we represent in our unassuming fashion the two important shades of public opinion now prevalent in our country.

B: Please don't jump to hasty conclusions by inferring that I hold a view 'contrary' to yours. Do you mean to say that I think the troops *should* be withdrawn? I mean nothing of the sort. I only maintain, tentatively of course, that the withdrawal of what few soldiers U. S. happens to keep in Korea will make no material difference to our security. And then, your talk of 'public opinion' really takes the biscuit. Do you honestly believe that we have a so-called 'public opinion'? We have, if you like, an undue amount of 'private opinion,' but not public. We do not know how to form one, or to analyze it when it is formed, still less to direct it. And what's the use, if you don't care to investigate it and turn it to good use? In this particular respect, we were much better off and better at it during the Military Government days. We have today what Robert Peel called "that great compound of folly, weakness, prejudice, feeling, right feeling, obstinacy, and newspaper paragraphs which is called Public Opinion"--and don't forget to add, gossip. Seoul is an island of its own. What is talked about with interest here sounds entirely unreal in the provinces, and what is felt to the quick in the countryside seems to the people of Seoul like some hearsay from remote lands. I exaggerate on purpose, but only on the right side. So don't bring up that damp squib about public opinion again.

A: So long as you realize that you are going off the track by your over-statement, I will not argue on that score. But you must admit that our Government's stand regarding the withdrawal issue has been both consistent and legitimate. Consider the matter in chronological sequence for the last half-year or so. On September 11 last Dr. Cho Byŏng-ok pleaded at Tokyo that U. S. Army must stay. President Rhee stressed the same on October 8. In response to an urgent motion on October 12 by forty-four Assemblymen calling for "the simultaneous and orderly withdrawal" of the two occupation forces, Government spokesman expressed strong opposition on November 18 to an "unconditional" withdrawal of U. S. forces. Though not official, Han-guk Democratic Party also expressed on November 19 a similar opposition to the withdrawal as being "improper" under the present situation. On November 20 the National Assembly passed a resolution, moved by ninety-nine representatives, on a request for the retention of U. S. troops by no less a majority than 88 votes to 3. You will also recall that, before the voting took place, Premier Yi Bŏm-sŏk had supported the resolution in his speech at the Assembly. On November 22 the Government decided at Cabinet Council to make a formal request to the U. S. Government for the retention of its troops. On November 24 President Rhee asked for assurance that the U. S. would not withdraw while the Communist menace was in existence. On November 26 Han-guk Democratic Party again reiterated its stand in corroboration to the President's statement. On November 30 Metropolitan Police Chief Kim Tae-sŏn warned the people not to be influenced by "Communist" agitators of troop withdrawal. On December 3 Colonel Goodfellow, unofficial representative of the President, told AP at Tokyo that immediate U. S. withdrawal would "mean civil war." On December 29 President Rhee made the following comment on the AP report from Tokyo on the arrival in Japan of some Seventh Division units: "The Korean Government is confident that the reported departure of some American Army elements from Korea is not in conflict with the best interests of both Korea and the U. S. . . . We have not requested that any specific number of American troops remain, but only ask that America keep enough of her armed strength here until this young Republic is certain of its abilities to cope with the existing dangers." On February 15 President Rhee called for abandonment of the American proposal to relegate Japan to a secondary strategic position in the event of war, adding that the U. S. withdrawal from the Orient would only "bring the potential enemy closer to America and shorten the time before Americans will be forced to defend their homes against a Communist attack." An AP report from Washington on May 18 revealed that Dr. Cho had appealed once more to the American people "for more arms and also a military agreement to assume our security after the American forces withdraw." On May 19 Foreign and Defense Ministers urged the U. S. in a joint statement to be mindful of the 'moral' obligation in regard to the situation in the Far East: "It is understood that the U. S. should be assured of the adequate defense for the Republic of Korea before they withdraw their forces from Korea." On May 28 Foreign Minister stressed the Government's hope that the U. S. would withdraw "only when the Korean Government and people require such withdrawal." On June 1 Premier Yi Bŏmsŏk again stressed that the military force of the Republic of Korea be raised to the level of the North Korean Army. What more evidence do you need to prove the consistency of our Government's stand? Surely our Government would not have reiterated its desires and arguments so often if it thought that it could dispense with the politico-military fact of U. S. occupation.

B: I do not doubt the legitimacy of our official stand in regard to the withdrawal issue, though I have some misgivings about its method of enunciating that legitimacy. As far as a layman is permitted to observe, the factual aspect of withdrawal leads one to believe that the U. S. Army moves by its own carefully planned policy, well worked out in advance. And in this sense, the withdrawal is already a *fait accompli*, which no amount of press statements can alter at this late stage. Without intending any irony, I am sometimes reminded of a quatrain by J. C. Squire when I hear of the way in which we urge this and dictate that to the U. S. Army and Government: "God heard the embattled nations shout 'Gott strafe England' and 'God save the King,' God this, God that, and God the other thing. 'Good God,' said God, 'I've got my work cut out.'"

A: Are you implying that the U. S. has something of the status of divinity?

B: I would not care to blaspheme to that extent, though in a way it might do us good to assume that, when it comes to the point, the Americans rig the game in favor of the angels! But seriously, don't you think we have had just about enough of this cajoling and browbeating of the poor GIs on the slightest provocation? To ask for the retention of U. S. troops when most of them have already gone, and the few remaining due to leave any day, is to show a streak of sentimentalism or of monolithic simplicity on our part, with little regard or tact for the feeling of the GIs. Notice in this connection the curious reticence of the U. S. commanders on every occasion of reported troop withdrawal. Last December when portions of the Seventh Division were found to be in Japan, AP reported: "General John D. Coulter, commander of the 24th Corps, grinned and said no comment when asked for details of the movement." U. S. Army Secretary Kenneth Royall, on the occasion of his flying visit to Korea, was equally evasive of comment on withdrawal issues. On April 12 INS reported from Tokyo that MacArthur's chief of staff had "no comment" to make on reports that U. S. troops in Korea would be transferred to Hawaii. The AP dispatch the following day was: "There was nothing to confirm the week-end rumors mentioning late this summer as the probable withdrawal time with 4,000 infantrymen slated for transfer to Hawaii." Again Brig. Gen. William L. Roberts "refused to comment," and his chief of staff, Col. William A. Collier, said: "At present I am in no position to either affirm or deny." If the American high-ranking officials do not fuss about the staying or the going of their troops, why should we? There has altogether been too many a public announcement from our ministerial rank and file about our "unprepared-ness." It merely helps to create more feelings of general instability. So much dust has been kicked up on this score that even the Philippine delegate to the U. N. Commission feels a 'moral' compunction to 'help' Korea by moving a draft resolution that the General Assembly or the Interim Committee be consulted before the withdrawal of U. S. 'troops,' now less than one regiment. Is not this indeed a case of straining at a gnat, while swallowing the camel? As to the consistency of the Government's stand, of which you make a strong case, I do not fully agree. I might borrow your very method of chronological sequence, not necessarily to bring out the discrepancies for the sake of bringing them out, but rather to point to a moral that we need more coordination in our official statements by curbing that human weakness for making statements. (I might add in passing that, when even Metropolitan Police Chiefs have a say in the matter of the withdrawal issue, one wonders where one is going to land some day when Korea might be faced with an acute shortage of paper through lack of ECA supply.) As you have already mentioned, forty-four members of the National Assembly signed an urgent motion on October 12, calling for "the simultaneous and orderly withdrawal" of the two occupation forces. On November 19 Mr. Cho Bong-am, a member of the Cabinet at the time, urged the "peaceful" withdrawal of the same. On November 20, when the Assembly passed the resolution requesting the retention of U. S. troops by eighty-eight votes to three, thirteen members walked out of the session and issued a counter-statement, to which eighteen more absent members subscribed two days later in a similar statement of protest. On December 19 AP reported President Rhee's confidence "that the reported departure of American troops from Korea constituted no threat to Korean security." On March 19, sixty-three Assemblymen, including Vice-Chairman Kim Yak-su, submitted a petition to the U. N. Commission urging "that the Commission is delegated with the vital mission of effecting a peaceful unification and democratic development of our fatherland by observing the actual withdrawal of all occupation forces in Korea." An AP report from Washington on April 20 disclosed that President Rhee had told a recent news conference that "the Korean Republican forces are sufficient to protect the security of the new nation and to repel any attack that might be made on it." On April 19 Defense Minister Shin Sŏng-mo stressed the same point. And yet on May 7 both President Rhee and Mr. Kim   Dong-sŏng made the stunning announcements, to which you have already referred. An AP dispatch from Washington on May 11 reported the opinion of some sources there that "the two Korean statements appear to contradict" the previous declarations. On May 31 Defense Minister Shin stated his confidence that our National Army possesses the necessary qualifications for "crushing any northern invasion in three days." Does that mean that we are on a par with the Northern Army, which, according to the joint statement of Foreign and Defense Ministers on May 19, is said to have been promised an armament to the teeth by Soviet Russia, complete with "20 patrol boats (fast destroyers), 100 fighters, 20 bombers, and 100 reconnaissance planes"? No wonder that Premier Yi Bŏm-sŏk, in a statement on June 1, should be compelled to urge that our military forces be raised to the level of the Northerners. I sometimes wonder how on earth we are going to man those destroyers and bombers and fighter planes, should the U. S. also, being the most generous of nations, decide to give them to us in the not distant future. Is mere will to patriotism enough to make those destroyers and bombers plough the deep blue sea and fly the stratosphere? It would be really gratifying to have such a romantic World War III for a change.

A: I readily admit that small nations like ours cannot afford to bluff, though the blame must partly be attributed to the bad tutelage and example of America and Russia in their collective bargaining at the U. N. But coming back to the point, I am rather relieved to discover that you did not after all quote as part of your 'counter-evidence' those eternal reiterations of Mr. Kim Ku advocating 'immediate' withdrawal and 'peaceful' unification by the principle of 'self-determination,' an argument, I may add, which comes out like water pumped over and over again through an artificial well.

B: There is no need to confuse the official and the unofficial. The venerable gentleman is at liberty to make what he considers to be 'oracular' pronouncements when and where he chooses. The trouble with the arguments set forth by him or by many of the Assembly members is that they are the advocacy of men whose political weakness still exempts them from the responsibility of taking practical decisions, and who, in a sense, find themselves still in the 'pre-political' stage, through which all must pass at one time or another. Again I exaggerate, but on the right side.

A: At any rate, you must admit that we are in need of some guarantee of security in the form of a potential Pacific Pact or a Military Alliance, or failing in both, at least a strong military aid from the U. S. That is what our President has been advocating all along.

B: Apart from the obvious fact that such strident demands would ultimately depend on the purse of the American taxpayer and the judgment of the policy-makers in Washington, it is incumbent upon us to put across such proposals through the accepted, cut and dry diplomatic channels. There is no necessity to carry on all our negotiations in a glass cage, open to public peering. Too often we are inclined to regard diplomacy as a matter of public announcements and table speeches, both of which are usually the outcome of self- dramatization before the backcloth of history and transience. Ah, "the expense of spirit in a waste of"--cocktail parties! (I.L.)

(Tuesday, June 7, 1949, *The Seoul Times*)

제3부
한국문학 英譯

MODERN KOREAN POEMS

Mountain Abode

Han Yong-un (1879–1944)

Forsake this dusty world, they said,
And I would achieve oblivion.
So I hewed the crags to build a hut,
And delved the rocks to dig a well;
The clouds are entertained as guests,
Who freely come and freely go;
And the moon, although no sentinel,
Keeps watch all night above the gate;
The song of birds my music is,
And the wind among the pines my lyre—
As they were wont from ancient times.

None but my little pillow knows
My rue for love of thee, which stays
And haunts me through the sleepless nights.

O solitude of the vacant heights!
Whence do you bring this silent grief?
Rather give me that tranquil grief
Without the song of nightingales!
O solitude of the vacant hills!

(Wednesday, November 5, 1947, *The Seoul Times*)

A Prayer

Cho Myŏng-hŭi (1894–1938)

My Lord!

When with your rod of destiny

You picked this maggot up,

And dropped it into the world,

You must no doubt have heaved

A sigh of contrariety.

And when this lump of disgrace

Wriggled on the earth,

Yonder radiant sun

Must indeed have scowled.

Oh what is to be done

With this contagious flesh?

Or where let flow

This polluted blood?

My Lord! If you design

Eternally to reject,

Rather bestow on me

The glory of the lightning,

I say, that glory of the lightning.

(Thursady, December 11, 1947, *The Seoul Times*)

Wild Flowers of the Mountains
   —After a Folk Song—

Kim So-wŏl (1902–1934)

In the mountains are blowing flowers,
There the flowers blow;
Autumn, spring, and summer through,
There the flowers blow.

In the mountains far and near,
In the mountains everywhere,
There the flowers bloom and blow,
So lovely, wild, and fair.

In the mountains are singing birds,
Where the flowers blow;
There they sing the seasons through,
Because the flowers blow.

In the mountains are blowing flowers,
And there the flowers wilt;
Autumn, spring, and summer through,
There the flowers wilt.

(Monday, January 24, 1949, *The Seoul Times*)

Sak-ju-ku-sŏng

Kim So-wŏl (1902–1934)

Three whole days by water and boat,
O three thousand distant leagues!
But farther and wearier on foot,
Over the mountains Sak-ju-ku-sŏng is three score leagues.

Even the swallows, drenched in rain,
Come back halfway, caught in the storm.
High are the mountains at evening hour,
And higher still at night.

Over the mountains is Sak-ju-ku-sŏng
Sixty distant leagues;
And at night in dreams some forty leagues,
When I travel there and back.

Being parted, for your presence I yearn;
Being absent, of your abode I dream.
Know you not how the birds do fly
North and south, desiring for home?

Yon cloud sailing above the fields,
Over what land shall it be this night?
Over the mountains is Sak-ju-ku-sŏng
Sixty distant leagues.

(Thursday, May 12, 1949, *The Seoul Times*)

Does Spring Come Also to These Ravished Fields?

Yi Sang-hwa (1901–1943)

Unto this land no more our own,
Does spring come also to these ravished fields?

Bathed in the sunlight shower,
I go, as if in dreams, along a lane
That cuts the fields like parted hair,
To where the blue of sky and green earth meet.

You heavens mute and silent fields!
I do not feel I have come here alone.
Resolve me whether I am drawn
By you, or beckoned by some other force.

The breeze that whispers into my ears
Is flitting my garment at every step;
And the hilarious lark behind the clouds
Is singing like a maiden beyond the hedge.

You bounteous green fields of corn!
Have you too washed your hemp-like plaits of hair
In the soft rain that fell late last night?
How cool and light my own head feels!

Lone as I am, my steps are cheery!
For the happy meandering brook
Dances past the thirsty fields
With rippling songs of self-sung lullaby.

Hand me a hoe,

That I may tread this rich soft-swelling earth

Until my very ankles weary,

With recompense of honest sweat.

Even as a child beside a river's brink,

My soul is fondly yearning for the infinite.

What is it you are craving for?

And whither in flight, so wild? Can you not tell?

Soaked in the smell of earth and corn,

I walk dizzy all day with limping steps

Between the green joy and the green sorrow;

Perchance the spirit of spring has come on me.

But long since have our fields been ravished;

Our very spring may soon be plundered.

Translator's Note:
　　Yi Sang-hwa is one of our most inspiring poets of the modern times. He was born into a family of noted talent and integrity. He studied at Chung-ang Middle School, Seoul, and later at Tokyo Foreign Language Institute, specializing in French. His poetic activity started well before he was twenty, his early twenties proving most productive.
　　He participated, both in deed and in writing, in the independence cause of our country, for which he was frequently imprisoned and always under police surveillance. The above poem, though in a tentative translation form, may be considered as an expression of his ardent feelings. Few of our poets have been as tongue-tied as Yi Sang-hwa.
　　Between 1935 and 1937 he was in China with his soldier brother in exile. On returning home, he suffered such tortures from the Japanese police that he never recovered his health again. He devoted his remaining years to school teaching and rehabilitating Korean poetry. Except for the few poems that had appeared in odd journals, his manuscripts were completely suppressed and destroyed by the Japanese immediately after his death.
　　Recently, his friends and fellow-poets erected a memorial tablet to his honor in Taegu, his native town.

(Thursday, March 25, 1948, *The Seoul Times*)

In the Glen of Ku-sŏng-dong

Chŏng Ji-yong (1902–1950)

Often in the glen
Are buried shooting stars.

Where at dusk at times
Noisy showers of hail accumulate,

Where the very flowers
Live in exile,

With no wind tarrying
Where once an ancient temple stood,

In the dim mountain shadow
A stag is seen to move over the ridge.

(Friday, November 8, 1947, *The Seoul Times*)

Stars

                Chŏng Ji-yong (1902–1950)

I lay me down with windows open,
For then I have a sky to own.

I put my glasses on again. This night
The stars look bluer, after the sun's eclipse.

For this night's banqueting of stars
I am arrayed in white, with a white bed.

All mundane love and wedlock are
But slovenly ado in the stars' view.

Turning over, from star to star
I navigate without a chart.

Each star is sprung from separate stub;
There's one that looks more sinewy;

Another like a newborn babe,
But faintly, faintly shimmering;

Another is in fever,
Red and trembling.
In the winds the very stars are swept;
So many wavering tremulous candle lights.

Washed in the cold water,
Sands of gold in the Milky Way!

Islands ever tumble below the mast,

When the stars look fondly to the harbor of our brows,

And the Great Bear

Leans in turning.

In the serene tragedy of the firmament

We even hold our breath.

For reasons that may be known in after life,

We each have nights of private vigilance.

Without a lullaby

I am lulled to sleep.

(Monday, March 22, 1948, *The Seoul Times*)

Sorrowful Image

                      Chŏng Ji-yong (1902–1950)

Are you at peace in rest this night?
How in rude and uncouth words have I come to be solicitous of your
    quotidian peace in the faintest of whisperings in my solitude?

Is there indeed no human speech that better matches your exaltation?

You who surely are at a greater and sweeter peace in rest than a drowsing dove
    or a drooping flower with closing petals as the shadow leans and lengthens,

Shall I tarry and dwell upon your eyes?
A pair of blue lakes, crystalline to the depths;
Has night been created to alight and plume its feathers upon those lakes?
Am I here to be submerged in those blue lakes, bold as the star of Venus?

Ah those delicately pressed lips!
Lest my unchecked thoughts lose all propriety, let me hold myself anew in
    sternness and explain!

Therein lies the cause, among sundry other such, for fearing you like a leopardess
    and holding you in awe and dignity.

If there is yet a sacred peak, unsoiled and untrespassed by human feet, such be
    your one and only nose of purity, made purer and whiter by your snow.
Wherefore, it is denied in sorrow but that you needs must ever inhale the fragrance
    of the alpine flora, even though the nether seasons flourish in luxuriance.

Looking up your forehead front in awe and piety, and down again your cheeks, I will
    tarry and contemplate your ears hidden and yet invisible beneath your ebony hair.

Seashells that I faintly remember having seen by the Ionian shores of Greece herself; though fashioned after the ever-hearkening shape and posture, still unknowable as to what they have been hearkening to;

A sea as smooth as oil, a blue sky above, and sands so white that the very gulls, alighted, were invisible to sight, in such places of distilled quietude, the shells never ceased to keep their whorled ears in silence, whence I awoke to the sensation of being a solitary traveler in this life.

This world, which is but an empty shell, be it overspread with a sky and circuited with seas, was in truth but a crusted shell of another world.

Inasmuch as there was no doubt of these ever-listening shells to be of another life and another world, how could I be but turn away in grief from this world and this transitory life?
The very winds blowing hither and thither had no meaning except of wronged injustices.

Even as I linger close by your ears, I know myself to be a mere wayfarer with a temporary stay in solitude.
For this night also your ears are in an open posture for the sake of listening only!
For in this very world of confusion I have observed the Ionian seas, as still as death, encircling your ears.

Let me now venture further and plunge into your secret depths.

As the fathomless sea hoards corals and countless mysteries, so you have in store an infinity of treasures.
I marvel indeed at the profusion of your rich treasures.

What rarity is your heart!
The Muses of old, molded by the immortal hands of Hellas, were not from birth

possessed of such hearts; wherefore, they spend today their eternity of sorrow in museums.

You are not of their kind.

Shall I compare your heart to a pot that spins in never-ending prolongation the sacred fire of life in platinous threads of finest make?

Or shall I compare it to a sanctuary that enshrines that eternal love which is the very stuff of heaven and earth?

The never-changing richness of bright-red hue is testimony thereof.

Yet when from time to time you open up your window to the vulgar world, your heart feels so readily its shame and indignity, that you withdraw into your innermost secrecy.

How bright and palpitating are your lung, liver and gall! How dense and poignant!

But it lies not within reason to discriminate them overmuch by colors.

And though there flow in the deep recesses streams of mysterious rivers, I will pass them by for other matters.

A pair of swelling breasts that may be well compared to some round hillocks of delicate curve and elasticity, over which the sun or the moon might be rising, and the silver-white hare drowsing or skipping.

Even as I am portraying you thus, I feel like a person wandering in a strange labyrinthine way.

But already you are gathered and collected in perfect poise and measure, with folded hands of ivory and tucked feet of grace.

And you have achieved your oneness in purity with wisdom, prayer, and soft breath.
And I cannot but meditate upon your posture and your surroundings, as I scrutinize

your state of perfection.

Reverting to my former thoughts in an eternal round, I say this world is ordained to be an unreality and an empty shell; how is it then that you are settled here in your stronghold of solitude?
And how indeed can you recline in rest upon your seat of translucent sorrow?

Because this vexes me to the utmost, I walk round and round your stronghold of solitude and keep watch, sighing, with the pale moon overhead, like a mongrel dog that cannot bark at darkness.

Inasmuch as I tremble with unhappy prognostics, I feel the dawn is not too far hence when you will draw apart because of your love and solitude and purification, stripped of your body of gorgeous graces, of all your beauty, virtue, and your luxuriant limbs.

At that break of dawn also, will you keep as ever the selfsame posture of hearkening like that white shell on the Ionian shores?

I will dedicate my last adornment of white lilies and resolve to take my departure by myself from the Ionian sands.

(Saturday, December 25, 1948, *The Seoul Times*)

Homeward
                    Chŏng Ji-yong (1902–1950)

The night mist closing upon the pavement
Burdens my shoulders with heavier weight.

The season's chill lips touch my temple,
And the street-lamps dim with tears.

Swallows are flown, and roses too in hiding;
My heart within puts on a mourning badge.

Listless steps follow the natural discretion of thirty years;
A shadow of ill omen, not of lamentation, stretches long.

O this nightly homeward plod in solitude!
Joyless routine, uncheered by the purple wine.

(Holograph Manuscript, dated August 24, 1947)

The Vertex

Yi Yuk-sa (1904–1944)

Lashed by the bitter season's scourge,
I'm driven at length to this north.

Where numb circuit and plateau merge,
I stand upon the sword-blade frost.

I know not where to bend my knees,
Nor where to lay my galled steps,

Naught but to close my eyes and think
Of winter as a steel rainbow.

(Friday, November 14, 1947, *The Seoul Times*)

The Fountain

                                Kim Ki-rim (1908–?)

The sunray's myriad fingers now
Have drawn with haste the sable velvet curtain of night.
And in the window stands my naked daffodil,
(O young Madonna), bathing in the fountain of light.

Beloved! Yesterday night
I did unfold to read in secrecy
My past year's crumpled littered memory.

Stroking the cold stiff back of Hope,
I called in whispers to stir from its sepulchral sleep
Within my breast, and mount on its broken wings.

But now, beloved, is the morn returned.
Pray quickly open wide my sickroom door.
Do you not see the fleecy clouds
Running like colts above the azure vault?

Let's to the lawn and wash in the sunbeam fountain
Our wounded wings, and tightening ourselves like leopards or eagles,
Swoop, as the wind, on this dull season crouching at our heels.

(Friday, November 21, 1947, *The Seoul Times*)

Rain

Kim Ki-rim (1908–?)

The countless hands, and hands, of the rain,
That lightly tap at the hard wall of darkness,
Stir up the spectral emotions of the asphalt breast.

In broad daylight we scorned the asphalt, saying:
"You dullard! Yet another kind of rock!"
But look at now his tear-bound face,
Dumbly staring into the sky.

Ruby, emerald, sapphire, amber,
Nephrite, jewel of the night,
All music of the neon-signs
Melting into the asphalt pools.

The cat-eyed tramcar,
Like the Titanic in the Atlantic,
Crosses the darksome sea of memory,
Scuttling our irreparable hope.

Listlessly hanging by their paper umbrellas,
As if on to their lifebuoys,
The women, the men,
So many fishes,
Swim past, swayed by the night,
And none to rescue them.

Night has run aground on the deep-sea reef;
The signals dart and flit about on the sea,

But all the radio stations are closed.

(Saturday, July 31, 1948, *The Seoul Times*)

Incantation of the Owl

　　　　　　　　Kim Ki-rim (1908–?)

Mother, shall I bring a microphone to your grave?

Dearest skull, will you revoke your ancient lullaby
And sing it into my crippled ears?

Oh the foolish sea, that knows not how to sing a lullaby.

The sea only
Is a perpetual grumbler,
Rebelling against darkness.

The sea incessantly
Gnaws at night with white teeth.

(Holograph Manuscript, 1950)

Dusk

Kim Ki-rim (1908–?)

Pray tell me, why stands the dark bridge there yet, by the waterless ditch, baring his back to the cold draught and his bony legs exposed to his thighs?

The poplars are shivering, shivering, beside the muddy waterway, his white flanks stripped bare. What merciless hand has denuded him of his green coat that kept his shoulders warm? The sparrows will no longer come to hide in his folds for their chatting of the day's endless gossip.

The sun having set, the homeless wind is again crouching under the bridge, sobbing. Houses creep into the gray of the evening, their bodies curled up like monstrous trumpet-shells, and then taking out their hollow chimney-pipes, they have a whiff of tobacco. What impudent-looking pipes are the chimneys!

Lest too big dreams surprise the village, the looming hills stalk near and keep watch over it, standing still and expressionless like Cossack sentries. Then suddenly small lamplights lean out of the windows of every house, doubtless to commune with the flying stars of the firmament.

(Holograph Manuscript, dated October 3, 1946)

Spring Comes without a Telegram

Kim Ki-rim (1908–?)

Inhaling the chilly mist of the distant dusk,
Along the silent stretching mountain slope,
The train comes crawling,
Rumbling, rumbling;
Today again the bridge is groaning something.

Well, spring has come like a thief by that train
Without even a warning telegram,
And with her tender motherly voice
Is waking the streams
Locked in sleep in valleys;
And now the red-faced smiling sun
Is busy strewing his parting kisses
Here and there
On the languishing eyelids of dusk.

Enwrapped in pale-blue smoke,
The poplars stand in row
On the white bank of the late afternoon,
Outspread like linen,
And are smoking like idle loafers.
O spring!
Though I do not recall you meeting me
Beside some riverbank to make me promises,
I am yet expecting something grand of you.

So again I turn today, with hoe on shoulder,

And watch the train crawling

By the silent stretching mountain-side,

Inhaling the chilly mist of the distant dusk.

(Friday, December 31, 1948, *The Seoul Times*)

Sun of My Life
             Yu Ch'i-hwan (1908–1967)

Shall not the bright sun shine
Above my head wherever I go?

Abiding by the ancient primitive laws,
Be it my fortune to sleep with the stars,
And to endure with the rain and the wind.

Grant me to love my life with zeal
And what besides thereto pertains;
Yet humbly I seek to be delivered
Of groveling pathos and humiliation.

Since to my enemies, and them
That fawn upon my enemies,
I have my righteous hate in store,

Even when the fearsome sun has stamped
Into my sockets his sunflower brand,
And I'm suddenly butchered like a beast,

What grudge and grievance should I bear
To you, O mighty sun of my life?

(Thursday, December 18, 1947, *The Seoul Times*)

Flag

Yu Ch'i-hwan (1908–1967)

Behold that voiceless shouting to the sea!
That handkerchief of ever-yearning heart,
Waving unto the distant purple sea!

Elected pathos, wavelike, flaps in the wind,
And on the staff of the pure and pointed thought
Sorrow outstretches, like a heron, its wings.

Ah! Can no one tell me who it was
That first knew thus to hang into the air
This grieving heart, the plight of being?

(Holograph Manuscript, 1947)

Head

Yu Ch'i-hwan (1908–1967)

Here in December in the land of northernmost Manchuria,

Unblessed by snow, and slashed by the dry ripping wind of the Amur,

Here at the cross-roads of a small stripped citadel town,

Are exposed high on stakes twin heads of whilom bandits;

Their dark purple faces shriveled up like withered children,

And their half-open eyes staring into the distant polar circuit

Of hills and rivers beneath the sunset shimmer of the bladed sky.

Know you now in death the taste of the Judgment of Law?

It is not that death is one of the four evils

But that the preservation of peace renders at times

Human life as cheap as a chicken or a cur.

Your life might well have proved an instant threat of my death,

So that to rule out force by means of force has ever been

The sanction of blood from times primeval.

Now as I pace along this wind-swept thoroughfare,

I am resolved afresh of the dogged ferocity of life.

You who housed your uncontrollable souls of treachery,

Close your eyes in peace! May merciful heaven

Cover this landscape of waste thoughts with deep, deep snow!

(Holograph Manuscript, 1948–1950)

Rock

Yu Ch'i-hwan (1908–1967)

Let me became a rock after death.

Neither tainted by pathos of love,

Nor moved by human mirth and wrath,

But as carved by the wind and the rain

In the sempiternal silence of passionless-ness,

Lacerated deeper and deeper,

Till at last my very life is obliterated;

Even as the sailing cloud,

Or the distant thunder,

A rock will I be,

Neither singing in dreams,

Nor crying with pain, though cleft in twain.

(Holograph Manuscript, 1950)

A Child's Fear

P'i Ch'ŏn-dŭk (1910–2007)

Mummy!

Should Daddy come alive some day,

How will he stir out of his mound,

With so much earth and turf to weigh?

Mummy!

How walk in that ghostly array,

When people will jest and mock around?

(Monday, November 17, 1947, *The Seoul Times*)

Life

P'i Ch'ŏn-dŭk (1910–2007)

If you're depressed in mortification,

Look up Mount Pukhan's blue sky, my friend!

For I have marked

The tiny heart's faint palpitation

In an egg of three days' incubation.

If by mishap you're crossed in love,

Go into statistics, my friend!

For I have marked

Life's sure and unmistakable move

As in the ticks of the second hand.

If you are tired of vegetation,

Visit the South Gate Market, friend!

For I have marked

The pulse's beat and the stir of life,

As certain as the earth's rotation,

In the egg of three days' incubation.

(Monday, December 22, 1947, *The Seoul Times*)

Sunflower

Sŏl Jŏng-shik (1912–1953)

Rather the sunflower for the sake of endurance,
Rather the sunflower for the sake of belief,
To salvage your future generations to come.

Let the bitter cruel sun
Parch the reindeer's throat,
And set the forest afire,
And make salty the fathomless sea.

The sunflower alone
Has denied your degradation.

When all the flowers were beguiled by the beauteous Cross,
And all the fruits relentlessly were trodden down,
That day of reenactment of the Original Sin,

When the pitiless sun
Held his iron sway over men,
And men in triumph sang over other men,
Whose shoulders, rebellious, sank beneath the yoke,

The sunflower alone
Has been coeval with the sun.

(Thursday, October 30, 1947, *The Seoul Times*)

Gong

Sŏl Jŏng-shik (1912–1953)

In what secretion have you sanctified
The lamentations of myriad living souls,
That you should crouch away from us
And ever keep your nightly vigils, so?

O heavy-curtained Silence!
Who was it broke your solemn dignity?
What power thumped at your back
To force your hollow choked reverberations?

If it is power, rather let flesh be slashed,
Our tumored flesh in dark imprisonment!
Ah, if it be power, carve our futile flesh!

Is freedom greater than its shadow?
Or is it the eternally lost cause of history?
O this armful of vacancy!
What is it we're caressing and stroking?

But heavy-curtained Sufferance!
Within your deeply caverned will,
Let live the people's endurance power,
And the strength to refuse all clamorous laws.

Because the people shall outlive my years,
Await the day of self-resounding freedom;
And because their lamentations outlast my span,
Ring out your broken murmurings silently.

(Thursday, March, 4, 1949, *The Seoul Times*)

Sunless Land

Sŏl Jŏng-shik (1912–1953)

Though harvests ripen, year to year,

This is a bootless land

Whose people stand

With their backs turned, row after row.

The streams may turn and flow

In search of our parching lips,

Flow they may, and yet

Our mouths are filled with sand,

And the land spread out in arid waste.

This we only know, know only,

That the land is always ours:

Though history chase us as the wind

That seeks the forests out,

This is our mother bosom earth

Over and yet again.

Knowing how the knuckles only grow

Of us that stroke the ploughshares,

Pointed bright like burnished spear,

Will you, great ox, ever abide

By your wisdom of sufferance?

Resembling shades crowd in hordes

Beneath the Namsan hills of everywhere,

Even as the winds, the drizzly winds,

That gather in the forests thick.

Though sweat may flow and flow,

This is a useless land,

A sunless land.

Bitten by white teeth, tumored and bruised,

Our torpid backs endure,

As the dumb ox endures,

Your fearful cruelty, hardly to be endured.

And for the fumy blood of resistance

October even hesitated

To let the frost descend

Upon this sunless land.

With swollen knuckles and finger-nails

Potatoes have been planted, one by one;

And yet to fill whose belly

Toils the boldly staring ox?

The Namsan woods in wrath are everywhere,

Insurgent as the stormy winds;

The ploughshares, stuck in earth, are flung aside,

As the deserted spear points,

Upon the wide outstretching land.

Though harvests ripen, year to year,

This is a bootless land

Whose people stand

With their backs turned, row after row.

(Monday, April 19, 1948, *The Seoul Times*)

With a Brew of the Bitter Sunflower Wine

Sŏl Jŏng-shik (1912–1953)

The month of August has returned

Whereof we must ever sing and grieve.

Shall we entwine a wreath to enshrine

Elsewhere our joyous virgin memories?

Or shall we, with a pot of home-brewed wine,

Make yet another riot and a shudder?

But come, happy month of August!

Let her recovered wings soar high! However, . . .

Ah!

The forest trees are felled;

Lo! The bleak hills in December's snow!

Though April's longed-for shower has come,

Whereof shall we procure the seeds

To redeem the forest's foliage green?

The radiant August sun, once risen,

Has branded his roundly burning stamp

Upon the broad breast of the nation:

It is the sunflower!

The flower for the parched and the thirsty:

It is the phoenix!

The flower for the people given to plight.

Another month of August has come round,

Which we must long endure and ever await.

With a wreath of entwined sunflower

Be it our lot to crown the people's crusades,

That shall go forth to battle from this day.

With a brew of the bitter sunflower wine

To quench your thirst, we shall await your return.

Let August settle down;

Fold we the recovered wings and embrace the wind.

The very hills and wastes of yellow earth

Are in freedom's shade beneath the wings of history.

Water ye the people's bitter sunflower!

Alone they who fear freedom,

Who rebel against life-giving thoughts and time,

Suffer defeat in the heavy shade of history.

Let August have faith in the shade of August:

And let the deathless people

Water the deathless flower of August,

The sunflower.

(Monday, August 16, 1948, *The Seoul Times*)

The Wrath of Heaven

    Sŏl Jŏng-shik (1912–1953)

From heaven

A voice was heard

In words recorded by Prophet Jeremiah:

In the tenth year of Jedekiah the Judaean king

When Nebuchadnezzar wielded power,

The alien hosts of Babylon

Encircled Jerusalem,

Because the pillars of Israel were rotted

And the people corrupt,

Imprisoning their own leaders.

From heaven

Another voice was heard admonishing:

In times of yore

I led you forth

That ye may live in the blessed

Land of flowing honey and milk,

Having led you forth from Pharaoh's land

To wander in the wilderness for six and thirty years,

And to sleep in the dew and swallow roots,

That ye may all be promised

The bounteous land of the Amorites;

And now ye bend

Your suppliant knees before alien powers,

Selling justice for silver pieces

And for the price of a pair of shoes,

Delivering your brothers in prison to the mercy of the Edomites;

I gave you

Rice in abundance

And also clean white teeth;

Wherefore bite ye at your own people?

Ye men of Gaza, pointing daggers at your brothers' throats,

And ye men of Damascus that trample

Over the hunger-stricken torsi of the poor,

Though ye build up marble columns

With wheat and barley

Plundered from the good, all-suffering people,

Ye will not prosper for three generations.

I will cover up at night

The fiery Orionid,

And have a ball of darkness rise at dawn;

And that ye may be blinded

Of your useless seeing eyes,

I will set fire to the walls of Gaza.

Dreading the simple righteous truth

As a fearsome lion, if ye hide

Behind the altar of Bethel,

Where father and son together

Finger the sweet flesh of the selfsame maiden

And offer her as sacrifice to the heathens,

Once more will I

Pelt down a rain of sands,

And else, truth greater than myself

Will itself become a sandstorm,

Whereupon your palms and soles
Will be sorely festered,
And your vineyards turn arid.

Wag not therefore your wily tongues,
Nor seek to amass riches,
Nor lick the honey from alien hands;
But regain your primeval senses.
And follow the steps of the people, poor and just,
And on the hills of Samaria, weep and repent.

And then,
Even in your dispossessed fatherland,
Virgin daughters of Israel will rise again,
For that they are the mothers of all being.

(Holograph Manuscript, 1948–1950)

Funeral Cortège

O Jang-hwan (1918–1948)

Into the moonlit night
Go, O funeral bier,
Tolling the sorrowful knell,

In the hooded sedan
With no mourners after,
Bearing my grieving heart.

This night once again
Tears welling unbidden
Drench the bright moonlight.

Funeral bier, O beautiful!
In the darkened forest
The nightingale's throat is choked in blood.

(Friday, Octobert 24, 1947, *The Seoul Times*)

Christmas

O Jang-hwan (1918–1948)

The piercing cries of chasers penetrate

The dark forest down to the mountain skirts;

And the hunted deer

Trickles his warm blood upon the snow.

The torch fires burn till late at night

Down the valleys, along the slopes,

And on the open hills.

These several days the huntsman and his hound

Have slept in the mountains, chasing after game.

This day again the young deer has espied

The chasers carrying on their shoulders

A leopard and a wolf.

Licking the wounds of his mother doe,

The young deer thinks

Only

Of the sleepless gushing spring in the dim valley,

And the white blooming herb in snow beyond the ravine.

At the perilous place and hour,

The temple gong is heard.

Let the dead bury their dead.

On either cheek

Of the slow returning deer

Are settled beads of dew;

And still the trickled blood is warm on the snow.

(Thursday, December 25, 1947, *The Seoul Times*)

The Way to Father's Grave

O Jang-hwan (1918–1948)

Beat in the fumy heat,
Among the seared pines,
Barren was the hilly path
That led to Father's grave,
Where red earth dyed my garment red.

O even thus far stretches up
The new-built road, where laborers
Are stooping under their gravel load.
At this bare height with wilted grass,
Where no cicadas sing,
My homeland folk are making yet
Another road that leads somewhere.

The dynamite reverberates
In the sequestered valleys and hills;
And a memorial tablet stands,
Long since unheeded, ruinous,
Before the village desolate.

Father! O departed!
Leaving this mound where death lies deep
On this red hill, unvisited,
And this, within my bosom, thus. . . .

What have I come to tell you here?
In the droughty heat of dry stream-beds,

Refractory was the hilly path

That led to Father's grave.

(Thursday, March 18, 1948, *The Seoul Times*)

At the Nok-dong Burial Ground

Kim Kwang-gyun (1914–1993)

Has he come thus far to be buried in this red clay?

Here are but row on row of desolate mounds,

Low-lying, turfless, and flowerless,

With no alder or hillock to adorn the view.

The rain-soaked tent sobs in the wind,

And the knell spreads one thin toll in the vacant field.

Clutching at his thirty-eight years of grief,

Has he at last disburdened his drooping shoulders?

Ah, must we part here, so, in equanimity?

The sounds of the hammer on the thick coffin

And the lowering chain

Pierce through my temple,

And the rain drips and drips

Down my tightened lips

And the small tomb-stone.

After-song:

Whither bound the waves of time,

Bearing his beauteous soul?

Some day, hence, when I'm overtaken,

Where shall we two rejoin?

(Holograph Manuscript, dated August 22, 1947)

Autumn Scene

Kim Kwang-gyun (1914–1993)

The fallen leaves are reminiscent of

The exiled Polish Government's paper notes,

And the autumn sky of the blasted city of D. . . .

The road is loosed like a creased necktie,

Whirled in the cataract of sunlight.

Leaving a thin line of tobacco smoke,

The two o'clock express crosses the field.

Between the bony poplar trees

The factory roofs expose their gleaming teeth,

And a crooked wire fence swings in the wind

Beneath a thin tissue-papered cloud.

Kicking the insects chirping in the grass,

Not knowing where to dump my thoughts forlorn,

I throw a stone into the vacant air,

Which, drawing a lonesome semi-circle, falls

Beyond the curtain of the leaning scene.

(Holograph Manuscript, dated August 23, 1947)

Primeval Morn

                        Yun Dong-ju (1917–1945)

Where the snow lies white,

Over the howling telegraph poles,

The voice of God is heard.

What revelation?

With haste,

When spring comes round,

Will I enact my sin,

And wake to pangs in store.

And after Eve's travail and toil,

Hiding my shame with fig leaves,

I will endure the sweat on my brow.

(Friday, December 24, 1948, *The Seoul Times*)

Counting the Stars at Night

Yun Dong-ju (1917–1945)

Up where the seasons pass,
The sky is filled with autumn.

In this untroubled quietude
I could almost count these autumn-couched stars.

But why I cannot now enumerate
Those one or two stars in my breast
Is because the dawn is breaking soon,
And I have tomorrow night in store,
And because my youth is not yet done.

Memory for one star,
Love for another star,
Sorrow for another star,
Longing for another star,
Poetry for another star,
And O! Mother for another star,

(Mother! I try to call each star by some such evocative word, names of school children with whom I shared desks, names of alien girls like Pae, Kyŏng, Ok, names of maidens who have already become mothers, names of neighbors who lived in poverty, names of birds and beasts like pigeon, puppy, rabbit, donkey, deer, and names of poets like Francis Jammes and Rainer Maria Rilke.)

They are as far away
And intangible as the stars.

Mother!

You too are in the distant land of the Manchus.

Because I have a secret yearning,

Seated on this star-showered bank,

I have writ my name thereon

And covered it with earth.

In truth, it is because the insects chirp

All night to grieve over my bashful name.

But spring shall come to my stars after winter's delay,

Greening the turf over the graves;

So, this bank that buries my name

Shall proudly wear the grass again.

(Thursday, December 23, 1948, *The Seoul Times*)

Another Home

Yun Dong-ju (1917–1945)

The night I came back home,
My bones that followed lay in the self-same bed.

The dark chamber was one with the universe,
And the wind blew down like a voice from heaven.

Looking into the bones
Quietly bleaching in the dark,
I know not whether it is
Myself that weeps, or my bones,
Or my beauteous soul.

The upright dog incorruptible
Barked all night at darkness.

He who barks at darkness
Must be hunting after me.

Let me go away, away,
Like a person pursued,
Unknown to my bones,
To yet another home of peace.

Translator's Note:
The poet was born in the land of the Manchus; according to his friends, he learnt the Korean language by reading the Bible in translation. After graduating from the Chosŏn Christian College in 1941, he went to Kyoto to continue his studies in English literature. While at the university there, he was arrested by the Japanese police as a suspected

Nationalist sympathizer. He died in prison at Fukuoka, Japan, on February 16, 1945.

(Thursday, May 18, 1948, *The Seoul Times*)

The Heat of Yellow Corn

Sŏ Jŏng-ju (1915–2000)

The stony streambed burns
Beyond the mud-cracked wall;
The heat of yellow corn
Evokes insidious crime.
Leaving the sharp sickle
Hanging on the shelf,
Whither, unseen, has Mother fled?

Where the mountain boar
Of the rocks has snorted past,
Leaving a bloody trail
On the path between the fields,
A leper sits and weeps,
In a red garment dressed.

Supine on the ground,
The serpentine woman,
Sweating and sweating,
Lays me prostrate
In a whirling daze.

(Monday, December 20, 1948, *The Seoul Times*)

The Leper

Sŏ Jŏng-ju (1915–2000)

The leper grieves
Over the sun and the blue sky.

When the moon shines on the cornfield,
He murders a child and eats,

And weeps all night his flower-red weeping.

(Monday, December 20, 1948, *The Seoul Times*)

Self-Portrait

Sŏ Jŏng-ju (1915–2000)

Dad was a serf,

Who seldom came home till late at night.

Home was guarded only by Granny,

Withered like the root of a leek,

And a flowering date-tree.

Big with child,

Mom would always long for sour apricots,

Just one.

Mom's brat was I,

With dirty finger-nails,

Under a rude lamp in the mud wall.

I, with bushy hair and bold-staring eyes,

Am said to take after Grand-dad on Mom's side,

Who, in the year of the insurrection,

Went to sea, so the story goes,

And never returned.

For three and twenty years

The wind has reared four fifths of me.

Ever and more the world has been a place of embarrassment;

Some have read a convict in my eyes,

And some an idiot in my mouth;

Yet will I repent nothing.

At each dawn I have noted

The dew of poesy settled on my brow,

Mixed always with some drops of blood.

I have come thus far panting

Like a cur in malady

With hung-out driveling tongue

In the sun and the shade.

(Thursday, December 30, 1948, *The Seoul Times*)

Midday

Sŏ Jŏng-ju (1915–2000)

Over the path between red flowers
Whose petals taste of drowsy death,

Over the serpentine ridges,
Writhing as if in opiate dream,
You run away and call me after.

And I pursue, holding in both my hands
The keen-scented blood trickling from my nose.

In the scorching midday calm, hushed as night,
We burn and sear along our two bodies.

(Thursday, May 12, 1949, *The Seoul Times*)

A Post-Card
—To Kim Dong-ni—

Sŏ Jŏng-ju (1915–2000)

Having had my hair newly cropped,
I look different from all the other poets.
The sky is good to laugh with my adamantine teeth,
And happy I am to see my nails thicken like tortoise shells.

My friend, we will no more of this idle talk
Of Philomels till after we meet at the nether world.
Why did we have to be so aristocratic
Like the slender-naped Li-Po?

Even the moonlit night of Paul Verlaine
I spend, twining ropes with Poktong the peasant boy;
And should I yet hear the songs of the nightingales,
I pledge to cut off my shameful ears.

(Holograph Manuscript, 1948–1950)

Mountain Swallow

Kim Ch'ŏl-su (1910–?)

You mountain swallow swallow in wearied sorrow having sought in circuitous flights to tarry once more among these native hills and valleys and villages only to forsake them beneath the September dusk closing upon the mountain barricades swallow swallow of the mountains are you?

Here are but mountain ranges melting afar each pointed ridge revoking dreams and dreams of home and of grieving remorse with sailing clouds and floating songs and wind-blown soul

Because of the season of autumn that is here with folded garments in silence and stealthy visitation now I must needs away again somewhere having waved my white handkerchief to the scenes of native hills and rivers O swallow of the mountains

What care I of presidents and kings in regal state and of commanding generals I know not but where the scarlet peppers ripen and redden each to each in clusters on the hill-slopes below the mountain barricades I squat on the fallen walls meditating upon the remembered warmth and freshness of native dawn

Point no more that gun at my breast for virtue sake nor raise that blue saber above my head but pray what trespasses have I been guilty of in my pre-existence to merit this pursuance and now this flight I a mountain swallow?

I of the herd of innocent sheep am I shaking and rubbing and rolling each to each being but one of the herbivorous people the people of little friends and guiltless folk if but ye will leave me be and play tied each to each on leash with the sheep

Ah how I yearn for the springs that return to this my land of native hills and streams with cravings for the dream-locked dusks descending upon the mountain barricades and walls of autumnal September thus and evermore longing with palpitating breast of a mountain swallow swallow I.

(Thursday, May 12, 1949, *The Seoul Times*)

The Demonstrations

Han Ha-un (1920–1975)

I feel like jumping into it,
I feel like jumping into it,

Plumb into that stream,
Into the whirlpool and the roar of the waves,
I feel like flowing with the hurrahing shouts.

Right ahead of the stream
Marches a blood-colored banner, while end on end
The hoarse-voiced people of Korea follow.

All healthy people, all by themselves,
Shouts and sea-roars, crying,
"Give us rice! Give us freedom!"

God! I feel like dashing myself against the sea-roars,
I feel like dying, I feel like dying;
The demonstrators march past while the leper weeps, standing.

(Holograph Manuscript, 1948–1950)

Annual Ring

Pak Mog-wŏl (1916–1978)

She that had sown the seed of sorrow departed nevermore to return, and year by year, as the season revolved, thin-drawn circles of the annual ring were traced in blood delicately round and round the graceful tree.
> (My lass, oh golden lass.)

The slender-naped lad was ever mute with only his black-pupiled eyes growing bigger and rounder, and the unforgettable northern dialect lingered with ever-deepening sorrow ringing and ringing in his ears. The annual ring reddened evermore.
> (My lass, oh golden lass.)

Now the lad has grown to man, his dreams and sorrows and years having flown with the galactic turning of the Milky Way. And still the thin-drawn lines of the annual ring are figured round the graceful tree in the distant forest.
> (My lass, oh golden lass.)

(Holograph Manuscript, 1950)

Beneath the Blue Sky

Pak Du-jin (1916–1998)

Come to me come quickly I say there is a fire sweet homes are ablaze the verdant hills aflame and the roseate flower gardens burning and the neighbors the goodly neighbors weeping had fled and scattered weeping leaving the houses empty.

The wolves are growling and the sheep trembling the wolves howling and growling are fighting with wolves tearing each other's flesh and blood trickling killing and being killed the wolves fighting with wolves shall meet with annihilation through wolves.

The night is bloody but the stars in heaven the stars abide and the sun rises yet wherefore I say come quickly we'll to the fields and dig up anew the ravaged land you and I and together we'll sow the seeds make green the hills and make roseate the flower gardens.

Tall evergreens we'll plant and also annual plants that flourish and decay by season coniferous pines and plums and peach trees we'll also plant and yet again wild roses and pinks and chamomiles we'll also plant awaiting their budding and their season of luxuriant blooming.

When golden birds haunt once more our green hills and the butterflies flutter and the honey-bees swarm into our flower gardens ah how you will rejoice with me the neighbors dispersed in sorrow shall reunite and then how you will rejoice with me dancing and rejoicing together the livelong day beneath the blue sky the deep-blue sky and between the roseate flower gardens where we will dance and sing and weep together rejoicing wherefore come quickly I say.

(Holograph Manuscript, 1950)

Mountain Lodge

Cho Ji-hun (1920–1968)

Beside the closed bamboo gate
The blossom petals are trembling.

The very sound of water soaks
Into this cloud-encircled lodge.

Drenched in the welcome shower,
The iris blades look fresh and cold.

A honeybee drones past
The sun-bathed paper screen.

The rocks squat apart,
Immovable and still,

And look proud beneath
Their green coat of moss.

In the soft vibration
Of a faint whirlwind,

The bracken sprouts
Roll up their fists.

(Wednesday, November 19, 1947, *The Seoul Times*)

Shedding of the Petals

Cho Ji-hun (1920–1968)

What if the petals be shed,
Should the breeze be blamed?

The stars hung beyond the bamboo-screen
Are put out one by one.

The distant hills loom nearer
After the Philomel's song.

Should the candle be blown
Now the petals are falling in flakes?

The shadows of the petals falling
Are dimly cast upon the lawn,

And the white paper-screen
Is faintly flushed.

Lest the frail mind
Of him who lives in refuge

Be revealed to the vulgar,
I have some natural fears.

These petals that are shed in the dawn
Prompt some listless tears.

(Holograph Manuscript, 1950)

VERSES FOR THE YOUNG

By Yun Sŏk-jung (1911–2003)

Half Past Four

A child went to a little store
Kept by a man wrinkled and hoar,
And said: "Sir, Mother asks the time!"
"Tell her, sweet one, it's half past four!"

"Exactly half past four, past four!"
On's way a drinking cock he saw,
So stood and gazed for quite a while.

"Exactly half past four, past four!"
Ere long a round anthill he saw,
So sat and gazed for quite a while.

"Exactly half past four, past four!"
Anon some dragonflies he saw,
So chased and ran for quite a while.

"Exactly half past four, past four!"
With jalap-flowers did he blow
Tra-la la-la-la till he saw
The sun sink suddenly red and low.

"Mummy, he says it's half past four."

The Postman and the Leaves

The children ran out from every door,
And Uncle Postman did implore:

"Give us letter, letters each!"
"None today! Out of the way!"
"Please, O Uncle, we beseech!"

The Postman tears some leaves and scatters:
"Here, then, take these leaves as letters!"

The children stoop for the letters green,
And Postman hies his way between
The rice-fields, and ere long unseen.

Day and Night

Even in broad daylight,
  If but you close your eyes,
    It'll be dark as night.

Even in darkest night,
  If but you close your eyes,
    Things you'll see in mind-sight,
      Clear as in broad daylight.

Shadow

O Shadow, Shadow,
You never get wet.
O for a coat of Shadow,
To walk on rainy days!

O Shadow, Shadow,
You never get caught.
O for a coat of Shadow,
To play in hide and seek!

O Shadow, Shadow,
You never get soiled.
O for a coat of Shadow,
To roll and roll on the ground!

Dew-drops

Night after night
The dewdrops fall
And spend the night
Upon the grass.

This day, the sun
Being hidden in cloud,
They're late to rise.

And lest they stir,
The breeze is soft
And birds are mute.

Child that Lost His Way in Snow

Walking upon the snow,

Crunch, crunch,

He heard the chicks under his feet.

Delighted with the sound,

Crunch, crunch,

Farther and yet farther he went,

Crunch, crunch,

Until at last he lost his way.

"Mummy," he cried, "Mummy!"

And Echo answered, "Mummy!"

Down he plumped upon the snow,

And burst out crying, tears astream;

When anon he saw a row

Of tiny footsteps on the snow.

"My steps, my steps!"

Up he rose, brushed off the snow,

Hied home, retracing his own steps,

Upon the silver snow,

Crunch, crunch.

Lotus Leaves

    The rain

    In vain

Exerts to wet the lotus leaves.

    The leaves

    Receive

And roll the drops in jewels and pearls.

The Train's a Fool

So as not to go astray,

He keeps only to his rails.

The train's a fool, say what you may.

Crossing a bridge over a river,

He screams and screams, for fear of falling.

The train's a fool, say what you may.

With the look of a mouth-organ,

He has no tune or song in him.

The train's a fool, say what you may.

Horsie that Sleeps Standing

O Horsie,
You who sleep standing,
Is it for someone you're waiting?

O Horsie,
You who sleep standing,
Is it you have a pillow wanting?

O Horsie,
You who sleep standing,
Is it of a journey you're dreaming?

O Horsie,
You who sleep standing,
Is it in punishment you're standing?

O Horsie,
You who sleep standing,
Why is it you're not answering?

Child and Acorn

A child was taken to a hill.
"What tree is that?" "An oak, my dear."
"Is't a strong tree?" "Not half, my dear."
"Does't grow naturally?" "O no."

Brother picked up an acorn to show:
"'Tis from this that the oak doth grow."
The child held it upon his palm,
And stared a while in solemn calm.

Where Do They Play?

Where do the stars play?
 In the blue sky.

Where do the gulls play?
 On the blue sea.

Where do we children play?
 On the green lawn.

Stream and Tree

O Stream,

You who down and down do flow,

Is it the sea you want to go?

O Tree,

You who up and up do grow,

Is it the sky you want to know?

Hempen Sandals and Wooden Clogs

An aged woman had two sons,
A sandal-maker and a clog-maker.
On rainy days, the elder son's
Hempen sandals would not sell;
On sunny days, the younger son's
Wooden clogs would not sell.
Day in, day out in solitude
She spent her hours in solicitude.

Said an old man of the village,
Moved to pity by her distress:
"On rainy days, your younger son's
Wooden clogs will surely sell,
And on sunny days, your elder son's
Hempen sandals just as well."

Not till she heard these cheery words
Did she exult, slapping her thigh:
"Good sir, you're right, upon my word!
I've worried for naught, how all absurd!"

Lullaby

Jingle, jingle, jingling bells,
Do not wake our Baby's sleep.
Around the donkey's jingling neck
Hang some pinecones in their stead.
    Upon our Baby blessings heap,
    Sweetly adream, sung to sleep.

Bow-wow, bow-wow, hairy dog,
Do not wake our Baby's sleep.
Let the willow's hairy catkins
Keep the front-gate in his stead.

Cuckoo, cuckoo, cuckoo clock,
Do not wake our Baby's sleep.
Plant a silent sunflower-clock
In the garden in its stead.

O Reindeer

O Elephant!

When there's a fire in our village,

Pray come and put it out for us.

O Bear!

When I have picked some chestnut burs,

Pray open 'em with your paws for me.

O Giraffe!

Those water lilies on the pond,

Will you pick some and give to me?

O Goat!

When I have finished with this book,

You shall have it for snack, I swear.

O Reindeer!

I wish you'd let me hang my hat

Just once upon your branching horns.

The Child and the Wind

The Wind stole in thro' the window and rapidly turned over the leaves of the picture book at which the Child was looking.

"Little Friend! Let us now put the book away, and go out and play."

The Child followed the Wind and spent the whole day out, flying the kite.

The Wind called again the next day. This day the window was closed tight.

He buzzed thro' the chinks, but there was no answer.

Turning round the back terrace, past the front garden, the Wind stepped on to the verandah.

"My word! The screens are also closed."

He happened to find a little hole in the screen, so he peeped thro' it.

"Dear me! This draught!"

The Mother immediately stopped the hole. Cough, cough.

The Child was heard coughing.

"Ah, he must have caught a cold yesterday."

Stepping over the dry pumpkin leaves, the Wind climbed over the fence, and went far far away.

SHORT FICTION

The Rock

Kim Dong-ni (1913–1995)

The wild geese were coming back, crying, from the northern sky. The autumn season was well on the way; the glow-worms were no more to be seen in the evenings, and the Milky Way was slowly moving to the middle of the sky. The destitute and the houseless, who would lie anywhere to pass their summer nights, did not welcome the sound of the wild geese.

Under a railway bridge in the suburb of a town was gathered a motley company of crippled beggars and lepers. Whether lying down with his feet wrapped in a straw-mat,

or squatting with a sack-cloth flung over his shoulders, each felt a fear for the coming season.

"Dammit! gettin' quite chilly these nights!" began an old cripple, lame of one leg.

"Chilly! Don't be jokin'. I feel all me limbs shrivelin' up," joined his neighbor, deformed in one arm.

Two beggar boys nearby were busy learning a street-ballad to be sung at the market:

> "A queer kettle o' fish was he,
> Though a son of a minister;
> Refused the offer o' governorship,
> And sold himself for a penny. . . ."

At this stage of the ballad, the instructor cut them short by a wave of his hand and began to sermonize:

"Lookie! boys! Correct gesture's the thing! Wheder yer stick out yer buttocks, or swing yer neck, or spit out at the right moment, everythin's got to be in time, pat like dat!"

After due preaching, the two boys began again:

"Who the devil is teaching you?

You do a better job yourself

Than I can ever hope to do!

You must've read the ancient books

Of odes and poems and chronicles

To be so learned in your lips;

You have the sage Confucius,

Besides the sophist Mencius,

At your tongue's end and finger-tips. . . ."

This time, every gesture and movement of the neck, the hand, the hips, and the shoulders, seemed to have turned out flawless; they all burst out laughing in apparent satisfaction.

Further below, where the lepers were gathered together, a fresh topic would crop up whenever the train roared past above their heads:

"Auntie, d'ye hear from yer son now and agen?"

The woman addressed as 'Auntie' shook her head silently. For a while, a heavy silence and a dark melancholy would enwrap them.

"By the by, they say the Japs'll kill all lepers and get rid of 'em that way."

"Soorly they won't kill innocent people like that," retaliated 'Auntie,' who had joined them recently from a village nearby.

"Gosh, the days be gettin' cold agen."

As the young man next to her murmured thus, Auntie was suddenly overcome with the thought of her son. Until last year she had a son and a husband to her credit.

Her son was called Sool-I. Though he was approaching thirty, he was still unmarried. But he had saved a sum of over a hundred odd *won,* which among his friends was an object of great envy. He had always said that he would get married when his odd savings reached another round sum of a hundred *won.* He would thus go without his favorite drinks, and even live through the winter without socks. He might well have led a humble and decent life with wife and kids around him, had not his mother been plagued with that cursed disease.

Sool-I had spent all his savings for his mother's medicine; and from the night he had flung away his last twenty *won* in drinking and gambling, he became an unhinged and desperate person. He would walk about with bloodshot eyes, cursing the villagers for no earthly reason, and picking up brawls. Several times he even tried to set fire to his mother's hovel. Early this spring, when fresh buds were appearing on branches, he suddenly disappeared, leaving no trace of his whereabouts.

Having lost the son, her husband became rougher day by day. Night after night he would come home drunk, and beat her. At times he would neglect for days to procure food for her. He never opened his mouth without cursing her to die:

"Quit livin', will yer? I can bury yer wid all me moight while I've got this much stren'th left in me!"

She would weep bitterly whenever such words were spoken. A few months back, when they had been turned out of their household service, he had built a mud hovel behind the village; and telling her to stay indoors, he would go about from house to house looking for odd jobs for the day, or engage himself on some errand for the village pub, and bring home scraps of remnant food, such as rice, and meat, which he would offer to his wife, clacking his tongue with pity and compassion:

"Fill yer belly at least."

It happened early this summer, when the barley ears were coming out, and when gruesome rumors were abroad among the villagers that a wolf had taken away a child in some distant village and that lepers were hiding in certain cornfields. The drunken husband came to look for his wife in the hovel. In his pocket was a parcel, wrapped in newspaper, of rice-cake poisoned with arsenic. It was growing dusky. His wife was sitting by the open straw-mat hanging, scraping an earthen bowl with a worn-out spoon for some dried-up morsels of bean-paste. She threw up a wry grimace to her husband as a sign of welcome, chasing away the swarming flies with her hands.

"U-hum!"

Her husband nervously felt for the parcel in his pocket. Even after entering the hovel, he sat watching her blankly for some time with dim drunken eyes, and then suddenly groped for the parcel again.

Holding the parcel in hand, she grinned back at him once again in apparent gratitude. But the next moment, she was dumbstruck by the bruised, reddish hue of the poisoned rice-cake, and was staring back at her husband with a fearful, accusing look.

From the distant hills the cuckoo-birds were heard singing.

Presently she understood everything and hung her head. Tears were flowing down her red-speckled face of tumor-ridden, corpse-colored flesh.

Her husband turned away in embarrassment, spat on the ground, and stood up:

"My cursed enemy ye're! Quit livin', will yer?" He spat again in apparent confusion, at a loss to save the situation.

The next day a whispering rumor got around among the villagers that, after she had been left by her husband, she did eat the poisoned food in sorrow and desperation, but that death did not come to her so easily, and that she had to go away for good, leaving behind in the hovel a heap of filthy mess that she had vomited of the reddish rice-cake.

The woman wandered through as many villages as her strength would permit. It was not so much because she found begging easier among the villages than in the market, as because she cherished the all but impossible hope of meeting her beloved son again in the course of her distant wanderings. In vain had she spent the summer months in begging and sleeping by the waysides. Her cherished dreams of meeting her son before autumn at the latest had all proved self-deceptive. These days she was even beginning to miss her husband. "I'll bury yer wid all me moight while I've got dis much stren'th in me bones." He who would urge her thus to die, she felt, would surely not refuse to build her a shanty to pass the winter in.

One day at last, driven by compunction, she set out to build for herself a tiny shed under the railway bridge by the side of a field. It was only a shed in name, because she had barely managed to prop up a few wooden sticks on which to hang some straw-matting. At best it might be expected to keep off the frost. But even this had cost her several days' labor. Her mouth, nose, and eyes were molested with the sand, her skin was chapped, and her bones within ached with pain. She lay in a daze for two whole days, groaning.

On the third day, the owner of the field came along and ranted at her in a frenzy:

"Clear this mess at once today, do you hear? Or I'll set fire to it myself!"

So saying in a thunderous voice, he disappeared. But she not only had no strength left to build another shed, but there was no other suitable spot in the vicinity; and she could not demolish the shed herself, even if it might incur the risk of being burnt down to the ground.

Furthermore, she refused to leave this spot under the railway bridge because there was a large rock located just outside the village on the way to the marketplace. Many legends were told of this rock: some called it "The Fortune Rock" or "The Wish Rock," because it gave one good luck and fulfilled one's wishes; others called it "The Tiger Rock," because it looked like a tiger in a lying posture. Several other names were attached to this famous rock. Women would come continuously throughout the year, and pray for their happiness. It was said that if one sat on the rock and scrubbed it all day with a small pebble, and if the pebble should get stuck fast to the rock, then, any wish would come true. Some women would even come with their food prepared, and rub for three days running. It was not only by the praying women folk that the rock was worshipped; but was also respected by the villagers, young and old, who came to play or rest, watching the praying folk.

Sool-I's mother proved no exception in being drawn to this rock. She too felt that she would meet her loving son again if she scrubbed it long enough. For several nights, evading the notice of the villagers, she had scrubbed it, calling her son's name.

It was about a fortnight after she had started rubbing the Wish Rock that she, either by pure accident or by the miraculous influence of the Rock, was given an opportunity to meet her son whom she had longed to see day and night. One morning when people were crowding together into the marketplace, she was about to enter a restaurant, with a gourd in hand, to beg for some food, when someone stopped her by her sleeve. She knew instinctively that it was none other than her son. She looked into his face with raised head. Her long white buckteeth showed themselves instantly.

He walked away, leading his mother by the hand. On the outskirts of the marketplace was an old wall in ruins, along which was a deserted footpath. Mother and Son sat on the footpath overgrown with autumn weeds.

"Mom!"

"Sonny!"

Tears flowed down their cheeks ceaselessly.

"How have yer bin livin', Mom? And where? My God!" Sool-I buried his head in her lap and howled in sorrow as if his heart would burst.

His mother was silent, exposing her long buckteeth only. Tears flowed as of old, even though her flesh was rotting away.

A red dragonfly came and sat on a wild buckwheat blossom among the weeds on the footpath; and a bright-striped snake was crawling into a crack among the stones of the ruined wall.

"I'll work hard and bring back money quickly, I swear. We'll live together. Wait for me. Don't die before I come back with some money."

With such words did the son plead to his mother, stroking her shoulders and arms.

They went back to the market. Sool-I emptied his pocket of all his cash and gave it to her, which amounted to some seven copper pieces. Promising to be back in a couple of days, he parted with her in front of a rice-cake shop.

The sun was already nearing the west. In the midst of the general confusion and hubbub of so many swarming bees—vociferous folk coming and going in haste, men driving oxen or carrying fuel, women tarrying with babies on their backs and large wooden bowls on their heads, boys wriggling past on bicycles, Japanese *hakamas* on rickshaws swaying this way and that, some chatting and laughing, others quarreling and gripping each other by the throat, and still others munching something or weeping—through such a scene of human disorder was Sool-I sauntering with heavy steps, alone.

"The bridge past the Wish Rock!" he was mumbling to himself as he walked through the crowd aimlessly, with downcast head and an empty rack on his back.

Now that he was in the marketplace after long absence, he was anxious to hear some news of his father also. But none told him anything certain: that he was said to be tottering about the streets, stricken with palsy, or that he was rumored to be engaged in menial labor at some inn or other, gasping with asthma. None had anything good to say.

Having once met her son, the woman began to miss him all the more. Everyday she was around in the marketplace. A week, a fortnight, a month passed; but the son, who was due to return "within a couple of days," did not appear.

More than ever before, she had only the Rock to rely upon. As long as the Rock remained on earth, she would sooner or later reunite with her son, and, fortune favoring her, be able to cure herself of the fatal disease. Such was her blind faith in the miracle of the Rock.

"Rain or snow, let me but worship the Rock!"

Thus she would drag her heavy body up the Rock to scrub it every night after the people had gone to sleep. But the miracle did not work so easily this time. It occurred to her that the Rock might be insensitive of her ardent devotion because she had shown it only in the darkness of the night. So from the following day she decided to show it at daytime, whenever people were not looking.

It proved extremely difficult, however, to escape the notice of the villagers during daytime. One day she was scrubbing the Rock, praying as usual, when suddenly she felt a rope round her neck, and the next moment she was aware of a precipitous fall. By the time she had been dragged like a dog up to the bridge, she was bleeding all over, having even lost her consciousness. When finally she was brought to herself again, she noticed that the villagers were bringing up water to the Rock and washing it.

Henceforth, whenever she passed by the Rock, she would only stand and stare at it blankly, as if her feet were stuck to the ground. To her the Rock was something infinitely desirable, and at the same time, an object of envy, longing, and bitter grudge, because she felt her whole fortune, good or ill, to depend upon it.

This day again she was returning from her day's wandering in the marketplace. It was already dusk. The surrounding hills, the stream, and the village were wrapped in the ashy twilight. With heavy steps and drooping head, she was moving along her accustomed route past the village, with a gourd in hand. Inside the vessel was a jumbled assortment of odd edibles, rice-cake, bean curd, persimmon, jelly, dates, candy, noodles, bean sprouts, and lopped heads and tails of fish. Now and again she would stand to look back, glance at her day's ration in the gourd, and then start walking again.

"Why didn't I ask 'em there and then to make sure?" she murmured several times.

She was thinking of a conversation, which she happened to overhear while begging for some jelly at a pudding-shop. An old man who was selling persimmons in front of the shop was talking with someone:

"Sool-I not out yet?"

"How so soon, wid a six month sentence?"

It was some such exchange of words that she thought she had vaguely overheard. She had hardly been attentive to their talk then, partly because her mind was preoccupied with the thought of acquiring some food at the shop, but chiefly because she had never dreamt that her son would be a topic of their conversation. But now that she was walking past the village with the Rock seen ahead of her at some distance, those words which had skimmed over her consciousness at the market suddenly flashed past her head and arrested her whole being. Yes, they were distinctly speaking of her son by name. The more she ruminated, the more convinced she felt of their reference to Sool-I.

His name still ringing in her ears, she hesitated for a moment, wondering whether she should go back to the marketplace; but after a glance at her gourd, she resumed her gait. Her body was aching with pain, her legs so stiff that she might fall any moment, and her head swimming dizzy as if in fever.

By the time she reached the Rock, the sun had already set, and darkness was spreading its wings over the fields far and near. Automatically she halted and raised her head to stare at the Rock, and then in the direction of her nightly shed. Just then, her eyes caught sight of a burning fire where had stood the familiar shape of the small shed. For a moment, she doubted her own eyes. She looked again; it was a fire after all. She stood in petrifaction. The flame was blazing even inside her closed eyelids. Open or shut, the fire was there palpably. Instantly she fell down on the Rock like a block of wood.

With hands that had already turned numb and senseless, she groped for the Rock. Hugging and caressing it, she began to rub her corpse-colored cheeks on it with a seeming calm of resignation.

A line of cold tears trickled down the Rock.

The next morning the villagers were gathered round the Rock. They were all spitting and cursing:

"Why, the filthy wretch's chosen this very spot to die in!"

"The leper's gone stiff hugging at the Wish Rock!"

"And defiled it, too!"

The two cheeks of the woman prostrate on the Rock were shining with smeared blots of dry tears.

(Thursday, December 9–Monday, December 13, 1948, *The Seoul Times*)

The Wing

Yi Sang (1910–1937)

That No. 33 is not unlike a brothel in its layout. Eighteen households jostle together in one block, shoulder to shoulder in a row, with the same screen and the same oven-hole. And besides, all the occupants are young like so many flowers. The sun never comes in, because the people do not take note of it. The soiled bedclothes that are hung out to dry on the wire line just below the eaves, serve as an excuse for keeping off the sunshine from the screens. Inside the dusky rooms the people are all asleep during the day. I do not know whether they sleep at night or not. I have no means of finding out because I myself sleep day and night. A hushed silence reigns over the eighteen households of No. 33 in the daytime.

This silence is broken towards the evening. As it grows dusky, the people take in their bedding. A hubbub of brisk activity begins in the eighteen households after the electric lights come in. Screens are opened and shut incessantly. Various smells come drifting to the nostrils, smells of grilled herring, and rice water, smells of face powder and soap. . . .

But what arrests one's attention in particular is their nameplates. There is indeed a communal single-flapped gate, detached from the block, for the eighteen households; but this has never once been closed so that it might just as well be part of the street. A street vendor can walk through it any time of the day. The occupants do not buy things at the gate; they have but to open their screens, and they can buy bean curds from their own rooms. It is thus pointless to have their eighteen nameplates in line on the gate. Each household has unwittingly adopted the custom of fixing its nameplate just above the screen beside some such nomenclature as "the Abode of All Endurance" or "the Abode of Happiness" in Chinese calligraphy.

It is in accordance with such tacit custom that there should be found above my own screen-door a name-card, not of myself but of my wife, about a quarter of the size of an ordinary playing card.

I have little contact with any of the fellow occupants. Nor do I exchange greetings.

With the exception of my wife, I have had no particular desire to speak to any one of them.

It is because I have felt all along that such an intimacy would hardly be any credit to my wife, so mindful am I of my love and honor for my wife.

Furthermore, it is because I know that my wife, like her name-card, is the most modest and most beautiful being in the whole of the eighteen households of No. 33. Among the many flowers crowded together in these eighteen establishments, my wife has ever been the one flower of unique beauty beneath the corrugated iron roof of this sunless quarter. It is therefore only natural that I should feel an indescribable embarrassment in my own existence that guards her, or rather, is dependent on her.

My room is never my permanent home. I have no home. But this room suits me well enough. Its temperature goes well with that of my body, and its dimness with my eyesight. I have desired it to be neither warmer nor cooler, neither lighter nor cozier. I have always felt thankful for my room for preserving what little I have desired in a room. I have been gratified with the feeling that I was after all born into this life for such a room.

But this was never a means of calculating my happiness or unhappiness. I have, as it were, never had the necessity to feel happy, or, for that matter, unhappy. If I just idled away my days and months with no specific aim in view, that was that, and nothing more to it.

Rolling about inertly in a room that fitted my mind and body like a tailor-made suit, with no such world of thought as happiness or unhappiness, was to me a mode of life greatly to be desired, one, as it were, of absolute ease and comfort.

This room of mine was the seventh from the gate. The "lucky seven" was not without significance. I cherished the number 7 like a medal. Who would have thought that this room, which was partitioned into two halves, was to be the symbol of my fate?

The outer section of our room does have some sunlight, which in the morning is about the size of a cloth-wrapper, dwindling in the afternoon into a handkerchief before it disappears. I need hardly point out that the inner half, which receives no sunlight, is my own quarter. I do not remember how we came to decide that the sunny half should be my wife's room and the darker half my own. Not that I have anything to complain of.

As soon as my wife goes out, I go into her room and open the window on the eastern side. I derive a unique pleasure from watching the sunlight bring out all sorts of gorgeous colors and patterns from the innumerable quaint toilet bottles on her toilet stand. I take out a small lens and play with it in the sun, burning soft sheets of toilet paper, which only my wife uses. Those all but brief moments of tension would prove an experience of fascinating thrill, as I would the sunlight focused on the tissue paper issuing a thin line of smoke up to my nostrils and eventually making a hole in it.

After a while, when this wearies me, I take out my wife's hand mirror and play with it also. A mirror is after all a toy, except when it is made to serve a practical purpose in reflecting one's own face.

This too wearies me in turn. My playful mood leaps at once from the physical plane to the mental. I discard the mirror and sit before my wife's toilet stand to watch those toilet bottles of variegated shape arrayed before me. They attract my being more than anything else in the world. I pick out one of them, open its lid slowly and bring it to my nostrils, killing my breath and softly inhaling its smell. As its exotic sensual smell penetrates into my lungs, I find myself closing my eyes. Distinctly it is a fragment of my wife's smell. Closing the lid again, I try to remember which part of her body issues forth this perfume. But it is very difficult to unravel because her smell is the sum total of these bottled scents and perfumes arrayed here.

Her room was always colorful, whereas mine was somber without a single nail on the wall; hers was decorated on all sides with gorgeous-colored skirts and vests hanging from many nails below the ceiling. The patterns on her garments were beautiful to look at. I would always imagine her torso and all her possible movements in these colorful skirts, and would feel not a little emotional disturbance.

And yet, I had no clothes myself. My wife never gave me any clothes. The corduroy suit I had on served me as pajamas, workaday clothes and my Sunday best. I had a jersey with high collars that served me as a vest all the year round. Both my suit and my jersey were dark-colored. It is my conjecture that this was doubtless to make them look clean as to save my wife the trouble of washing as much as possible. I would spend my days in quiet contentment, dressed in my soft pants with elastic bands around the waist and the thighs.

Meanwhile, the handkerchief-shaped sunlight has gone, but my wife is not home yet. Partly with fatigue as a result of my afternoon play, and partly from my desire not to be found in her room, I retire into my quarter. It is dim and gloomy. I roll into bed and go to sleep. My bedding, which has never once been folded up, receives my body perfectly as if it were a part of myself. Sometimes I sleep well; but now and again my whole body aches with such pain that I find it impossible to fall asleep. On such occasions I choose any odd subject to meet my needs of speculation. Wrapped in my slightly damp bedclothes, I have made many a discovery, written many a dissertation, and composed many a poem. But no sooner do I fall asleep than all the feats of my wild imagination melt away like soap into the sagging stagnant air that fills my room, and when I wake again I invariably find myself to be nothing but a membrane of nerves, no better than a pillow stuffed with buckwheat chaff in a cotton cover.

There is one thing in life, which stirs my hate: bedbugs. They pester me all through the year; even in winter they never fail to visit me in twos and threes. If I have any worry, it is that caused by my hatred of these insects. When they have bitten, I scratch and scratch to the point of bleeding and smarting. Doubtless it is a peculiar sensation of pleasure. Then I fall into a deep sleep.

Never once, however, have I chosen to reach any positive conclusion in my silent meditation in bed. It is because I have never had the necessity to. Even if I were to arrive at some conclusive point, I would have to consult with my wife on it, in which case I would only be an object of her rebuke. It is not that I am afraid of her rebuke, but that I simply can't be bothered with it at all, whether in living up to my potential capacities as a decent social creature or in being considered worthy of my wife's scolding.

Like a lazy animal, I was content to wallow in my very sloth. If possible, I wished to be relieved of this meaningless human bondage.

I was a stranger in human society. To me everything in life was a misfit.

My wife washes her face twice a day. And I don't even once. Sometimes at three or four in the morning, I find myself standing blankly in the moonlit yard as I return from the lavatory. That is why I hardly ever meet with any of the occupants of the eighteen households. Nonetheless, I remember the faces of nearly all the young women in the block. They were all without exception inferior to my wife in beauty.

Her first toilet of the day, which takes place around eleven, is comparatively simple. But her second one around seven in the evening is more complicated. She wears better and smarter dresses in the evenings than during the day. But she has her outings at all odd hours.

Is it because she has some regular job or other? There is no knowing on my part. If she had no work, she would have little occasion to go out so often any more than I. But she not only goes out often but has many guests. And on days when she has guests coming continuously, I have to stay in bed in my room all day long, deprived of the pleasure of playing with the lens or of enjoying the perfume of her toilet bottles. On such occasions I would deliberately assume an air of melancholy. My wife would then give me money—a fifty-cent silver coin. Much as I liked to receive these coins, I would never know how to spend them, so that I would just leave them about by my pillow, and in due course they added up to quite a decent sum.

Noticing this one day, my wife bought me a saving-box in the shape of a miniature safe. I dropped my coins into it one by one, and my wife kept the key. I remember putting some more occasional coins into it. I continued to wallow in my sloth. Some time after I discovered it to be unusually light, when quite coincidentally I happened to notice a small pimple-like hairpin, hitherto unseen on her coiffure. Was the one an evidence of the other? Be that as it may, I had no further occasion to handle the saving-box again. I could hardly be bothered to stir my inertia with such things.

When my wife had guests in her room, I could not sleep so soundly as on rainy days. On such occasions I would ask myself why she had so much money to spare.

Presumably, her guests were unaware of the fact that I was just across the screen partition; without any sign of hesitation they would crack such outspoken jokes as I myself would hardly have ventured to exchange with my own wife. But this much at least could be said for those small companies who surrounded my wife that they had had enough decency in them to make it a rule to leave soon after midnight. Some of them did indeed seem to show little breeding, that they would on the whole make up for their shortcomings by jovialities over food which they would order for entertainment.

Though I started wondering what my wife's profession could possibly be, it was difficult enough to make the right conjecture with my poor imagination and limited store of experience.

My wife used always to wear new socks only. She also did the cooking. Though I had never seen her do it myself, I gathered as much because she would regularly bring my daily meals to my own room. Since there were only two of us in the family, there was no shadow of a doubt that my wife was personally responsible for the preparation of my meals.

But never once did my wife invite me to her room; eating and sleeping as I always did in my own room. Nor for that matter did I ever enjoy my meals, so plain were they, though I would in all passivity munch away whatever was given me, as a chicken or a puppy would be fed. It was not without a secret sense of self-pity that I ate my grub. I saw myself getting thinner and paler every day, with visible signs of physical debility. I became so bare-boned on account of malnutrition that I found myself hardly able to endure the physical pain of sleeping through a night without hurting over and over again.

And so lying in bed I was led to scrutinize in my mind the source and origin of that money which was so readily available to my wife, and at the same time, to speculate in my naïve fashion on the nature of that food which I could smell through the cracks of the screen partition between her room and mine. I was not to sleep soundly in any case.

At last I realized. The money, which my wife had to spend and to spare, must surely be that given to her by those unknown visitors of hers, who to me were no more than foolish and despicable people. But why they should give her any money at all or that she should receive it of them was beyond my conception of custom or etiquette.

Would it be but a mere formality? Or would there be something more to it in perhaps a form of remuneration or reward? Did my wife strike them as some pathetic creature that deserved their compassion?

As I pursued such never-ending thoughts, I would feel more and more confused. Whatever conclusions I might seem to have reached before dozing off to sleep were to me but misgivings of the distasteful kind; and yet never once did I bring myself to ask her directly in order to clear my own doubts. It was not only because I could not really be bothered to bestir myself from that torpor, but also because, waking again after a snatch of sleep, I would find myself in a state of complete mental blank, oblivious of all that had gone before, as if I were born an entirely new person.

On departure of her guests, or on returning from her outing, my wife would change into a simple dress, and visit my room. Raising my blanket, she would endeavor to comfort me with some articulate words whispered into my ears. With a faint smile, neither derisive nor painful nor sincere, I would look into her beautiful face. She would smile back sweetly. But rarely did I fail to catch that glimpse of sorrow lurking behind her expression.

She would surely be aware of my hunger, but she never offered to serve me the remnant of the food in her room. Since this was undoubtedly out of her sincere respect for me, I would gladly feel reassured in my mind, hungry though I might be. Not that I ever had the presence of mind to recall her whispered words. I would merely note time and again the dull gleam of the silver coin below the lamplight by my pillow.

How many coins by now would be saved in that miniature safe? I never brought myself to lifting it to see. With no specific desire or end in view, I would but mechanically drop the coins into it through that buttonhole of a chink.

Just as it remained a perpetual mystery to me why her visitors should leave her money, so it was ever an unresolved question as to why my wife should leave those odd coins in my room. Even if I were to admit to myself of a certain indifferent pleasure in receiving money from her, it did not amount to no more and no less than that momentary sensation, trivial in itself, of feeling the coins between my finger-tips for that brief span of time as I would pick them up to drop into the saving-box hole.

For some reason or other I threw the saving-box one day into the lavatory. A considerable number of coins must have been contained in it, though I could by no means be certain of the exact number.

To think that I was living on this earth, which was being whirled through the infinite spaces of cyclonic wind, was to create in me a feeling of vacuity. Ah! How I yearned to be relieved of this vertigo of existence on this busy earth.

The very act of dropping silver coins into the box had become something wearisome after such harassing thoughts in bed. I secretly wished that my wife would take charge of the whole thing, since I had no use whatsoever for either the box or the money whereas they would in reality be of use to her. But she did not take it into her room. At times I would wonder whether I should take it myself and leave it in her room, but then it would invariably happen that her room would be full of guests, and I would never have the opportunity of seeing her in private. So I came to decide upon the disposal of the box by dropping it into the latrine.

In solemn gloom I expected my wife to pick up a fuss. But she never cast any reflections on my rash act. Not only did she remain silent but she still continued to leave money by my pillow. The silver coins made quite a heap in no time.

I started meditating again in bed that it was perhaps a sort of pleasure pure and simple that I derived from the money, whether it be left by my wife's guests [*The translator's holograph manuscript leaves off at this point.*]

Editor's Note:
"Yi Sang" was the pen name of Kim Hae-kyŏng (1910–1937), a literary genius who left many episodes revealing his idiosyncratic personality. He died young from tuberculosis. Several of his stories, including the above one, are considered to be autobiographical.

[The above fragmentary translation of the story remains only in the translator's holograph manuscript, and has never been published.]

제4부
현대영시 번역

T. S. 엘리어트 (T. S. Eliot, 1888-1965)

荒蕪地 (*The Wasteland*)

第一部 埋葬

四月은 殘忍한 달이라
荒廢한 땅에서도 라일락은 크고
追憶과 情欲을 뒤섞으면서
잠 든 뿌리를 봄비로 깨우쳐 준다.
三冬은 차라리 따스했거니
大地를 忘却의 白雪로 덮어 주고
빼마른 감자낱의 가냘픈 목숨을 이었었거니.
여름은 또 난데없이 스타안벨거세의 湖水를 건너
묻어오는 소낙비로 우리를 놀라게 하면
두리기둥 廻廊에 발을 멈췄다가
비가 들면 햇볕 속을 庭園으로 가서
커피를 마시면서 한 時間쯤 이야기를 했드니라.
난 아라사 사람 아니애요. 出生은 리투아니야이지만 純獨逸血 統인걸요.
그리구 어렸을땐 四寸되는 皇太子집에 같이 있었는데
썰매를 태 줬을땐 참 무서웠어요.
"마리! 마리! 꼭 부짭어" 하드니만 쏜살같이 미끄러져 내리드군요.
山에서야 정말 自由스럽지요.
밤에는 늦도록 책을 읽구요 겨울엔 南쪽으로 避寒가지요

이 돌밭에 뻗어난 가지는 무엇이며
악착하게 얽힌 뿌리는 또 무엇이란 말이냐?
사람된 者여 너는 알기는커녕 짐작도 못하리니
뜨거운 햇빛 아래 나무그늘도 귀또리의 慰安도
돌틈을 새는 물소리도 없는 이곳에

네가 아는 것 다만 산산이 부셔진 形象의 조각조각.
오직 그늘이란 이 붉은 바위 밑 뿐이니
(어서 이 붉은 바위 그늘로 들어오려므나)
그러면 나는 너에게 알려주리라.
아침에 너를 뒤딸른 그림자나
저녁에 너를 막아서는 그림자와는 다른
한줌 흙속에 묻힌 무서움을 보여주리라.
  바람은 시원하게
  故鄕으로 부는데
  愛蘭의 우리 님은
  어데 있기 못오뇨?
"당신은 昨年 처음으로 저에게 히아씬쓰를 주셨지요.
그래서 모두들 저를 히아씬쓰 아가씨라 부릅데다."
―그러나 이슬에 젖은 머리를 흐트린채
한 아름 꽃을 안은 너와 더부러
히아씬쓰 꽃밭에서 밤 늦게 돌아왔을 때
나는 말도 못했고 눈마자 멀어
生死도 意識도 없었드니라
그저 물끄러미 寂然한 燈心을 凝視했드니라.
바다는 거칠고 쓸쓸도 허이.

有名한 占術家 쏘쏘쓰트리쓰 女史는
毒한 感氣를 알았지만 여전히
귀신같이 맞히기로 全 歐羅巴에 소문이 자자하고
한벌 靈妙한 카아드를 가졌는데 그의 말이다.
여기 뽑은 당신 카아드는 물에 빠진 페니키아 뱃사공의 卦요
(보라! 그의 눈은 眞珠로 化했나니.)
이것은 벨라돈나 巖穴의 淑女인데
萬古 風浪의 女性.
그리구 이것은 지팡이 셋 짚은 사나이 그리구 이것은 바퀴

그리구 여기 나온 것이 애꾸눈 商人인데
이 空白의 카아드는 그가 등에 지고 가는 것이지만
나는 보아서 안 될 것입네다.
絞殺當한 사나이는 보이지 않습니다. 물 조심하세요.
數 많은 사람들이 圓을 그려 뺑 뺑 돌고 있군요.
또 오세요. 혹시나 저의 親舊 에쿠이토온 夫人을 만나시거든
天空圖를 내 몸소 가져간다고 傳해 주세요.
요지음은 하도 때가 險惡하니깐요.

虛妄한 都市
겨울 아침 누루무레한 안갯 속을
倫敦橋 위로 밀려가는 數 많은 群衆
나는 짐작도 못했드니라 주검이 저만치 많은 生命을 앗아갔다고는.
이따금 가쁜 한숨을 내쉬면서
앞만 보고 가는 사람들.
언덕길을 올라서 윌리암 王街로 내려서면
울려오는 聖 마리아 울노스 敎會의 鐘 소리가
아홉점 마즈막 자즈러지는 소리를 친다.
거기서 나는 親舊를 만나 붙잡고 소리를 쳤다.
"스텟쯘 君! 이 사람 마일리 海戰에서 生死를 같이 하던 친구여!
자네가 去年 마당에 심어둔 屍體가
이젠 싹틀때도 되지 않았나? 올해쯤 꽃이라도 피지 않을까?
아 이 사람! 사람의 친구 개란 놈은 아주 멀찌기 하게!
그놈이 발톱으로 후벼낼지도 모르겠네!
그대! 僞善의 讀者여!—나의 同類—나의 兄弟여!"

第二部 將棋

몸을 포긴 椅子는 눈 부신 玉座와도 같이
大理石 바닥 위에 빛나고

사이로 金빛 큐피돈이 기웃거리는

(또 하나는 날개로 눈을 가리운)

주렁주렁 열린 葡萄넝쿨을 彫刻한

두 기둥 사이로 천장까지도 닿는 거울은

일곱 갈래로 된 燭臺의 불빛을 反映하고

테불에 反射된 불 빛은

緋緞 佩物쇨에서 쏟아져 나온

寶石의 燦爛한 光彩와 마주치며

마개 뺀 象牙色 琉璃 瓶속에는

女子의 恍惚한 여러가지 香臭가 어리어

香油 가루粉 물粉—感覺은 香氣에 괴롭고 어지럽고 醉하고

窓에서 흘러드는 산뜻한 바람에 香氣는

길게 일렁이는 촛불을 키우면서 위로 떠오르며

촛불의 거림은 反射鏡을 그슬러

우물반자의 무늬 위에 설레인다.

그리고 구리火箸로 집어 넣은 굵다란 海水에 쩌른 火木은

暖爐앞 五色 大理石 기둥 새에서 유자빛 푸른 빛으로 피어 올라

거기 彫刻된 海豚이 그 슬픈 光線속에서 헤엄친다.

古風의 맨틀 위에는

窓밖으로 숲 景致를 내다보듯

무지스런 임금에게 凌辱을 當한

필로멜의 幻生이 그려저 있으니

아직도 그림 속 꾀꼬리의 맑은 목청은

왼 沙漠을 울리며 여전히 울건만

俗된 衆生은 여전히 貪淫하니

더러운 귀에는 그저 "쩍 쩍"하고 들릴뿐이다.

그리고 그밖에도 시드른 낡은 時代의 그루터기가

壁에 걸려있으니 凝視하는 肖像은

앞으로 수그린듯 끼웃거리고 에워싼 房안을 고요히 한다.

층층계에서 발소리가 들려온다.

불빛 아래 빗어내린 女子의 머리털은
불꽃처럼 퍼져
말할듯 타오르다가는 또 무서울만치 고요해진다

"오늘밤엔 내 神經이 아주 異常해요. 정말이예요. 가지 마세요.
이얘길 하세요 왜 이얘길 안 하세요? 하시라닌깐!
당신 맘속은 도무지 알수없어요 생각을 하세요."

나는 생각노니 우리는 지금
죽은이가 뼈를 잃은 쥐구먹에 있나보오.

"저 소린 무엇예요?"
　　　門틈에 바람 소리.
"저것은 또 무엇이예요? 바람이 뭘 한단말이예요?"
　　　아무것도 아무것도 아니야.
"당신은
아는 것이 없어요? 보는것도 記憶하는것도 없어요?"

나는 記憶하노니
그의 눈은 眞珠로 化했느니라.
"아니 당신은 살았는거요 죽었는거요? 머리속엔 아무것도 없단 말예요?"
그러나
아, 저 셰익스피어처럼 떠받드는
검둥이들의 흥청대는 가락이라니―
기막히게 맵시 있고
기막히게 聰明한.
"이제 난 뭘 할가요? 뭘 해요?
나는 이대로 튀어나가 거리를 걸어볼테여요.
머리랑 이렇게 풀어헤친채. 그리구 來日은 뭘 할가요?
두고 두고 난 뭐하면 좋아요?"

             열時엔 더운물.
비가 오면 네時에 닫혀진 自動車를 타고
그리구 한판 將棋를 뒤고나면
감기지 않은 눈을 감고 門에 녹크를 기다릴뿐

릴의 남편이 軍隊에서 돌아올 무렵에
나는 아주 露骨하게 말했는걸
—여러분 時間입니다 빨리 해주십시요—
앨버트가 日間 돌아오니까 너 몸단속 좀 해야쟎나
이[齒] 해박으라구 주고간 돈 어디 썼느냐구
물어볼게닌깐 으레. 분명히 주었어 내눈으로본걸.
릴! 죄다 빼버리구 참한걸루 다시 해 박우
보기숭해 죽겠어——이런 말투랬다우 거짓말아냐.
그래서 나두 "정말 그래" 하구 맞장구를 쳤어.
너 딱한 앨버트 생각도 좀 해봐
四年이나 軍隊사릴 했으니 실컨 재미도 보구 싶을거야
그런데 네가 받어주지 않으면 나설 사람이야 얼마든지 있다고 했드니
으흥 그래? 하구 실룩거리길래 내말이 過히 틀리지 않을게라구 했지.
그랬드니 그럼 대강 짐작이 간다구 눈총을 주겠지.
—여러분 時間입니다 빨리 해주십시요—
내말이 귀에 거슬리거던 좋을대루 하라고 쏘아주면서
너는 매인 몸이지만 남이야 골라잡을수도있단다.
그건 또 그렇다 치드라두 앨버트가 너를 버리는 날엔
미리 일러주지 않은 탓이라곤 아예 입밖에두 내지마러.
그렇게 늙어뵈는 상파대기 조곰은 부끄러워 할 줄도 알아야 한다고 일러줬드니
(나이는 겨우 설흔하나 이면서)
언짢은 얼굴로 하는말이 人力으로 못하는 노릇 어떻거란 말이야
그걸 지우랴고 먹은 丸藥 때문인걸
(허긴 벌서 다섯이나 나왔는데 막내이 조오지 땐 죽을번 했어)
藥局主人은 괜찮을게라구 했지만

그걸 먹은 뒤로는 영 몸이 전같지 않다구 하겠지.
그래서 네가 어수룩한 바보란거야
거봐 앨버트가 자꾸만 건디리는것 어떻거람
어린애 낳기 싫은걸 뭣하러 結婚하느냐구 해줬지
—여러분 時間입니다 돌아가 주십시요—
그러자 고댐 空日 앨버트가 돌아오든 날
돼지 뒷다리를 장만해놓구
뜨끈뜨끈할때 같이 맛보자구 나를 저녁에 불렀겠지.
—時間이 다 됐읍니다 어서 돌아가 주십시요
—時間이 다 됐읍니다 어서 돌아가 주십시요—
빌, 또 만나. 루, 잘자요. 메이, 좋은 꿈꾸어
안녕, 안녕, 잘 가요, 조심들 해.
안녕히 주무세요. 貴婦人들, 안녕히 주무세요. 안녕히들 주무십시요.

第三部 火敎

江을 덮었든 張幕은 걷히우고
마즈막 간당거리는 나무잎이 濕한 江기슭에 나려앉는다.
바람은 蕭條히 黃土 벌판을 불고 水靈은 어디론지 떠나버렸다.
고이 흐르라 情든 템스여 나의 노래가 끝날때 까지.
물 위엔 빈 瓶도 쌘드위치 꺼풀도
비단 손수건도 馬糞紙 箱子도 卷煙토막도
또 무슨 여름밤의 證據品도 보이지 않는다. 水靈은 어데론지 떠나버렸다.
都心地 重役들의 호강스런 子弟들도 그들과 함께
杳然히 行方을 감추었다.
나는 리만 湖畔에 앉아 울었드니라.…
고이 흐르라 情든 템스여 나의 노래가 끝날때까지.
고이 흐르라 情든 템스여 나는 울지도 불지도 않으리니.
그러나 등뒤에는 一陣 寒風에 白骨이 덜걱이고
귀에서 귀로 속사기는 嘲笑의 킥키거림이 들려온다.

어느 땐가 荒凉한 겨울 夕陽에 瓦斯 탱크 뒤를돌아

濁한 運河에 낙시를 드리우고

難破한 兄王과

그보다도 앞선 父王의 죽엄을 슬퍼했을때

더러운 뱃대지를 江기슭에 끌면서

소리없이 풀밭을 기어가든 한마리의 쥐.

濕地 위엔 헐벗은 屍體가 딩굴고

몬지 쌓인 다락 골방엔

해마다 쥐 발에 뒤채이는 白骨이 있다.

그러나 이따금씩 내 뒤에서는

봄이 오면 쓰위니氏를 포오터夫人에게로 태워다 주는

모터와 고동 소리가 들려온다.

포오터 母女가 쏘다 水에 발을 씻는날 밤의

아―皎皎 明月이여

아―둥근 집웅아래서 合唱하는 어린이들의 노랫소리여!

트윗 트윗 트윗

쩍 쩍 쩍 쩍 쩍 쩍

그다지도 무지하게 劫奪했든고

테리우

虛妄한 都市

겨울날 누우런 안개 속에

수염이 주렁주렁한 쓰머너의 商人 유제니디스氏는

호주머니에 한오큼 乾葡萄와

倫敦入港 運賃及 保險料 賣主負担의 船荷證書와 書類로 賣買되는 入荷案內書를 지니고

쌍스러운 佛語로 나를 請하여

캐논街 호텔에서 점심을 하고

週末에는 首都호텔에서 놀자고 했다.

저녁때 눈과 등이 책상에서 기지개를 키며 도라다 볼때
人間의 엔진이 털털거리는 택시처럼 待機할때
비록 눈은 멀었을망정 두가지 生의 中間에서 날뛰는
쭈그러진 女子의 젓가슴을 갓인 늙은 사나이
나 티레씨에스는 보노니
모두다 집으로 발걸음을 재촉하고
먼 바다에서 뱃사람이 돌아오는 黃昏
茶詩間 대여 도라온 타이피스트는 이제야 아침설거지를 하고
暖爐에 불을 피우곤 통조림 飮食을 느려놓는다
窓 밖에 위태로이 널린 속옷을 마지막 夕陽이 물드리고
밤에는 寢臺로 쓰는 디밴 위에는
양말짝이며 슬맆퍼며 단속옷 콜세트가 쌓어있다.
쭈그러진 젓가슴의 늙은 사나이 나 티레씨애스는
이 光景을 보며는 其余는 於此可知라
나도 함께 約束한 손님을 기다린다.
이윽고 나타난 그는 여드름이 한창인 젊은 사나이
一個 小住宅事務所의 書記 눈매가 당돌하고
배운것은 없으나 제딴에는
부래드포드 巨富의 씰크햇트 처럼 自信이 있다.
저녁은 먹었고 女子는 나른하니
때는 알맞다고 짐작을 하는지라
은근히 달래보면 女子는
반기지도 않지만 뿌리치지도 않는다.
얼굴에 핏기를 돋구어 決心을 하고 달겨든다.
이윽고 더듬는 손이 反抗을 만나지 않으니
사내의 虛榮이 應待를 바라지 않기에
女子의 無關心을 도로혀 반긴다.
(그러기에 티레씨애스 나는 일찌기
테에베스 城壁下에 앉아 嘆息도 하고
賤한이들과 地獄을 거닐기도 하며

寢臺 兼한 디밴 위에 行해지는 모든 것은 미리 當했느니라.)
사내는 마지막으로 사랑의 키쓰를 주고
더듬어 내리는 층층계엔 불이 없었다....
女子는 도라서서 잠시 거울을 보고
愛人은 그저 보낸둥 만둥
생각아닌 생각만이 머리에 떠오른다.
"이젠 끝났으니 한짐 덜었다."
얌전한 女性이 어리석음에 빠져
새삼스레 혼자서 房을 거닐다간
自動式 손으로 머리를 쓰다듬고는
蓄音機에 레코드를 건다.

"이 音樂이 나를 따라와"
스트랜드 빅토리아 女王街로 올라오는구나.
아 都市여 都市여 나는 이따금
템스 밑바지의 술집을 지나면서
구슬픈 만도린의 노랫소리와
낮술 먹는 漁夫들의 말소리 구둣소리를 듣는데
그 옆엔 殉敎者 매그누스의 聖堂이
흰빛 금빛 이오니아의 燦爛한 榮華를 黙示한다.

江은
기름과 타마유의 땀을 흘리고
배는
썰물과 더부러 떠나가는데
넓고
붉은 돛은
바람을 받아 육중한 돛대를 돈다.
배는
떠가는 통나무를 물결로 적시면서

狗島를 지나 그리니지 水道를 잡아든다.
  어화 어여우 상사뒤야
  어화 어여우 상사뒤야

櫓를 젓는
엘리사베스와 레스터
고물[船尾]은
붉은빛 금빛을 씨운
조개 모양
날뛰는 물결은
兩岸에 출렁이고
西南風은
흰 塔들의
鐘소리를
불어내린다.
  어화여루 상사뒤야
  어화여루 상사뒤야

"電車와 먼지 쓴 나무.
하이버리에서 나고
릿치몬드와 큐우에서 몸을 버리고
릿치몬드 江上
좁은 나무뱃 속에서
두 무릎을 추켜들었다네."

"발은 무어게이트에 있고
가슴은 발바닥으로 밟혔어라.
한고비 風波를 겪고 난 다음
男便은 눈물로서 '새 出發'을 盟誓하였다.
"어찌 내가 나무래랴 참지 참아."

"마아게트의 모래톱
나는 無에 無를
連結할 따름.
더러운 손의 갈라진 손톱.
나의 겨레는
希望도 갖지못한 불상한 겨레."
　　　에헤야 에

이윽고 칼타고에 나는 왔도다.

타노라 타노라 타노라
오 主여 그대 나를 責하시니
오 主여 그대 責하시니

타노라.

第四部 水死

죽은지 보름만인 페니키아 뱃사공 풀리버스는
갈매기의 우름도 怒한 바다도
남고 밑지는것도 잊어버렸다.
오직 물밑에서 潮流가
무언지 속삭이며 뼈를 집어 올렸다.
白骨이 물속으로 오르내릴때
그는 지나간 靑春과 老年을 다시 겪었다.
조곰식 물매미[渦]로 끌려가면서.
信仰이 다르다고 묻지를마라
오 그대 바람쪽을 노리면서 키[舵]를 잡는 者여
풀리버스도 그대처럼 얌전하고 키가 컸던 것을 잊지 말아라.

第五部 雷語

땀 쩌른 얼골들을 붉은 햇불이 지나간 다음

山庭에 서리같은 沈默이 깃들인 다음

山庭에 서리같은 沈默이 깃드린 다음

돌밭에 괴로움을 겪고 난 다음

웨치는 아우성과 아우성

獄과 宮闕과 먼 산을 넘어서 울려오는

봄 우뢰의 震動이 사라진 다음

살았든 그분은 이미 죽었고

살았든 우리들은 이제 죽어간다

가까스루 참어 가면서.

여기는 물은 없고 바위뿐이라

물이 없고 바위와 모래뿐인 길

길은 물 없는 바윗산을

구비 구비 돌아오르는데

물만 있다믄야 발을 멈춰 목을 추기련만

바위틈에서는 머물지도 생각지도 못한다

땀은 말르고 두 발은 모랫속에 밝힌채

물만 있다믄야 바위틈을 새는

산은 잇몸이 헐어 침도 못 뱉는 입과도 같은 산은

앉도 서도 눕도 못할 곳

마침내는 寂寞도 없어

매마른 우뢰소리만 일고

또한 孤獨도 없어

갈라진 흙담 門 앞에

비웃고 으르대는 붉은 얼골들

    물만 있고

    바위가 아니라면

바위도 있고

물도 있다믄야

물

샘물

바윗틈에 고인 물

물소리 만이래도 있다믄야

매미[蟬] 소리가 아닌

마른 풀잎의 노래도 아닌

바윗틈을 새는 물소리만 있다믄야

그러나 거긴 오직 산새가 소나무에서

뚝뚝뚝 물방울 소리같은 노래를 할뿐

물 소리는 없다.

저 언제나 너의 곁을 걸어가는 第三者는 누구냐

세여보면 너와 나 단 둘뿐인데

고개를 들어 흰 길을 바라보면

언제나 너의 곁을 훨훨 따라가는

사낸지 女子인지도 알수없는

고동색 만토를 뒤집어 쓴 또 하나의 사람

―그녀의 저쪽을 가는 사람은 누구냐?

하늘 높이 사뭇치는 저 소리는 무엇이냐

嘆息하는 어머니들의 흐느끼는 소리

처늬를 쓰고 曠漠한 벌판을 우줄우줄 걸어가면서

나직이 地平線이 뺑 돈 갈라진 땅바닥에

뒤를 이어 쓰러지는 저의들은 누구냐

山 넘엔 또 무슨 都市가 있길레

보래빛 저녁하늘에 發砲하고 改革하고 爆發하는게냐

문허지는 塔들

예루사렘 아테네 알렉싼드리아

비에나 론돈

虛無하고나

안악네가 칠칠한 머리를 바짝 동혀쥐고

그것으로 깽깽이 音樂을 키고

어스름이 짙으면 얼골이 흡사 갓난이인 양

박쥐는 시커먼 壁을 꺼꾸로 기여내리고

空中에 倒立한 塔들이

때를 알리는 追憶의 鐘소리와

빈 독과 廢井에서 反響하는 空虛한 소리 소리

山속에 버려진 이 洞窟 흐릿한 달밤에

바람만이 설레이는 빈 禮拜堂 곁

허무러진 무덤 위에 속사기는 풀잎.

빈 廳엔 窓이 없어 門짝만 찌걱이는데

白骨이야 사람을 害칠 리 있으랴.

번쩍하는 한줄기 번갯불 속에

대들보 위에서 한마리 숫닭이

꼬꼬오 울 뿐이다. 그리곤 무더운 바람이

휙 일어 비방울이 떠러진다.

간지스 江물은 바닥이 들어나고

타는 나무잎이 비를 기다리는데

먹장구름이 먼 히마라야 峯머리로 몰려든다.

密林은 죽은듯이 쭈그리고 있는데

드디어 우뢰는 입을 띠었다

"다—"

"다타—" 그러나 우리는 무엇을 주었든고?

벗이여 가슴을 뒤흔드는 피

平生을 自重해도 避할수 없이 한 刹那에 降服해버리는

울컥 나오는 이 무서운 大膽

이것만으로 단지 이것만으로 우리는 살아왔으나
그렇다고 죽은 뒤 行狀에 남을것도 아니요
착한 거미가 줄을 처주는 碑銘이나
빈 房에서 瘦瘠한 辯護士가 開封하는
遺書에 울을것도 아니다.
"다—"
"다야드밤" 단 한번 돌아가는 열쇠 소리를
나는 들었노라.
우리는 各各 自己 監房에서 열쇠만을 생각한다.
열쇠만을 생각하면서 밤이 올때마다
우리는 스스로 獄囚임을 깨닫는다
바람결에 傳해진 風聞이 잠시
滅亡한 코리오레이너쓰를 蘇生시킨다.
"다—"
"담야타" 돛과 櫓에 익은 손에는
배가 반가히 많고
바다는 고요하니
請했든들 그대 마음도 欣喜雀躍
반가히 내 손에 따를것을

　　　나는 물가에 앉아
荒廢한 벌판을 등지고 낚시를 드리웠드니라
나는 다시 한번 나의 땅을 바로 잡을꺼나?

倫敦橋는 문허진다 문허진다 문허진다 문허진다
그리하야 그는 淨化하는 火中으로 다시 몸을 던졌다.
어느날에 나는 제비처럼 되랴—오 제비야 제비야
廢塔에 幽閉된 아키텐의 王子
나는 이 斷片으로서 나의 破滅을 버티었으니
너의들의 비위에 맞을것이다. 히어로니모는 또다시 發狂했다.

"다타— 다야드밤 담야타"

"샨티— 샨티— 샨티—"

譯者의 말

一九二二年에 發表되자마자 끊임없는 絶讚과 지나친 非難의 對象이 되어 온 이 長篇詩는 三十代 엘리오트의 傑作일뿐만 아니라 現代 英詩의 모나리사이다. 詩文學의 낡은 形式을 깨트리고 김빠진 浪漫의 言語와 感情을 淸算하였다는것만이 이 作品의 功績은 아니려니와, 그 짙은 律調와 纖細한 뉴안쓰로 말미암아 爛熟한 西歐 中産 文化의 崩壞를 警告하고 슬퍼하는 作家의 輓歌的 詩才는 마치 希臘神話의 오-피우쓰와도 같이 뒤를 도라보지 않으면 안될 運命을 가진것이라 引用과 暗示로 表現된 많은 語句와 故事를 細密히 解說치 않고는 차라리 理解에 困難한 作品이라 할수 있다.

이 作品에 對한 批判的 解說도 重要하려니와 原文을 고대로 우리말로 옮겨놓아 보는것도 意味없지 않으리라고 생각된다. 勿論 詩作生涯에 있어서 여러번 '發展的 解消'를 한 엘리오트인 만큼, 이 作品이 그의 最高峰이라는 것도 아니요, 現代 英詩가 이로써 終結을 지운것도 아니요, 今年度 노벨 文學賞을 그가 받게 되었다는 뉴-스 價値를 爲해서 새삼스레 <荒蕪地>를 紹介하랴는 것은 더욱 아니다. 現代 英詩가 이런 過程도 밟은 일이 있었다는것과, 八·一五를 지나 三年半이나 되는 南朝鮮의 오늘의 精神的 心理的 雰圍氣가 차라리 四十年前 <荒蕪地>의 時代性을 아직도 벗어나지 못했다고 느껴지는 理由와, 그리고 朝鮮現代詩에 多少라도 糧食이 됨직도 하다는 信念에서 이 長篇詩를 飜譯해 본것이다. 四百三十줄 나머지 되는 原詩의 뜻과 줄에 忠實하도록 우리말로 譯했을 따름이니, 朝鮮詩로서 어색한 點은 讀者諸賢이 고쳐서 읽으시기 바란다.

끝으로 이 詩를 飜譯한 수고의 절반은 高麗大學英文科學生 金致逵(宗吉)君에 돌려야 함을 여기서 讀者에게 밝혀 드리고자 한다. 비록 '共譯'이라는 表示는 君의 謙遜이 許諾치 않으리나, 이태동안 한 敎室에서 英文學을 공부하면서 筆者는 언제나 君의 말에 對한 感覺과 詩的 洞察力에 놀랐던것이고, 이 飜譯文에도 到處에 君의 말솜씨가 숨어있는 것을 多幸으로 여기는 바이다. (1948년 12월) (<新世代>, 4권 1호, 1949. 1. 25. 발행 '新春號')

故 李仁秀 敎授의 <荒蕪地> 翻譯 肉筆原稿

[打字者註: 다음은 20行 x 20字 民衆書館原稿用紙 30枚에 故 李仁秀 敎授가 肉筆로 적은 그의 <荒蕪地> 翻譯과, 잇대어 同一한 原稿用紙 8枚에 걸쳐 亦是 肉筆로 적은 <譯者註>이다.]

I. 죽은이의 埋葬

봄 四月은 殘惡한 달이기에
죽은 땅에서 라일락을 길러내고
追憶과 情欲을 뒤섞어 버므리며
잠 자는 뿌리를 봄비로 깨우다.
겨울은 우리를 품속에 안어
忘却의 눈(雪)으로 땅을 덮어주며
빼마른 球根으로 가냘픈 生命을 이여 주었건만.
여름은 난데없이 스타안벨거세의 湖水를 넘어
묻어오는 소낙비와 더부러 우리를 쫓았거니.
우리는 나무 밑에 몸을 의지했다가
볓을 마지하야 庭園에 들어가서
커피를 마시면서 이야기하고 한 時間을 보냈었다.
난 露西亞사람 아니애요. 出生은 리투아니아이지만 純獨逸血統인걸요.
그리구 어렸을제 四寸되는 皇太子집에서
쏠매를 태주마고 할젠 무섭드군요.
마리 마리 꼭부짜버 하고 四寸은 소리치드니만
쏜살 같이 내려가드군요.
山에선 정말 自由스러워요.
난 밤 늦도록 讀書하는 버릇이 있에요.
겨울엔 南쪽으로 가지요.

이 돌무더기에 박힌 뿌리는 무엇이며

뻗친 가지는 무엇이냐?

人子여 너히는 말도 못하고 짐작도 못하리니

햇살이 쬐이고

죽은 나무 그늘지지 않고

귀뜨래미 慰安을 주지 않으며

타는 돌에 물소리 아니들리는 이곳에

너히가 아는것은 다만

조각조각 부셔진 形象의 부스러기뿐이러라.

다만 그늘은 이 붉은 바위 밑 뿐이니

(어서 이 붉은 바위 밑 그늘로 들어서라)

아침에 너히 뒤를 껑충거려 쫓아오는 그림자도 아니고

저녁에 네 앞길을 막어스는 그림자도 아닌

다른것을 너히에게 나는 보여주고저 하노라.

한줌의 흙 속에 든 무서움을 알려주리라.

  바람은 시원하게

  故鄕으로 부는데

  愛蘭의 님이여

  어데 있고 아니 오느뇨?

"당신이 一年前에 하이야씐쓰를 첨 주셨지요.

사람마다 나를 하이야씐쓰 아가씨라 합데다."

―그러나, 이슬 젖은 머리를 드리워

한 아름 꽃을 안고

밤 늦게 나와 같이 하이야씐쓰 꽃밭에서 돌아왔을제

나는 말도 못하고 눈(眼)마자 바로 뜨지 못했으니

生死의 意識조차 잃어

光明의 심지 沈黙만 들여다 볼 뿐이었습니다.

  바다는 거칠고 쓸쓸도 허이.

有名한 占術家 쏘쏘쓰트리쓰 女史는

毒한 感氣를 앓었지만 如前히

귀신같이 맞히기로 所聞이 全歐羅巴에 藉藉하고
靈妙한 카아드를 한벌 가진 분이다.
그의 말이다.
여기 뽑은 당신 카아드는 물에 빠진 페니키아의 뱃사공이요
(보라! 그의 눈은 眞珠로 化했나니).
이것은 벨라돈나 岩下의 淑女인데
風浪 많은 말썽의 女性이라.
이것은 지팽이 세개 짚은 사나입니다.
그리고 이것은 바퀴.
여기 나온 것은 애꾸눈 商人인데
빈(空) 카아드는 그가 등에 지고 가는 것이지만
나는 보아서 안될것입니다.
絞殺當한 사나이는 보이지 않습니다.
물 조심 하세요.
數 많은 사람이 圓을 그려 뺑뺑 돌고 있군요.
또 오세요. 或시나 나의 親舊
에쿠이토온 夫人을 만나시거든
내가 몸소 天空圖를 가져 간다고 傳해주세요.
요지음은 때가 하 險惡하니깐.

虛無의 都市
겨울 아침 거뭇노란 안개 밑에
론돈 다리 위를 밀려가는 數많은 사람.
나는 몰랐더니라
죽엄이 저리 많은 목슴을 채 간 줄을.
숨 가뿐 한숨을 이따금씩 내쉬며
발치만 보고 건너 가더라니.
언덕 길을 올라 윌리암 王街로 내려스니
聖 마리아 울노스의 鐘樓는 때를 찾아
아홉번 울리는 마지막 죽어가는 소리를 치다.

거기서 나는 知舊를 만나

부짢고 소리쳤다.

"스텟쯘 君! 마일리 海戰에서 生死를 같이하던 親舊여!

자네가 지난해에 마당에다 심어둔 屍體가

쌌이나 트기 始作했나? 올에는 꽃이 필가?

또는 때아닌 서리에 얼어버렸나?

아— 사람의 벗, 개란 놈은 멀지기 警戒하게!

놈이 발톱으로 파 후벼 낼걸세!

讀者여! 너는 僞善者 나와 같은 同志다."

Ⅱ 將棋 한 판

앉은 자리는 눈부신 玉座와도 같이

大理石 위에 빛나고

體鏡은 기둥사이로 천장까지 뻐쳐

葡萄 주렁주렁 익어가는 넝쿨에 감겨있는데

黃金빛 큐피돈이 끼웃거려 내다보다.

(또 하나는 날개로 눈을 가렸다.)

일곱 갈래 燭臺의 불빛은 二重으로 거울에 비취이며

테불에 反射되는 光彩는

貢緞 佩物函에서 쏟아저나온

그의 寶石 번득이는 燦爛과 混化되다.

마개 열린 象牙色琉璃의 瓶속에는

그의 異國的인 混爛한 香臭가 숨어있고

香油 가루粉 물粉의 恍惚한 香氣는

感覺을 麻醉하고 어지럽게 잠그다.

窓에서 흘러오는 산뜻한 바람에

香氣는 흔들리어 긴 燭불을 굵게 하고

거림은 反射鏡을 그슬리어

우물반자의 무늬를 흔들다.

구리 火箸로 집어던진 굵다란 火木은

五色 大理石의 기둥사이에서

푸르게 피여올라 유자 빛이 되고

헤엄치는 海豚의 彫刻을 구슬프게 비춰이다.

古風의 맨틀 위에는

窓밖으로 수풀 景致를 내다보듯

한幅의 그림이 필로멜의 幻生을 알려주니

殘酷한 임금은 어찌도 그리 무지하게 凌辱했드뇨.

그러나 그림속 夜鶯의 聖스러운 목청은

왼 沙漠을 쨍쨍 울리여

끊임없이 울건만

俗된 衆生은 如前히 쫓느니

더러운 귀에는 "쩍 쩍" 하고 들릴 뿐이라.

그 밖에도 시드른 時代의 화상이

포기 포기 壁에 걸려 있으니

노려보는 肖像이 끼웃끼웃 하면서

방의 沈潛을 에워싸고 지키다.

層層階를 오르나리는 발자욱 소리 들려오다.

빗어내린 그의 머리 끝은

불꽃처럼 불빛 속에서 퍼져

말할 듯 潤氣있고도 성낸듯이 잠자코 말이 없다.

"오늘밤엔 내 神經이 야릇해요. 정말이애요.

가지 마세요. 이애길 하세요.

웨 이애기 안 하세요? 제발 이애기 좀 하시라닌깐.

무엇을 생각하세요? 무엇을요? 무엇을?

당신 맘속은 도무지 몰르겠어요. 생각하세요."

나는 생각노니 우리는

죽은이가 白骨을 잃어버린 쥐구먹 속에 있느니라.

"저 소린 무엇이어요?"
　　　門 밑에 바람소리.
"지금 저 소리는요? 바람이 뭘 해요?"
　　　아무것도 아니야 아무것도 아니야.

"당신은 아는 것이 없어요?
보는 것도 없어요? 記憶조차 없어요?"

나는 記憶하노니
그의 눈은 眞珠로 化했더니라.
"살았소? 죽었소? 머리속에 아무것도 없단 말이요?"
그러나

아—아—아— 셰익스피어같은 숨가쁜 흔들음악.
기막히게 맵시 있고
기막히게 才幹 있어.
"이젠 뭘 할가요? 뭘 해요?
나는 이대로 거리로 튀여 나갈테예요
머릴랑 이대로 드리우고.
來日은 뭘 할가요? 두고 두고 뭘해요?"
　　　열時 되면 더운 물.
흐린 날엔 네時에 車를 덮고.
그리고 將棋 한판 된 다음
꺼풀 없는 눈을 감고 門 두달기는 소리를 기다릴 뿐이다.

릴의 男便이 軍隊에서 나올 무렵에
나는 얼버무리지 않고 分明히 말했는걸
"어서 어서 들일 時間이 다 돼 갑니다."
앨버트가 日間 돌아오니 몸단속 좀 하구랴
이 해박으라고 주고 간 돈

어떻게 썼나 물어 볼거니깐 으레.

주고 말고 해. 내가 옆에서 내 눈으로 본걸.

릴! 죄다 빼버리구 멋지게 다시 해 박우

보기 숭해 죽겠서.

男便 말투가 이랬다우 거짓말 아냐아.

나두 옆에서 同感이라구 했지머.

앨버트의 딱한 立場도 생각해 봐

四年이나 軍隊살이 하다 오면

한바탕 느러지게 놀랴 할텐데

안해가 대꾸않으면 헐 사람 많다고 내가 말했드니

그래? 하구 코대답을 하겠지.

내 말이 過히 틀리쟎다고 두고 보자고 뻣댔드니만

그럼 내가 뉘한테 치사할지 알겟노라 하면서 눈총을 주겠지!

"어서 어서 들일 時間이 다 돼 갑니다."

내 말이 귀에 거슬리면 좋을대로 하라고 쏴주면서

너는 매인 몸이지만 남은 골라 잡을수 있는 것이고

萬若에 앨버트가 딴 女子와 가까워진다면

豫告 안 했단 말일랑 하지도 말라 하고선

그렇게 古物 같은 상파대길 하고

부끄럽지도 않느냐고 타일렀드니만

(나이는 겨우 설흔하나 밖엔 안됐는데)

잔 언짠한 얼골로 하는 말이

내가 人力으로 못한 노릇이라 하면서

지이량으로 먹은 丸藥 때문이라 하겠지.

(허긴 벌서 다섯이나 낳는데

끝에 애 조오지 때는 죽을 걸 살아난 셈이야)

藥房主人은 괜찮을거라 했건만

그後론 영 몸이 달라졌다고 하겠지!

아이우 어수룩한 바보야! 하고 나는 빈정대면서

거봐 앨버트가 자꾸만 건디리면 할수있나

어린애 낳기 싫으면 뭣하러 結婚하느냐고 타일럿거든.
"어서 어서 들일 時間이 다 됐읍니다"
그러자 고댐 空日 앨버트가 집에 돌아온 날
돼지 뒷다리를 料理해 놓고
뜨끈뜨끈한 맛을 같이 보자고 날 저녁에 招待했드군.
"어서 어서 들일 時間이 다 됐습니다"
"어서 어서 들일 時間이 다 됐습니다"
빌 또 만나세 루 좋은 꿈 꾸어 응
메이 잘 자요 안녕 안녕
또 보세 잘들 가 잘들 가
안녕히 주무세요 貴婦女들 안녕히 주무십시요
안녕히들 주무십시요.

III 불의 說敎

江의 天幕은 걷어지다.
마지막 매달린 나무잎 손가락은
젖은 江기슭에 가라앉다.
바람은 소리없이 荒土를 쓸어가고
江물의 精靈은 자최조차 없어지다.
고이 흐르라 情깊은 템스여 내 노래 끝일때 까지.
물에 떠가는것 빈 瓶, 쌘드위지 종이쪼각,
비단 손수건, 마분지 상자짝, 담배 꽁초,
아무런 여름밤의 證據物도 보이지 않어.
물의 精靈은 떠나갔다.
都心地 重役들의 호강스런 子弟도 동무삼아 떠나가고
住所조차 남기지 않았다.
리만의 물가에 앉어 나는 울었드니라….
情든 템스여 고이 흐르라 내 노래 끝일때까지
情든 템스여 고이 흐르라 내 노래 길지 않고

요란치도 않으리니,
그러나 등 뒤에서는 찬바람과 더부러
白骨이 덜걱거리고
귀에서 귀로 퍼져가는 嘲笑가 들려오다.
쥐 한마리 풀속으로 뱃대기를 끌고
물기슭을 기여가는데 때마츰
겨울 夕陽에 나는 瓦斯탕크 뒤를 돌아
흐린 물 고인 運河에서 낙시질 하며
破船한 兄 王의 신세를 생각하고
兄 앞서 돌아가신 임금 아버님을 슬퍼하다.
젖인 개골창에 내둥구는 헐벗은 屍體
몬지 쌓인 집웅밑 좁은 광에 던저
해마다 쥐발에 걸려 덜걱대는 白骨.
그러나 이따금씩 내 뒤에서는
自動車와 고동소리 들려오니
봄이 되면 스위이니君이 포오터夫人을 찾는것이라.
아— 밝은 달은 포오터夫人과
그의 따님을 비처주니
母女는 쏘다물에 발을 씻다.
아— 둥근 집웅에서 울려오는 合唱隊의 노래소리여!

트윗 트윗 트윗
쩍 쩍 쩍 쩍 쩍 쩍
그리도 무지하게 劫奪했든고.
테리우

虛無의 都市
겨울 낮 거뭇노란 안개 밑에서
쉬염 주렁주렁한 쓰머너의 商人 유제니디스氏는
호주머니에 乾葡萄 한줌과

론돈 入港 運賃保險料 負擔濟 船荷證書
書類로 賣買되는 入荷案內書를 지니고
상쓰러운 佛語로 니를 招待하는데
캐논街 호텔에서 점심을 같이 하고
週末에는 首都호텔에서 놀자고 하더라.
자줏빛 저녁때에 눈과 등이 冊床에서 돌아볼제
人間의 機械가 기다리는 택시처럼 두군대며 기다릴제
눈 먼 老翁 티레시애쓰 나는
주름 잡힌 젖가슴을 달고
두 生命 가운데서 脈動하나니

자줏빛 저녁때에 모든 것을 目睹하다.
저녁때는 집으로 돌아갈 길을 催促하고
바다에서는 뱃군을 불러들이니
타이피스트도 茶時間 대여 돌아와
아침설거지를 하면 暖爐에 불을 피어
통조림 飮食을 食卓에 準備하다.
窓 밖에는 마지막 夕陽에 빛우워
말러가는 속옷이 危殆롭게 널리여
밤이면 寢臺되는 디밴 위에는
양말, 슬립퍼, 단속곳, 콜세트가 어지럽게 싸여있다.
쭈구러진 젖가슴의 老叟 티레시애쓰 나는
이 光景을 보자마자 남저지를 豫探하였도다—
나도 함께 約束한 손님을 기다렸다.
때마츰 여드름 더덕더덕한 젊은 사내 들어스니
厥公은 적은 住宅事務所의 書記요
눈세가 날카롭고 배운데는 없으나
부래드포드 富豪의 씰크햇트 처럼
自信이 滿滿한 靑年이라.
食事는 끝났고 女子는 倦怠와 疲勞를 느끼는 차니

機會가 좋다고 생각되는지라.
愛撫로써 달래보나
바라는배 아니연만 구태여 막을배도 아니라.
決心한바 있어 핏기운 도두어 直時로 달겨드다.
더듬는 손을 말리지 아니하니
公의 虛榮心이 應對를 要치 않으므로
無關心을 도로혀 歡迎할 뿐이니라.
(그러기에 티레시애쓰 나는 일직이
티이브스 城壁 밑에 웅그려 앉어도 보고
賤한 者와 더부러 地獄을 거닐기도 하였나니
寢臺 兼한 이 디밴 위에서 모든 것을 미리 當했느니라.)
그는 作別하는 愛護의 키쓰를 하나 붙히고
갈 길을 더듬어 내려오니 層階는 캉캄하더라.

愛人을 보낸둥 만둥
女子는 돌아서서 暫時 거울을 보니
생각 아닌 생각이 머리속을 시쳐가다
"자 이젠 그만저만 끝났으니 해치워 시원하다."
아름다운 女性이 어리석음에 빠저
다시금 호을로 房을 거닐면
自動式 손으로 머리를 쓰다드므며
留聲機에 소리판을 걸다.

"이 音樂이 물결을 타고 나를 따라와"
스트랜드로 빅토리야 女王街로 올라오다.
아 都市여 都市여
나는 가끔 가끔

템스 下街 술집을 지나면서
만도린의 구슬픈 소리와

낮술 먹는 漁夫들의 말소리 구두소리를 듣다.
그 옆엔 殉敎聖者 매그누스의 聖堂이
흰빛 금빛 이오니아의 絶妙한 榮華를 黙示하다.

    江은
    기름과 타마유의
    땀을 흘려
    배는
    썰물과 더부러 떠나가며
    넓고
    붉은 돛은
    바람에 불려 무거운 돛대를 돌다.
    배는
    떠가는 화목을 씻어
    狗島를 지나 그리니지 水道를 나리다.
    어화어여루 상사뒤야
    어화어여루 상사뒤야

櫓를 젓는
엘리사베스와 레쓰터
고물(船尾)은
붉은 金을
씨운 조개 모양
날뛰는 물결은
두 기슭에 출렁 출렁
西南風은
흰 塔
鐘 소리를
불어 나리다.
    어화어여루 상사뒤야

   어화어여루 상사뒤야

"電車와 몬지 끼인 나무.
하이버리에서 낳고
릿치몬드와 큐우에서 몸을 버려
릿치몬드 江 우에서
좁은 보오트 바닥에 누어
두 무릎을 들었더니."

"발은 무어게이트에 있고
가슴은 발바닥에 밟혔나니
그 風波 겪은 다음
男便은 눈물로써 '새 出發'을 盟誓했지.
어찌 나는 나무래랴 참지 참아."

마아게트 모래톱
나는 虛無에 虛無를
連結할 따름.
더러운 손에서 깎어 낸 손톱.
나의 겨레는
希望조차 잃은 불쌍한 겨레."
   에헤야 에

이윽고 칼타고에 나는 왔도다

불타며 불타며 불타며 불타며
主여 나를 집어 내시니
主여 집어 내시니

불타며.

IV 水中魂의 노래

죽은지 보름되는 플리버쓰 페니키아의 뱃사공은
갈매기의 노래와 우렁찬 波濤소리와
남고 밑지는 셈속을 잊어버렸다.

바다속 물결이 속사기며 그의 뼈를 집어올려
뼈는 오르나려 화방수로 들어스며
靑春과 老衰의 過程을 다시 한번 밟었다.

믿음의 달름을 묻지를 말라
바퀴를 돌리며 바람쪽을 우러러보는 너히들이여
너히와 다름없이 키도 크고 美男이든 플리버쓰를 잊지 마라.

V 우뢰의 외침

땀 난 얼골에 붉은 횃불 지난 다음
山庭의 서리같은 沈默이 지난 다음
돌밭에 괴로움이 지난 다음
웨치는 아우성
牢囚와 宮闕과 먼 山을 넘어
울려오는 봄 우뢰의 震動이 지난 다음
살었든 그 분은 이미 죽었고
살었든 우리들도
가까스로 참어가며 이윽고 죽어간다

여기는 물이 없고 바위 뿐이니
물 없는 바위와 모랫길
길은 山속으로 굽어 올라가는데
물도 없는 바위山이라

물만 있다면 발을 멈춰 목을 추기련만
바위틈에서는 머물지도 못하고 생각조차 하염없어
땀은 말러 발은 모래에 박혔으니
바위틈에 물이나마 있었던들
이(齒)가 헐어 뱉지 못한 입과 같은 죽은 山
여기야 앉도 스도 눕도 못할 곳이니
山에는 沈默조차 없어
비도 없는 마른 雷聲 뼈에 맺힐 뿐
山에는 孤獨조차 없으니
핏대 올린 성낸 얼골이
뭃어진 土담집 門간에서 嘲弄하며 으르대다

    물만 있고
    바위가 아니라면
    바위도 있고
    물도 있고
    물
    샘
    바위틈에 고인 물
    물소리락도 있다면
    매미소리와
    마른 풀에 바람소리 아니고
    바위를 흐르는 물소리라면
    山새가 소나무 사이에서 노래하는 곳
    뚝 뚝 뚝 뚝 뚝 뚝 뚝
    그러나 물은 없다

너희 옆을 언제나 걸어가는 저 사람은 누구냐?
세어 보면 너와 나 단 둘 뿐인데
고개를 들어 흰 앞길을 보면
언제나 너히 옆에 또 한 사람이

사나인지 女子인지도 몰르건만

고동색 만또를 두르고 가만가만 걸어가

―너희 저쪽에 가는 이는 뉘란 말이냐?

하늘 높이 들려오는 저 소리는 무엇이냐

멀리서 나는 어머니의 痛哭소리

처네 쓰고 曠野 벌판을 우줄거려

하늘 지쳐 끝나는 地平線만 보며

짜개진 땅에 쓰러지는 저히들은 누구냐

山 넘어스면 무슨 都市냐

자줏빛 하늘에 와르르 뭃어지고 터지는 改革의 소리

쓰러지는 塔

예루사렘 아테나 알렉싼드리아

비에나 론돈

虛無

아낙네가 칠칠한 검은 머리를 죄여 잡아

머리칼에다 깽깽이 音樂을 키다

자줏빛 저녁노을에 간난애인 양

박쥐는 휘휘 날며 퍼더기더니

검은 壁을 꺼꾸로 기여내려

空中엔 塔이 물구나무를 서

追憶의 鐘을 時間 마춰 흔드니

빈 독이나 물 없는 우물에서 울려오는 노래소리라.

山골에 廢墟된 이 굴 속

흐릿한 달빛에 禮拜堂 옆

허무너진 무덤 위에서 풀은 노래하다

禮拜堂은 비여 窓조차 없고

바람만 모여들어 門짝이 흔들리다.

마른 白骨이야 害칠 理 없어

다만 숫닭 한 마리가 上梁보에 앉어
꼬꾜 꼬— 하고 우니
번개가 치다.
그리고 비 묻은 바람이 일다.

강가의 江물은 빠저
시들은 나무잎이 비를 기다리는데
거문 구름이 멀리 히마반트 山줄기 위로 몰려든다
密林은 沈黙 속에 허리를 쪼그리고 있는데
드디어 雷聲이 터지다.
　　"다—"
　　"다타—" 우리는 무엇을 주었느냐?
벗이여 내 가슴을 흔드는 피
한 刹那에 降服하는 이 무서운 大膽이란
一生을 두고두고 操心한들 收拾 못 할것
이것 이것만으로써
우리는 살어 왔으니
이 事實은 우리의 行狀에도 나오지 않고
情 많은 거미가 幕처주는 碑文에도 없고
빈 房에서
빼마른 辯護士가 開封하는 遺言狀에도 없느니라
　　"다—"
　　"다야드밤" 나는 들었나니
열쇠가 한번 돌고 한번만 도는 것을
우리는 열쇠만 생각하고
各其 獄 속에서 열쇠만 생각나니
어시어 어둔 밤에 囚人임을 確認하며
虛空에 뜬 所聞이 暫時
沒落한 코리오레이너쓰의 기운을 붓돋다.
　　"다—"

"담야타" 배는 마음대로
돛과 櫓에 익숙한 손에 놀아
바다는 고요한데
님의 마음 請했던들
操縱하는 손에 順應하야 脈搏치며
반가웁게 承諾하였으런만
荒蕪 벌판을 등지고
물 기슭에 앉아 고기를 낚는 나
내 땅을 다시 한 번 다사려 볼거나?
론돈 다리는 무너지다 무너지다 무너지다
"그리하야 그는 洗練의 불 속으로 몸을 더저"
"언제나 나는 제비처럼 되랴"
―아 제비야 제비야
"아키텐의 王子는 廢墟된 塔 속에 있어"
나는 이 破片을 주어 뫃아
나의 滅亡에 對備하였나니
그렇다면 나는 너히들 비위에 맞을걸.
히어로니모는 다시금 미쳤다.
"다타―. 다야드밤. 담야타.
　　샨티― 샨티― 샨티―"(끝)

[以上이 400字 原稿紙 30枚에 故 李仁秀 敎授의 肉筆로 담겨 있는 그의 <荒蕪地> 飜譯이며, 다음은 亦是 400字 原稿紙 8枚에 걸처 그의 肉筆로 적혀 있는 註釋이다.]

NOTES (譯者註)

標題(Epigraph)

Nam Sibyllam. . . .

    Jury는 아래와 같이 英譯한다:

"Yes, indeed, I myself have seen at Cumae with my own eyes a Sibyl hanging in a cage, and when the boys said to her, 'Sibyl, what do you wish for?' she answered, 'I wish to die.'"

    原文은 羅馬의 諷刺詩人 Petronius의 文集 *Petronii Arbitri Satyricon* 에서 引用한 一節. Gaius Petronius는 暴君 Nero의 寵愛를 받아 暴君의 享樂을 提供하는 總責任者(Elegantiae arbiter)이였으나 叛逆의 罪로 몰려 A.D. 66年頃에 血管을 끊어 自殺한 사람이다.

    Cumae는 Italy의 西南地方 Campania에 있는 古都市로 여기에 Sibyl(巫女)이 있었다고 傳한다.

    Sibyl은 古典神話에 나오는 豫言者로 그 數爻는 文獻에 따라 달르니 Plato는 하나를 말하였고 其他 둘, 넷, 열을 指名한 文獻도 있거니와 中世紀 때 修道僧들은 열둘까지 셌다고 한다. 그 중 Cumaean Sibyl(이름은 Amalthea)이 가장 有名하니 이가 곧 Aeneas를 地獄으로 案內한 Sibyl이다. Apollo가 무슨 所願이든지 成就시켜준다 하기에, Sibyl이 한줌의 모래를 쥐어들고 이 모래알 數爻 만큼 오래 살게해달[라]고 해서 千年을 살게 되였는데 不幸히도 그때에 永遠의 靑春을 달라 하지 않았기 때문에 老衰를 免치 못하야, 結局 肉體는 미이라가 되여 구경꺼리가 되여버리고 목소리만 남아 未來를 豫言하는 使命을 갖게 되였다고 Aeneas에게 말하는 대목이 *Aeneid* 第六卷에 나온다.

    Sibyl은 그의 豫言을 希臘語로 棕櫚(palm) 잎에 적는다하야 'Sibylline leaves'라는 말이 있다. 이 引用文에 나타나는 Sibyl의 말도 Greek로 되어 있다.

    그런데 Eliot가 이 故事를 標題로 삼아, 靑春을 가질 運命이 못되는 Sibyl로 하여금 "내 차라리 죽고 싶어 하노라"고 말하게 한다는 것은 *Waste Land*를 一貫하는 죽엄의 테-마를 解得하는데 뜻 깊은 것이라 하겠다. 또 한편 Sibyl이 한줌의 모래를 쥐어 들었다는 故事가 L. 30, 'I will show you fear in a handful of dust,'와 詩想에 關聯이 없지 아니 하겠다.

Pound, Ezra (1885–1972): 美國 詩人. Idaho州 出生. 十五歲에 Pennsylvania 大學에

入學하여 三年 동안 比較文學을 硏究 (1900–1903), Hamilton College에서 硏究를 繼續 (1903–5), 1906年에 Pennsylvania 大學에서 A.M. 學位를 받은 다음 Romance Languages를 가르치다가 1908年부터 歐羅巴 各國에 流浪 現在에 이르름 (1908年 에 Italy; 1908–20年 London에 있다가, 1920–24年 Paris로 옮기고 1924年 以來 다시 Italy에 定住). 近年 그의 美國文化, 政治에 對한 反感이 極端化하야, 大戰中 Fascism의 代辯者로 猛烈한 宣傳放送까지 하야 戰爭犯罪者의 陋名을 쓰기에 이르렀다 함.

Pound의 詩作發展의 過程은 獨特한 것이 있으니, *A Lume Spento* (1908), *Personae* (1909), *Exultations* (1909)等의 初期詩集에서 이미 새로운 律調를 發見하여 該博한 學識과 獨創精神을 融合하는데 成功하였으며 *Canzoni* (1911), *Ripostes* (1912)等을 거쳐서 Imagism, Vorticism과 같은 新詩 運動을 일으켰고, *Sonnets of Guido Cavalcanti* (1912), *Cathay* (1915)等의 譯詩集을 通하야 Provence 詩, 漢詩의 精神을 英詩에 받아 들이려 애썼다. 要는, Eliot가 말한바와 같이 Pound는 古今東西의 詩作品을 널리 耽讀하여 "verse as speech"와 "verse as song"을 並有하는 rhythm과 form을 찾는데 애썼고, 果然 *Lustra* (1916), *Hugh Selwyn Mauberley* (1920)같은 中年作에는 놀랄만한 成果를 거두었다고 하겠다. 그의 後期作 長篇詩 *Cantos*는 이미 七十餘章이나 發表되었으나 [卽 I-XVI (1925), XVII-XXVII (1928), *A Draft of XXX Cantos* (1930), *Eleven New Cantos*: XXXI-XLI (1934), *Cantos* LII-LXXI (1940)] 아직 未完成 作品으로, 完成하면 約 百章이나 될 計劃이라 하며 Dante의 <神曲>과도 비길 수 있는 Human Comedy를 構想한 것이라 한다. 果然 *Cantos*가 詩로서 作家 自身이 期約한 바와 같은 劃期的 作品이 될지 또는 後世의 웃음꺼리로 남을지는 알바가 아니로되, Pound의 奇想天外하고도 駭怪罔測한 手法은 現代詩에 미치는 影響이 크고, 親舊 Eliot 自身은 勿論이려니와 Hart Crane (1895–1932), Archibald MacLeish (1892–1982) 같은 美國詩人들도 배우는 바가 많다.

il miglior fabbro (伊) = the better craftsman. Dante가 煉獄篇 第二十六章 L. 117에서 Arnault Daniel을 讚揚하여 "fu miglior fabbro del parlar materno" (Norton의 英譯: "[This one] was a better smith of the maternal speech....")라고 한 말을 Eliot는 自己의 先驅者인 Pound에 適用한 것이다.

Eliot는 일찍부터 *Ezra Pound: His Metric and Poetry* (1917)를 發表하여 Pound의 獨創的 手法과 律調를 밝힌 일도 있었고 또 1932年에는 손수 Pound의 詩選集을 엮어 序文을 부쳐 Pound의 英詩에 이바지한 功勞를 指摘했다. 特히 다음의 個人的 讚辭를 參照:

"A man who devises new rhythms is a man who extends and refines our sensibility; and that is not merely a matter of 'technique.' I have, in recent years, cursed Mr. Pound often enough; for I am never sure that I can call my verse my own; just when I am most pleased with myself, I find that I have caught up some echo from a verse of Pound's. . . .
He has enabled a few other persons, including myself, to improve their verse sense. . . . I cannot think of any one writing verse, of our own generation and the next, whose verse (if any good) has not been improved by the study of Pound's."

허긴 Eliot도 中年以後부터는 獨自的 發展을 한 作家이며 Pound를 끝끝내 追從한 것은 아니다. 例를 들면 *After Strange Gods* (1934)에서 Eliot는 Pound의 *Cantos*에 나타나는 地獄을 評하야 다음과 같이 論하는 一節이 있다:

"And I find one considerable objection to a Hell of this sort: that a Hell altogether without dignity implies a Heaven without dignity also. If you do not distinguish between individual responsibility and circumstances in Hell, between essential Evil and social accidents, then the Heaven (if any) implied will be equally trivial and accidental."

Eliot가 道德觀에 立脚하야 Pound를 評한 一節로 두 詩人 間에 自在하는 價値觀의 差異를 明示하는 批判이라 할 수 있겠다. 그러므로 여기서 確實히 밝혀야 할 것은, Eliot가 Pound를 한 詩作의 'fabbro'로서 尊敬하는 것이고 *Waste Land*에 內包된 價値觀이 Pound의 그것과 同一하다는 것을 意味하지는 않을 것이다. [역자주미완]

T. S. 엘리어트 (T. S. Eliot, 1888–1965)

바람 부는 밤의 狂想曲 (*Rhapsody on a Windy Night*)

열두 時.
달빛의 綜合 속에 놓인
거리 막바지까지,
記憶의 底層과
그 明晳한 關係와
限界와 精密을 溶解하는
月夜의 呪文을 속삭이면서,
내가 지나가는 個個의 街燈은
終焉의 북을 울리고,
어둠의 空間을 通하여 深夜는
시들은 제라니움을 뒤흔드는 狂人처럼
記憶을 뒤흔든다.

한 時 半,
街燈은 침을 튀겼다.
街燈은 중얼거렸다.
"저기 쓴웃음처럼 열려진
門 틈으로 새어나는 불빛 아래
너를 보고 躊躇하는
女子를 보라.
그의 치맛자락이 찢기고,
흙에 더럽혀지고,
눈구석이 꼬부라진 핀처럼
쌜룩하지 않으냐"고 街燈은 말했다.

記憶은 뒤틀린 물건들을

쓸어 올린다.
世界가 모질고 흰
그 骨格의 秘密을 暴露한 것처럼
반지런히 닳고 닳은
뒤틀어진 나무가지를 海邊에 쓸어 올린다.
工場 마당의 탈난 彈條
彈力을 잃은 채 硬直하고 오그라진
금시 부러질 形態에 쓸은 녹.

두시 半.
"下水道에 납작 엎드린 저 고양이가
혀를 사르르 내밀어
겨튼 바터 찌끼를 貪食하는 것을 보라"고
街燈은 말했다.
그렇게 自動的으로 兒孩의 손이 사르르 나와서는
埠頭를 굴러가는 장난감을 집어 포케트에 넣었다.
兒孩의 눈 뒤에 나는 아무 것도 볼 수 없었다.
불빛 비치는 커튼을 뚫고 드려다 보려는 눈들을
나는 거리에서 보았다.
그리고 어느날 午後
등어리에 딱쟁이가 붙은 늙은 게 한 마리를
물웅덩이에서 보았다.
내가 내민 막대기 끝을 그놈은 꽉 물었다.

세시 半.
街燈은 침을 튀겼다.
街燈은 어둠 속에서 중얼거렸다.
街燈은 콧노래를 불렀다.
"저 달을 보라.
달은 怨恨을 품지 않는다.

달은 가냘픈 눈으로 눈짓한다.
달은 눈 구석으로 微笑짓는다.
달은 풀의 머리를 쓰다듬는다.
달은 제 記憶을 잃어버렸다.
退色한 瘢痕이 제 얼굴에 금을 넣는다.
달의 손은
먼지내와 香水내를 풍기는 종이 薔薇를 비튼다.
그의 腦髓를 스치고 지나가는
모든 밤의 냄새와 더불어
그는 외롭다."
追憶은
그늘진 말른 제라니움과
틈새에 낀 먼지로부터 온다.
街路는 밤나무 냄새로부터 온다.
커튼 친 房 속의 女人의 體臭로부터
廊下의 卷煙으로부터
빠의 각테일 냄새로부터 온다.

街燈은 말했다.
"네時,
문 위에 番號가 있다.
記憶아,
열쇠는 네가 가졌느니라.
조그만 등불이 층층대에 동그라미를 편다.
올라가거라.
침대는 비었다. 칫솔이 壁에 걸렸다.
신발일랑 문 밖에 벗어 놓아라. 자거라. 살 준비를 해라."

칼의 마지막 도림.

T. S. 엘리어트 (T. S. Eliot, 1888–1965)

聖灰 水曜日 I (*Ash Wednesday* I)

내 다시 돌아서기를 바라지 않으므로,
내 바라지 않으므로,
이 사람의 才操와 저 사람의 力量을 貪내어
내 돌아서기를 바라지 않으므로,
내 이미 그런 것을 애써 바랄 양으로 애쓰지 않아
(늙은 독수리가 무엇 때문에 날개를 펴랴?)
무엇 때문에
凡庸한 一生의 사라진 힘을 슬퍼하랴?

積極的인 瞬間의 부질없는 榮譽를
내 다시 알기를 바라지 않으므로,
내 생각지 않으므로,
단 한가지의 참된 一時的인 힘을
내 알지 못하리라는 것을 알고 있으므로,
나무가 꽃피고 샘이 솟는 곳에
내 목을 축이지 못하므로,
모두가 다시 虛無이어라—

時間은 언제나 時間이고,
空間은 언제나 空間이며 空間으로 그치고,
現實은 다만 한 때의 現實이고,
한 空間에 그치는 現實임을 내 알고 있으므로,
모든 것이 이제의 모습대로 마련 된 것을 내 기뻐하며,
내 그 聖스러운 얼골을 斷念하며
그 목소리를 斷念하노니,
내 다시 돌아서기를 바랄 수 없음이라.

따라서 내 기뻐하고
기뻐할만한 것을 構想해야만 되나니,

우리에게 慈悲를 드리우시도록 하나님께 빌며
내 홀로 지나치게 論議하고
지나치게 說明하는 이런 것들을
내 잊어 버리도록 비노라.
내 다시 돌아서기를 바라지 않으므로
이미 저지른 일 다시 되풀이해선 아니 됨을
이 말로써 報答할지어다.
우리에게 審判이 너무 苛酷하지 않기를 비노라.

이 날개는 날기 위한 날개가 아니고
虛空에 퍼득일 쪽지에 지나지 않으므로
이제와 空氣가 아주 졸아들고 바싹 말라
意志보다 더 졸아들고 말랐나니,
關心을 가지면서도 無關心하도록 우리를 이끄소서.
가만히 앉아 있도록 우리에게 가르침을 주소서.

이제 우리의 죽음을 期해 우리들 罪人을 爲해 祈禱하오.
이제 우리의 죽음을 期해 우리들을 위해 祈禱하오.

G. M. 홉킨스 (Gerard Manly Hopkins, 1844–1889)

봄과 落葉 (*Spring and Fall*)
―어린 少女에게―

마가레트야,
金山에 잎이 진다고 슬퍼하느냐?
사람에 따른 것인 양, 나뭇잎을
너 亦是 어린 마음에 아낄 줄을 아느냐?
아, 가슴에 年輪이 박히면,
於焉間 그런 光景에도 冷淡해지고,
가랑잎 世界 되어 낱낱이 져도,
한숨 하나 허술히 쉬지 않으리라.
그러나 눈물겨워 까닭을 짐작하리라.
아이야, 이름이 무엇인들 어떠랴.
슬픔의 根源은 다 한가지라.
가슴이 듣고 靈魂이 짐작한 바를
입과 理智가 表現한 적이 없나니,
이것이 사람이 타고 난 咀呪로다.
네가 슬퍼함은 마가레트이니라.

G. M. 홉킨스 (Gerard Manly Hopkins, 1844–1889)

별을 헤는 밤 (*The Starlight Night*)

별을 보아라. 우러어 우러어 하늘을 보아라.
아, 드높이 앉아 있는 불 사람들을 보아라.
저 밝은 都市하며 저 둥근 城砦를 보아라.
어두운 숲 속 깊이 숨은 金剛 寶石 窟, 妖精의 눈알들!
黃金이며 산 黃金이 흩어진 싸늘한 灰色 마당!
바람에 쏠린 白光! 불꽃 타오르는 虛空의 白楊!
農場 마당에서 놀라 푸드득 날아오르는 비둘기의 깃!
그래, 그래, 모두 다 흥정거리이고 寶物이지.

사렴! 값을 매기렴! 무엇을? 祈禱와 忍從과 喜捨와 盟誓려니—
보아라! 보아라! 爛漫한 果園의 꽃가지 같은 端午의 祝祭를.
보아라! 노란 가루 뽀오얀 버들강아지의 三月 꽃밭을.
아니, 이 하늘은 穀倉이러니 그 안에는 놀라움이 있어,
반짝이는 울 너머 새 新郞 그리스도가 집에 있도다.
그리스도와 그의 어머니와 聖者의 무리가 있도다.

G. M. 홉킨스 (Gerard Manly Hopkins, 1844–1889)

필릭스 랜덜 (*Felix Randal*)

馬蹄鐵쟁이 필릭스 랜덜이 마침내 죽었단 말인가?
骨格이 壯大하고 씩씩하게 잘 생긴 그의 體軀가
病에 시들시들 하다가는, 너댓 가지 致命的인 病毒이 모조리
한 몸 속에서 싸우는 통에 그만 精神조차 맑지 못하던 것을―
내 몸소 監視해 오던 내 任務도 끝났단 말인가?

病魔가 그를 잡았었거니, 처음엔 가슴을 치며 咀呪도 하더니만,
塗油의 式典도 다 끝나면서부터는 마음을 돌렸더니라. 하기야
몇 달 前부터 우리의 貴한 죽음의 猶豫와 贖罪를 내 빌어
그에게 바친 以後로는, 더 한層 純眞한 마음이 생기기도 했건만,
아, 어쨌든 그의 生前의 모든 잘못을 하느님은 두고 두고 풀어 주시길―

이렇게 病者 수발을 하면, 病者나 우리나 情이 들고 마는 것을―
童心의 필릭스, 불쌍한 필릭스 랜덜, 내 그대에게 慰安을 가르쳤고,
惻隱에 그대 눈물도 가시었거니, 그 눈물에 내 마음이 얼마나 아팠던가.

그대 젊음이 한창이던 때, 불 기운 무서운 어수선한 대장간에서
同僚들과 더불어 줄기차게 번득이며 굴리는 편자를 희뿌옇고 덩치 큰
馬車 말에 신기던 때 그대가 豫想턴 것과는 이 얼마나 다른 노릇이냐?

W. B. 예이츠 (William Butler Yeats, 1865–1939)

第二의 降臨 (*The Second Coming*)

넓어만 가는 螺旋을 그리며 돌고 도는 매는
매부리꾼의 목소리를 듣지 못하는도다.
萬事가 갈피없이 흩어져 中心이 감당을 못하니,
收拾 못할 無秩序가 世上에 방사(放肆)하며,
피에 흐린 潮水가 터져
到處에 純潔의 儀式은 沈沒하다.
善하고 貴한 者 確信을 잃고,
惡하고 賤한 者 熱狂에 氾濫하다.

分明히 무슨 黙示가 가까웠나보다.
第二의 降臨이 틀림없이 오나보다.
第二의 降臨! 말이 떨어지기가 무서워라.
드디어 地魂의 무서운 그림자가 눈앞에 어른거리다.
沙漠의 曠野 어딘가에서
人頭에 獅子의 몸통을 가진 怪物이
太陽처럼 無慈悲한 허연 눈깔을 부릅뜨고
끔찍한 다리로 어슬렁대며 기어오는데,
성난 沙漠의 猛禽 그림자가 어지러이 휘돌다.
어둠이 다시 내려 캄캄해지다. 그러나
바위같이 잠들었던 二千年의 歲月이
흔들리는 搖籃에 가위 눌린 듯 깬 것을 나는 아노라.
바야흐로 제때를 만나 태어날 양으로, 베들레헴으로
어슬렁거리며 기어가는 사나운 짐승은 무엇이냐?

W. B. 예이츠 (William Butler Yeats, 1865–1939)

비잔티움으로 뱃길을 뜨다 (*Sailing to Byzantium*)

이곳은 늙은이의 나라가 아니어라.
젊은 男女는 雙雙이 팔을 끼고 노래하며,
나무 속의 새들은 —죽어가는 世代인줄도 모르는지— 우짖고,
鰱魚 뛰오르는 瀑布水하며, 鯖魚 우글거리는 바다하며,
물고기나 짐승이나 새나 모조리 기나긴 여름철에
배에서 낳고 죽는 모든 것을 讚美하누나.
뭇사람은 저 肉感의 音樂에 興겨워,
不老의 知性이 물려준 거룩한 遺蹟을 돌보지 않는다.

늙은 사람이란 하찮은 존재이니,
허수아비 말뚝에 걸쳐진 누더기 같아라.
그러기에 靈魂이 손뼉 장단을 치고 노래하며,
조만간 썩어 버릴 衣裳 누더기 조각조각을
목청껏 노래하여야만 되느니라. 그러나 靈魂이
노래를 배울 길이란, 스스로의 壯麗를 아로새긴
遺蹟을 공부하는 것 뿐이러라.
그러므로 나는 마침내 뱃길을 떠나
비잔티움의 聖都를 찾아 왔노라.

아, 聖堂 壁의 金色 모자이크처럼
神의 聖火 속에 서 있는 哲賢들이여,
聖火에서 내려와 나를 에워싸 돌며
내 靈魂의 스승이 되어 노래를 가르쳐 주오.
나의 가슴을 앗아 가시오.
情欲에 역겨워 하며 죽어가는 짐승에 억매여
가슴은 스스로의 本分을 모르는구나.

永生의 精妙가 되도록 나를 收拾해 주오.

한번 自然을 벗어나면 나는 다시금
自然 生物에서 肉身의 모습을 빌지 않으련다.
차라리 希臘의 金工 名匠들의 技巧를 본받아
金襴 물리고 鍍金한 노리개가 되어
졸음에 겨운 皇帝의 無聊를 풀고,
或은 金 가지에 얹혀 노래하여
비잔티움의 貴男 貴婦人들에게
지난 것과 지나가는 것과 앞날에 올 것을 알려주리라.

W. B. 예이츠 (William Butler Yeats, 1865–1939)

肉體와 靈魂의 對話 (*Dialogue of Self and Soul*)

I

靈魂: 旋回하는 옛 層階로 그대를 召喚한다.
    가파르게 오르는 階段과
    비바람에 무너져가는 塔上의 胸墻과
    별이 쏠리는 숨가쁜 밤 空氣와
    그리고 北極을 가리키는 별에 마음을 集中하라.
    헛되이 헤매는 모든 思索을 가다듬어
    모든 思索이 終結하는 그 地域을 凝視하라.
    어둠과 靈魂을 區別할 사람 그 누구랴?

肉體: 내 무릎에 찬 이 聖스러운 長劍은
    名匠 사토가 만든 칼이라
    아직도 옛날과 다름없이 날이 시퍼렇고
    몇 百年 동안 녹 한 점 슬지 않아 거울같이 맑다.
    비단에 꽃을 繡 놓은 저 古風의 刺繡는
    아마도 어느 宮女의 옷자락에서 찢어 온 것인 듯,
    나무 칼집을 칭칭 감고 동여매었으니
    삭은 실올 바랜 빛이나마 아직도 곱고
    칼을 잘 지녀 준다.

靈魂: 젊음을 버린 지 오랜 사나이가
    사랑과 싸움의 象徵物들을 惟想 속에서
    그리워한들 무슨 보람 있으랴.
    오로지 想像力이 塵俗을 超脫하고
    理智가 定處 없이 헤매면서
    하찮은 이것 저것에 끌리지 않을 때,

그대는 太初의 밤을 생각할 것이고,
　　　生死의 罪惡으로부터 救濟 받으리라.

肉體: 三代孫 몬타시기가
　　　五百年 前에 이 칼을 달구었느니라.
　　　어디서 마련된 刺繡인지 알 길 없으나
　　　가슴의 보랏빛 꽃무늬가 칼을 감쌌으니
　　　나는 이 모든 것을 낮의 象徵으로 삼아
　　　밤을 表象하는 塔에 對備코자 하노라.
　　　그리하여 虎班의 權利로써
　　　다시금 罪를 犯할 特權을 要求하노라.

靈魂: 後生의 地域에는 그러한 빛남이 넘쳐 흘러
　　　마음의 그릇 안에 고이게 되고, 따라서
　　　사람은 듣고 보고 말하는 官能을 다 잃게 되지.
　　　'實在'와 '蓋然', '知者'와 '被知者'를
　　　知性은 分揀치 못하게 되니,
　　　天國으로 간다는 뜻이 여기에 있네.
　　　죽은 뒤에야 赦罪가 있을 것을 생각하니,
　　　내 혀는 돌처럼 굳어 버리고 마는군.

II

肉體: 산 사람은 눈이 멀어, 떨어지는 것만 마실 뿐.
　　　개천이 더러운들 대수로울 것이 무엇이며,
　　　내가 다시 되푸리하여 산들 무슨 상관이랴?
　　　자라나는 동안 겪어야 하는 아픔과
　　　어린 시절 느끼는 수치심을 견디어 내렴.
　　　미숙을 벗어나 성숙에 이르는 과정의 고통과
　　　성년에 이르고도 미완의 상태인 자신의
　　　어설픈 모습을 직면하는 괴로움을 견디어 내렴.

뜻을 이룬 成年이 敵들에 둘러싸인들 대수랴.
악의에 찬 눈길로 노려보는 거울이
그의 눈에 비춰 주는 그 冒瀆스럽고
뒤틀린 형상을, 하늘의 이름을 걸고라도,
그가 어찌 피할 도리가 있겠나? 그 형상이
자신의 형상일 수밖에 없음을 깨달을 밖에—
명예를 위해 겨울 바람 맞으며 서 보더라도
그러한 도피에 무슨 보람이 있겠는가?

나는 몇 번이고 삶을 되푸리하여도 좋아.
설령 올챙이들이 우글거리는 개굴창—
장님이 다른 장님들을 두드려 패는
수렁에 빠져 허우적대는 것이 삶일지라도—
아니면, 영혼의 반려자가 되지 못할
한 교만한 계집을 만나 구애하는 동안,
한 사나이가 도리없이 빠질 어리석음의 수렁,
수렁 중에서 제일 潤澤한 수렁에 빠지더라도.

나는 행위나 사고에서 일어나는 모든 일을
그 근원까지 파고 들어감에 만족하노라.
分數를 가늠하고, 分數대로 나를 容恕할 밖에—
나 같은 사람이 뉘우침일랑 버리면
크나큰 기쁨이 가슴 속으로 흘러드니,
우리는 웃고 노래를 부를 수밖에—
모든 것이 우리에게는 祝福이고,
눈에 보이는 모든 것은 축복을 받도다.

해럴드 몬로 (Harold Monro, 1879–1932)

쓰라린 祭壇 (*Bitter Sanctuary*)

I
女子는 門間房에서 행랑살이를 한다.
羽緞 裝置物은 니코틴에 절어가는데,
손님들이 두고 간 寫眞은 빛이 바래가고,
女子는 草綠빛 덧窓 틈새로, 意識을 잃으러
한사코 들어오는 사람들을 살핀다.

여자는 번지러운 唐紅빛 얇은 입술을 핥기도 하고,
손톱으로 앞니를 쑤시기도 한다.
여자는 머리를 내밀고 새로 온 손님을 맞기도 하고,
문 앞에서 기다리란―무슨 苦痛이람?― 말도 한다.

II
더위는 무거운 땅을 잠궈 버리어
들리는 소리마다에 힘을 주었다.
生命이 아직 땅 위에 서 있게 만드는 곳에서
男子는, 痲醉된 채, 再生을 바라 呻吟하면서
門에 기대어 선다.
집에서는 인기척이 어렴풋이 들려온다.
뚜쟁이 한사람. 덧窓 뒤에서 킥킥대는 소리―

III
醉한 눈은 番號를 찾아 읽으려 앞으로 기울고,
손마디로 두드리는 소리와 감긴 혀로 씨부렁대는 소리.
男子는 깨어날 수도 없고, 잠을 이룰 수도 없다.
길 건너편에 뻗어 있는 흰 壁 위에
보일 듯 사라지는 運柩車의 그림자가 어른거린다.

IV

바야흐로 門이 활짝 열린다.

남자: "방이 남아 있소?"
여자: "당신 苦痛의 境界線을 넘었수?"
남자: "내 肉身이 헛되이 내것 아닌
　　　　꿈 속에 누워 있기를 바란다네."
여자: "잠의 盞을 들라지요."

V

깡마른 팔뚝과 앙상한 손가락, 게슴츠레한 파란 눈,
감기는 긴 눈썹, 떠 있는 虛空 가장자리에 매달린
보름달처럼 부풀어오른 눈꺼풀.
무슨 希望이 있겠나? 무엇이 두렵겠나? 눈을 뜨고,
아직 남아있는 肉身 혹은 永遠을 보는 것 아니라면.

아, 그러나 아직 반은 살아있는 얼굴이
은근한 눈길을 던지며 콧소리로 말을 건다.
여자: "낯빛이 안 좋군요. 외로우신가 보아.
　　　　내 하늘나라로 가까이 오지 않을래요?"
남자: "나는 돌이 되어 가는 중이야."
여자: "나도 그랬으면! 나도 제발 그랬으면!"
그러자 흰 옷 입은 下人들이 盞을 채운다.

VI

온 世上에 새날이 오면,
커피를 들고 오는 문지기 下人들을 보아.
풀밭 위의 牧童들을 보아. 그리고
몸단장하는 나리님들과 마나님들과
농사꾼들과 장사꾼들과 거품 이는 都市들을 보아.

그러나 이제 저 不幸한 남자는 낯선 방들을
더듬어 가다가 발을 헛딛고는 비틀거리네.
어둠이 휘덮는 밤을 그가 피할 수 있을까?
빛이 한 가닥 새어 들어 올 틈새가 어디 없을까?

VII

한번 그 房에 들어서면 헤어날 길이 있을까?
荒廢한 무덤 속에서 깊이 잠들어 있는
사람들도 있다고 말들을 하지.
어떤 이들은 얼굴들에 둘러싸여 흰 침대에 누워 있기도 하고,
어떤 이들은 世上을 헤매다가 영영 집을 찾지도 못한다지.

T. E. 흄 (T. E. Hulme, 1883–1917)

가을 (*Autumn*)

가을 밤 싸늘한데,

내 밖을 나섰더니
불그레한 달이 있어
낯 벌건 農夫처럼 울을 넘어다 보더라.
말은 걸지 않고, 나는 고개만 끄덕였다.
周圍에는 想思에 잠긴 별들이 있어
都會地의 아이들처럼 얼굴이 야위었더라.

T. E. 흄 (T. E. Hulme, 1883–1917)

템스 江畔 (*The Embankment*)
　　―사무치는 겨울 밤 어느 零落한 紳士가 부른 幻想曲―

내 한때는 깡깡이 켜는 솜씨에 恍惚하여도 보고,
딴딴한 鋪道에 번득이는 금빛 발꿈치에 홀려도 보았더니,
이제 나는
따뜻함이 詩의 眞髓임을 아노라.
아, 주여, 별이 좀 먹은
저 하늘의 해묵은 담요를 말아주소서.
두 다리를 뻗고 내 몸을 덮겠나이다.

D. H. 로런스 (D. H. Lawrence, 1885–1930)

熱帶 (*Tropic*)

太陽, 어두운 太陽,
시커먼 텅 빈 熱을 뿜는 太陽,
타는 대낮의 무서운 暗黑의 太陽.

보아라, 내 머리털이 까맣게 타 오그라진다.
보아라, 내 두 눈이 짙은 누렁으로 변해 간다.
黑人 모양으로—
北녘 거품 이는 牛乳가
내 血管 속에서 까맣게 엉기는 것을 보라.
乳香처럼 향기롭다.

검고 부드러운 기둥,
볕에 탄 사람들,
부드러운 잔등, 日光을 呼吸하는 입,
노오란 金싸락 같은 눈들,
硫黃처럼 摩擦하고 危險하고 爆發할 것만 같은.

바위, 어두운 熱氣의 물결,
어두운 熱氣의 물결, 바위여, 치켜라.
垂直으로 치켜라.

내 眼界를 橫斷하여 일렁이며 上昇하는
검은 熱氣의 洪水에 比한다면,
저 水平으로 구비치는 물이란
대체 무엇이란 말이냐?

D. H. 로런스 (D. H. Lawrence, 1885–1930)

除夜 (*New Year's Night*)

오늘밤 드디어 말하거니와, 너는 이제 나의 것이다.
너는 내가 祭物로 산 한 마리의 비둘기.
오늘밤에 나는 그것을 죽인다.

여기 내 품안에 나의 발가벗은 祭物이 있다.
죽음이여, 그대는 듣는가, 나는 이제
高價로 산 나의 祭物을 품에 안아 바치노라.

그 女子는 내가 가진 全部보다 값진 한 마리 銀빛 비둘기.
나는 이제 그 女子를 옛 嚴酷한 神에게,
나를 모르는 神에게 바친다.

보아라! 그 女子는 흠 하나 없는 멋진 비둘기. 나는
모든 것, 나의 이 世上에서의 最後도, 自負도, 힘도,
모든 幸福도, 女子를 위해 犧牲시킨다.

모든 것, 모든 것은 祭壇에 놓였다! 죽음이
매처럼 휩쓸어 내린다. 神이 祭物을 받는 것이다.
나는 榮光을 누린 것이다.

D. H. 로런스 (D. H. Lawrence, 1885–1930)

南國의 밤 (*Southern Night*)

솟아 올라라, 너 시뻘건 것아.
올라서, 달이라 불려지거라.

오늘밤은 모기가 무는구나,
追憶과도 같이—

追憶, 북녈 생각,
따갑게 찌르는 뿌연 世界, 나의 故鄕이
이 밤 속으로 파묻혀 간다.

月出이란
이 시뻘건 咀呪를 말함이냐?

솟아 올라라, 너 시뻘건 것아.
느릿느릿 치밀어라, 피처럼 검게.
고요한 별들의 밤 膜일랑 사뭇
찢어 버려라.

얼룩이 진
赤點.

D. H. 로런스 (D. H. Lawrence, 1885–1930)

平和 (*Peace*)

문간에 平和라고 쓰여져 있다.
溶岩으로—

平和, 굳어버린 시커먼 平和.
山이 불을 뿜을 때까지
나의 가슴은 平和를 모르리라.

이글거리는 견딜수 없는 溶岩,
철철 넘치는 불 琉璃마냥 이글거리다 못해,
莊麗한 구렁이처럼 山을 내려 바다 쪽으로 걸어간다.

숲과 都市와 橋梁은
燦爛한 溶岩의 발길 아래 다시 사라지고,
橄欖나무 뿌리 밑 數千尺 낙소스,
지금은 橄欖나무 잎사귀가 數千尺 불타는 溶岩 밑에 있다.

門間에 용암으로 굳어버린 시커먼 平和.
內部엔 白熱하는 溶岩, 결코 평화롭지 않으니,
마침내 터져 나와 땅을 뒤덮고 메마르게 할 테지.
그래서 다시 바위가 될 때 까지—
暗灰色 바위가 될 때 까지—.

그것을 平和라 하느냐?

D. H. 로런스 (D. H. Lawrence, 1885–1930)

뱀 (*Snake*)

뱀 한 마리가 내 물통에 와 있었어. 그날은
날씨가 하도 더워 나는 잠옷 차림으로
그리로 물을 마시러 갔었지.

커다랗고 무성한 캐롭나무의 이국적 향기 감도는 짙은 그늘 아래
나는 물병을 들고 층계를 내려갔지만, 거기 서서 기다리고 또
기다릴 수밖에 없었어. 그 놈이 먼저 물통에 와 있었기 때문이지.

그늘진 흙담 갈라진 한 틈새로부터 그 놈은
누른빛 축 늘어진 물렁 배를 길게 늘여 돌 물통에 걸친 채,
돌바닥에 모가지를 드리고 쉬고 있었어.
水栓에서 맑은 물이 조금씩 방울져 떨어지는데,
그놈은 一字로 째진 입으로 조금씩 마시고 있었어.
곧은 잇몸 사이로, 축 처진 긴 몸 안으로 조용히
물을 넘기는 중이었어.

누가 나보다 먼저 물통에 와 있었던 거야.
그래서 나는 나중에 온 이처럼 기다렸어.

물을 마시다가 그놈은 머리를 처들더군. 마치 소가 하듯.
그리고 물끄러미 나를 보더군. 물 마시며 소가 하듯 말야.
그리고 입술 사이로 둘로 갈라진 혓바닥을 낼름거리고는,
잠시 생각에 잠겼다가, 다시 머리를 숙여 좀 더 마시더군.
뜨거운 大地의 內臟에서 나온 흙빛 금빛 몸뚱아리가—
시실리의 七月 어느 날, 에트나는 煙氣를 뿜는데.

내가 받은 教育이 나에게 속삭였어.
저놈을 죽여야 한다고—
시실리에선 검은 뱀은 無害하지만, 누런 놈은 毒이 있다지.

또 내 안에 있는 목소리가 말하더군. "네가 사내라면
당장 막대기를 집어 들고 저놈을 때려 죽이란 말야."

그러나 내가 굳이 고백해야 하나? 얼마나 그놈이 마음에 들었고,
그놈이 조용히 마치 손님처럼 내 물통에 물을 마시러 왔다가,
목을 축이고 나서는, 평화롭고, 차분하고, 고마운 줄도 모른 채,
大地의 이글거리는 속으로 돌아간 것이 얼마나 기뻤는지—

내가 겁이 많아서 그놈을 죽이지 못한 것일까?
내가 괴짜라서 그놈에게 말하고 싶었던 걸까?
내가 영광스레 느낀 것은 내 겸손 때문이었나?
참말이지 나는 영광이라고 느꼈어.

그러나 아직도 그 목소리:
"네가 겁내지만 않으면, 그놈을 죽일 걸!"

그런데 나는 정말 겁이 났어. 아주 무서웠어.
그런데도 나는 훨씬 더 영광스레 느껴지더군.
그놈이 그 은밀한 大地의 어두운 문을 나와
내게서 善心을 기대했다는 사실이 말야.

그놈은 마음껏 물을 마신 다음
마치 술에 취한 사람처럼 꿈꾸듯 머리를 처들었고,
그리고는 갈라진 밤처럼 검은 혓바닥을 허공에 날름댔는데,
제 입술을 핥으려는 것 같았어.
그리고는 神이 하듯, 볼 생각도 없으면서, 허공을 휘둘러 보고는,

천천히 머리를 돌리더군.
천천히, 아주 천천히, 깊은 꿈속에 잠긴 듯,
그 느리게 구불구불 감기는 긴 몸을 끌며
갈라진 벽을 타고 기어오르기 시작하더군.

그리하여 그놈이 그 무서운 구멍에 머리를 넣고,
어깨를 늘어뜨리고 천천히 기어 올라 조금씩 들어갈 때,
그 무서운 검은 구멍으로, 그 암흑 속으로, 애써 들어가며
온 몸을 사라지게 하는 것에 대한 공포가, 거부감이,
그놈이 완전히 사라지고 나자, 나에게 덮쳐 왔어.

나는 주위를 둘러보고는, 물병을 내려 놓고,
되는 대로 생겨 먹은 막대기를 집어 들어
그 물통을 향해 소리나게 던졌어.

그놈이 맞은 것 같지는 않았는데,
채 못들어간 그놈의 몸 부분이 불쌍하게 후들대다,
번개처럼 잠시 꿈틀거리더니, 그 검은 구멍 속으로,
壁面에 입술처럼 갈라진 大地의 틈으로 사라지더군.
끓는 고요한 대낮에 나는 넋을 잃고 그 틈만 보았지.

그런데 나는 불현듯 뉘우쳤다네.
얼마나 졸열하고, 비겁하고, 천한 짓이었냐 말야!
나는 나를, 빌어먹을 교육의 가르침을, 경멸하였네.

그리고 나는 앨버트로스를 생각하였고,
내 뱀, 그녀석이 다시 돌아와 주기를 바랐네.

왜냐면 그놈이 나에겐 무슨 제왕처럼 보였거든.
땅 밑에서 왕관이 벗겨 귀양살이 하는 제왕—

언젠가는 다시 왕관을 쓰게 될 제왕 말일세.

해서 나는 生命의 군왕 중의 하나와
함께 할 수 있는 기회를 잃었고,
언젠가는 속죄해야 할 것이 있으니,
그것은 옹졸함— 바로 그것일세.

에즈라 파운드 (Ezra Pound, 1885–1972)

어쨌든 그들은 싸웠지 (*Those Fought in Any Case*)
―戰歿勇士의 記念碑를 세우기 爲하여―

어쨌든 그들은 싸웠더니라.
어쨌든 鄕村을 防衛한다고
皆中에는 믿었기에.

냉큼 武裝한 이도 있어,
冒險을 위한 이도 있어,
卑怯을 두려워 한 이도 있어,
非難을 두려워 한 이도 있어,
실컷 虐殺이나 해보겠다고 想像한 이도 있어,
나중에 깨달은 바 있었거니와,
虐殺欲을 맛보고 무서워한 이도 있어.

祖國을 위하여 죽은 이도 있어,
―달지도 않았고 壯하지도 않았지만―
늙은이의 거짓말에 속아
눈에까지 찰락말락 地獄에 빠져 거닐다가
속임수를 깨닫고 다시 故鄕에 돌아왔으나,
故鄕은 欺瞞과 疊疊의 背信,
묵은 거짓과 새로운 破廉恥,
古來의 遺物 高利貸金業,
그리고 公席의 詐欺漢으로 가득하더라.

千古에 없던 膽力이며 千古에 없던 浪費 였어라.
젊은 피와 끓는 피,
붉은 두 뺨과 늠름한 體軀,

千古에 없던 不屈의 精神,

千古에 없던 정직,
이제껏 듣지도 못하였던 幻滅,
갖은 히스테리와 狂亂, 塹壕속의 懺悔,
죽은 자의 배에서 터져나오는 哄笑.

헤아릴수도 없이 죽었구나,
―겨레의 精華도 있었겠지―
이빨 빠진 할멈을 위해,
부스럼 투성이 文明을 위해.

純直한 입으로 빙긋 웃는 魅力,
흙 속에 파묻힌 聰明한 눈들,

수백 개의 깨진 石像들을 위해―
破損된 몇 千 券의 冊들을 위해―

지그프리드 써쑨 (Siegfried Sassoon, 1886–1967)

臨終 (*The Death-bed*)

스르르 잠이 들자 周圍를 둘러싸
鐵壁같이 튼튼한 고요가 쏟아져 오는 걸 느꼈다.
떠도는 琥珀빛 光線처럼 흐늑흐늑하고
잠의 날개를 타고 오르며 떠는
고요와 安全. 무거운 肉體의 기슭에는
달빛도 없는 죽음의 물결이 혀를 내밀다.

누구인지 입에다 물을 대주어,
그는 힘없이 삼켰다. 앓는 소리와 함께
그는 피빛 黃昏을 지나 暗黑 속으로 떨어졌다.
負傷이라 일컫는 痲藥 같은 두근거림과 아픔도 잊었다.
    물— 둑을 넘어 푸르게 흘러내리는 잔잔함.
    물— 하늘이 비쳐주는 좁은 뱃길.
    배는 새처럼 삐걱이고, 그 가장자리에는
    여름 꽃과 빛깔이 알록달록 비친다.
    물결에 노를 맡기고, 한숨을 쉬며 잠이 들었다.

한 줄기 바람과 함께 밤이 病棟에 찾아 들고,
바람에 불린 커튼은 번득이는 곡선으로 부풀었다.
밤— 흐려져 가는 눈에, 떠가는 구름의 亡魂 속에서
반짝이는 별들은 보이지도 않았다.
물에 잠겨 가는 그의 눈 속에는, 보라, 당홍, 초록의
怪異한 빛깔이 범벅이 되어 어른거리다 사라졌다.

비— 어둠 속에 주루룩 비 내리는 소리가 들렸다.
香氣와 淡淡한 音樂이 뒤섞이고 있었다.

수그린 薔薇 꽃송이에 내리는 따스한 비―
숲 속으로 배어드는 후둑이는 소나기―
우레 뒤에 휩쓸어 오는 거센 비가 아니라, 목숨을
부드러이 천천히 씻어 내리며 방울져 돋는 平和.

몸을 움직여 꿈틀거려 보았다. 그러자 苦痛이
어슬렁대며 먹이를 찾고 있던 猛獸처럼 튀어나와,
그가 더듬던 꿈을 無慈悲한 발톱과 이빨로 뜯어발겼다.
    그러나 그 옆에 누가 와 있었다.
    怪物이 사라지자 그는 부르르 떨며 누워 있었다.
    바짝 다가선 죽음이 그를 물끄러미 凝視하였다.

燈을 많이 밝혀 들고 그의 침대에 둘러서렴.
너희의 눈길과 따스한 피와 삶의 意志를 그에게 주렴.
말해 보렴. 깨워 보렴. 아직 살려낼 수 있을지 몰라.
젊은 사람이잖아? 戰爭을 嫌惡했는데, 왜 죽어야 하지?
惡毒한 老兵들은 無事히 戰勝의 끝장을 보는데 말야―

그러나 죽음은 對答했다. "내가 그를 골랐거든."
그래서 그는 죽었고, 여름밤은 고요하였다.
寂寞과 平穩, 그리고 베일처럼 드리워 내린 잠.
이윽고 먼 곳에서 아득하게 울려 오는 砲聲.

H. D. (H[ilda] D[olittle], 1886–1961)

더위 (*Heat*)

바람아, 더위를 찢어 헤쳐라,
더위를 베어 젖혀라,
갈가리 찢어발겨라.

이 텁텁한 空氣에
實果는 떨어질 수가 없어—
배의 꽃맺이를
몽그시 내밀어 부풀리고
葡萄 알을 동글게 하는 더위 속으로
實果는 떨어질 수가 없어.

더위를 뚫어라.
쟁기로 갈아 헤쳐서
너의 길 양편으로
젖혀 놓아라.

이디스 씨트월 (Edith Sitwell, 1887–1964)

間奏曲 (*Interlude*)

이 더웁고 검푸른 대낮의 어둠 속에
말 한 마디, 빗방울처럼 뚝 떨어진다.

주렁주렁 머리 위에 열린 익은 과일처럼
새의 노래는 空中에 매달린 듯도 싶어,

황금방울새 화살같이 어른거리는데,
무르익은 따스한 빛이 몰래 쪼아 먹는다.

그늘 속에 노래를 감춘 새처럼
나의 발에도 깃털이 돋는다.

이슬 맺힌 푸른 가지와 과일을
나는 그대에게 물어 나른다.

이 코오뉴코피어의 豊饒 속에서라도
땅벌 빛 알록진 트랫머리에 다시 꽂으려

네 뜨거운 입술에 이슬방울이 떨어지면
새의 피도 네 푸른 脈 속에서 뛰놀 듯한다.

이디스 씨트월 (Edith Sitwell, 1887–1964)

비엘지바브 卿 (*When Sir Beelzebub*)

때마침
비엘지바브 卿이
地獄의 호텔에서 牛乳葡萄酒를 請했는데,
―그곳은 옛날 프로서피나가 墜落한 고장―
바다의 波濤는 憲兵隊 制服처럼 푸르러,
―배멀미로 女給을 놀라게 했지―
그에게 럼酒를 바치는 者 이미 없거늘,
하늘 水平線만은 河馬처럼 鈍感한지라,
黃泉 고개를 넘는 알프레드 테니슨 경에게
冥福의 祈願을 바치기에는 階梯가 좋아,
榮譽로써 桂冠詩人에게 딴죽을 걸 양으로
― 故人은 古典의 律調로 점잖게 걷지―
卿을 삼가 追悼한다는 趣旨로 連判 捺印한
禁酒運動 宣傳工作隊員들의 빛바랜 陳情書가
차디찬 꽃다발이 되어 故人의 머리 위에 얹히다.
때마침 비엘지바브 卿은 럼 酒를 달라고 號令하는데
밸라클라바의 옛 戰場처럼
溶岩은 지붕에서 터져 나오고,
바다의 푸른 制服 뻣뻣한 長斫개비 憲兵隊는
이를 制壓하느라 全力을 기울이다.

윌프레드 오웬 (Wilfred Owen, 1893–1918)

더 큰 사랑 (*Greater Love*)

입술이 붉다 한들, 戰死한
   英國人들 입맞춤에 얼룩진 돌만큼 붉진 않아.
사랑을 주고 받는 이들의 多情함도
이들의 純粹한 사랑 앞에선 오히려 羞恥일 터.
아, 사랑아, 내 대신 감긴 눈들을 보노라면
   너의 눈도 부질없어.

너의 날렵한 姿態도
   劍이 후빈 팔다리 같은 아찔한 떨림은 없지.
하느님도 關與치 않는 것처럼
저기 아무렇게나 딩구는 팔다리 같은—
저들의 熾熱한 사랑은 마침내
   저들을 마지막 衰弱, 죽음으로 억눌렀나니.

너의 音聲이 곱다 한들,
   —창살 버틴 골방으로 속삭이며 부는 바람처럼—
너의 말소리가 多情하고,
부드럽고, 쾌청한 저녁처럼 맑은들,
이제는 아무도 듣지 못하는 저들의 音聲만은 못해.
   기침하던 저들의 애달픈 입을 흙이 메워 버렸거든.

가슴아, 너는 한 번도, 銃彈을 맞아 커진
   가슴들처럼 뜨겁고, 크고, 가득한 적이 없었어.
너의 손이 희다 한들,
火焰과 우박처럼 쏟아지는 銃彈을 헤치며
너처럼 十字를 긋던 손들이 더 희었더구나.

마음껏 울어 보렴. 그래도 저들은 꼼짝도 않을 걸.

허버트 리드 (Herbert Reed, 1893–1968)

크라나크 (*Cranach*)

그러나 옛날 한때에는
참나무 잎들과 멧돼지들도 있었는데—
안토니오, 안토니오,
지난 날의 傷創에서 피가 흐르누나.

우리는 실버타운에 와 있어.
템스 강변 테라스에 앉아 치즈와 절인 양파를 씹으며
江바람이나 좀 쏘일까 하는
素朴한 抱負로 우린 여기 와 있어.

정다운 템즈 江아, 나룻배는 레다의 白鳥처럼
네 가슴 위를 미끄러져 가는구나.
工場들은 가녀린 몸매를 자랑하는
巧慧한 裸身의 계집들처럼 보드라운 깃털을 끄덕이네.

로버트 그레이브스 (Robert Graves, 1895–1985)

歲月 (*Time*)

渺茫한 바다는 大理石 絕壁을 때려
해묵은 바위 조각을 갈아
조약돌 꽃을 피어낸다.

廣漠한 季節이 들판을 헤매는 중,
알록달록한 꽃 봉오리들이
대리석 조약돌처럼 솟는다.

꽃의 아름다움은 죽음을 슬퍼하는 歲月―
조약돌의 아름다움 또한
삶에 지친 歲月이라.

피어나는 꽃이나, 아니면 歲月과 渺茫이
꽃처럼 알록지게 깎은 보드라운 조약돌을
禮讚함은 쉬운 노릇.

時間이란 흐르는 것― 流液처럼 흐르며 달래
頑强한 자물통과 녹슨 돌쩌귀를
柔軟함으로 이끌지.

나 또한 拒逆할 수 있으랴? 歲月이 낳는
사랑스런 쌍둥이, 老年과 幼年을,
서글픈 아득함에 묻으면서―

그 해묵은 感謝를 어찌 아니 表하리요?
老年을 宜當 피어나는 꽃으로 보고,
어린 時節을 조약돌로 보면서―

세실 데이 루이스 (Cecil Day Lewis, 1904–1972)

죽음에 바치는 序曲 (Overtures to Death)

I

깃털이 나듯 나무는 本能的으로 싹을 틔우고,
여름날은 점점 길어지고, 聖誕節에 눈 내리고,
宮闕에는 哨兵들이 지켜 서는
이 世上에 태어 난 우리들에게

그대는 우리들의 부모들이
잊을 수도, 容恕할 수도 없는 자—
客地에서 財産이나 축내는 망나니,
아니면 寸數가 먼 親戚과도 같았소.

家庭用 聖經에서 그대 이름을 우리는 보았지만,
不淨탈까 食事 때나 공부할 때엔 입에 안 올렸소.
그러나 때때로 敎會에서는
사람들이 그대를 위해 祈禱하는 것도 같았소.

우리는 그대가 멀리 海外에 사는 걸로 짐작했소.
그래서 이따금 침대에 조용히 누워,
몰아치는 波濤의 들이키는 숨소리를 들으며,
우리는 그대를 생각해 본 적도 있었소.

얼마 뒤 그대는 大戰 때에 많은 功을 세웠다고
어른들이 하는 이야기를 우리는 엿들었소.
비록 그대는 錦衣還鄕은 아니 하였으나,
우리는 到處에서 그대의 이름을 보았소.

집안 살림이 如意치 못하게 되자,

한때는 그대가 큰 人氣를 끌었다오—
白紙手票를 서슴지 않고 떼어주고
理解 깊은 웃음으로 반겨주는 아저씨 같았소.

우리들 중에는 그대를 찾아가려고
飛行機나 빠른 自動車를 타는 이들도 있었고,
病院을 歷訪하는 이들, 邪惡한 길에 드는 이들,
별 점을 쳐 보는 이들도 더러 있었소.

그러나 이제 어느 때고
한밤에 그대가 우리를 찾을 듯하니,
庭園으로 통하는 미닫이 門쪽을 보면서
우리는 若干 다른 角度로 그대를 그려 본다오.

집이 초라하고 나무 기둥이 말라 썩어가는 걸
우리는 뻔히 알고 있다오.
迎接이 변변치 못하나, 오는 그대를 막을 길도 없으니,
우리가 흠잡힐 일이나 없었기를 바랄 뿐이라오.

이제 와서 허둥대며 大淸掃를 할 겨를도 없고,
부서진 자물쇠를 고칠 틈도 없으니,
우리는 壽衣가 드리워진 이 應接室에 웅크려 앉아
처음이자 마지막일 그대의 노크를 기다릴 뿐이요.

III

이 보시오, 내 아무리 大膽하기로소니,
臨終의 자리나 戰場에서 뭇사람이 當然히 認定하는
그대의 威力을 어찌 하찮게 여길 수 있겠소?
深夜 三更에, 아니면 來訪客과 對話를 나눌 때,
그대가 내 腹中에서 時針처럼 똑딱임을 느끼는 내가
설령 원하는 바일지라도, 그대보다 더한 試鍊이

있을 수 있다 믿으며 나 自身을 속일 수는 없었소.
서로 낯익은 사이지만, 그대와 나는 相剋이니,
싸움은 피할 도리가 없소. 그러나 내 非難의 상대는
그대가 아니라, 이 자리에 없는 敎唆者라오. 그대의
權限과 근기와 술수를 내가 가벼이 대하는 듯하다면,
窮地에 몰려 發惡하는 쥐, 아니면 두 醫師를 籠絡하는
精神病者, 아니면 차분하게 자리잡은 圓周를 향해
공연한 是非를 거는 點 정도로나 생각해 주구려.
  그대는 여러 모습으로 우리들 앞에 나타났소.
蒼白한 神父로, 검은 낙타로, 徵集되어 服務하다
勳章을 수여받은 中士로, 두 번째 찾는 幼年期를
떨게 하는 未知의 恐怖로, 아니면 착한 소년 소녀들을
축복하는 보석처럼 반짝이는 常綠樹를 보여 주려
그토록 敬虔하게 걷어 올리는 徽章으로도 말이요.
그대가 萬人을 平等하게 만든다고는 합디다만,
한 썩은 지역구에서 다른 지역구로 그대가 곧바로
옮겨 놓은 特權階層에겐 별 意味가 없는 말이었소.
空虛하고 차가운 우리들 처지에, 무덤을 共有하는
별 볼 일 없는 平等論者들을 부러워 할 것도 없소.
강박에 몰린 이 時代에 그대를 '平和'라 부르는 자는
幸福하오. 數百萬을 죽게 만드는 '平和'가 그대 아니오?
  草原에 내린 이슬이 野生花처럼 피어나듯
잠간 동안의 慰安이 있고, 忍冬草의 꽃망울이
향기 머금은 한 철 지키려 매달리고, 고혹적인 肉身의
아름다움이 성큼 다가오는 시간의 걸음을 절게 하고,
꽃잎 나부끼는 사랑의 입술이, 落照의 情炎에 타오르는
구름처럼, 서서히 다가오는 그림자를 遲延시키더라도,
그대는 마음을 편히 가져도 좋으리니, 오래잖아
그것들은 다 그대의 얼굴빛을 띠게 될 것이외다.
  끝장은 당신이 보고야 마는 것. 허나 어쩔 것이요?

敗北感에 미쳐 날뛰며, 그대가 앞질러 仲裁해 주기를
强要하려는 陰謀를 꾀하는, 죽음의 意志를 부추기는
저 犯罪의 下手人들을 말이요―
그대의 망나니 走狗 노릇을 하는 저들이야말로,
굶주리고 불기 없는 방에서 스스로 목숨을 끊는 자,
이끼 낀 運河 검푸른 물가에 고개 떨군 억죄인 가슴들,
무모한 狂亂의 총알에 때 아니게 지는 어린 꽃송이들,
쇳덩이를 핥은 듯 우리 앞날을 短縮하는 검은 서리처럼
내리는 恐怖― 이 모두를 책임져야 할 자들이오.
이 보시오, 내가 그대를 아무렇게나 대접한다면,
그자들이 그대를 하찮은 것으로 만들었기 때문이오.
그대는 자연의 일부이나, 그들은 자연을 逆行하는 자들이오.
우리가 살아 있는 동안 그대의 平穩을 원하리오마는,
제멋대로 주제넘게 날뛰는 그대의 下手人들을 상대로
우리가 치르는 전쟁은 삶 자체이니, 패할 수가 없소.

루이스 맥크니스 (Louis MacNeice, 1907–1963)

聖誕節에 題한 牧歌 (*An Eclogue for Christmas*)

A: 험악한 계절에 자넬 만나네그려.
B: 험악한 종소리가
   울리며 다른 모든 생각을 몰아내는 것 같으이.
A: 싫증에 겨운 달력은 해마다 되풀이 되고,
   나사에 기름이 말라 밸브도 검게 타 막혔으니,
   당뇨병 걸린 문명의 당분과다증은   5
   生과 문학의 신경을 썩어 문드러지게 하누만.
   그래서 異國 산골 벽지에서 구세주가 탄생하심을 알리는
   번쩍이는 색종이와 허식의 꾸밈을 해마다 꺼낼 때면
   나는 자네를 찾아 오네. 지겨운 삶의 되풀이에 절은 자네는
   지난 날의 어릿광대 놀음의 현기증에서 벗어난 사람이니—   10
B: 나와 닮은 자네가 나를 찾는 게 갈못일세.
   내 고장에 자네의 도피처가 될 만한 곳이 없고,
   어떤 측량지도에도, 자네의 도시들과 도시가 낳은 생각이
   무너질 때, 자네를 구해 줄 지점은 바늘 끝만큼도 없네.
   차라리 나처럼 제 자리에서 죽는 게 나아.   15
   어딜 가보나 나쁜 건 다 마찬가지야. 본능이 부르는 데로
   다시 돌아가서 밤거리의 고양이와 택시 소리나 듣게.
   아니면 유성기를 틀고 위인들의 말소리나 엿듣게.
A: 해마다 듣는 장단 소리와 하와이안 기타의 재즈에 지쳐
   바둑판 무도장에서 맴을 도니, 내사 폭탄과 진흙과 독가스에서   20
   멀리 떨어진 것도 같으이. 버터처럼 매끄러운 유선형의
   고급 요부에 허리를 감겨 말을 더듬었나니,
   희부옇게 가리워진 조명은 거슬리게 휘돌고 빙빙 감아들어—
   香油에 번지르르한 멋쟁이 장난감—
   世紀의 순진한 시절에는 한량 주인공 노릇을 도맡아 했고,   25

피카소의 모델이 되어 검푸른 수평선의 바다를 끼고 앉았었건만,
　　　이제 나는 부서진 단면으로 걸러지고 조각이 나서
　　　假線의 연필 그림, 실속 없는 負債투성이,
　　　나의 실재와는 아무런 상관이 없는
　　　畵家의 칼로 긁어낸 抽象으로 살아왔지.　　　　　　　　　　　　　　　30
　　　내 살과 내 얼굴을 제대로 지니는 것도 허락이 안 되어,
　　　그들은 나를 抽象化하고 分析하여 순수한 형상,
　　　하나의 象徵, 하나의 混成畵, 낡은 기법의 프로필로
　　　만들었으니, 하여튼 영혼과 육체는 아니었지.
　　　그래서 나는 이 싫증나는 음악을 틀어 놓아　　　　　　　　　　　　　35
　　　사색을 파기하고 자동기계가 되고 싶은 걸세.
B: 시골에도 내가 두려워하는 인간이 많네.
　　　다 죽은 뱃대기에 맥주를 들이붓는 자, 갖은 種子의 개를 몰고
　　　휘파람 불며 떨치고 다니는 사십 줄에 든 아낙네들,
　　　언덕길, 밭길, 로마인들이 닦은 길, 들국화 핀 방천길, 할 것 없이　　40
　　　서슴없이 활보하면서도, 그들이 넘나드는 장벽은 그들의 오만을
　　　둘러싼 철조망에 비하면 아무 것도 아님을 깨닫지 못하는 사람들—
A: 또 도시에서 차를 몰 때, 가슴을 철렁 내려앉게 만드는 사람이 둘—
　　　하나는 차를 멈춰 길가에 대라고 유인하는 여자,
　　　또 하나는 마음 놓고 속도를 내려 바른 발을 뻗고 앉았을 때,　　　　45
　　　움켜쥐고 꽉 밟아 요란한 급정거 소리로 정지시키는 남자.
　　　여자는 겨울 바람을 조롱하듯 비단 양말을 신었고,
　　　남자의 흰 지팡이는 장님의 表迹이라.
B: 시골에선 아직도 여우사냥이 성행하지. 겨울비에 젖은 지방에 가면
　　　회색 몰이꾼이 들에 혜겼고, 황혼은 야만시대의 영웅들을 火葬하는 듯　50
　　　옛 하늘에 붉은 연기를 뿜어, 공장의 검은 연기가 한 쪽을 가리면,
　　　또 한 쪽에는 주홍색 달이 무뚝뚝한 딱불이 촌놈처럼
　　　鐵가지 나무 사이로 멀리서 우리를 비웃으니,
　　　이것이 부드러운 옛 慰撫의 달이런가.
　　　우리는 마치 구석기시대의 인간이기라도 한 듯,　　　　　　　　　　55

앞날의 빙하시대나 징기스칸을 맞이할 걸세.
A: 바야흐로 새 鑄貨를 만들 때가 되었네. 사람들은 늙어 버려,
　　찍히고 손때 묻고 주머니 들락거리느라 반들거리게 됐지만,
　　이런 偶然 속에 사는 것이 獨自의 生命인 줄로만 생각하고,
　　不可思議한 精神의 流通手段에 지나지 않음을 전혀 몰라.　　　　　　　60
B: 思考하지 않는 精神 — 그런 것이 있을 수 있다면 —,
　　機械的인 理性, 변덕스런 正體性,
　　이런 制約을 직면할 수 있고 움츠려 들지 않는다면 —
A: 行商人의 양철 장난감은 鋪道위에서 움직거리지만,
　　태엽이 감긴 때문인 줄은 모르지. 차라리 그것이 나아.　　　　　　　　65
　　우리처럼 태엽이 감겼다가 풀리는 걸 알기보다는 —
B: 그러나 到處에 個性의 捏造가 되풀이 되고 —
A: 化粧粉을 서리처럼 바르고 毛皮를 휘감은 낡은 얼굴들.
B: 뻐드렁니 農事꾼은 곱사등 담을 넘어다 보고.
A: 地方 巡廻하는 장사치는 뒷간에서 익살 피우고.　　　　　　　　　　　　70
B: 世上 萬事도 끝장이 된 모양이야. 땅은 매말랐으니.
A: 지나친 精密도 아무런 보람이 없어.
　　街路燈은 다시금 켜졌고, 가스, 전기, 하수도,
　　끊임없이 改善되는 文明의 利器는 便利할 대로 便利해졌지.
　　쇠락해 가는 로마가 別莊과 下水道를 改善했듯 말야 —　　　　　　　75
　　(防音 잘 된 도서관과 一定하게 유지되는 溫度라니.)
　　街路燈은 밝고, 붉은 불은 어둠에 묻힌 쇠붙이 창자,
　　긴 鐵管들의 塹壕를 말없이 表識하고,
　　고트 족이 다시금 山에서 벌떼처럼 내려오기 前에는
　　압축공기 굴착기의 요란한 소리는 그치지 않을 걸세.　　　　　　　　80
　　그렇더라도 우리로부터 자라난 이 거대한 有機體에는
　　痲醉시키다가 落葉처럼 지는 아름다움이 아직 있어,
　　道路의 安全地帶마다 하얀 공이 달처럼 떠있고,
　　都市 안개는 흐릿한 琥珀처럼 가르릉 소리로 옹알대고,
　　雄壯하게 굽은 길에 列 지어 휘돌아 가는 높은 버스들은　　　　　　　85

　　　　菊花처럼 아름다운 노오란 불빛으로 입맞춤을 하지.
　　B: 시골 나으리들은 변함이 없으리니, 성난 상황과
　　　　정신적 自蔑感에 종전과 다름없는 상태로 죽음을 맞을 터.
　　　　매가리 없이 消滅하는 그들의 삶은 끊임없이 稀釋되는 毒,
　　　　의미없이 반복되는 精神 상태의 연속임을 證明할 것일세.　　　　　　　　　　90
　　　　偶像이 追放되면, 이미 그들은 살 수가 없을 것이고,
　　　　아무도 存續하지 못하리니, 私有財産 부스러기와,
　　　　발발이와, 水仙花와, 毒이 되고 고름이 되는 좋은 것들과,
　　　　다리 휜 椅子와, 銀 집게로 집어내는 각설탕과,
　　　　年年歲歲 울리는 晩餐을 알리는 요란한 종소리—　　　　　　　　　　　　　95
　　　　이런 것들 없이 그들이 도대체 어찌 살아간단 말인가?
　　　　아니면 곡식 창고 지붕에서 떨어져 내리는 빗방울이
　　　　累積되는 證據가 되지 못한다면 어찌 할 것인가?
　　　　시골에 사는 자의 唯一한 特權이 그런 것들일진대—
　　A: 재즈로 板子를 대고 굽두리한 우리들은?　　　　　　　　　　　　　　　　　100
　　　　黑人이 뱀장어처럼 꿈틀대며 춤을 추고,
　　　　粉紅빛 넙적다리가 수레바퀴살처럼 번쩍이는 劇場에
　　　　구경을 가는 우리들은? 그 모든 뚜벅걸음, 익살스런 걸음걸이 춤,
　　　　맥고모자에 벙거지를 뒤집어 쓴 광대들의 곤두박질 해학과
　　　　요술쟁이의 깝치고 뒤집는 재주를 우리가 벌써 다 아는데—　　　　　　　105
　　B: 國家가 領地의 담을 헐어 버리면 우리는 어쩌지?
　　　　私有 遊獵地와 漁場이 없어지고, 멧갓[山坂]은 모조리 伐採되고,
　　　　얼굴 表情은 指針盤이 되어 웃지도 찌푸리지도 못하게 된다면?
　　A: 킬킬대는 기관총이 젊은이의 손에 놀아나, 아파트, 俱樂部, 美粧院,
　　　　神父의 巢窟, 할 것 없이 射擊練習의 表的이 되면 어쩔 것인가?　　　　110
　　　　어떻게 될 것인가? 우리 文明이 오랫동안 갇혀 있던 풍선처럼—
　　B: 올 것은 오고야 말아. 賣笑婦와 어릿광대가 그 통에 한 몫 볼 테지.
　　　　꿈을 꾸지 않으니, 이것들이야 잃을 꿈인들 있겠나?
　　　　政權이 바뀌는 날에도 이것들이야 적어도 제자리를 찾아가겠지.
　　　　그러나 한 가지는 있을 법 하지 않네.

A: 자기도취는 금물일세.   115

제 몸을 뜯는 독수리가 되진 말게. 높은 산언덕에 웅크리고 앉아

벗어진 목에 냉혹한 抽象을 휘감고 있다가,

벌판에 떨어져 구겨진 제 屍身을 뜯으려 내려오는 독수리 말야.

劇場과 映畫館의 시끌덤벙한 저편에서 여태껏 들어보지 못한

노래가 들려오는 것 같군.

B: 마님은 銀 집게를 맵시 있게 들어   120

각설탕을 집으면서 하시는 말씀― "이 以上 더 어떻게 해요?

延命을 위해서라 한들 달리는 못하겠어요."

A: 나 역시 달리는 못하겠네. 오늘 저녁 좌석이나 예약해 둘까?

B: 나는 거름 냄새 못지않게 기억으로 충만한

農場 주변이나 거닐어 보겠네.   125

A: 영웅숭배자 노릇 하는 나를 기쁘게 해 주었고,

개성 있는 사람 구실 하는 나를 즐겁게 해 준,

전문가이건 비전문가이건, 모든 예능인의 묘기에

나는 싫증이 나도록 한번 빠져 보려네.

B: 다시 한번 우리 스스로를 속여 보세. "所願은 成就된다"는   130

옛 공상가들의 거짓말로―

A: 그리고 내 죽기 전에

그 화려한 조명등 아래 마음껏 돌았으면―

B: 그리고 英國의

高原地 풀밭, 윌트셔의 草原과 롱마인드 地方에서[1]

내 발이 공처럼 풀 위에 튀고, 얼굴은 바람에 화끈대고,

눈썹은 바람에 찔리는데, 허연 돌바위 같은 羊들이   135

내 인간적 虛勢를 눌러 주었으면―

A: 쌕소폰과 실로폰,

모든 탁월한 기교에 대한 예찬, 畵廊에 즐비하게 전시된 화폭들,

滄海에 펄럭이며 바람을 타는 돈 많은 사람 소유의 요트의 돛,

---

[1] 원고정리자 註: 윌트셔 초원(the Wiltshire Downs)은 잉글랜드 동남부에 소재하는 나무들이 없는 고원지대이다. 롱마인드(Longmynd)는 웨일즈 변경 가까이 슈롭셔(Shropshire)에 소재하는 고원이다.

화덕에 구어 낸 스테이크의 기막힌 맛—
B: 덧없는 이 모두가
제비의 날렵한 날개처럼 영원한 것이라면 얼마나 좋으련.   140
그럼 또 만나세. 잊지 말게. 오늘은 聖誕祭— 解釋은
자네 하기에 달렸네만, 오늘 아침 救世主가 誕生하셨다네.

W. H. 오든 (W. H. Auden, 1907–1973)

西班牙 1937년 (*Spain, 1937*)

모든 過去는 어제의 것.
貿易航路를 따라 中國까지 퍼지는 膨脹의 言語.
計算臺와 石塚의 普及.
어제는 端陽한 氣候에서 日光時計를 보기.

어제는 傳票에 依한 保險料의 査定   5
地官을 불러 우물터를 잡기.
어제는 수레와 時計의 發見이며 騎馬의 訓練.
어제는 航海者의 번거로운 世界.

어제는 妖精과 怪物의 退治.
골짝을 眈眈히 노려보는 독수리같은 要塞.   10
숲 속에 지은 禮拜堂.
어제는 天使와 怪物을 彫刻하는 일.

돌기둥 法廷에서 異端者를 審判하기.
어제는 술집에서 벌어지는 神學의 論戰.
그리고 샘물에서 이루어지는 奇蹟的인 治癒   15
어제는 妖魔들의 밤 饗宴. 그러나 오늘은 鬪爭.

어제는 動力과 터어빈의 施設.
植民地 沙漠에 鐵道의 敷設.
어제는 人類의 根源을 論하는 歷史的 講義.
그러나 오늘은 鬪爭.   20

어제는 希臘語의 絶對的 價値를 믿고,

英雄의 죽음에 幕이 내리고,
어제는 落照에 바치는 祈禱와 熱狂者의 禮拜.
그러나 오늘은 鬪爭.

소나무 사이에서 놀란 詩人이   25
或은 줄기차게 쏟아지는 瀑布水 노래를 들으며,
或은 斜塔 곁 낭떠러지에 우뚝 서서 혼자 하는 말,
"아, 나의 꿈이여, 나에게 뱃사람의 幸運을 다오."

學者는 器械를 드려다 보며
인간 세계 아닌 영역, 번식하는 세균,   30
이미 식은 巨大한 木星을 관찰한다.
"그러나 내 벗의 生命을 나는 묻노라, 묻노라."

그리고 貧者는 불 없는 宿舍에서 夕刊新聞을 떨구며
툴툴댄다. "우리 삶은 하루하루가 損失이야.
推進者이며 組織者인 歷史를 우리에게 보여 다오.   35
淸明한 江물 歲月을 보여 다오."

그리고 뭇 國家는 아우성에 아우성을 보태어,
사사로운 이윤을 챙기고, 은밀한 밤의 공포를
불러 오게 만드는 삶을 부추긴다.
"너희가 한 때 海綿의 都市國家를 세우지 않았더냐?   40

"상어와 호랑이의 거대한 軍國主義 帝國을 길러
다부진 뱁새의 兵營을 設立하지 않았더냐?
仲裁하거라. 비둘기 되어 내려오거라. 아니면, 차라리
무서운 아버지로든, 溫良한 技師로든, 어쨌든 강림하거라."

그러면 삶은—呼應할 餘力이 있으면—   45

가슴과 눈과 肺腑에서, 都市의 商店과 廣場에서 對答한다.
"아니외다. 내사 推進者가 아니외다.
적어도 아직은 아니외다. 그대에게는 아니외다.

"내사 그대에게 굽실거리는 자, 술친구, 어수룩하게
속아 넘어가는 자이외다. 그대 하는 일이 곧 나이외다.　　　　　　　　　　50
내사 착해지라는 그대의 盟誓요, 그대의 웃음꺼리이외다.
내사 그대의 事務的인 언성이요, 그대의 중매꺼리이외다.

무엇을 提案하시려오? 正義의 都市를 建設하라고요?
그렇게 하지요. 同意해요. 아니면 自殺同盟, 그 낭만적인
죽음 말이요? 좋아요. 受諾하고 말고요. 왜냐하면 나는　　　　　　　　　55
그대의 選擇이요, 決定이니까. 내가 곧 西班牙 아니오?"

허다한 사람들이 그 소리를 들었노라.
먼 半島에서, 고요한 平原에서, 외딴 漁夫의 섬에서,
그리고 썩은 都心地帶에서 이를 들었노라.
그리하여 갈매기 떼처럼, 꽃씨처럼, 候鳥의 몸이 되었노라.　　　　　　　60

不義의 땅으로 밤을 새워 알프스 굴 속을 달리는
긴 急行列車에 그들은 가시풀처럼 엉기어 갔노라.
그들은 바다를 건너 떠갔노라.
그들은 재를 넘어 生命을 바치러 왔노라.

무더운 아프리카에서 꼭지처럼 떼어, 創意에 넘치는　　　　　　　　　　65
歐羅巴에 저토록 無謀하게 접붙인 강파른 땅 조각,
江물로 새겨진 저 高原地에서는
우리들의 熱病의 모습이 매섭고 칼날 같더라.

내일 당장, 아니면 미래.

제4부 현대영시 번역　　**437**

疲勞와 包裝꾼들의 동작에 대한 硏究, 70
放射線의 모든 옥타브들의 단계적 探索.
來日은 섭생과 呼吸에 의한 意識의 확장.

來日은 浪漫的 인 사랑의 再發見.
가마귀를 撮影하고, 自由의 믿음직한
그림자 아래에서 모든 재미를 보고, 75
來日은 가장행렬 기획자와 樂土의 날.

來日은 젊은이들의 것, 爆彈처럼 터지는 詩人들의 것.
湖畔의 散策과 완벽한 교감의 겨울.
來日은 여름 노을에 郊外를 달리는
自轉車競走. 그러나 오늘은 鬪爭. 80

오늘은 불가피하게 늘어나는 죽음의 機會.
殺人의 현실에서 意識的으로 용인한 罪惡.
오늘은 진부한 허섭스레기 팜플렛과
지루한 회의에 소비한 精力.

오늘은 그때그때의 慰安과 나눠 피는 담배. 85
곳간에서 즐기는 촛불 밑 화투놀이,
거칠은 音樂會와 남자들의 농담. 오늘은
몸 버리기 전에 더듬어 얻는 快感 없는 抱擁.

별들은 죽었고, 짐승은 눈을 감았다.
우리에게 맡겨진 건 오직 이 하루. 90
歲月은 짧고, 歷史는 패배자를 향해
탄식을 할 망정, 돕거나 容恕는 못한다.

W. H. 오든 (W. H. Auden, 1907–1973)

無名의 市民 (*The Unknown Citizen*)

    JS/07/M/378의 英靈을 爲하여
    祖國은 삼가 이 人理石 記念塔을 세움

統計局 調査에 의하면, 그는 公民으로서
何等의 汚點이 없었다는 사실이 判明되었고,
그의 品行에 關한 모든 調會는, 비록 그 表現은 낡았으나,
現代的인 의미에서 그는 聖人이었음에 意見이 一致한다.
그는 弘益社會에 一生을 바침에 餘念이 없었기 때문이다.   5
戰爭期間을 빼놓고 그는 隱退할때까지
職場을 工場에 두어, 한번도 罷免된 일이 없었고,
雇傭主인 <퍼지> 發動機 有限會社에 좋은 成績을 남겼다.
그러나 무슨 유별난 견해가 있어 同僚를 背信한 적도 없었으니,
勞組의 기록에 의하면 그는 組合費를 忠實히 納付하였다 한다.   10
(報告에 의하면 그가 속했던 勞組는 健全한 것이었다.)
社會心理 調査員들이 한 조사 결과에 따르면,
그는 同僚間에 評이 좋았고, 술도 한잔씩은 할 줄 알았다.
그는 날마다 신문도 열심히 사 읽었고, 廣告에 對한 그의 反應도
다른 사람들과 조금도 다름이 없었으리라고 言論界는 確信한다.   15
그의 名義로 加入된 保險證書를 보면, 그의 保障은 완벽했고,
保健證에는 한번 入院하여 치료받고 退院한 事實이 적혀있다.
그가 月賦制度의 長點을 完全히 理解하고, 現代人의 生活必需品인
축음기와 라디오와 자동차와 냉장고를 소유하였다는 사실은
「生産者 調査部」만 아니라 「生活改善會」도 確證한다.   20
輿論調査部員들도 滿足스럽게 느낀 것은
그가 그때그때 옳은 意見을 主張하였다는 사실이니,
平和時에 그는 平和를 부르짖었고, 戰時에는 출정하였던 것이다.
그는 結婚해서 人口에 다섯 자식을 더해 주었으니, 이는

優生學者의 언명에 依하면, 그 世代의 부모에게 가장 적합한 숫자였다. 25
또 교사들 말로는, 그는 子女 敎育에 대해 어떤 간섭도 하려 든 적이 없었다.
그는 자유로웠던가? 그는 행복하였던가? 이런 질문은 語不成 說이리니,
만약 무언가 잘못되었다면, 우리 귀에 틀림없이 들어왔을 것이기 때문이다.

스티븐 스펜더 (Stephen Spender, 1909–1995)

貧民窟의 小學校 敎室 (*An Elementary School Classroom in a Slum*)

거센 물결에서 멀리 멀리 떨어진 이 아이들의 얼굴들.
뿌리 없는 海藻처럼 흩어진 머리칼은 蒼白한 얼굴을 덮어,
키 장다리 少女는 머리를 무겁게 수그리고,
쥐 눈깔을 한 少年은 종이처럼 파리하다.
아비의 오래된 身病을 如實히 말해 주는 비틀린 뼈
앙상한 不運의 相續者가 冊床에서 글을 배운다.
침침한 敎室 뒷줄에 숨어 앉은 순하고 여린 아이 눈동자엔
나무 속 다람쥐와 노는, 이 房과는 다른 꿈의 房이 어린다.

누루죽죽한 壁에는 褒賞狀이 걸려 있고,
沙翁의 頭像은, 먼동 튼 하늘에 구름이 개어,
文明의 象徵, 둥근 지붕처럼 온 都市를 내려다 본다.
鐘樓와 꽃방천의 티롤 산 기슭. *아낌없이 보여주는 地圖는
세상이 어떤지 온 세상에 알린다. 그러나 이 아이들의 世界는
地圖에서는 볼 수 없는 窓 밖의 世界인지라, 아이들의 將來는
안개로 그려지고, 납덩이 하늘로 封合이 된 좁은 골목은
江과 곶과 별처럼 숱한 단어들과는 멀기만 하다.

*[寬厚한 地圖는 解說된 世界를 表彰하건만
이곳은 아닌 딴 이름을 주다.
꽉도 적은 몇몇 사람에게는 이 窓이 참되여
世界와 말과 손짓하는 나뭇잎이 慰安을 주다.
이 젊은 生命들에게는 旅行의 꿈이 罪스럽고 아슬하다

組織된 거짓 속에서 비틀리여
웃음이 아니면 미움으로 돌아가는 生命들에게는

아무래도 沙翁은 罪가 많으리.
그네들의 무더기 사이에서 어린이들은……]

안개에서 끝없는 밤으로 얄미웁게 돌아가는
옹색한 굴속의 生命들에게 沙翁은 아무래도 몹쓸 존재.
地圖는 나쁜 垂範이 되어, 배들과 태양과 사랑이
도적질로만 誘惑하리. 破碎된 돌무더기위 이 아이들은
뼈가 드러나 보이는 살가죽을 뒤집어쓰고, 유리알 같아 낀
강철 테 안경은 파쇄 무더기의 깨진 병 조각과도 같아.
안개 낀 빈민굴이 그들의 시간과 공간의 전부이러라.
그러니 최후의 심판처럼 큰 빈민굴로 그들의 지도를 메워라.

우리들 將來에 걸쳐진, 戰爭을 숨기는 煙氣처럼
童孩心의 위 虛空에 列을 지어 이 房에 늘어선
未亡人 設立者, 歷代機長들의 이 肖像畵가
아아 美는 말과 보람이 있어라
色갈진 壁과 境을 깨뜨려 뚫고 나오다 하고
아우성 친다면 또 모를레라.
兒童들은 山길을 올라가는 汽車에 탄 몸과도 같아라.
눈앞에 펴지는 골작 골작의 푸른 世界와
꽃 香臭에 무거운 綠陰의 여름을
이 時間은 가르쳐 주다.

스티븐 스펜더 (Stephen Spender, 1909–1995)

君主의 最後[的] 理論 (*Ultima Ratio Regum*)

銃은 돈의 窮極의 理論을
납의 글자로 봄 언덕 위에 가로새긴다.
그러나 올리부 나무 밑에 쓰러저 죽은 靑年은
虎視耽耽하는 그들의 눈에 띠이기에는
너머나 어렸고 너머나 어리석었다
차라리 그는 입맞훔의 標的이 될 것을
生前인들 드높은 工場 고동이 그를 부른 적 없었고,
食慾의 유리짝門이 回轉하야 손짓한일도 없었다
그의 이름이 新聞에 난 적도 없었거니와
世上은 우물 같이 깊숙하니 黃金을 갖추고
死者를 에워싸 古來의 障壁을 守直하였으니
그의 一生은 株券 時勢의 風聞처럼 空漠하게도 겉돌았다
아아 봄바람이 나무의 꽃닢을 떠러트리든 어느날 이던가
그는 너머나 가벼히 帽子를 내던졌다
담장이 꽃 없는 담壁에는 銃이 도쳤고
機關銃의 忿怒는 瞬息間에 풀을 베였고
旗빨과 나뭇닢은 손과 가지에서 우수수 떠러졌다
트위이드의 캡帽子는 뻐꾹채의 풀 속에서 썩었드니라
생각해보라 그의 一生을
雇傭問題나 호텔의 宿泊簿나 公報綴로 본다면 아무런 價値도 없건만
생각해보라 一萬개의 銃알에서 單 한개가 사람을 죽이느니라
물어보라 世界여 죽엄이여
올리브 나무 그늘에 쓰러진 저리도 젊고 어리석은者의 죽엄에
그만한 大量消費가 必要하였든가?

찰스 매지 (Charles Madge, 1912–1996)

星座가 만남 (*In Conjunction*)

이제 별들은 激流를 이루어 蒼穹을 휘감아 도는데
괴로움과 기쁨의 表情을 띠운
몇몇 가지 일이 또렷히 正確하게 그리워지다
星座의 運動을 틀림없이 알리는
날개 도친 流星은 밤 집을 떠나가다
비틀린 그림자가 드높은 半球에 가득 차니
이에 우리는 平和를 結論지워 感謝의 祭物을 올리다
그러나 戰爭의 猛禽은 우뢰 소리도 없이 납덩이 지붕에 웅크려 앉아
銀河水의 빛나는 가슴패기에 어른거리는 그림자도 없다
悲劇의 運命이 지워진 四方刑으로 굳은 이 집 밖에는
寂寞의 高木 밑에 저녁이
天宮에서 나리는 安息의 저녁이 옛 싸움터를 슬퍼하고
警鐘과 높슬은 쇠와 戰歿英靈 사이에서 우리를 지켜주는
저녁이 祝福을 기다리고 있다.

조지 바커 (George Barker, 1913–1991)

여름의 牧歌 (*Summer Idyll*)

때때로 여름철이 되면
大地는 姙娠하여 黃金빛으로 몸이 무거워지고
가지는 늠름히 드리워 휘어지고
잘잘 흐르는 葡萄糖 시내에 물은 붇고
꽃은 金빛 캐무풀라지인 양 共謀하는 여름을 감추어 주건만
시내 밑바닥에는 겨울이 차게 흘러
穀食 속에는 굶주림이 쌌처럼 차게 숨었나니
豊富 밑에 缺乏이 웅쿠려 困窮이 씨앗이 되어
가난이 휘인 가지를 잡아다리다

綠陰 우거진 여름 옷을 입혀도
모서리에 뼈는 앙상히 불거지다
芳菲한 봄 王國을 누리게 하여도
가슴패기 밑 빈 虛空에는
貧困이 惡辣한 幽靈의 꽃처럼 피어 오르다
靈魂의 눈알을 억눌르고
앙상한 肉體의 器官을 억눌르고
사랑하며 살아가는 몸부림과 기쁨과 生을 억누르는 底力은
千深의 바다처럼
견디어야 하므로 차라리 견디기 어려우니라

때때로 여름이 暫時라도 壓力을 덜어주면
여름 薔薇 꽃숭이처럼 탐지게
江물에서 沐浴하고 나오는 사람도 있어
落照에 토끼를 몰이하고 풀밭에서 노리하고
休紙나 여름 벌레처럼 公園에 흩어져

딩굴며 땀에 촉촉이 젖었다가

저녁에 巡視나 園丁이나 警官들에게 몰려

이제 내 꿈꾸드시 安息과 새옷과 現金을 꿈꾸는 이도 있어

花園은 季節의 勳章을 차고

處女出演하는 계집처럼 華麗하다

빛나는 珊瑚 사이를 떠가는 바다의 侍體와 같이

사람들은 꽃밭 사이를 徘徊하야

스치는 香臭에 쓸리우며 純潔한 美에 眩惑하다

젊은 女性을 裸體로 하는 여름은 그들의 우퉁도 벗기다

많은 사람이 뱃노리하며 여름 江을 올라가

그늘진 물속에 손가락을 잠그면

손가락도 江물을 따라 올라가다

물속 그림자에 江기슭이 무삼 必要 있으리요

고른 果實처럼 얼골만 수그리고 손을 드리워 올라가다

얼골이 비춰이며 寺院과 建築會社는 사라지다

귓청을 뚫을 듯 들려오는 베에토벤 音樂에 웨일스의 메아리는 사라지는데

여름은 地中海를 불어와

곱디고운 白鳥와도 같아라

딜런 토머스 (Dylan Thomas, 1914–1953)

태양 없는 곳에 (*Light Breaks Where No Sun Shines*)

太陽 없는 곳에 볕발이 뚫고 드다
바다가 흐르지 않은 곳에
가슴의 潮水가 밀물 드다
腦 속에 반디 불을 켠
깨진 幽靈같은 볕발의 물건들이
뼈를 덮지 않는 살 속으로 列지어 나오다

허벅다리 사이의 촛불이
젊음과 씨를 녹이여 늙음의 씨름 태우다
씨가 쌌트지 않은 곳에
사람의 열매는
無花果처럼 빛나는 별 속에서 주름을 펴다
촛농이 없는 곳에 초는 털을 나타내다

눈알 뒤에서 먼동이 트다
頭蓋骨과 발꾸락의 兩極에서
疾風같은 티는 바다물같이 쏠리다
울도 말뚝도 없는
天宮의 噴油井은 끝까지 내뿜어
微笑를 띠우며 눈물같은 기름을 叡智하다

眼窩에 가리우는 어둠은
새캄한 달처럼 地球의 兩極을 돌다
햇살이 뼈를 비취이다
치위가 없는 곳에 疾風은
살을 저미는 듯 겨울 옷을 벗기다

봄 아지랑이가 눈까풀에 아른거리다

볕발이 秘園에 뚫고 들어
비에 젖어 추군히 내음새 풍기는 思索의 尖端을 비취이다
論理가 消滅하는 곳에
大地의 秘密은 눈을 뚫고 쌌터
피는 太陽에 躍動하고
빈 터 위에서 새벽은 멈추다

데이비드 개스콘 (David Gascoyne, 1916–2001)

假想 人物 (*The Supposed Being*)

입을 想像하면
짙은 빛 꽃송이가 꽂혀있는 다문 입술.
꽃잎은 터져서 거품을 이루고
샛노란 雄蕊는 겨눈 화살과 같고
뾰죽하니 돋친 꽃술 끝은
불과 물의 交叉點을 가리키는 信號가 되어
그 무서운 情熱은
놀란 눈초리와 手顫症의 손과 痙攣하는 얼굴의
通行人을 숨가쁘게 하며
그 言語는 새까마
우리가 한번도 써보지 못한 言語이다

눈을 想像하면
속눈섭 아롱아롱하여 잠에 깊이 젖었고
이마 밑 눈알은 바위틈의 샘과도 같아
밀려오는 바다의 거센 波濤에
떨면서도 굶주린 듯 毒살스럽고
물결의 날카로운 발톱에 할퀸 듯이
눈알은 눈꺼풀에 깎이고
햇빛에 그슬린 눈꺼풀은
새파란 핏줄 고운 손으로 부벼지다
바위에 불이 붙어
눈동자는 그 뜨거운 불꽃에
아지랑이가 끼다

손을 想像하면

손톱과 갸름한 손가락 뼈는
새의 柔弱한 다리뼈와도 같아
손 끝은 분홍빛 꽃 봉오리의 끝과 같이
싸늘하고 神秘스러운 空氣를 더듬어
바위의 表面같은
皮膚 밑의 피를 나타내다.

젖가슴을 想像하면
世上의 끝
바다 없는 海邊의 조개와 같아
한자루의 칼을 들고 무찌르는 것도 같아
손으로 뜯어 놓을 빵과도 같아
아직 情欲에 꿈틀거리지도 않고
아직 목마른 입에 빨리지도 않고
아무런 動作도 없는 젖가슴을 想像하면
가슴은 무서웁게도 고요하고
밤속 섬에 갇힌 듯이 사랑과 죽음을 다같이 두려워 해

性을 想像하면
허벅다리 사이의 殘忍과 恐怖
꺼멓게 벌어진 틈사구니
닐름대는 불꽃의 숯 자취
性은 X字와도 같아
모든 過去의 表識이며 足跡이 되고
鬱悶의 숲속과
不可思議의 밤 山을 비쳐 줄
횃불이 되다.

그리고 全體의 存在를 想像하면
만질 수 있는 肉體가 꿋꿋이 섰고

눈에 보이는 實在的인 四肢가
햇빛에 비쳐 움직일 때도 있고
瀑布水 밑에 엎드린 돌바위처럼
또는 그 위에 불거진 돌바위처럼
어둠 속에서 죽은 듯이 靜止할 때도 있건만
그러나 結局
이 같은 存在는 나의 肉眼에 보이지 않고
내 손의 觸覺으로 어루만지지를 못하니
그 女性의 存在는
모든 矛盾이 共存하는 곳
어둠이 光明이고 實在가 虛無인 곳
世界가 꿈속의 꿈인 곳에 있을 따름이다

제5부
창작 시, 희곡

Variations on the Theme of Despair:
Before and After August, 1945

—BEFORE—
I. Morning Prayer in the Desert

The leafless tree of Knowledge gives no shade,
Being hung with only bitter fruits. Sitting
Thereunder should we plan to journey shadeward
Before this sun of sorrow rolls o'erhead?
Or should we greet the fierce inheritance
In solemn calm? Consider by what course
We've reached this valley in the desolation,
And of the bitter sun-trodden shrubberies
Our caravan of hopes and coming glories
Has trailed across Your hard horizon, kept
The vigils of the night, abiding by
Your laws of pilgrimage and sacrifice
And now, what have You given? What reward?
For us with nerves enslaved and shrunken loins,
There is no choice between despair and joy;
The question is: how shall we set in order
This chaos, our grieving heart and memory?
You who have given us power in the sun,
Will You, O God, forsake us in this toil?

II. Descent from the Mountains

Walking downhill the meandering path of Grief,
Treading with sored refractory feet the stones
Of dried stream-beds, I never found relief

In th'incidental songs birds, the groans
Of haunted, lost mankind without belief
Humming their figured bass in well-known tones.

Then past a mud-hut crouching to the earth
Beside a fruitless orchard long forsaken,
I went, desiring water, rest, and mirth.
"In vain!" the hermit cried. "Comest thou to waken
Afresh th'insinuating smell of dearth?
Of thee my longer-for peace shall not be shaken!"

Last to a learned city came and saw
A host of dessicated souls astray
Along dumb streets, each ay a closed door,
And stagnant ponds—the swans had flown away,
Seeing no promised vision of thy Law,
O God, I must to sea; here is no stay.

III. Chorus of the Spirits that Appear in a Woman's Daydream

1st Spirit:
We are the creatures of day-dreams.

2nd Spirit:
We come to every woman-born
Who, winter and spring, at times forlorn,
Sit by the ancient fountain-streams
Of regret, dreaming of glories past
And joy in deep-sea Memory cast.

3rd Spirit:

We also come, both first and last

To lovely women who have wept

For causes that have taken flight,

Who, grieving at Life's given plight,

Have learned to be in sorrow adept.

1st Spirit:

To those we also come who know

What creative misery is, who go

From mood to mood, snatching beauty,

As a famished soul its craven Deity.

All:

We are the spirits that confirm

The eternal doubts of Man whose term

Of life must end in self-fold darkness

And gnawing grief in all its starkness.

    (Surrounding the woman)

So here we come in twos and threes,

Crowding her dreams by slow degrees.

For dream she must and dream she will

Of us who hold and turn the Mill

Of Destiny that grinds to dust,

Alike all hopes, all pains, all lust.

1st Spirit:

What we dictate is absolute

2nd Spirit:

Because we are the stern statute

3rd Spirit:
Of hidden remorse and discontent.

All:
What we dictate she must assent.

—AFTER—
IV. Monologue of a Scarecrow

The wind blows down the barren hills, bearing
The wailing cries of all-suffering pines.
And here I stand on bamboo crutches, staring
At vacant space, and Time's secret designs.
The patient tillers of the soil have reapt
Their harvest and gone; only the stubs in lines
Bear witness to their bent backs in summer's heat.
This sterile patch of earth on which they heapt
Such care and toil, now trespassed by the feet
Of starved crows! Who be the tenant now?
I see men swayed by shouts of false deceit,
Blinded by naïve dreams of power. But how
Shall these children of poverty await
Their blessings peace? Shall they be forced to bow
To alien thoughts and philosophies of hate?
Here is no abiding love, but merchants' greed,
Impostors' strut, and scholars' hot debate,
And coughing foxes with their holes, to feed
Upon the noxious flesh of the beguiled.
When shall arrive the sower with the seed
Of futile frondage to redeem this wild?

And the peace-maker who shall mediate

Between the hostile father and the child?

Lost erring souls, seek to alleviate

The anguish of your unresolved belief

By faith, not make-believe, in future fate.

The patriots back from exile will relieve

Your burdened souls, and guide your feet. O ye

That trample without direction, cease to weave

Your patterns of ambition! Learn to be

Firm on your soil, and love humility.

(From *Grove of Azalea*, Edited by Y. R. Pyun (卞榮魯), 國際出版社, 1947, pp. 13~18)

LOVE AT PHILLIPPI

A Conversational Melodrama in Three Acts

Characters of the Play

Mark Lorayne

Claudia Lorayne, *his wife*

Michael Lorayne, *their son*

Charles Hilary

Joy Hilary, *his sister*

Eleanor Anderson

Julian Anderson, *her son*

Margaret Anderson, *his sister and fiancée of* Charles

Dr. Duncan Stuart

Anthony Pearsall, *Solicitor*

Brigit, *the maid*

A Woman

Veronica, Joe, Mac, Oliver, Ben, *some of the people of the Circus "Marco Polo"*

Place: London

Time: Present [around 1940]

Act I, Scene i: One afternoon in December

       ii: Later in the same afternoon

Act II, Scene i: Evening, the same day

       ii: Later in the same evening

       iii: Still later, in the small hours

Act III, Scene i: Late morning, the next day

       ii: One afternoon in late September, some nine months after

Note on the Setting:

A big window in the center. Two doors: one on each wall. One door leads to the hall, presumably, and the other to the other parts of the house. The usual drawing- room-furniture (but the minimum amount). A fireside. A pale violet light through the window.

Anthony: *Aged about 37. "Tall, dark and handsome" fits his outward appearance well enough. Inwardly, a man who is always aware of the effect he is making, a man who is well versed in "the art of living." Somber nature.*

Claudia: *About 34–35. Also possesses, in her way, a theatrical sense of the world. Endowed with fully developed physical beauty. Conscious of her youthful appearance and good proportion. Loves company—for fear of being bored when alone.*

Act I, Scene i

The living room at Mrs. Lorayne's house; one winter afternoon. Rising curtain reveals Anthony and Claudia, smiling and holding hands. Anthony speaks—seriously. Claudia continues to smile.

Anthony: So today's your birthday!

Claudia: Yes, Anthony, and what about it?

Anthony: The day when one designs to turn over a new leaf, and you—

Claudia: I object, Anthony, I'm doing no such thing; I hate revolutions. Besides, I hate the imagery of turning over a new leaf: it reminds me not of a Shakespeare folio but rather of those miniature diaries with inch-wide spaces in which you are expected to record your soul's diurnal round. You can roll your cigarettes in inch-wide slips of paper but not your soul.

Anthony: You don't let me finish my sentence. I don't care two hoots whether you like the imagery or not, but I repeat, you're going to turn over a new leaf— with my help.

Claudia: You mean you'll bleach my soul and wash my dirty linen for me? How sweet! I should adore to roll round nonchalantly in your back-in-a-day dry cleaning machine.

Anthony: Oh shut up, Claudia. I'm in earnest.

Claudia: Yes, in deadly earnest. (*Pensively*) You always are when alone with me.

Anthony: Because I'm always thinking of your future happiness.

Claudia: Happiness is a thing one cannot plan.

Anthony: But one can guess it and I mean to do it for you.

Claudia: But where is the person who is going to be happy with me? One cannot be happy all by oneself: alone one can only cry—like the voice in the wilderness. (*Pause*) Oh, solitude, the enemy of happiness! (*Pause*)

Anthony: Do I in any way make you happy?

Claudia: Yes, in many ways. (*Smiling*) Do I you?

Anthony: (*Peeved*) Must you counter-question me now?

Claudia: (*Unheeding*) Do I?

Anthony: Yes, of course.

Claudia: Well, that's splendid. Our balance sheet of love is perfectly satisfactory. No sign of overdraft on either side. I hate overdrawing whether from a bank or from a heart.

Anthony: You exasperate me just when I—

Claudia: (*Amused*) Yes, of course, exasperation is a sign of love!

Anthony: Oh well, you can just take the words out of my mouth and chew them to your own taste and—

Claudia: You won't care two hoots—always two hoots! I love to bait you Anthony because you never care two hoots about being baited.

Anthony: Claudia, you're being frivolous. I know you dangle your frivolity before meas a sort of bell to keep the camel in good spirits; but if I, the camel, stopped walking the tinkling bell would not tinkle any more.

Claudia: Don't be bitter, Anthony. I never said you were a camel!

Anthony: But you've repeatedly implied it with your abstract smile whenever I've brought forward the facts—the legal facts—of your open road to a new life.

Claudia: Divorce and remarriage? Like having old teeth pulled out and replacing them with new ones?

Anthony: There you go off again. Why should you be so unkind to me when my only desire is to make you happy?

Claudia: (*Quietly*) I'm not worth all that of your valuable attention.

Anthony: That's for me to decide. (*Pause*) To me you are the living symbol of hesitant beauty, the beautiful and therefore the un-nameable tree, which stands on the other side of the lake of my heart and casts its long shadow on the water.

Claudia: But Anthony, the shadow of your anonymous tree would not be falling that way, if the sun were not setting beside it. Think what that means. I have the sun behind me and tread my own dim shadow. It's my birthday today and I'm getting old.

Anthony: If only you would let bygones be bygones!

Claudia: (*Teasingly*) But you don't know what pleasure I derive from sniffing round like a dog over the buried bone of Memory!

Anthony: And if only you were less conscious of the pastness of your life!

Claudia: But you don't know what pleasure I derive from counter-balancing your excessive belief in the future-ness of life!

Anthony: But why must you do that, counter-balance me, as you call it?

Claudia: Because I'm generally fond of you and because my life would not be so full without you. (*Pause*) To me you are the high tide, which fills my heart with water to the brim of its dyke and covers up its skeletoned and criss-cross structure. (*Smiling*) It sounds a bit selfish if you like. But then love is a peculiar alchemy of selfishness and unselfishness. That's what makes it so sweet and so bitter alternatingly.

Anthony: (*Pause*) Dearest Claudia, there are moments when I am simply overwhelmed with the desire to possess you, to announce to the world that you are mine.

Claudia: But don't I let you sometimes announce to yourself that I am yours—in every possible way?

Anthony: Yes, thank God. But that's not enough.

Claudia: Thank yourself. What more do you want?

Anthony: Oh Claudia, don't pretend that you like living in this neutral territory of spiritual widowhood! Will you not accept my love for you for what it is worth? We could be happy together, if only you would dare the consequences.

Claudia: Your solicitation of my happiness is a simpler affair than my acceptance of it. For my happiness depends as much on you as on Michael's future. The change from motherhood to wifehood is not so easy as you would like to think. And Michael will feel it more acutely than I, in all probability. Besides, I would not particularly care to dare now; I have suffered much, perhaps unnecessarily, through over-daring. It's not that I cannot dare. (*Amusedly*) I could if I wished put my handkerchief round my eyes, like your goddess of Justice, and pick my lot that way. But then the awful thing is that I'll have to undo my handkerchief and see what I've picked and live up to it whether I will or no.

Anthony: You know Michael better than I do, I suppose. I know the choice rests with you. But the fact is that I'm haunted by the silent flow of your life. Is there no way in which I can arrest that silent flow, or at least put up something in the stream so that I can hear the water running?

Claudia: Yes, you can and you do.

Anthony: How?

Claudia: By coming closer to me.

Anthony: (*Pause*) May I kiss you?

Claudia: If you wish.

They kiss. While they are kissing, enter Michael followed by Dr. Stuart. Michael is between 18 and 20. Dr. Stuart is a man of between 40 and 45, plump is he, slightly bald, wearing glasses. Dr. Stuart is absorbed in his own words, but Michael sees them. As soon as Claudia and Anthony hear his voice, they separate. Dr. Stuart is a man who realizes that "life is but the intermediary voice who will not say so because he has too great a sense of humor. And his sense of humor extends, ever, to his bubbling mind and restless movement. A man of many gestures; and a voice, which has an unusual number of pitches and modulations. Michael is a creature of many moods, which he cannot control himself. He is young: beyond that, there is nothing to be said about him, because he is what "youth" does.

Dr. Stuart: So you see, my boy, virtue also is a punctured and dried-up bladder, only fit to be hung up on the ceiling of an Oriental apothecary, something which will delight immensely the casual eye of an Occidental traveler wandering with his inevitable wallet of curiosity, the camera. (*Seeing Claudia and Anthony*) Oh hallo, it's only me, and Michael.

Michael: Good afternoon, Mr. Pearsall.

Anthony: Hallo, Michael.

Claudia: Dr. Stuart is in his sour mood again. He most probably wants a drink.

Dr. Stuart: My dear Claudia, you misapprehend me. I was only saying something quite to the point because Michael happened to tell me that he had a peculiar dream last night and I was telling him how all dreams are peculiar in that they debunk our good breeding. That's what the night will do for you: you build your castle of all the cardinal virtues during the daytime, but then comes the night bringing in its dark blanket the tidal force of your libido which will flood your castle and raise it to the ground.

Anthony: (*Unheeding*) (*To Michael*) Your mother and I have been talking about you.

Michael: (*Calmly*) In audible language?

Dr. Stuart: (*Turning to Anthony*) But you're not listening, Anthony. You and I, the family solicitor and the family doctor, ought to be like Siamese twins always giving each other moral support and always going together like salt and pepper. (*Turning to Claudia*) Tell me, Claudia, which is the more important of the two? Salt? Or pepper?

Claudia: Don't be facetious, Doctor.

Dr. Stuart: Ah, the perfect table-manner of Claudia's. (*Drinks*) (*Turns to Michael*) Now that I come to think of it, I never asked you what your dream was.

Anthony: Quite like you—discoursing on the nature of virtue without even hearing what the dream was about.

Michael: Nor do I intend to tell it in public.

Dr. Stuart: Oh come, this is not in public.

Claudia: What was it, Michael dear?

Michael: Mother, do you really wish to hear it?

Claudia: Yes, of course.

Michael: (*Pause*) Well, I saw a person with his coat collar turned up, looking remarkably like Father getting off a taxi in front of our house; and the taxi was funny enough drawn by a milkman's horse—it was very early in the morning, and somehow I hadn't gone to bed yet and was looking out of the window. He and the taxi-driver got out together, and the driver was dressed in white, like a dairyman. But as they opened the front gate, the white cap of the dairyman turned black, and he then looked just like a postman. I shouted after Father, but my voice failed, and I choked and woke up.

Claudia: (*Laughs*) Oh Michael! (*But ceases to laugh immediately*)

Dr. Stuart: (*Taking off his spectacles*) A most surrealistic dream, Michael. Quite a usual phenomenon, I believe.

Anthony: I wish you didn't always have to be funny, Doctor.

Dr. Stuart: Pepper complaining of the salt, eh?

Claudia: Michael, has this dream been troubling you much today?

Michael: Yes, in a funny sort of way.

Dr. Stuart: (*Pouring himself a drink*) I notice you've recently been making hard attempts to read *The Odyssey* in the original, Michael. You've not by any chance reenacting the part of Telemachus in your own surrealistic dream-Greek, are you? I know Greek does often behave funnily, especially Greek stories.

Anthony: Don't be absurd, Doctor. This isn't a Greek story.

Dr. Stuart: Always the legal mind—never seeing the funny side of things! Anthony, I hope you realize that judges often have bald heads under their wigs.

Claudia: Like you!

Dr. Stuart: Quite right, but I wear no wig, that's the difference.

Michael: Mother, I wonder why Joy isn't coming. Do you think she will come after all? Ought I to ring up her music teacher and find out whether she is still there or not?

Claudia: Oh, I'm sure she'll come, Michael dear.

Dr. Stuart: About your dream, Michael. There probably is an element of forecast truth in it. I remember when your father said good-bye to me seven years ago, he said it in such a way that it sounded like "We'll meet again some day." (*He drinks.*) All told, he wrote about three letters to me.

Claudia: (*Bitterly*) Yes, he wrote only to you.

Dr. Stuart: His first letter came about a year after he left England, written in one of the Greek islands. He said that he was on his way to Athens. I then expected a letter from Athens but none came. One characteristic of Mark's letters was that he never described the places he visited. Six months later he was apparently near the Persian Gulf. Then there was a long gap; eighteen months after I got a letter from somewhere, I forget now, on the Indian side of the Himalayan range. He said he was thinking of crossing the mountains into Chinese Turkestan or Tibet. In that letter he said a great deal about you, both imaginary and well wishing.

Michael: (*Excitedly*) Yes, go on.

Dr. Stuart: There is nothing much to go on. That was the last of your father. If it took him three years or more to get to where he wanted, and if he was not crushed in one of those avalanches, it would take three years to return home. Quite logical, isn't it? I often thought it symptomatic that he stopped writing as he did then. It meant that he was not going any further—if anything, coming back.

Anthony: Non sequitur, that is, if ever anything is.

Dr. Stuart: Don't be so Anglo-Saxon, Anthony, in spite of your Latin tags. The legal mind is a one-track mind and never comprehends the subtlety of the human logic. Take the question of divorce for instance—

Anthony: What do you know about marriage and divorce?

Dr. Stuart: (*Ignoring him*) The one human problem which the law should not meddle in. The law court generally dodges the issue of divorce and cheapens it to just another piece of legal news to the delight of the penny press. My remedy is that divorce should be handled by a jury of poets and novelists and doctors—like myself—who know after all how the human blood stream runs.

Claudia: Won't you include clergymen in your jury?

Dr. Stuart: No. Let them continue to deal with marriage and death only—the two celestial matters in man's life. Divorce and birth are earthly matters.

Claudia: Charming. Why don't you write your version of the Platonic Republic?

Anthony: Oh, the bachelor who knows all the remedies for the remaking of the world! History has had too many of them already!

Exit Michael in exasperation. Claudia and Anthony look towards Dr. Stuart.

Dr. Stuart: I did begin it once, as a matter of fact, but on second thought I gave it up because I was afraid of being called a Utopian idealist, which would have plagued my medical vocation straight away. (*He drinks.*) After all, what ordinary person—who discredits a doctor in any case—would believe in the diet sheet made by a Utopian idealist? (*Looking round*) I say, where the devil is Michael?

Anthony: He walked out whilst you were talking your drivel about divorce and what not. I nearly stopped him to apologize, but on second thoughts. . . .

Dr. Stuart: On second thoughts you let him go. Just as well. Young people should not be interested in drivel; it's only the grown-ups like we three, the incurable trio, who wallow in drivel, a sort of dirty story in fancy dress.

Claudia: He went out to meet Joy, I think.

Dr. Stuart: Oh, is she coming? Good. We'll be able to hear her play some good music for a change.

Anthony: (*Cynically, in a declamatory tone*) Dr. Duncan Stuart, everyone who comes to this house does so to entertain you, is it not so? You manage somehow to get something for nothing from each of them.

Dr. Stuart: No, not quite. I've got nothing from you. But then you're a lawyer and see to it that you never give anything for nothing. That's why I'm so often peeved with you—in my fashion.

Anthony: I don't care a hang whether I displease you or not. But consider Joy for instance. She may not necessarily want to play when she is here: she may come here for other reasons.

Claudia: You don't know Joy well enough to suppose such things, Anthony.

Dr. Stuart: No, no, Claudia. It's just the lawyer's way of saying that he wishes to goodness I would clear out so that he can talk to you in private.

Claudia: O shut up, Doctor. You're really getting uncontrollably wild.

Dr. Stuart: Yes, yes, I know. I must learn to muffle my tongue of indiscretion to suit my graying hair. Ripeness is all, as someone said.

Anthony: With you it seems to be all sourness. That's what confirmed bachelorhood will do for you.

Dr. Stuart: Not quite my fault, Anthony. I never confirmed it myself—other people, especially women, did the job for me. (*Piano is heard.*) Listen. Joy must be here.

Claudia: Bach's Prelude in E minor.

Anthony: (*Cynically*) Yes, I know. The well-tempered moral prescriptions on the pianoforte for the warped mind!

Dr. Stuart: Shut up, for Heaven's sake.

Claudia: I remember how Mark, in our first days of marriage, made me play this piece again and again. It is sad and brief.

Dr. Stuart: Brevity is Beauty's first cousin, Claudia.

Claudia: (*Continuing dreamily*) Each time he would say that it was like a shooting star in the black of night—as bright and yet intangible as its momentary flashing line. (*By this time the first half of the Prelude is finished and Presto begins.*) Listen to the Presto. (*After the Presto finishes*) He would say that was the movement of the celestial elements. And then the fugue—the movement of the human elements. (*The Fugue begins; pause until it ends*)

Dr. Stuart: (*Dreamily*) I wonder how that would sound on a harpsichord.

Anthony: (*Bitterly*) What, that awful instrument which sounds so much like a barrel organ? (*Anthony's statement is ignored.*)

Claudia: Doctor –

Dr. Stuart: (*Absent-mindedly*) Hhm.

Claudia: Do you think that Michael too will be like Mark—always walking on the thin edge of the world? Things like this playing of the E Minor Prelude and Fugue sets me thinking all over again. I can't bear the thought, Doctor. What if, after all these years, my effort to solidify his roots just crumbles to naught! I don't want Michael to be like his father, both for his sake and Joy's.

Dr. Stuart: And for yours? You are, as they say, in a tough spot. Not wanting someone to do something or other is so much harder than wanting them to do it—which is bad enough—you ought to write a sequel to Schaupenhauer, entitled *The World as the Will's Failure.*

Anthony: (*Annoyed*) That's an insult to Claudia—and indirectly to me. If anybody, you should be the author of such a book, not Claudia.

Dr. Stuart: (*Dryly*) Well, I could write it for her as her literary ghost.

Claudia: (*Amused*) No, we'll compromise. We'll make it a joint authorship.

Anthony: Anything to snub me and to leave me out of the tête-à-tête!

Dr. Stuart: Oh come, don't be on edge all the time. You ought to know by now that it doesn't pay to be sulky with Claudia and jealous of me; because she doesn't like sulkiness and I'm not worth being jealous of.

Enter Maid.

Maid: Mr. Charles Hilary to see you, Madam.

Claudia: I didn't expect him.

Dr. Stuart: Oh, he's probably come to fetch his sister.

Claudia: Show him in.

Exit Maid.

Anthony: (*Still querulous*) I say, Dr. Stuart, if you are so fond of music as all that, why don't you go more often to concerts instead of always hanging about here for Claudia or Joy to play to you?

Claudia: (*Interrupting*) Forget it, Anthony. It's not because he's got no money or is stingy.

Dr. Stuart: (*Taking no notice of Claudia's remark*) For the simple reason that I like to hear my music unofficially. Music and multitudes do not always go together. (*Declaiming after another drink*) O solitude, the one ally of human happiness!

Enter Charles Hilary, aged about 24; rather effeminate, but with a touch of cruelty somewhere—as effeminate people very often are.

Charles: Good afternoon, Mrs. Lorayne.

Claudia: Hallo, Charles. What chance brings you here?

Charles: Oh, just paying my respects.

Claudia: How nice. It's foggy out, isn't it?

Charles: And cold, too. (*Grinning*) Funny how the cold creeps in through one's sleeves and trouser-legs.

Dr. Stuart: (*Animated*) And don't forget, through your nostrils, too.

Charles: Yes, of course. The foggy atmosphere sort of makes you hesitant about breathing deep and the cold sort of creeps through your nose, surreptitiously, as it were.

Dr. Stuart: And through the soles of your shoes, too. I have a theory that the feet are the coldest part of the human body. Remember the death of Falstaff? How Mistress Quickly felt his stone-cold feet?

Charles: Yes, I suppose it's quite likely, in spite of the rug, which I suppose was over him. (*Turning to Claudia*) Mrs. Lorayne, I was just wondering whether my sister has been here?

Dr. Stuart: (*Breaking in*) No, she hasn't been here—since last week when you fetched her back.

Charles: Really?

Dr. Stuart: Well, I live here and I ought to know!

Charles: Of course, I forgot that. I'm so absent-minded you know. Oh, that reminds me. I have a couple of friends waiting for me outside. I really think I ought to be getting along Mrs. Lorayne.

Claudia: Poor souls, waiting outside in this cold! Ask them to come in for a warm-up.

Charles: You don't mind? That's terribly nice of you. I'll call them in. (*Exit*)

Anthony: (*Furious*) Ridiculous! To say that she's not here when she might be walking into this room at any moment!

Dr. Stuart: (*Pacifying him*) Keep your wool on, Anthony—or rather your wig. Doctors can tell lies too, you know, not only lawyers. I'll pop in and tell Joy and Michael not to come in here because we're only drinking cocktails and reciting limericks. (*Exit*)

Anthony: (*Looking after him*) And talking to spineless and probably reckless youths! I don't know, Claudia, how you put up with all these fatuous people.

Claudia: Have moral courage, my dear Anthony. Even though you don't care two hoots about such people.

Anthony: Can't you forget those two hoots?

Claudia: No, because I want to remember you, Anthony.

Enter Charles, with Julian and Margaret Anderson. Julian is a blasé youth of about 27, wearing a moustache. But there is fire in his eyes. Willful nature. Will not speak, unless spoken to. Has a tendency to scorn company as a means of enjoyment. Margaret, aged about 22, is talkative, shallow and self-assertive. She wears a fur-coat. General Introductions.

Claudia: Come to the fire, won't you, and what about a cocktail?

Margaret: I'd adore one.

Charles: (*Aside*) I say, do you think you ought to, Margaret?

Margaret: Of course, I ought. I'm not in the nursery, Charlie.

Charles: (*Still aside*) All right, not so loud. If you absolutely must...

Margaret: You don't mind, do you, Duckie?

Enter Doctor

Dr. Stuart: (*Excited*) Ah, the younger generations come to cheer up the older. I'll introduce myself. Name, Duncan Stuart. Profession, ex-doctor.

Margaret: What do you mean by "ex-doctor"?

Dr. Stuart: It means that I can now live in leisure and comfort because I've at last acquired a certain number of perfectly healthy patients who desire my regular medical attention which is nothing more than informal visits in fortnightly cycles.

Margaret: How delightfully pleasant it must be to have so many visitors in your engagement book!

Charles: (*Flustered*) Oh, Dr. Stuart, this is my fiancée, Margaret Anderson, and her brother Julian.

Dr. Stuart: Margaret, Margaret. I like that name immensely.

Margaret: Do you really, Doc? Charlie does too, don't you, Duckie?

Julian: (*Cynically*) Yes, he likes the name as much as the person, I believe.

Margaret: Oh, don't be nasty, Julian. (*To the Doctor*) He's got a sinister tongue, Doctor.

He enjoys saying the worst about everybody, you know. Partly due to his giving up school early, as I say. He left school much earlier than I did, you know, and he's always got that inferiority complex whenever he meets my boyfriends who have been to the university—like Charlie.

Dr. Stuart: (*Mildly*) You're lucky to have had such a good education yourself, Margaret.

Margaret: Yes, I know, Doctor. But then I sometimes think that education isn't everything, either. You've got to have the power to size people up, don't you think?

Dr. Stuart: Quite, quite.

Margaret: And that intuition doesn't necessarily come with education, does it? That's why I think Shakespeare is so much greater as a writer than Bacon, don't you? Because Shakespeare has intuition, and Bacon only education.

Dr. Stuart: Yes, and it obviously follows, doesn't it, that Shakespeare couldn't have been Bacon, as some of the modern unintuitive scholars have maintained, isn't that so?

Margaret: Yes, I never thought of that.

Julian: (*Grinning*) No, that's because you have so much intuition.

Margaret: Well, Julian, it's not nice manners for a brother to flatter his own sister in front of other people like that. Can I have another cocktail, Doctor?

Dr. Stuart: Let me pour it out for you.

Margaret: (*Drinking*) And I think also that my picking Charlie as my future husband was not, all said and done, such a bad choice. Do you, Doctor? He's a bit on the quiet side, but I always think, don't you, that husbands should be quiet, because you have to live with them more or less your whole life. And, after all, when you really want a merry evening now and then, you can always invite your friends and relatives, like Julian, who has a very loud voice. Charlie titters, but Julian guffaws. I always find it interesting to compare the two men who are and will be so near to me.

Dr. Stuart: Oh, absolutely, yes.

Julian pokes her in the side.

Margaret: Be quiet, Julian. Do you know, Doctor, I like you very much. You don't mind my being frank like this, do you?

Dr. Stuart: Oh, no, of course not. I'm flattered, Margaret. In fact, may I call you Peggy for short? I feel that we shall be great friends. When you get married and have babies, I'll come and help you at your confinement.

Margaret: Oh, Doctor, you shouldn't say such things in public.

Dr. Stuart: Business is business, you know.

Margaret: Haven't I seen you before somewhere, Doctor? I seem to know your face.

Dr. Stuart: Now, where could that have been, I wonder?

Margaret: I'm pretty good at remembering faces. That reminds me. Would you believe it: we were at the Circus the other afternoon, and as true as I am sitting here, the man at the box office looked just like Michael's father. (*Anthony and Claudia, who have been in the background, come forward, on hearing this.*) Charlie denies it absolutely, but then I'm generally right in these matters.

Dr. Stuart: (*Calmly*) Had you seen him before?

Margaret: Only in a photo which Joy showed to me not long ago. She'd got it from Michael. The face somehow reminded me of D. H. Lawrence—you know, the man who writes those dirty books. Joy is very fond of Michael, you know, but he never takes her out to dances or theaters or circuses—funny for a young boy and a bit unfair to her, don't you think?

Dr. Stuart: (*Still calmly*) Yes, Michael is a bit on the quieter side. (*Brightening up*) But then you like quiet men, don't you?

Margaret: Not too quiet, though. And Michael's got curly hair. I like men to have straight hair like Charlie.

Dr. Stuart: Mine used to be straight, but I haven't got much of it left now.

Margaret: (*Apologetically*) Oh, with elderly gentlemen like you, it's different. I suppose when Charlie's your age he'll go bald too.

Charles: (*Fed up*) Really, Margaret, we didn't come here to hear your suppositions and predilections and dislikes. We came to look for Joy.

Margaret: Julian did. I didn't. (*Cheekily*) Besides I can say what I like, when I like, can't I? I prefer to talk. Let Julian do the chasing of his mates.

Julian: (*Furious*) Oh, hold your tongue, and mind your own blasted business.

(*Embarrassed*) Well, really, I think we ought to be getting along.

General farewells.

Margaret: Well, goodbye, Doc. Come on, Charlie.

Dr. Stuart: Goodbye, Peggy. Such a charming personality you've got. Be good to Charlie, won't you?

Exeunt Julian and Margaret.

Charles: (*Embarrassed*) I'm awfully sorry to have butted in like this. It was frightfully nice of you to ask us in. (*To the doctor*) You know they're my guardian's children.

Voice of Margaret: Come on, Charlie. We'll be late for the flick.

Exit Charles.

Anthony: (*Furious*) Well, I'm damned. Of all the impudence that Man was ever capable of—

Dr. Stuart: Yes, I always said that Man was the only impudent animal of God's creation.

Anthony: I don't know how Joy can put up with people like that.

Dr. Stuart: (*Dreamily*) Oh, the hapless Friday, when God created man, and man in turn destroyed his Lord. (*Pause*)

Anthony: Well, Dr. Stuart. You remain here and pray for the sins of man. I'll go and look for the facts of their sinning, preferably the legal ones.

Claudia: Oh, Anthony, dear, you mustn't leave me so soon. (*Plaintive*) Stay for dinner if you can, and comfort my entangled heart.

Anthony: Doctor will do that for you. But I shall continue to think of our future in the light of this afternoon's talk. Au revoir. (*Exit*)

Dr. Stuart: (*Reflectively*) Perhaps Margaret did see Mark. It is incredible, but then Mark is incredible. (*Enter Michael and Joy, unnoticed by Doctor. Joy, about 18, is a susceptible nature, i. e., she is what other people make her. She has beauty, but it has not yet been cultivated—in the beauty-parlor sense of the word.*) But Michael mustn't know, Claudia.

Michael: What mustn't I know?

Dr. Stuart: Oh, caught again. I meant the metaphysical significance of Shakespeare's phrase 'much ado about nothing.' Feel any the wiser, Michael?

Michael: You mean metaphorical, and not metaphysical. I know you—the eternal metaphor-maker of our household, always telling lies and mending them with wit.

Joy: (*Very sweetly*) Oh, that's Nuncle's pet theory that we should enter life through the stage door and not through the box-office.

Claudia: Hello Joy darling. You played marvelously.

Dr. Stuart: Ah, but you should see her hands when she plays. The human hand! The most amazing thing out of God's bag of tricks. It can milk cows as it can milk the yellow keyboard! And then look at my hands—shuffling, clumsy, stump-fingered and skinny—but they've brought enough babies into this world!

Joy: Yes, Nuncle's hands are restless hands, always pouring drink with one hand and drinking it with the other.

Dr. Stuart: Oh, Claudia, I said to Joy a while ago that she ought to call me Nuncle as the fool did King Lear and we laughed because we both knew that she was no fool and I no king. No matter, though. (*Turning to Joy*) Joy, darling, it's a pity your name is not Margaret because I know such a good poem about Margaret.

Michael: Not a Limerick, I hope.

Dr. Stuart: No, it was written by one Jesuit poet with the name of Hopkins. Listen.

(*Recites*) Margaret, are you grieving
        Over goldengrove unleaving?
        . . . .
        Ah! As the heart grows older
        It will come to such sights colder
        By and by, nor spare a sigh
        Though worlds of wanwood leafmeal lie;
        And yet you will weep and know why.
        Now no matter, child, the name:
        Sorrow's springs are the same.

> Nor mouth had, no nor mind, expressed
>
> What heart heard of, ghost guessed:
>
> It is the blight man was born for,
>
> t is Margaret you mourn for.

I once set it to music for exclusive copyright recitations by myself. I'll sing it to you one day when I am in a good mood.

Joy: Have another glass, and please be in a good mood, Nuncle, now.

Dr. Stuart: A brilliant suggestion, Joy, darling. Lear would always listen to his fool, you know. Even while his giant heart was being crushed under the wheel of fire. (*Drinks.*) Come, Claudia, let us retire to where the piano is.

Claudia: (*Lingering behind*) Oh, my Joy, if only I could tell you now day and night my thoughts of love and fear, for you are spinning round you like a spectral disc of white flame. My blessings on you both.

Exeunt Claudia and Doctor

Joy: Oh Michael, I wish I had a mother like yours. You wouldn't know what it means to have no mother—

Michael: Do you know what it means to have no father?

Joy: Having no mother is like having only summer and winter of the four seasons. The fingers, which mould my heart, are either icy-cold—like my guardians'—or red hot—like yours. I have no intermediate experience corresponding to the thawing of the spring earth or the coloring of the autumnal leaves.

Michael: But supposing one had to tread perpetually the thawing earth, to feel one's boots becoming heavier and stickier and to see the stirring roots and the growing bulbs—but no flowers as yet! Or supposing one were to watch continually the autumnal beauty, the gradual unleaving of the grove, the beauty of the decaying, if you like, but yet never to see the positive hour of complete decay and death, never to see the trees as pure lines or as Bach's fugues, the rustling colorless leaves being still reluctant to leave their branches and making them look like half-bald heads or moth-eaten muffs, thin here and thick there. . . . Look at Dr. Stuart or Mr. Pearsall or, for that matter, look at Mother. X-ray them, and they will be full of maladies, which their   lukewarm flesh seemingly covers up.

Joy: Ah Michael, we have no right to judge or misjudge our fathers and mothers and their contemporaries. We are what they have made us and what we make ourselves. And for you and me, all that matters is what we make each other.

Michael: Yes, Joy, you're right again. You are my only rectifier, my only—

Joy: Hush, the Doctor is singing. (*Dr. Stuart continues to sing till the end of the scene.*)

Michael: Yes, merry people singing sad songs! Oh, why should music be the assembling hall of sad and merry people alike?

Joy: You're sad, Michael. You must not be sad. Because when the wind of sadness sweeps you off into the crowded Highway of Restless Thought, I am left behind in desolation like the Solitary Reaper, but without a field to reap before me.

Michael: Sweet Joy, you must not say such things, stand so on the cliff of desperation. I am, after all, like a ridiculous kite, which you happen to fly. If it weren't for your sweet-smiling face in this winter desolation, I would scorn the flat earth, which looks flatter still from the air, and jump into the sea, and as the Irish would say, have a clean burial.

Joy: But you are not just a casual person, Michael. You are the one who makes me look up to the air and the fire-folk of the sky, Michael, even in the broadest of daylights.

Michael: What is love? And who are you? That the cauldron of my heart should be burning like this, even on the coldest of days of London's violet fog? Does it mean a birth of some new life, which God will let us preserve? Or is it just another of His many ways of preparing us for an unknown calamity? You and I. What pattern are we making with our countless threads of interlinked emotions?

Joy: I do not care what pattern I make, so long as I make it with you, Michael.

Michael: You and I, we are like two figures in a picture from which the background has been taken away, or like two birds of passage flying together over the vast ocean, unaware of their destination.

Joy: What care I of destinations or backgrounds? It is enough to live—with you.

Michael: Yes, it is enough to live—with you—like two blades of grass, sprouting from the same root, in a vast savanna of greenness.

Curtain

Act I, Scene ii

Afternoon of the same day—later; behind the Circus "Marco Polo"; scene laid in proscenium, so as to produce the effect of closeness and oppressiveness; stage shows the cross-section of a caravan, divided in the middle into two compartments with a communicating door. In the one compartment sit Joe, Ben, Mac, Oliver playing poker. In the other is seated Mark, writing, known in the circus by some other name, and nicknamed "The Hermit." In each compartment there is a small electric fire.

Joe: looks after the animals; about 45; American-born
Ben: about 30; a trapeze performer; of sunny temperament, but easily clouded
Mac: about 50; the clown; Irish; has a tendency to be bored
Oliver: about 40, the conjuror; thin and agile; nondescript person

Of the four, Joe appears to have the most vitality—shown by his robustness, clumsiness, etc. The others, no doubt, are equally lively in public life, but not so in private. Similarly, Joe's language is less refined than the others', because he has no occasion to need the "public" language.

After each game the poker-players change seats to be near the fire in turn. Throughout the scene is heard the clinking of coins, etc. And even while the dialogue is proceeding, cards are being shuffled, dealt out, and so on. All are fond of talking in their own way.

Joe: A copper chip.
Ben: Me too—just to sweeten the pot.
Mac: Being Irish, I, er,

Oliver: You raise?

Mac: (*Decisively*) Right to Heaven—by 4d.

Joe: Oh yeah? You'll sink to Hell. This toime by *my* judgment.

Oliver: I'm in. (*Beseechingly*) Give us another drop, will you, Joe?

Joe: No. Dhef'nitely not! (*Pointing to* stove) Ye're got da fire. Ye can't 'f licker as wal.

Mac: Enough of that, surely. On with the game.

Joe: (*Continuing*) 'N it's gotta last till tonight, ain't it?

Mac: (*Quietly*) Yes, Oliver, it's going to be a cold night. I can feel it in my bones. On with the betting.

Joe: Aw right. Be pashunt, Mac. (*He bets, and Ben also.*)

Oliver: How many cards? (*Deals as they answer.*) None? Three? Two? Me too. (*Looking at cards he bets*) One.

Joe: 6d. with my blessing kiss. (*Kisses the coin*)

Ben: I'm out.

Joe: (*Grinning*) Loike fish outa water?

Mac: 6 and 2.

Oliver: (*Flinging cards on the table*) No, dammit.

Joe: (*With glee*) A dhuel, eh? Between you and me. Wal. Make it 12.

Mac: I'll see.

Joes: Straight.

Mac: Well, well. (*Putting down his own*) Here's Queen of Sheba with two others on the roof, calling for Solomon's stable boy—that's you, Joe.

Joe: Eh, none of yer rhude noises. Rake in me money but don't spit out them worrds.

Mac: That's meant to be a compliment, my good Joe.

Joe: Compliment my foot— (*In a commanding voice*) Cum ahn, change for the fire.

All change seats. Cards are shuffled and dealt out, play continues, while in the next compartment Veronica enters and looks, for a moment, at Mark writing. Veronica is about 30, a trapeze performer. She is much quieter than the other circus people; quieter because she seems to be more interested in discovering a new "scheme of life," one that would go deeper than her mere "tricks of the trade." Mark is a pale-faced bearded man about 45 or older; he has "a lean and hungry look."

Veronica: (*Whimsically*) What are you writing? Love-letters?

Mark: (*Calmly*) You wouldn't understand.

Veronica: I would—if it's a love letter.

Mark: It's not a love letter.

Veronica: What then?

Mark: You wouldn't understand.

Veronica: Am I so ignorant? May I look? (*Stoops*)

Mark: Look here, Veronica, I'm not in a playful mood. Kindly remove yourself to the next room.

Veronica: (*Hurt*) I will go if you tell me what it is you are writing. I'm not so ignorant as all that.

Mark: Who said you were ignorant?

Veronica: Why, you! You've been saying it ever since we came to London—at least implied it.

Mark: Well, we shall be leaving here tomorrow.

Veronica: (*Regaining her caprice*) And then you won't imply any more that I am ignorant and so on?

Mark: (*Annoyed*) Woman, can't you see that you are disturbing my work?

Veronica: Your work? What work? That letter? Who is it to?

Mark: Oh well then—it's a letter to the editor of—of any newspaper you like—or a letter to Somerset House or anything you like. Feel any the wiser? Now clear out.

Veronica: I will. Don't be so shirty. (*As she goes into the next compartment, Ben starts up with pleasure.*)

Ben: Darling, you've brought me luck. I'm winning.

Joe: Gels never bring me luck! Lost agin. (*To himself*) So durned shure I'd win, I wis.

Mac: (*Gently and teasingly*) Yes, you'll never go to heaven because you're always so sure of yourself.

Joe: Neether wul yuh! Gawd 'n his host doesn't need no clowns loike ye: they don't need no jokes and grimaces and made-up faces up there. Yuh were born for hell.

(*Laughing raucously*)

Mac: At least I say my prayers for forgiveness.

Ben: (*To Veronica*) You stay right here by me and see how I win again.

Joe: Hey! None av yer gallavantin', man. If ye play, play seriously.

Oliver: Glory be.

Mac: Getting a Royal Flush?

Oliver: No. (*Flinging down his cards*) Just a collection of odd tit-bits! don't join up at all with anything. (*Turning to Joe*) Somebody give me a cigarette.

Joe: I dunno how ye manage to be a smoker without nivver buyin' a packet of yer own. (*Handing him a cigarette*) Here. I jine in the bettin'.

Ben: Right.

Joe: (*Turning to Veronica*) Lissen. I don't moind if yuh jist watch. But don't yuh dhare look into me hand and then help Ben behind me back. 'Cos that'll spile the whole fun av ut, see?

Veronica: As if I ever did such a thing.

Joe: No, but understand that this is speshully a man's game see?

Veronica: A man's game indeed. A gambler's game, you mean.

Mac: Stop talking and get on, fuss-pot.

Joe: I ain't fussin' but if I play I loike to play accordin' to the rules of the game, see? which is more'n you kin say fur yerself, Mac! You Irish cheat wherever you have a chance.

Oliver: So one should—(*Pleased with himself*) conjuring being my profession.

Joe: I wasn't talkin' to yuh. Cheatin's yer job, I know that on'y too well.

Oliver: All the same you waste too much time talking, get on, get on.

Mac: Yes, let's make it a rule that from now on anyone who starts quarrelling in the middle of the game pays 6d. fine. Agreed? Right.

Ben: (*Dealing cards*) Two for you, three for you, and two for me.

Joe: Four.

Mac: Four and four.

Ben: Four and four and three.

Joe: Make it 1s/2d.

Mac: Raised by 6? Right. Another 6.

Ben: Shall I go in, Veronica?

Veronica: Please yourself.

Joe: Hey, that'll do. Hurry up, what d'ye say?

Ben: No.

Joe: O.K. I'll see you. Six.

Mac: Four magnificent bullets. Come on. Premium! (*Raking in the money*)

Oliver: What good luck I wasn't in.

Ben gives the premium but Joe hesitates.

Joe: Mac, I'll give ye a dhrop of me licker instead of premium. What d'ye say?

Mac: I don't mind. (*Oliver pokes at Mac.*) Provided you give one to Oliver also.

Oliver: Come along, be a sport.

Joe: Aw right. I calc'late I'll have to, luck guy.

Ben: How about the lady of the party?

Joe: I tell yer this is a man's game!

Mac: But it's a Christian's game, too, see Joe? Remember that God's all the time looking upon us and in His bright eyes we're all born civilized, see Joe?

Joe: I ain't no civilized genelman, so Gawd won't pay no attenshun to a guy loike me.

Mac: That's blasphemy, man.

Joe: Gawd! You sound like straight out av Pilgrim's Progress—so pie!

Veronica: I don't want any drink.

Joe: See, she don't want none.

Mac: (*Restraining Veronica*) It doesn't matter whether she wants any or not. You've just got to be Christian and offer her a glass, a small one will do. And God will simply love you for it.

Joe: (*Pouring drink*) Sich a fox, ain't yer? Allus ready with yer answer, I dunno why you don't pour it out yerself if yer're so keen on bein' Gawd's darlin' 'n whatnot. Here, Veronica.

Mac: That's the stuff. Now we're friends, Joe, aren't we?

Joe: Frens, My foot. After persecutin' me loike that. Cum ahn. Move round the fire now. Yu've baked yerself long enough. Yuh kin do the rest of yer bakin' when ye're in Hell.

As they are moving round, enter a woman who goes by the name of Mary, aged about 30. She is wearing a costume with a cheap sort of fur round her neck. Coatless, blue with cold.

Mary: (*Having already come in*) May I come in?

Joe: Wot, more women? I'm goin' broke today, aw right.

Mac: Cummon in Lassie, and warm yourself. Cheer up, Joe. Women brighten like— like flowers in a room.

Joe: Naw, not wid me.

Oliver: Why, do they give you the creeps?

Joe: Naw. But they gimme what must be the eighth plague of Egypt.

Mary: Gosh, it's cold out and foggy—like a Turkish bath—only cold. (*With a professional* look) How is everyone today?

Joe: Jist bloody.

Mary: Good.

Joe: Good for yuhs but bad for me.

Mary: Feeling gloomy? What you need is a pretty little petticoat like me to cheer you up.

Mac: He's lost a bit so he's sulking furiously.

Game continues.

Veronica: You look blue with cold.

Mary: I feel blue for several reasons—with cold, and with jealousy, seeing everybody walking out of shops with enormous Christmas parcels.

Veronica: Let me make you some hot tea.

Mary: That would be marvelous. Thanks ever so much.

Veronica: Not at all. Mac, where is your teapot?

Mac: Oliver broke it yesterday, thanks to his butterfingers!

Oliver: (*Protesting*) Well, you told me to clean the spout, didn't you? So when I finished cleaning I just lifted it by the spout up to the light to see whether it was clean enough, and pop goes the thing like a guillotined head.

Veronica: (*To Mary*) I shan't be long. (*Exit.*)

Ben: (*Laughing*) And even our conjurer couldn't put together the broken teapot again!

Oliver: Listen, Ben, my boy, I don't like professional criticisms. Supposing I said to you, "Why can't you fly over the Tower Bridge on your trapeze?" Would you like it?

Mary: (*Readily*) Of course he would, wouldn't you, Duckie? (*Fondles Ben*)

Ben: Just a tick, you're distracting the game, Mary.

Joe: (*With glee*) I'll say she isn't. Won at last! (*Draws in money.*)

Mac: Now, will you take back what you said about women—bringing bad luck to you?

Joe: By Jingo, no. I still gotta make up fur another 3/-.

Mary: (*To Ben*) Will you come for a stroll with me tonight?

Ben: Shush, you.

Mary: Will you, my shy pet—my daring young man on the flying trapeze?

Joe: (*To Ben*) Are yuh playin' or ain't yer? Mebbe ye're playin' women instead av cards, eh?

Mac: Mary, Joe's in a good mood just now. Ask him for a warm up, he's bound to give it.

Mary: Has he got any drink, really? Such a sweet soul!

Joe: Hey, who sed it wis for yuhs?

Mac: Come on, Joe. Don't you remember what I said before?

Joe: I disremember nothink.

Mac: Besides, the whole point about drink is that it is the one thing that God has given us mortals that we can share equally and enjoy together, so that God may love us all equally and we may in turn glory him together.

Joe: You make me sick. Yuh'd never ought to have jined the circus. Yuh'd ought to have jined the army.

Oliver: What army?

Joe: The Salvation Army, you silly ass. (*Laughs.*)

Mac: Never you mind about my mischoice of profession—that's God's business. But give Mary a drop, I say.

Joe: Aw right. The way you insist on making me feed everyone, anyone'd tink I wis the haugs'-herd.

Oliver: Come on, be a sport, Joe.

Mac: Be a Christian sport.

Joe: It's gotta last the hull night yer know. Still I'll give her a wet if she gives us furst a song—a kinda chanty to put us all in a good temper so that they won't nag me so much.

Mac: Well, she's got to drink before she can sing, you know. Everybody does that.

Oliver: Like them useless chairmen who in the middle of a dinner get up after a sip and say, "Ladies and Gentlemen."

Mac: Quite right.

Mary: (*Receiving the glass*) Ta. Not much of a voice but—(*She sings. As she sings, she makes amorous signs to Ben. Ben looks awkward.*)

> He flies through the air with the greatest of ease—
> That daring young man on the flying trapeze.
> His movements are graceful, all girls he can please,
> And my love he has stolen away, pom, pom.

Joe: Why, cus. This was for Ben. (*Turning to Mac*) Ain't you noticed that, Mac? Be fair, Mac.

Mac: Don't be jealous. Songs also, like drinks, are shared equally by everyone who shares them. You heard it, didn't you? Pretty, eh?

Joe: Purty, my Gawd! Stale, like last year's Christmas cake.

At this point Veronica enters into Mark's compartment with teapot. Simultaneously Anthony Pearsall enters into the other. Joe and company are dumbfounded for a moment by this strange intrusion.

Veronica: (*With forced cheerfulness*) Still writing? Or worse, just thinking?

Mark: (*Matter-of-factly*) Neither.

Veronica: Or dreaming, which is worst of all? Sitting there like a broken pillar, dreaming on the ruined glory! (*With a changed voice*) Will you have some tea?

Mark: No thanks.

Veronica: You look as if you're waiting for somebody.

Mark: Waiting is my nature. It is part of my congenital sloth.

Anthony: (*In another compartment*) Is there a gentleman in this circus who goes by the name of Mark Lorrayne?

Meanwhile the poker-players are continuing.

Oliver: No. There is no such person in our circus.

Joe: You to bet, Ben.

Ben: Chip.

Anthony: Are you sure that there is no one of that name?

Oliver: I am. Aren't you, Mac?

Mac: (*Teasingly*) The Son of Man is never sure about anything!

Joe: Cum ahn, Mac. Ye're playin', not preachin'.

Veronica: I wish you'd tell me what you're doing in your head.

Mark: I'm just adding up the fortune of the circus and myself and seeing where we all stand.

Veronica: I still don't believe it, seeing that you never reveal the whole truth about yourself. (*As she says this she goes into the next room.*) Well, here is the tea, everybody.

Mac: Ben, pull out the cups, they're behind you.

Oliver: Veronica, do you know somebody called Mark Lorrayne in our bunch?

Mark starts up, hearing this, like a guilty person.

Veronica: No.

Oliver: (*With triumph*) Personally I think it must be a name coined by someone who wanted to do this gentleman in; our circus is called Marco Polo, you know.

Joe: Now, ain't that clever av ye? (*Sneeringly*) Yuh sittin' there twiddlin' yer paws, and spoutin' out yer 'personally' this and 'personally' that. Nobody exceptin' yerself ain't interested in yer opinions. At this rate we'll nivver get on to the game.

Ben: Ask The Hermit if he knows who Mr. Mark Lorrayne is.

Mark: (*Opening the door*) Yes, will you come in here, please? (*Anthony does so.*)

Joe: How the devil is The Hermit to know what we don't know?

Oliver: Well, it was just a suggestion on Ben's part, just as I made a suggestion.

Mac: The Hermit is quite likely to know more than you, Joe, for the simple reason that a human being knows more than a chimp generally.

Joe: D'ye mean that I am a chimp?

Mac: (*Suavely*) I wouldn't put it so bluntly.

Joe: Yeh? But chimps don't insult each other loike yuh do. It's only those who pretend to be human bein's that insult others—loike yuh.

Mac: Let's have some tea.

Tea drinking and game continue.

Mark: You'll excuse those people there. You see, in the circus world it is the animals who are tame and the human beings wild.

Anthony: I understand perfectly well, the phenomenon being quite a common one.

Mark: That is their form of relaxation after the strain of public entertainment. I may remark that they are in actuality most subdued people.

Anthony: They store up their bubbling energies for public occasions, I presume.

Mark: Precisely.

Anthony: (*After an awkward pause*) My name is Anthony Pearsall.

Mark: Mine is—Gordon Sellinger—but really Mark Lorrayne.

Anthony: (*Taken aback*) So you are the very gentleman I am looking for. (*Pause*) Tell me, Mr. Lorrayne, why did you join the circus? (*Pause*) I ask you purely as a point of interest. I am not implying that you should not have done so. (*Pause*) You see I have heard quite a lot about you and your personality.

Mark: (*Acidly*) Indeed. That sounds most ominous. By personality you probably mean a great deal of gossip, true as well as legendary. For it's only in gossip, scandal and such like that one meets with the bare essence of that otherwise subjective bogey called personality.

Anthony: You are a much-traveled man, are you not?

Mark: In my fashion, yes. For instance, I met this circus in an obscure part of Serbia, some eighteen months ago, and I thought it would be a cheap way of traveling from place to place. I do very little work actually—merely the behind-the-desk part of the circus and it suits my errant nature.

Anthony: I still do not understand why you should have chosen this mode of life.

Mark: I am an opportunist; beyond that there is nothing to understand.

Anthony: (*Critically observing Mark*) So Claudia says.

Mark: (*After a pause; scanning Anthony*) Does Claudia know of my existence here?

Anthony: Not as a definite fact.

Mark: And you came round to ascertain it?

Anthony: I had a purely personal motive in coming here, Mr. Lorrayne.

Mark: Can I help you in any way?

Anthony: I shall be precise, Mr. Lorrayne, and say 'yes.' About Claudia.

Mark: What about Claudia? I thought you said it was about yourself.

Anthony: Well, about both of us then.

Mark: Oh, pardon my indelicacy.

Anthony: (*After a slight pause; seizing his opportunity*) I beg you to understand that it is no longer reasonable for me or for anyone else to discriminate between Claudia's life and mine.

Mark: (*With an empty smile*) You mean you are married to her?

Anthony: Not quite. Legally she is still your wife.

Mark: Well?

Anthony: (*With an air of disinterestedness*) And she has not yet cast aside that outward bondage. She has of course her reasons for acting thus—perhaps it is sentiment or perhaps it is sheer inertia. Be that as it may—

Mark: Be that as it may, there is no need for you to be so discursive. What would you have me do?

Anthony: Understand that I have been responsible for her happiness for some time and will continue to be so—though personally I would not like to prophesy *who* will be responsible for her *unhappiness.*

Mark: I flatter myself that I do my best not to be in the way of Claudia. I have been in the city for about four weeks now—

Anthony: During which time you could have done plenty, which could not be undone! Is that what you mean?

Mark: You're a man of understanding!

Anthony: It is my business to understand the labyrinth of human entanglements.

Mark: Aha. You are a man who writes apologies for the sins of men?

Anthony: I am a solicitor.

Mark: Indeed? Most opportune! (*After a slight pause*) I have been writing my will this afternoon—a somewhat pleasant pastime to my thinking.

Anthony: So I have often been told. Will-making seems to have a unique effect on people; because it combines the double pleasure of loving and hating simultaneously. And the way Wills are treated with the utmost exactitude is positively heathen.

Mark: Your remark reminds me of the way in which the Tibetans dispose of their dead: they cut the body and give it to the vultures—the live preying on the dead. And they have a special class whose profession is to cut the body—I forget what they are called. (*After a pause; with a twitch of the mouth*) Perhaps you would like to be my executor?

Enter Veronica. Veronica has been suspicious since Anthony's arrival, and has been trying to hear their conversation.

Veronica: Would you like me to bring some drink for you—and the distinguished guest you have here?

Mark: (*Feeling the interruption*) Kindly knock before you enter.

Anthony: No thanks, not for me.

Mark: (*Turning to Anthony with false joviality*) I think the solemnity of the occasion lends itself to some form of celebration. I find the occasion solemn not because I have just composed my Will but because you, Mr. Pearsall, have stooped so low as to look for me here.

Anthony: I come to bury Caesar, not to praise him.

Mark: And bury you shall, Mr. Pearsall. (*Mark hands over the Will to read. Anthony automatically receives it, though he probably feels some doubt as to Mark's ulterior motive. Mark produces bottle and two glasses, pours drink out. To Veronica*) It will not be necessary for you to remain here. (*Veronica exit, hurt.*)

Ben: Come on, Veronica, darling, what is the matter, walking up and down?

Joe: She's got the jitters about somethin' or other—loike the lions. When they walk up and down, as true's I'm sittin' here I know they wann me to feed 'em.

Ben: (*To Veronica*) Sit here and bring me luck.

Mary: Don't I bring you luck, sweetie?

Mac: Apparently not. Ben's been loosing, and Joe's winning. Joe, she must be your lucky star.

Joe: Me locky star is me own winnin' instink and no other thin'.

Mary: Oh chum, you don't dislike me, do you?

Joe: (*After looking at her dispassionately*) Ye know, Mary, ye oughter grow yer hair long—loike the Mary Magdalene of the Boible. Long tresses'd soot yer swell.

Mary: But you don't dislike me as I am, do you?

Joe: (*Again irritably*) Oh Ben, get that dame outta here—I caant concentrate. Ben, she thinks ye'er swell. (*With coarse humor*) Why don't yer do somthink about it?

Mary: (*Angrily*) Mind your own business, I can look after myself.

Joe: Oh yeh? It don't look that way.

Oliver: Stop quarrelling.

Joe: (*Shouting*) I ain't quarrellin'.

Oliver: You are.

Joe: Oh shuks. It's yuhse makin' all the shindy.

Oliver: With whom?

Joe: Wid me.

Oliver: I was just telling you not to quarrel.

Joe: Wid whom?

Oliver: With her. You're old enough to be her father.

Joe: I get yer. Actin' the paw-stunt for her? (*Cynically*) Say, why don yer take the gal out then and give her a bellyful of eats—yeh, and take yerself along fer company?

Oliver: (*Losing his temper*) I'm not your sort, you crude ox. (*Jumps up. Mac intervenes, pacifying.*)

Mac: Come on, you two. Pay me 6d. each—regulation!

Joe: Wot reg'lashun!

Mac: Anyone who quarrels and delays the game pays 6d. penalty.

Joe: I wasna fightin'. Jist talkin' loud.

Mac: Come on, if you don't hurry, I'll make you pay 6d. extra. (*Receives money, and giving it to Mary*) Here, Mary, the tip's for you. You proved a worthy Helen of Troy, getting these two all hot and bothered.

Anthony: (*Having read the Will*) Well, Mr. Lorrayne, you put me in an awkward position. I did not come here to deal with your business. Rather I came to deal with Claudia's and mine.

Mark: But I assure you they both come to the same thing. (*Anthony looks unconvinced.*) Besides, now you've read it, you cannot help but be my Executor.

Anthony: I hope you're not blackmailing me.

Mark: (*Ignoring Anthony*) There is one thing I want to ask you. How is my son, Michael? (*Spoken slowly*)

Anthony: He has fallen in love with a sweet girl called Joy Hilary, and goes about, as it were, cross-gartered.

Mark: Joy Hilary!

Anthony: Joy is a young and tender maiden—like the center of a cabbage, I always tell her—and she studies music. They are both made for each other, so it seems, and like the twin eyes, they move together.

Mark: (*Slowly*) In the light of your remark I should just like to add a clause to what I have already written.

Anthony: (*Indifferently*) As you please. We shall have to have some testators.

Mark: Naturally. (*Goes over to the door and opens it. Calls.*) Mac, Joe. Just come in here for a moment. (*They do so, and Oliver and Veronica follow.*)

Mary: (*Persuasively*) Come out with me, Ben, eh?

Ben: (*Timidly*) I don't know.

Mary: No one will know where you are.

Ben: Veronica will.

Mary: She won't worry if you do come with me.

Ben: It depends on how she's feeling.

Mary: She's upset about something or other—not about you, though. I'll see you later, eh?

Ben: I tell you I don't know.

Mary: I'll wait for you. (*Tenderly*) My shy boy. You don't have to be shy with me. You can put your head on my round, soft bosom, and tell me all your heart-breaking feelings. I shan't mind. It's foggy and cold outside, but I know how to make you feel all summery, with kissing and cuddling. Promise to come?

Ben: I don't know. Go away. (*Exit Mary.*)

Mark: (*In next compartment*) I want you to be my testators.

Joe: Tea tasters?

Mac: Shut up, Joe.

Mark: I have made my will.

Joe: So soon, Hermit? What'll yer do if yer change yer mind later?

Oliver: Why, man, write another, of course.

Joe: Waste av toime, that'd be.

Mark: After I've signed, will you sign?

While they are signing, Ben comes to the next room, and draws Veronica aside.

Ben: What's the matter with you, Veronica?

Veronica: (*Cuttingly*) None of your business.

Ben: I hate to see you like this.

Veronica: Leave me alone. (*Ben wanders back.*)

Joe: Gee, this yer reel name—Mark Lorrayne?

Oliver: There, what did I tell you? I knew that it was a variation on our circus, Marco Polo.

Joe: (*Shutting him up*) Yeh, only conjurors loike yuh would make Marco Polo and Mark Lorrayne the soime ting.

Mac: (*To Mark, with a kindly smile*) I say always, you mustn't hurry yourself to heaven. Take things leisurely, I say! In heaven, the angels take things very leisurely, and we've got to be practiced while we're upon this earth in taking things leisurely, too.

Mark: (*In a friendly tone*) Why are you telling me these things?

Mac: Just speaking in generalities. That's all. You can't rush into heaven. There, even the saints and angels tread softly!

Joe: (*With glee*) That's 'cos in heaven, if they thump they're afraid of fallin' through the floor, which is made very thin on purpose.

Mark: Thank you, that's all. You can go back to your game now. (*They go out.*)

Anthony: Events have turned so unexpectedly that I really don't know what to say. What I wanted to say I haven't said and I fear I've done all the wrong things.

Mark: (*Cynically*) Mr. Pearsall, for a solicitor, that is rare, indeed. (*With triumph*) I told you I was an opportunist.

Anthony: You must have had some foreknowledge of my coming.

Mark: Empirically speaking, yes—as a rheumatic person knows the coming of rain.

Anthony: (*After a pause*) I daresay we shall meet again in the near future.

Mark: Yes, at Phillipi.

Curtain

Act II, Scene i

Later in the evening on the same day; flat of Charles and Joy Hilary. The stage is divided into two sections. The larger is the living room, the smaller Joy's bedroom. When the curtain rises, the stage is dark. Enter Joy, followed by Michael. The living room light is switched on, revealing among other furniture a piano and a gramophone.

Joy: (*Taking off her hat*) Here we are, Michael.

Michael: (*Also taking off his hat; in a faintly echoing tone*) Yes, here we are.

Joy: (*With concern*) Why? Are you sorry that we have come in? Would you rather have gone on walking—in that fog?

Michael: (*Absent-mindedly*) I wish you were living at the other end of the world, so that I could go on walking forever to reach you. A lifetime's walking! *That* would be indeed "a zealous pilgrimage."

Joy: (*Goes to her room, takes off her coat, throws it on the divan, and returns.*) That would be an unreal journey, Michael.

Michael: (*Continuing in the same vein*) No. Walking is real. The unreality comes when the body's walking is at an end. "But then begins another journey in my head, to work my mind when body's work's expired." *There* is someone who knew what he was talking about.

Joy: Well?

Michael: For, don't you still hear the echo of our feet, even though we have now stopped clicking our way along the pavement? And, do you not hear distinctly the throbbing of your heart, now that your body has come to a deadlock?

Joy: (*Softly*) I know that mine throbs—for another reason.

Michael: What?

Joy: A mortal reason, one that is sufficient to keep me hopping from one day to the next.

Michael: Name it.

Joy: Being a mortal reason, let it be unnamed, and let it be guessed at. (*Pause*)

Michael: Yes, love is an act of conjecture!

Joy: Ours, too?

Michael: (*Unaware of her question*) And the garden through which all lovers roam, like the Garden of Eden, is laid in the subtle realm of potential chaos. Where man walks, there creeps the serpent.

Joy: (*Archly*) Could we not keep the serpent out of our garden?

Michael: By putting up a fence round it, as it were? Men have been known to build fences round their gardens—adding poles, year by year, as they add candlesticks on their birthday cakes. But by trying too keep the serpent out, they have managed to shut themselves all round away from their neighbors. (*In a heavier tone*) Joy, God knows I love you, but, but I do not think that our love is going to outlive the serpent or our neighbors.

Joy: What do you mean?

Michael: I have walked through tonight's foggy streets, the city's deep trenches, and felt the emotions of an ant toiling through his sunless corridors, and I have seen in the narcotic bulbs of street-light the squint of some palsied monster, prophesying death, reclining.

Joy: Whose death?

Michael: Ours, perhaps.

Joy: Must we talk of such unreal things as death? (*In a sad voice*) Is it because I am unreal—so?

Michael: (*With a sigh*) You're real enough to be sure, like Pippa who passes singing.

Joy: Is it then your love for me, which is unreal?

Michael: To call it unreal would itself an unreal act. For my love for you is like a stick that is half submerged in the translucent water of your mind—it is bent and yet is not so. (*Pause*) To reconcile the psychological and the physical facts—that is the difficulty.

Joy: If you choose to create that difficulty!

Michael: That choice is not within me. I feel it was made years ago, that tiny crack which makes the avalanche, perhaps even before I was born.

Joy: (*Entreatingly*) Can't you let go the past?

Michael: If you let go the past, the past will come to you unexpectedly, like a ghost.

Joy: (*With exasperation*) The past! The past! Always the past! Where is the present, where am I? You have talked enough about your past. Your father, for instance. What is the use of going up and up the stream, like a salmon? It will only tire your mind.

Michael: It is my nature, unfortunately.

Joy: Michael, that is no excuse, surely. You are sometimes too naïve for words. (*Pause*)

Michael: (*Feeling his irrelevance*) I must go home.

Joy: Oh Michael, you've just come in. Have I annoyed—

Michael: (*Shouting*) No, damn it. It's I who have annoyed—you, the present.

Joy: (*Calmly*) Don't shout at me, Michael. It's not nice. (*Pause*)

Michael: (*With forced calm*) I suppose I sound like a braying ass!

Joy: (*Slightly relieved*) You certainly don't sound like a bleating lamb.

Michael: (*With disgust*) What the hell!

Joy: (*Pityingly*) What *is* the matter, Michael?

Michael: I ought to be put in a bag and drowned in water, as they do unwanted cats.

Joy: (*With genuine amusement*) Yes, put your melancholia in a bag and I'll throw it into the sea; and the sea-demons shall feed upon it—

Michael: To the tune of the mermaid—your tune!

Joy: Me, a mermaid? (*Regaining self-assurance*) Let me play to you.

Michael: No. Don't open the piano. The white keyboard will remind me too much of the white waves on which you will ride. And then, you would be too far away, and the sea's roar will swallow all my shouting! Be near me, where I can touch you.

Joy: I am.

Michael: And yet you are not.

Joy: Why?

Michael: Because we meet, as it were, at a tangent only.

Joy: No more?

Michael: No more!

Joy: No more!

Pause

Michael: No, not with you. You will always have your music to fall back upon.

Joy: (*In a temper*) O yes. A fallen angel will always have his hell to fall back upon.

Michael: What do you mean? You are misunderstanding me.

Joy: I mean nothing.

Michael: What the hell!

Joy: Precisely. What the hell, as you say. I shall always have my music to fall back upon. I will show that I have. (*Defiantly puts on Delibes' 'Maid of Cadiz' on the gramophone.*)

Michael: (*After an awkward pause, dryly*) Good night. (*Exit*)

Joy: (*After another pause, looking after him, shouts.*) Michael. (*Rushes out.*)

Stage empty while music goes on; a few moments after, while the music goes on, enter Margaret, ushered in by Charles; Julian follows. Margaret and Charles in good spirits, Julian calmer than they.

Margaret: (*Singing with the record*) Tra la la la, etc. (*Gets hold of Charles and dances round the room. Charles responds willingly.*) "If music be the food of love, play on!" (*Addressing the gramophone*) Play on! (*They dance until record stops.*)

Charles: (*In a sing-song voice*) Darling, the gramophone is a machine! It stops automatically when the record is finished.

Julian: Like my salary at the end of the week.

Margaret: (*Sentimentally*) Oh, play it again, my sweet Charlie.

Charles: I must have a drink first, and then a kiss—and I must kiss you while my mouth is still wet.

Julian: Go easy, man. You've had enough. And I may tell you in parenthesis, you've kissed her enough too.

Margaret: Come, Julian, don't be so stingy with the bottle. Charlie, I will kiss you before you drink too. (*She does so. Pointing to the gramophone, in a dreamy voice*) Wouldn't it be marvelous to be able to sing like that soprano! People would be rushing up to me for autographs, and Charles would be looking after my fan mail. Oh boy, oh boy!

Charles: Yes, and I'll see to it that those who write too intimate letters will have their due answers in the mordant vein. (*Drinks. Suddenly realizing that the gramophone has been playing, he knocks at Joy's bedroom door, opens it, and sees no one.*) Good heavens. Who the devil has been playing the machine? Where is she?

Julian: (*Calmly drinking*) She's not in?

Margaret: (*Still sentimentally*) Aren't you going to play the record again, darling?

Charles: (*Absent-mindedly*) No.

Margaret: (*Archly*) You breaker of promises. Like all men! Give me back the kiss, then, which I gave you.

Charles: (*Again whimsically*) The kiss you took, you mean. Girls' kisses are taken, never given.

Margaret: Oh, yes. Girls may take kisses; but men, when it comes to the point, take something far more important than kisses.

Charles: What, lipstick?

Julian: (*On the point of losing his temper*) Shut up, Peggy.

Margaret: I wasn't talking to you. By the way you shout at me, anybody would think that I was saying something that touched only you in particular.

Julian: (*To Charles, with an uncomfortable grin*) She becomes dangerous when she starts yapping. I know her. It's by her yapping that she has always managed to get more from life than I ever have.

Margaret: What a brother! Running down the family when run down himself.

Charles: (*Whimsically*) Never quarrel in front of your fiancée. Bad policy, that. Let me put you on the merry track again. (*Kisses her.*)

Margaret: Thank you, darling. (*After the kiss*) Your breath smells like the smell one whiffs when one passes a fishmonger's.

Julian: There, what did I tell you? She does yap, doesn't she?

Charles: (*With false levity*) Darling, didn't you know? That is the smell of love when it is welded with whisky.

Margaret: I didn't mean to be nasty to you, darling, but Julian's rawness somehow gets me mixed up! Always!

Charles: Now, now don't run down the family, pet, as you said yourself.

Julian: (*Drawing Charles aside*) I say, what can have happened top Joy?

Charles: Lost in the fog, I suppose.

Margaret: Play that song again, Charles, my angel.

Charles: (*Perversely*) On what? I have lost my harp, (*Shrugs*)

Margaret: (*Splitting her sides with laughter*) Yes. You're so funny! Better to have an angel like you, with no harp but with a sense of humor, than an angel like Julian who ahs got a harp but no strings, having plucked them too hard with his claws, which resemble a gardener's tool rather than a human hand.

Julian: Listen, you, Duchess of Sauciness, either you or I have to clear out of this flat.

Margaret: (*Fondling Charles*) Whose side will you take up, Charles, if we quarrel?

Charles: I'll defend the weaker sex!

Margaret: That's bound to be Julian.

Julian: Hay, none of that flirtatious bribery.

Margaret: (*Not heeding Julian*) Oh, Charles, your knees are awfully hard.

At this point, enter Joy, looking cold and disheveled. Momentary silence. Charles starts up, pushing Margaret away.

Margaret: (*Putting on a ready smile*) Hello, Joy.

Julian: Hello, Joy.

Margaret: Been out in this cold, without even a coat?

Joy gives some vague answer.

Charles: (*His mood suddenly darkening*) Where have you been all day? (*With genuine concern*) You look pale, Joy. What on earth have you been up to? (*In a self-pitying tone*) I—we—have been looking for you since this afternoon.

Joy: (*Annoyed*) I was at my music teacher's. You ought to know by now that I go there every Saturday afternoon. (*Retires to her room, and Charles follows.*)

Margaret: (*To Julian*) She looks awfully worried about something, doesn't she?

Julian: (*No answer*)

Margaret: (*Louder*) Doesn't she, stone-face?

Julian: (*Flaring up*) Stop pestering me. Your clattering will not improve her pale look.

Margaret: Can't I talk?

Julian: Damn your char-womanish tongue.

Margaret: (*Also flaring up*) How dare you treat me like that? (*Slaps Julian's face.*) You drunken beast!

Julian: (*Stares at her for a moment with contempt; then takes seat away from her, and speaks *slowly, with forced calm.*) Beast as I am, I will not bite back. For there are some dogs which are more civilized than the ladies who lead them on leash.

Both keep sulkily silent.

Joy: (*In the next room*) What do you want?

Charles: Where were you this afternoon, after your music lesson?

Joy: (*After a pause, dryly*) At Michael's.

Charles: I thought so!

Joy: Thought what?

Charles: (*Ignoring her*) And you said that you were not there when we called.

Joy: (*With a sneer*) Don't be absurd.

Charles: (*In an accusing voice*) You lied to me!

Joy: You must have had too many glasses.

Charles: You lied to your own brother!

Joy: You're being childish.

Charles: (*Stares at Joy.*)

Joy: What if *I did* lie to you? Of course you're my only brother! There is something sacrosanct in the fact of being my only brother. (*Passionately*) I wish to God I had another brother so that you would not be able to extract so much juice out of that dear phrase of yours, "Your own brother," or "My only sister."

Charles: (*Taken aback slightly*) Do you realize what you're saying?

Joy: By God, I do. It's just a coincidence that Mother and Father died before a child was born, that's all. (*Charles is dumbfounded.*) Leave me alone, Charles.

Charles: And who was here just now, before we came in? I noticed you were having a merry time by the way you left the gramophone on.

Joy: (*Quietly*) Merry time indeed!

Charles: (*Shouting*) Who was here, I say?

Joy: Michael.

Charles: What was that sneaking rat doing here in my flat?

Joy: (*After a pause*) I never imagined that you could be so low, Charles. If Michael is a sneaking rat, you're the slime on which it crawls.

Charles: (*Striking her*) You wretch. Giving your body and soul to that bastard. (*Slams the door. Exit into the living room.*)

Joy collapses on to her bed; instantaneously Margaret and Julian, who have heard her bursting cry, start up like rabbits in a field.

Charles: I want a drink.

Julian: (*Snatching away bottle*) No, you don't, you swine.

Margaret: (*Pulling Charles aside*) What is the matter with you, shouting at her like that? Shall I go and calm her down?

Charles: (*After a pause*) No, leave her alone. It's not your business.

Margaret: (*Annoyed*) All right, don't be rude.

Charles: Let's go to some place or other where we can drink the night out.

Julian: (*Disgusted*) Have you got no sense of decency? Leaving Joy in that state, and going out to enjoy yourself?

Charles: Enjoy myself! I don't drink for enjoyment.

Julian: You drink as a gesture of pride! If so, it's a mighty rotten gesture.

Charles: All right then, if you don't want to come, don't.

Charles pulls Margaret by the arm, and exit. Margaret looks behind for a moment, but is dragged out. Julian looks after them with scorn, then suddenly feels himself lost, looks towards Joy's door, and pauses with his head drooping. Suddenly, walking towards her door, he knocks. No answer. He knocks again.

Julian: (*Opening the door*) May I come in?

Joy: (*Scrambling up*) If you wish.

Julian: Here is a small drink. Take it. It'll brighten you up.

Joy: Thank you. (*Takes it.*)

Julian: I shall not be so indelicate as to ask you what happened. Perhaps he drank a bit too much.

Joy: (*Resigned*) I'm used to his spasmodic outbursts of passion. All his frustrated emotions he accumulates and then from time to time empties them on me as if I were his dustbin.

Julian: Never mind. I know what it is like—to be struck by one's own sister or brother as the case may be—and for no earthly reason, either.

Joy: It's not *that* in particular that I mind so. (*Adjusts her hair and dress.*)

Julian: No, leave your hair as it is. It looks beautiful enough; long and disheveled hair goes well with your Boticelli face.

Joy: (*Vaguely smiling*) Thank you, Julian, you're always so kind to me.

Julian: (*Pouring out drink for both*) Don't call it *my* kindness. Call it rather the temperate quality of your nature. Here's to you! "Shall I compare thee to a summer's day? Thou art more lovely and more temperate. Rough winds do shake the darling buds of May, And summer's lease hath all too short a date." (*Drinks.*) You see, I've swallowed the rest of the sonnet all for you.

Joy: With that ready honey-tongue of yours you could aspire to any position in the world!

Julian: That's just where you're wrong. I have an awful confession to make—to you and to you alone. For which purpose I have been looking for you all day. Hear it patiently.

Joy: What is it?

Julian: (*After a pause*) The long and the short of it is that I am going away—or rather, running away. I don't know where I'm going, but that I'm going is a certainty. (*Pause*) The reason is a simple one. That I am just fed up, an ailment which is common enough, of course, among most of us, whose daily function consists of thinking in terms of hope and living of those of boredom. (*Pause*) My bag is all packed though no one knows about it—not even Mother. There only remains for me to say good-bye to you and buzz off. Only one request to make: you are not supposed to know that I am going. You're only supposed to know that I have gone when the news becomes public.

Joy: (*Dumbfounded and hesitant*) I had no idea that you also were—

Julian: I was what?

Joy: I don't know.

Julian: I know that you think I am being foolish because I do myself.

Joy: I just don't know what to say.

Julian: I don't want you to say anything! Don't start thinking that I am a pitiable wretch and all the rest of it. (*In a fresh tone*) By God I shall be glad to walk out of the house early tomorrow morning and down the street to the station, like a stray dog. (*Pause*) And like a stray dog I shall have only one thing to regret: Why doesn't Joy love me, when I love her so?

Joy: (*After a pause, with a frown*) I love Michael.

Julian: Lucky boy, he. (*Drinks.*)

Joy: I hate to make you suffer on account of me.

Julian: (*Declaiming*) Oh, I shall forget about Michael as soon as I leave London. And when I am gone I will think of London only as a city that nestles you, as sand and mud are known to nestle gold. And every memory of the city will lead up to you. (*Seriously but laughingly*) For instance, the memory of the beautiful curve of Regent Street will always remind me of the beautiful line of your body.

Joy: (*Forgetful for a moment of her sadness*) How absurd you are!

Julian: But then you'll admit that love performs sometimes strange gymnastics.

Joy: Yes, I'll admit that. (*Drinks.*)

Julian: (*After a pause*) Michael must be a strong personality to attract you so.

Joy: (*Frowning and slowly*) But he gives me so much strenuous emotions besides love, as tonight for instance, that I feel often at a loss. I am scorched by his very intensity. With him I am lacerated by two seemingly distinct activities—love's progress and its regress.

Julian: And yet you love him?

Joy: In my ineffectual way.

Julian: It's he who is ineffectual, not you.

Joy: (*Almost to herself*) Why must he always arrest and paralyze? Why must he stop and consider? And make me stop and consider too?

Julian: I don't know, Joy. I'm not Michael. (*As if to seize the opportunity*) You must not yourself stop and consider while I am here.

Joy: (*Smiling*) I'm sorry.

Julian: I love you, Joy, with all the heat of the sun—even in the darkest of winter nights. Let your red and my burning lips meet, and from where they meet let us draw on our bodies the whirling circles of supple passion of love. (*Pause; softly*) May I kiss you?

Joy: (*Bewildered*) I--I don't know.

Julian: (*Kissing her passionately*) There *is* nothing to know—when the curtain of night is falling upon us slowly, like spring rain.

Curtain

Act II, Scene ii

In the living room at Mrs. Lorayne's house; the same evening; no time has elapsed since Act II, Scene i; the lighting should, probably, be concentrated on the people only—the rest (background, etc.) being dimmed almost to darkness.

Claudia: (*Accusingly*) What made you return to the house you walked out of seven years ago? Not for pleasure, I hope—though I ought to know by now that your conception of pleasure differs somewhat from mine.

Mark: No, not for pleasure, but for purification. I've come to see—

Claudia: Oh! You may have come and in due course you may see, perhaps more than I'd like you to, but you will not conquer. I'll see to that. And what do you mean by purification? If you remember, you left Michael and me seven years ago for that very reason—for purification, as you call it. Did you not discover, during your wanderings in the wide world, any spiritual surgeon who could handle your case? And have you returned now because you expect to find him here, in this clinic?

Mark: I've returned, not because I expect anything, but because I've always kept to a straight path. (*With a slight twitch of the mouth*) The earth is supposed to be round, like a racecourse. And you're bound to come to where you started from if you keep a straight course. I'm no Columbus, but that's what I've done.

Claudia: Very pretty! But no ordinary person can keep a straight course in this life, though he might in the next. Only extraordinary people can do that! And I have never pretended to be anything but ordinary. Your purification! Yours—never anybody else's. How absurd that you should be perpetually washing your hands—like Lady Macbeth. Only not so convincing as she, because you do it when you're awake and she when asleep.

Mark: I admire your levity, Claudia, perhaps because it conceals your gravity; and perhaps because you realize now that the actual reason of my returning is of little importance and that what matters is the event itself. (*Reflectively*) Even that will not matter in the long run—for us who have suffered and seen the perpetual Grinner, squatting before us wherever we have been.

Claudia: I never consider what may happen in the long run, nor about my suffering. I do not beg for alms or sympathy with a cardboard placard on my breast, saying, "I have suffered," though, in your eyes, no doubt, such a placard would be as glittering as God's decoration on mankind.

Mark: You have not seen what I have seen.

Claudia: Nor you what I have seen. You went out of your way to look for Death. To me Death came. You have never given birth to death. I knew that I did not want that child, and I knew that that child would not be able to bring us together again. You knew that too. Otherwise why did you leave the country as you did? You left apparently to purify yourself, to stock-take your burden of the mystery in the auction-room of your imagination! And I was left behind with the real burden—the burden of my own dead body. You like the overtones of things, and so I'm left only with the undertones.

Mark: Is that meant to be an accusation?

Claudia: Not exactly. Men were born to be unwise, and women to endure the toll of their un-wisdom. We are both like flies in a room, which do not know how they got into it—with the slight difference that when you see the shaft of sunlight outside, you dash your head on the window-glass trying to get out, and I turn the other way trying to settle down. Not that I ever begrudge that tribulation: first you and then Michael. My life has not been entirely pointless. I made you happy while you chose to remain happy. And now there is Michael to look forward to.

Mark: Now that you mention Michael, I may as well tell you that the chief reason of my returning was to see Michael. After all, he is the only visible symbol of our once untroubled happiness—

Claudia: (*Interrupting*) The shivered fragments of which you have buried in the urn of your memory, hoping that Michael in time will play the archaeologist in digging up the subterranean happiness and sanctifying it into a museum piece!

Mark: (*Almost to himself*) Yes, I have thought about him all these years. Michael has been with me wherever I have traveled—below the vigilant sphinx, among the cursing muleteers of rocky Greece, under the Celestial Mountains of the Black Gobi, and sometimes also looking on the Persian Gulf he has stood beside me.

Claudia: It's like you to think about him when you are certain that there are several continents to separate you from each other. Perhaps you left because you wanted to dream your cerebral dreams and contemplate your heart's downstream journey, commonly known as heredity.

Mark: You will never know why I left, because, although you knew me better than anyone else, you also in time took everything, including happiness, for granted. You always expected your tap of life to run: you never heard the hissing noise, which often came out of it, instead of water. Michael will know the cause of my action. He will not take up the prosecutor's role: he will cross the river of unknowing that separates you and me, and pacify our spirits clamoring for their pounds of flesh. And I have come to see him.

Claudia: You leave nothing untried—that's your method. Your thoroughness is inhuman. It's because you're inhuman that you go about practicing cruelty both to yourself and to others around you—like Death. (*Impassioned*) You are Death.

Mark: (*Quietly*) Yes, I smell of mortality.

Claudia: No, that's not what I mean. You do not understand the human un-logic, my logic. You only understand the logic of death. The desert is your only possible home. Wherever you go, you carry with you your own desolation: you spread your carpet of sterility at sunset, and by the next morning, there is no sign of life beneath that carpet. And Michael shall not be squashed under that carpet.

Mark: But you will let me see him?

Claudia: (*Ironically*) To show how well I have educated him for the last seven years, all on my own? And should he meet your approval, for you to carry him away from me?

Mark: No, there will be no abduction, because abduction is not what I want.

Claudia: The fact is that you never did know what you want.

Mark: The fact is that I shall not know what I want until the occasion for wanting has passed—until I have seen Michael and said good-bye to him.

Claudia: (*Shouting*) Then why in the name of all the seraphim don't you just see him and say good-bye without making so much fuss?

Mark: To one who has not measured the wearied steps of pilgrimage, the awful moment of treading on the threshold of the Holy Temple cannot be imagined. Seven years of futility and doubt, and I have decided to see Michael once again, and now that I am on the point of drawing the curtain of my doubts, I do not know what vista of landscape is going to open up. I shall know after I have seen him—when the negative of my desire has been developed into a photograph, be it good or bad.

Claudia: Oh how men fear the moment of birth—the moment when the formless fluid of their imagined passion takes shape in the mold of Reality! And how invariably they are disappointed—while we are relieved—at the realization of their expectations! I warn you, Mark, that you will be disappointed when you see Michael. Your cloud of unknowing will thicken and so will Michael's.

Mark: That is an impossibility.

Claudia: Oh, Mark, when will you cease to deceive yourself?

Mark: Tonight. (*Handing out his Will*) Here is my last Will and Testament and (*sneeringly*) dying men are supposed to be honest. You will peruse this document of denunciation in your leisure, I hope, and consider perhaps the tricks that Death plays sometimes with his sickle.

Claudia is dumbfounded. Enter Dr. Stuart in his dressing gown. As the Doctor enters, Mark automatically retreats slightly so that he is not visible to the Doctor.

Dr. Stuart: (*Not noticing Mark*) Ah, Claudia! A mentally unemployed man like myself has no excuse for sleeping during the night. I neither work to warrant fatigue nor have a bedfellow whom it is my duty to entertain. Tossing the night alone in a wide bed is no fun for a man—that's meant surely for women in confinement. Claudia, you look surprised! Have I shocked your sense of modesty? (*Seeing Mark, aghast*) Good God, who is here? The dead come alive? "Pray do not mock me: I am a very foolish fond old man." But you're Mr. Mark Lorayne! I am genuinely sorry for my intrusion.

Mark: (*Stepping forward and smiling*) "No cause, no cause." And you're Dr. Stuart. You have not changed a bit, except that you seem to have acquired more flesh!

Dr. Stuart: (*Regaining his animation*) Ah yes, life is pleasant. I give nothing and receive everything, and I get plump on it. But you seem to have got thinner—in spite of your bushy wilderness round your chin. Beware of thinness, as I used to say in my capacity as a doctor, thin people as a rule are found either to scorn their own nature or to distrust other people's—

Claudia: Do shut up, Doctor. (*Stopping him from drinking*) And don't drink so much. It's too late.

Dr. Stuart: Pardon, sweet Claudia! (*Turning to Mark*) You know I adore Claudia—she loses her temper just at the right moment.

Mark: I am heartily glad that your attention to Claudia is as sedulous as ever.

Dr. Stuart: One advantage of being a family doctor is that when he has looked after the health of the family, say, for about ten years, the family then looks after his in turn—until he dies, maybe. I have practically become a part of this household. (*Suddenly recollecting himself*) But really, what brings you back to this master-forsaken house?

Mark: (*Dryly*) Ask Claudia.

Dr. Stuart: Ah, there. That's certainly a reason enough. Claudia, I say, is worthy of being visited by kings. I'm glad you did not forget that during your seven years' silent existence. (*Seeing the Will on the table*) What's this, what's this? (*Pause; in a husky voice*) Does, does it frighten you too—"the eternal silence of the infinite spaces"?

Mark: You must not pay such undeserved compliments.

Dr. Stuart: (*Raising his wine glass, and looking through it*) For my part, it is the perpetual clamor of this little head (*Pointing to his own*) that drives me to this alcoholic fountain of "peace without honor."

Mark: I am leaving with the circus tomorrow. This time for good—and I thought I would pay my last tribute to Claudia.

Claudia: Funny sort of tribute!

Dr. Stuart: (*Almost to himself*) So were with the circus after all!

Claudia: Why didn't you tell me that before? Like you! Either I have to find you out or else you have to take me with a surprise.

Dr. Stuart: But my dear Claudia, why should he tell you where he is? A spiritual bankrupt does not tell the world of his whereabouts, lest his Eumenidean creditors, servants of Death, pursue him! Besides why shouldn't he be with a Circus? After all, the world is split into three sorts of people, and we have got to fit into one of them by hook or by crook: one, the overworked minority who have to entertain the majority; two, the contented majority who always crave to be lulled by them; and three, the very unhappy few who are left to entertain themselves!

Claudia: I don't understand your buffoonery.

Dr. Stuart: Buffoonery is a degraded form of soliloquy, a thing that the buffoon himself swallows like pills, not chews.

Claudia: (*Still with apparent disgust*) But why the Circus?

Mark: You would not understand me even if I told you. Mr. Anthony Pearsall didn't!

Claudia: (*Surprised*) Anthony! So you saw him?

Mark: He came to see me.

Dr. Stuart: Lawyers are quick in the uptake, but they are born misunderstanders, because they demand the cause of things, whereas the real clue to human nature is in the effect—in the fact that Mark does go about with a Circus.

Mark: Thank you for finishing my sentence for me—

Dr. Stuart: You mean, snatching it away from you.

Mark: You understand me, Doctor.

Dr. Stuart: You flatter me, Mark. And at the same time you snub Claudia by saying so— which is not quite chivalrous of you.

Claudia: I do not expect chivalry from Mark. He gives it all to his own soul, and can't spare any for other people.

Dr. Stuart: Oh, come! (*Pacifying her*) Don't start accusing and tearing the human heart at this hour of the night. (*With eyes brightening*) Do you know that the human heart contains as much gall as blood? Funny that! It took even me, a doctor, with surprise. And guess what is the best antidote to gall? Alcohol, of course. That's the only moral justification for alcohol.

Mark: (*With approving smile*) Yes, don't be vague, and you're supposed to get Haig.

Dr. Stuart: (*With animation*) Ah, you win the bargain there—my soul is yours.

Mark: You seem to sell your soul at a remarkably cheap price!

Dr. Stuart: I was born cheap. It is my clothes that make me look expensive: as Shakespeare would say, "A tailor made me." Ever seen me naked? By the Spirit of Polonius you will see the truth of my estimation then. (*Finishing his glass*) I swear by the spirit of Polonius because I am convinced that he and no one else did the Guardian Angel stunt at my birth. Imagine Polonius, plump, like me, with an accidental pair of wings like a moth's, hardly strong enough to sustain his weight in the air, and yet having to flutter about whilst I, the combined essence of starkness, clumsiness, ugliness and cheapness was being pushed out into the narrow and hard bed of a world. I have always wanted to see this particular angel, and subsequently entered the medical theater in the hope of witnessing my patron doing his usual stuff. The snag is that it is hard to think about old Polonius whilst the primitive life-and-death drama of the mother and her parting flesh is going on. You know, I still don't know why these little brats should be coming into this world. In fact, nothing is more mysterious to me than the advent. Other people think that departure—death—is mysterious. What I question is the advent—birth.

Claudia: Men were never meant to understand that mystery—it's the prerogative of women.

Dr. Stuart: (*Still to himself*) Advent, advent! What is advent?

Mark: Are you suggesting that I should tell you why I have come back tonight?

Dr. Stuart: Oh, no. You—pardon my wet glove—come as a dead man, an already dissected corpse on the operating table of God, this earth, awaiting the report of His diagnosis, poetically called "The Sound of the Trumpet."

Mark: I came to see Michael, Doctor.

Dr. Stuart: You came to betray Claudia once and for all.

Mark: You too forbid me to see Michael?

Dr. Stuart: I never forbid. People never obey doctor's orders in any case. I merely warn.

Mark: That's what Claudia was doing just before you came along.

Claudia: (*Impatiently*) Oh, what's the use of talking like this when Michael might be coming back any moment from his walk and surprise us all here?

Dr. Stuart: That's right.

Enter Michael from behind. Michael stands dumbfounded for a moment.

Dr. Stuart: (*Quietly*) The brute fact will come from behind us unnoticed and surprise us while we are consulting each other as to how we shall cross the tight-rope that hangs over the torrent of dark Reality.

Michael: (*Overcome with emotion*) Father!

Mark: Michael!

Dr. Stuart: Claudia, you and I are no longer wanted—now that the dress-rehearsal, for Mark, is over. Let us retire. I feel awfully tired.

Dr. Stuart and Claudia start to go out. As she passes Michael, Claudia looks at him for a moment beseechingly.

Dr. Stuart: (*Looking towards Michael also*) Poor Michael, he too has to come back, for the dew will rust men as well as swords. (*Exeunt both.*)

Michael: (*Bursting with emotion*) Oh, Father!

Mark: (*Calmly*) Do not try to bring all your feelings to your tongue. That will merely add to your confusions and famish your expectations. I know how words fail us when our hearts are tear-bound, as I know how breath fails us at great altitudes. (*Pause*) I am glad to see you again.

Michael: You bring me, Father, that aching joy which I have been craving for these many years.

Mark: I too have waited long for this moment.

Michael: But I knew, I knew that you would come back—and tell me why you ever left us. Seven years age I was too young to desire that knowledge. Today I long to be delivered of that dilemma.

Mark: Your mother's first question, when she saw me tonight, was why I returned, which is not the same as your asking why I left to begin with.

Michael: But she was not expecting you as I was. That's why.

Mark: (*Rather self-pityingly*) She was remote, almost indifferent. I felt as though I were the faded snapshot of a new undesirable acquaintance, brought out by mistake.

Michael: Mother's mind is never indifferent, only distilled and hushed—like a lake.

Mark: Like a lake, she is not vexed by any ancient world-wave of the sea, perhaps to her advantage.

Michael: Life to her is not a matter of diving deep into the sea to look for the coral bones of drowned sailors. Like a lake, she is content to reflect the silent mountains that surround her, and to hearken to the picnic-making weekenders who, with tinkling teacups, scoop out their indoor philosophy that they preserve in their frigidaire chests like homemade ice-cream. She knows that life consists of little things and detached moments of minor hopes and pleasures.

Mark: That knowledge came with Time!

Michael: Time was ever the torturing Rack of Man, and Oblivion his Executioner. (*Remembering suddenly*) But you do not tell me yet why you left us seven years ago.

Mark: Michael, before I answer that overwhelming question let me ask you a question first. Do you know, Michael, that there are two twilights in a day, the dawn and the dusk, and that both are marked by the confused singing of certain birds—and that such a bird is Man? Do you know that the twilight, whether morning or evening, is the hour when one life pants to be delivered into another, when light and darkness groan together in a single dream-dimensioned bed, when the parti-colored jester of birth-and-death sits on the throne like a judge, shuffling the evidence of pros and cons as though they were a pack of fortune-telling cards? Do you know that you are in that dawn, and I in that dusk, and that therefore we must speak together—like birds?

Michael: I know the hour, Father. It is then that one has such damnable dreams whose howling wind of indifference one cannot howl back because one's voice has turned traitor.

Mark: It is well that you should know the hour. It is then that we muse on what we have done and contemplate our future actions in the light of our past actions: it is then that our remembered love turns into sorrow, and that we plan to betray with an infinitely suffering kiss the one we have loved, and that the mind craves to be delivered of the body it has violated.

Michael: Is it then that the flame of our happiness flickers and casts certain mobile and monstrous shadows on the domed concave of our skulls?

Mark: Yes, it is the hour, Michael. And for those who have woken in this half-dawn there are only two ways of meeting the day: either by going out and hanging oneself, like Judas, or by setting out on a journey in search of the vision of Protracted Death among the hungry rout of alien dream-cattle—in short, by weeping bitterly, like Peter.

Michael: And you took the second course! I would have preferred the method of Judas, Father.

Mark: (*Thoughtfully*) Perhaps you're right. But then I wanted to consider my resolutions—and irresolutions.

Michael: And what judgment did you pluck from your reconsiderations in what the grammarians call the historic present tense?

Mark: That you are the fruit of my violation of Claudia's innocence.

Michael: Are you sure, Father?

Mark: And that man's happiness is none other than the detached worship of an act of violence while it lasts.

Michael: Why do you tell me these things?

Mark: Because I want you to remember that Claudia and I were once happy together.

Michael: Will I have to remember that even in the presence of Joy?

Mark: (*Does not answer.*)

Michael: Father, you do not know Joy. She is the one person in the presence of whom I should like to forget everything else.

Mark: Remember that I too once felt like that towards Claudia.

Michael: (*With great passion*) Remember! Remember! Damn memory then.

Mark: Damn memory, and you damn what distinguishes man from beasts and trees.

Michael: But Mother has never told me to remember such things.

Mark: Because mothers, by their very nature are concerned with what is to come: and because it is the fathers who have to remember what has gone by. They look before, but we look after and pine for what is not.

Michael: What do you mean, Father? Mother also pines in secret, more than she would like to admit.

Mark: No, that is something different. It is rather fear for the coming danger of life, while ours is the despair of the foregone certainty of death.

Michael: Explain, Father, do not hold me up in this anguish.

Mark: Women are like Nature, in that they accept unwittingly the two laws of nature, death and change. They unknowingly suffer the innocent death of the spirit which we inflict on them, and suffer the sea change of strange girlhood to rich motherhood. They move with the movement of nature, flowing and changing ceaselessly like water and seasons. But we, the guilty souls, do not move with them: we hate change: we feel the after-vacancy of all changes and long for rest and changeless eternity.

Michael: But what has this to do with your leaving seven years ago?

Mark: Claudia, the young girl, needed me and I needed her—and we were happy. But Claudia the mother was no longer the same person as Claudia the girl. Time passed, ten years, twelve years, covering our happiness with earth, in which Claudia had discovered her new love-object but I had lost mine. In her love-world I was no longer relevant. Was it my own imagination's undoing or was it hers? I did my best to avert my eyes from looking at the change as change, until one early summer-night I made my last effort to recapture my Claudia, the Claudia I had created twelve years before. But she knew that it was doomed to failure, like a foregone conclusion. She said pityingly that I was being adolescent and silly, but that she would willingly play her part towards reconciliation. To me her words "adolescent" and "silly" sounded as if she meant "hypocritical" and "bestial."

Michael: Now I remember that early summer night. I was waiting and waiting for her to come and kiss me goodnight, but she did not come, and I fell asleep, waiting.

Mark: Next morning I resolved on a journey, which would take me to some distant country.

Michael: Next morning I discovered that she had not slept that night: she was looking pale and disheveled and older than she had ever looked before. For the first time I ate my breakfast alone that morning. When I was finishing she came down and sat beside me, mute, watching me eating, then hugged me tight. I could feel her jumping heart and hear her choking throat. And then I felt on my head through the hair the hottest tears that I have ever felt. She said in a husky voice, "You will not leave me!" I automatically answered, "No." Throughout the day all my senses were concentrated on those wet spots where the tears had dropped. That day I did not go bathing, because I did not want to cool those warm spots, but came home early to find Mother still in her dressing gown. The faint perfume on her dressing gown I still remember. I could tell it any day anywhere.

Mark: A few days later I packed and left.

Michael: I remember that day too. All night the rain had been falling, falling silently, and I could hear the muffled voices of your friends expressing, I supposed, their last conjectural reasons for your sudden departure. I wished I could come down and listen to their conversations, because I too did not know why you were leaving. And I dared not ask Mother, because she was sleeping. This time she slept while I watched. And I thought it mean of her to sleep like that. It made her seem like servants—servants who, like Macbeth's porter, will give anything for sleep. Dawn came with the blackbirds and the trot of the milkman's horse. Then I dozed and was surprised by Mother, who entered, saying, "Not up yet? This day of all days?" That day Dover Harbor looked especially dingy and wet everywhere, and the sea wind-swept and black and white as in winter. When I finally felt your hard bristly face on my cheeks, I felt like green hay being cut before its time by a blunt scythe.

Mark: No matter now: the past is dead and gone, cold as the deep-sea current and as dark, even though our Memory, the fish, swims in it.

Curtain

Act II, Scene iii

Same night; about three o'clock; scene same as Act I, Scene ii. Joe, Oliver, Mac still playing poker; Veronica walking to and fro, with a shawl over her; play continues even while they are speaking.

Mac: I would go to bed if I were you, Veronica, instead of fretting like that in the cold at this unearthly hour.

Oliver: (*To Veronica*) Make some tea, then, and keep yourself warm.

Veronica: I am tired of making tea! My fretting is no worse than your gambling.

Oliver: All right then, don't! I was only thinking of your cold.

Joe: She's ole enough to a'ter 'erself. Yuh jist look a'ter yer bettin'. Gawd, I wush we had some av that stuff now. Three o'clock in the morning is jist the toime fur a wet. If on'y yuh hadn't kep on forcin' me to give it away loike that.

Mac: You've had enough to keep your head swimming to the North Pole and back.

Joe: (*Protesting with triumph*) I ain't dhrunk, Mac! Licker can't kill a fella loike me.

Mac: Oh, I know that! Your belly is like the Black Sea—it can hold any amount of water or alcohol.

Joe: Full house! My winnin'. Yeah, sure I kin hold any amount a' dhrink. But the wondher is that I ain't got no belly loike a beer-barrel loike yuh have. (*Laughs raucously*)

Cards shuffled

Mac: (*To Veronica*) Poor Ben! You ought to have been nicer to him.

Veronica: What the hell am I to do if he always sticks to me like a leech?

Mac: Six. Life isn't worth all that. If he sticks to you, let him stick to you. But you mustn't think of him as a leech, when he sticks to you, think of him rather as a fellow-slave who needs your help.

Veronica: (*Sharply*) He can get whatever help he needs from that—that night bird of his!

Oliver: Now, now. Don't let your thoughts get so harsh. I'm in.

Joe: Me too. Shure, if Ben 'ud been here, it 'ud have made a better game, that's sartin.

Three's a bit too foo.

Veronica goes into Mark Lorayne's compartment, waits.

Oliver: Cards? Three, three, three for me too. You know, Mac, it's all very well for you to talk like that to Veronica. But women are a funny lot.

Joe: Not 'arf so funny as men loike yuhs. Four.

Oliver: Eight. I remember being smitten by a Spanish woman in Buenos Aires about six years ago. It was just her smiling mouth. I'm always on the lookout but I still haven't found another like it. The smile went straight thro' my eyes, my head, and then right down my back to my toes, I felt. Sometimes when I close my eyes, I picture just that seductively smiling mouth—red lips and white teeth.

Joe: Yeah? Loike the smile of the Cheshire Cat, I 'spect.

Oliver: Do you know, Mac, as I get older, I seem to see why the Ancient Greeks went so mad over a woman!

Joe: In the Southern countries, they are speshully fond of women!

Oliver: But imagine, just one woman!

Mac: Yes, my boy, it's what we Catholics call Original Sin!

Joe: Py chimney Christmas! There yuh go off agin! Jist as the conversashun gits int'restin', and poisonal, yuh brin' art yer favrite trump card and shut everybody's marf.

Oliver: (*Dreamily*) Personally, I am always dreaming to meet one day a woman—like Shahrazad—who would tell me stories and stories for the rest of my life—it would be such a change from all the women I have ever met, who invariably expect me to do the talking.

Joe: Cum ahn. We ain't in the Arabian Nights: this is London, man. Le's git back to the playin'. Where were we? Yuh to bet, Mac.

Enter Mark Lorayne; Veronica starts up and stares at Mark Lorayne with accusing look.

Mark: (*After a pause*) What on earth are you doing here?

Veronica: Waiting for you.

Mark: What mischief are you up to now?

Veronica: What mischief have you been up to?

Mark: I?

Veronica: You! Yes, you. Visiting your old home? It must have been a delightful evening for you. (*Pause*) I heard what you and your friend were saying this afternoon.

Mark: (*Taking off coat*) I scorn to answer you.

Veronica: Is that all you have to say?

Mark: I have nothing more to say.

Veronica: (*Pleading*) Not even to say you are sorry?

Mark: Sorry for whom?

Veronica: For me!

Mark: You waste enough sympathy on yourself; you don't need my sympathy poured on you as well.

Veronica: (*Bursting out*) You beast.

Mark: It's all too late for shouting, Veronica.

Veronica: Yes, it is indeed. Why didn't you tell me before that you were already married and had a son as big as a cow?

Mark: It's all too late for shouting, I keep telling you.

Veronica: You hypocrite! Deceiving me when it suits you.

Mark: I have never deceived you.

Veronica: It's always me, isn't it? It's I who deceive myself, isn't it?

Mark: I have always tried to prevent you from building your petty hopes on me.

Veronica: You never make any demands on me, do you? You are such a saint! You've soiled my body! Isn't that making demands on me?

Mark: It's all too late for shouting.

Veronica: I will shout so long as my voice allows me to shout! (*With self-pity and helplessness*) I give in to every demand you make on me—every demand, do you hear? And you just shake me off when you have the kernel, as if I were a nut and nothing more.

Mark: Woman, your body was defiled by other lecherous potato-fingers long before I came to your rescue. And I rescued you because your soul still had something of that flashing sword of innocent beauty. And now, even that is gone. Instead you are full of daggers.

Veronica: Go on. Say that I am not worth a brass farthing.

Mark: I will not be made part of your clash of animate wills.

Veronica: You lump of cold arrogance. Go and rot to death in a charnel house. Words, words, nothing but words: that's all you can do, argue yourself to death, as if God would not punish you because you think you can excuse yourself by arguing. Your breath stinks of the ashes of burnt bodies.

Mark: None is more aware of it than I, Veronica.

Veronica: Aware of this and aware of that! You can take that awareness to your grave and it won't make life any the easier.

Mark: It will make death easier.

Veronica: Have an easy death, then. (*Exit*)

Mark: I will have an easy death. (*Walks into next compartment.*)

The poker-players next door have naturally heard what has been going on, and are feeling lost. Then as Mark unexpectedly opens the door, they all start up, especially Joe.

Joe: (*Putting on an air of disinterestedness*) Hallo Hermit!

Mark: Still up?

Mac: Yes, we are all up still, sons of the nocturnal hag, rustling like a brood of mice!

Joe: (*Having found in Mac's words an opportunity of diverting his attention*) E-e-e-eh, keep them harrd wurrds fur yer confeshunals, this ain't no place fur'em.

Mark: I want to join you in your playing.

Joe: Shure! Wid pleasure! 'Ere, cum and sith 'ere betune Mac and meself.

Mac does so; pause.

Mac: I told her to go to bed.

Oliver: She'll get over it!

Mark: We all get over things—sooner or later.

Joe: (*Dealing out cards*) Gawd, I wish I had somethin' to dhrink.

Mark: You'll find some in my cupboard. Bring it here.

Joe: Really, that's greath! (*Rushes out*)

Oliver: You are behaving funnily today.

Mark: We all behave funnily—sooner or later.

Oliver: Don't keep repeating and twisting my words. It's annoying.

Mark: What's that pistol doing on the table?

Oliver: (*Grinning with pleasure*) It's just Joe's stake. At one time he was losing heavily to me tonight and had to hand it to me as a £1 stake. He's got it back now, but he still owes me eight or nine bob.

Joe: (*Returning with bottle*) Here we are! Le's all dhrink this clear divil's brew—as clear as any lake-wather—and furgit about iviry bleedin' worry av the world! (*Pouring it and regaining courage*) Hermit, ye're all tempramental-like tonight. Anythink gone wronk?

Mark: No. Everything is just as it should be.

Mac: Now that's the greatest ailment you can possibly have. We Catholics think that if everything is just as it should be, there is definitely something wrong with the person who thinks that.

Joe: Yeah, Cath'lics are a snaky lot. They wriggle roun' and roun' wid cunning loike a serpent and finish up by havin' everythink their own bleedin' way. I don't wondher why it's so diff'cult fur a blunt fella loike me to git into heaven 'cos the place is heavily patrolled by all the arty-crafty saints and martyrs.

Oliver: Restrain yourself, man.

Joe: Shuth yer marf. (*Having recovered his defiant mood with his drinking*) I kin talk me black head off if I loikes. And I wol talk so long as me pump's goin's aw right.

Mac: Quiet, Joe. Pour me another drop. (*Then drinking, to Mark*) You have another glass too. Drink is the only clue to oneself when one is woolgathering, whether in temper or out of it. What is the point of all, really, quarreling, like Gulliver's dwarfs over this soft cow-pad called Life? Decidedly the dung stinks if you stick your nose into it looking for the so-called germs of Life.

Joe: Nobody ain't stickin' no nose into nothink, Mac! Why mist ye talk av them dirty things when we've got dis clean licker, as clean as any dew in summer-mornin'?

Oliver: Stop eulogizing on the cleanness of it, because it won't sstay clean long after you've gulped it down. (*Giggles*)

Joe: I don't partic'larly care for yer fiddlestick humor, see, Oliver? It may please yuh 'cos yuh's as thin as a fiddlestick yerself. But it don't please me, see?

Mark: Hadn't we better start playing?

Joe: (*Apologetically*) Shure! Yuh to bet, Oliver me fiddlestick!

Oliver: Six.

Mac: Make it ten.

Mark: Twelve.

Joe: O.K.

Oliver and Mac: All in.

Joe: Cards? Two for you. One for you. Three for you. Three for me. Chip.

Oliver: Chip and four.

Mac: Chip and twelve.

Mark: Chip and twelve—and four.

Joe: Yuh're up and up loike me temper! I ain't in. Gawd, wot a pot, thick as the divil's soup.

Oliver: I'll see you.

Mac: Make it twenty-four.

Mark: See you.

Oliver: No.

Mac: Flush.

Joe: Gawd, wot bloody luck. Yer deal, Oliver. And none av yer cheatin' neither. We're all wide awake, see?

Oliver shuffles.

Mac: (*Continuing in his former vein*) Poor Veronica! She doesn't realize, of course, that we are all like a lot of buttercups whose shining faces may have to be splodged any time, any day, with those mucky droppings from mid-air, and that when the cow-pad falls upon us unfortunately, we shall have to sustain it—put up with it—as best as we can, like Atlas of old whose misfortune was to hold up this earthy earthy globe.

(*Momentary pause*)

Joe: Listen, Mac, I dunno why ye keep talkin' abaht that cow-dung av yers—speshully when nobody kin folla yer meaning! Veronica is to be pitied, we all knows that. But she ain't 'arf so wretched as some av the women I've known: a woman who dies in child-birth, furr instance. I knows that 'cos I saw it wid me own eyes—wan me wife died more'n ten years ago in Noo Yoik. Wan I think av her, I think perraps most av these 'poor' wailin' women are just sham, somehow. (*Suddenly aware of the silence*) Come ahn, yuh've shuffled enoff. Yuh'll wear out them cards if ye keep on. Deal now. Kindly rimimber them cards are mine: no one in this room ever supplies wid cards, exceptin' meself.

Oliver: No one is so fond of cards as you are, that's why.

Joe: I on'y play pashunce wid 'em—wal, I mean, most o' the toime.

Mac: (*Blasé tone*) Yes, this is a funny world, by God—

Joe: You mean funny peculiar or funny ha-ha?

Oliver: Both, you silly parrot!

Mac: And Man who inhabits it—a funny beast—because he does not realize the filthiness of his body until he has tried to wash his own linen and the greediness of his belly until he has attempted to do his own cooking. I pass.

Mark: Six.

Joe: In fur six.

Oliver: O.K.

Mac: Right.

Oliver: Cards? Three, two, two, three fur me.

Joe: Hey, put that third card back. You took it from the bottom. I saw you do it.

Oliver: I didn't.

Joe: You lying toad.

Oliver: I didn't, I tell you.

Joe: (*Starting up*) Put it back or I'll make a blancmange out of yer jelly-eyes.

Oliver: I didn't, you—bullying ox.

Joe: What, you crawling insect! Callin' me names, eh? Put it back or I'll shoot yuh. (*Holds up pistol.*)

Mark: (*Jumping up and snatching away pistol*) Stop dawdling! It's all too late for shouting, you gypsy beggar. (*Shoots himself*) Mac, will you bury me? (*Dies*)

Mac: For the Love of Mary! What have you two done! (*After long pause, crosses himself.*)

Joe: It was his (*meaning Oliver's*) blasted fault! Idiot! (*Pause; feeling body*) Is all stiff, dammit, loike a dead rabbith. Gawd, who's gonner look arter our box-office and the advertisin'? (*Pause; to Oliver who with fear has fled to one of the corners of the room*) Come ahn, yuh sniveling fox, help me stretch 'im outh. Say, Mac, was he talking to me when he said somethink abaht it's all too late for shouting, you gypsy beggar? (*Spoken softly*)

Mac: Yes, I'll bury you, Mark.

Curtain

Act III, Scene i

Next Morning; in the living room of Claudia's house; rising curtain reveals Claudia and Dr. Stuart seated; the one staring at a morning paper with a frown of helplessness, the other looking into space, blankly meditating; red lighting from the window.

Claudia: (*Putting down the paper, after a pause*) Oh what am I to do?

Dr. Stuart: (*With an air of matter-of-factness*) Pack up and go south! (*Then in a soft voice, reciting*)

>To Sorrow,
>I bade good-morrow,
>And thought to leave her far behind;
>But cheerly, cheerly,
>She loves me dearly;

> She is so constant to me, and so kind. . . .

(*Then suddenly declaiming*) How the hell am I to know what you should do, when all I know is that Mark's death, as far as you are concerned, is like a bad anachronism?

Claudia: Not so with Michael! He is shattered to bits! What is he going to do?

Dr. Stuart: No earthly use worrying about that, Claudia! The older generation can never predict what the younger will do. One thing is quite certain, however, and that I am always telling you: If you care at all in this world, you are bound to be betrayed sooner or later.

> All this the world well knows; yet none knows well
> To shun the heaven that leads men to this hell.

Pardon these quotations: I don't mean to be flippant! I usually quote poets when I am up against a situation that I cannot cope with, because, to my great relief, the major incompetence of great poets helps me forget my own minor incompetence!

Claudia: Oh, Doctor. What will be the outcome of all this?

Dr. Stuart: Several things! One: You will drown in the sea of sorrow and become flat like an oyster, and your compressed heart will gradually turn into a pearl. Two: I shall continue to adore you despite your oyster-like despair. Three: History will continue to march despite you and me; for others have begun it, and therefore others must finish it, thank God! And it, History, will continue to litter our basket, the head, and the eye-socket, with red-hot headlines of stream-lined political movements, greasy news of cardinal virtues and deadly sins, and copyright viewpoints of our knowing neighbors who think in abstract terms and prophesy in concrete ones.

Claudia: Was it my fault after all?

Dr. Stuart: There was nothing you could do to save Mark from his folly. You know, Claudia, he was a sentimentalist about life, which accounts for his unsentimental death. With me it is the reverse: being a sentimentalist about death, I still seem to be living all right—for the most part unsentimentally.

Claudia: But why did he have to shoot himself like that?

Dr. Stuart: Mark, I imagine, did not particularly care for queuing up in front of Death's dark hall. (*Enter Michael, unnoticed by Dr. Stuart.*) And what's the use of saying whose fault it is? When you trip and break a beautiful vase, is it the foot's fault or the hands? Just persuade yourself to the brute fact that Hymen, the heavenly housekeeper who runs the Palace of Matrimony, often confuses wedding sheets with winding sheets—seeing that they're both white.

Michael: (*With forced calm*) That's because Hymen is a fussy old busybody.

Dr. Stuart: (*With animation*) Well-done, Michael. Nothing like cynicism to whip off catastrophe—a sort of victory by double-crossing one's own doom.

Michael: Mother, I want to speak to you, in private.

Dr. Stuart: All right, I'll retire if you want me to.

Claudia: (*Entreatingly*) No, don't go.

Dr. Stuart: It's all right, Claudia. I think I know what he's going to say, almost word for word. If walls have ears, I am such a wall—standing mute between two worlds, this and the next, and between two hearts, yours and Michael's, hearing both voices simultaneously and suffering for both! (*Turning to Michael*) But Michael, my boy, I strongly recommend that you and Claudia should pack up and go south—away from this befogged city, where every roof emits from its organ-pipes the droning smoke of huddled tepidity. (*Soliloquizing*) Ah, the winter smoke of London—the pulverized testimony of the after-funeral psychology of its inhabitants, sipping tea over the sulky fire while their singing heads are filled with snatches of the traffic noise and the organ sound of the burial service. Yes, Michael, follow the swallow and go south, I say. I have been trying indirectly to persuade your mother to do the same but she won't listen—sorrow has stopped her ears with cotton wool. (*Exit*)

Michael: I will follow the swallows—if they will tell me why Father has prescribed himself the leaden potion of suicide.

Claudia: (*With a mixed feeling of terror and pity*) Oh, Michael, don't say such terrifying nonsense.

Michael: (*Softly*) Mother, what are we to do?

Claudia: (*Also softly*) Nothing. Let time decide.

Michael: Father let time decide—for seven years. And what has it come to!

Claudia: Nothing.

Michael: Oh, what have you done?

Claudia: I? Nothing. It is what he has done—to you.

Michael: To me?

Claudia: To you.

Michael: Why?

Claudia: Because you will now leave me and follow his footsteps, because from now on you will not ask me what to do but him.

Michael: How do you know?

Claudia: I am your mother, and ought to know.

Michael: Know what?

Claudia: That men place their duty towards the dead before their love for the living. And you are such a man now, or think—

Michael: Or think that I am!

Claudia: Which is the same. There comes a time when sons cease to listen to their mothers and listen instead to bodiless voices—duties, books, ideas, abstract passions and beauties—in short, when they take death more seriously than life.

Michael: (*His mood clouding*) Well?

Claudia: And want their mother's support in so doing and—

Michael: (*Breathless*) And?

Claudia: End by killing their mother's love for them.

Michael: (*Impassioned*) Mother, you're driving me I know not whereto. You're drawing a route on the map of my doom, which I do not comprehend as yet. Father has departed for good, with a certainty, which surpasses every doubt. But he has left with me an imperfect knowledge of what preceded that certainty and I do not know yet what it is.. Until yesterday he was too far away—like the distant sea-surge in an empty shell—and last night he was too near—like a blinding flashlight.

Claudia: It was ever a characteristic of your father that he only revealed to you the final results of his thoughts and emotions. I remember that somber evening in November when he uttered his love for me with the finality of a sudden applause—which overwhelmed me almost to the verge of pitying him. But then, after he left me, I recapitulated in my memory the course of the preceding months, the slow-coming spring and the gentle summer, during which time he used to come and go, with the ease and the dispassion of a sea-gull. And remembering all this, the landscape of my heart suddenly swayed like a field of undone harvest.

Michael: (*Eagerly*) And?

Claudia: A few days later we were married. I was still very young—only sixteen.

Michael: Yes, go on.

Claudia: And fled from the winter into the South of France.

Michael: Following the swallows, as Dr. Stuart keeps urging?

Claudia: And we received the benediction of the sun. For days on end I used to meditate on the Van Gogh picture, comparing him to the Cyprus tree—

Michael: Oh! To have that evergreen blood of the Cyprus tree!

Claudia: And myself to the yellow cornfield.

Michael: Golden, like your hair.

Claudia: All that's gone now.

Michael: But go on, Mother, what then?

Claudia: In April, the year after, we returned to London. I was heavy with you.

Michael: Heavier now!

Claudia: London looked tawny after France and scrubbed—

Michael: Like a collier's face after a bath.

Claudia: The redecoration of the house was hardly finished, but we managed to settle down upstairs. Dr. Stuart hurried down from the north and took up temporary abode in the house to look after me.

Michael: Then temporary, now permanent!

Claudia: A fortnight later, amid cataleptic despair, I was delivered, thanks to his devotional attention. I still remember the sickly smell of that bedroom, partly of my own body and partly of the new paint. After you I swore to myself secretly that I would not have another child.

Michael: (*After a pause*) Must love always come to that?

Claudia: To what?

Michael: Bearing in hysteria, and thereafter swearing in secrecy.

Claudia: Love comes to that, Michael, even as Alph, the sacred river flows to meet the sunless sea.

Michael: (*Bursting out*) No more, Mother. Father has told me already of that unholy region where the water is neither fresh nor salt, having merged in secret mud.

Claudia: I was right, was I not, in saying that he only tells you the end of the tale?

Michael: No, Mother, it is a tale which, like a circular chain, has no beginning or end. And it is a chain to be worn round one's neck, not as an ornamental necklace but as a millstone.

Claudia: You are being over-meditative, Michael.

Michael: Father has told me much!

Claudia: Words of betrayal behind my back!

Michael: (*Bursting out*) You have no right to say so.

Claudia: Nor had he any right to come back and stir up the mud and dregs that had settled at the bottom of my otherwise clear conscience.

Michael: Your shrill bitterness will not rouse him now. For I do not think that any silk-tearing cries of birds are heard on the banks of Hell's Acheron.

Claudia: What do I care if my shrillness touches him or not? I'm only concerned with you.

Michael: What if I am concerned with him?

Claudia: (*Unable to contain herself any longer*) Michael, you mustn't, you mustn't desert me now.

Enter Anthony with a seemingly triumphant air.

Anthony: Good morning. (*No response*) A most unexpected domestic scene. (*An awkward pause, in which he seems to sum up the situation*) I expected Michael to be weeping, not you, Claudia.

Michael: (*In a flat tone*) You expect an awful lot, Mr. Pearsall.

Anthony: (*With forced joviality*) Do I? Why, is it so hard to make you weep? I always thought you were such a tender soul, ready to weep for the whole world at a moment's notice. (*In a serious tone*) I may expect a lot! But I don't make a song about it as you do. The incantation of nothingness happens to be your hobby, not mine.

Michael: It is my affair, whatever hobby I indulge in.

Anthony: (*Loudly*) Is it also your affair to make Claudia miserable?

Claudia: (*Impatiently*) Oh, please! (*Exit*)

Michael: It is not my affair to make anybody miserable, except myself.

Anthony: (*In a mimicking tone*) "For the greatest crime of man is that he was born." Is that what you're driving at? If so, you had better let it go. It is no earthly good, clinging on to a vicious circle. If you do—like every Jack and Jill—you're bound to tumble after it.

Michael: How paternal of you to give me this advice. But I knew it before you told me.

Anthony: Good, how understanding of you!

Michael: An exploited slave like myself ought to have a keen insight into the one who has exploited him.

Anthony: How exploited, may I ask?

Michael: By calculation.

Anthony: Not by love? For I love your mother, this side idolatry.

Michael: Your love is nothing but a calculation.

Anthony: (*Shouting*) And boy, your love is nothing but a speculation, a soft-boiled projection of your vague egg-like willfulness.

Michael: You're not at your best, Mr. Pearsall, when you lose your temper, and let loose your emotions, like potatoes out of a sack.

Anthony: (*Swallowing the insult*) I saw your father yesterday afternoon.

Michael: So he told me.

Anthony: He was making his Will.

Michael: What luck for you.

Anthony: He had a peculiar way of splitting up his fortune. He divided it equally into four parts and left it to Claudia, you, Dr. Stuart, and the Circus. He left the house to Claudia on condition that she does not sell it and leaves it to Joy whenever she chooses.

Michael: (*Surprised*) Joy? How did he know of her?

Anthony: I told him about her.

Michael: My compliments on your presence of mind.

Anthony: And lastly, he left his library to you—in fact, everything that is in his study, he made it quite clear.

Michael: Did you not remind him to leave my mother to you?

Anthony: What infernal impudence you sometimes have! Unless you get rid of that impudence, you will never grow out of your adolescence.

Michael: Indeed. (*Exit woodenly as he sees Dr. Stuart entering*)

Dr. Stuart: (*Entering*) Claudia! Claudia! So you are here too--to give the funeral oration? Just itching to make use of your legal eloquence?

Anthony: Good morning, Doctor. I wouldn't be so bitter if I were you. You are a man of fortune now. Nothing like good fortune to hang misanthropy with!

Dr. Stuart: But, of course, my fortune is not nearly as great as yours, Anthony.

Anthony: Still malcontent? It's a moral crime, you know, to suffer from that desire which breeds further desire—it's like having diabetes.

Dr. Stuart: Quite jovial this morning, aren't you? (*Softly*) It seems that Joy has disappeared.

Anthony: (*Surprised*) Disappeared?

Dr. Stuart: Her brother just rang me this moment to ask me if she was there.

Anthony: (*Trying to shake his astonishment off*) She might be coming here, of course, to play the funeral march for you! (*Then feeling the irrelevance of his callous remark*) But I must say young people behave most unexpectedly!

Dr. Stuart: The prerogative of youth! Hush!

Enter Michael

Michael: I fetched this pistol from Father's desk. The damn thing is getting rusty. (*Polishing it*) This is mine now, Doctor. Father has left it in his will, (*in a louder and harder voice*) according to Mr. Pearsall, whose authority I have no reason to doubt.

Dr. Stuart: Now, now, Michael, no need to polish that thing now.

Michael: Can you tell me, Doctor, why he has left this ugly thing to me?

Dr. Stuart: Protection against thieves, I suppose.

Michael: (*Suddenly rising voice*) Quite right, Doctor. It is a protection against thieves who creep into the innermost shrine of our household, Mother's heart, as a worm does into a fruit.

Dr. Stuart: (*Surprised*) What on earth do you mean?

Anthony: (*Calmly*) It's all right. Michael's contracted his family fever—hysteria.

Dr. Stuart: Who is the thief of Claudia's heart? Do you mean myself?

Anthony: Let Michael ask himself.

Michael: (*Pointing pistol at Anthony*) Yes, my God, and my answer will be leaden and explosive.

Dr. Stuart: (*Protecting Anthony*) Calm yourself, Michael. Don't be so sudden and pointed.

Michael: (*Shouting*) Go away, Doctor.

Anthony: (*Calmly*) I should step aside, Doctor, Michael apparently wants it to be a duet, not a trio.

Dr. Stuart: I don't mind duets, so long as you keep harmony.

Michael; go away, Doctor.

Anthony: What Michael wants seems to be counterpoint, not harmony.

Enter Charles in haste

Charles: Good God! (*Seeing the situation, he halts suddenly.*)

Dr. Stuart: (*Stepping forth*) Come, Michael. Put away that toy now. Toys are things to play with in solitude, not in company! There now. Don't you see, child, that your desperation will lead your mother—and joy—but to one doom, the ocean-roar of darkness?

Michael: (*Self-castigating*) I am a fool and a coward, who has rushed into the bog of my own incomprehension. The more I struggle, the deeper I sink. And there is but one remedy for such fools, to be drowned in their own folly.

Dr. Stuart: (*To Charles*) Now what are you here for? Wasn't telephoning enough?

Charles: No, telephoning is not enough! I had to come and ascertain the truth of your answer.

Dr. Stuart: Are you insinuating that I told you a lie on the telephone?

Charles: No, but she is quite capable of telling me a lie when she chooses to: she might very well be here and yet I might be told the contrary, as I was yesterday.

Dr. Stuart: All right, don't be so impatient. Talk to me alone, if you must. Do you mind, Anthony? And Michael? Charles has something to say to me, in private.

Exit Anthon; as Michael is going out,

Charles: (*With sudden resolution*) No, let Michael stay. For I think he is in some way responsible for her action too.

Michael: (*Turning*) Whose?

Charles: Whose! Good God! How you can say such innocent words in such an indifferent tone, as though you had nothing to do with her. It's my sister I am talking about!

Michael: What about your sister?

Dr. Stuart: Can't you see, Charles, you will be making things far worse than they already are, if you insist on dragging in Michael as well?

Michael: Things can't be worse than they already are.

Charles: Precisely.

Dr. Stuart: (*Sighing in despair*) Oh well then.

Michael: What is it that I am held responsible for?

Charles: (*Slowly and emphatically*) I will tell you without ado—Joy has eloped.

Michael: Eloped?

Charles: Yes, eloped! (*Louder*) What servant-girls call "run away."

Dr. Stuart: (*Impassioned*) I still say 'no.' (*Almost despairing*) Just wait and see. Can't you young people wait? Is it so impossible, waiting?

Michael: (*Quietly*) That's what Mother said. Do nothing and let time decide.

Dr. Stuart: (*To Charles*) But I don't know why you should say that Michael is responsible for her present action.

Charles: Maybe not wholly, but at least partly.

Michael: Will you tell me more exactly what happened?

Charles: It's you who should tell us more exactly what happened last night! (*Pause*)

Dr. Stuart: (*Softly*) Were you nasty to her?

Michael: (*After a pause, quietly*) I was. Some uncontrollable wind had swept me off my guard like a leaf off its branch and rolled me about on the stone pavement of Obscure Emotions, so that I did not know what I was doing or saying. (*Quietly*) But soon I will cease to be blown about, for the Eternal Road-sweeper will gather me up.

Dr. Stuart: What do you mean, Michael?

Michael: (*Shouting*) Accuse me while you can to your heart's content. It was my fault! Say everything that I deserve. Now! Here!

Charles: (*Taken aback by Michael's passion*) Well, I did not mean to say that it was entirely your fault. It was my fault as well.

Michael: How so? Who else can betray her, besides myself? If to love is to be betrayed, as I know it is, she could not be betrayed except by me!

Charles: Young man, you need not make yourself so exclusive! I love her too. (*Slowly*) She is my only sister.

Dr. Stuart: Never mind about that. But for heaven's sake, tell us, dispassionately, what exactly happened.

Charles: (*After a pause*) I wasn't quite sober last night. I made her miserable over nothing, and myself too. Then I lost my temper and went out with Peggy, leaving Julian with her.

Michael: Julian!

Charles: This morning, when I returned home, I found her out. Soon after, Margaret telephoned me to say that Julian had disappeared suddenly, complete with baggage. (*Pause*)

Dr. Stuart: How about her things?

Charles: Partly gone, partly remaining. (*Pause*) What are we going to do about it?

Dr. Stuart: You go home and wait. Listen to me for once, wait and see! I still can't believe that it is true.

Michael: (*Calmly*) As you used to say, Doctor, I believe it because it is incredible.

Dr. Stuart: I will not have you insult Joy like that, Michael. (*To Charles*) You go home and wait. You've made quite enough mischief already. Why you couldn't believe me on the phone, I really can't tell. At least I can. But still I say, you should have believed me, Charles. Now go home and wait! Will you? (*Almost pushes him out.*)

Michael: (*After a pause; quietly and passionately, throughout*) I do not blame Joy. What right have I to blame her? God only knows it is wrong to blame anybody! For why should one life be necessarily at the expense of another?

Dr. Stuart: (*Quietly*) Will you forgive her, Michael? You must forgive her. Forgive that you may be also forgiven.

Michael: Forgiving is God's business. Man's business is only to imagine. And I can well imagine that, in the forests of the night, no natural woman or son of woman could dare think of anything else but the tiger, tiger, burning bright, and his fearful symmetry.

Dr. Stuart: Michael, listen to me. Don't, for the love of God, be blown away by the gust of your own void implications! Michael, do you hear? You have heard nothing certain yet.

Michael: I have heard enough to know that the passion-fruit which Joy has borne on her branches and which I, having no subtle sinews of the tiger, have been afraid to reach, would have been shaken off violently sooner or later. We all live by mutilation, sooner or later.

Dr. Stuart: Will you listen to me, I say? For my sake, for Joy's sake, for God's sake!

Michael: May God grant her a clear vision of that mountain-happiness which she has now begun to unfold! And may God punish me if I should dull that vision like a murky mist.

Dr. Stuart: (*Striking Michael, unable to control himself*) Wretched boy, when will you cease to be so obstinate! Can't you listen to what I may have to say? Will you never come out of that cocoon of yours, that cobweb of hysteria?

Michael: (*Softly*) Yes, Doctor, I shall not be hibernating long in the frozen dust. For I no longer have my summer to dream upon. (*Pause*) Today's Sunday, is it not?

Dr. Stuart: Yes.

Michael: Day of Rest! (*Pause*)

Dr. Stuart: (*Wiping forehead*) It looks more like a Day of Unrest.

Michael: (*Going towards door*) It is that too.

Dr. Stuart: (*Anxiously stopping him*) Where are you going?

Michael: I am going to tell my mother what has happened.

Dr. Stuart: (*Softly*) Will you remember to tell her, that it is the first time in my life that I have slapped anybody's face?

Michael: Yes, I'll tell Mother everything. (*Exit*)

Dr. Stuart: (*Soliloquizing*) Oh, the lying coward that I am! If only Charles had not come! Meddling fools—all of us! Myself—more than others! (*Sitting down and wiping his glasses*) Clustering together like a lot of flies on a piece of meat lying on a butcher's counter! What business had any of us to be here? Poor Claudia! And wretched Joy!

A shot is heard. Dr. Stuart starts up, drops his eyeglasses, which break.

Dr. Stuart: Oh, my God! Fireworks in solitude!

Claudia and Anthony rush in.

Claudia: Where is Michael?

Dr. Stuart: He said—he was going to you—to tell you everything that's happened.

Claudia: Oh for the love of the Sacred Heart! (*Rushes out by the other door.*)

Dr. Stuart: (*Holding Anthony back*) Don't go. I've dropped my eyeglasses and broken them. I can't see! Help me see, Anthony!

Claudia's wailing heard.

Anthony: How about Claudia?

Dr. Stuart: Quick! Don't leave her alone! Bring her here. Quick! (*Anthony rushes out. From here, Dr. Stuart speaks dead-slowly. Groping at seat*) God, what a dim, evil world! (*Claudia's crying continues.*) Let the actors act: let them shoot with finality, wail with sorrow and rush to and fro with excitement! But let the spectators sit and suffer: let me sit with dimmed eyesight and await the consequences. Wait and see! Was I saying? Yes, I will follow my own words. Knot the loose ends of your obscure sufferings, Duncan Stuart, tie up tight your liver, squat like a cat on the chair, and wait! Wait!

Enter Claudia, led by Anthony.

There now, Claudia, sit down—like a piece of wet cloth dropped from the air like this *(Mimicking with his handkerchief)*—and weep.

Claudia: Oh, Doctor! Oh, Anthony!

Dr. Stuart: Ah, there! I can just—dimly—see your torpedoed body sinking, sinking, getting gradually compressed, tighter, tighter, ready to become an oyster with a pearl therein.

Pause

Anthony: (*To Dr. Stuart softly*) A shot through his head!

Dr. Stuart: Ah, my boy Michael's third eye was a bull's eye, then and deep-set too! Deep-set eyes are sorrowful eyes!

Pause

Anthony: What happened?

Dr. Stuart: (*Dead-slowly*) Let me see, what happened? Very simple, very simple! I slapped my boy Michael to life, and I slapped him back to death; with a pause of some nineteen or twenty years in between. During which time, I suppose, he, poor boy, got caught in the groove of the screw's turn, unexpected and relentless.

Another pause

Claudia: (*At last pulling herself together*) What then must I do now?

Dr. Stuart: Pack up and go south.

Claudia: Will the South be any the better now?

Dr. Stuart: Oh yes, sorrow in the south—melted grief, your grief—is not the same as that in the North—frozen grief, my grief.

Anthony: Claudia, you had better go and calm yourself.

Enter Joy—with a small attaché-case—slowly, looking tired and guilty, i. e. comparative calm mixed with restlessness. As she stands at door, there is a momentary deadlock.

Claudia: Oh, Joy! We are lost! (*Exit, led by Anthony.*)

Dr. Stuart: Like a couple of errant sheep.

Pause

Joy: Where is Michael?

Dr. Stuart: At his father's funeral. (*Pause*) Come nearer, darling. I can't see you well. I've broken my spectacles. Come nearer. (*Holding her face*) Comfort yourself, Joy.

Joy: (*Falling on his lap*) You must forgive me—I need your forgiveness rather than your comforting. I came back to beg for Michael's forgiveness, Claudia's, yours.

Dr. Stuart: Talk to me now. As you have seen, Claudia is not herself. Tell me everything. I'll understand.

Joy: I have so many woeful telegraph messages in my submerged heart that my tongue only stutters—in dots and dashes.

Dr. Stuart: Speak! I will follow you, Joy, as I always have done and will. Where were you this morning?

Joy: I went out early to see the sun rise along the Thames.

Dr. Stuart: And did you notice how the sun gradually sucks up the cold mist of the gray dawn and how, as it rises, the buildings, the trees and the river-banks literally thaw and sweat—as I am doing now?

Joy: What's the matter—your face looks like a stone!

Dr. Stuart: Continue your story.

Joy: (*After a pause*) I was not alone. I was with Julian.

Dr. Stuart: Michael would not mind you being with Julian.

Joy: But when I got to the station, without even seeing the sunrise, I was running away with him.

Dr. Stuart: Nothing wrong in running away, Joy, darling!

Joy: No, but once I started running away, I couldn't run away quick enough.

Dr. Stuart: But what made you return?

Joy: In the train, I happened to read in this morning's paper of the death of Michael's father. Then I realized how wrong I had been about Michael last night. Michael knew that something was going to happen, he kept telling me. And it did happen.

Dr. Stuart: And when you were returning, leaving Julian to go his way, did you feel yourself that something was going to happen today?

Joy: I don't know. But I was right in coming back, was I not? Why aren't you answering? Where is Michael?

Dr. Stuart: I told you before.

Joy: Was the funeral so soon?

Dr. Stuart: So soon!

Joy: (*Crescendo*) How long will Michael be there? I want to speak to him. How long? How long? Answer me!

Dr. Stuart: Ever so long.

Curtain

Act III, Scene ii

Late September one early afternoon some nine months later; in the living room at Claudia's house; some change in the setting; a few suitcases in the middle; when curtain rises, the stage is empty, piano heard. The playing is much more "advanced," the music being much more florid than that of Act I, Scene i. Telephone starts ringing. Dr. Stuart rushes in. Pale blue light comes from the window.

Dr. Stuart: Damn the telephone. Can't even hear music nowadays without being interrupted by this awful atmospheric noise of the twentieth century. (*Mimicking*) Trrrrr! Trrrrr! Like some fantastic cockroach, screaming to be picked up and be relieved of its ugly message. (*Picking up*) Hallo. Yes, speaking. Oh, hallo Charles. This is a surprise! I thought you had disappeared from the earth for good. Wait! I can't hear you very well: Joy's practicing. Just a moment. (*Rushes out: piano stops; returns*) Hallo, Charles. How are you? A hectic time? You have lots to tell me? Good! I like people to have lots to tell about themselves—especially young people.

People should talk more when they are young and less when old! You will be here in about an hour's time? Excellent. Of course not! Joy's fine. Practicing hard. She'll be delighted to see you. Of course not! What? Not answering your letters? It just means that she is too busy to do anything—that's all! Claudia is leaving this afternoon for Italy. Yes. Very soon! I doubt if she'll be able to stay till you arrive here! So am I. All right, I'll explain. I am glad to hear your voice again. I will be waiting for you! Goodbye.

Enter Anthony with cases—in a good humor.

Anthony: Anybody for me?

Dr. Stuart: Of course not.

Anthony: Not even a goodbye for me from someone?

Dr. Stuart: No, I say. Are you so anxious to be said good-bye to over the phone? If so, I can go out and ring you up, just to please you. Of course, that happens to be my idea of hell: to be rung up, so that the moment that contraption starts ringing, the whole universe has to stop instantaneously—my thinking, Joy's playing! That reminds me—

Anthony: (*Smiling*) Don't knock down Claudia's cases. (*Exit Dr. Stuart. Anthony starts inspecting the luggage, whistling. Dr. Stuart returns.*) You seem all flustered today.

Dr. Stuart: That's because you're leaving!

Anthony: Oh come! Let's not be ironical now. After all, I am leaving, as you say, and we shan't be together again for some time. (*Pause*) I hope you will write occasionally.

Dr. Stuart: To say how wretchedly I am faring without your paternal solicitation of my well-being?

Anthony: You know, Doctor, when you are upset or annoyed about something or other, your words distinctly smell of that tang which one smells in a cow's breath! And I know the reason why.

Dr. Stuart: Why?

Anthony: Because you chew people's words too much—and make honest hay into savory cud!

Dr. Stuart: Honest hay is a dried up affair—not unlike you, in fact; therefore it should be chewed and enriched and made into cud. I wonder why Joy's not playing.

Anthony: Probably helping Claudia with her packing.

Dr. Stuart: (*Sharply*) The maid does that!

Anthony: You are certainly determined to make a musician out of her. 'Art for art's sake! Art before life!' There's a guiding star for you!

Dr. Stuart: I don't need a guiding star.

Anthony: The three Magi did.

Dr. Stuart: Their slaves and their donkeys needed that bearded carrot of the sky more than they did, I am sure of that.

Anthony: Ha! Are you suggesting that you are comparable to the Magi?

[The pages for the concluding part of the play are illegibly damaged.]

부록

Insoo Lee and His Cloud Cuckoo Land

Gregory Henderson
(New York, 1967)

The first touches of spring, invading the Hudson River Park in front of my eyes, full of its susurrant pigeons to which our white-haired neighbor has just fed bread crumbs mixed with birth-control pills, stirred an odd corner of my memory and brought, after labored search, out of the bookcase a copy of a Korean response to spring Seoul met eighteen years ago, in 1949.

Time has moved fast over Korea's cities. And, I think, compared to Europeans and even to Americans, Koreans are not especially prone to looking back: with good reason, perhaps. Korean culture seems now to lack the nostalgia the earlier Chosŏn dynasty *shijo* once had. Nearly half of Seoul's present population had not even been born into the land eighteen years ago and one wonders, a bit nervously, how many of her present swollen multitudes could even remember the city of 1949—hardly a quarter, surely; perhaps a good deal less. With the towers of the Vietnam-fattened *chaebŏl* (*zaibatsu*) crowding Chung-gu and Chongno-gu, why look at the past's receding—and far grimmer—shores? Yet spring is here, stirring memory with desire, and the Seoul of 1949, immortally evoked by the late Insoo Lee in his "Inside Cloud Cuckoo Land," somehow cries out for resurrection.

As does the soul of a friend. We have left him in the past, Insoo Lee, shadowed, in the end, by mistake and tragedy. But we must admit, we who knew him, that none of us have found his like again. Wherever one met his students from Koryŏ University, there was praise, even awe. No other companion endowed the murk of the earlier Myŏng-dong tearoom with the assured coruscations of Bloomsbury wit as he did. Who else would have dared fit the then new shoots of a reviving Korean language to the awesome intricacies of Eliot's *Waste Land*? Or write that superb *tour de force* on Cloud Cuckoo Land?

Translations are not prophetic, after all. Yet Lee's *Waste Land* was. The Seoul of

"Cloud Cuckoo Land" was seeing the departure of the last American combat troops within five weeks. "Inside a year we shall have invasion," my friend Ha Kyŏng-dŏk told me, gravely, his face ashen. And within a year, the prophecy was complete. Korea became the world's newest—alas, not the world's last—wasted land. And fate, so intricately bound up with character, decreed that the blight should spread to the life of Insoo Lee himself. Something of the bitterness and despair he had so artfully evoked bade him feel in late June 1950, that when the feet of his former friends—American and Korean—had gone they would not return. Knowing his unmatched eloquence in English, the Communist invaders came to his Seoul house and half lured, half forced him to demean his gifts to their propaganda. A refugee and exile in Pusan myself, I heard with heavy heart his voice behind their English broadcasts. But what had been cynicism in his view of 1949's spring turned to disgust in 1950's summer when the Cloud Cuckoos were replaced with Communist birds considerably more malign—and with him in their nest. Knowing his danger, he yet stayed behind and gave himself up to the re-conquering U. N. forces, admitting his guilt but in a desperate quest for mercy.

He did not find it. When I saw Seoul again, he was in jail and my day of return allowed no time to search him out. Others pled in vain against what was then becoming a mounting personal drama. The defense minister, Shin Sŏng-mo, whose power was then next only to President Rhee's, had been Lee's intimate friend in former years when the two had been Korean souls alone in London. Caught in a world of encompassing recrimination, Shin felt that any move of his to save Lee would be laid to personal ties he dared not invoke. Shin himself came to insist on the extreme penalty. Abandoned, Lee was then killed by his own countrymen. A decade later, Shin, long in obscurity, died of shock in the wake of the April revolution. In the strong tides of that time, there were few to remark his passing and none to note that the drama in which he had played had now come full circle. Again, Koreans seem not a very nostalgic people. But it was still a pity that something so richly Sophoclean met so little response in a land of ancient and sensitive literary traditions. Lee would himself have been the first to have located these meanings and given them the expression they cried out to have. But then, he had no successor.

He was not a hero, of course; his ghost would be the first to agree with our inability to confuse him with an epic of loyalty like Admiral Yi Sun-shin. He was not a man of religion or of patience, or, perhaps, even of faith. He did not live in a simple, clear-cut age but faced times and values which he found complex. The ambivalence he felt toward what he saw led, perhaps inexorably, toward his fate once the pincers of North against South began to close. But this same ambivalence was a mainspring of his art and of his spirit as a human being—brilliant, wayward, the expression of a bruised confidence in life; yet a humanist, one not without a strong touch of gallantry. And in this spirit he actually stood shoulder to shoulder with many of the best minds of his age, especially in the West. Only they were not exposed; at least not as he was.

As I was saying, when spring knocked at these recollections, I had no idea why Cloud Cuckoo Land rose from the ashes of the past, more like some quixotic phoenix than like a well-bred English cuckoo. (Are Greek Aristophanic cuckoos well bred, we wonder? Perhaps not.) I asked myself, sitting Hudson-side, what occasion I should seek to excuse this reminiscent excursion up-river. Should I perhaps try to find the date of Lee's birth or of his death by which, somehow, to pin this memorialization? Then I felt it better not to inquire into these things. Birth and death and even the spring of each year come only once. But the genius of a man should be green the months around. Let us pick any date to remember him—and the past world his bright words and dark fate evoke.

(Friday, April 28, 1967, *The Korea Times*)

Editor's Note:
The writer of this memoir, Mr. Gregory Henderson, worked for the United States Embassy in Seoul till the Korean War broke out, and later worked for the United Nations. Later on, he taught at Tufts University. When he contributed this memoir to *The Korea Times* for its "Thoughts of the Times" column, he was working for the United Nations Institute for Training and Research in New York.

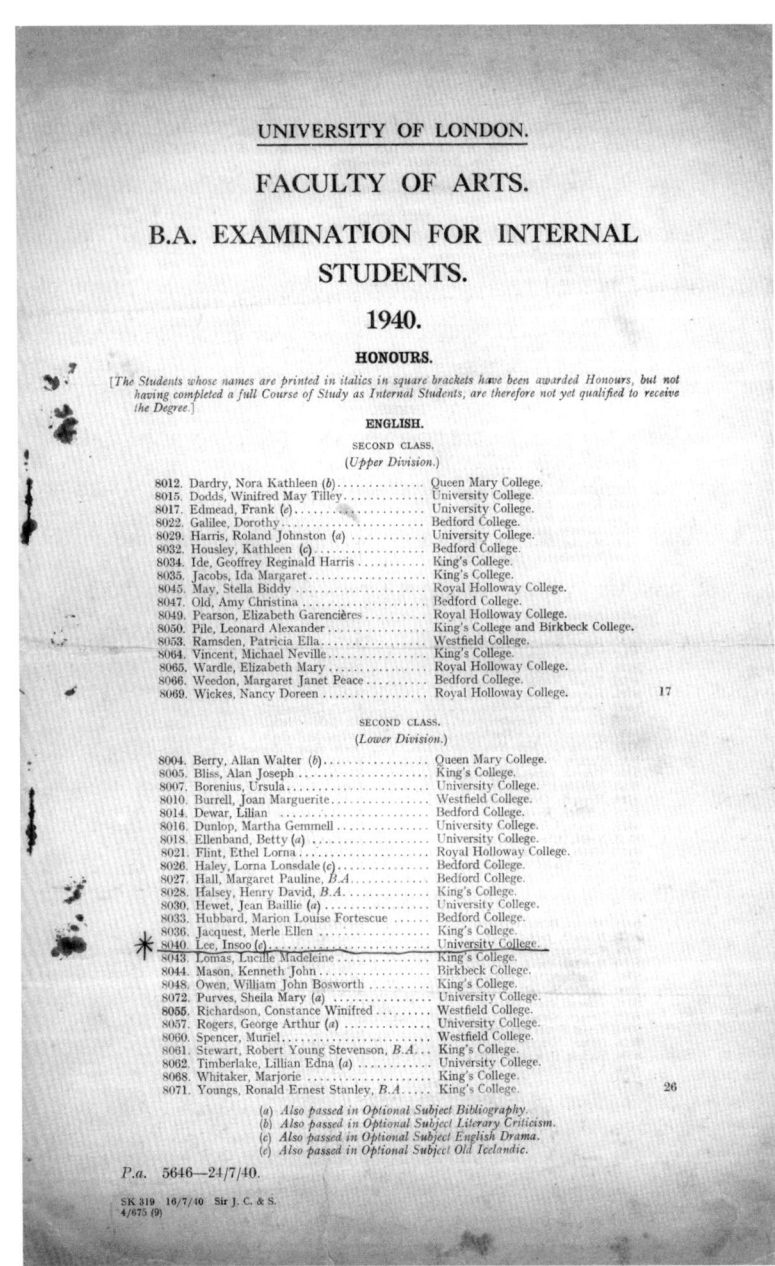

List of Recipients of B. A. Honours Degree, 1940, University of London

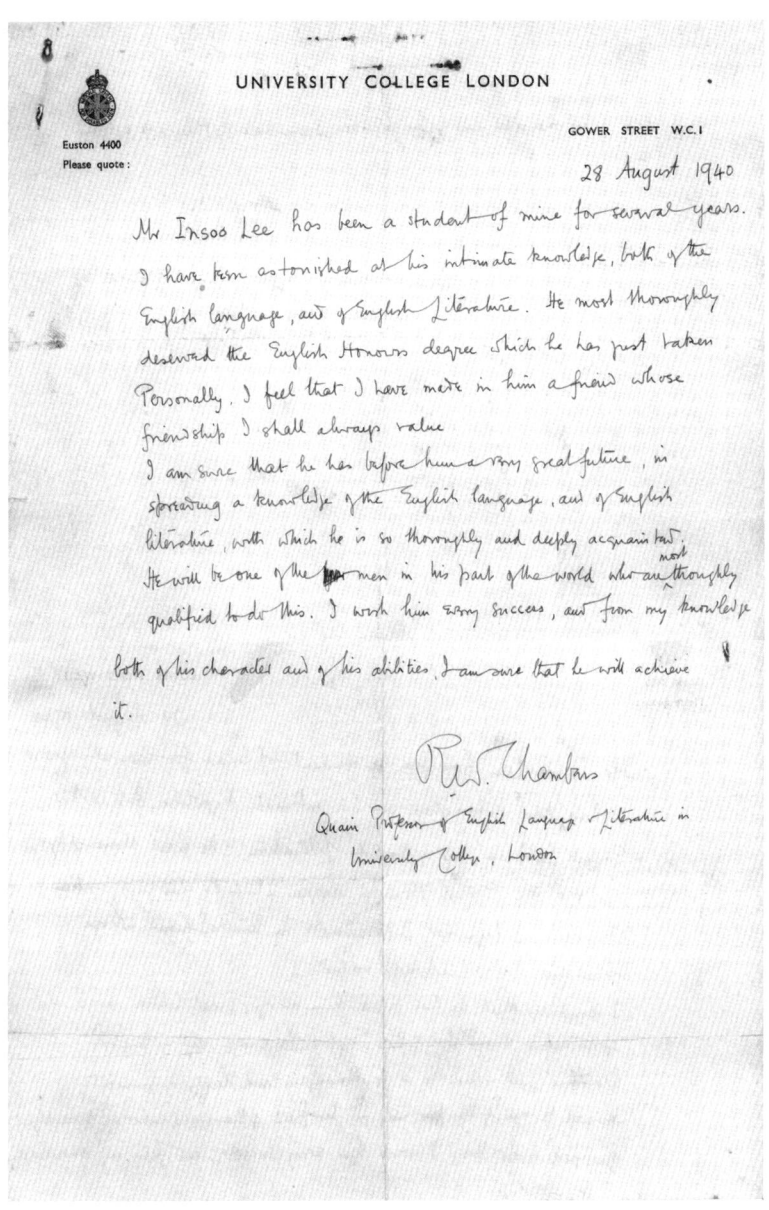

Testimonial of R. W. Chambers, Quain Professor of English, University College, London

UNIVERSITY COLLEGE, LONDON

GOWER STREET, W.C.1

TELEPHONE: EUSTON 4400
PLEASE QUOTE:

10 Marine Terrace,
Aberystwyth.

29th August, 1940.

Dear Mr. Lee,

    I sent off a letter to you immediately I received yours, but the posts are so delayed it may not have reached you before you left for Liverpool. In case it did not, I am sending you this, which I hope will be forwarded to you in any case.

    I have been very much impressed during the years you have been with me both by your extraordinary command of the English language and by your very wide knowledge of English literature. When you return to your home you will be one of the few men in the Far East who are thoroughly equipped not merely for school but also for University teaching in English. As such you will, I am sure, have a most distinguished career open before you. I wish you every success for a long and prosperous life and I am sure that it will be a most useful one.

    I hope you will let me know from time to time how you are getting on, and I shall always, so long as I am alive, be glad to testify to your very high character and very great abilities.

                              Yours ever,

                              R. W. Chambers
                              Professor of English Language & Literature

Insoo Lee Esq., B.A.,
11 Fitzjohns Avenue,
London, N.W.3.

Letter from R. W. Chambers, Professor of English,
University College, London

GOWER STREET, W.C.1

TELEPHONE: EUSTON 4400
PLEASE QUOTE:

Department of English

28 August 1940

Mr. Insoo Lee attended my classes throughout his course at this College, & impressed me from the beginning with the rapidity, & later with the completeness, with which he entered into an understanding of English Literature. He is one of the ablest students of foreign birth who have ever studied in this Department, & is well qualified either to pass on his knowledge of English to others or to use it in other ways than teaching. His steadiness & persistence of character should also help him in his chosen career, & I wish him every success.

Edith C. Batho, M.A., D. Lit.
Reader in English Literature in
the University of London

Testimonial of Edith C. Batho, M. A., D. Lit.,
Reader in English Literature, The University of London

[Edith C. Batho's Testimonial Typed]

Department of English
28 August 1940

Mr. Insoo Lee attended my classes throughout his course at this College, and impressed me from the beginning with the rapidity, and later with the completeness, with which he entered into an understanding of English Literature. He is one of the ablest students of foreign birth who have ever studied in this Department, and is well qualified either to pass on his knowledge of English to others or to use it in other ways than teaching. His steadiness and persistence of character should also help him in his chosen career, and I wish him every success.

Edith C. Batho, M. A., D. Lit.
Reader in English Literature in
the University of London

Biographical Note on the Author

Insoo Lee was born in 1916, at Kurye, South Chŏlla Province, Korea, in a family with scholarly heritage. His early education, including high school and the first year at college, was in the field of commerce. His passion for literary studies, however, made him withdraw from the college he was attending and go to England to study English literature. He matriculated in the University of London in 1934, and the next year, he passed the Intermediate Examination for Internal Students in English, Latin, French, and German, thence proceeding to the B. A. Honours degree course in English, with German as subsidiary subject. In 1937, he passed the B. A. Honours subsidiary subject in German language and literature, and in 1940, he passed the B. A. Honours Examination for Internal Students in English language and literature.

Having completed his baccalaureate, he returned to his homeland, and taught English at a high school for five years till he became an instructor of English at Posŏng College in 1945. With the rise of the college to the status of a university in 1946, he was appointed Associate Professor of English language and literature at Koryŏ University, where he taught until the outbreak of the Korean War. While teaching at Koryŏ University, he also served as the Editor of *The Seoul Times*, the first Korean newspaper in English.

Upon the outbreak of the Korean War in June 1950, he was taken by the North Korean Army, and was forced to work for them as an interpreter in the interrogation of the captive U. S. Army officers, and also to do radio broadcast in English propagating the communist cause in the war. When the U. N. forces retrieved Seoul in September 1950, he surrendered himself to the U. N. command, and remained in the custody of the U. S. Intelligence, until he was relegated to the Korean Army and put on trial. He was sentenced to death at a court martial, and was executed in November 1950.

After Compiling Our Father's Writings

More than five decades are gone since our father met his untimely death in the late fall of 1950. They say time flows like a rapid stream, but remorse and embarrassment weigh down heavily on us as we recall how long we have neglected the long overdue task of putting together the records of the intellectual probing that our father went through in his brief life.

Half a century is buried in the past, along with people's memory of his love of learning and the tragic end of his life. But his voice is still heard in the lines he wrote; and although we have been deprived of our father's physical presence for so many years, the kind of loneliness coming upon those not blessed with paternal love has not been our lot. The crumbling leaves where his handwriting fades as time passes have always been with us, watching us, who have gradually acquired bits of knowledge that have enabled us to read what he wrote. Without his physical presence, our father has always been near us, making us feel both proud and guilty—proud for being his offspring, and guilty over neglecting to cultivate whatever gift he may have left in us as parental legacy.

As we make this confession, our memory goes back to the days when our mother carried the box containing her husband's typescripts and manuscripts wherever she had to move during the war. She would wistfully turn the leaves bearing our father's translations of Korean poems, and we grew up reading the lines he wrote. Each stroke of his handwriting was like his breath, and we knew, although too young to realize it, that our mother's lifelong dedication to the memory of our father would make us walk, though in limping steps and with much tardiness, on the path which he once trod.

The book consists of two parts: prose essays in English, and translations of modern Korean poems and stories. Most of the essays were published in *The Seoul Times*, the first Korean daily newspaper in English, for which the author worked as Editor. These essays, written in the late 1940s, reflect the turbulence of the times following the liberation of the country in 1945, up to the outbreak of the Korean War in 1950. Most of his translations of Korean poems were also published in *The Seoul Times* from 1947 to 1950, when the journal ceased to be in print upon the outbreak of the war. Of the two stories included in this volume, "The Rock" by Kim Dong-ni was published in *The Seoul Times* in 1948, but the translation of the other story, "The Wing" by Yi Sang, was not completed, and remains in fragmentary manuscript.

Grateful acknowledgement is due to the Korean Culture and Arts Foundation for having granted a subsidy for the production of this volume.

The late Mrs. Anna Blyth, our father's teacher and benefactress, who spent several years of arduous academic training and financial support for our father's education, would have been much comforted to see this book finally in print.

(Sung-Il and Sung-Won Lee)

李仁秀의 年譜

1916년 3월 15일. 전남 구례군 용방면 용강리 571번지에서 白村 李炳浩의 장남으로 출생.

1933년 3월. 경기도립상업학교 우등 졸업.

1933년 4월. 경성고등상업학교 입학.

1933년 10월. 경기도립상업학교의 은사 Anna Blyth부인의 권유로 영국에 유학하기 위해 위 학교를 중퇴하고 도영.

1934년 9월. 런던대학교(University of London) 입학시험(Matriculation)에 합격 (시험과목: 영어, 수학, 라틴, 불어, 독일어)

1935년 6월. 런던대학교 정규등록학생(Internal Students)으로서 학위 취득을 위한 중간시험(Intermediate Examination)에 합격 (시험과목: 영어영문학, 라틴, 불어, 독일어). 이 시험에 합격함으로써 독어독문학 부전공으로 런던대학교의 영어영문학 전공 우등 학사학위 (B. A. Honours in English) 과정에 진입.

1937년 6월. 우등 학사학위 (B. A. Honours) 취득을 위한 부전공으로 독어독문학 시험에 합격.

1940년 6월. 런던 대학교 정규등록학생을 위한 영어영문학 전공 우등 학사학위 시험에 합격. (B. A. Honours in English Language and Literature, University College, London)

1941년 4월. 귀국하여 중앙고등보통학교 영어 교사로 임명.

1945년 10월. 보성전문학교 영어 강사로 임명.

1946년 9월. 보성전문학교가 고려대학교로 승격함에 따라 고려대학교 영문학과 부교수로 임명.

1950년 11월 7일. 한국전쟁 발발 직후 북한군에게 억류되었고, 그들을 위한 영어방송을 한 죄목으로, 1950년 9월 수도 탈환 후 군법회의에 회부되어 사형을 언도받고 처형됨.

아버님의 文集을 펴내며

덧없이 흘러가는 세월 속에서 색이 바래어 가는 원고지 다발마다에서 흐려만 가는 아버님의 육필을 접할 때마다 마음 속에 이는 죄책감과 자괴심을 억누르지 못하면서 허송한 세월이 부끄럽기만 합니다. 어머님께서 저희 형제들이 영문학을 공부하는 것을 굳이 막지 않으셨던 것은, 비록 아버님만큼의 학문을 이룩하지는 못할지라도 그 그늘 밑에서 못 다 받은 아버님의 사랑과 훈도를 어렴풋이나마 느껴보라는 뜻이 숨겨져 있었음을 뒤늦게 깨달았습니다. 전란중에 이곳 저곳으로 옮겨 다니며 어려운 생계를 이어가시는 중에도 아버님의 원고를 담은 상자들은 늘 우리 곁을 떠나지 않았음을 새삼 기억하게 되는 것은, 어머님의 가슴에 담긴 지아비에 대한 그리움 뿐만 아니라 언젠가는 자식놈들이 아버지의 글을 읽으며 그 숨결을 느낄 날이 오지 않겠는가 하는 기대감 때문이었다는 깨달음도 뒤늦게 찾아 왔습니다. 서양 속언에 "늦게라도 하는 것이 아니 하는 것보다는 낫다"는 말이 있는데, 이 말을 위안으로 삼으며 뒤늦게 아버님의 문집을 내어 드리는 것에 대한 부끄러움을 억누르려 합니다.

이 문집은 저희 아버님이 한 사람의 영문학도로서 하고저 하였던 바를 일목요연하게 보여줍니다.

제1부에 포함된 다섯 편의 글들은 순전히 영문학에 관한 것들입니다. 그중에 두 편의 글―"T. S. 엘리어트의 古典主義 文學論"과 "近代英詩 小史"―은 안타깝게도 미완으로 남아 있으나, 남아있는 그 상태로도 영문학 연구의 향방을 제시한다는 점에서 충분한 의미가 있습니다. 완결된 세 편의 논문들 중, "영문학에 반영된 20세기 前半의 思潮"는 20세기 영문학을 시대 사조의 큰 흐름 속에서 읽어 내려한 점에서 큰 의미를 담고 있는 논문입니다.

제 2부는 영문으로 쓴 연설문, 논설문, 수필들로 구성되어 있는데, 그 대부분은 아버님께서 한국 최초의 영문 저널이었던 *The Seoul Times*의 주필로 있으면서 쓴 글들입니다. 2008년 미국에서 출판된 *Inside Cloud Cuckoo Land: The Voice of Korea* (The Association for Textual Study and Production, Troy, Alabama)에는 들어있지 않은 글이 두 편 있는데, 그 하나는 1948년 파리에서 개최된 UN 총회에 새로이 탄생한 대한민국의 대표로 참석하여 만국의 대표들 앞에서 대한민국을 주권국가로 인정해 달라는 호소를 한 장면박사의 연설문입니다. 당시 국가의 지도자들―특히 인촌 김성수 선생―의 하명을 받아 아버님께서 며칠 밤을 새워가며 쓰신 연설문인데, UN 본부의 서류보존실에 보관되어

있던 타자본을 저희 조카인 김정권(누이 성윤의 장남)이 사본을 입수하여 보내주어 다시 세상에 빛을 보게 된 글입니다. 그리고 또 한 편은 이승만 대통령 시절에 국방장관으로 있던 신성모씨를 대신하여 대한민국의 해군 창설의 역사와 의미를 역설한 글인데, 아버님이 비운을 맞게 되는 직접적 원인을 제공한 장본인을 위해 쓰신 글이라는 점에서 실로 아이러니의 극치를 보는 것 같습니다.

제3부는 한국 현대문학작품들의 영역을 담고 있습니다. 특히 한국현대시의 백미라고 일컬어질 수 있는 작품들을 최초로 영역하신 것들인데, 그후 한국시 영역의 귀감으로 자리매김을 한 것으로 알고 있습니다. 산문 작품 번역으로는 김동리 선생의 "바위"가 완역으로 남아 있고, 이상의 "날개" 영역은 미완으로 남아 있는 것이 안타깝습니다.

제4부는 현대영시를 우리말로 번역하신 것들을 정리하였는데, 원고를 보면 미처 말을 가다듬지 않은 상태로 남아있습니다. 아버님의 초역을 그대로 싣는 것도 의미가 있지 않을까 생각도 해 보았지만, 독자들을 위해서는 역시 말을 가다듬어 활자화하는 것이 독자들에 대한 예의일 것 같아 원시를 참고하여 아버님의 초역과 너무 멀지 않은 것으로 말을 가다듬었음을 밝힙니다.

마지막으로 제5부는 창작시 한 편, 그리고 아버님이 영국에서 공부를 마치고 귀국선을 타고 긴 항해를 하실 때, 무료함을 잊기 위해 쓰셨다는 희곡 한 편이 들어 있습니다. 안타까운 것은 마지막 한 두 장이 훼실되어 작품의 결말이 어떠한지를 알 수 없다는 사실입니다. 그러나 남아있는 것만으로도 작품의 전체적 윤곽은 짐작할 수 있기에 실었습니다.

육신은 오래 전에 소멸되셨으나, 남겨 놓으신 원고와 타자본들을 뒤늦게 정리하며, 한 권의 책으로 엮어 드림으로써 지난날의 나태에 조금치라도 용서받기를 바라는 마음으로 이 책을 펴냅니다.

2020년 3월
성일, 성윤, 성원 아룀

정리

이성일(李誠一) 연세대학교 영문학과 명예교수
이성원(李誠元) 서울대학교 영문학과 명예교수

한국에서의 영문학
1940년대 한국 사회와 문화

1판 1쇄 발행 2020년 6월 19일

지 은 이 | 李仁秀
정　　리 | 이성일·이성원
펴 낸 이 | 김진수
펴 낸 곳 | 한국문화사
등　　록 | 제1994-9호
주　　소 | 서울특별시 성동구 광나루로 130 서울숲 IT캐슬 1310호
전　　화 | 02-464-7708
팩　　스 | 02-499-0846
이 메 일 | hkm7708@hanmail.net
홈페이지 | hph.co.kr

ISBN　　978-89-6817-892-4　93840

· 잘못된 책은 구매처에서 바꾸어 드립니다.
· 이 책의 내용은 저작권법에 따라 보호받고 있습니다.
· 책값은 뒤표지에 있습니다.